VOID

Library of
Davidson College

**The GATT—Law and International Economic Organization**

Kenneth W. Dam

# The GATT

Law and
International
Economic
Organization

The University of Chicago Press
Chicago and London

STANDARD BOOK NUMBER: 226-13495-4
LIBRARY OF CONGRESS CATALOG CARD NUMBER: 75-93088
THE UNIVERSITY OF CHICAGO PRESS, CHICAGO 60637
THE UNIVERSITY OF CHICAGO PRESS, LTD., LONDON

© 1970 BY THE UNIVERSITY OF CHICAGO
ALL RIGHTS RESERVED. PUBLISHED 1970
PRINTED IN THE UNITED STATES OF AMERICA

# Contents

| | | |
|---|---|---|
| **Preface** | | **xiii** |
| **List of Abbreviations** | | **xvii** |
| **Part 1** | **Introduction** | |
| **Chapter 1** | **Some Themes to Be Developed** | **3** |
| | LEGALISM VERSUS PRAGMATISM | 3 |
| | SUBSTANTIVE RULES VERSUS PROCEDURES | 4 |
| | ECONOMIC THEORY | 5 |
| | CHANGING CIRCUMSTANCES | 6 |
| | CONFLICTING VALUES | 6 |
| | CLARIFYING THE COMMON INTEREST | 7 |
| | ATTACKING PROBLEMS PIECEMEAL | 8 |
| | PREDILECTIONS | 8 |
| **Chapter 2** | **The Drafting of the General Agreement** | **10** |
| | THE ITO AND THE GATT | 10 |
| | U.S. VIEWS ON GOALS AND MEANS | 12 |
| | DIVERGENT GOALS | 13 |
| | THE INTERNATIONAL ENVIRONMENT | 15 |
| | THE INSTITUTIONAL FRAMEWORK | 15 |
| **Chapter 3** | **A Preliminary View of the General Agreement** | **17** |
| | TARIFF CONCESSIONS | 17 |
| | THE MOST-FAVORED-NATION PRINCIPLE | 18 |
| | NONTARIFF BARRIERS | 19 |
| | THE PROCEDURAL AND INSTITUTIONAL FRAMEWORK | 21 |
| | THE ADDITION OF PART IV | 22 |

## Part 2 — The Technical Arrangements: Tariffs

### Chapter 4. The GATT Tariff System — 25

- THE SPECIAL STATUS OF TARIFFS — 25
- TARIFF STRUCTURE — 27
- TECHNICAL PROVISIONS ON TARIFFS — 30
  - Bindings — 30
  - Schedules — 31
  - Tariff Surcharges — 32
  - Rectifications or Modifications — 34
  - Specific Duties — 35
  - Fixed Official Values — 37
  - Conversion of Specific to Ad Valorem Duties — 38
  - Miscellaneous Technical Provisions — 39
- INTERNAL TAXATION ON BOUND ITEMS — 40
- PREFERENTIAL ARRANGEMENTS — 42
  - Preferences in Existence on 10 April 1947 — 42
  - The U.K. Waiver — 45
  - The Utility of Reporting Procedures — 47
  - Other Preferential Arrangements: The U.S.-Canadian Automotive Products Agreement — 48
  - Australian Preferences for Less-Developed Countries — 52

### Chapter 5. Tariff Conferences — 56

- THE PROVISIONS OF THE GENERAL AGREEMENT — 57
- RECIPROCITY — 58
- BILATERAL VERSUS MULTILATERAL NEGOTIATIONS — 61
- ABORTIVE PROPOSALS FOR REFORM — 64

|  |  |  |
|---|---|---|
|  | THE KENNEDY ROUND | 68 |
|  | Exceptions | 69 |
|  | Agriculture | 70 |
|  | Nonlinear Countries | 71 |
|  | Disparities | 73 |
|  | Sector Discussions | 76 |
|  | The Results of the Kennedy Round | 77 |
|  | RULES, OBJECTIVES, AND PROCEDURES | 77 |
| Chapter 6 | **Technical Tariff Negotiations** | **79** |
|  | RETALIATION AS AN ENFORCEMENT SYSTEM | 79 |
|  | "OPEN SEASON" NEGOTIATIONS | 81 |
|  | The Procedures for "Open" Season Negotiations | 82 |
|  | The Definitions of "Substantially Equivalent Concessions" | 87 |
|  | The Impact of Part IV | 91 |
|  | "OUT-OF-SEASON" NEGOTIATIONS | 95 |
|  | THE SIGNIFICANCE OF ARTICLE XXVIII RENEGOTIATIONS | 97 |
|  | ESCAPE CLAUSE NEGOTIATIONS | 99 |
|  | ARTICLE XVIII NEGOTIATIONS | 107 |
|  | ARTICLE II:5 NEGOTIATIONS | 108 |
|  | ACCESSION NEGOTIATIONS | 108 |
|  | SUMMARY | 111 |
| Part 3 | **The Technical Arrangements: Nontariff Barriers** | |
| Chapter 7 | **Internal Taxes** | **115** |
|  | INTERNAL TAXES VERSUS TARIFF DUTIES | 116 |
|  | THE SCOPE OF THE PROHIBITION | 117 |
|  | BORDER ADJUSTMENTS FOR DOMESTIC TURNOVER TAXES | 121 |
|  | DIRECT TAXES | 124 |
|  | EXCHANGE TAXES | 125 |
|  | THE FEDERAL STATE PROBLEM | 127 |
|  | INTERNAL TAXES IN THE KENNEDY ROUND | 129 |
|  | THE GATT RECORD | 131 |

viii    Contents

| | | | |
|---|---|---|---|
| Chapter 8 | **Subsidies** | | **132** |
| | SYMPTOMS AND CURES | | 133 |
| | | Exchange Rates | 133 |
| | | Agriculture | 134 |
| | | Economic Development | 135 |
| | SUBSIDIES VERSUS TARIFFS AND QUANTITATIVE RESTRICTIONS | | 135 |
| | SUBSIDIES IN THE CONTEMPORARY WORLD | | 137 |
| | PRODUCTION SUBSIDIES | | 141 |
| | EXPORT SUBSIDIES | | 142 |
| | | Primary Products | 142 |
| | | Nonprimary Products | 144 |
| | REPORTING REQUIREMENTS | | 146 |
| | TRADE NEGOTIATIONS | | 147 |
| Chapter 9 | **Quantitative Restrictions** | | **148** |
| | THE STRUCTURE OF THE GATT RULES | | 150 |
| | THE ROLE OF THE INTERNATIONAL MONETARY FUND | | 152 |
| | THE PERVERSE INFLUENCE OF THE GATT RULES | | 157 |
| | THE OEEC APPROACH | | 157 |
| | THE EEC APPROACH | | 161 |
| | CONSULTATION AND WAIVER PROCEDURES | | 163 |
| | RESIDUAL RESTRICTIONS | | 165 |
| Chapter 10 | **Antidumping and Countervailing Duties** | | **167** |
| | THE DUMPING PROBLEM | | 167 |
| | EXPERIENCE UNDER ARTICLE VI | | 172 |
| | THE ANTIDUMPING CODE | | 174 |
| | COUNTERVAILING DUTIES | | 177 |
| Chapter 11 | **Administrative Barriers to Trade** | | **180** |
| | FORMALITIES | | 181 |
| | MARKS OF ORIGIN | | 186 |
| | VALUATION | | 187 |
| | HEALTH AND SANITARY REGULATIONS | | 192 |
| | TECHNICAL CONVENTIONS | | 195 |
| Chapter 12 | **Government Procurement** | | **199** |
| | MOTIVES FOR PROCUREMENT RESTRICTIONS | | 200 |

|  |  |  |
|---|---|---|
|  | RESTRICTIVE TECHNIQUES | 202 |
|  | EXPERIENCE IN OTHER ORGANIZATIONS | 205 |
|  | The OECD | 205 |
|  | The EEC | 206 |
|  | The EFTA | 208 |
|  | A ROLE FOR THE GATT? | 208 |
| Chapter 13 | **Border Tax Adjustments** | **210** |
|  | THE GATT GROUND RULES | 210 |
|  | PRESENT TRENDS AND OMENS | 213 |
|  | THE ECONOMIC UNDERPINNINGS OF THE GATT RULES | 214 |
|  | PROSPECTS AND POSSIBILITIES FOR AMENDMENT | 216 |
| Part 4 | **The GATT and the Broad Economic Problems of Our Time** |  |
| Chapter 14 | **Less-Developed Countries** | **225** |
|  | THE HAVANA CHARTER | 225 |
|  | ARTICLE XVIII | 227 |
|  | THE PANEL OF EXPERTS AND COMMITTEE III | 228 |
|  | Tariffs | 229 |
|  | Quantitative Restrictions | 231 |
|  | Internal Taxes | 232 |
|  | State Trading and Import Monopolies | 233 |
|  | Other Restrictions | 233 |
|  | THE ACTION PROGRAMME | 233 |
|  | PART IV OF THE GENERAL AGREEMENT | 236 |
|  | THE TRADE AND DEVELOPMENT COMMITTEE | 242 |
|  | INTERNATIONAL COMMODITY TRADE | 244 |
|  | PREFERENCES | 247 |
|  | OTHER ACTIVITIES | 255 |
| Chapter 15 | **Temperate Agricultural Commodities** | **257** |
|  | THE AGRICULTURAL PROVISIONS OF THE GENERAL AGREEMENT | 258 |
|  | THE GATT VERSUS AGRICULTURAL PROTECTION | 260 |

x    Contents

|  |  |  |  |
|---|---|---|---|
| | | EXPORT SUBSIDIES AND CONCESSIONAL SALES | 266 |
| | | THE INTERNATIONAL GRAINS ARRANGEMENT | 271 |
| Chapter 16 | | **Regional Economic Arrangements** | **274** |
| | | THE DETAILED RULES OF ARTICLE XXIV | 276 |
| | | Paragraph 4 versus Paragraphs 5–9 | 276 |
| | | The Common External Tariff | 277 |
| | | Elimination of Internal Barriers | 279 |
| | | Elimination of Internal Quantitative Restrictions | 280 |
| | | Interim Agreements | 282 |
| | | TRADE CREATION AND TRADE DIVERSION | 283 |
| | | Internal Tariffs | 284 |
| | | Quantitative Restrictions | 286 |
| | | External Tariffs | 287 |
| | | Preferential Arrangements | 288 |
| | | APPLICATION OF ARTICLE XXIV | 290 |
| | | SOME THOUGHTS ON REFORM | 291 |
| Chapter 17 | | **Market Disruption and Cotton Textiles** | **296** |
| | | THE DECISION ON MARKET DISRUPTION | 297 |
| | | THE LONG-TERM ARRANGEMENT IN COTTON TEXTILES | 300 |
| | | IMPLEMENTATION OF THE LONG-TERM ARRANGEMENT | 307 |
| | | THE HONG KONG SYSTEM | 309 |
| | | CRITICISMS BY LESS-DEVELOPED COUNTRIES | 311 |
| | | THE COTTON TEXTILES ARRANGEMENT AS PRECEDENT | 313 |
| Chapter 18 | | **State Trading** | **316** |
| | | CENTRALLY PLANNED AND MARKET ECONOMIES | 317 |

|  |  | THE CONTENT OF THE GATT PROVISIONS | 321 |
|---|---|---|---|
|  |  | Nondiscrimination | 321 |
|  |  | Tariff and Other Concessions | 323 |
|  |  | Quantitative Restrictions | 328 |
|  |  | THE GATT EXPERIENCE | 328 |
|  |  | Central Plan Countries | 328 |
|  |  | Market-Economy Countries | 329 |
|  |  | THE EEC EXPERIENCE | 331 |
| Part 5 |  | **The Institutional Arrangements** |  |
| Chapter 19 |  | **The GATT as an International Organization** | 335 |
|  |  | INTERSESSIONAL PROCEDURES | 336 |
|  |  | THE SECRETARIAT | 339 |
|  |  | PROVISIONAL APPLICATION | 341 |
|  |  | AMENDMENT OF THE GENERAL AGREEMENT | 344 |
|  |  | ACCESSION | 345 |
|  |  | NONAPPLICATION BETWEEN PARTICULAR CONTRACTING PARTIES | 347 |
| Chapter 20 |  | **Dispute Settlement** | 351 |
|  |  | THE RANGE OF DISPUTE SETTLEMENT PROCEDURES | 353 |
|  |  | RIGHTS AND REMEDIES | 356 |
|  |  | PROCEDURAL LIMITATIONS ON RETALIATION | 364 |
|  |  | SUBSTANTIVE LIMITATIONS ON RETALIATION | 367 |
|  |  | THE URUGUAY-BRAZIL PLAN | 368 |
|  |  | THE REFORM OF GATT PROCEDURES | 373 |
| Chapter 21 |  | **The Institutional Environment: The UNCTAD and the OECD** | 376 |
|  |  | THE UNCTAD | 378 |
|  |  | THE OECD | 385 |
| Appendix |  | **Text of the General Agreement** | 391 |
| Index |  |  | 469 |

# Preface

In reading the literature on international organization, I have been struck by the relatively small proportion devoted to the problems of organization itself. And I have frequently been depressed by the inability of the international community to organize itself peaceably and effectively. From these twin observations grew the conviction that the scholarly community could better serve the cause of world order by discussing the nature and problems of international organization, rather than by being lured so frequently into discussing the policies followed by the international organizations and by their member states and into offering advice to decision makers.

Organization presupposes rules, and the law is preeminently about rules, both substantive and procedural. As a lawyer, I have therefore been led to ponder the relevance and utility of rules in the organization of the world community. This book poses a number of questions about the efficacy of different kinds of rules, particularly procedural rules, that have been used in the organizing of the international community.

As a teacher in a law school in the United States, I have preferred, and indeed have been forced by the habits engrained by the "case method" of instruction, to pose these questions within the context of a single international organization, the General Agreement on Tariffs and Trade. The GATT provides a particularly attractive framework for an inquiry into the use of rules in international organization. The General Agreement itself is a complex set of rules. The procedures of the GATT are highly developed. Countless agreements have been entered into by the contracting parties over the years. And economic problems lend themselves to more elaborate rules than do political problems.

As a book about rules, this is, of course, a book about law. For all the lip service paid to the notion of a "rule of law" in international affairs, law is in disrepute in the international community. The General Agreement was in part an outgrowth of the "rule of law" idea. But curiously enough there is perhaps no international organization in which law is viewed as such a hindrance to progress as in the GATT. Both the enthusiasm for the "rule of law" in certain legal circles and the rejection of law in GATT circles is, as I hope indirectly to show, based on a simplistic view of the nature of law and of its functions.

Adoption of the vehicle of a case study has required me to go in considerable detail into a number of current economic questions, such as the role of trade in development, the growing autarky in temperate agricultural products, the effects of border tax adjustments, and the like. Those who are interested in current events and those who are specialists in international economics are urged to recognize the peculiar perspective under which those problems are treated here. Fascinating as the various economic problems are, I have conscientiously endeavored to avoid the temptation to focus upon them and have attempted, no doubt with some lapses, to stick to the fundamental theme of the role of rules in dealing with those problems.

A number of people in governments and in international organizations have been consulted and have given freely of their time and insights. Since the discussions were conducted in confidence, discretion commands that I thank them collectively and anonymously. But I cannot refrain from expressing my personal gratitude to Walter Hollis of the Legal Advisor's Office of the U.S. Department of State, who reviewed the manuscript. From his wealth of experience in GATT matters, which goes back to that organization's beginning, he gave me indispensable assistance in analyzing, and indeed in finding, the historical record (in that mimeographed nightmare that is the GATT document system). I am also grateful to Gerard Curzon, who gave me many helpful comments on the manuscript and whose excellent book on the GATT[1] provided me with much useful information and insight (although the book's appearance nearly led me to abandon this project). I am also indebted to Robert Aliber and John

1. *Multilateral Commercial Diplomacy* (London: Michael Joseph, 1965).

David Stoner, who commented upon portions of the manuscript. I hasten to add that the remaining oversights and mistakes are mine and that the opinions expressed, if not always original, are at least my own and are not to be attributed to any of those who have helped me.

Chapter 16 of this book is based upon an article published in the *University of Chicago Law Review,* volume XXX (1963), pages 615–65. Chapter 19 was preprinted, in a slightly different form, in the *Journal of World Trade Law,* volume III (1969).

The Rockefeller and Ford Foundations provided much-appreciated financial assistance. Carol Stitt assisted in the search for documentation. I was particularly fortunate to have the benefits of the legal and editorial talents of Charles Bush during much of the writing process. Perhaps my greatest debt is to the students of the University of Chicago Law School, who cheerfully endured dozens of hours of classroom discussion of draft chapters.

KENNETH W. DAM

*Chicago*
*October 1968*

## Abbreviations

| | |
|---|---|
| EEC | European Economic Community |
| EFTA | European Free Trade Area |
| GATT | General Agreement on Tariffs and Trade |
| ICC | International Chamber of Commerce |
| ICITO | Interim Commission for the International Trade Organization |
| IMF | International Monetary Fund |
| ITO | International Trade Organization |
| OECD | Organization for Economic Co-operation and Development |
| OEEC | Organization for European Economic Co-operation |
| OTC | Organization for Trade Cooperation |
| UNCTAD | United Nations Conference on Trade and Development |

# PART 1

Introduction

# 1 Some Themes to Be Developed

This book is a study of how legal rules have been and can be used in the organization of international life. The emphasis is on the development of international institutions dealing with economic problems. It is in one sense a case study, since a single international body, the General Agreement on Tariffs and Trade, is the main focus of the analysis. The experience of other regional and international institutions will nevertheless be examined to the extent that such institutions perform tasks similar to those of the GATT.[1]

The choice of the GATT is explained, if not justified, by a double circumstance. The GATT is the most "legal" of international institutions, consisting some would say simply of a legal document—the General Agreement—setting forth mutual rights and duties and not constituting an organization at all. At the same time, its secretariat and, to a large extent, its contracting parties have followed a consciously pragmatic policy of downplaying to the maximum extent possible the legal character of the institution and always attempting to reach "practical" solutions to problems.

This book has no single conclusion. Nor is the analysis pursued from a single and unvarying point of view. Nevertheless, a number of themes recur with such regularity, as attention shifts from one field of GATT activity to another, that they deserve to be set out for independent examination.

### Legalism versus Pragmatism

The first theme is the tension that exists in the GATT between the poles of what may be called "legalism" and "pragmatism." By "legalism" is meant at one level the tendency to view the General Agreement on Tariffs and Trade as

1. Both the institution and the underlying legal document bear the name of the General Agreement on Tariffs and Trade. The convention will be followed of referring to the institution as the "GATT" and the legal document as the "General Agreement."

nothing more than a legal document. At another level, "legalism" is used here to refer to an approach to the drafting of international agreements under which draftsmen attempt to foresee all of the problems that may arise in a particular area (such as, let us say, the elimination of quantitative restrictions) and to write down highly detailed rules in order to eliminate to the greatest extent possible any disputes, or even any doubts, about the rights and obligations of each agreeing party under all future circumstances. By "pragmatism" is meant an approach to the drafting and administration of international agreements under which emphasis is placed on mutual agreement on objectives, and rules concerning rights and obligations are considered formalities to be avoided whenever possible.

Under this analysis, legalism and pragmatism are simply two opposed tendencies and not positions fully subscribed to by any of the participants in the drafting and administration of the General Agreement. One is nevertheless struck by the extent to which "legalism" was dominant in the drafting of the original General Agreement and some of the amendments to it, and the extent to which "pragmatism" has governed the interpretation and administration of the General Agreement by the GATT secretariat and by some of the most influential contracting parties.

## Substantive Rules versus Procedures

In analyzing the tension between legalism and pragmatism within the framework of the GATT, one may observe how those leaning toward one pole view those leaning toward the other with suspicion, the legalists deploring the lack of respect for legal obligations manifested during the first twenty years of the GATT's history, and the pragmatists dismissing out of hand the "legal" approach and "lawyers." It may be observed that this latent dispute between the proponents of the two approaches is a false one. Within the GATT context, legalism and pragmatism alike rest upon a single, naïve view of the law. Both view law as substance—as substantive rules prescribing rights and obligations for all parties for all future problems. Legalists view substantive rules as inherently desirable—and the more detailed and comprehensive, the better. Pragmatists are more likely to view detailed and comprehensive substantive rules as obstacles to the accomplishment of commonly held, long-term objectives.

This jointly held view of the nature of law tends to obscure the importance of procedures—or, if you will, of the legal process. Law is not solely, or even primarily, a set of substantive rules. It is also a set of procedures, adapted to the subject matter and designed to resolve disputes that cannot be foreseen at the moment when those procedures are established. Perhaps more important than serving to settle disputes, law viewed as procedures and process serves to identify the common interest in complex situations and to formulate short-term policies for the achievement of long-term objectives.

Ironically enough, the importance of legal procedures and the insufficiency of substantive rules alone are more clearly recognized in domestic legal systems than in the primitive and decentralized international legal order, where nation-states cannot easily be fined or jailed for failure to live up to substantive obligations. To take a simple example, although much time is given to defining particular crimes in domestic legal systems, it is generally recognized that the procedures of courts, police, prisons, and sentencing and parole systems are far more important in determining the crime rate than are the definitions contained in the statute books. Similarly, if domestic commercial legal systems are able to set forth highly detailed rules about the rights and duties of merchants, this is in part because those most complex and highly sophisticated institutions known as the courts exist not only to coerce where necessary, but also to focus the attention of the parties on the crux of their dispute, to provide a framework for pacific resolution of that dispute, and, where the substantive rule is not perfectly clear in advance, to assist in identifying the common interest of all parties currently or prospectively concerned. Courts are supplemented and complemented by other institutions designed to resolve disputes and to help achieve common objectives, such as arbitration panels, independent legal advisors, and—where new problems arise or circumstances change—legislatures.

Part of the history of the GATT is in fact a movement away from the naïve view of law that held sway for many years and toward an interest in procedures. The legalists found that substantive rules requiring the abolition of trade barriers did not make much difference, and the pragmatists found that good will and ingenuity could achieve little in the way of reducing trade barriers and promoting international trade unless those qualities were accompanied by procedures for identifying underlying economic problems that made barriers inevitable, for promoting staged multilateral moves toward the liberalization of trade barriers where it was difficult for any one contracting party to move alone, and for providing governments with a mechanism or an excuse to do that which they wanted to do but were unable to do because of domestic pressures. The second theme thus concerns the GATT's progress toward breaking down the false antithesis between legalism and pragmatism through increased interest in, and recourse to, procedures for achieving defined goals.

## Economic Theory

Another recurring theme is the extent to which the rules of the General Agreement and some of the pragmatic decisions taken within the GATT fail to take account of the teachings of economic theory. Part of the reason for this failure is that some of the most significant theoretical work, notably the theory of the second-best with its subtheory of customs unions, did not find its way into the technical economic literature until the 1950s and is only now appearing in popular discussions of international economic problems. But if it were merely that the secretariat and the old GATT hands in the national delegations have tended to be innocent of economic theory, the point would not be worth examining. What *is* important is that both the legalistic and the pragmatic approaches have tended to focus attention on questions that we now know, through the work of economists, are essentially irrelevant to the achievement of the GATT goal of freer trade. Some of the more precise rules in the General Agreement appear old-fashioned today. Certain procedures will be suggested that should tend to focus attention more readily on the issues that the economists tell us are crucial.

### Changing Circumstances

The problem of adaptation of legal rules to new problems is still another theme. The problems discussed in GATT meetings today have little in common with those that dominated the meetings of the early years. Economic development of the less-developed countries was strictly a secondary topic in those years, and such matters as market disruption and border tax adjustments were rarely mentioned. Here the pragmatic approach deserves a good many more stars than does the legalistic approach. The history of the GATT suggests that its growth as an institution and the development of its procedures can be attributed in large part to the necessity of responding to new challenges.

### Conflicting Values

Constantly changing circumstances would not present such a challenge to the GATT if all the contracting parties shared a common view of their precise objectives. Then common policies and programs might be thrashed out. But the fact is that contracting parties have differing views of the function of international trade. Some countries, notably the United States, are primarily interested in the economic efficiency of international trade. Trade tends to promote the international division of labor, to allocate limited resources, and thereby to raise the standards of living in all trading countries. From this perspective all of the GATT's work should be directed toward eliminating as many as possible of the barriers to international trade.

This view has been shown to be somewhat simplistic with the development of the theory of the second-best, which shows that in a world with many trade barriers it is not possible to say a priori whether the elimination of a particular barrier will lead to greater efficiency. Rather, the effect of that elimination will depend upon the circumstances. Nevertheless, those who place economic efficiency first in their scale of values can easily adjust to the "new criticism," and the more sophisticated have already done so.

A great many countries do not, however, place economic efficiency first in their scale of values. For less-developed countries the primary value is economic development, by which most of them mean industrialization. These countries view international trade as important only insofar as it can contribute to industrialization, and within the GATT context they have often been more concerned to assure that GATT obligations to eliminate trade barriers do not interfere with their industrialization plans than they have been to promote trade for the sake of efficiency. More recently these countries have been interested in promoting international trade, but only international trade within the context of special discriminatory rules assuring that such trade contributes to industrialization—often at the expense of the efficiency that another, nondiscriminatory, kind of international trade regime would provide.

Still other countries prefer other values, such as self-sufficiency, for reasons of national defense or nationalistic sentiment. And some countries believe that, autarkic goals aside, the protection of domestic industry against the ravages and vicissitudes of international trade is more important than either efficiency or the industrialization of less-developed countries.

If countries could be easily classified by the order in which they rank such values, the problems facing the GATT would be clearer of analysis, if not easier of solution. But governments, being, as they are, institutions representing many conflicting tendencies, are often unsure of the order of values that they hold. Or, even if they see clearly, they may not act consistently. Domestic pressures may require them to act in favor of one value while professing another. Many countries, for example, preach freer trade as a means of maximizing economic efficiency while they pursue autarkic and protectionist goals in such politically sensitive fields as agriculture and cotton textile manufactures.

## Clarifying the Common Interest

The confusion that results from this welter of conflicting values among, and even within, governments tends to favor immobility. An institution like the GATT should therefore attempt not only to resolve this conflict in values but to aid governments in clarifying the common interest of all the members of the international trading community. Neither rules nor mere pragmatic improvisation can do that. But the GATT has been able to contribute to the clarification process in certain areas, and it may be that procedures can be worked out that will increase the effectiveness of the GATT in this domain.

## Attacking Problems Piecemeal

A theme of quite a different order that recurs with dismaying regularity is the difficulty of attacking problems piecemeal. Of all the problems faced by the international trading community in the past twenty years, it is hard to think of a single one with respect to which the GATT was able to deal with all the dimensions. Quite aside from the obvious fact that most international trading problems have their roots in domestic economic problems over which the GATT can have no jurisdiction, the GATT lacks the competence to deal with all the international aspects of most trading problems.

To be more specific, GATT has no jurisdiction over monetary matters; in a world with fixed exchange rates, monetary phenomena lie behind many, if not most, trade barriers. For less-developed countries trade and aid are obviously closely related, but the GATT exercises no jurisdiction over aid. Since it is difficult to disassociate problems in particular products from the overall international economic position of participant governments, it is a circumstance of considerable importance that the GATT has little or no influence over vast sectors of international economic activity, notably trade in invisibles (including shipping, insurance, and tourism) and capital transactions. And even where the GATT has competence, it has to share that competence with other international institutions, whether they be United Nations organizations such as the United Nations Conference on Trade and Development, contractual institutions such as international commodity agreements, or other institutions such as the Organization for Economic Co-operation and Development and the European Economic Community.

## Predilections

The foregoing are the themes that will recur. In addition, the writer has certain predilections of which the reader should be aware. The most important of these is a belief in the value of an international trade organization that seeks to improve the conditions of trade for the international community as a whole, whether that organization be the GATT or another. The writer is therefore interested in the preservation and improvement of the GATT, pending the emergence on the international scene of a more effective organization with a similar perspective.

The goal of increased efficiency through international trade is sufficiently important (although in many cases outweighed by goals of distributive justice, equality of opportunity, and avoidance of undue social hardship) that in considering most international trade problems it is highly useful to identify the prospective policy that would maximize economic efficiency before preferring some other policy. As Ragnar Nurske has observed, "The world is not rich enough to be able to despise efficiency."[2]

A major objection to both the purely legalistic and the purely pragmatic approaches is that they attempt to avoid the conscious identification of policies maximizing economic efficiency. This identification is a more complicated job than might appear. On a theoretical plane, it is no longer taken for granted, as it was by the drafters of the General Agreement, that all customs unions lead to efficiency, or that all preference lead to inefficiency. And on a more practical plane, it can be argued, and has been argued in connection with the GATT Cotton Textiles Agreement, that the imposition of certain trade barriers will lead in the long run to more efficiency than will an attempt at outright prohibition of such barriers. These are a few examples of the difficulty of identifying those policies that lead to efficiency. It is no wonder that, when values other than efficiency must also be put in the balance, discussions of international policy matters all too frequently become superficial and confused.

2. "International Trade Theory and Development Policy," in *Economic Development for Latin America,* ed. Howard S. Ellis (New York: St. Martin's Press, 1961), p. 234.

# 2 The Drafting of the General Agreement

The emergence of the GATT as the central international trade institution of the postwar period was a development that none of the countries participating in the drafting of the General Agreement had anticipated. Nevertheless, the GATT can be said to be a product of U.S. planning and a reflection of certain views that dominated the thinking on trade matters of U.S. diplomats in the 1940s. To begin our study of the GATT, we must examine briefly the history of the drafting of the General Agreement, emphasizing the U.S. views that played such a large role in that history.

## The ITO and the GATT

The GATT can trace its origin to the work of a number of U.S. State Department officials during World War II. Those officials sought, however, a much grander institution, which was to be called the International Trade Organization. Negotiations concerning the form and function of the ITO were first held on a bilateral basis with the British. The results of those bilateral negotiations were incorporated in a pamphlet entitled *Proposals for Expansion of World Trade and Employment,* the first published version of U.S. plans.[1] Thereafter, the United States elaborated the *Proposals* into a draft charter, which was amended in successive conferences from 1946 to 1948 in London, New York, Geneva, and Havana.[2] The final version, drawn up in Havana in March 1948, became known as the Havana Charter.

---

1. Department of State Publication 2411, Commercial Policy Series 79 (1945); reprinted in *Department of State Bulletin,* XIII (1945), pp. 912, 929.
2. The original U.S. draft charter was published in pamphlet form, *Suggested Charter for an International Trade Organization of the United Nations,* Department of State Publication 2598, Commercial Policy Series 93 (1946).
   After meetings of the Preparatory Committee of the United Nations Conference

Meanwhile, the General Agreement had already been drawn up in Geneva in October 1947. It was in origin a trade agreement designed to record the results of a tariff conference that was envisioned at the time as being the first of a number of such conferences to be conducted under the auspices of the ITO. In order to assure that the tariff concessions it recorded would not be undercut by other trade measures, however, the General Agreement incorporated many of the commercial policy provisions of the ITO draft charter. When it became clear that the Havana Charter[3] would not be ratified by the United States, the General Agreement became the founding document for an international institution, and the GATT assumed the commercial-policy role that had been assigned to the ITO.

Although the General Agreement as it now stands has been amended to include most of the commercial policy amendments added to the draft charter at the 1948 Havana meeting, it does not include the substantive chapters of the Havana Charter, "Employment and Economic Activity," "Economic Development and Reconstruction," "Restrictive Business Practices," and "Inter-Governmental Commodity Agreements." Nor does it include any of the Charter's organizational or procedural provisions. What was carried over to the

---

on Trade and Employment in London in late 1946, there was published a "London Draft" of the projected ITO Charter, *Report of the First Session of the Preparatory Committee of the United Nations Conference on Trade and Development*, U.N. Document E/PC/T/33 (1946); reprinted as *Preliminary Draft Charter for the International Trade Organization of the United Nations*, Department of State Publication 2728, Commercial Policy Series 98 (1946). The "London Draft" was modified by the Drafting Committee of the Preparatory Committee in New York in January and February, 1947. *Report of the Drafting Committee of the Preparatory Committee of the United Nations Conference on Trade and Employment*, U.N. Document E/PC/T/34/Rev. 1 (1947). The resulting "New York Draft" became the basis for modifications by the Preparatory Committee in meetings in Geneva from April to August, 1947. *Report of the Second Session of the Preparatory Committee of the United Nations Conference on Trade and Employment*, U.N. Document E/PC/T/186 (1947); reprinted as *Draft Charter for the International Trade Organization of the United Nations*, Department of State Publication 2927, Commercial Policy Series 106 (1947).

The Preparatory Committee having completed its work, the "Geneva Draft" was still further amended in meetings of the full Conference and its various committees and subcommittees in Havana from November 1947, to March 1948. *Reports of Committees and Principal Sub-Committees of the United Nations Conference on Trade and Employment*, U.N. Document ICITO 1/8 (1948); *Final Act and Related Documents of the United Nations Conference on Trade and Employment*, U.N. Document E/Conf. 2/78 (1948).

3. The text is set out in Clair Wilcox, *A Charter for World Trade* (New York: Macmillan, 1949), pp. 231–327. A useful "Analysis of Charter Text" is found in William Adams Brown, *The United States and the Restoration of World Trade* (Washington: Brookings Institution, 1950), pp. 391–557.

General Agreement was essentially the chapter "Commercial Policy," and even there some provisions were somewhat altered.[4]

## U.S. Views on Goals and Means

Although the General Agreement contains neither the institutional provisions nor all the substantive provisions of the Havana Charter, it contains most of the provisions on commercial policy supported in the 1940s by U.S. diplomats. The General Agreement is therefore a sufficiently direct expression of U.S. views on the appropriate form of concerted international action in the commercial policy area that it cannot be understood without an examination of those views.

The views of U.S. diplomats of the postwar period may, for convenience, be analyzed in terms of the substantive goals sought and the means chosen for the achievement of those goals. On the substantive level U.S. negotiators sought to achieve the goals of free, nondiscriminatory trade—goals that ever since the appointment of Cordell Hull as secretary of state had dominated U.S. thinking on commercial policy.[5] Simply stated, the U.S. position was that, in general, nontariff barriers should be abolished forthwith and that all tariffs should be reduced through international negotiations.

The U.S. view of the means best calculated to achieve these substantive goals was equally important. Oversimplified only slightly, it was that all nontariff barriers should be flatly prohibited within the framework of a comprehensive code governing world trade. This codification would limit severely the right of individual governments to interfere with the free flow of private trade. Transgression of the code would be an unlawful act. The role of the international body that would be the institutional expression of the code would be to interpret

---

4. Paragraph 1 of Article XXIX of the General Agreement provides, however, that the contracting parties "undertake to observe to the fullest extent of their executive authority the general principles" of certain of the chapters of the Havana Charter. This provision was to apply only until acceptance of the Havana Charter, and, although the provision is still technically in force, it appears to be de facto a dead letter, except insofar as it may be authority for using the Havana Charter to clarify certain points of interpretation of the General Agreement.

5. Hull's philosophy was that free, nondiscriminatory trade was essential to world peace: "I have never faltered, and I will never falter, in my belief that enduring peace and the welfare of nations are indissolubly connected with friendliness, fairness, equality and the maximum practicable degree of freedom in international trade" (*Economic Barriers to Peace* [New York: Woodrow Wilson Foundation, 1937], p. 14). Undersecretary of State Sumner Wells agreed: "One of the surest safeguards against war is the opportunity of all peoples to buy and sell on equal terms and without let or hindrance of a political character" ("Address on 'Our Foreign Policy and National Defense' to the Foreign Affairs Council, Cleveland, September 28, 1940," in *War and Peace Aims of the United Nations*, ed. Louise W. Holborn and Hajo Holborn [Boston: World Peace Foundation, 1943], pp. 29–30).

and, if need be, to enforce the code; its role would thus be not unlike that of a court determining whether crimes have occurred.[6] Except perhaps in the area of trade negotiations, the organization's role in persuading member governments to adopt more responsible trade policies and in providing a framework for the accommodation of divergent viewpoints and for the mediation of disputes would be strictly secondary. The code would lay down the law, and the members would be law-abiding.[7]

The weakness of the U.S. views lay not so much in the substantive goals sought as in the combination of those goals with a code-of-law approach. The United States might have been able to achieve its substantive goals, but not by means of the promulgation of a code purporting to abolish, in one stroke, restrictions other than tariffs. The considerations that doomed U.S. trade diplomacy of the postwar period are the subjects of the next three sections.

## Divergent Goals

As an initial problem, the United States faced opposition to its substantive goals from many other countries, which were determined, or at least felt forced, to continue existing trade restrictions. In many cases the motives of those countries had little to do with conventional protectionism. Among major considerations were the protection of overvalued currencies, the inability or unwillingness to remove wartime controls, the need to put millions of unemployed to work, whatever the efficiency of their output, the desire to protect national economic plans from the vicissitudes of international trade, the drive for economic development through the creation of import substitution industries, and the pursuit of international political objectives through preferences for some trading partners and discrimination against others. Views on the role and organization of international trade differed profoundly between deficit

6. The notion that an international trade agreement should be a legal code was knowingly fostered by the U.S. government. For example, Secretary of State Dean Acheson characterized the Havana Charter as "the first comprehensive code of international law to govern trade policies" ("Economic Policy and the ITO Charter," *Department of State Bulletin,* XX [1949], pp. 35–40).

7. A State Department official explained, "The ITO Charter . . . would establish a code of principles and rules of fair dealing that countries voluntarily agree to follow in their conduct of trade with each other." Admitting that the ITO "can work only if the nations of the world want it to work," the official, nevertheless, went on to say that the "democratic countries have shown their will to cooperate in economic matters." As proof he offered the following: "Fifty-four countries, representing widely different economic systems, have agreed upon the text of the ITO charter, the most comprehensive code of commercial conduct ever formulated" (Norman Burns, "The American Farmer and the ITO Charter," *Department of State Bulletin,* XX [1949], pp. 215, 220).

and surplus countries, developed and underdeveloped countries, market-economy and planned-economy countries, and so forth.

The code that the United States sought could, however, only be put into effect by common agreement. Consequently, the U.S. draft of this code was shot full of holes, first at home by the need to permit continuation of certain U.S. protectionist policies,[8] then abroad by the British insistence on continuing the imperial preference arrangement (which involved discrimination by Commonwealth countries in favor of one another) and on retaining the right to use quantitative restrictions to protect the shaky pound sterling, and finally at the drafting conferences by countries that differed profoundly from the United States in their view of the role of the state in international trade. The result was a grotesquely complicated document that included a multitude of detailed compromises and that all too often saw a free-trade principle followed immediately by an exception authorizing trade restrictions.

The attempt to negotiate a detailed code was in no small measure responsible for the failure of the ITO. U.S. public opinion, suffering from a reaction against the disappointing first few years of the operation of the United Nations and expressing shock at the compromises that had been necessary to arrive at a trade agreement with the rest of the world, responded unfavorably to the Charter. *Fortune* captured the prevailing mood with an article entitled "How the U.S. Lost the ITO Conferences"[9] and an editorial subtitled "The Charter is all exceptions." The editorial railed, "Every nationalistic trade-control device now in use, and every excuse for using it, is somewhere in this document invoked and permitted."[10] In 1950 the Truman administration finally decided not to seek the Congressional approval that it had announced would precede U.S. acceptance of the Charter. The ITO was dead.[11]

8. The U.S. Department of Agriculture insisted on an exception to the rule against quantitative restrictions to permit the United States to continue to support domestic agricultural prices at higher than world market levels. See Richard Gardner, *Sterling-Dollar Diplomacy* (Oxford: Clarendon Press, 1956), pp. 149–50.
9. Michael A. Heilperin, September 1949, p. 80.
10. "The ITO Charter," July 1949, p. 61. The editorial also stated: "It is a wretched compromise. . . . [It] merely registers and codifies the worldwide conflict between freer trade and economic nationalism. As the lawyers say, it gives the decision to the nationalists and the language to Mr. Hull. . . . The greater part of the charter consists in exception, enumerating all the ways in which governments so inclined can flout the objectives and control their own trade. . . . It is one of the most hypocritical state documents of modern times" (ibid.). *Fortune's* concluding appraisal of the Charter: "a meaningless document with everybody's name on it" (ibid., p. 62). See also Phillip Cortney, *The Economic Munich,* (New York: Philosophical Library, 1949).
11. The U.S. State Department tried to bury the news in a subordinate clause: "The interested agencies have recommended and the President has agreed, that, while the proposed Charter for an International Trade Organization should not be resub-

## The International Environment

A second consideration that doomed U.S. trade diplomacy of the postwar period was that a code-of-laws approach was ill adapted to the nature of the international economy and to the international financial system. The code was to operate in an uncontrolled environment in which the quantity, content, and direction of world trade was constantly changing as a result of natural economic forces. This trade instability was exaggerated in the postwar period. Prewar trading patterns had been destroyed, and postwar patterns had not been definitely established (partly as a result of the impact of the cold war on trade between western and eastern Europe). The trend toward raw material and agricultural self-sufficiency in developed countries had accelerated. And inflation was occurring at sharply different rates in different countries.

The international financial system was not designed to permit major changes to occur smoothly without direct controls on trade. Monetary reserves were concentrated in only a few countries. The remaining countries had no reserves to fall back upon when imports threatened to exceed exports. The international community was committed by tradition and by the Articles of Agreement of the International Monetary Fund to a financial regime under which adjustments in exchange rates were permitted, but only as a last resort. Small and frequent changes in exchange rates, which were precisely what was needed to deal with most payments imbalances, were considered incompatible with the rules of the international financial system.

Nevertheless, adjustments had to be made, and, with exchange rate fluctuations largely ruled out, it was folly to think that some countries would not resort, code or no code, to direct controls over trade. The system of fixed exchange rates was in fact so firmly grounded in the mores of the international financial community that prior resort to trade controls was considered a condition to devaluation. Thus, even if the United States had been able to obtain full agreement to its substantive goals, few countries could have adhered scrupulously to the code in the postwar period.[12]

## The Institutional Framework

A third problem inherent in the U.S. approach was that the United States failed to appreciate the need for an appropriate institutional framework and placed its faith almost entirely in substantive agreement. To be sure, the U.S. negoti-

---

mitted to the Congress, Congress be asked to consider legislation which will make American participation in the General Agreement more effective" ("Future Administration of GATT," *Department of State Bulletin,* XXIII [1950], p. 977).

12. True, resort to direct controls on trade could have been greatly reduced by exclusive recourse to exchange controls, but that is merely a way of saying that the trade code could have been circumvented in practice.

ators were sensitive to the need for an international organization; that is why they sought to establish the ITO. But in the area of commercial policy, they tended to see the organization's primary purpose as the application and enforcement of substantive rules of law. As Secretary of State Acheson argued, "No code of laws is worth very much without an authoritative body to interpret it and administer it."[13]

What was needed was not an enforcement agency, but rather, in view of the differences that divided countries and of the economic and financial environment of international trade, an institutional framework within which countries might examine the particular circumstances of specific trade problems, thereby, if possible, identifying their common interest and working out mutually acceptable solutions. Since the different policies pursued by different countries reflected competing values, it was important to create procedures for clarifying the common interests of the various trading countries and for establishing the impact of specific commercial policies.

The ITO was not primarily designed to fulfill that function, and the GATT as it came into being was, of course, totally unequipped to do so. To a certain extent, however, the institutional handicap has been overcome. In one of the happiest examples of ingenuity in the history of international organization, the GATT has risen above the legalistic confines of the text of the General Agreement and has improvised numerous procedures. These procedures have gone a long way toward overcoming the original weaknesses of the U.S. approach.

13. Dean Acheson, "Economic Policy and the ITO Charter," *Department of State Bulletin* XX (1949), p. 626.

# 3 A Preliminary View of the General Agreement

The bulk of this book consists of a detailed analysis of the General Agreement and of the GATT as an institution. Before proceeding any further, however, a summary of the main principles of the General Agreement may serve to make that analysis more approachable, if not less technical.

## Tariff Concessions

The General Agreement was in its origin an agreement on tariffs, and it is fair to say that the GATT has had its primary significance in the field of tariff negotiations. The GATT has provided the framework for six major tariff conferences, the most recent of which was the Kennedy Round, concluded in 1967.

Although the General Agreement does not specify the rules to be followed in tariff conferences, the legal bargains struck in those conferences find their meaning in the Agreement. No contracting party is required to lower any tariff, or even to refrain from raising any tariff, in the absence of special agreement. Such tariff *concessions* are normally made only in tariff conferences and, under the principle of *reciprocity,* only in return for reciprocal concessions from other contracting parties. Once a tariff concession is made on a particular item, that item is *bound* against increase above the agreed level (Article II).[1] An item may be bound at any level, but, since the purpose of the tariff negotiations is to reduce tariffs, the level of binding will normally be below the rate theretofore applied.

Just as a tariff on a bound item may not be raised above the level of binding,

1. The references in this chapter to particular articles of the General Agreement are intended only for orientation and therefore are not exhaustive. Nor is there any attempt to lead the reader through thickets of paragraphs and subparagraphs. For more detailed analyses of specific provisions, the reader is directed to the later chapters.

so a contracting party making a tariff concession is committed, except as otherwise specifically provided, not to impose other duties or charges that would tend to undercut that concession (Article II). Moreover, a great many of the substantive provisions of the General Agreement are designed to assure that other types of trade measures, including those of a nonfinancial character, do not operate to offset the effect of tariff concessions.

Contracting parties are required not only to abide by tariff concessions but also to apply those concessions to all contracting parties and not just to the contracting party with which the concession was negotiated (except in the case of certain preferences). This latter requirement, found in Article II, has the effect of a most-favored-nation obligation, although another most-favored-nation clause of broader applicability, to be discussed below, is found in Article I.

In order to prevent the system of concessions from becoming too rigid a yoke on the commercial policies of contracting parties, the General Agreement contains a number of provisions designed to provide flexibility. Under certain conditions contracting parties may withdraw operative concessions, so long as new, compensating concessions are made (Article XXVIII). And if an operative concession leads unexpectedly to serious injury to a domestic industry, the contracting party affected may be able to take advantage of an escape clause in order to withdraw that concession. In the absence of any agreement providing otherwise, the contracting party to which the concession was originally granted is then entitled to withdraw equivalent concessions (Article XIX). The justification for these provisions is that they encourage governments to make concessions that would not normally be made if concessions were permanently and irrevocably binding.

## The Most-Favored-Nation Principle

In addition to the most-favored-nation principle inherent in Article II, the General Agreement contains in Article I a most-favored-nation clause that applies to all tariffs, whether or not covered by a concession, and also to all other rules and formalities applying to importation and exportation. This latter most-favored-nation clause, which is normally the subject of references to "the" most-favored-nation clause, is in many ways the cornerstone of the General Agreement.

Insofar as the most-favored-nation principle applies to tariffs, it is subject to two major exceptions. First, certain specified preferential arrangements are excepted. The U.S. negotiators found in the late 1940s that the most-favored-nation principle was acceptable only on condition that a number of arrangements already in effect, under which certain countries offered certain other countries special tariff benefits, were left undisturbed. The most important was the British Commonwealth system of imperial preference, but a number of other preferential arrangements were "saved" by the General Agreement's "grandfather clause" (Article I).

Second, customs unions and free-trade areas are excepted from the most-favored-nation clause. The explanation here is that, although they are technically incompatible with the most-favored-nation principle and are undeniably discriminatory, such arrangements are, or at least once were, thought to constitute a movement toward the GATT goal of freer trade (Article XXIV).

The application of the most-favored-nation principle to nontariff restrictions on trade (see particularly Article XIII) is also subject to certain exceptions, one of which concerns special situations involving the administration of quantitative restrictions imposed for balance-of-payment purposes (Article XIV).

## Nontariff Barriers

Although the General Agreement may have its primary significance in the field of tariffs, enough has already been said to indicate that nontariff barriers to trade are not ignored. The philosophy of the General Agreement is, however, quite different in the case of nontariff barriers. Whereas a contracting party is not required to lower tariffs in the absence of special agreement, the general principle with respect to nontariff barriers is one of immediate abolition. As a corollary to this principle, the General Agreement makes no general provision for negotiations on the reduction of nontariff barriers.[2] Such negotiations were, however, included in the Kennedy Round of "trade negotiations." As might have been expected, those negotiations were not outstandingly successful. Contracting parties following practices inconsistent with the General Agreement sought concessions from other contracting parties as reciprocity for the abolition of those practices, whereas contracting parties adhering to the General Agreement argued that the principle of immediate abolition took precedence over the principle of reciprocity.

Since nontariff barriers can assume widely varying forms, and since in many cases there can be honest disagreement not only on whether a given measure should be termed a nontariff barrier but also on what the "abolition" of that measure should entail, the General Agreement includes no general provision on nontariff barriers. Rather, each type of nontariff barrier is treated separately.

Where a prohibitory approach is deemed feasible, as in the case of quantitative restrictions, contracting parties are simply prohibited from introducing new measures and required to eliminate forthwith existing measures (Article XI). But such a prohibitory approach is not feasible for all types of trade measures

2. See, however, Articles IV(d) and XVII.

that may inhibit imports. Various financial measures, to take only one set of examples, are considered consistent with free trade, despite the fact that they inhibit imports to a greater or lesser extent. A "trade barrier" effect is thought to arise from these financial measures only if the charge is inordinately high or if there is some kind of discrimination in its imposition or administration. Thus, the relevant provisions of the General Agreement must be regulatory and not prohibitory in character.

The regulation of permissible financial measures takes several forms. Internal taxes are not to be imposed at a higher rate on imported goods than on domestically produced goods (Article III). Antidumping and countervailing duties are permitted only in certain prescribed cases and even then are limited to amounts deemed sufficient in the circumstances to accomplish a few approved objectives (Article VI). And fees charged by customs officials are limited to the approximate cost of customs services (Article VIII).

Nontariff barriers that are other than financial in character raise a variety of problems. With respect to some measures, such as domestic legislation and regulations concerning sales, purchases, transportation, and distribution, a "trade barrier" effect arises only if there is discrimination against imported goods, and it is considered sufficient to prohibit such discrimination (Article III). But with respect to other measures, such as requirements concerning marks of origin, the source of any "trade barrier" effect is hard to pin down, and quite general language is necessary (Article IX). In some instances the General Agreement even regulates nontariff barriers by setting out affirmative rules, such as the rule requiring the prompt publication of laws, judicial decisions, and regulations concerning imports (Article X).

Still other types of nontariff barriers are thought too complicated or controversial to be subjected to the prohibitory approach. In the case of production subsidies that tend to reduce imports, the General Agreement does not go beyond a general requirement of notification and consultation designed to reduce subsidization (Article XVI). And, although the U.S. diplomats who shaped the overall structure of the General Agreement viewed state trading as a nontariff barrier, they had to content themselves with requiring state trading agencies to use market factors in making decisions with respect to purchases and sales (Articles II:4, III:4, and XVII).

Quantitative restrictions were the most important nontariff barriers at the time the General Agreement was drafted, and it is therefore not surprising that they are the subjects of very complex provisions. Most of the complexity stems, however, from the fact that the General Agreement undercuts its general prohibition of quantitative restrictions with three major exceptions. The most important exception is that quantitative restrictions may be maintained for balance-of-payments purposes (Articles XII–XV). The second is that quantitative restrictions may be used in support of certain domestic agricultural programs, particularly those which, by raising domestic prices above the world market price, tend to create an incentive for importation (provided that domestic production or marketing is similarly limited) (Article XI). And the third is that less-developed countries are permitted under certain circumstances to impose quantitative restrictions in furtherance of their economic development programs or in response to foreign exchange problems attributable to their peculiar status (Article XVIII).

The General Agreement also deals with barriers to the free flow of international commerce that operate on the export, rather than the import, side of the transaction. Here the philosophy of immediate prohibition is generally operative (Article XI). But the export equivalent of the tariff—that is, the export subsidy—is treated differently from the tariff. Export subsidies of primary products are subject to special rules designed to prevent one country from obtaining an undue proportion of world trade, and other forms of export subsidies are subject to more stringent limitations (Article XVI).

## The Procedural and Institutional Framework

The commercial policy provisions of the Havana Charter came to the General Agreement stripped of the procedural and institutional framework of the ITO. The General Agreement has, however, a number of articles of a nonsubstantive character. They are largely limited to provisions that were thought necessary in 1948 for the General Agreement to function as a continuing multilateral agreement, and do not include ones that might have been inserted if it had been contemplated that the General Agreement would become the founding document of an international organization.

On the procedural level, aside from the special consultation procedures that accompany certain substantive provisions and aside from the provisions on tariff negotiations, the General Agreement contains a general provision on consultation and another on "Nullification or Impairment" (Articles XXII and XXIII). The latter provision constitutes the heart of the GATT remedies section and characterizes the decentralized nature of the GATT system. A violation of the General Agreement—for example, the nullification of a concession—leads not to the imposition of punitive measures, but rather to the creation of a mere right on the part of injured contracting parties to withdraw concessions (or other GATT obligations) running to the offending contracting party. This remedy underscores the basic principles that the General Agreement is to represent for each contracting party a balance of advantages and that, in the crucial area of tariffs, concessions need be made only in return for equivalent reciprocal concessions.

On the organizational level, one finds in the General Agreement no provision for a secretariat or for any subsidiary organs. The only recognized body consists of representatives of the contracting parties. An editorial device permits, however, a distinction between the contracting parties acting jointly and those parties acting merely in their individual capacities: the former are mandatorily referred to as the (upper case) "CONTRACTING PARTIES" (Article XXV).

The General Agreement also includes a number of organizational provisions of the kind that one might find in either a long-term agreement or a founding document; these provisions cover such matters as amendments, withdrawal, and accession (Articles XXX, XXXI, and XXXIII). Also included is a less common kind of provision permitting individual contracting parties to refrain from applying the General Agreement in their dealings with particular acceding contracting parties (Article XXXV). A system of provisional accession has developed outside the framework of the actual provisions of the General Agreement.

## The Addition of Part IV

Most of the provisions described above were found in the original General Agreement. Some were added in revisions, notably those that followed the Havana Conference and a major review of the General Agreement in 1955. The mid-1960s saw, however, the addition of a new class of provisions, reflecting partly a surge of interest in the trade problems of less-developed countries and partly institutional competition stemming from the 1964 United Nations Conference on Trade and Development.

These provisions, constituting a new Part IV, do not change the content of the first three parts in any decisive way. Nevertheless, they reflect a more active, less prohibition-oriented approach to the problem of reducing barriers to trade, and they alter the central notion that tariff concessions are to be products of arm's-length bargaining. Less-developed countries are no longer to be required to offer "reciprocity" in tariff negotiations with developed countries. And with respect to items of export interest to less-developed countries, developed countries are to accord high priority not only to the elimination of nontariff barriers, but also to the reduction of tariffs (Article XXXIII).

# PART 2

**The Technical Arrangements: Tariffs**

# 4 The GATT Tariff System

The General Agreement draws a fundamental distinction between tariffs and other forms of restrictions. Tariffs (and related charges) are the sole form of trade restrictions that are not considered incompatible with the GATT system. All the other forms are, as a matter of principle, to be eliminated forthwith. To be sure, there are many minor exceptions with respect to nontariff restrictions, and in addition there are certain grounds on which a contracting party may continue to impose certain types of barriers temporarily. The balance-of-payments dispensation for quantitative restrictions is the leading example. But for tariffs the legal situation is the reverse. Nothing in the General Agreement requires any contracting party to take a single step in the direction of reducing tariffs.

Since the GATT system for tariffs differs radically from the GATT system for nontariff measures, tariffs will be examined in detail first. After an introductory exploration, in this chapter, of the GATT tariff system, tariff conferences and nontariff barriers will be examined in succeeding chapters.

## The Special Status of Tariffs

Since nothing in the General Agreement prevents a contracting party from increasing existing tariffs or introducing tariffs on currently duty-free items, any such limitation upon the liberty with respect to tariff items must come from a special agreement. Such a special agreement is called, in GATT jargon, the "binding" of a duty rate.

The intent of the CONTRACTING PARTIES to reduce tariffs through tariff concessions, particularly in rounds of tariff negotiations, is clear. While other barriers are in principle to be abolished forthwith, once and for all, the reduction of tariffs remains a goal to be accomplished over time through mutually advantageous agreements among particular contracting parties, with complete elimination more of a distant glimmer than a goal. The goal of tariff reduction

25

did not appear so clearly in the terms of the original General Agreement as it now does as a consequence of amendments resulting from the 1955 Review Conference. The original lacunae resulted from the circumstances of the drafting of the General Agreement. It was to be merely the first of a series of multilateral trade agreements entered into under the auspices of the International Trade Organization. The ITO Charter provided that "[e]ach Member shall, upon the request of any other Member or Members . . . enter into and carry out . . . negotiations directed to the substantial reduction of the general levels of tariffs and other charges on imports and exports . . . on a reciprocal and mutually advantageous basis."[1]

As a consequence of the addition of Article XXVIII bis to the General Agreement at the 1955 Review Conference, similar language now appears in the General Agreement itself. The new language is, however, both clearer on the longer-term goal and less binding. A contracting party, unlike an ITO member, is not required to "enter into and carry out [tariff] . . . negotiations." On the other hand, there is a fairly straightforward statement of intention:

> The contracting parties recognize that customs duties often constitute serious obstacles to trade; thus negotiations on a reciprocal and mutually advantageous basis, directed to the substantial reduction of the general level of tariffs and other charges on imports and exports and in particular to the reduction of such high tariffs as discourage the importation even of minimum quantities, and conducted with due regard to the objectives of this Agreement and the varying needs of individual contracting parties, are of great importance to the expansion of international trade.

To that end, the CONTRACTING PARTIES are empowered to sponsor such negotiations from time to time.

In attempting to explain and justify the grounds for this distinctive treatment of trade barriers that take the form of duties and charges, one encounters a mélange of historical accident, pragmatic judgment, and myth. To the extent that tariff reduction is coupled with most-favored-nation treatment (as has been the case more often in theory than in practice during the lifetime of the GATT), one can isolate a few economic principles that may partially justify that difference in treatment. But economics does not provide the real explanation for the differential treatment. First of all, simple tradition was important in favoring tariffs. Tariffs evoked the golden days before World War I when tariffs were the principal protective device. Other barriers, such as quantitative restrictions, reminded the draftsmen of the gloomy interwar period and were considered by Cordell Hull and his intellectual disciples to have been contributory causes of World War II.

Second, pragmatic considerations played their part. It was clear that there was not the slightest chance that the community of nations would agree to the

1. Havana Charter, Art. 17:1.

outright abolition of tariffs. The same was true of many other barriers, but there were devices available for agreeing in principle to abolition while continuing the barriers in practice; the balance-of-payments exception on quantitative restrictions is the most notable example. Balance-of-payments problems, to consider the example a little more deeply, could be related to quantitative restrictions. Those restrictions had tended to grow out of balance-of-payments difficulties in the interwar period, even though they had come in many cases to be used for protectionist purposes. By contrast, tariffs had always been used primarily for protectionist (or revenue) purposes. The device of the empty agreement was therefore not so easily available for tariffs as for quantitative restrictions.

Third, it was generally thought that tariffs alone lent themselves to reduction through negotiations. The draftsmen believed that tariffs of particular countries on particular items could be equated and that they could therefore be reduced through mutually advantageous bargains. Other barriers were viewed as more difficult to equate in a bargaining situation and therefore more difficult to reduce over time in bargaining rounds. Experience tends to bear out the wisdom of this view as to the "bargainability" of various barriers. Nevertheless, as we shall see later, the GATT has largely limited negotiations, at least until the Kennedy Round, to tariffs, and there have never been concerted attempts to devise comparable negotiation procedures for nontariff barriers. Even more important, the notion that tariffs lend themselves especially well to reduction through negotiations is to be attributed partially to the rather naïve fashion in which tariff reductions tend to be measured. By unwritten agreement, tariff reductions have tended to be measured by the amount of existing trade covered by the tariff item and the extent to which the percentage duty is reduced, rather than by that which is economically more important: namely, the extent to which the existing duty, by protecting domestic industry, forecloses potential imports, and a given change from one percentage rate to another tends to reduce that protective effect. It is not clear that this reduction of protective effect cannot be equally well measured, or equally poorly measured (to speak frankly), in the case of nontariff barriers. The use of negotiations to attempt to reduce nontariff barriers was undertaken, in a limited degree, in the Kennedy Round, and will be discussed later in that context.

## Tariff Structure

Not only does the General Agreement fail to impose any limitation on the level of the tariffs, but it also fails to impose any limitation on their structure—that is to say, on the relationships among various levels of duties on various tariff items of a single country's schedule. On the plane of pure principle this lacuna is curious, even though regulation of the structure of tariffs was probably never seriously considered by anyone connected with the drafting of the General

Agreement or the Havana Charter. But the wide diversity of tariff levels in particular countries contrasts oddly with the condemnation of multiple exchange rates that one finds enshrined in the Articles of Agreement of the International Monetary Fund, a condemnation indirectly ratified by the General Agreement in its requirement in Article XV that contracting parties join the IMF or enter into an exchange arrangement with the CONTRACTING PARTIES. The IMF condemnation is further confirmed in the General Agreement by the suggestion in the interpretative notes that multiple exchange rates may constitute a subsidy[2] or involve a violation of the fees and formalities provisions of Article VIII.[3] But the impact on trade may be quite as dramatic in a structure of tariffs in which some items enter duty-free and others are subject to very high tariffs as in the case where the same price relationship between the two kinds of items measured in the importing country's currency is established by means of multiple exchange rates. Furthermore, tariffs on imports coupled with the absence of export duties, or indeed with a subsidy conforming to Article XVI, are analogous to multiple exchange rates with differential rates for import and export transactions. To be sure, tariffs cover only imports of goods on current account and not other parts of the spectrum of international transactions influenced by exchange rates, such as invisible or capital transactions. But it is precisely in the area of current imports of goods that multiple exchange rates have been used to achieve what are essentially commercial-policy objectives.

The range of differences in the tariff structures of particular countries can be quite considerable. Even after the first three rounds of GATT tariff negotiations, some 8 percent of U.S. imports involved duties over 30 percent (ad valorem or equivalent), while about 50 percent involved duties of 10 percent or less. Since higher duties tend, on the whole, to restrict trade more than lower duties, these statistics tend to underestimate the burden that higher rates impose upon trade. And where tariffs are prohibitive in their level, the statistics tend to ignore them. After the first three rounds of tariff reductions, a substantial number of items (amounting however to only $500,000 of imports) were subject to duties of more than 90 percent; there is no sure way of knowing how important those ultrahigh-duty items may have been in their effect on trade.[4] It is clear, nevertheless, that the United States imposed a system in which importers of some items were able to pay at the official exchange rate, the items being duty-free, while other importers had to pay varying surcharges in the form of tariff duties that were sometimes 90 percent or more above the official exchange rate. The point is not, of course, that differential tariffs are the same

2. Interpretative note, Ad Art. VI, paras. 2–3 (note 2).
3. Interpretative note, Ad Art. VIII, para. 1.
4. U.S. Tariff Commission, *Operation of the Trade Agreements Program*, 5th Rep. (1952), p. 106.

as multiple exchange rates. Multiple exchange rates involve a number of problems, particularly of an administrative character (for example, the understating of receipts by exporters) not involved in differential tariffs. Nevertheless, the complete inattention in the General Agreement to tariff structures reflects a tendency to approach trade problems piecemeal, a tendency no doubt fully justified by the bargaining considerations and the historical context that shaped the Agreement.

The freedom granted contracting parties to raise tariffs so long as those tariffs have not been specially bound in tariff negotiations also contrasts with the prevailing dogma that exchange rates are to be fixed once for all. In fact, exchange rates are, to use the current expression, subject to the system of the "adjustable peg," which means that they are pegged at a certain level, but the level is adjusted from time to time by devaluations and, more rarely, by revaluations. Under this dogma exchange rates are not to be varied except in extraordinary situations where, for "structural" reasons, there is no hope of returning to equilibrium at existing exchange rates. Influenced by these rules of the international monetary system, governments have turned increasingly in recent years to imposing tariff surcharges that involve across-the-board increases of most if not all tariffs by a certain ad valorem percentage. Such surcharges differ from devaluations mainly insofar as they do not involve exports or invisible or capital transactions. Import surcharges are preferred to quantitative restrictions by the countries facing payments imbalances because they are thought to have a less distorting effect on trade and to be easier to administer than direct controls. Interestingly enough, balance-of-payments difficulties that would be sufficient to justify quantitative restrictions are not a justification for tariff surcharges to the extent that any of the items subject to the surcharge have been bound in GATT tariff negotiations.

Since in practice no country can accede to the General Agreement without making certain tariff concessions, all tariff surcharges are subject to review by the CONTRACTING PARTIES; and inasmuch as there is nothing in the treaty that can be used to justify such surcharges, a waiver by the CONTRACTING PARTIES, or no action at all, is the inevitable outcome. In recent years Ceylon, Chile, Peru, and Uruguay have secured waivers, under Article XXV, of the obligation under Article II:1 not to raise duties above bound rates.[5]

As we shall see, Canada and the United Kingdom were able to maintain their surcharges in flagrant violation of Article II:1 without the benefit of a waiver, although both had to undergo rather probing consultations.[6] To some

5. The CONTRACTING PARTIES to the General Agreement on Tariffs and Trade, *Basic Instruments and Selected Documents* (hereafter cited as *Basic Instruments*). Ceylon: 14th Supp. (1966), p. 31; 11th Supp. (1963), p. 60; 10th Supp. (1962), p. 35. Chile: 8th Supp. (1960), p. 29. Peru: ibid., p. 56; 7th Supp. (1959), p. 37. Uruguay: 10th Supp. (1962), p. 51.
6. On Canada, see ibid., 11th Supp. (1963), p. 57.

degree the GATT has recognized the relationship between tariff surcharges and devaluations by making the informal approval of surcharges by the IMF a prior condition of a waiver (although the source of the IMF-approval requirement is no doubt the analogous IMF role in passing on the balance-of-payments need for quantitative restrictions). And by requiring annual reviews of the status of the surcharges, the General Agreement has perhaps had a marginal influence over their use. Nevertheless, it may be said in general that parties using tariff surcharges have not found the GATT an impediment and have moreover been able to escape from the kind of retaliation that would normally flow, under Article XXIII, from a less generalized increase in duties.

The failure of the General Agreement to deal with either tariff levels or tariff structures outside the context of special agreements among particular contracting parties to bind certain rates is not surprising. The considerations that led to treating tariffs as fundamentally different from other barriers to trade also led the draftsmen of the General Agreement to take a hands-off attitude toward the general tariff policy of contracting parties. The fundamental decision was to leave the level of tariffs to the contracting parties' own discretion, but also to encourage reduction through mutually advantageous tariff agreements and to stipulate that tariffs be applied in a nondiscriminatory fashion under the most-favored-nation clause.

**Technical Provisions on Tariffs**

Since the General Agreement relies on specific agreements among contracting parties to reduce particular tariffs rather than on a general condemnation of tariffs, the technical provisions of the General Agreement with respect to the form of the agreements, remedies against nonperformance, possibilities of suspending tariff concessions previously made, and the like take on considerable importance. In an important sense they constitute the heart of the General Agreement. In part this is due to the historical circumstance that the General Agreement was originally, before the demise of the ITO, merely a trade agreement setting forth the results of the first round of tariff negotiations, determining the legal content of the concessions made, and, in its Part II, assuring that nontariff barriers would not undercut the tariff concessions made.

## Bindings

The basic concept in the GATT tariff negotiating system is the "binding" of customs duties on particular items in the tariff schedules of individual contracting parties. Interestingly enough, the terms "binding" and "bound" do not appear in the General Agreement. But the need to have a central term for this basic concept has led to the almost universal use of "binding." This term is used interchangeably with "tariff concession."

A given rate of customs duty on a particular item is "bound" when an agreement has been reached with respect to it. Basically there are three types of bindings: (1) agreements to lower a duty to a stated level; (2) agreements not to raise a duty above its present level; and (3) agreements not to raise a duty above a specified higher level. (The term "binding" is sometimes reserved for the last two categories, but the more inclusive usage will be followed here.) But there are also other possible forms of bindings. The most common are agreements to convert a particular specific duty to an ad valorem duty. The ad valorem rate is thereby bound, and, assuming that the new ad valorem rate is considered by the parties to have approximately the same protective effect as the former specific duty, this form of agreement can be assimilated to the second category.

The foregoing three-part classification is not quite the empty exercise in categorization that it might appear. A fair number of disagreements have arisen and a number of pronouncements have been made on how far, for example, an agreement not to raise a given duty should be considered adequate compensation for a negotiating partner's agreement to lower another given duty. Nevertheless as we shall see later in the discussion of tariff conferences, the negotiating character of the binding of tariff items tends to make such pronouncements pointless and to render the three-part classification of little practical value.

## Schedules

Bound rates are included in a schedule, which under Article II:7 becomes an integral part of the General Agreement. There is in theory one GATT schedule for each contracting party (for example, Schedule XX for the United States). In practice there is a separate schedule for each contracting party after each major round of tariff negotiations, and from time to time these separate schedules are consolidated for each contracting party. The GATT Schedules are to be distinguished from national tariff schedules. The former set forth only bindings. The fundamental obligation with respect to a bound duty is, of course, not to raise it beyond the level agreed upon. It was early established that contracting parties are free to reduce tariffs below the bound rate. A decision of the CONTRACTING PARTIES adopting that rule in the course of dealing with a related problem thereby rejected a formalistic view that incorporation of a binding in a schedule which was an integral part of the General Agreement meant that the specified rate had to be applied unless the schedule was unanimously amended pursuant to the amendment provisions of Article XXX.[7] The bindings are, it is true, an integral part of the General Agreement, but they are

---

7. Ibid., Vol. II (1952), p. 11. The decision was specifically that a margin of preference on an item included in a schedule is not bound against decrease.

to be interpreted as maximum, and not minimum, rates. This interpretation is supported by the language of Article II:1, requiring that products subject to tariff concessions be exempt from "ordinary customs duties in excess of those set forth and provided for" in the Schedules.

A bound duty may not be increased above the level bound even where it can be demonstrated that no increase in protection would result; an example of such a situation would be the replacement of an existing quantitative restriction (which if used for balance-of-payments purposes may well have been lawfully imposed) by a tariff increase.[8] Nor may a bound duty be raised as part of an across-the-board increase, however temporary.[9]

## Tariff Surcharges

The principle that a bound duty may not be raised as a part of an across-the-board increase is subject to a major limitation in practice. As has been seen, temporary import surcharges imposed for balance-of-payments purposes, although clearly unlawful, have been tolerated by the GATT. In recent years both Canada and the United Kingdom have been able to impose substantial import surcharges without benefit of a waiver. In the Canadian case the CONTRACTING PARTIES recognized that the surcharges were "inconsistent" with Article II and recommended that they be "eliminated expeditiously." Canada was "requested" to report subsequently on the action taken.[10] In the case of the U.K. 15 percent ad valorem surcharges, a decision was never reached by the CONTRACTING PARTIES in plenary session. Although the United Kingdom reported the surcharges to the GATT, the discussion was confined largely to reviews of the situation by a working party.

The increasing preference for import surcharges over quantitative restrictions as a technique for dealing with balance-of-payments problems, particularly where the imbalance is viewed as temporary, casts doubt on the rationality of the General Agreement distinction that permits the quantitative restrictions but purports to prohibit absolutely the surcharges. The reactions of the GATT to import surcharges imposed in recent years, particularly by Canada and the United Kingdom, is an implicit rejection of that distinction. Aside from the failure of the CONTRACTING PARTIES to take concerted action with respect to Canadian and U.K. surcharges, individual contracting parties do not appear to have withdrawn concessions in retaliation against the surcharges, as they would have been permitted to do under Article XXIII.[11]

---

8. Ibid., 7th Supp. (1959), p. 37 (Peruvian Import Charges); ibid., 3d Supp. (1955), p. 26 (French Special Temporary Compensation Tax on Imports).
9. Ibid., 7th Supp. (1959), p. 37 (Peruvian Import Charges).
10. Ibid., 11th Supp. (1963), p. 57.
11. The right to withdraw concessions under Article XXIII was specifically recog-

A veiled suggestion that the OECD countries are dissatisfied with the GATT distinction is to be found in the recent Report of Working Party No. 3 of the Economic Policy Committee on the Balance of Payments Adjustment Process, a report which was hailed in the press as a cornerstone of international economic cooperation on a par with the General Agreement. After indicating that both forms of barriers have not only the vice of restricting trade, but also that of "imped[ing] the re-establishment of a more balanced demand and/or competitive position in the country concerned," the Working Party continued in the bland language that characterizes the report:

> The type of measures authorized under international agreements as appropriate for dealing with balance of payments difficulties is the imposition of quantitative restrictions. In some cases, however, countries have seen advantages in resorting, as an alternative, to the temporary imposition of surcharges on imports. Further consideration might need to be given to the relative disadvantages of these methods and to the appropriate safeguards governing their use in differing circumstances.[12]

A consideration of the nature of surcharges and quantitative restrictions tends to confirm the OECD view that there is no a priori basis for preferring quantitative restrictions to surcharges. Across-the-board surcharges leave the source of imports to the interplay of market forces, whereas quantitative restrictions, even under a global quota, require some kind of administrative determination that may in practice result in discrimination on the basis of origin. Even if quantitative restrictions are administered in a way that forecloses any discrimination on the basis of nationality (through, for example, a first-come, first-served basis for allocating licenses), they are much more likely than tariff surcharges to discriminate against low-cost sources of foreign supply in favor of high-cost sources of foreign supply and thereby undercut the efficiency goal of international trade.

It should be noted that the argument for surcharges in place of quantitative restrictions as devices for combating payments imbalances is quite similar to the argument for tariffs rather than quantitative restrictions as the principal instrument of commercial policy. The General Agreement is thus in a sense internally inconsistent. While preferring tariffs to quantitative restrictions in principle, it has preferred quantitative restrictions to tariffs in the case of the dominant cause of trade restrictions in the postwar period. The principal argument for quantitative restrictions over surcharges—that the former can be used more selectively and thus restrict a smaller volume of trade—is hardly a suffi-

---

nized by the CONTRACTING PARTIES in the Canadian case (ibid., 11th Supp. [1963], p. 57).

12. Working Party No. 3 of the Economic Policy Committee of the Organization for Economic Co-operation and Development, *The Balance of Payments Adjustment Process* (1966), p. 24.

cient basis for reversing the traditional GATT preference for tariffs over quantitative restrictions. At most, such an argument tends to lead one to prefer selective import surcharges—which were in fact what Canada used—to across-the-board surcharges.

## Rectifications or Modifications

The binding of a duty precludes not only direct measures to increase the rate of duty above the bound level, but also any indirect measures that may tend to have the same effect. Indirect measures may be thought of for convenience under two headings: (1) measures involving tariff schedules; and (2) measures involving nontariff matters. As to the former category, the General Agreement says only that bound items are to "be exempt from ordinary customs duties in excess of those set forth and provided for" in the GATT schedule in question. The problem of interpretation of this language is to distinguish those adjustments to a contracting party's national tariff schedule that are purely formal in character and therefore do not tend to undercut the implicit guarantee to foreign suppliers involved in a binding, from those adjustments that, even if attributable to purely administrative considerations, tend to undercut that implicit guarantee.

To forbid all changes of whatever character in national tariff schedules once the item in question appeared in a GATT schedule would tend to paralyze the administration of national tariffs. Changes of nomenclature, for example, are necessary to keep tariff administration up to date with changes in technology and commercial practice. So long as nothing more than nomenclature is changed, the substance of the international agreement that the binding represents is not undercut. Similarly, changes in nomenclature that tend to standardize usage among countries, such as adoption of the so-called Brussels nomenclature, should be welcomed insofar as the effect is not to increase protection. In order to permit these and other minor changes in schedules without the necessity of the involved negotiations that, as we shall see, are required when bound duties are increased above the level bound, the CONTRACTING PARTIES have adopted differential procedures for those schedule changes that are called rectifications (or "rectifications of a purely formal character") and those that are called modifications. Where a rectification is involved, the GATT schedule in question may be amended without the necessity of consulting with the contracting party that originally negotiated the binding or with any other party. Modifications to the GATT schedule, on the other hand, may only be made after the appropriate negotiations specified by the General Agreement have been carried out.[13] However, since changes in nomenclature may be used to

13. For the procedures on certifications relating to rectification and modification, see *Basic Instruments,* 12th Supp. (1964), pp. 20, 22; 8th Supp. (1960), p. 24.

disguise increases in rates, a contracting party does not have carte blanche to make changes without going through GATT channels. Under the procedure adopted in the Turkish case, the revised nomenclature must be distributed to the contracting parties, and, in the event that any objection is lodged, consultations with the objecting government must be undertaken.[14]

Most updating of tariff schedules, even if consisting mainly in changes of nomenclature, also involves changes in rates of duty. Even purely technical changes often cause certain kinds of products to fall into different classifications and consequently to become dutiable at higher or lower rates than before. Even if the lower rates cancel out the higher rates on the whole, they are not likely to do so for each affected contracting party.

In any event, the General Agreement does not provide for such equilibrating changes without negotiations; on the contrary, Article XXVIII, as will be seen later, is specifically designed to serve as a framework for those changes of rates on bound items that "endeavour to maintain a general level of reciprocal and mutually advantageous concessions not less favourable to trade than that provided . . . prior to such negotiations." The negotiations under Article XXVIII resulting from technical changes can often be complex and time-consuming. Negotiations lasting a number of years resulted from the U.S. Tariff Classification Act of 1962, which was a technical revision of the U.S. customs system designed to establish "a more logical arrangement and terminology better adapted to present-day trade, to the elimination of classification anomalies, and to simplification of the determination and application of tariff classifications."[15] Because the delay involved in completing negotiations is often incommensurate with the injury to affected contracting parties, the CONTRACTING PARTIES have rather freely granted waivers to permit the implementation of technical changes in national tariff schedules before Article XXVIII negotiations have been completed.[16]

### Specific Duties

Specific duties have given rise to special problems in connection with technical

---

14. Ibid., 3d Supp. (1955), p. 127.
15. Ibid., 12th Supp. (1964), p. 57.
16. *Basic Instruments.* Greece: 8th Supp. (1960), p. 51. New Zealand: 9th Supp. (1961), p. 42; 6th Supp. (1958), p. 34. Turkey: 9th Supp. (1961), p. 49. United States: 12th Supp. (1964), p. 57. Since a change in a GATT schedule is an amendment of Part I of the General Agreement, unanimous acceptance is required by Article XXX. For a reflection of the dissatisfaction with the delays that have been incurred in securing unanimity, see *Basic Instruments,* 15th Supp. (1968), p. 57. A procedure will probably be worked out for putting rectifications and modifications into effect automatically within thirty days of a decision of the CONTRACTING PARTIES if no objection is filed. See GATT Document L/2975 (Feb. 19, 1968).

changes. The two principal difficulties have involved the upward revision of specific duties in times of inflation and the conversion of specific duties into ad valorem duties. As an importing country's prices rise, specific duties, being by definition calculated in terms of a certain amount of local currency per physical unit of imports, tend to lose their protective value (and also their revenue-yielding capacity in real terms). An upward revision to keep pace with inflation would not therefore usually increase their protective effect.

The General Agreement contains a special provision, Article II:6, granting a limited power of revision of bound specific duties. The fundamental limitation of this provision is that the power may be exercised only if there has been a devaluation of the local currency of at least 20 percent, measured in terms of the change in the par value accepted or provisionally recognized by the International Monetary Fund. Thus, inflation will not always justify an increase in specific duties on bound items; rather, the inflation must result in a devaluation of not less than the prescribed percentage. The requisite reduction in par value must, however, be carried out consistently with the Articles of Agreement of the International Monetary Fund. But even assuming compliance with the foregoing requirements concerning the nature of the devaluation, the CONTRACTING PARTIES must still decide (by a majority vote under Article XXV) that such adjustments "will not impair the value of the concessions provided for the appropriate Schedule [i.e., tariff bindings] or elsewhere in this Agreement, due account being taken of all factors which may influence the need for, or urgency of, such adjustments."

The imposition of this further requirement gives rise to two questions about the drafting of the General Agreement. The first is why a devaluation should be a prerequisite to revision of specific duties if the CONTRACTING PARTIES are satisfied that the revision in question does not impair any concessions. The answer would appear to be that a majority vote is not considered an adequate safeguard.

The second question is why a 20 percent devaluation is made the decisive element, given the tendency of such a requirement to exclude a number of upward revisions of specific duties which would be necessary to preserve the duties' protective effect. The 20 percent devaluation requirement might exclude apparently justified upward revisions either where the devaluation is of less than 20 percent or where, as is not uncommon, the country in question has chosen to try to live with an overvalued currency rather than resort to devaluation. One can surmise that the 20 percent devaluation requirement is a device for discouraging upward revisions of specific duties, given the danger that they may result, even unintentionally, in increasing levels of protection.

A more subtle point, however, concerns the comparative methods of calculating specific and ad valorem duties. If a country applying specific duties to certain items and seeking to increase those duties had previously taxed the items by means of ad valorem duties, the increase in price levels measured in terms of the local currency would not have permitted an increase in the amount of the duties collected (measured in units of local currency) in the absence of inflation in the countries of origin of the items. Or to put the point another way, even an ad valorem tariff normally fails to maintain its protective effect when prices in the importing country inflate more rapidly than prices in the exporting country and there is no change in the relationship between the official values of the two countries' currencies. The inflexibility of the ad valorem tariff in such a situation results from the fact that, pursuant to the "actual value" provisions of Article VII, the base for the assessment of ad valorem duties is normally a price in the foreign currency, which price is converted to local currency in accordance with the terms of Article VII:4 at a rate of exchange recognized by the IMF. To permit an upward valuation of specific duties in the absence of a devaluation would thus normally be to favor specific duties over ad valorem duties, a favoritism that not only would be unjustified by any special characteristics of specific duties, but also would run counter to the general trend toward use of ad valorem duties in the contemporary world.

The question remains, however, why a devaluation should have to be not less than 20 percent to justify upward revision of specific duties. After all, a 10 percent devaluation, assuming it reflected changes in relative price levels, would in principle coincide with a proportional diminution of the protective effect of a specific duty. Here one seems to detect the twin policies of avoiding too frequent revisions of specific duties and of discouraging the general use of specific duties.

### Fixed Official Values

A special variant of the upward revision problem arises where the duties in question are ad valorem in form but specific in substance. Some countries have adopted tariffs that are stated in percentages rather than in units of currency, but in which the base is a fixed value determined in advance by legislation or regulation rather than a flexible value computed in the manner prescribed by Article VII. Since the duty payable (measured in local currency) per unit of goods imported does not vary with the actual value of the goods, this kind of duty is in substance a specific duty and as such tends to lose its protective effect in times of inflation. Readjustments of such duties are usually accomplished through an upward revision of the official base rather than through an increase of the ad valorem rate, although in principle either kind of revision could be used to maintain the protective effect. Mixed duties of this character would appear to be inconsistent with the proscription in Article VII of assessment based "on arbitrary or fictitious values." The CONTRACTING PARTIES have nevertheless granted waivers to upward revisions of the official values in certain cases. The inconsistency with Article VII is of less consequence, it should be noted, so long as Part II of the General Agreement is only provisionally applicable. Under the Protocol of Provisional Application, Article VII is applicable only "to the fullest extent not inconsistent with existing legislation."[17] In any event, the CONTRACTING PARTIES have on two different occasions specifically authorized Uruguay to increase the *aforos,* or fixed values, in the Uruguayan Schedule to the General Agreement, although not to the full extent of the 763 percent increase in the number of pesos per U.S. dollar which had occurred in the official exchange rate.[18]

## Conversion of Specific to Ad Valorem Duties

A different kind of problem associated with specific duties involves the conversion of specific duties to ad valorem duties, a process that has become a common element of tariff reform because of increasing recognition of the inadequacies of specific duty systems, particularly in times of inflation. The conversion is usually intended to establish an ad valorem rate equal in protective effect to the specific duty replaced. Insofar as the conversion accomplishes this result, it need not impair—as a matter of economic fact—the value of a concession. Nevertheless, the position followed in these cases has been that "there is no provision in the General Agreement which authorizes a contracting party to alter the structure of bound rates of duty from a specific to an ad valorem basis" and therefore that such a conversion requires negotiations under Article XXVIII.[19] This position is somewhat strange because there is nothing in Article II that would require the duties incorporated in the GATT schedule to be applied as such. Article II requires only that bound items "be exempt from ordinary customs duties in excess of those set forth and provided for therein." The official position seems justified, however, because the conversion of specific to ad valorem duties carries with it a sufficient risk of increased protection, or at least creates a sufficient risk of a dispute over whether protection was increased, that it is not unreasonable to place the burden of undertaking negotiations upon the party electing to make such a change in its national tariff schedules rather than upon the contracting party finding itself injured thereby.

The risk of a dispute is increased by the circumstance that for many items any conversion is bound to be somewhat arbitrary. Wherever goods falling within a given specific duty classification vary in value, the corresponding ad

---

17. See discussion in chapter 19, on "The GATT as an International Organization," infra.
18. *Basic Instruments,* 13th Supp. (1965), p. 20; 10th Supp. (1962), p. 34.
19. Ibid., 3d Supp. (1955), p. 127, 128. See also 7th Supp. (1959), p. 112.

valorem duty varies with the value of the imported goods. If, for example, a specific duty classification system imposes a $1 duty on certain kinds of goods, some of which have a value of $4, some $5, and some $6, the corresponding ad valorem rates range from 25 percent through 20 percent to 16.7 percent. In making the conversion, a single ad valorem percentage must be chosen for the classification as a whole. If any rate higher than 16.7 percent is chosen, those countries that are the source of the high value goods will consider that the effective rate of duty on their goods has been increased. To the importing country any rate of duty below 25 percent will tend to reduce the effective rate of protection on low value goods, and any rate of duty at the lower end of the 16.7 percent–25 percent range may tend to reduce total revenue from the duties.

Aside from the inherent arbitrariness of any conversion, there is also the possibility that a particular conversion may be a veiled attempt to adjust the effective rate of protection to a level that the specific duties provided, not on the date of conversion, but rather at some earlier time. This risk arises from the difficulty of making specific duties keep pace with inflation, a difficulty that is a principal source of dissatisfaction with specific duties. An attempt to revise the specific duties upward indirectly in the process of converting to ad valorem duties may occur where a direct upward revision of specific duties would be impossible for want of a 20 percent devaluation. Alternatively, it may occur where a direct revision would be possible but a veiled upward revision in the course of conversion is seen as an easier or otherwise more desirable alternative.

### Miscellaneous Technical Provisions

Among the other kinds of indirect increases in protection on bound items that are prohibited by Article II are changes in the "method of determining dutiable value" and changes in the "method . . . of converting currencies" (Article II:3). Either technique, if permitted, could obviously have a drastic effect on the value of concessions previously granted. Both prohibitions are closely related to the provisions of Article VII, which limit the methods of valuation and of exchange conversion that contracting parties may choose. The question of exchange conversion is also related to the provision of Article XV:9(a), which states that "nothing in this Agreement shall preclude . . . the use by a contracting party of exchange controls or exchange restrictions in accordance with the Articles of Agreement of the International Monetary Fund or with that contracting party's special exchange agreement with the CONTRACTING PARTIES." Changes in methods of converting currencies that take the form of exchange controls or exchange restrictions and are authorized by the Fund Agreement or by a special exchange agreement with the CONTRACTING PARTIES are thus exempted from the provisions of Article II:3. This would apparently be true even if the effect of a change in conversion methods would be to "frustrate the intent of the provisions of [the General] Agreement" under Article XV:4.[20]

## Internal Taxation on Bound Items

In addition to being free from customs duties "in excess of" those set forth in the GATT schedules, bound items are to be "exempt from all other duties or charges of any kind imposed on or in connection with importation in excess of those imposed on the date of [the General] Agreement or those directly and mandatorily required to be imposed thereafter by legislation in force in the importing territory on that date" (Article II:1). This provision constitutes a recognition of the obvious fact that a tariff is just one kind of tax and what matters to the exporter is the level of taxes in the importing country (particularly in relation to the level of taxes borne by competing domestic products in the importing country), whether or not those taxes are denominated tariffs. A binding of tariffs would be meaningless if other forms of taxation on imports could be varied at will. In order to deal with this problem, the General Agreement imposes, through the language set out above, a standstill on further taxation on bound items. The provision that other duties or charges that were not imposed on the date of the General Agreement may be imposed thereafter only if such imposition is "directly and mandatorily required . . . by legislation in force . . . on that date" is intended to limit the discretion of administrative authorities operating under broad delegations of authority from their legislatures. Unless legislation places a duty on the administrative authorities to impose a particular duty or charge, there may be no such imposition under the standstill provision.

The reference to "other duties and charges" is intended to be "all-inclusive." That was the understanding at the Review Session when it was decided to amend Article II to add the language, "including charges of any kind imposed on the international transfer of payments for imports."[21] The technique used by the Review Session Working Party to give effect to this general understanding of the "all-inclusive" character of the provision (that is to say, the specific reference to one kind of charge) is an exceptionally clumsy method of drafting, but the views of this Working Party are presumably entitled to considerable weight. It should be noted that the Working Party also indicated that " 'charges of any kind' do *not* include ordinary commercial charges for effect-

20. See generally Ervin Hexner, "The General Agreement on Tariffs and Trade and the Monetary Fund," *International Monetary Fund Staff Papers,* I (1951), pp. 432, 452–59.
21. *Protocol Amending Part I and Articles XXIX and XXX,* § C(b) (i); *Basic Instruments,* 3d Supp. (1955), p. 209. The entire Protocol was, however, subsequently abandoned for want of unanimous acceptance (15th Supp. [1968], p. 65).

ing the international transfer of payments for imports."[22] Since these commercial charges are imposed by nongovernmental parties, the question should no more arise than it would in the case of any other private charges, such as those made by private customs brokers, because the General Agreement is directed at action by states, not individuals. That some confusion might remain on this fundamental jurisdictional point is suggested, however, both by the refusal of the majority of the Group of Experts on Restrictive Business Practices to take a position on the question whether the "nullification and impairment" provisions of Article XXIII can apply to action by private cartels[23] and by the opinion uttered by the minority of that group that those provisions of Article XXIII are applicable.[24] In any event, the appropriate interpretation of the language concerning "other duties or charges of any kind" would appear to be that it applies to all governmental impositions, subject of course to the general exception (already discussed) of Article XV:9(a) concerning "exchange controls or exchange restrictions" consistent with the IMF Articles of Agreement or a special exchange agreement.

The general prohibition against "other duties and charges of any kind" on bound items would be unworkable if it were not for three major exceptions contained in Article II:2. The trend of taxes is upward, throughout the world, and it would be impracticable to immunize imported goods from this trend. What is crucial from the trade point of view is that there should be no discrimination in the imposition of internal taxes on imported and domestic goods of a particular type.

The first major exception, contained in subparagraph (a) of Article II:2, permits the imposition on bound items of a "charge equivalent to an internal tax imposed consistently with the provisions of paragraph 2 of Article III in respect of the like domestic product or in respect of an article from which the imported product has been manufactured or produced in whole or in part." It should be observed that the effect of this exemption, read in the light of Article I, is to make clear that the rules respecting discriminatory internal taxation are neither more nor less strict for bound items than for unbound items.[25] The other two exceptions to the prohibition of duties and charges on bound items relate to "anti-dumping or countervailing dut[ies] applied consistently with the provisions of Article VI" and to "fees or other charges commensurate with the costs of services rendered," thereby giving legal status to national antidumping laws and to cost-keyed fees for inspections and similar services.

22. *Basic Instruments,* 3d Supp. (1955), p. 209 (emphasis supplied).
23. Ibid., 9th Supp. (1961), p. 172.
24. Ibid., p. 177.
25. See discussion in chapter 7, "Internal Taxes," infra.

## Preferential Arrangements

The framers of the Havana Charter and the General Agreement regarded the most-favored-nation clause and the principle of tariff reduction through mutually advantageous negotiations as the two main bases of the GATT system. In the end the most-favored-nation clause had to give way, however, to a major exception for existing preferential tariff arrangements. The exception for preferences found in Article I is the result of an Anglo-American compromise. The United States had made elimination of all preferences a major principle of its policy for the post-war organization of world trade. The chief goal of the U.S. policy was elimination of the imperial preference system established at the Ottawa Conference of 1932. Under that system, pairs of Commonwealth countries exchanged reciprocal preferences. In most cases the United Kingdom was one of the parties to the arrangement, and not all Commonwealth countries granted all other Commonwealth countries preferences. Although the United States was able to secure British approval of various statements on the desirability of fully nondiscriminatory trade, notably in the Atlantic Charter and the U.S.-U.K. Mutual Aid Agreement, the British refused in the end to agree to the abolition of imperial preference, and an exception had to be written into the Havana Charter and the General Agreement.[26] In the course of the negotiations, a number of other preferential arrangements were granted exemption from the most-favored-nation clause. The General Agreement ultimately did little to reduce the number of preferential arrangements, although the tariff bargaining procedures had an indirect effect of reducing the economic impact of existing preferences on particular items. The effect of seeking to outlaw preferences was, ironically enough, to write a permanent exemption into the General Agreement for most existing preferential systems.

## Preferences in Existence on 10 April 1947

The failure of the U.S. attempt to secure the abolition of existing preferences rendered desirable a legal formula to prevent increases in the degree of preferences. The traditional most-favored-nation clause was designed only to preserve uniformity of treatment and contained no language dealing with the control of preference levels. Three basic formulas were available for adoption. The least restrictive was the proposal put forward by the Australian delegation, which would have permitted increased margins of preference if arrived

---

26. Richard Gardner has eliminated any need to recount this crucial story of mid- and postwar diplomacy. The reader is referred to his detailed and perspicacious account, *Sterling-Dollar Diplomacy* (Oxford: Clarendon Press, 1956), pp. 107–9, 150–61, 270–71, 348–61.

at in GATT tariff negotiations.[27] The most restrictive was the U.S. proposal contained in Article 18 of the Suggested Charter. Under this proposal the "elimination of preferences" would have been a specific goal of tariff negotiations, and this goal would have been achieved by a provision that "all negotiated reductions in most-favored-nation import tariffs shall operate automatically to reduce or eliminate margins of preference. . . ."[28] The third position, which was in fact the position adopted, was to bind margins of preference existing on a particular base date (in most cases the commencement of the first round of tariff negotiations, 10 April 1947).

The binding of margins of preference, although tolerably consistent with the watered-down goal of "elimination of discriminatory treatment in international trade" set forth in the Preamble of the General Agreement, was nevertheless a fundamental decision. Preferences were thereafter to be treated differently from tariffs. Contracting parties were to retain unlimited discretion to increase duties on unbound items, but preferences on unbound items were to be frozen.

The technical apparatus devised to assure the maintenance of preferences at no higher than existing levels was to divide GATT schedules into two parts. The parts were in fact separate columns indicating for each item in the first column the nonpreferential rate bound in GATT negotiations (called the most-favored-nation rate) and in the second column the preferential rate bound in GATT tariff negotiations. It was thereupon provided in Article I:4 that the margin of preference on any item might not exceed (1) the maximum margin of preference specifically provided for in the schedule; (2) if no maximum margin of preference was provided for in the schedule, the difference between the most-favored-nation rate provided for in the schedule and the preferential rate provided for in the schedule; (3) if neither a maximum margin of preference nor a preferential rate was provided for in the schedule, the difference between the most-favored-nation rate provided for in the schedule and the preferential rate actually in force on 10 April 1947; (4) if none of the three—a maximum margin of preference, a preferential rate, or a most-favored-nation rate—was provided for the schedule, the difference between the most-favored-nation and preferential rates actually in force on 10 April 1947 (whether or not the item in question was mentioned in a schedule).

The margin of preference is the absolute difference between the applicable most-favored-nation and preference rates.[29] If the two rates are ad valorem

27. William A. Brown, Jr., *The United States and the Restoration of World Trade* (Washington: Brookings Institution, 1950), p. 75.
28. *Suggested Charter for an International Trade Organization of the United Nations,* Department of State Publication 2598, Commercial Policy Series 93 (1946).
29. Interpretative note, Ad Art. I, para. 4.

rates (expressed either as two different figures or as a fractional relationship), it is the absolute difference expressed in percentage points ad valorem which is decisive. Consequently, in the case of unbound items, a reduction of a certain number of percentage points ad valorem in the most-favored-nation rate permits a reduction of an equal number of percentage points ad valorem in the preferential rate. To take an example, if the most-favored-nation and preferential rates are on the reference date 50 percent and 25 percent respectively, and if the most-favored-nation rate is subsequently reduced in GATT negotiations to 30 percent, the preference rate can be reduced to 5 percent (and not just to 15 percent, which would be the result if the proportional difference rather than the absolute difference were decisive).

In the case of specific duties the absolute difference (measured in currency per unit) between the most-favored-nation and preferential rates is decisive. Thus, if the most-favored-nation and preferential rates are on the reference date $5.00 and $2.50 per ton respectively, and if the most-favored-nation rate is subsequently reduced to $3.00 per ton, the preferential rate can be reduced to $0.50.

The rule that it is the absolute rather than the proportional margin that is decisive is also operative when the most-favored-nation duty is raised. This point is of practical importance, since a margin of preference is automatically bound against increase where neither the most-favored-nation nor the preferential rate is bound against increase.

Although the absolute difference formula was chosen over the proportional difference formula because of asserted difficulties in calculating proportional differences,[30] and although the framers of the General Agreement perhaps saw no further implications at the time, employment of the absolute difference formula has an important consequence in the case of specific duties, which are fairly prevalent in Commonwealth tariff schedules. In the inflationary years that have followed the signing of the General Agreement it has become necessary, as we have seen, for many countries to revise their specific duties upward. But if, to take the prior example, the most-favored-nation and preferential rates are on the reference date $5.00 and $2.50 per ton respectively, and if because of a subsequent quadrupling of the local price level the most-favored-nation rate is correspondingly increased to $20.00 (the increase being permitted either because the item is unbound or because there is a devaluation meeting the terms of Article II:6), the preferential rate must be increased to $17.50 (and not just to $10.00). The effect of the rule in the years that have followed the signing of the General Agreement has thus been to reduce the importance of preferences—in the illustration, from a 50 percent preference ($2.50/$5.00) to a 12.5 percent preference ($17.50/$20.00).

30. The CONTRACTING PARTIES to the General Agreement on Tariffs and Trade, *Analytical Index* (Second Rev. 1966), p. 3 (hereinafter cited as *Analytical Index*).

The automatic binding of preferences not only has the effect in times of inflation of automatically reducing the effectiveness of preferences in specific duties, but also has the collateral effect of frequently freezing most-favored-nation rates. Clearly, this indirect effect may result where there is a GATT binding of a preferential rate. But even where the preferential rate is not bound, the same consequence may occur as a matter of political fact. Given the political relationships existing between preference-giving and preference-receiving countries, it is not always easy to increase preferential rates. This indirect effect of the margin-of-preference rule is particularly marked where the preferential rate is in fact a zero rate. In order to raise the most-favored-nation rate, the preference-giving country must impose duties for the first time on imports from the preference-receiving country.

### The U.K. Waiver

The United Kingdom, with its traditional system of duty-free imports from Commonwealth countries, particularly of foodstuffs, found itself in a difficult situation as a consequence of the margin-of-preference freeze. Where inflation had caused specific duties to lose their protective effect, or where imports from non-Commonwealth countries had begun to create politically unacceptable competition for U.K. producers, the United Kingdom found itself in an intractable situation, even though in many cases the most-favored-nation rates were not bound. The U.K. government, seeking a GATT waiver, explained that it had the power to raise tariffs on imports from non-Commonwealth countries but that the imposition of tariffs on then duty-free imports from the Commonwealth would require special legislation which, given the emotional as well as institutional bonds among Commonwealth countries, would create serious political difficulties. Such legislation would create a question of principle of major dimensions, it was explained, even though no products were in fact imported from the Commonwealth under the tariff classifications in question.

The European countries that were exporters to the United Kingdom of the agricultural products principally in question challenged the U.K. waiver request, arguing among other things that the United Kingdom should be prepared to grant concessions on other items to the extent that it increased margins of preference on the items in question. The United Kingdom responded by referring to a principle that had theretofore received little mention in GATT deliberations and that was grounded in economic learning rather than in the text of the General Agreement; this was the principle of "substantial diversion of trade." The increase sought in preference margins was not inconsistent with the purpose of the margin-of-preference freeze, the United Kingdom argued, because no substantial diversion of trade would occur; that is to say, imports into the United Kingdom from non-Commonwealth countries would not be replaced by imports from Commonwealth countries when tariffs were increased on the imports from non-Commonwealth sources. The United Kingdom was not then importing the items in question from Commonwealth sources, and under the economic circumstances an increase in preferences would not be likely to change this situation.

To put the argument in slightly more technical terms, the increase in preferences would not be inconsistent with the goal of freer nondiscriminatory trade, because it would not involve a shift of production from relatively lower-cost non-Commonwealth sources to relatively higher-cost Commonwealth sources (using "cost" in each case to refer to real resources expended by producers). To be sure, the U.K. government conceded, the effect of the tariff increases would be to reduce imports from non-Commonwealth sources and to increase domestic production in the United Kingdom (and in that sense would be inconsistent with the goal of freer trade by shifting production from lower-cost foreign sources to higher-cost domestic sources). But such a result would not be inconsistent with the General Agreement. The items in question were unbound, and the cornerstone of GATT tariff doctrine had always been that each contracting party was to have absolute discretion with respect to unbound rates. To limit the United Kingdom's discretion with respect to certain unbound items simply because it happened to grant preferences on those same items would be to discriminate against the United Kingdom.[31]

This argument was accepted by the CONTRACTING PARTIES and was reflected in the terms and conditions of the waiver granted.[32] The waiver was narrowly drawn to apply only to the situation complained of, and it required the United Kingdom to consult with all contracting parties requesting consultations and claiming "a substantial interest in the trade in the item in question" and the likelihood of a substantial diversion of trade. If in the course of the consultations it should be agreed that there was "no likelihood of a substantial diversion of trade," the waiver was to be applicable. If there should be no such agreement, the United Kingdom would be entitled to arbitration by the CONTRACTING PARTIES. In the case of such arbitrations the CONTRACTING PARTIES were to reach one of three conclusions:

    (i)  that there is no likelihood of substantial diversion,
    (ii)  that there is likelihood of substantial diversion, or
    (iii)  that the evidence is not sufficient for them to determine whether or not there is likelihood of substantial diversion.[33]

31. On the circumstances of, and the negotiations for, the U.K. Waiver, see *Basic Instruments,* 2d Supp. (1954), p. 96; U.S. Tariff Commission, *Operation . . .,* 7th Rep. (1954), p. 27.
32. The terms and conditions of the waiver are set out in *Basic Instruments,* 2d Supp. (1954), p. 20.
33. Ibid., p. 20, 22.

If they found "no likelihood of substantial diversion," the waiver was to apply; if they found "likelihood of substantial diversion," the waiver was not to apply; and if they found the evidence insufficient "to determine whether or not there is likelihood of substantial diversion," the waiver was to apply unless the CONTRACTING PARTIES were subsequently to find within a reasonable time (not to exceed one year) that "substantial diversion of trade" had resulted from the increase in the margin of preference, in which case the waiver was to cease to apply.

To assure that this mechanism would operate, the United Kingdom was required to distribute trade statistics not only to "contracting parties [appearing] . . . to the United Kingdom likely to have a substantial interest," but also to the GATT secretariat for redistribution to all contracting parties so that contracting parties not contacted by the United Kingdom would be in a position to judge whether or not they in fact had a substantial interest. In addition, annual reports of action under the waiver were to be filed.[34]

## The Utility of Reporting Procedures

These reporting duties are of great importance, and it is unfortunate that similar procedures have not been imposed in all cases where they might be useful. The mere announcement of a change in tariff policy may suffice to give a large country with a well-staffed ministry of foreign commerce the opportunity of discovering for itself the probable impact of that change on its exports, but a small country will not always be so fortunate. It is not simply a question of looking at the export figures for the item in question. Rather, a complicated assessment of the competitive position of different countries may be necessary. Given the pressures of time on small ministries and considering the fact that GATT responsibilities in smaller countries may devolve on diplomats who are located in Geneva and who have neither economic training nor access to staff assistance, parties seeking waivers should be prepared to justify their proposals in economic terms (as, for example, along the lines of the substantial diversion of trade analysis used in the U.K. case) and to present not only bare summaries of prior imports but also sufficient economic data to suggest what

---

34. The waiver was amended two years later to permit the United Kingdom to take similar action with respect to those bound rates which, under the provisions of the Agreement, "it was free . . . to increase" (i.e., bound rates affected under Article XXVIII either by a renegotiation of the United Kingdom's own tariff schedule or by a withdrawal of U.K. concessions in connection with a renegotiation of another contracting party's schedule) (*Basic Instruments*, 3d Supp. [1955], p. 25). In 1962 a panel of the Council of the CONTRACTING PARTIES recognized a further restriction on the U.K. waiver; namely, that the United Kingdom might not increase preference margins unless it was able to establish a need for such action in the near future. GATT Document L/1749 (11 April 1962).

the impact of the waivers might be. To be sure, analysis would still be required in each country to determine whether the assertions made were correct, but the requisite inquiry would be more likely to be carried through if the countries concerned were not required to start from scratch.

The exception to the most-favored-nation clause for preferences existing on 10 April 1947 (and also the exception for customs unions) engendered in 1947 a movement to establish a similar exception for free trade areas. This movement was led by France, Syria and Lebanon, who were apparently hopeful of working out arrangements among French territories similar to imperial preference,[35] and it succeeded at the Havana Conference with the amending of what is now Article XXIV of the General Agreement. Article XXIV has in the past two decades been a magnet for a host of proposals (to be discussed in chapter 16) for "dressed up" preferential trading arrangements, which even with their trimmings do not satisfy the elaborate formal requirements of Article XXIV but have nonetheless normally been granted waivers. This has caused a shifting of attention from Article I to Article XXIV, which has in turn caused a turning of inquiry even further from the essential question of diversion of trade.

## Other Preferential Arrangements:
## The U.S.-Canadian Automotive Products Agreement

A number of preferential arrangements that have involved only a few products and that have not even been presented as free trade areas have nevertheless been accorded waivers by the GATT—in part, it would appear, because these arrangements have been seen as analogous to ones already exempted under Article I. Included in this category have been the Australian waiver on certain imports from Papau–New Guinea,[36] the U.S. waiver on imports from the Trust Territory of the Pacific Islands,[37] and the Italian waivers on imports from Libya and Somalia.[38]

One important case where a waiver was granted to a preferential arrangement that could not possibly be passed off as a good faith attempt to conform to Article XXIV involved the 1965 U.S.-Canadian Automotive Products Agreement. There the principle established in the U.K. preference waiver case re-

35. See Helmut Steinberger, *GATT und regionale Wirstschaftszusammenschlüsse* (Cologne and Berlin: Carl Heymanns Verlag, 1963), p. 96.
36. *Basic Instruments,* 8th Supp. (1960), p. 28; 5th Supp. (1957), pp. 34, 114; 4th Supp. (1956), pp. 14, 82; 2d Supp. (1954), pp. 18, 93.
37. Ibid., Vol. II (1952), pp. 9, 173.
38. Ibid., 13th Supp. (1965), pp. 24, 127; 10th Supp. (1962), p. 45; 9th Supp. (1961), p. 40; 7th Supp. (1959), pp. 34, 118; 4th Supp. (1956), p. 99; 3d Supp. (1957), p. 21; 1st Supp. (1953), p. 14; Vol. II (1952), p. 10.

ceived an interesting application. The U.S.-Canadian Automotive Products Agreement involved the elimination of customs duties between the United States and Canada on new automobiles and automobile parts imported for use as original equipment. Canada, unlike the United States, extended the duty-free treatment to all contracting parties and therefore did not require a waiver. The United States, forced by the circumstances to argue the merits of the agreement as a preferential arrangement, contended that the arrangement was not intended to, and given the nature of the demand for automobiles and the structure of the automobile industry in North America would not, reduce imports from third countries. Despite the 6.5 percent tariff on the importation of foreign automobiles into the United States (which the United States hoped to reduce by 50 percent in the Kennedy Round), no contracting party would "suffer trade damage," the United States representative assured.[39]

Acting on this assurance, the CONTRACTING PARTIES conditioned the future use of the waiver by the United States upon the application of procedures similar to those applied in the U.K. waiver case. Both the substantive test and the methods of enforcement differed somewhat, however. In the U.S. case the question to be resolved was not whether there would be "substantial diversion of trade," but rather whether there would be a "significant diversion of imports." It is not clear to what extent a difference in substance between these two formulas was intended. The methods of enforcement in the U.S. case were less elaborate than in the U.K. case. Although the United States was required to enter into consultations with any contracting party so requesting on the grounds "(i) that it has a substantial interest in the trade in an automotive product in the United States market, and (ii) that the elimination of customs duties by the United States on imports of that automotive product from Canada has created, or imminently threatens to create, a significant diversion of imports of that automotive product from the requesting contracting party to imports from Canada," the United States was required neither to take the initiative of commencing such negotiations nor to distribute the kind of information from which other countries could determine their particular interest.[40]

These procedural differences could perhaps have been justified by the circumstance that in the U.S. case the products in question were determined in advance and were produced by a limited number of large countries, whereas in the U.K. case a waiver was sought for products to be determined by the United Kingdom at its own discretion in the future. Nevertheless, the failure to require a detailed analysis and justification, adequately supported by statistics and other relevant evidence and capable of being examined by other countries' experts, appears, at least insofar as one can judge from the report of the

39. Ibid., 14th Supp. (1966), p. 187.
40. Ibid., p. 37.

Working Party,[41] to have caused the GATT discussions to pass in a doctrinal fog that made it impossible for other countries to identify their national interest with precision. Surely the precedent is not a fortunate one for future preferential areas where the contracting parties concerned will not consist solely of a few major countries with great experience and sophistication in foreign commerce.

One other aspect of the U.S.-Canadian Automotive Products Agreement warrants passing attention. The benefits of the reduction in duties were not intended to flow to consumers. The agreement is a rather singular one, for only automobile manufacturers, and not individuals, are permitted to make duty-free importations. Indeed, the representatives from both the United States and Canada took pains to point out that the granting of duty-free treatment would not result in lower prices (except perhaps as a consequence of increased efficiency).[42] From the point of view of the proponents of the waiver, the unlikelihood that the U.S. and Canadian importers—all large automobile companies—would pass on the benefits of the tariff reduction to consumers tended to show that there would be no trade diversion. On the other hand, from the point of view of the domestic U.S. and Canadian critics of the agreement this aspect revealed a kind of tariff disarmament that was hardly consistent with the overall goals of GATT and with the free-trade ideology in general. Although the arrangement would not be trade-diverting in the sense of replacing third-country production by production within the two agreeing countries, it would create trade only in a very limited sense. While imports into the United States from Canada, or vice versa, might increase, and while this trade might indeed involve some rationalization of production between the two countries, the arrangement was not expected to lead to the lower prices that are a raison d'être of international trade. It can thus be said that while the case against the waiver was very weak (unless one adopts a legalistic, absolutist approach to preferences), the case *for* the waiver was also rather weak.

But if the consumers in the United States and Canada had reason to complain of the agreement, it is not so clear that it was the role of an organization such as the GATT to defend those consumers' interests. One may, however, suspect that if the GATT waiver exercise had been more serious and more penetrating, and if, to take the suggestion one step further, there had been an independent international body to examine from an overall point of view the implications of the agreement, there might have been more vocal and effective criticism of the preferential arrangement within the United States and Canada. It is not unlikely that effective analytical work at the international organization level would have an indirect influence both in improving the quality of political

41. Ibid., p. 181.
42. Ibid., p. 187, 189.

discussion within the individual contracting parties and in furthering the goal of economic efficiency which the GATT as an organization has in common with the market economy systems of the individual contracting parties.

Whatever the indirect effects of better GATT procedures might be, the precedential value of the U.S. waiver is important at this particular juncture in economic history where less-developed countries are turning increasingly to preferential arrangements in their search for commercial policy solutions to the seemingly intractable problems of economic development. Two kinds of preferential arrangements have been urged in response to the problems of underdevelopment: (1) preferences by developed countries in favor of less-developed countries; and (2) preferences by less-developed countries in favor of one another. Both proposals will be considered at length in chapter 14. For the present discussion it is important only to note that in many cases these proposals will not achieve their most important goal—that of industrialization—unless there is a substantial diversion of trade. It is intended in many of these plans that exports by less-developed countries should replace exports by developed countries, which would mean a loss of efficiency in the world trading system (the replacement of relatively efficient production sources by relatively inefficient production sources).

That fact need not call for out-of-hand condemnation of these plans. Efficiency is only one of the goals of the economic system and of international trade, and there are many countries that regard industrialization as a more important goal than efficiency. Nevertheless, it is in the interest of each member of the trading community, developed or undeveloped, industrialized or not, to know how far the adoption of these kinds of preferential schemes would reduce efficiency. Loss of efficiency would be a real cost. This cost might fall primarily on developed countries that were willing to bear the burden, but it might also fall on less-developed countries. In the case of preferential arrangements among less-developed countries, for example, where tariffs would be removed as against other less-developed countries but not as against developed countries, imports of industrial products from the less-developed country partners, measured in the real terms of exports necessary to pay for these imports, might cost more than imports from developed countries. But whether the costs in real terms would be only costs to the world as a whole or also costs to particular less-developed countries, they would have to be put in the balance with the goal of industrialization—however difficult the weighing process might be in the determination of which kinds of preferential arrangements deserved support. Such supposedly minor matters as procedures, reporting requirements, analyses by independent international secretariats, and the like therefore take on great importance.

## Australian Preferences for Less-Developed Countries

One must consequently view with disquiet and regret the failure of the CONTRACTING PARTIES to make significant use of the opportunity presented by the Australian application for a waiver to permit the granting of preferential rates to less-developed contracting parties. This 1966 waiver was viewed as a test case, the first partial and tentative step toward introducing a system of preferences for imports into developed countries from less-developed countries. The precedent established by this waiver was thus to be of more than ordinary importance.

Under the waiver Australia was permitted to introduce a system of preferences on imports from less-developed countries of specified goods.[43] The list had been chosen on the basis of "competitive need," and items that individual less-developed countries were able to export at competitive prices were excluded from the benefits of the preferences.[44] To assure that Australian industry would not be too severely injured by new imports (and collaterally to limit diversion of developed country exports), most items on the preference list were subject to tariff quotas; once the quotas (which were global quotas for the less-developed countries as a group) were exceeded, the higher most-favored-nation rate would be applied. The waiver was open-ended in the sense that Australia was permitted to "vary at any time the list of goods, the rates of duty and the size of quotas."[45]

These preferences had two potential effects from the point of view of world efficiency. The preferences could have permitted relatively efficient production sources in less-developed countries to replace relatively inefficient production sources in Australia; in that case the preferences would have been trade-creating and consistent with the free trade ideal. In view of the "competitive need" criterion that had been applied in selecting the list of products and countries and in view of the use of tariff quotas, this trade-creating aspect of the preferences could have been expected to be modest. The preferences could, on the other hand, have permitted the displacement of relatively inefficient production sources in nonpreferred exporting countries. Whatever values might have been served by this "trade diversion," the result would neither have contributed to world efficiency nor have been consistent with the free trade ideal. Although the tariff-quota device would also have helped to limit this trade diversion, it is

---

43. Ibid., p. 23.
44. Statement by the Rt. Hon. J. McEwen, Deputy Prime Minister and Minister for Trade and Development, in the [Australian] House of Representatives on 19th May, 1965 (mimeographed document), p. 12.
45. *Basic Instruments,* 14th Supp. (1966), p. 23, 25.

likely that Australia—a country depending in large measure on a relatively small number of primary products[46]—expected a good deal more trade diversion than trade creation. On the other hand, it is possible that Australia did not expect any substantial change in trade patterns as a consequence of the preferences. This seems to have been the burden of criticisms to the effect that the Australian preference offer was "entirely cynical"—that it was made with the intention of winning friends in the favored countries with a device that would be of "little immediate material benefit" to those countries.[47]

Whatever the probable impact of the preferences, the GATT procedures established were poorly designed to determine whether or not the scheme would either be of any value to the recipient countries or, more important in view of the precedential value of the waiver, contribute to world efficiency. The Working Party does not appear to have addressed itself to the latter question in any systematic way, although it had the list of proposed products and preferential tariff levels and was well placed to require Australia to produce the information that would have been a prerequisite to a judgment on that question. The waiver provides, however, a limited control on trade diversion: namely, a requirement that Australia must notify the CONTRACTING PARTIES before (1) adding to the list of goods, (2) reducing the rate of any duty, (3) removing any quota limitation or increasing the size of any quota, or (4) ceasing to grant preferential treatment to any less-developed contracting party. If any contracting party "considers that such action threatens substantial injury to its trade with Australia in the relevant goods," it may demand consultations. The consultations are to be carried on "with a view to arriving at a mutually acceptable settlement." If such a settlement cannot be reached, the complaining party's claim of a "threat" of "substantial injury" may be considered by the CONTRACTING PARTIES. In the event that the CONTRACTING PARTIES find that such a threat exists, "Australia shall not take such action but may take other action which conforms with any recommendation made by the CONTRACTING PARTIES, or alternatively, may remove the relevant good or goods from the [preference list]." In addition, if any contracting party subsequently considers that "its trade with Australia in any product is suffering substantial injury" as a consequence of any action taken under the waiver, that contracting party may demand that Australia engage in bilateral consultations "with a view to arriving at a mutually satisfactory settlement."[48]

Under neither the pre-action nor the post-action procedures, however, is

46. Ibid., p. 23, 24.
47. See "Australia's Trading Transformation," *The Economist*, CCXVII (1965), p. 863.
48. *Basic Instruments*, 14th Supp. (1966), p. 23.

there a substantive norm for judging the content of a "mutually acceptable settlement." The absence of such a norm may be thought desirable in the case of post-action disputes, where there is no possibility of recourse to the CONTRACTING PARTIES; but such an absence is more serious in the case of pre-action disputes, where a recommendation of the CONTRACTING PARTIES may be sought. The procedures seem to suggest that the avoidance of any "threat" of substantial injury to nonpreferred exporters is to be the guiding principle for the CONTRACTING PARTIES in arriving at their decision. Such an interpretation is consistent with the goal of improving world efficiency, but the whole procedure—with its emphasis on bilateral consultation and its lack of concern with independent fact-finding—is surely poorly designed to identify and clarify the common interest of the world trading community.

Any general preference scheme for less-developed countries, even in a single product, may well involve elements of both trade creation and trade diversion. The important question is that of the balance between these two tendencies. It would be fully as unwise to condemn all new preferences that contain some elements of trade diversion as, under the formal GATT system, to condemn all new preferences whatever. What is needed is a substantive standard for weighing these divergent effects and, perhaps even more urgently, an institutional system for developing the necessary information, hearing the views of all parties concerned, and identifying and clarifying common interests of all members of the international trading community.

Common interests are perhaps more difficult to discern in the context of the problem of less-developed countries than in the context of other problems of world trade. But those interests are not necessarily absent in the former context. Certainly the willingness of the developed countries to pay for massive foreign aid programs suggests a worldwide interest in the industrialization of the less-developed countries. If that willingness is an accurate indication, a consensus may develop that particular kinds of preference arrangements are in the common interest even if, on balance, they tend away from world efficiency. At the same time it should not be overlooked that many kinds of preferential arrangements would likely lead to little further industrialization while at the same time compromising seriously the efficiency-creating function of international trade. Without prejudging any of the policy questions of that sort, one can observe that the GATT procedures on preferences are poorly designed to lead to the intelligent discussion of such questions in the context of concrete proposals for particular preference arrangements.

In addition to the GATT discussions arising out of Australia's application for a waiver, discussions have been carried on in the GATT, the UNCTAD, the OECD, and other organizations on the advisability of a system of general preferences by developed countries as a group in favor of developing countries as a group. These discussions will be reviewed in chapter 14. It should be noted here merely that, given the high level of generality that has characterized most of these discussions, it is a pity that in the Australian waiver case the GATT missed an opportunity to analyze carefully what effects a particular, limited preference scheme for less-developed countries might have on world efficiency and the promotion of industrialization.

# 5 Tariff Conferences

The GATT is perhaps best known for its sponsorship of tariff conferences or, to use the popular term, *rounds* of tariff negotiations. Six such conferences have been held. The first was held in Geneva in 1947, and the General Agreement was drafted to embody the results of that round. Subsequently, major tariff conferences were held in Annecy, France, in 1949 and in Torquay, England, in 1951; these conferences were primarily designed to facilitate the accession of countries that had not participated in the Geneva Round, but at Torquay original contracting parties also negotiated inter se. Another round, rather minor in dimensions because of congressional limitation of the U.S. negotiating authority, was held in Geneva in 1956.[1] In the 1960s two further rounds were held in Geneva. Unlike some of the former rounds, which had become known by the names of the locales in which they were held, these two rounds became known by the names of the men whose efforts seemed most important in bringing them into being. Thus the 1960–62 conference was referred to as the Dillon Round; the 1964–67 conference, the Kennedy Round.

These six rounds of tariff negotiations (from the Geneva Round in 1947 to the Kennedy Round in 1964–67) have resulted in the reduction of world tariff levels to a degree that probably would have surprised the most sanguine proponents of the ITO. In 1955 the U.S. Commerce Department calculated that the "actual average ratio of United States tariff collections to dutiable imports" had been reduced from nearly 30 percent at the end of World War II to about 12 percent in the mid-Fifties. Although some of this reduction was due to the effect of inflation on specific duties, most of it was attributed to GATT negotiations.[2] In 1965 a U.S. trade negotiator said that the "average of all

1. Major negotiations were also held in 1955, but these were concerned almost entirely with the accession of Japan.
2. "The Role of the United States Tariff and the Effects of Changes in Duty Rates," in Staff for the Subcommittee on Foreign Trade Policy of the Committee on Ways

dutiable U.S. imports has been lowered from a high of 59.1 per cent in 1932 to 26.4 per cent in 1946 to less than 12 per cent today."[3] And at the conclusion of the Kennedy Round, the chief U.S. negotiator announced that the GATT secretariat had made preliminary estimates that the [Kennedy Round] agreement covered more than forty billion dollars in world trade, that 70 per cent of dutiable imports of the major participants were affected, that two-thirds of the tariff reductions were 50 per cent or more, and that the nations making concessions accounted for 75 per cent of world trade.[4]

Of course, the effect of these tariff reductions on the promotion of world trade is problematical. No one has yet devised a satisfactory method of determining the economic effect of tariff reductions, since that effect depends upon essentially unmeasurable factors such as the elasticities of supply and demand, and since some tariff reductions merely represent the removal of "water" from earlier tariff levels. Even after the fact, it is difficult to isolate the impact of tariff reductions from all of the other factors affecting the rate of importation. Statistical analyses of the differential rate of change in imports of products on which tariffs are cut and those on which tariffs are not cut tend to show, however, that tariff reductions do have a substantial economic effect.[5]

## The Provisions of the General Agreement

Until the addition of Article XXVIII bis in 1957, the General Agreement contained no provisions on tariff conferences. This anomaly, like many others involving the GATT, is to be explained by the GATT's early association with the ITO. The General Agreement was intended to be the expression of the results of a particular tariff conference, not the authority and rules for further such conferences. The ITO was to sponsor tariff conferences, and the necessary authority and rules were contained in Article 17 of the chapter on commercial policy of the Havana Charter.

The Havana Charter rules were used, however, even after it became clear that the ITO was a failure. The CONTRACTING PARTIES simply adopted those

and Means of the U.S. House of Representatives (ed.), *Foreign Trade Policy* (1958), p. 216. See also U.S. Tariff Commission, *Operation of the Trade Agreements Program,* 5th Rep. (1952), p. 12.

3. Address by the Hon. W. Michael Blumenthal, Deputy Special Representative for Trade Negotiations, at the 43rd Annual Luncheon of the National Council of American Importers, New York City, Thursday, September 16, 1965 (mimeographed document), p. 2.

4. Address of W. M. Roth before the National Conference on the Kennedy Round, 7 July 1967, p. 2. (mimeographed document)

5. See Gerard Curzon, *Multilateral Commercial Diplomacy* (London: Michael Joseph, 1965), pp. 81–85.

rules with minor changes for each successive conference.[6] Likewise, the provisions of Article XXVIII bis are essentially consistent with the Havana Charter rules. There are two principal differences. One, which is of limited importance, is that, whereas the Havana Charter imposed an obligation upon members to enter into tariff negotiations upon the request of any other member, the General Agreement imposes no such obligation.[7] The other is that, whereas the Havana Charter required negotiations on a *selective product-by-product* basis, Article XXVIII bis provides, in the alternative, for the use of "such other multilateral procedures as may be accepted by the contracting parties concerned."

It was only after Article XXVIII bis was added that the CONTRACTING PARTIES, in the context of the Kennedy Round, made their first major departure from the system that had been used since the first round of negotiations. They were able to do this without amending the General Agreement, for the essence of the change was precisely to reject the selective product-by-product method in favor of a multilateral procedure termed the *linear* or *across-the-board* method.

These two methods will be discussed in detail later, but two points should be observed now. First, the consistent use of the selective product-by-product method in the first five rounds coincided with serious disagreements over the efficacy and fairness of that method. Second, it is open to question whether adoption of the linear method constituted a fundamental change in the negotiation process or only constituted a change in form.

## Reciprocity

Although under the Havana Charter members were required to negotiate, they were not required to reach agreement. Indeed, the Charter language emphasized that "no Member shall be required to grant unilateral concessions, or to grant concessions to other Members receiving adequate concessions in return," and that negotiations "will afford adequate opportunity to take into account the needs of individual countries and individual industries."[8]

With the elimination in Article XXVIII bis of the Havana Charter's duty to negotiate, the right of a contracting party to refuse to make concessions other

---

6. See e.g., the rules for the Torquay Round, *Basic Instruments,* Vol. I (1952), p. 104, and the rules for the 1956 Geneva Round, ibid., 4th Supp. (1956), p. 79.

7. Paragraph 2(b) of Article XXVIII bis waters the obligation of the Havana Charter down to a statement that "contracting parties recognize that in general the success of multilateral negotiations would depend on the participation of all contracting parties which conduct a substantial proportion of their external trade with one another."

8. Art. 17:2.

than in the pursuit of its own self-interest became even clearer. Language was nevertheless added to Article XXVIII bis to make clear that negotiations are to be "on a reciprocal and mutually advantageous basis," and that "[n]egotiations shall be conducted on a basis which affords adequate opportunity to take into account . . . the needs of individual contracting parties and individual industries . . . and . . . all other relevant circumstances including the fiscal, developmental, strategic and other needs of the contracting parties concerned."[9]

This permissive approach to the content of tariff agreements is often referred to under the heading of *reciprocity*. From the formal legal principle that a country need make concessions only when other contracting parties offer reciprocal concessions considered to be "mutually advantageous" has been derived the informal principle that exchanges of concessions must entail reciprocity.

Reciprocity as a concept is nowhere defined in the General Agreement, but it is nonetheless one of the most vital concepts in GATT practice. For example, when less-developed countries contended that GATT tariff negotiations were of no value to them because they needed to retain high tariffs for revenue purposes and for the protection of infant industries and therefore had nothing to offer as reciprocity, the CONTRACTING PARTIES added a new Part IV, containing the statement (which many would regard as the key provision of Part IV) that the "developed contracting parties do not expect reciprocity for commitments made by them in trade negotiations to reduce or remove tariffs and other barriers to the trade of less-developed contracting parties." (Article XXXVI:8). But the CONTRACTING PARTIES did not furnish a definition of reciprocity.[10]

With the growing popularity in GATT circles of the concept of reciprocity, a customary method for measuring reciprocity developed. The heart of this method was the concept of *trade coverage*, which referred to the annual volume of imports within the tariff classification to which the concession in question applied. The custom grew up of attempting to balance the trade coverage of concessions made by each party to a particular negotiation.

The notion of measuring tariff concessions solely in terms of trade coverage is, of course, absurd, for such a measure ignores the depth of cuts. The effect is like trying to measure the area of a rectangle by taking the rectangle's length

---

9. Additional language is contained in paragraph 3 of Article XXVIII bis to make clear that less-developed countries are not required to reduce tariffs needed for economic development or revenue purposes.
10. An interpretative note contains what is in form a definition of the phrase "do not expect reciprocity" but in substance a statement of little value. The statement explains merely that "the less-developed contracting parties should not be expected, in the course of trade negotiations, to make contributions which are inconsistent with their individual development, financial and trade needs, taking into consideration past trade developments" (Ad Art. XXXVI, para. 8).

and ignoring its width. Percentages of reduction tend to be ignored. The absurdity of trade coverage as a measure of reciprocity is illustrated by the fate of the provision, presently located in paragraph 2(a) of Article XXVIII bis, that the "binding against increase of low duties or of duty-free treatment shall, in principle, be recognized as a concession equivalent in value to the reduction of high duties." This principle has never been fully followed in practice, because high-tariff countries have demanded more from low-tariff countries in return for major reductions than mere promises not to raise existing duties. The low-tariff countries have consequently been in the forefront of certain efforts, which we shall examine shortly, to change the GATT tariff negotiation system.[11]

The foregoing example suggests that, at least in tariff conferences, negotiators may use trade coverage as a measure of reciprocity less in determining what concessions to grant than in justifying their actions to their domestic publics. Because they operate under close congressional scrutiny, U.S. negotiators are particularly anxious to give the impression that the amount of trade coverage on concessions received is not less than the trade coverage on concessions granted, and, indeed, they attempt to make this demonstration for each major trading partner and for each major sector of economic activity. For example, at the end of the 1960–61 negotiations the Department of State published a report that led off with a chart showing that the United States had received concessions on $1,140.4 million of U.S. exports, while making concessions on only $946.0 million of U.S. imports. The chart also showed that in terms of trade coverage the United States had outnegotiated each of its major trading partners: the EEC by $750.2 million to $597.4 million, the United Kingdom by $197.5 million to $185.2 million, and Canada by $75.1 million to $64.5 million.[12] The body of the report, although referring to ad valorem percentages of cuts, gave a prominent place to trade coverage, showing that concessions received had a larger trade coverage than concessions granted in the agricultural, fishery, and industrial sectors.[13]

---

11. An attempt by Brazil, at the time of the Review Conference, to secure the adoption of a formal measure of the value of tariff concessions was defeated. Overriding the advantage of certainty that such a measure would offer was, felt the majority of the Review Session Working Party, the disadvantage that "the measurement of concessions in monetary terms might not be equitable when the economic effects of customs duties are unequal because of differences in the economic structures of the countries concerned" (*Basic Instruments,* 3d Supp. [1955], p. 205, 219).

12. *General Agreement on Tariffs and Trade: Analysis of United States Negotiations: 1960–61 Trade Conference* (1962), I, p. iii.

13. See e.g., ibid., pp. 1–26. A similar form of trade-coverage presentation was used by the U.S. State Department in its summary of the Kennedy Round. A footnote was added, however, indicating that "in the course of the negotiations" trade coverage, depth of reductions, and "numerous other factors were considered in evaluating the balance of concessions—the height of duties, the characteristics of

Used mainly to pacify mercantilist sentiments at home, the concept of trade coverage may nevertheless have a feedback effect on negotiations. U.S. negotiators may, for example, at times be so preoccupied with the need to show a net balance on trade coverage that they will accept lesser percentage reductions in exchange for an increase in the number of tariff classifications subject to concessions. Moreover, as we shall see in the next chapter, the trade coverage concept tends to exercise a hypnotic and rigidifying role in technical tariff negotiations between rounds.

## Bilateral versus Multilateral Negotiations

When the United States was preparing its proposals for an international trade organization, State Department trade experts debated at length the relative advantage of bilateral and multilateral negotiations.[14] The decision to create an international trade organization reflected a decision in favor of the latter. Bilateral negotiations under the prewar Reciprocal Trade Agreements Act had been considered slow and limited in scope, and it was thought that these defects could be remedied by negotiations within a multilateral framework.

A close examination of GATT tariff negotiations prior to the Kennedy Round suggests, however, that the multilateral character of those negotiations can easily be overemphasized. On all but one occasion, conferences commenced as networks of bilateral negotiations. Meanwhile, the GATT as an institution tended to function much like the New York Stock Exchange or the Chicago Board of Trade, providing a forum in which bilateral agreements might be reached in accordance with procedures laid down centrally.

The only occasion on which multilateral negotiations were successfully arranged was the accession of Japan to the General Agreement. On that occasion the United States granted concessions to six contracting parties; those six contracting parties granted concessions to Japan; and Japan granted concessions to the United States.[15]

An index of the bilateral character of GATT tariff negotiations prior to the Kennedy Round was the *principal supplier* rule. Under this rule requests for concessions on a particular product were normally to be made by—and only by—the principal supplier (that is, exporter of the largest volume) of that

---

individual products, demand and supply elasticities, and the size and nature of markets" (*General Agreement on Tariffs and Trade: Report on United States Negotiations: 1964–67 Trade Conference* [1967], I, p. iii n. 1).

14. E. F. Penrose, *Economic Planning for the Peace* (Princeton: Princeton University Press, 1953), pp. 87–103, gives some of the flavor of these debates. Similar debates were going on within the British government.

15. U.S. Tariff Commission, *Operation* . . . , 8th Rep. (1955), pp. 84–85.

product.[16] Actually, the principal supplier rule was simply a formal codification of an economic principle inherent in the nature of bilateral negotiations. A country pursuing an unconditional most-favored-nation policy and engaging in bilateral negotiations is for two reasons unlikely to grant a concession to a country that is not the principal supplier of the product in question. First, adherence to an unconditional most-favored-nation policy makes it unlikely that a country will be able to obtain economic compensation for a single concession from two different countries on two different occasions (since any second country from which economic compensation might be sought will already be receiving the benefits of the concession). Second, between the principal supplier and a lesser supplier of a particular product, the principal supplier has more to gain from, and consequently will normally give a greater reciprocal economic compensation in return for, a concession on that product. (Nevertheless, contracting parties that are not principal suppliers have sometimes been prepared to grant a quid pro quo for recognition that they have "initial negotiating rights," for the purpose of Article XXVII, with respect to concessions originally granted to another contracting party.)

The principal supplier rule served to reinforce as well as to reflect the bilateral character of pre-Kennedy Round trade negotiations. This effect resulted from the following circumstances: The basic assumption of the GATT tariff negotiating system was that each party to a particular negotiation would be in a position both to grant and to receive concessions. The principal supplier rule provided in effect that only countries that were the principal suppliers of products were in a position to receive concessions. Therefore, the principal supplier rule operated to exclude from meaningful tariff negotiations a large number of countries, namely, those countries that were not the principal suppliers of any products. One may note in passing that countries that were not the principal suppliers of any products included most of the less-developed countries.

Although the early GATT tariff rounds with but one exception began as networks of bilateral negotiations, they ended as exercises in multilateralism. Application of the most-favored-nation clause had the effect of creating, with respect to each bilateral agreement that was concluded in a round, a greater or lesser "spill-over." At the end of the bilateral phase of a round, individual con-

---

16. See, e.g., the third rule for the 1956 Conference: "Participating countries may request concessions on products of which they individually, or collectively are, or are likely to be, the principal suppliers to the countries from which the concessions are asked. This rule shall not apply to prevent a country not a principal supplier from making a request, but the country concerned may invoke the principal supplier rule if the principal supplier of the product is not participating in the negotiations or is not a contracting party to the General Agreement" (*Basic Instruments,* 4th Supp. [1956], p. 79, 80).

tracting parties thus knew both that, under Article II:1, they were entitled to the benefits of concessions made to all other parties and that they were required to accord the benefits of their own concessions to all other parties. And with this knowledge came a period in which requests and offers previously made were reshuffled, as countries tried to strike a balance in the global effect of concessions received and concessions granted.

The effect of this last-minute balancing, which constituted the only truly multilateral element of the negotiations, may have been to increase tariff reductions, for certain contracting parties were induced to grant additional concessions in order to assure that concessions from which they stood indirectly to benefit would not be withdrawn. But the opposite may also have been the effect. A contracting party, finding that one of its concessions indirectly benefited a contracting party that had not made a reciprocal concession to it, was sometimes tempted to withdraw the original concession.

On balance, the possibility of making these last-minute adjustments probably contributed to greater tariff reduction than would have occurred if the pre-GATT system had been continued. At the time of the making of original offers, contracting parties could take into account the possibility of later requesting reciprocal concessions from countries obtaining indirect benefits. By contrast, under the pre-GATT system a country normally negotiated with only one other country at a time and therefore was unwilling to offer concessions leading to a major spill-over of benefits.[17]

In addition to permitting requests for additional concessions in the final balancing of accounts, the simultaneous bilateral negotiations that characterized GATT tariff conferences permitted individual contracting parties to offer bindings on particular items to more than one other party and thereby to obtain greater compensation than they would have obtained in isolated bilateral negotiations. Greater compensation implies, of course, a lower overall level of tariffs.[18]

In retrospect, it seems probable that the most important advantage of GATT negotiations prior to the Kennedy Round over negotiations in the pre-GATT period was simply that the holding of major tariff conferences led to an increase in the number of bilateral negotiations. Each time a major round of tariff negotiations took place, all the major commercial contracting parties par-

17. It must be recalled that even prior to the GATT nearly all major commercial countries followed an unconditional most-favored-nation policy (subject, of course, to certain rather well-defined preferential arrangements that were in any event continued under the General Agreement).
18. A country that is the direct beneficiary of a concession has, however, greater rights under Article XXVIII (as a "contracting party with which such concession was initially negotiated") and perhaps also under Article XXIII than has a country that is an indirect beneficiary.

ticipated. As we have seen, such participation was mandatory under Article 17 of the Havana Charter; and even after the Charter became de facto a dead letter, full participation normally occurred.[19]

By contrast, during the pre-GATT period negotiations to reduce tariffs were relatively rare. Even the United States, with the authority granted by the Reciprocal Trade Agreements Act, entered into only thirty-two bilateral agreements in the thirteen years from 1934 to 1947, whereas it negotiated with twenty-two countries in the first GATT round alone.[20] The number of bilateral tariff-reduction agreements entered into by other major commercial countries in the pre-GATT period was surely much lower.[21]

## Abortive Proposals for Reform

Even if the GATT system was an improvement over the pre-GATT system, a reform movement gained momentum within the GATT during the 1950s and eventually resulted in the adoption of the linear method employed in the Kennedy Round. The major impetus for this reform movement was dissatisfaction with the predominantly bilateral character of tariff negotiations—a dissatisfaction stemming from two sources.

First, low-tariff countries found that bilateral negotiations placed them in a weak bargaining position. Since their tariffs were already low, they had little to offer high-tariff countries in compensation for major reductions of the latter's tariffs. As we have seen, the GATT as an institution attempted to offset this weakness by adopting a rule that in its eventual form in paragraph 2(a) of Article XXVIII bis provided that "the binding against increase of low duties or of duty-free treatment shall, in principle, be recognized as a concession equivalent in value to the reduction of high duties." However, so long as reductions were to occur through bilateral negotiations and individual contracting parties were to remain the judges of whether bilateral agreements were "mutually advantageous" under paragraph 1(a) of Article XXVIII bis, this rule was—at least in the view of the low-tariff countries—without influence.[22]

19. France threatened to boycott the 1956 Conference (*Basic Instruments,* 4th Supp. [1956], pp. 74, 75–76), but in the end participated in at least a nominal way (U.S. Tariff Commission, *Operation* . . . , 9th Rep. [1956], pp. 73–74).
20. U.S. Tariff Commission, *Operation* . . . , 1st Rep., Part II (1948), pp. 6–15, 61.
21. The Commonwealth countries entered into a number of preferential agreements as part of the imperial preference system, but these negotiations were not hampered by any spill-over produced by the most-favored-nation clause.
22. In preparation for the 1956 Tariff Conference, the CONTRACTING PARTIES appended to the rule the following statement: "This rules takes account, *inter alia,* of the position of countries which, whilst maintaining low or moderate duties on all or most of the products from their principal suppliers, find their exports or potential exports generally impeded by high rates of duties" (*Basic Instruments,* 4th Supp. [1956], p. 79, 81). The low-tariff countries protested that this additional statement

Second, some of the trappings of bilateral negotiations gave support to domestic protectionist forces in various countries. The protectionist view of tariff negotiations was that a reduction in one's own tariff schedule involved a detriment that could be counterbalanced only by a reciprocal reduction in another country's tariff schedule. Bilateral negotiations reinforced this view by appearing to set two countries against each other as opponents and to hold out the prize of securing a larger reduction in an opponent's tariff than in one's own tariff.

The GATT vocabulary even today fits this image perfectly: an original tariff reduction is a "concession," whereas a reciprocal reduction is "compensation." Even the word "round" suggests a competition in which one side must "win," a boxing match with two parties locked in combat. As we have seen, this view of tariff negotiations is further engrained by the practice customarily followed by U.S. and some other negotiators of claiming a string of "victories" after every tariff round.

The protectionist view of tariff negotiations is, of course, in sharp contrast to the view traditionally held by most economists, a view that prevailed among noneconomists as well in the latter half of the nineteenth century.[23] Under the economists' view the reduction of a tariff is a benefit to the country making the reduction. Tariff reduction raises the standard of living by lowering prices to consumers, contributes to the competitiveness of local industry by lowering the cost of imputs, and improves the allocation of resources by shifting production from relatively inefficient, import-competing industries to relatively efficient, export industries. If one concentrates on these aspects of tariff reduction, tariff negotiation becomes a joint, cooperative effort.[24]

One of the grave defects of Cordell Hull's Reciprocal Trade Agreements Program was that it secured domestic political support for tariff negotiations mainly by reinforcing the protectionist view of those negotiations. Hull's instinct was sound insofar as it rested upon the notion that the willingness of the United States to reduce its own tariffs could be used as a bait to secure reductions from other countries, which in the 1930s were generally reluctant to act. But the mystique of reciprocity and the mechanics of the product-by-product

---

was only a "recognition of the special problems" of low-tariff countries and that the "rule in itself affords no solution of these problems and the position of the countries concerned will only be improved to the extent to which the rule is effectively applied" (ibid., p. 74, 79).

23. For a contrast between these two ways of viewing tariff reductions, see Harry G. Johnson, "An Economic Theory of Protectionism, Tariff Bargaining, and the Formation of Customs Unions," *Journal of Political Economy,* LXXIII (1965), pp. 256–82.

24. For a discussion of the "two faces" of the doctrine of reciprocity, see John W. Evans, *U.S. Trade Policy* (New York: Harper & Row, 1967), pp. 29–32.

method were strengthening their hold on the U.S. imagination at the same time that successive GATT tariff rounds were beginning to exhaust the possibilities for further reduction under the existing system.

Two different approaches to tariff reduction were under active consideration in the early 1950s: the Low Tariff Club in the Council of Europe and the French Plan in the GATT. These two proposals, although similar in their rejection of bilateral negotiations, reflected different philosophies and therefore attracted somewhat different constellations of political support.

The Low Tariff Club, receiving its initial impetus from the low-tariff countries, sought to reduce high tariffs while leaving low tariffs unchanged. This objective, which implied a complete rejection of the notion of reciprocity, was to be accomplished by the imposition over a three-year period of a ceiling on tariffs. At the conclusion of the three-year period, tariffs on trade among parties adhering to the plan were not to exceed 25 percent on finished goods and food products, 15 percent on semifinished goods, and 5 percent on raw materials. The Low Tariff Club was designed to be a first step in the integration of Europe, although the possibility that non-European countries might adhere to the plan was not excluded.[25]

The French Plan, which became known as the GATT Plan to avoid confusion with the Low Tariff Club being considered by the Council of Europe, was oriented more toward the harmonization of tariffs than toward the reduction of high tariffs, although it had the attractive quality for low-tariff countries of requiring more rapid tariff reductions by high-tariff countries than by low-tariff countries. The French Plan, as revised after technical discussions within the GATT, provided for the classification of tariffs into ten "sectors." Each participating country was to reduce the average incidence of duties within each sector over a three-year period by 30 percent, subject to the following qualification: A demarcation line was to be established for each sector; the percentage of required reduction for each participating country within each sector was to be as much less than 30 percent as the average incidence of the country's duties in the sector was less than the amount indicated by the demarcation line. Thus, low tariffs were to be reduced by a lesser percentage than were high tariffs, and very low tariffs were not to be reduced at all.[26]

Although adoption of the French Plan would have served to reduce tariffs, the essence of the Plan was tariff harmonization; that is, reduction of the disparity between high tariffs and low tariffs. This French idea was to play an important role, as we shall see, in the Kennedy Round negotiations.

The French Plan had the attractive quality of substituting automatic reduc-

25. Council of Europe, *Low Tariff Club* (1952), pp. 25–26.
26. *Basic Instruments,* 2d Supp. (1954), p. 67.

tion for the uncertainties inherent in the doctrine of reciprocity while at the same time preserving a certain degree of the flexibility that was a justification for the system of bilateral negotiations. If a contracting party felt that, for reasons of national interest or of domestic politics, it could not reduce a particular tariff, the average incidence rule would permit it to compensate for the exclusion of that tariff from the general reduction by a larger-than-averge reduction of other tariffs within the sector in question. As in bilateral negotiations, contracting parties would retain a degree of sovereignty over their tariff structures; but in contrast to bilateral negotiations, this retained sovereignty would not be permitted to interfere with general tariff reductions.

Although a majority of the contracting parties favored adoption of the French Plan for the 1956 Geneva Tariff Conference, the opposition of the United States and the United Kingdom blocked any change. This setback did not, however, cause an abatement in interest in seeking an alternative to the system of bilateral negotiations. The success of the European Economic Community and subsequently of the European Free Trade Area in reducing internal tariffs in accordance with an automatic formula not unlike the French Plan tended to strengthen U.S. interest in the adoption of some such across-the-board method. The EEC proposal in the Dillon Round to reduce its Common External Tariff by a uniform 20 percent[27] forced U.S. negotiators to reconsider the question, but no action was taken because of a belief that across-the-board negotiations were inconsistent with the terms of the U.S. Congressional mandate.

When the Kennedy Administration proposed a further round of tariff negotiations in 1962, the draft Trade Expansion Act sent to the Congress authorized both a 50 percent reduction of most tariffs and, implicitly through the legislative history, across-the-board negotiations. Congress passed the act, and the Kennedy Round was launched amid high expectations in the United States that the abandonment of the old product-by-product method and the adoption of what came to be known as the "linear" method would revolutionize the process of tariff negotiating.

In retrospect, it is interesting to note that the Kennedy Administration, either through a failure to understand the implications of linear tariff cuts or through an excess of political guile, led Congress to believe that, as Undersecretary of State Ball promised the Senate Finance Committee, there would be "full reciprocity for every concession that the United States makes."[28] Congress acted on this belief by providing that "trade agreements" should afford "mutual trade

---

27. See U.S. Department of State, *General Agreement on Tariffs and Trade: Analysis of United States Negotiations: 1960–61 Tariff Conference* (1962), I, p. 9.
28. Hearings before the Committee on Finance of the U.S. Senate on the Trade Expansion Act of 1962 (87th Cong., 2d Sess., 1962), p. 2250.

benefits."[29] The administration's position and the exclusion by Congress of certain products totaling some 12 percent of U.S. imports from the scope of the negotiating authorization[30] were implicit disavowals of the across-the-board method and first steps back toward the product-by-product method. As we shall see, at nearly every crucial turn of the Kennedy Round negotiations, decisions were taken, either by the United States or by its principal negotiating partners, that compromised the across-the-board method and carried the GATT back toward the product-by-product method.

## The Kennedy Round

In adding Article XXVIII bis to the General Agreement, the CONTRACTING PARTIES had foresightedly prescribed that negotiations might be carried out either on a "selective product-by-product basis" or "by application of such multilateral procedures as may be accepted by the contracting parties concerned." The decision to depart from the product-by-product method could therefore be treated as any other change in the rules. The final decision to proceed with linear reductions was taken at a ministerial meeting in May 1963,[31] after long and heated discussions over a period of months among the members of a Working Party on Procedures for Tariff Reductions.[32] The ministers delegated the task of preparing detailed rules to a Tariff Negotiations Committee composed of representatives of all participating contracting parties; a set of rules was adopted at a meeting of that committee on the ministerial level in May 1964.[33]

29. 76 Stat. 872 (1962), 19 U.S.C. § 1801 (1964).
   Reciprocity is said to be incompatible with an across-the-board cut of a given percentage by all countries because even if reciprocity is sought on an overall basis rather than on the basis of "every concession," high-tariff countries are unwilling to accept a given percentage cut in a low tariff as the equivalent of an identical percentage cut in a high tariff. At least this is the view of low-tariff countries.
   U.S. negotiators later disavowed any intention to require separate and identifiable reciprocal concessions for all concessions granted. The chief U.S. negotiator explained that one had to take a broader view of reciprocity: "A proper appraisal of the benefits gained and given in a trade negotiation necessarily involves a composite judgment based on the nature and volume of trade subject to concessions, an evaluation of the potentials thereby created for future trade expansion, and on the depths of the concessions made." (statement of William M. Roth before Subcommittee on Foreign Economic Policy of the Joint Economic Committee, 11 July 1967 [mimeographed document], p. 11).
30. The estimate of 12 percent was made by the U.S. delegation to the GATT. See GATT, Document L/1982 (14 March 1963), p. 5
31. *Basic Instruments*, 12th Supp. (1964), p. 36.
32. These discussions are summarized in GATT Document L/2002 (30 April 1963).
33. *Basic Instruments*, 13th Supp. (1965), p. 109. On the Kennedy Round generally, see John B. Rehm, "The Kennedy Round of Trade Negotiations," *American Journal of International Law*, LXII (1968), p. 403.

Interestingly enough, the shift from the product-by-product method to the linear method was not accompanied by a deemphasis of the principle of reciprocity. The first principle in the 1963 Resolution was:

> A significant liberalization of world trade is desirable, and . . . for this purpose, comprehensive trade negotiations, *to be conducted . . . on the principle of reciprocity,* shall begin at Geneva on 4 May 1964, with the widest possible participation.[34]

Only in the fourth principle was the linear method mentioned for the first time.

The various meetings beginning in 1962 and ending with the final adoption of the rules in 1964 revealed certain unexpected limitations of the linear method. In the end the Kennedy Round negotiations became a hybrid of the product-by-product and linear methods. In order to understand the nature of the negotiations as they finally developed, it is useful to review the many departures that were made from a strict across-the-board approach.

## Exceptions

The linear method presupposed that all countries would reduce tariffs by the prescribed percentage on all items. If some countries excluded certain items from the scope of the linear reductions (that is, if they tabled "exceptions" with respect to certain items), other countries would inevitably be forced to weigh concessions received and concessions granted much as under the old product-by-product method. But exceptions were politically inevitable. Congress had, as we have seen, tied the U.S. negotiators' hands, and it was clear that many other countries wanted to exclude certain products. Two possibilities existed for reconciling, at least partially, exceptions with the linear method, but both were rejected.

One would have been to construct a list of common exceptions. This was rejected because, as a practical matter, such a list would have had to include all items excepted by any contracting party and therefore to be very long. Moreover, such a list might have been inconsistent with the linear method insofar as some contracting parties excepted items constituting a larger percentage of their imports than did other contracting parties.

The alternative would have been to prescribe a certain maximum percentage of total imports (broken down perhaps by categories of imports) that might be covered by each national exceptions list. The problems associated with constructing a common exceptions list would thus have been avoided. But this alternative was rejected because it was felt that any "quota" for exceptions would, in Parkinsonian fashion, be filled automatically, as each country sought to minimize concessions granted.

The decision was made to call for "a bare minimum of exceptions which shall

---

34. Ibid., 12th Supp. (1964), p. 47 (emphasis supplied).

be subject to confrontation and justification." Since the term "bare minimum" was not defined, some contracting parties treated the exception lists as bargaining devices, tabling many exceptions and then offering to reduce the number as other contracting parties did the same. Only Austria, Denmark, Sweden, and Switzerland tabled no exceptions, and their offers to make reductions without exceptions were made subject to reciprocity.[35] In the end some items were withdrawn from the 50 percent cut in order to enable certain countries to achieve reciprocity vis-à-vis the EEC.[36] Although the lists were not published, the EEC list was known to be rather long; since the Community had to construct a list satisfactory to each of its six member states, there was a tendency to cumulate the exceptions demanded by those member states. The EEC experience may be noted as an illustration of the difficulties that would have faced the GATT in constructing a common exceptions list for all contracting parties.

The device of confrontation and justification was designed to deal with the danger that exceptions lists might be used as bargaining tools and to keep exceptions to the agreed "bare minimum." Each country was to justify its list in detailed discussions with each of its major negotiating partners. Some sessions of that character were held, but it is unclear whether the number of exceptions was significantly reduced. What is clear is that the process of tabling exceptions lists and then haggling over them served to focus the attention of contracting parties on individual products and to lead negotiators to view the reciprocity principle in a traditional manner.

### Agriculture

In addition to excepting individual products, it was decided after extensive discussions to treat the agricultural sector specially. This special treatment was thought to be justified by the high frequency of quantitative restrictions and other nontariff barriers in agriculture, a circumstance that tended to make tariffs irrelevant to determining international trade flows for agricultural products.[37] In part, the dispute about agriculture reflected a difference between

---

35. GATT Document INT(66)447 (May 1966), p. 4.
36. Jean Rey, "Successful conclusion of the Kennedy Round," *Bulletin of the European Economic Community,* VI (1967), p. 7.
37. Quantitative restrictions and nontariff barriers created difficulties with respect to not only agricultural products, but also a broad range of industrial products. To the extent that the exports of a particular contracting party faced nontariff barriers in one or more major markets, the danger existed that that contracting party would feel compelled to limit its participation in the full 50 percent across-the-board reduction in order to achieve reciprocity. The GATT attempted to meet the difficulties in this area by including nontariff barriers in the scope of the Kennedy Round negotiations (*Basic Instruments,* 12th Supp. [1964], p. 36, 47; ibid., 13th Supp. [1965], p. 109, 111). Whereas in former rounds the term "tariff negotiations" had been used, the term "trade negotiations" was adopted. See, e.g., The CONTRACTING PARTIES to

the national interests of the two major protagonists, the United States and the EEC. The United States was a major agricultural exporter, and its negotiators were committed politically to the Congress to making the successful conclusion of agricultural negotiations a condition for any concessions on industrial products. The EEC was for many agricultural products a major importer and was pursuing a conscious policy of seeking agricultural self-sufficiency.[38] The United States, although maintaining that the general linear rules should apply to agricultural tariffs of major significance, was successful in seeking the adoption of "acceptable conditions of access" as the goal of agricultural sector negotiations. "Acceptable conditions of access" was open to the interpretation that the United States sought a guarantee of a certain percentage share of the EEC market, a guarantee that would have been difficult to reconcile with the linear method if not also with the most-favored-nation clause.

In the end, all agricultural products were excluded from the linear negotiations. Cereal, meats, and dairy products were the subjects of special discussions oriented toward the creation of international commodity arrangements, and the remaining agricultural products were dealt with through specific offers—that is to say, through product-by-product negotiations.[39]

### Nonlinear Countries

If all countries had had approximately the same ratio of agricultural exports to other exports, the exclusion of agriculture from the linear negotiations would not have been so serious. The export receipts for some countries were, however, dependent almost solely on agricultural products. Australia, New Zealand, and South Africa argued that they should be excluded entirely from the linear negotiations, because they would be unable to achieve reciprocity if they were forced to cut tariffs on industrial and consumer goods while receiving only whatever uncertain benefits might emerge from the agricultural negotiations.[40] They had a particularly appealing case because the ministers had been unable to agree in their 1963 and 1964 meetings upon the rules that were to govern the attempts to secure "acceptable conditions of access." Moreover, even if tariffs on agricultural products were ultimately reduced by 50 percent, non-

---

the General Agreement on Tariffs and Trade, *The Activities of the GATT: 1964/65* (1965), p. 17 (hereafter cited as *The Activities of GATT: 1964/65*). This nontariff barrier aspect of the Kennedy Round was, however, much less successful than was the tariff aspect.

38. See generally Kenneth W. Dam, "The European Common Market in Agriculture," *Columbia Law Review,* LXVII (1967), pp. 209–65.

39. Since the agricultural negotiations in the Kennedy Round raised many problems peculiar to that area, further discussion of those negotiations will be deferred to chapter 15, "Temperate Agricultural Commodities," infra.

40. *Basic Instruments,* 13th Supp. (1965), p. 109, 112.

tariff barriers imposed by agricultural importers might deprive agricultural exporters of the benefits of that reduction.

Canada too argued that its heavy dependence on agricultural exports required its exclusion from the linear negotiations. It added (without any reasoned public explanation) that its proximity to, and extensive trade relations with, the United States precluded its cutting tariffs as deeply as the United States cut U.S. tariffs.

As a response to these arguments, a special category was constructed in which Canada was lumped with Australia, New Zealand, and South Africa. These contracting parties were referred to as "countries with a special economic or trade structure such that equal linear tariff reductions may not provide an adequate balance of advantages." Accordingly, they were to be permitted to negotiate on a product-by-product basis, outside the framework of the linear negotiations, so that they might secure "a balance of advantages based on trade concessions by them of equivalent value"; that is, reciprocity.[41]

The establishment of a category of nonlinear countries, as they came to be called, necessitated that the linear negotiations of the Kennedy Round be accompanied by product-by-product negotiations on a wide variety of products. These products included not only the nonlinear countries' exports (which were principally agricultural and therefore largely outside the scope of the linear negotiations in any case), but also those countries' imports. Since the nonlinear countries were relatively high-income countries, the establishment of a nonlinear category had substantial consequences for the negotiations of the linear countries.

Also excluded from the linear negotiations were the less-developed countries as a class.[42] They were to participate through affirmative offers, and they were not to be required to table their offers until they had learned to what extent agricultural products of particular export interest to them were affected by the exceptions filed by linear countries.[43] The addition of the less-developed countries to the nonlinear category would no doubt have occurred in any event on the theory that those countries had special economic structures, but its actual occurrence was compelled by the provision of Part IV that developed countries do not "expect reciprocity" from less-developed countries (Article XXXVI:8).[44]

The categorization of the less-developed countries as nonlinear countries tended to create additional complications in the calculation of global advantages

41. Ibid.; *The Activities of GATT: 1964/65,* pp. 18–19. Greece and Portugal were also included in this category, apparently because they were unwilling to participate on any other basis and because they could not easily be fitted into the category of less-developed countries, a separate nonlinear category.
42. *Basic Instruments,* 13th Supp. (1965), p. 109, 112.
43. GATT Information Services, *Press Release 922* (22 March 1965).
44. See discussion in text, supra, at note 10.

to be derived from linear cuts, particularly as there were so many less-developed countries. In the end, only sixteen countries (counting each member state of the EEC separately) participated in the Kennedy Round as linear countries, while thirty-six were in the nonlinear category.[45]

Disparities

Even the exclusion of agriculture and of excepted items would have left the sixteen linear countries with the great bulk of their industrial products subject to the linear cut. But an EEC proposal threatened to discard the central notion of a 50 percent across-the-board cut. This proposal, which was based on the tariff harmonization ideas of the earlier French Plan and which sought to draw support from the low-tariff countries, was designed to reduce the amount of dispersion in the tariff schedules of different countries. The U.S. tariff schedule, argued the EEC, had a wide range of duties, including many extremely high ones; and a general 50 percent reduction would leave those high duties with a strong protective effect. By contrast, the EEC tariff schedule showed a small degree of dispersion (as a consequence, it should be noted, of the averaging of national tariffs that took place in the creation of the EEC's Common External Tariff), and a general 50 percent reduction would, argued the EEC, destroy the protective effect of all EEC duties. Ergo, the United States would have to reduce its high duties by more than 50 percent if the EEC was to achieve the reciprocity that was the central principle of negotiations. In short, tariff harmonization would have to accompany tariff reduction.

The EEC argument was subtle and arguably inconsistent. In response to the U.S. argument that a high degree of tariff dispersion necessarily reflected many low duties as well as many high duties, the EEC asserted that the low U.S. duties were so low as to be only a small deterrent to trade. The dispute became intense and tangled, with each side advancing statistics based on different weightings of tariff categories to show that on average its duties were lower.[46]

45. Hearings before the Subcommittee on Foreign Economic Policy of the Committee on Foreign Affairs of the U.S. House of Representatives on the Foreign Policy Aspects of the Kennedy Round (89th Cong., 2d Sess., 1966), pp. 27–28.
Of the thirty-six in the nonlinear category, four—Argentina, Iceland, Tunisia, and the United Arab Republic—participated in the Kennedy Round as a way of paying the entrance fee for accession. To this extent, Article XXVIII bis negotiations and Article XXXIII negotiations were merged. Another of these thirty-six, Poland, a state-trading country, made a specific offer; therefore, negotiations with it were necessarily on a product-by-product basis (*The Activities of the GATT: 1964/65*, p. 21).
46. At one point a leading U.S. negotiator, seeking to show that statistics varied with the "bases used and the method of calculation," said that he had seen "at least five reputable comparisons of United States and EEC average tariffs, with spreads ranging up to six per cent, and with first the EEC and then the United States having the highest level" (Remarks by the Hon. W. Michael Blumenthal, Deputy Special

There was also a good deal of debate over the economics of tariff reduction. In the U.S. view, the EEC argument failed to "take into account the fact that the reduction of a high rate of duty might lead to a greater increase in trade than the same percentage reduction in a lower rate of duty."[47]

The EEC proposal initially stipulated that tariffs be reduced by "50 percent of the extent to which they exceeded a target ad valorem rate which would be the same for all contracting parties other than less-developed countries but would be different for the main commodity groups . . . say, free entry for raw materials, say 5 percent for semi-manufactured products and say 10 percent for finished products."[48] At the May 1963 meeting, the United States argued that this formula would drastically lower the average tariff reduction in the Kennedy Round.[49] The GATT ministers were thereafter unable to arrive at more than a pretense of agreement on the EEC proposal. The ministers' resolution stated that "in those cases where there are significant disparities in tariff levels, the tariff reductions will be based upon special rules of general and automatic application," but it left to the Trade Negotiations Committee the task of selecting the "criteria for determining significant disparities in tariff levels and the special rules applicable for tariff reductions in these cases."[50] This formula for procrastination was further complicated when the ministers accepted a statement of the chairman of the meeting, the Swiss representative, that the tariff disparities that were to be considered significant were those that were "meaningful in trade terms."[51]

After the May 1963 meeting the EEC gave its disparities proposal a new form. A disparity would have existed under the amended proposal if at least one of the three principal linear participants (that is, the United States, the

---

Representative for Trade Negotiations, at a Round Table Sponsored by the Institute for International Relations, Rome, Italy, Saturday, March 12, 1966 [mimeographed document], pp. 5–6). For a comparison of statistics based upon a simple average rate, upon an average rate weighted by imports, and upon a median rate, see Address by the Hon. W. Michael Blumenthal, Deputy Special Representative for Trade Negotiations, at a meeting of the Carl Schurz Association, Bad Godesberg, Federal Republic of Germany, Wednesday, March 16, 1966 (mimeographed document), p. 4.

47. GATT Document L/2002 (30 April 1963), p. 15. On the economic issues, see Robert E. Baldwin, "Tariff-cutting Techniques in the Kennedy Round," in Baldwin et al., *Trade, Growth, and the Balance of Payments* (Chicago: Rand McNally & Co., 1965), pp. 68–81; Richard N. Cooper, "Tariff Dispersion and Trade Negotiations," *Journal of Political Economy,* LXXIII (1964), pp. 597–603.

48. GATT Document L/2002 (April 30, 1963), p. 2.

49. "GATT Ministers Reach Agreement on Tariff Negotiating Procedure," *Department of State Bulletin,* XLVIII (1963), p. 993.

50. *Basic Instruments,* 12th Supp. (1964), pp. 36, 47–48.

51. GATT Information Services, *Press Release 847* (5 May 1964), p. 2.

United Kingdom, and the EEC) had imposed a duty at least twice as high as the duty imposed by another linear participant (principal or otherwise) on the same item, provided that in the case of manufactured products the former duty had been at least ten percentage points higher than the latter duty.[52] In the case of the existence of a disparity thus defined, the high-duty country would have reduced its tariff by 50 percent, while low-duty countries would have reduced their tariffs by a lesser percentage. The degree of reduction by the low-duty countries would have depended upon the breadth of the disparity and would have averaged about 25 percent.

Adoption of the amended EEC proposal, which was opposed not only by the United States but also by Switzerland and certain other relatively low-tariff countries, would have led, in the words of the Swiss representative, to "paradoxical" if not "absurd" consequences.[53] Under that proposal the effect of a declaration of the existence of a tariff disparity would have been to lower the degree of tariff reduction by the low-tariff countries rather than to increase the degree of tariff reduction by the high-tariff country. (In part, the EEC disparity formula was forced into this mold by the U.S. negotiators' lack of authority to grant concessions of more than 50 percent.) This effect would have weighed most heavily on the major exporters of the item in question. These major exporters would, however, most likely have been not the high-tariff countries, but rather some of the low-tariff countries, since only a country that is an inefficient producer, and therefore not a major exporter, of a particular item is likely to feel the need for a high tariff on that item.[54]

A concrete example may serve to illustrate the point. Prior to the Kennedy Round, the U.S. duty on many types of watches was above 50 percent; the EEC duty on comparable items, below 15 percent. Under the amended EEC proposal the EEC could have claimed a disparity against the United States on watches and thus have reduced its duty by only about 25 percent instead of the normal linear figure of 50 percent. This smaller cut by the EEC would not have harmed the United States, since the latter did not export watches in significant quantities. The smaller cut would, however, have harmed Switzerland, which was a major exporter to the Community. In effect, Switzerland would have been denied the benefits of a full 50 percent duty cut in one of its major markets simply because the United States happened to have a high duty on the item in question.[55]

The impact of the EEC disparities formula on the Kennedy Round negotia-

52. The amended EEC proposal was apparently not published. The description in the text is taken from Baldwin, p. 74.
53. GATT Information Services, *Press Release 847* (5 May 1964), p. 3.
54. See GATT Document INT(66)493 (July 1966), p. 3.
55. The example is drawn from Baldwin, p. 76.

tions would thus have been to cause linear participants to make a product-by-product assessment of the extent to which invocations of the disparities principle by other linear participants had upset the global balance of concessions granted and concessions received and had thereby made necessary a renegotiation of the exceptions lists. Since, according to U.S. calculations, adoption of the EEC proposal would have resulted in the applicability of the disparities principle to 1,200 out of 2,300 industrial tariff items,[56] it is not unlikely that the entire Kennedy Round would have been converted into a product-by-product negotiation.

No agreement was reached at the May 1964 ministerial-level meeting of the Trade Negotiations Committee. The proposed 50 percent across-the-board cut became only a "working hypothesis," and it was agreed that "ultimate agreement on tariff reductions in accordance with the application of this hypothesis is linked with the solution of other problems arising in the negotiations, for example, tariff disparities."[57] The Kennedy Round commenced with no agreement on the disparities question. The failure to agree was tantamount to a decision to treat each alleged disparity in ad hoc fashion and therefore was a powerful incentive to product-by-product negotiations.

### Sector Discussions

Once the negotiations started, it quickly became apparent that there were certain industrial sectors in which there was almost no likelihood that all the major participants would agree to a 50 percent across-the-board reduction. The reasons for the hesitancy to make the full reduction in these sectors were diverse and complex, ranging from a rapidly changing world competitive situation in textiles to special tariff administration problems in chemicals. To prevent difficulties in these sectors from distorting the negotiations in other sectors and to provide a framework for specialized bargaining, it was decided to initiate "sector discussions" on aluminum, chemicals, pulp and paper, steel, and textiles among countries with a special import or export interest in those products.[58] Here again, attention was shifted from linear reductions to product-by-product negotiations. Unlike the product-by-product negotiations in former rounds, however, these discussions involved—at least in theory—not haggling about the "trade coverage" of individual products, but rather an attempt to understand and deal with each industry as a whole.

56. "Breakthrough," *Newsweek,* 9 March 1964, p. 68.
57. *Basic Instruments,* 13th Supp. (1965), pp. 109–10.
58. GATT Document INT(66)447 (May 1966), p. 4; *Tenth Annual Report of the President of the United States on the Trade Agreements Program,* House Document No. 449 (89th Cong., 2d Sess., 1966), p. 10.

## The Results of the Kennedy Round

The final weeks of the Kennedy Round developed into an extremely complex exercise in which each participant, whether linear or nonlinear, adjusted its exceptions and percentages of reduction in a quest for global reciprocity.[59] In the end, 30 percent of the dutiable imports of the major participants were left untouched by tariff reductions, and approximately one-third of the reductions on the remaining imports were of less than the full 50 percent. Just as in earlier rounds the principle equating the binding of a low tariff with the substantial reduction of a high tariff had failed to survive intact the realities of tariff bargaining, so in the Kennedy Round the across-the-board principle was seriously compromised.

## Rules, Objectives, and Procedures

The Kennedy Round experience suggests that rules alone cannot determine the content of tariff negotiations, particularly so long as the principle of reciprocity exercises such a powerful influence on negotiators. But it would be a mistake to conclude that the right kind of rules cannot exercise a beneficent influence on the outcome of negotiations. Advance agreement on objectives may play a particularly important role. The agreement that a 50 percent cut should be the working hypothesis of the Kennedy Round negotiations, for example, deserves major credit for the reductions that were in fact made in those negotiations. Although the U.S. and EEC exceptions lists and the EEC disparities proposal were said by some to evidence bad faith, the 50 percent principle was a convenient and appealing expression of a commonly held goal—the reduction of tariffs to a point where they would be of minor importance in determining international trade patterns.

Some of the new procedures followed in the Kennedy Round also exercised a beneficial influence on the outcome of the negotiations. The sector discussions, for example, introduced a valuable multilateral element and enabled the participants, if not to transcend the limitations of the reciprocity principle, at least to arrive at detailed understandings of the industries concerned and of the compromises possible. Indeed, special arrangements worked out in the chemical and steel sector discussions helped to draw the negotiations away from the brink of complete collapse.[60]

---

59. A number of specific issues not discussed here became important. One dealt with the American Selling Price system of valuation, which is discussed in chapter 11, "Administrative Barriers to Trade," infra.

60. Communauté économique européene, *Dixième rapport générale sur l'activité de la Communauté* (1967), point 312.

The precedent of sector discussions may in the future provide a key to further progress toward tariff liberalization. The former director general of the GATT, Wyndham White, has suggested that future tariff negotiations could usefully take the form of attempts to reach global free trade in particular industries.[61] Whether this could be done in a single sector is doubtful: the elimination of all tariffs in a particular industry generally does not by itself satisfy the principle of reciprocity, and the members of the world trading community have yet to show any disposition to deemphasize that principle. But perhaps reciprocity could be achieved by linking two or three sectors together in a single "package."

Although the device of holding a major tariff conference every four to five years has served the cause of trade liberalization well in the past, the very success of the Kennedy Round, coupled with that round's unprecedented length and complexity, may have seriously reduced the incentive for further such conferences. Trade liberalization in the future may therefore depend upon finding some simpler, more limited framework for tariff bargaining, perhaps along the industry lines suggested by Wyndham White.

Whatever the scope of future negotiations, more thought needs to be given to devising procedures that will facilitate agreement on tariff liberalization. The Kennedy Round experience indicates that the reciprocity notion is so deeply imbedded in the psychology of national governments and in the traditions of the GATT that any attempt to conjure it away by rules is futile. Rather, the challenge will be to work out procedures that will harness that principle in the direction of trade liberalization. At certain crucial points in prior rounds, the director general stepped in to suggest "packages" of concessions, which, by making it possible for all parties concerned to achieve reciprocity, helped to break deadlocks in the negotiations. In the period after the Kennedy Round, when national enthusiasm for major tariff conferences can be expected to be low, the GATT secretariat may be able to play a useful role by suggesting to the major contracting parties special ad hoc "packages" of concessions that will provide the reciprocity that those contracting parties have made the prerequisite of tariff reductions.

61. GATT Document INT(66)576 (Oct. 1966), p. 3.

# 6 Technical Tariff Negotiations

Most GATT tariff concessions are made in periodic rounds of trade conference negotiations, discussed in the immediately preceding chapter. Equally important from the legal viewpoint, although not statistically so frequent, are tariff concessions in a number of different kinds of technical tariff negotiations taking place between, and outside the central framework of, trade conference negotiations. Also important are the technical tariff procedures for the withdrawal or modification of tariff concessions. To a substantial extent these two classes of tariff changes occur as part of the same technical negotiations. It is in the process of renegotiating existing tariff concessions that most of the extraconference bindings occur. Consequently, in order to understand technical tariff negotiations, it is essential to consider the legal nature of a tariff binding and, in particular, the ways in which a duty may become unbound.

## Retaliation as an Enforcement System

The essence of the GATT system lies not in the abstract legal relationships created by a tariff concession but rather in the enforcement mechanism. Under Article XXIII the principal sanction for an increase of a duty in violation of a binding is the suspension by interested contracting parties of concessions made to the offending contracting party. There is no punitive sanction for nonperformance of the promise implicit in a tariff concession. The consequence of nonperformance is thus merely the reestablishment, at the option of an interested party and subject to the approval of the contracting parties, of the preexisting situation (although the retaliatory suspension may be on items not originally negotiated with the offending contracting party).

This brief reference to the enforcement question is intended not only to suggest the essential nature of tariff bindings, but also to provide a useful perspective for understanding the unique nature of the GATT tariff system. The system rests, as the Preamble states, upon the notion of "reciprocal and mutually advantageous" arrangements directed to the substantial reduction of tariffs. The rules in the General Agreement are designed to preserve whatever balance of advantages is arrived at in the course of negotiations, with a bias toward preserving that balance at the lowest tariff level possible.

The goal of achieving and maintaining a relatively low tariff level has resulted in a system that contrasts sharply with the international law of treaties and the domestic law of contracts in the world's major legal systems. Public international law and domestic contract law tend to view agreements as binding even when one of the parties no longer regards continued performance of the agreement to be in its interest (although the two bodies of law give some recognition to the principle of *rebus sic stantibus,* under which an agreement is not held binding if the circumstances have fundamentally changed in a way that was not anticipated by the parties at the time of the making of the agreement). This indicates that, with many obvious exceptions, domestic contract law and public international law are more concerned with assuring that commitments made are carried out than with promoting the making of agreements in the first place.

The GATT has a special interest in seeing that as many agreements for the reduction of tariffs as possible are made. Enforcement of bindings is important in the GATT insofar as such enforcement gives contracting parties the confidence necessary to rely upon tariff concessions offered by other contracting parties. But because of the economic nature of tariff concessions and the domestic political sensitivity inherently involved in trade issues, a system that made withdrawals of concessions impossible would tend to discourage the making of the concessions in the first place. It is better, for example, that 100 commitments should be made and that 10 should be withdrawn than that only 50 commitments should be made and that all of them should be kept.

The best guarantee that a commitment of any kind will be kept (particularly in an international setting where courts are of limited importance and, even more important, marshals and jails are nonexistent) is that the parties continue to view adherence to their agreement as in their mutual interest. The principal tariff functions of the GATT, beyond the sponsoring of rounds of tariff negotiations, are therefore (1) to prevent contracting parties from upsetting the balance of advantages by unilateral withdrawals of concessions, (2) to maintain the general level of liberalization already achieved by assuring that retaliatory action by other contracting parties is not greater than necessary to reestablish the balance of advantages and does not set off further rounds of retaliatory action, and (3) to establish procedures for original withdrawals of concessions and for subsequent retaliatory withdrawals so that disputes among contracting parties do not destroy confidence in the GATT system.

Thus, the GATT system, unlike most legal systems (including public international law), is not designed to exclude self-help in the form of retaliation. Rather, retaliation, subjected to established procedures and kept within prescribed bounds, is made the heart of the GATT system.

The essentially multilateral nature of the GATT system creates some special problems in using retaliation as an organizing principle. So long as the most-favored-nation rule is observed, it is difficult to limit the effects of retaliation to the trade of the contracting party initially withdrawing a concession. If contracting party A withdraws its concession on item X, contracting party B, finding its exports to A endangered, may decide to withdraw its concession on item Y. But if B imports item Y from both A and contracting party C, and if B adheres to the most-favored-nation principle, C will find that its exports to contracting party B are faced with a higher tariff, and C may in turn decide to retaliate. The possibilities for an "unraveling" of the interwoven, interdependent system of tariff bindings are readily apparent. Some additional controls must therefore be placed on retaliation if the web of bindings resulting from a round of multilateral tariff negotiations is not to come apart gradually as a consequence of a few initial decisions to withdraw concessions.

## "Open Season" Negotiations

In order to induce extensive tariff concessions in the initial 1947 round of GATT tariff negotiations, the duration of what was called the "firm validity" of concessions was limited to three years. Under the original arrangement all tariffs were therefore to have become open for renegotiation on 1 January 1951. Convinced that the common interest required that ground already gained be held, the CONTRACTING PARTIES agreed to extend the period of firm validity of the schedules then in effect (including schedules amended since the original round) to 1 January 1954.[1] The period of firm validity was subsequently extended to 1 July 1955,[2] and to 1 January 1958.[3] On each occasion it was possible for an individual contracting party not to sign the declaration of continued firm validity and thereby to remain free to renegotiate its concessions at any time under Article XXVIII, but this entailed granting other contracting parties the same right of renegotiation.

In the course of deciding upon the second of these three extensions, the CONTRACTING PARTIES were forced to take account of objections from countries that found too confining the resulting quasi-permanent firm validity of commitments made some years before. The only result was, however, a state-

1. *Basic Instruments,* Vol. II (1952), p. 30.
2. Ibid., 2d Supp. (1954), pp. 22, 61.
3. Ibid, 3d Supp. (1955), p. 30.

ment that the CONTRACTING PARTIES had in the past examined "with sympathy and understanding" requests made "in exceptional circumstances, to modify certain bound rates of duty," and that there was "no reason to believe that contracting parties will be less ready in the future than they have in the past to consider requests of this kind."[4]

The uncertainty of the periodic renewal procedure and the indefiniteness of the statement made at the time of the second extension led the 1955 Review Session Working Party to reconsider the entire question and, thereupon, to propose an amendment to Article XXVIII, which was subsequently adopted by the CONTRACTING PARTIES. As the Working Party observed, there were three principal possibilities: (1) to extend the firm validity of the schedules indefinitely; (2) to extend their firm validity from time to time; and (3) to provide for automatic extensions of their firm validity by three-year periods, "with greater flexibility in the right to renegotiate and in the procedures for negotiation, both during the periods of firm validity and at the end of each period."[5]

The working party chose the third alternative. Schedules were to be automatically extended at the end of each third-year period (dating from 1 January 1958) or such other period as might be chosen by a two-thirds vote of the CONTRACTING PARTIES. To give contracting parties the opportunity to renegotiate particular concessions, however, provisions were to be made for two types of technical tariff negotiations. We may call the two types "open season" negotiations and "out-of-season" negotiations.

### The Procedures for "Open Season" Negotiations

"Open season" negotiations conducted under amended Article XXVIII may lead to modifications or withdrawals of concessions in two situations. First, a contracting party may elect at a date not earlier than six months, nor later than three months, prior to the termination date of one period of firm validity to modify or withdraw a concession in its GATT schedule on the first day of the following period of firm validity.[6] Second, a contracting party may elect at any time during one period of firm validity to reserve the right to take such action at any time during the following period of firm validity (Article XXVIII:5). In the second situation notice of such an election gives other contracting parties the reciprocal right to modify or withdraw concessions originally negotiated with the electing contracting party. The purpose of the

---

4. Ibid., 2d Supp. (1954), pp. 61, 62–63. The CONTRACTING PARTIES had in 1948–49 granted Pakistan and Brazil permission to enter into negotiations to modify concessions they had granted on certain items in their schedules.
5. Ibid., 3d Supp. (1955), pp. 205, 216–17.
6. Interpretative note, Ad. Art. XXVIII, para. 1:3.

strict rule of reciprocity that is applied to elections to reserve the right to modify or withdraw a concession at any time during a following period of firm validity is obviously to dampen the incentive for making such elections as a matter of course in order to gain flexibility with regard to future tariff changes. Any flexibility that may be gained in this manner is at least partially offset by the insecurity (with respect to tariffs) that the electing country's exporters must face. It should be noted in this regard that any reservation of the right to negotiate during a following period of firm validity applies to the entire GATT schedule in question and not just to certain items. This means that all contracting parties that have ever negotiated concessions with the reserving party gain the right to renegotiate those concessions.[7]

"Open season" negotiations must be carried on not only with the contracting party with which the concession was originally negotiated, but also with any other contracting party deemed by the CONTRACTING PARTIES to have a "principal supplying interest." The CONTRACTING PARTIES are to determine that a contracting party has a "principal supplying interest" only (1) "if that contracting party has had, over a reasonable period of time prior to the negotiations, a larger share in the market of the applicant contracting party than a contracting party with which the concession was initially negotiated," or (2) if that contracting party "would, in the judgment of the CONTRACTING PARTIES, have had such a share in the absence of discriminatory quantitative restrictions maintained by the applicant contracting party."[8] As a further limitation, the CONTRACTING PARTIES may not determine that more than one contracting party has a "principal supplying interest," except that they may specify two contracting parties "in those exceptional cases where there is near equality."[9]

One might conclude, if one read Article XXVIII literally, that the number of contracting parties with which it would be necessary to carry on negotiations would therefore never be more than three and would rarely be more than two. As a practical matter, negotiations may often be required with a number of contracting parties. It early became a common practice of some contracting parties to negotiate for the recognition by other contracting parties that the former had "initial negotiating rights" in concessions already granted by the latter to third parties. When such rights were granted, the grantee became contractually entitled to be treated as a "contracting party with which [a] concession was initially negotiated" under Article XXVIII and hence to

7. *Basic Instruments,* 3d Supp. (1955), p. 205, 218.
8. Interpretative note, Ad Art. XXVIII, para. 1:4.
9. Ibid. One major exception to this rule exists for exporters of one or very few products. If the item in question "constitutes a major part of the total exports" of a contracting party, even though that contracting party is not the leading exporter of that item, the CONTRACTING PARTIES may "exceptionally" designate it as having a "principal supplying interest."

be an Article XXVIII negotiating partner in the event of modification or withdrawal of that concession. In some cases a number of contracting parties may have received initial negotiating rights, and therefore the Article XXVIII negotiations may be truly multilateral.

The use of the linear method in the Kennedy Round created certain conceptual problems in determining, for the purposes of Article XXVIII, the contracting party with which a linear reduction was initially negotiated. At the session of the CONTRACTING PARTIES following the conclusion of the Kennedy Round, this lacuna in the conceptual apparatus of Article XXVIII was bridged by a recommendation that, for the purposes of Kennedy Round concessions, "a contracting party shall, when the question arises, be deemed for the purposes of the General Agreement to be the contracting party with which a concession was initially negotiated if it had during a representative period prior to that time a principal supplying interest in the product concerned." The recommendation did not foreclose the possibility that a contracting party that had no such principal supplying interest could negotiate to be recognized as having such initial negotiating rights.[10]

The identity of the negotiating partners in "open season" negotiations is thus prescribed by the General Agreement with great precision, although left subject to a certain residual discretion in designated situations. By comparison, the selection of the contracting parties that must be consulted is somewhat more within the discretion of the CONTRACTING PARTIES. Here the classification is defined as including those contracting parties that have a "substantial interest," a term left undefined in the General Agreement. An interpretative note indicates that contracting parties having a "substantial interest" include "only those contracting parties which have, or in the absence of discriminatory quantitative restrictions affecting their exports could reasonably be expected to have, a *significant share* in the market of the contracting party seeking to modify or withdraw the concession."[11] The notion of "significant share" is surely at least as indefinite as that of "substantial interest." The consequences of the ambiguity are not serious, however. According to an interpretative note, it is not intended that the designation of additional contracting parties for consultation "should have the effect that [the applicant] should have to pay compensation or suffer retaliation greater than the withdrawal or modification sought."[12]

Although Article XXVIII contemplates that the CONTRACTING PARTIES will determine the parties having principal supplying interests and substantial in-

10. *Basic Instruments,* 15th Supp. (1968), p. 67; GATT Document L/2867 (13 Oct. 1967); Interpretative note, Ad Art. XXVIII, para. 1:5.
11. Interpretative note, Ad Art. XXVIII, para. 1:7 (emphasis supplied).
12. Interpretative note, Ad Art. XXVIII, para. 1:6.

terests, that cumbersome procedure has been simplified by a decision of the CONTRACTING PARTIES which makes this determination a question in the first instance for the affected contracting parties. A contracting party claiming an interest in a concession that is to be modified or withdrawn under Article XXVIII, may seek recognition of that interest by the applicant contracting party. If that claim of interest is recognized, "the recognition will constitute a determination by the CONTRACTING PARTIES of interest in the sense of Article XXVIII:1."[13] Only if the claim is not recognized is recourse to conventional procedures required.[14]

Although the carrying on of negotiations is to be distinguished from consultations, it is not clear to what extent the two exercises are to differ. Perhaps a single meeting will suffice as consultation. It is clear, on the other hand, that negotiations are to be carried out with a view to an "agreement." The content of that proposed agreement is in general a question for the negotiating partners, but the General Agreement does lay down certain guidelines. The parties are to "endeavour to maintain a general level of reciprocal and mutually advantageous concessions not less favourable to trade than that provided for in [the General] Agreement prior to such negotiations" (Article XXVIII:2). Since the individual country schedules are integral parts of the General Agreement, this provision means that the powers granted by Article XXVIII are to be used only to reshuffle the applicant's concessions in such a way as to maintain roughly the same overall level of protection on items subject to concessions, and are not to be used to increase the overall level of protection. This balance may be achieved by "compensatory adjustments"; that is to say, by new or increased concessions in compensation for the withdrawal or modification of other concessions.

The importance of this provision cannot be overemphasized. Having once made tariff concessions, contracting parties are to "endeavour" thenceforth to maintain the new lower level of tariff duties. In return for this limitation on action, they are to have considerable flexibility in altering the structure of their tariff schedules. This solution is a promising compromise between, on the one hand, the desirability of holding parties to their bargains and, on the other hand, the pragmatic end of providing flexibility in order to encourage further lowering of tariffs and the need for a respectable, lawful escape valve for governments torn between external commitments and unmanageable protectionist pressures at home.

In addition to helping to preserve each new advance made and thereby creating a "ratchet effect" in the tariff negotiating process, Article XXVIII

13. GATT Document L/635 (31 May 1957), p. 2.
14. See, e.g., the procedures for the Article XXVIII open season negotiations in 1957, ibid.

also makes clear that parties that decide to restructure their tariff schedules need not necessarily be subjected to punitive retaliation. The maintenance of the overall schedule at a level "not less favourable to trade than that provided . . . prior to such negotiations" is to be accomplished by "reciprocal and mutually advantageous concessions." It is not the applicant country alone that is to maintain its overall level of tariffs; rather, all of the contracting parties concerned are to "endeavour" to achieve that result.

The measurement of the compensation that is to be offered by the applicant in the form of new or increased concessions to offset the withdrawal or modification of other concessions raises some difficult and fundamental problems. It is usually considered in original tariff negotiations that the equivalence of reciprocal concessions between two contracting parties is to be judged by those contracting parties alone. A logical corollary would seem to be that it is up to the contracting parties involved to determine the adequacy of compensatory adjustments in Article XXVIII negotiations. An interpretative note nonetheless indicates that the adequacy of compensatory adjustments is to be "judged in the light of the conditions of trade at the time of the proposed withdrawal or modification, making allowance for any discriminatory quantitative restrictions maintained by the applicant contracting party."[15] This standard is, of course, considerably less than a formula of mathematical exactitude, but it departs, particularly in its insistence that the effect of discriminatory quantitative restrictions be taken into account, from the principle applied in original tariff negotiations.

Since negotiations need not result in agreement, the General Agreement allows contracting parties to fall back on the remedy of self-help. If agreement is not reached before the commencement of the next period of firm validity, or (since extensions of time are frequently given) within the period of any extension, the applicant is free to carry out the proposed changes. Both negotiating and consulted contracting parties are correspondingly free to withdraw "substantially equivalent concessions." The withdrawn concessions must have been initially negotiated with the applicant. Similarly, if agreement is reached in the negotiations but a contracting party that must be consulted is not "satisfied," that contracting party may also withdraw "substantially equivalent concessions initially negotiated with the applicant contracting party." In each case the retaliatory withdrawal is to take place within six months of the initial withdrawal and following thirty days written notice to the CONTRACTING PARTIES. Unlike retaliatory withdrawals envisaged in certain other provisions, notably Articles XIX and XXIII, no special authorization of the retaliatory measure is required (Article XXVIII:3).

15. Interpretative note, Ad Article XXVIII, para. 1:6.

## The Definition of "Substantially Equivalent Concessions"

The elaborate procedures of Article XXVIII, although well designed to insure deliberation before action, nevertheless leave open a number of questions. The most important involve the definition of "substantially equivalent concessions." In seeking a definition of this term an interpretative note to paragraph 1 of Article XXVIII may be relevant, even though the "substantially equivalent concessions" language appears in paragraph 3 of that article. This interpretative note (which was considered above in connection with compensatory adjustments) states that retaliation is not to be "greater than the withdrawal or modification sought, judged in the light of the conditions of trade at the time of the proposed withdrawal or modification, making allowance for any discriminatory quantitative restrictions maintained by the applicant contracting party."[16] As far as disputes over the appropriateness of retaliatory withdrawals are concerned, this interpretative note gives the CONTRACTING PARTIES some benchmarks, but it does not address itself directly to the problem of the appropriate technique to be used for comparing the equivalence of reciprocal tariff concessions. At the stage of initial negotiation of concessions (under Article XXVIII bis) and even in the course of Article XXVIII negotiations, this matter can safely be left to the negotiating parties to determine as they deem appropriate. But when a dispute arises and a decision must be reached by the CONTRACTING PARTIES or a subsidiary body, the question is squarely faced.

The problem of defining "substantially equivalent concessions" arose in the so-called chicken war between the United States and the European Economic Community. In that case the negotiations were conducted under Article XXIV:6, which requires that if, when a customs union is in the process of formation, any bound rate of duty is to be raised above the bound level, negotiations must be initiated under the procedures of Article XXVIII. In the course of constructing the EEC system for poultry, a concession previously granted by the Federal Republic of Germany to the United States was withdrawn. The dispute that arose between the United States and the EEC about the appropriate extent of the U.S. retaliatory withdrawal of concessions under Article XXVIII reflected certain typical attitudes that have developed among the contracting parties in measuring concessions.

The dispute centered on the quantity of U.S. imports of poultry into the Federal Republic of Germany that were affected by the action of the EEC. A panel was established with the following terms of reference:

> To render an advisory opinion to the two parties concerned in order to determine: "On the basis of the definition of poultry provided in . . . the Common Customs Tariff of the European Economic Community, and on

16. Ibid.

the basis of the rules of and practices under the GATT, the value (expressed in United States dollars) to be ascribed, as of 1 September 1960, in the context of the unbindings concerning this product, to United States exports of poultry to the Federal Republic of Germany."[17]

The panel took the actual figures for U.S. exports of poultry to the Federal Republic of Germany during the most recent twelve months for which figures would have been available on the chosen base date, adjusting those figures to reflect discriminatory quantitative restrictions in effect in the Federal Republic of Germany during that period. The panel, compromising between the relatively high figure claimed by the United States and the relatively low figure claimed by the EEC, arrived at $26,000,000 as the extent of U.S. exports.[18] The United States thereupon proceeded to suspend concessions on potato starch, brandy valued at more than $9.00 per gallon, dextrine and soluble or chemically treated starches, and automobile trucks valued at $1,000 or more.[19] These items were chosen because they were imported almost entirely from the EEC (only $1,000,000 of imports from third countries were involved), and because the total amount of U.S. imports totaled $24,000,000—that is to say, almost exactly the amount of U.S. exports of poultry to the Federal Republic of Germany.

As has been previously argued, measuring the value of a concession solely by the quantity of imports entering under the tariff item to which that concession applies is absurd. Whatever considerations of convenience may support its employment in the major tariff conferences, such an approach is extremely misleading where only a single tariff is involved. It ignores a complementary factor—the number of percentage points ad valorem by which the tariff is raised in the modification or withdrawal of the concession. Of course, where a concession is withdrawn and not merely modified, it is not possible to measure the rate change because, the concession no longer being in effect, the Article XXVIII applicant is thereafter free to alter the tariff rate at will and without further negotiations. But the fundamental weakness of the trade coverage approach is that it ignores what is really important—the extent to which the protective effect is increased in raising the tariff by a certain percentage.

This increase in protective effect will have only a very loose relation to (1) the quantity of trade preceding the increase and (2) the percentage in-

17. *Basic Instruments,* 12th Supp. (1964), p. 65.
18. GATT Document L/2088 (21 Nov. 1963). See Herman Walker, "Dispute Settlement: The Chicken War," *American Journal of International Law,* LVIII (1964), p. 671.
19. U.S. Tariff Commission, *Operation of the Trade Agreements Program,* 16th Rep. (1966), pp. 46–47.

crease. The quantity of trade preceding the increase will have depended upon the protective effect of the original tariff, and this protective effect will have had little necessary relation to the nominal ad valorem rate. For one product a 10 percent tariff will have been prohibitive; for another product a 50 percent tariff will not have prevented the elimination of an inefficient domestic industry. The protective effect will have depended upon such factors (in addition to the ad valorem percentage) as the relationship between world prices and domestic prices and the importance of price in determining purchases. Similarly, the percentage increase will not necessarily indicate much about the increase in protective effect. In industries where demand is highly elastic, a very slight increase in the tariff may be sufficient to reduce imports drastically.

What would be preferable to the volume-of-imports criterion would be an indication, however inexact it might be, of the extent to which imports might be expected to decline as a result of a particular tariff increase. Admittedly, such a measure would involve a good deal of guesswork. It would, however, be a great improvement upon the criterion of the volume of imports prior to the tariff increase. Obviously such an approach is more workable for the modification than for the withdrawal of concessions.

It should be noted that all of the foregoing comments on valuing retaliatory withdrawals of concessions apply mutatis mutandis to the measurement of compensatory adjustments in the applicant contracting party's schedule. It is clear that, for example, a 5 percent increase of a tariff covering $1,000,000 of imports need not be equivalent in effect to a decrease of 5 percent in another tariff covering $1,000,000 of imports.

One may speculate about the reasons underlying the use by the contracting parties of such a naïve measure of the value of concessions. Although estimates of the reduction in imports to be expected might be uncertain and might give rise to disputes between the parties, the certainty offered by using pre-increase import figures alone is patently deceptive. One might suppose that the pre-increase import figures are simply shorthand figures, used to explain matters to an untutored public but failing to reveal the arcane calculations made by the experts behind closed doors. Such a supposition no doubt contains a grain of truth, but it attributes entirely too much merit to the scientific quality of the discussions that actually take place. The history of the poultry war dispute would seem to verify this thesis. Likewise, the reports by the U.S. Tariff Commission on the Trade Agreements Program reveal not a more sophisticated approach, but rather a compulsion to demonstrate the approximate equality of the total volumes of imports involved in reciprocal grantings or withdrawals of concessions or in compensatory adjustments within a single schedule. In discussing the Article XXVIII negotiations held at Torquay, for example, the Tariff Commission reports:

The countries that negotiated under Article XXVIII at Torquay modified or withdrew concessions they had granted to the United States at Geneva or Annecy on products which accounted for United States exports valued at approximately *100 million dollars* in 1949. In exchange for these modifications or withdrawals, these countries granted the United States compensatory concessions on products the United States exports of which were valued at approximately *102 million dollars* in 1949.[20]

What perhaps happens in practice is that in the case of retaliation an attempt is made to pick items involving the same volume of trade as the items on which concessions have been withdrawn or modified and to raise the tariff by an amount estimated to have approximately the same trade effect. Of course, the appropriate trade effect to aim at is difficult to judge where the applicant has withdrawn and not merely modified its original concession. Similar rough guesses of trade effect are perhaps also made in the case of compensatory adjustments. In the latter case, however, the necessity of securing agreement to the change on the part of the affected contracting parties tends to act as an automatic limitation on the freedom of action of the applicant contracting party. It may therefore be sufficient to rely, as in the case of initial negotiations under Article XXVIII bis, upon the judgment of the contracting parties concerned as to the relative value of the withdrawn or modified concession and the compensatory adjustment. Where retaliation is involved, the retaliating party is no longer in the position of needing the assent of any negotiating partners, and there may consequently be more freedom of action. In a dispute about the appropriateness of a particular retaliation (in the event, for example, of a challenge under Article XXIII), it is necessary to have some neutral standard for determining whether the retaliation consists of "substantially equivalent concessions." Thus, the absence of a definition of that term in the General Agreement may sometimes be regretted. The absence of such a definition increases the danger of a reciprocal retaliation by the contracting party that acted initially (although such a reciprocal retaliation would presumably be subject to the procedures of Article XXIII).

Nevertheless, disputes do not appear to have arisen often in connection with Article XXVIII negotiations. At least they have not reached the stage of consideration by the CONTRACTING PARTIES. We have previously considered the major dispute on the record—the poultry dispute between the United States and the European Economic Community—and there a panel, limited to determining one issue in the dispute, was able to bring about a settlement of the entire dispute. On the other hand, if it is preferable to let the negotiating parties choose the method of determining the relative value of their reciprocal con-

---

20. U.S. Tariff Commission, *Operation* . . . , 5th Rep. (1952), p. 11 (emphasis supplied).

cessions, then it may be better not to have a clear rule on the meaning of "substantially equivalent concessions." Any formula that might be adopted in disputes would be likely to have an effect upon the outcome of negotiations. Being able to predict what would happen if the dispute settlement procedures of the GATT were used, the parties would tend to arrive at an agreement anticipating that eventuality. Risk as to outcome may sometimes increase the desire to settle.

## The Impact of Part IV

A further complication concerning the standards to be used in Article XXVIII negotiations arises where one of the contracting parties is a "less-developed contracting party" within the meaning of Part IV of the General Agreement. Under paragraph 8 of Article XXXVI, it is agreed that "the developing contracting parties do not expect reciprocity for commitments made by them in trade negotiations to reduce or remove tariffs and other barriers to the trade of less-developed contracting parties." Although it might be supposed that this language does not apply to Article XXVIII negotiations since those negotiations are not normally intended "to reduce or remove tariffs and other barriers to the trade of less-developed contracting parties," an interpretative note states clearly that paragraph 8 shall apply "in the event of action . . . under Article XXVIII."[21] In addition, under Article XXXVII:1(a), the developed contracting parties are required, "except when compelling reasons, which may include legal reasons, make it impossible," to "accord high priority to the reduction and elimination of barriers to products currently or potentially of particular export interest to less-developed contracting parties." Here again an interpretative note makes clear that this provision is to be applicable in Article XXVIII negotiations.[22]

It is none too clear what application the language of Part IV is to have in Article XXVIII negotiations, since such negotiations are normally designed to lead merely to the rearrangement of duties in such a manner as to maintain what that article calls "a general level of reciprocal and mutually advantageous concessions not less favourable to trade than that provided . . . prior to such negotiations." Some indication of the possibilities is provided, however, by an examination of the waiver granted to Peru in 1965. Peru sought to increase its rates of duty not just on certain items but on all items. Its goals were to reduce certain kinds of imports for development purposes and, at least the circumstances suggested, to place itself in a better bargaining position with its partners in the Latin American Free Trade Area. Since it sought to increase

21. Interpretative note, Ad Art. XXXVI, para. 8.
22. Interpretative note, Ad Art. XXXVII, para. 1(a).

duties before entering into any negotiations, it needed a waiver from the CONTRACTING PARTIES with respect to all bound items.

The working party charged with investigating the request proposed that the CONTRACTING PARTIES should suspend the provisions of Article II in order to permit Peru, which had in fact already put the new tariff schedule in operation, "to maintain in effect the increased rates of duty provided in its new tariff pending completion of negotiations under Article XXVIII of increased rates of duty bound in [the Peruvian Schedule]."[23] On the subject of the incompatibility of the proposed Peruvian action, and the requirement of Article XXVIII that the applicant contracting party's overall level of protection not be increased, the working party contented itself with the following paraphrase of the Peruvian position, which relied upon the then new provisions of Part IV set out above:

> The Peruvian delegation was prepared to comply with the procedures of Article XXVIII on the understanding that the negotiations be conducted in the spirit of Part IV of the General Agreement, which the Peruvian Government as well as those of a number of contracting parties interested in such negotiations had agreed to apply *de facto*. In particular, the Peruvian delegation referred to the Note to paragraph 8 of Article XXXVI.[24]

What the Peruvian delegation apparently sought was an understanding that, even though Peru would not make compensatory adjustments for its tariff increases by lowering other tariffs, the developed contracting parties would not exercise the power granted in paragraph 3(b) of Article XXVIII "to withdraw . . . substantially equivalent concessions initially negotiated with the applicant contracting party" (or would not, at minimum, withdraw concessions to the extent that would be permissible if the applicant were a developed contracting party). In response to a question, the Peruvian representative stated that his delegation "would be in a position to offer reductions of duties contained in the new tariff, if necessary."[25] This answer amounted to a statement that not all the items in the new tariff were permanently nonnegotiable, but it did not represent any commitment to maintain the same general level of tariff duties.

The waiver granted to Peru left the relationship between Article XXVIII and Part IV murky. It purported to be a waiver solely of the provisions of Article II and not of any of the provisions of Article XXVIII; indeed, the waiver decision implied that a waiver would not have been required had the tariff increase taken place in the "open season" and been put into effect after

---

23. *Basic Instruments,* 13th Supp. (1965), pp. 129, 131–32.
24. Ibid., p. 129, 132.
25. Ibid.

the completion of Article XXVIII negotiations. Paragraph 1 of the waiver decision conditioned the waiver upon entry by Peru into negotiations and consultations "pursuant to paragraphs 1–3 of Article XXVIII."[26] The waiver decision made clear, in paragraph 2, that Article XXXVI:8 was to be applicable to the negotiations and that "other contracting parties, negotiating with Peru, likewise accept the principle enunciated in Article XXXVI:8 as applicable to the negotiations."[27] Thereupon followed a most inaptly worded paragraph 3, in which the intention was nevertheless revealed to permit Peru to increase its overall tariff level without suffering extensive withdrawals of concessions by the developed contracting parties:

> The negotiations and consultations mentioned above shall be related to the concessions to be offered by the Government of Peru as compensation for the modifications and withdrawals and to any requests made by interested contracting parties for other or additional compensation with a view to reaching a satisfactory adjustment consistent with the requirements of paragraph 2 of Article XXVIII and to the establishment of a new Schedule. . . .[28]

This application of Part IV is fundamentally inconsistent with the freer trade goal of the GATT. At best it can be viewed as an exception necessary to enable less-developed countries to deal with their balance-of-payments or development problems, but for that purpose a special procedure focusing on the balance-of-payments or development needs of the applicant contracting party would be preferable.[29]

The fundamental distinction between the application of Article XXXVI:8 in Article XXVIII tariff negotiations and in other tariff negotiations is that in other tariff negotiations referred to in Article XXXVI:8, the application of Article XXXVI:8 does not lead to an increase in tariff levels. In tariff negotiations under Article XXVIII bis, for example, Article XXXVI:8 merely excuses the less-developed contracting parties from reducing tariffs as "reciprocity" for reductions in tariffs by the developed contracting parties. Similarly, in tariff negotiations under Article XXXIII, the application of the "no reciprocity" principle merely means that less-developed countries acceding to the General Agreement are permitted to make a reduced number of tariff concessions as part of their "entrance fees." Apart from tariff negotiations under

26. Ibid., p. 27, 28.
27. Ibid.
28. Ibid.
29. The Peruvian delegation admitted that Peru did not appear to have any balance-of-payments difficulties (ibid., p. 129). As for development needs, Article XVIII would appear to provide the appropriate procedures. See discussion in text, infra, at note 66.

Article XXVIII, the only tariff negotiations that are specifically mentioned in the interpretative note to Article XXXVI:8 and that may involve an increase in the overall level of duties are tariff negotiations under Article XVIII. But Article XVIII, unlike Article XXVIII, specifically contemplates increases of duties for the purpose of encouraging development and is available only to "a contracting party, the economy of which can only support low standards of living and is in the early stages of development." Moreover, the application of Article XXXVI:8 in Article XVIII negotiations has the effect of limiting, rather than encouraging, increases in duty levels. The right of less-developed countries to withdraw or modify concessions under Article XVIII is not subject to a duty to maintain the general level of concessions as in Article XXVIII.[30] The application of Article XXXVI:8 in Article XVIII negotiations therefore would tend primarily to reduce the extent of retaliation by the developed countries.

It must be observed, however, that Article XXVIII negotiations sometimes led to increases in tariff levels (not only by less-developed countries, but also by developed countries) even prior to the adoption of Part IV. In the 1955–56 negotiations between France and the United States, for example, France announced its intention to increase the rate of duty on unsweetened fruit and vegetable juices from 10 percent to 30 percent; as compensation France offered, and the United States accepted, a commitment not to seek additional compensation for the previous U.S. withdrawal, made pursuant to the provisions of Article XIX, of a tariff concession on bicycles.[31] Similarly, Pakistan announced in its 1955–56 negotiations with the United States that it intended to withdraw, in whole or in part, four of the five concessions it had previously negotiated with the United States. As compensation Pakistan bound its existing duty-free treatment of wheat, bound against increase its existing margin of preference on canned vegetables, and bound three other duties at rates *above* existing effective rates (although below statutory rates).[32] Thus, although in purely numerical terms there were more bindings in the Pakistani schedule than before, and although the negotiations gave the appearance of conforming to the letter of paragraph 2, the clear influence of the Pakistani negotiations was to move toward an increase in effective tariff levels. One may conclude that Article XXVIII negotiations have not always been carried out in a spirit compatible with the injunction of paragraph 2.

30. Article XVIII:7 requires the less-developed country only to make "every reasonable effort" to offer compensation for the concession to be modified or withdrawn.
31. U.S. Tariff Commission, *Operation* . . . , 9th Rep. (1956), pp. 89–90.
32. Ibid., pp. 94–95. Brazil was able to accomplish something similar to the Peruvian Part IV increase by a more roundabout maneuver. See *Basic Instruments*, 5th Supp. (1957), pp. 36, 122; 9th Supp. (1961), p. 36.

## "Out-of-Season" Negotiations

Article XXVIII:4 provides that "out-of-season" negotiations for the modification or suspension of a concession may be carried out at any time, assuming that authorization has been obtained from the CONTRACTING PARTIES. This authorization may be granted, however, only "in special circumstances," and the rules for such negotiations are less favorable to the applicant contracting party than those for "open season" negotiations.

No definition is given in the General Agreement or in the interpretative notes of the "special circumstances" under which the CONTRACTING PARTIES may authorize "out-of-season" negotiations. It is not clear whether, for example, the term "special circumstances" contemplates an emergency making negotiations necessary before the next "open season" or merely contemplates that the applicant should, in one way or another, be in a special position. That the provision contemplates a certain degree of time pressure might be inferred from the requirements in the interpretative notes that the CONTRACTING PARTIES make their decision on the application within thirty days, and that, in the absence of an extension of time by the CONTRACTING PARTIES, the negotiations be completed in sixty days.[33]

On the other hand, certain other stipulations in the interpretative notes suggest that Article XXVIII:4 is intended primarily to benefit particular classes of contracting parties. Contracting parties that depend "in large measure on a relatively small number of primary commodities" and that rely "on the tariff as an important aid for furthering diversification of their economies or as an important source of revenue" (that is to say, most less-developed countries) are placed in a special category. The CONTRACTING PARTIES "shall" authorize such contracting parties to carry on "out-of-season" negotiations "unless they consider this would result in, or contribute substantially towards, such an increase in tariff levels as to threaten the stability of the Schedules to this Agreement or lead to undue disturbance of international trade." The reason given for such special consideration is somewhat disingenuous—that requiring such contracting parties to negotiate only under the "open season" provisions "might cause them at such a time to make modifications or withdrawals which in the long run would prove unnecessary."[34]

Even if it may be deduced from the language of the interpretative notes that less-developed countries are entitled to invoke Article XXVIII:4 whenever they wish to further "diversification" (a term that presumably refers primarily to the protection of infant industries) or to increase revenues, the requirement

33. Interpretative note, Ad Art. XXVIII, paras. 4:1, 4:3, 4:4. In fact, the time for negotiations is normally extended.
34. Interpretative note, Ad Art. XXVIII, para. 4:2.

in paragraph 4(a) of Article XXVIII that the negotiations "be conducted in accordance with the provisions of paragraphs 1 and 2 of this Article" nevertheless suggests that "out-of-season" negotiations may not be used to raise the general level of tariffs. This limitation derives from the requirement in paragraph 2 that "the contracting parties concerned shall endeavour to maintain a general level of reciprocal and mutually advantageous concessions not less favourable to trade than that provided for" prior to such negotiations. With respect to "out-of-season" negotiations as with respect to "open season" negotiations, however, this limitation has probably been sharply undercut by adoption in 1964 of Part IV and particularly of Article XXXVI:8.

Another class of contracting parties that are entitled to benefit from the provisions for "out-of-season" negotiations consists of those contracting parties that have "bound a high proportion of [their] tariffs at very low rates of duty and to this extent [have] less scope than other contracting parties to make compensatory adjustment."[35] It should be noted that low-tariff countries, unlike primary commodity countries, are not entitled to the benefit of the doubt on the question of whether "special circumstances" exist that justify "out-of-season" negotiations. Rather, low-tariff countries benefit from the "out-of-season" provisions in the sense that they are entitled to make smaller "compensatory" decreases in other tariffs to offset increases in bound tariffs. An explanation, although not a justification, of this anomaly is that New Zealand, at the time the CONTRACTING PARTIES were debating the permanent application of tariff schedules, placed special emphasis on the fact that it had not increased its tariffs since 1934 and therefore had very few products on which to offer concessions.[36]

The CONTRACTING PARTIES have granted authorizations to conduct "out-of-season" negotiations to contracting parties that are neither primary commodity nor low-tariff countries. "Special circumstances" were found, for example, when Canada wished to revise and modernize its textile schedule, when Norway wished to complete the conversion of its specific duties to ad valorem duties, when Denmark wished to make certain tariff increases coincide with the relaxation of quantitative controls on the items in question, and when the United States simplified its tariff classification.[37] The concept of "special circumstances" has thus been quite broadly interpreted.

The rules for the conduct of "out-of-season" negotiations are somewhat less favorable for the applicant than the corresponding rules for the conduct of

35. Interpretative note, Ad Art. XXVIII, para. 4:5.
36. U.S. Tariff Commission, *Operation* . . . , 7th Rep. (1954), p. 81.
37. *Fourth Annual Report of the President of the United States on the Trade Agreements Program* (1960), pp. 60–61, 100–101; *Basic Instruments,* 12th Supp. (1964), p. 57.

"open season" negotiations. In "open season" negotiations the applicant is entitled to proceed with the modification or withdrawal of the concession even if it has failed to reach agreement with its negotiating partners. (Of course, the negotiating partners may proceed with retaliatory modifications or withdrawals of concessions.) In "out-of-season" negotiations an applicant that has failed to secure such agreement may not proceed with the modification or withdrawal of the concession in question without first referring the matter to the CONTRACTING PARTIES. The CONTRACTING PARTIES are thereupon to submit their views to the parties primarily concerned. If, after reference to the CONTRACTING PARTIES, agreement is still not reached, the applicant may modify or withdraw the concession (subject to the principle of retaliation), "unless the CONTRACTING PARTIES determine that the applicant contracting party has unreasonably failed to offer adequate compensation." Thus, in "out-of-season" negotiations the CONTRACTING PARTIES have a residual supervisory role in assessing the extent of compensation offered by the applicant.

One might suppose that the purpose of this residual supervision is to offset the permission granted low-tariff contracting parties to offer less compensation than that normally required. The history of the drafting negotiations suggests, however, that the purpose of the special permission granted to low-tariff countries is to offset the residual supervision. In any case, it should be noted that the special difficulties of low-tariff countries in Article XXVIII negotiations are only one aspect of their weak position, already discussed, in all kinds of tariff negotiations.

### The Significance of Article XXVIII Renegotiations

Renegotiations of GATT schedules under Article XXVIII have proved to be a very important and staple item of business in the GATT. Such renegotiations have been numerous, even if the volume of trade covered has sometimes been small. In 1955–56, eighteen contracting parties were engaged in "open season" negotiations, and two more were engaged in "out-of-season" negotiations under informal procedures of the sort that were employed prior to the amendment of Article XXVIII.[38] In contrast, the United States entered into trade agreements with only twenty-one countries in the regular round of tariff negotiations conducted during the same period at Geneva.[39] In the course of the Article XXVIII negotiations, other contracting parties withdrew or modified concessions on some $30,000,000 of exports from the United States and also granted compensatory concessions on the same volume of U.S. exports.[40]

38. U.S. Tariff Commission, *Operation* . . . , 9th Rep. (1956), p. 84–102.
39. Ibid., p. 58.
40. *First Annual Report of the President of the United States on the Trade Agreements Program,* House Document No. 93 (85th Cong., 1st Sess., 1957), p. 5.

These figures on volume are, of course, smaller than the comparable figures for the regular Geneva round of tariff negotiations; U.S. concessions at Geneva covered, either directly as a result of negotiations or indirectly under the most-favored-nation clause, imports into the United States of more than $653,000,000.[41] During the period from July 1960 to June 1962, the United States entered into fifty-five separate negotiations with twenty-eight other contracting parties or acceding countries. Article XXVIII provided total or partial authority for thirty-five of these negotiations, whereas Article XXVIII bis provided authority for only fifteen, despite the fact that the "Dillon Round" was conducted during that period.[42] To be sure, the volume of trade covered by the Article XXVIII bis negotiations probably dwarfed the volume covered by the Article XXVIII negotiations. From the legal and institutional point of view, however, renegotiations under Article XXVIII are of great importance.

Article XXVIII negotiations are much more frequently held and generally involve much greater volumes of trade than other kinds of technical tariff negotiations. (Article XXIV:6 customs-union negotiations sometimes involve greater volumes of trade, but even they are conducted under the rules of Article XXVIII.) Of the fifty-five agreements entered into during the 1960–62 period, five were based in whole or in part on the escape-clause provisions of Article XIX, three on the inconsistent domestic decision provisions of Article II:5, and one on the customs-union provisions of Article XXIV:6.[43]

Article XXVIII has also had a considerable importance for less-developed countries in their relationships with developed countries. During the 1960 "open season," for example, Ceylon, India, and Indonesia each renegotiated concessions with fifteen developed countries without renegotiating concessions with any less-developed countries; at the same time Turkey and Peru renegotiated concessions with eighteen and ten developed countries respectively, while renegotiating concessions with only two less-developed countries.[44] Furthermore, by obtaining waivers under Article XXV:5 to put revised schedules into effect pending the completion of Article XXVIII negotiations, less-developed contracting parties (and sometimes developed contracting parties) have been able to raise tariffs on certain items for considerable periods of time without making compensatory adjustments and without provoking retaliatory increases by other contracting parties. Brazil, for example, received a waiver in 1956 to put into effect, pending the completion of Article XXVIII negotiations, a

41. U.S. Tariff Commission, *Operation* . . . , 9th Rep. (1956), p. 61.
42. Ibid., 14th Rep. (1962), pp. 5–8.
43. Ibid.
44. Staffan B. Linder, "The Significance of GATT for Under-Developed Countries," in *Proceedings of the United Nations Conference on Trade and Development* (1964), V, p. 523.

major revision of its tariff schedule involving increases on many bound items.[45] The revision, embodying the increases but making no provision for compensatory adjustments, went into effect early in 1957.[46] The waiver provided for optional, temporary suspensions of certain concessions pending the completion of negotiations, but of all the contracting parties affected only Finland took advantage of this provision.[47]

## Escape Clause Negotiations

Although Article XXVIII is the primary provision of the General Agreement granting contracting parties the possibility of freeing themselves from the restrictions involved in a tariff binding, another important provision with the same purpose is the "escape clause" of Article XIX. This provision of the General Agreement has received considerably more publicity than has Article XXVIII. Whether considered in terms of frequency of invocation or in terms of volume of trade affected, however, Article XIX is considerably less important than Article XXVIII. Such importance as it has derives mainly from the fact that, unlike the normal situation under Article XXVIII, the invocation of Article XIX usually leads to an increase in tariff levels.

Article XIX, as its popular name implies, is intended to provide the possibility of "escape" from tariff concessions that as a result of changed circumstances are causing or threatening "serious injury to domestic producers . . . of like or competitive products." Such injury, it should be stressed, warrants Article XIX relief only when it is "a result of unforeseen developments." The General Agreement escape clause can thus be analogized more directly to the doctrine of "changed circumstances" in international law than can the provisions of Article XXVIII. But the scope of Article XIX would not appear to be limited by the doctrine of *rebus sic stantibus*. Its justification is that the presence of such a clause encourages cautious countries to enter into a greater number of tariff bindings than would otherwise be the case. If one is to criticize the presence of such a provision, the criticism must be that the escape clause is invoked so frequently and so abusively that reliance on it by contracting parties more than offsets its favorable effect. As we shall see, the escape clause has been invoked relatively seldom, and therefore it is doubtful that a case for deletion of this safeguard clause can be made out.

Article XIX differs from Article XXVIII in a number of respects. First, whereas Article XXVIII can be used to renegotiate a number of unrelated

---
45. *Basic Instruments*, 5th Supp. (1957), p. 36.
46. *Third Annual Repart of the President of the United States on the Trade Agreements Program* (1959), p. 38.
47. Linder, p. 527.

concessions or even an entire tariff schedule,[48] Article XIX can only be invoked for a single concession at a time, or at most for several related concessions concerning a single industry. The volume of trade involved in an Article XIX proceeding therefore tends to be, on average, smaller than that involved in an Article XXVIII negotiation.

Second, whereas changes in tariff schedules effected under Article XXVIII are permanent, increases introduced by the invocation of Article XIX are in principle temporary. Under Article XIX a concession may be suspended, withdrawn, or modified only "to the extent and for such time as may be necessary to prevent or remedy" the injury resulting from the concession. A working party once stated that "action under Article XIX is essentially of an emergency character and should be of limited duration." It went on to emphasize that a "government taking action under that Article should keep the position under review and be prepared to reconsider the matter as soon as this section is no longer necessary to prevent or remedy a serious injury."[49] Although most of the tariff increases that have been made under Article XIX have in fact never been rescinded, a point of legal significance must not be overlooked: once the emergency has passed, the contracting party that originally negotiated the concession (and perhaps also contracting parties that have, under paragraph 2, a "substantial interest as exporters of the product concerned") may demand that the concession be reinstated and may invoke the dispute-settlement procedures of the GATT if no action is taken.

A third difference between Article XIX and Article XXVIII is that under Article XIX there is no necessity for the applicant contracting party to offer a compensatory adjustment in its tariff schedule. Rather, it is assumed that the balance of concessions will be reestablished by the retaliatory suspension of substantially equivalent concessions (or "other obligations"). There is no provision in Article XIX equivalent to the injunction found in Article XXVIII:2 to maintain the preexisting general level of concessions. Nevertheless, a compensatory adjustment is sometimes made. Thus the United States, when it invoked Article XIX to withdraw its concession on dried figs, granted Greece, at the latter's request, compensation in the form of other concessions on Greek imports into the United States. Turkey, the other contracting party affected by the U.S. action on dried figs, preferred to take its compensation entirely in the form of withdrawals of concessions on U.S. exports to Turkey.[50]

48. *Basic Instruments*, 9th Supp. (1961), pp. 36–37.
49. The CONTRACTING PARTIES to the General Agreement on Tariffs and Trade, *Report on the Withdrawal by the United States of a Tariff Concession under Article XIX of the General Agreement on Tariffs and Trade* (1951), p. 29 (hereafter cited as *Report on the U.S. Withdrawal*).
50. U.S. Tariff Commission, *Operation* . . . , 8th Rep. (1955), p. 56.

A fourth difference involves the timing of action and the procedures that must be followed under each of the two articles. While contracting parties may take advantage of Article XXVIII only at transition points between successive periods of continued application (unless "special circumstances" justify "out-of-season" negotiations), Article XIX may be resorted to at any time. On the other hand, whereas no justification need be offered for recourse to "open season" negotiations under Article XXVIII, recourse to Article XIX is subject to several substantive requirements.

These substantive requirements, which are set forth in paragraph 1(a) of Article XIX, deal with both injury and causation. The injury, which may be either actual or threatened, must be to "domestic producers of like or directly competitive products." Thus, Article XIX may be invoked where imports of a new type of product injure existing domestic production (that is, of an established and directly competitive type of product), but it may not be invoked where the only factor present is the foreclosure to domestic producers of the market in a new type of product. This point was emphasized in the report of the working party in a widely discussed Article XIX case involving the withdrawal by the United States of a concession on women's fur felt hats and hat bodies:

> Any proposal to withdraw a tariff concession in order to promote the establishment or development of domestic production of a new or novel type of product in which overseas suppliers have opened up a new market is not permissible under Article XIX but should be dealt with under other provisions of the Agreement, such as Article XVIII [sic]. On the other hand, it may be permissible to have recourse to Article XIX if a new or novel type of imported product is replacing the customary domestic product to a degree which causes or threatens serious injury to domestic producers.[51]

Causation must be established under each of three interrelated but different standards. First, the injury must be a result of the concession sought to be suspended; that is to say, there is no right to take action under Article XIX if the injury would have occurred in any event.

Second, the injury must be a "result of unforeseen developments." This second causal standard raises difficult problems of proof and judgment, because negotiators presumably anticipate the possibility of injury to domestic producers whenever they lower tariffs. In a case involving the importation of women's fur felt hats and hat bodies into the United States, the unforeseen development was a style change in favor of velours. The members of the working party (except for Czechoslovakia, the other disputant) agreed that the mere fact that hat styles had changed did not constitute an unforeseen devel-

---

51. *Report on the U.S. Withdrawal,* p. 21.

opment, since any negotiator must reasonably anticipate a change in women's fashions. They also agreed, however, that "the United States negotiators in 1947 could not reasonably be expected to foresee that this style change in favour of velours would in fact subsequently take place, and would do so on as large a scale and last for as long a period as it in fact did."[52] This suggests that the "unforeseen developments" requirement envisages the presence of very particular changed circumstances and not merely of a general economic change.

The third causal standard to be applied—which a U.S. lawyer might term "proximate cause"—involves "increased quantities" of imports. The product covered by the tariff concession must be imported "in such increased quantities and under such conditions as to cause or threaten" the requisite injury. (It is not clear what the language "under such conditions" adds to the concept of "increased quantities"; perhaps factors such as price and quality are to be taken into account.) The term "increased quantities" has been construed, relying on the language of Article 40 of the Havana Charter, to include "cases where imports had increased relatively to domestic production, even though there might not have been an absolute increase in imports as compared with a previous base period."[53] It is more doubtful that the requirements of Article XIX are met by an absolute increase in quantities which, because of an even greater increase in consumption, represents a decrease relative to production. Even if the "increased quantities" causal standard can be said to be met, the relative increase in domestic production may negate the idea of "serious injury."

In spite of their rigorous and complicated nature, these substantive requirements tend to be relatively innocuous in practice as a consequence of the operation of a procedural rule. In the U.S. withdrawal case, the working party—in order to uphold the U.S. action against a complaint from Czechoslovakia—held in effect that the burden of proof is on the complainant to demonstrate that the suspension of a concession under Article XIX is not justified. Given the nature of tariff bindings, the inaccessibility of facts about the injury caused to another contracting party by a tariff concession, and the exceptional nature of Article XIX, this reversal of what would appear to be the logical burden of proof seems somewhat surprising. To be sure, the working party did not speak in terms of the burden of proof, but this lack of clarity does not appear to have represented an attempt to engraft any nuances onto the rule to be followed. The working party stated:

> Moreover, the United States is not called upon to prove conclusively that the degree of injury caused or threatened in this case must be regarded as serious; since the question under consideration is whether they are in

52. Ibid., p. 12.
53. *Analytical Index,* p. 102. See also *Basic Instruments,* Vol. II (1952), pp. 39, 44–45.

breach of Article XIX, they are entitled to the benefit of any reasonable doubt. No facts have been advanced which provide any convincing evidence that it would be unreasonable to regard the adverse effects on the domestic industry concerned as a result of increased imports as amounting to serious injury or a threat thereof; and the facts as a whole certainly tend to show that some degree of adverse effect has been caused or threatened. It must be concluded, therefore, that the Czechoslovak Delegation has failed to establish that no serious injury has been sustained or threatened.[54]

Whatever distinctions may be made between the burden of coming forward with evidence and the burden of convincing the working party, it is clear that the effect of this procedural rule is to permit much freer access to Article XIX relief than might appear possible from the language of that article, particularly since—as any student of the lengthy proceedings under the U.S. domestic escape-clause provision can attest—evidence on injury and causation in this kind of case is often indefinite.[55]

Article XIX contains certain stipulations on procedure which are in many ways analagous to the procedural provisions of Article XXVIII:4. Notice in writing to the CONTRACTING PARTIES must be given. Thereupon the moving contracting party must afford the opportunity of consultation to "those contracting parties having a substantial interest as exporters of the product concerned." Article XIX contains, however, no definition of the term "substantial interest," and perhaps one is therefore entitled to refer to the definition of that term in the interpretative note to Article XXVIII, even though that note was added to the General Agreement after the drafting of Article XIX. The Article XXVIII definition requires, it will be remembered, consideration not only of actual export figures, but also of the effect of "discriminatory quantitative restrictions."[56] Interestingly enough, Article XIX, unlike Article XXVIII, leaves room for a refusal to consult the contracting party with which a concession was originally negotiated if that contracting party no longer has a "substantial interest as [an exporter] of the product concerned."

The possibility that the withdrawal of a concession may not require consultation with the contracting party with which the concession was originally negotiated underlines the fact that the GATT is an institution and not merely a complicated set of contractual relationships. In this respect it is also noteworthy that a contracting party seeking relief under Article XIX must be prepared to consult with the CONTRACTING PARTIES, even though agreement has been reached with the contracting parties having a substantial interest. Here again the reality of the situation differs somewhat from the legal theory, because

54. *Report on the U.S. Withdrawal*, p. 23.
55. See, e.g., George Bronz, "The Tariff Commission as a Regulatory Agency," *Columbia Law Review*, LXI (1961), pp. 468–77.
56. Interpretative note, Ad Art. XXVIII, para. 1:7.

it is difficult to envisage the circumstances under which the CONTRACTING PARTIES might be led to demand consultation if the contracting parties having a substantial interest were satisfied.

If agreement is not reached in the course of consultation, the moving contracting party may nevertheless proceed with the suspension of the concession in question. If it does, the affected contracting parties are entitled to suspend "substantially equivalent concessions or other obligations under [the General] Agreement the suspension of which the CONTRACTING PARTIES do not disapprove." No provisions specify the procedures to be followed in connection with the review by the CONTRACTING PARTIES of retaliatory action, but the language quoted indicates that a presumption is to be exercised in favor of the acts of individual contracting parties.

In addition to the foregoing procedure, a special emergency procedure is provided for "critical circumstances, where delay would cause damage which it would be difficult to repair." In such circumstances the suspension, modification, or withdrawal may be made forthwith, provisionally, and without consultation. Consultation must, however, follow the taking of such action. Contracting parties affected by such "provisional" action may suspend forthwith "such concessions or other obligations as may be necessary to prevent or remedy . . . injury," provided that here too "delay would cause damage difficult to repair." Although this emergency provision for retaliation has the attractive quality of granting a kind of rough justice, its justification is somewhat elusive. It is rather difficult to conceive of any irremediable damage that might result from a failure to retaliate immediately, since by assumption retaliation under the GATT is designed to reestablish a reciprocal balance of concessions rather than to protect the industries of the retaliating party. Of course, the right to retaliate at any time strengthens the hands of affected contracting parties in the consultation process, and thus may tend to temper the protectionist fervor of contracting parties seeking Article XIX relief.

Both original and retaliatory suspensions of concessions under Article XIX may raise certain delicate problems involving the most-favored-nation clause of Article I (and the related principle in Article II:1). Must a tariff increase be applied to all contracting parties equally? In the case of original suspensions, there seems to be no strong argument for the nonapplication of the most-favored-nation clause, even if the injurious imports come from a single country. The general arguments against discriminatory tariffs apply as fully to Article XIX increases as to any other increases. In the case of retaliatory suspensions, however, the only contracting party injured if the most-favored-nation clause is not applied is the contracting party invoking Article XIX. If one views retaliation as punitive in character, one may be prepared to declare the most-favored-nation clause inapplicable for retaliatory increases. Furthermore, application of the most-favored-nation clause to retaliatory increases would carry with it the danger of chain reactions of further tariff increases by third countries.

This distinction between original and retaliatory suspensions of concessions appears to be written into Article XIX. Paragraph 3(a), dealing with retaliation, speaks of suspension of "the application [of concessions] to the trade of contracting party taking such action." The quoted language is conspicuously absent in paragraphs 1(a) and 1(b), dealing with original suspensions. It may be noted that the quoted language is also missing from paragraph 3(b), dealing with emergency retaliation before or during consultation; the justification for requiring most-favored-nation treatment in the case of emergency retaliation but not in the case of ordinary retaliation is that it is only in the latter case that the CONTRACTING PARTIES have the opportunity to pass upon the retaliatory action and thereby upon the appropriateness of not applying the most-favored-nation clause.

The interpretation that Article XIX of the General Agreement envisions the application of the most-favored-nation clause to original suspensions and emergency retaliation but not to ordinary retaliation is supported by an interpretative note to the similar treaty language of Article 40 of the Havana Charter. That interpretative note distinguishes between paragraph 3(a) on the one hand and paragraphs 1(a), 1(b), and 3(b) on the other:

> It is understood that any suspension, withdrawal or modification under paragraphs 1(a), 1(b) and 3(b) must not discriminate against imports from any Member country, and that such action should avoid, to the fullest extent possible, injury to other supplying Member countries.[57]

Although a similar interpretative note is not found in the General Agreement, the identity of the treaty language of the Charter and that of the General Agreement tends to justify reference to the Charter note.

A final difference between Article XIX and Article XXVIII is that Article XIX provides the possibility of suspending both tariff concessions and other kinds of GATT obligations. This possibility extends both to original and to retaliatory action. Paragraph 1(a), dealing with original action, refers to "obligations incurred by a contracting party under this Agreement, including tariff concessions," while both paragraph 3(a), dealing with ordinary retaliation, and paragraph 3(b), dealing with emergency retaliation, refer to the suspension of "concessions or *other obligations*" (emphasis supplied). Frequently Article XIX action has resulted in the introduction of restrictions, notably quotas,

---

57. Havana Charter, interpretative note, Ad Art. 40. Further support for most-favored nation treatment in the original suspension of concessions may be found in a report of an ad hoc committee on agenda and intersessional business, GATT Document L/76 (13 Feb. 1953), p. 2. The CONTRACTING PARTIES did not have occasion to consider this document.

rather than in the suspension of concessions.[58] For example, in 1958 the Federal Republic of Germany introduced licensing arrangements on imports of coal, even though no tariff concession had been granted on that item.[59]

One interesting aspect of Article XIX is that it permits withdrawals of concessions when injury is being caused or threatened, not to producers in the withdrawing country, but rather to producers in a country granted a tariff preference by the withdrawing country. This unusual provision tends to strengthen the position of members of preferential arrangements and runs counter to the predisposition against preferences to be found in the General Agreement.

In spite of the inherent danger of any safeguard clause in a trade agreement, the GATT escape clause has been invoked relatively infrequently. The United States has invoked it the most often, but it has done so only fourteen times, and the concession was restored or the restriction suspended in four of those cases. In four other cases a compensatory adjustment was made to offset, at least partially, the tariff increase.[60] To the extent that a compensatory adjustment is made, the total effect of an Article XIX invocation is analogous to that of an Article XXVIII invocation. Australia has invoked Article XIX eleven times; Greece, three times; Austria, Canada, and the Federal Republic of Germany, twice each; and France, Italy, Nigeria, Peru, and Rhodesia-Nyasaland, once each.[61]

The total number of invocations of Article XIX, thirty-nine, pales beside the total number of concessions that have been negotiated in the regular rounds of tariff negotiations. Some 45,000 concessions were granted in the original Geneva round, 5,000 in the Annecy round, 8,800 in the Torquay round, and so forth.[62] Moreover, some of the items on which concessions have been suspended have involved relatively small volumes of trade. The case to which the GATT has given the most publicity, the U.S. withdrawal of a concession on fur felt hats and hat bodies, involved less than $2,000,000 of imports.[63]

One may conclude that the GATT escape clause is a useful safety valve for protectionist pressures and does not undercut in any serious way the advantages

---

58. The cases collected in *Analytical Index*, pp. 104–8.
59. *Third Annual Report of the President of the United States on the Trade Agreements Program* (1959), p. 52. It is not entirely clear that the General Agreement permits imposition of quantitative restrictions on unbound items, since it could be argued that, where an item was unbound, a tariff increase would be feasible and therefore there is no need for "emergency action" under Article XIX.
60. *Analytical Index*, pp. 106–7. The statistics in the text are as of the preparation of the *Analytical Index*, which was published in 1966.
61. Ibid., pp. 104–6.
62. U.S. Tariff Commission, *Operation . . .* , 4th Rep. (1951), p. 59.
63. *Report on the U.S. Withdrawal*, p. 9.

of the GATT tariff negotiating system. Insofar as the escape clause is a political "prerequisite" to the membership in the GATT of certain contracting parties—most notably, the United States[64]—the argument in its favor is even stronger.

Safeguard clauses are common in economic treaties. The Treaty of Rome, creating the European Economic Community, has what would appear to be a wide-open safeguard provision, Article 226:

> 1. In the course of the transitional period, where there are serious difficulties which are likely to persist in any sector of economic activity or difficulties which may seriously impair the economic situation in any region, a Member State may ask for authorization to take measures of safeguard in order to restore the situation and adapt the sector concerned to the Common Market economy.
>
> 2. At the request of the State concerned, the Commission shall by an expedited procedure immediately determine the measures of safeguard which it considers necessary, specifying the conditions and particulars of application.
>
> 3. The measures authorized under paragraph 2 may include derogations from the provisions of this Treaty, to the extent and for the periods strictly necessary for the achievement of the objects referred to in paragraph 1. Priority shall be given in the choice of such measures to those which will least disturb the functioning of the Common Market.

Despite the fact that EEC member states are required to reduce all tariffs on imports from other member states and therefore do not have the option, always available to GATT contracting parties, of making no concessions on sensitive items, EEC member states have not made extensive use of Article 226. The Commission has restricted authorizations to a few commodity items, such as sulphur, silk, and lead and zinc, and for these items the safeguard measures have primarily been limited to aiding Italy, the least industrialized of the member states.[65]

## Article XVIII Negotiations

Article XVIII, entitled "Governmental Assistance to Economic Development," contains certain provisions on tariff negotiations. Under Section A of that article, a less-developed contracting party—that is to say, any "contracting party the economy of which can only support low standards of living and is in

---

64. The U.S. negotiators at the Geneva and Havana Conference listed the presence of an escape clause in the GATT as one of the "prerequisites" to U.S. acceptance (Clair Wilcox, *A Charter for World Trade* [New York: Macmillan Co., 1949], p. 183).

65. Commission of the European Economic Community, *Eighth General Report on the Activities of the Community* (1965), pp. 49–50; *Ninth General Report on the Activities of the Community* (1966), pp. 52–53.

the early stages of development"—is entitled to modify or withdraw concessions whenever it "considers [such action] desirable, in order to promote the establishment of a particular industry with a view to raising the general standard of living of its people."[66] There is no need, however, to go into the intricacies of the procedures involved, which are not greatly different from those of Articles XIX and XXVIII. The provision has remained a dead letter.[67] While the reasons for this nonuse are not absolutely clear, it may be noted that by 1955, the date when the provision was engrafted onto Article XVIII, the practice of renegotiating tariff concessions under Article XXVIII was already well established. Moreover, Section B of Article XVIII gives less-developed countries the more tempting right to use quantitative restrictions in combatting balance-of-payments difficulties.

### Article II:5 Negotiations

Another provision of the General Agreement which can serve as a basis for tariff negotiations is paragraph 5 of Article II. That paragraph is designed to deal with the problem that arises where a "court or other proper authority" of a contracting party rules that under domestic law a product "cannot be classified . . . so as to permit the treatment" indicated in a GATT schedule. Any contracting party may raise the matter with the concession-granting party, and, if the latter agrees that the ruling in question has the effect of denying the treatment indicated in its schedule, these two contracting parties, "together with any other contracting parties substantially interested," are to negotiate "with a view to a compensatory adjustment of the matter." The words "compensatory adjustment" indicate that the concession-granting party is to offer a new concession in compensation for the one that has in effect been withdrawn. Article II:5 has been of particular importance to the United States in view of that country's relatively extensive system of administrative and judicial review of the decisions of customs officials. During the period from July 1960 to June 1962, for example, the United States concluded trade agreements under that provision with the Benelux countries and Italy and was negotiating such an agreement with France.[68]

### Accession Negotiations

Tariff negotiations may also take place under the accession procedures of Article XXXIII, even though that article does not refer to tariff negotiations.

66. See also Art. XVIII:18.
67. Secretariat of the U.N. Conference on Trade and Development, "The Developing Countries in GATT," in *Proceedings of the United Nations Conference on Trade and Development* (1964), V, pp. 458–59.
68. U.S. Tariff Commission, *Operation . . .* , 14th Rep. (1962), pp. 6–8.

Article XXXIII states that a government may accede to the General Agreement, and thereby become a contracting party, "on terms to be agreed between such government and the CONTRACTING PARTIES."

As a practical matter, accession under Article XXXIII requires negotiations between the acceding government and such contracting parties as may demand negotiations, the thought being that the acceding government must be prepared to give up something in return for the privilege of receiving rights in all prior concessions made by contracting parties among themselves.

Article XXXIII is not, however, the only GATT provision dealing with accession. Where the territories of newly independent states were formerly within the "international responsibility" of existing contracting parties, and where the latter had already accepted the General Agreement with respect to the territories, such newly independent states may accede under Article XXVI:5(c). Negotiations are not thought necessary under Article XXVI:5(c), since the territories of the newly independent states have already been receiving the benefits of the General Agreement and since concessions may already have been made on behalf of those territories by the sponsoring contracting parties.

The difference between legal postures of countries becoming contracting parties under each of these two articles may be less marked than might appear. In point of fact, countries acceding under Article XXXIII are likely to have already been receiving most of the indirect benefits of prior concessions among GATT contracting parties, as a consequence either of most-favored-nation clauses contained in bilateral trade agreements or of general most-favored-nation policies pursued by individual contracting parties.

In the case of a newly independent country formerly under the control of a contracting party, the decision to accede under one or the other of the two articles may depend upon the extent to which the latter made concessions on behalf of the former. By acceding under Article XXXIII, the newly independent country may be able to avoid such prior concessions, but only at the expense of paying an "entrance fee" in Article XXXIII tariff negotiations. Despite charges to the contrary, most colonial contracting parties did not make extensive concessions on behalf of their colonies; in the original GATT negotiations in 1947 the United Kingdom made no concessions at all on behalf of its colonies. Consequently, a large majority of newly independent contracting parties have acceded under the sponsorship procedures of Article XXVI:5(c).[69] This situation may change with the adoption of Part IV; as we shall see, Part IV may have the effect of making "entrance fees" nominal for less-developed acceding countries.

Countries acceding to the General Agreement under Article XXXIII are

---

69. Secretariat of the U.N. Conference on Trade and Development, "Developing Countries," p. 436. See also the discussion of accession in chapter 19, "The GATT as an International Organization," infra.

required, as we have seen, to pay "entrance fees" to countries that are already contracting parties in exchange for the benefits that the former are to be legally entitled to receive under Article II:1 (whether or not they have been receiving such benefits de facto). In addition, accession negotiations are often conducted simultaneously with several acceding countries, and in such situations concessions may be requested by one acceding country from another acceding country in order to compensate for benefits to be received under the most-favored-nation clause by the latter from concessions made by the former to existing contracting parties.[70] Finally, accession negotiations often lead to the making of concessions by contracting parties to the acceding parties, and in return for these concessions the acceding parties are expected to grant still further concessions. For an illustration of the resulting complexity, one may consider the statement on "entrance fees" that was included in the rules for the accession negotiations that took place as part of the Dillon round of regular tariff negotiations:

> In granting tariff concessions, acceding governments will take into consideration the indirect benefits which they will receive from the concessions exchanged between contracting parties at earlier conferences and those which will result from new negotiations among contracting parties. Similarly, all the participating governments will be expected to take into consideration the indirect benefits which they will receive from the negotiations between the acceding governments themselves and between them and the contracting parties.[71]

"Entrance fees" are somewhat more imposing in theory than in practice, particularly for less-developed countries. Where acceding countries have already received the indirect benefits of prior concessions made among GATT contracting parties, those contracting parties have little to hold out as advantages of membership in the GATT and therefore cannot demand much as a quid pro quo. However that may be, Professor Staffan B. Linder, analyzing the Cambodian accession negotiations held during the Dillon Round, finds that Cambodia entered into only five trade agreements. He finds, moreover, that in three of those agreements Cambodia received new concessions, an indication that "the 'fee' paid could not have constituted more than a token charge." Linder concludes that "on the whole, the accession negotiations appear to be ritualistic rather than substantive" where less-developed countries are concerned.[72]

The ritualistic element in less-developed country accession negotiations is

---

70. An analogy may be drawn to the final balancing of accounts in a round of regular tariff negotiations. See the discussion in chapter 5, "Tariff Conferences," supra.
71. *Basic Instruments,* 8th Supp. (1960), p. 114, 116.
72. Linder, pp. 527–28.

almost certain to become even more dominant with the entry into force of Part IV. According to the interpretative note to paragraph 8 of Article XXXVI, that paragraph, which contains the statement that developed countries "do not expect reciprocity" from less-developed countries, applies to Article XXXIII accession negotiations. To be sure, the renunciation of reciprocity by developed countries merely means that less-developed countries "should not be expected, in the course of trade negotiations, to make contributions which are inconsistent with their individual development, financial or trade needs, taking into consideration past trade needs." When one considers the accordionlike character of the notions of "development, financial [and] trade needs," however, one is led to conclude that any remaining "substantive" element in accession negotiations is, in the case of the least developed countries, likely to disappear.

Accession negotiations would still be of significance if certain countries in the middle stages of development were to accede to the GATT. Mexico, for example, not yet a contracting party, is the most developed country in Latin America, the possessor of convertible currency, and a "graduate" of the U.S. foreign aid program. So too accession negotiations might be important for the accession of certain Eastern Bloc state-trading countries, although the negotiations would take a special form in view of the limited role assigned to tariffs by those countries.

## Summary

Leaving aside the major rounds of tariff negotiations, such as the Kennedy Round, there are six principal kinds of tariff negotiations conducted within the framework of the GATT: (1) Article XXVIII "open season" negotiations; (2) Article XXVIII "out-of-season" negotiations; (3) Article XXIV:6 customs-union negotiations based on Article XXVIII rules; (4) Article XIX escape clause negotiations; (5) Article II:5 renegotiations following decisions of courts and other authoritative bodies; and (6) Article XXXIII accession negotiations. Some of these, notably Article XXVIII "open season" renegotiations, are staple items in the GATT agenda and have a substantial effect on trade. Even if the Kennedy Round had lowered tariffs to the point where no further major rounds of tariff negotiations were necessary or useful, the GATT as an institution would still have considerable importance in tariff negotiations. All these six kinds of tariff negotiations can be expected to remain important, and it is essential that a healthy, viable organization be available to provide facilities for them and to emphasize that their bilateral nature does not indicate the world trade community's lack of a common interest.

# PART 3

**The Technical Arrangements: Nontariff Barriers**

# 7 Internal Taxes

A tariff duty is a tax. But the General Agreement makes a fundamental distinction between tariff duties and other taxes, usually called internal taxes. This distinction gives rise to two kinds of problems. First, where a country elects to impose a tax at the point of importation but does not call the tax a tariff, is the tax to be considered a tariff duty or an internal tax? Second, in view of the fact that tariff duties and internal taxes may have the same effect on imports, what are the rights and duties under the General Agreement in respect of those taxes that are deemed to be internal taxes? These questions may arise in either of two contexts. First, an increase in an internal tax affecting a bound item may be said to give rise to "nullification or impairment" of the tariff binding under Article XXIII. In that event the problem is not, properly speaking, one of nontariff barriers, but rather one of the scope of rights and obligations arising from a tariff concession.[1] Second, the residual rights and duties concerning internal taxes, above and beyond those rights and duties arising from tariff concessions, may come into question whether or not the item in question is bound. It is this latter problem that is the subject of this chapter.

In view of the similarity between tariffs and internal taxes, the regulation of internal taxes is obviously of great importance. The General Agreement takes up the question in Article III, immediately following the most-favored-nation clause of Article I and the tariff schedule provisions of Article II, and thereby indicates the priority position accorded the problem of internal taxes. The crucial internal tax provisions of Article III are paragraphs 1 and 2. The arrangement of these two paragraphs is important insofar as it gives rise to ambiguities concerning the content of the limitation on the use of internal taxes. Paragraph 1 sets forth a general principle applicable not only to internal taxes but also to internal legislation and regulations in general. Paragraph 2 deals

---

1. See discussion in chapter 4, "The GATT Tariff System," supra.

with internal taxes in particular and is divided into two sentences, only the second of which refers to paragraph 1.

## Internal Taxes versus Tariff Duties

On the question of the distinction between tariff duties and internal taxes, paragraphs 1 and 2 appear to assume that everyone knows the difference. These paragraphs thereby seem to place decisive weight on the classification chosen by the taxing state. It is true that an interpretative note makes clear that a tax levied on both imported and "like" domestic products is an internal tax even though levied on the imported goods at the time of importation.[2] But where "like" products are not involved, the interpretative note gives no guidance. That the draftsmen did not intend to make form alone controlling is indicated by a Havana Conference subcommittee report that, in considering the Havana Charter provisions from which Article III is derived, opines that certain Chilean, Lebanese, and Syrian charges are

> import duties and not internal taxes because according to the information supplied by the countries concerned (a) they are collected at the time of, and as a condition to, the entry of the goods into the importing country, and (b) they apply exclusively to imported products without being related in any way to similar charges collected internally on like domestic products. The fact that these charges are described as internal taxes in the laws of the importing country would not in itself have the effect of giving them the status of internal taxes under the Charter.[3]

This interpretation with its emphasis on absence of taxes on corresponding domestic production has, of course, the paradoxical result of freeing from any control (other than possible "binding" in tariff negotiations) local charges that are denominated internal taxes by the domestic legislature when, because there is no related tax on domestic production, the discrimination is absolute, while prohibiting such charges when, because there is a tax on corresponding domestic production, the discrimination is only partial.

The ambiguities inherent in Article III came to the surface early in the history of the GATT when a challenge by France and the United Kingdom against a special Greek "contribution" levied on certain imported goods necessitated a determination whether the levy was an "internal tax [or] other internal charge" under Article III or an import duty under Article II. The Panel on Complaints threw up its hands. Without even indicating the criteria for making the determination, it recommended that the CONTRACTING PARTIES defer a decision pending receipt of "additional information" on the "tax system . . . its

---

2. Interpretative note, Ad Art. III.
3. *Analytical Index,* p. 21.

form and its method of application."[4] The Greek government eliminated the "contribution" shortly thereafter as a part of a 50 percent currency devaluation, and the opportunity to cast some authoritative light on the distinction between an internal tax and a tariff was missed.

## The Scope of the Prohibition

Despite the failure of the General Agreement to define the key terms, a challenged tax is in most cases conceded to be an internal tax rather than an import duty, and therefore the only important question is the substantive content of the General Agreement's rules on internal taxes. It should be noted that, as a matter of principle, two kinds of problems might arise in this context. First, an internal tax might involve discrimination against imported goods in favor of domestic goods insofar as imported goods were taxed more heavily than domestic goods. In that event, the economic impact of the internal tax would be essentially the same as that of a tariff. Second, even though domestic and imported goods were equally taxed and therefore no discrimination existed, the internal tax might nevertheless constitute a burden on international commerce insofar as it increased the cost, and thereby decreased sales, of imported goods. To be sure, sales of domestic goods would also be decreased. The effect of the nondiscriminatory tax would simply be to lower consumption of the taxed item.

For rather obvious reasons, the General Agreement does not attempt to deal with the second problem. Taxes are a fact of life in every country, and it would be impracticable to give an international body reviewing power over the incidence of the domestic tax burden as among different products. Because of interproduct competition, however, the line between the discriminatory and nondiscriminatory tax is not so clear. If product A is imported and product B is of domestic origin, and if an internal tax is levied on product A but no tax (or a lower tax) is levied on product B, the impact will be discriminatory in fact, although not in form.

Discriminatory internal taxes are dealt with in paragraph 2 of Article III. The structure of that paragraph warrants attention. There are two sentences. The first prohibits discriminatory taxes on "like" products: imported products are not to be "subject, directly or indirectly, to internal taxes or other internal charges of any kind in excess of those applied directly or indirectly, to like domestic products." This sentence does not, it should be noted, outlaw every tax that is discriminatory on its face. A tax applying to imports only is not unlawful if another, but different, internal tax imposes an equal or greater burden on like domestic products.

4. *Basic Instruments,* 1st Supp. (1953), p. 48, 50.

The second sentence of paragraph 2 deals with all other internal taxes—that is to say, it governs the problem of internal taxes that, because "like" products are not involved, are discriminatory in fact but not in form. This sentence is phrased in quite general terms. It purports to impose an additional rule above and beyond the rule contained in the first sentence of paragraph 2. Commencing with the word "moreover," the second sentence prohibits internal taxes applied "in a manner contrary to the principles set forth in paragraph 1" of Article III. Paragraph 1, however, does not set forth "principles" but only states that internal taxes should not be applied "so as to afford protection to domestic production." Moreover, the scope of the second sentence of paragraph 1 is considerably restricted by an interpretative note that states an internal tax meeting the requirements of the first sentence of paragraph 2 would fail to conform to the second sentence thereof "only in cases where competition was involved between, on the one hand, the taxed product and, on the other hand, a directly competitive or substitutable [domestic] product which was not similarly taxed."[5]

A typical example of nondiscriminatory internal taxation of one product in order to protect a domestic industry producing another product is the taxation of oleomargarine to protect local dairy production. This common form of protective internal taxation, however, probably cannot be considered to violate Article III. That would appear to be the proper interpretation of a laconic account of the discussions in the working party that dealt with Article III at the Review Session. The Swedish delegate sought to have an interpretative note adopted which would have made clear that the second sentence of paragraph 2 did not prohibit internal taxes "which, while perhaps having the effect of assisting the production of a particular domestic product (say, butter) are directed as much against the domestic production of another product (say, domestic oleomargarine) of which there is a substantial domestic production as they are against imports (say, imported oleomargarine)." The discussion revealed that the Swedish delegate was primarily interested in establishing that "the system of levying internal fees on home-produced and imported raw materials for oleomargarine manufacture, as well as on imports of oleomargine, in order to help in the stabilization of the marketing of butter" was consistent with Article III. Such a statement, the Swedish delegate pointed out, had been included in a report of a subcommittee at the Havana Conference. The report of the working party states only that it "took note of the Swedish statement."[6]

What is one to conclude? The nondiscriminatory taxation of oleomargarine as a means of discriminating in favor of domestic butter production may have been seen as a kind of "gentlemen's agreement" exception to Article III, justi-

5. Interpretative note, Ad Art. III, para. 2.
6. *Basic Instruments,* 3d Supp. (1955), p. 205, 210.

fied only by its prevalence in international trade. But it is hard to go beyond that to say that any kind of nondiscriminatory taxation of one product to protect a domestic industry producing another product escapes the proscription of Article III. Such an interpretation would rob the second sentence of paragraph 2 of most if not all of its meaning. At most the second sentence would then be applicable only to the situation in which the taxed product was not produced domestically in substantial quantities and therefore the tax affected only imports. But neither the proscription of paragraph 1 against use of internal taxes to "afford protection to domestic production" nor the interpretative note previously cited concerning the relationship between the first and second sentences suggests such a limited construction.[7]

A number of other important points of construction concerning Article III have been clarified. The principal question has concerned the effect of the Protocol of Provisional Application. Article III, like the other provisions of Part II, does not prohibit contracting parties from continuing to apply measures that were in effect on 30 October 1947 (or on the date of the applicable protocol of accession). This means that discriminatory internal taxes in effect on that date may be continued, although the extent of the discrimination may not be increased. The question of interpretation has been whether the differential between the tax on domestic products and the tax on imported products is limited absolutely or only proportionally. In many countries, particularly less-developed countries, inflation has caused the price level to double and redouble since 1947, and the "absolute differential" interpretation would prevent these countries from continuing to accord the same protective effect to domestic products. To take a simple example, a product that in 1947 cost ten units of local currency and was taxed 10 percent in the case of local production and 20 percent in the case of imports involved at that time a tax of one unit of currency more on the imported product than on the domestic product. If in the meantime local prices have increased by ten times, the price of the domestic product is now one hundred units, and a limitation of the tax differential to one unit would involve a tax preference for the domestic product of only 1 percent in place of the old tax preference of 10 percent (calculated on the price of the domestic product). To maintain the same protective effect therefore would require a proportional, and not just an absolute, increase in the differential.[8]

It should be observed, however, that even a proportional increase may not afford precisely the same protective effect. The protective effect of a tax is a

---

7. The original U.S. view on this question is reflected in U.S. Tariff Commission, *Report on the Havana Charter for an International Trade Organization* (1949), pp. 27–28.

8. The analysis is, of course, the same as that for the application of the absolute and proportional differential approaches to tariff preferences.

complicated matter. To maintain the same protective effect that a tax had on 30 October 1947 may require more or less than a proportional increase on the imported product at the time there is an increase on the domestic product. Among factors that are of importance are changes in the interim in the price of the local product, the price of the imported product, the exchange rate, the general price level, and, most problematical of all, consumer tastes. But one can venture the proposition that a proportional increase is likely to come closer to preserving the same protective effect than is an absolute increase.

Since protective effect cannot be readily measured, even with the fullest information, an international body like the GATT is probably wise to opt for one or the other of these two alternatives. Since the purpose of the relevant provisions of the Protocol of Provisional Application is to permit contracting parties provisionally to preserve existing nontariff protection, the proportional standard is more appropriate than the absolute standard. But the alternative chosen need be no more than a guideline. There is no reason to preclude a contracting party that considers itself injured by a less-than-proportional tax increase from bringing forth data sufficient to satisfy the CONTRACTING PARTIES that the increase serves, in the words of paragraph 1, "to afford protection to domestic production" beyond that afforded on 30 October 1947. Similarly, a state should be free to increase its tax on an imported product more than proportionally if it can bring forth data sufficient to satisfy the CONTRACTING PARTIES that the proposed increase does not afford increased protection.

Whatever conclusions economic analysis may suggest, the GATT formulated a position at an early date in the Brazilian Internal Taxes case. Brazil, faced with serious inflation, had raised internal taxes on most items in order to reduce consumer demand. The tax on liquors, for example, had been increased sixfold. Since the preexisting 100 percent differential between taxes on imported and domestic liquors had been maintained, the effect of this sixfold increase had been to increase the absolute differential by six times. Brazil contended that the Protocol of Provisional Application did not forbid the proportional increase; among the points raised was that the Protocol is phrased in terms of "legislation" in effect on 31 October 1947, and the Brazilian legislation in effect on that date required that the tax on imported liquors be twice that on domestic liquors. The Brazilian delegate further argued that the first sentence of paragraph 2 had to be read in the light of paragraph 1, particularly in view of the interpretative note to paragraph 2 (which refers to paragraph 1), and that since paragraph 1 states generally that internal taxes are not to be applied "so as to afford protection to domestic production," the real question was whether the maintenance of the 100 percent differential in the course of the general increase of internal taxes constituted an increase in "protection to domestic production."⁹ The Brazilian delegate was not able to rally the majority of the working party to his view; thus a precedent of sorts was established for the absolute differential interpretation.¹⁰

The Brazilian interal taxes decision also put a stamp of approval on two subsidiary points of interpretation. Neither point was expressly endorsed by a majority of the working party, but both seemed indispensible to the general conclusion reached.¹¹ The first of these two points is that the first sentence of paragraph 2 does not have to be read in the light of the "afford protection to domestic production" test of paragraph 1.¹² This means, the question of pre-existing discrimination under the Protocol of Provisional Application aside, that discrimination in internal taxes between "like" imported and domestic products may not be justified on the ground that no protective effect is established. Although this interpretation has the advantage of keeping the issue on a simple, legalistic level, equality is an elusive matter in practice. As the discussion below of the U.S. taxation of distilled spirits will show, it is often difficult to determine whether imported and domestic products are treated equally without considering whether the tax has a protective effect.

In addition, the Brazilian decision implicitly approved the view that the absence of imports of a taxed product is not a defense under paragraph 2, since "the provisions of Article III were intended to prevent damage and not merely to provide a means of rectifying such damage."¹³ Under this interpretation internal taxes that tend to preclude potential imports are just as forbidden as are taxes that tend to reduce existing imports.

## Border Adjustments for Domestic Turnover Taxes

An ambiguity of great practical importance in view of the prevalence of multistage turnover taxes in the world concerns the content of the antidiscrimination rule envisaged by paragraph 2. In the case of a multistage turnover tax applied to manufactured products, for instance, the internal tax on imports is applied only at the final stage, but the internal tax on like (first sentence of paragraph 2) or competitive (second sentence) domestic products is applied at each stage of

9. U.S. Tariff Commission, *Operation of the Trade Agreements Program,* 3d Rep. (1950), p. 37.
10. *Basic Instruments,* Vol. II (1952), pp. 181, 183–85.
11. It can further be said that Brazil in effect adopted these views by agreeing to change its internal tax structure (see ibid., p. 186), and in the interim to negotiate compensatory measures, see U.S. Tariff Commission, *Operation* . . . , 7th Rep. (1954), p. 38.
12. *Basic Instruments,* Vol. II (1952), p. 181, 184. See Interpretative note, Ad Art. III, para. 2.
13. *Basic Instruments,* Vol. II (1952), p. 181, 184.

the manufacturing process (including the acquisition of raw materials) at which purchases and sales occur. The issue of construction thus becomes the following: May the internal tax imposed on imports be higher than the internal tax imposed on domestic products at the comparable stage of manufacture in order to compensate for internal taxes imposed on the domestic product at prior stages?[14]

At the Review Session the German delegation sought to have an interpretative note adopted that would have made clear that under the language of the first sentence of paragraph 2 the internal tax on domestic products (to be compared with the internal tax on the imported products) is "the overall charge, including the charges borne by like domestic products through being subjected to internal taxes or other internal charges at various stages of their production (charges borne by the raw materials, semi-finished products, auxiliary materials, etc. incorporated in, and by the power consumed for the production of, the finished products)."[15] Views were sharply divided on the advisability of such an interpretative note. The United States, with no multistage turnover tax, advanced the rather formalistic argument that, since only a domestic final product is competitive with an imported final product, only the amount of the domestic tax at the final stage should be applied to the imported product. But other countries, with multistage turnover taxes, argued that such an interpretation would discriminate against them in favor of countries that levied domestic taxes only at the final stage. The controversy was settled by the rejection of the proposed interpretative note coupled with the adoption in the working party report of the essentially meaningless statement that it was "understood that the principle of equality of treatment would be upheld in the event of a tax on imported products being challenged under the consultation or complaint procedure of the Agreement."[16] Since the very question before the working party was in effect the definition of equality of treatment, the working party's diplomatic formula was hardly useful.

The ambiguity touched on by the German proposal suggests a more fundamental inadequacy of paragraph 2. That provision does not really take account of the phenomenon of border tax adjustments designed to offset multistage turnover taxes levied on domestic products, even though its language is certainly broad enough to include such adjustments. Rather, paragraph 2 seems to be directed toward single-stage consumption taxes.

To understand the full complexity of the problem, one must distinguish be-

14. See the description of the *Vorbelastung* in the German countervailing tax in ibid., 1st Supp. (1953), pp. 53, 55–56.
15. Ibid., 3d Supp. (1955), p. 205, 210.
16. Ibid., p. 205, 211.

tween the two major types of multistage turnover taxes: *cascade* and *value-added*. The cascade tax involves the imposition at each sale of a levy based on the full value of the product at the time of the sale. If the product changes hands five times, a levy is paid five times, each time on an increasing base. The cascade tax favors integrated firms and causes the effective rate of tax on finished domestic products to vary sharply with the degree of integration of various firms in the industry in question.

The value-added tax also involves the imposition at each sale of a levy based on the full value of the product at the time of the sale, but the taxpayer is entitled to subtract from the amount thereby fixed the total amount of value-added taxes paid at all previous sales. No matter how many times the product changes hands, the aggregate tax burden after the final sale will remain the same.

The cascade tax presents the most obvious difficulties. Let us assume for the moment that the German position at the Review Session was correct and that the tax burden on imported products should reflect the multistage taxation of domestic products. What method of calculation of the tax on imported products is then compatible with paragraph 2? The tax imposed on any particular product may vary from manufacturer to manufacturer, particularly where some firms are integrated and others are not. It may thus be impossible to avoid imposing a greater tax on imported products than on some domestic products, unless some imported products are to be granted a preference over domestic products.

Since adherence to the principle of value added insures that the aggregate tax burden on any particular domestic product after the final sale will always be the same, the value-added tax appears to permit easy calculation of the offsetting tax on imported products. But a substantial percentage of international trade involves semifinished products, and a given domestic product manufactured by an integrated firm may not at a semifinished stage have been subjected to any turnover tax at all (particularly if the domestic firm is fully integrated and therefore no domestic sale has occurred). The domestic firm will of course eventually pay a tax on the value theretofore added if it sells the finished product domestically, but not if it sells that product abroad.

By contrast, the sale abroad of a finished product made from an imported semifinished product may or may not result in a refund of the internal tax originally imposed on the imported semifinished product. And even if in the latter case a refund is granted, the imported product bears a greater burden than does the product produced by the integrated domestic firm, this burden being equal to the interest on the funds involved between the time the tax is paid and the time it is refunded.

The problem of such border tax adjustments merits extensive treatment because it is one of the problems in economic relations among developed market economies that may be expected to become more important as the Kennedy Round tariff reductions become fully effective and that is not satisfactorily dealt with by the General Agreement. In this chapter we have discussed only the question of the compatibility of such border tax adjustments with the internal tax provisions of Article III. The more general questions will be discussed in chapter 13.

## Direct Taxes

In the light of the multitude of taxes and charges imposed by governments (turnover taxes, income taxes, exchange charges, etc.), it is important to determine which kinds of internal taxes are subject to paragraph 2. This question of interpretation, it should be noted, applies both to the form of the tax on imports and to the form of the tax on domestic products. Paragraph 2 speaks of "internal taxes or other internal charges" to which "products of the territory of any contracting party imported into the territory of any other contracting party" are "subject, directly or indirectly." Such "internal taxes or other internal charges" are not to be "in excess of those applied, directly or indirectly, to like domestic products." Since paragraph 2 speaks of "products" being subject to tax, it appears that so-called indirect taxes (turnover taxes, sales taxes, etc.) are envisaged. Such an interpretation is consistent with the general economic assumptions of the drafters of the General Agreement; they thought that indirect taxes were fully shifted to the purchaser in the price of the good, while direct taxes (principally income taxes) were not shifted at all but rather were fully absorbed by the seller. (This assumption will be more fully explored in chapter 13.) Does the reference to subjecting "products" to internal taxes "directly or indirectly" mean, however, that income taxes are to be swept within the purview of paragraph 2?

The answer to that question appears to be negative. In the first place, the terms "directly" and "indirectly" do not refer to 'direct" and "indirect" taxes. On the contrary, a tax applying 'directly" to "products" is an indirect tax, while a tax applying "indirectly" to "products" is a direct tax. This terminological anomaly can be resolved by switching one's perspective. The traditional tax terminology has in mind taxpayers, not producers: an income tax is measured by the income of the taxpayer and is therefore called a direct tax, while a sales or turnover tax is assessed on the value (normally sales value) of a product and therefore applies only indirectly to the taxpayer. It appears moreover that the phrase "directly or indirectly" in paragraph 2 was substituted for "in connection with" in order to conform the English to the French text and that there was no intent to suggest a technical distinction between kinds of taxes. The position that paragraph 2 applies only to indirect taxes is seconded by a statement in the reports on the Havana Conference indicating that the article of the Havana Charter that became Article III of the General Agreement did not apply to income taxes.[17]

This exclusion of direct taxes from the scope of Article III means not only that a domestic income tax may not be offset by any tax on imported products, but also that an income tax levied on importers or foreign sellers need not offset any domestic tax. The latter point is important because taxes on the local income of foreign sellers are common and are frequently limited only by the requirement that the foreign seller have a "permanent establishment" in the taxing country. In addition, such taxes are often calculated on a different basis from taxes on local enterprises.

## Exchange Taxes

The direct-indirect tax dichotomy does not provide a key to the problem of the application of Article III to various kinds of fees and charges imposed by governments in connection with the importation of goods. Two principal classes of such charges should be distinguished: first, customs fees concerning expenses incurred in assessing duties, inspections, validation of documents, and the like; and second, fees and charges imposed on exchange transactions. The former class is treated specially in Article VIII, where the general limitation is that such fees and charges "shall be limited in amount to the approximate cost of services rendered and shall not represent an indirect protection to domestic products or a taxation of imports or exports for fiscal purposes." The latter class, exchange fees and charges, presents more troublesome questions. The General Agreement does not, in general, concern itself with exchange questions. Under the existing division of institutional labor, such questions are for the International Monetary Fund. This division of authority is not entirely satisfactory, at least conceptually, because trade measures and exchange measures are often alternative means for reaching the same protectionist end. A tax on the foreign exchange required to import goods may be just as effective as a tax on the goods themselves.

At the Havana Conference a subcommittee proffered the following interpretation of Article 18 of the Havana Charter, the equivalent of Article III of the General Agreement:

> The Sub-Committee considered that charges imposed in connexion with the international transfer of payments for imports or exports, particularly the charges imposed by countries employing multiple currency practices, where such charges are imposed not inconsistently with the Articles of Agreement of the International Monetary Fund, would not be covered by Article 18.[18]

17. *Analytical Index,* p. 19.
18. *Analytical Index,* pp. 19–20.

The subcommittee went on to make clear that if a multiple currency practice took the "form of an internal tax or charge, such as an excise tax on an imported product not applied to the domestic product, that practice would be precluded by Article 18."[19] In other words, form was to control, and a tax that purported to be an exchange tax was not to be subject directly to the provisions of Article 18.

Nevertheless, one has to consider the general clause of Article XV:4, which provides that "contracting parties shall not, by exchange action, frustrate the intent of the provisions of this Agreement." This puzzling provision indicates that, at least at the limit, a residual control of exchange practices rests in the CONTRACTING PARTIES. But to what extent are the specific provisions of the General Agreement applicable to exchange practices? Article XV:9 provides that nothing in the General Agreement "shall preclude . . . the use by a contracting party of exchange controls or exchange restrictions in accordance with the Articles of Agreement of the International Monetary Fund." But beyond that exemption for IMF-conforming exchange action remain the above-quoted provisions of Article XV:4. "Frustrate" seems to be the key word. According to an interpretative note, the "word 'frustrate' is intended to indicate, for example, that infringements of the letter of any Article of this Agreement by exchange action shall not be regarded as a violation of that Article if, in practice, there is no appreciable departure from the intent of the Article."[20] The problem treated by the interpretative note—a violation of the letter but not the intent of an article—is, however, the inverse of the exchange problem—a possible violation of the stated intent (to assure, under paragraph 1, that taxes are not "applied . . . so as to afford protection to domestic production") but not the letter of Article III:2. There are no important precedents in the application of Article XV:4 which provide guidance. In 1952 the Panel on Complaints dealing with the Greek special "contribution" was of the view that a violation of Article XV:4 might arise "even if it were found that the tax did not fall within the ambit of Article III."[21] With the settlement of the dispute, the Panel on Complaints was freed from the necessity of clarifying its interpretation.

One way for the GATT to approach the exchange tax problem would be to seek the intent of the taxing government. The decisive question would be whether, under the general principle of paragraph 1, the purpose of the exchange tax was "to afford protection to domestic production." The procedures of the International Monetary Fund provide a precedent for the employment of an intention test. Exchange taxes that cause "an effective buying or selling

19. Ibid.
20. Interpretative note, Ad Art. XV, para. 4.
21. *Basic Instruments,* 1st Supp. (1953), p. 48, 50.

rate" to differ from "parity by more than one per cent" constitute multiple currency practices under Article VIII:3 of the Articles of Agreement of the Fund and therefore have to be approved by the Fund.[22] In reviewing such exchange taxes, the Fund seeks to determine whether there are present balance-of-payments reasons, since it believes that "the use of exchange systems for non-balance of payments reasons should be avoided to the greatest possible extent."[23]

In considering the usefulness of an intention test for the GATT, certain differences between the IMF and the GATT should be observed. Consultations between the IMF and governments are much more thorough and extensive than are consultations between the GATT and governments. This difference can be attributed in part to the fact that the role of the GATT in such fields as internal taxes tends to be viewed as that of a quasi-judicial institution applying legal rules. So long as that is viewed as the role of the GATT, attempts to apply an intention test to determine the lawfulness of measures taken by contracting parties will be just as doomed to failure as are attempts by the courts of a given state to apply an intention test to determine the constitutionality of acts of the executive of that state. There is no reason, however, why the role of the GATT as an institution should not involve the affirmative task of reducing exchange taxes that constitute nontariff barriers to trade. In that event, it would be possible for the appropriate GATT authorities to explore the purpose of such exchange taxes in probing, confidential consultations with the authorities of the contracting parties concerned. And if this suggestion has merit, there is no reason why its application could not be extended to all questions concerning internal taxes. In each case the basic question under Article III:1 is whether or not the internal tax is "applied . . . so as to afford protection to domestic production." The more specific provisions of the first sentence of paragraph 2 provide a shorthand test for taxes applicable to "like" imported and domestic products. But in situations coming under the second sentence of paragraph 2 and hence falling equally under paragraph 1, the question may inevitably become one of protectionist intention rather than of protectionist effect. It must not be overlooked in this connection that any tax on imports discourages those imports pro tanto and hence provides in some measure protection for domestic products.

## The Federal State Problem

Federal states may have some difficulty in complying with Article III, since their constitutions delegate to constituent states a jurisdiction to tax that is

22. International Monetary Fund, *Selected Decisions of the Executive Directors*, 3d Issue (1965), p. 91.
23. Ibid., p. 81, 82.

exercisable without supervision by the federal government. Since only the federation, and not the constituent states, is normally a contracting party, the responsibility of the federation for discriminatory acts of the member states presents a troublesome question.[24] Discriminatory tax statutes imposed by the constituent states may be just as effective as other measures for excluding imports, but the federal government may be constitutionally unable to suppress the discriminatory activity.

Article XXIV:12 establishes the basic test of a federal state's responsibility:

> Each contracting party shall take such reasonable measures as may be available to it to ensure observance of the provisions of this Agreement by the regional and local governments and authorities within its territory.

This "reasonable measures" test has received a special interpretation in the case of internal taxes. Here again the interpretative note distinguishes between the "letter" and the "spirit" of Article III. Where the local government measure is "inconsistent" with the letter but not the spirit of Article III, the central government is not required to "repeal . . . existing national legislation authorizing local governments to impose internal taxes . . . if such repeal would result in a serious financial hardship for the local governments or authorities concerned." It should be noted, in passing, that if the local government tax is sufficiently protectionist to foreclose exports, it will yield little revenue, and therefore repeal of national legislation will presumably be required. In the case of local government measures "inconsistent with both the letter and spirit of Article III," contracting parties are permitted "to eliminate the inconsistent taxation gradually over a transition period, if abrupt action would create serious administrative and financial difficulties."[25]

The interpretative note is badly drawn for a number of reasons. First, it permits central governments of states that are not constitutionally federal states to avoid responsibility whenever "serious financial hardships" or "serious administrative and financial difficulties" are involved. A second objection is that it purports to be an interpretation of paragraph 1. It therefore appears not to apply to the discriminatory treatment of "like" products under the first sentence of paragraph 2, a result that can only be termed curious. But the interpretative note is wobbly on the point, because it speaks of measures that are inconsistent with "Article III" rather than merely with paragraph 1. The erratic

---

24. See generally John H. Jackson, "The General Agreement on Tariffs and Trade in United States Domestic Law," *Michigan Law Review,* LXVI (1967), pp. 250, 297–311; "National Power to Control State Discrimination against Foreign Goods and Persons," *Stanford Law Review,* XII (1959), p. 355; Lawrence F. Ebb, *Regulation of International Business* (Saint Paul: West Publishing Co., 1964), pp. 761–68.

25. Interpretative note, Ad Art. III, para. 1.

wording of the note may be taken, however, as indicating that the first sentence of paragraph 2 is, contrary to the view of the working party in the Brazilian Internal Taxes case, in some sense subordinate to paragraph 1. For example, the interpretative note suggests that when it is not clear whether "like" products are being treated equally, one may take into account whether or not the tax on imports is being "applied . . . so as to afford protection to domestic production."

## Internal Taxes in the Kennedy Round

Internal taxes can be and have been discussed in the periodic GATT trade negotiation rounds. But it was not until the Kennedy Round that internal taxes bulked large in the negotiations. The two principal items were the U.S. system of assessing taxes on imported distilled spirits, and taxes maintained by certain countries, notably in Europe, on U.S. automobiles. These two kinds of taxes warrant examination, for they reveal certain difficulties in the application of the principle of equal treatment of "like" products.

The United States statute taxing distilled spirits, principally whisky, purports to be nondiscriminatory. The tax is nine dollars per gallon, whether the liquor is produced domestically or imported. The problem arises in the definition of a gallon. The tax is imposed on the *proof gallon* if the spirits are 100 proof or higher (that is, if they contain 50 percent or more alcohol by volume) and on the *wine gallon* if the spirits are below 100 proof. Unlike the wine gallon, which is a standard U.S. gallon of 231 cubic inches, the proof gallon is not a fixed volume. Where the spirits are higher than 100 proof, one calculates the number of proof gallons by determining how many standard U.S. gallons of 231 cubic inches would be involved if the spirits were diluted to reduce the proof count to 100. Since spirits of 100 proof or above are taxed purely in proportion to their alcoholic content, whereas spirits of 100 proof or below are taxed on their volume, the consequence of the system is that the tax per unit of alcohol increases as the proof count descends. To put the point somewhat more colorfully, the tax is paid on the water as well as on the alcohol when the spirits are below 100 proof.

The tax statute is of course not discriminatory on its face. The protectionist element enters only when one considers the commercial patterns of the liquor trade and the time of imposing the tax. Most whiskey, for example, is about 86 proof in the bottle sold to the consumer. But the tax on domestic liquor is imposed at the moment the liquor is withdrawn from bond. At that point the water necessary to bring the proof count down to drinking level has not yet been added, and the liquor is over 100 proof. Assessment is therefore made on the basis of proof gallons. Imported liquor, on the other hand, is assessed at the moment of importation, when it is normally already in the bottle in which it will be sold to the consumer. It is therefore assessed on the basis of wine gallons. The consequence is that, in practice, imported bottled spirits bear a substantially higher rate of tax than do domestic spirits.

Although the U.S. system was vigorously attacked in the Kennedy Round, no agreement was reached in this portion of the nontariff barrier negotiations.

Does the system of assessment violate Article III? The U.S. Court of Customs and Patent Appeals held that it did not in *Bercut-Vandervoort & Co.* v. *United States*.[26] The court relied on the formal equality between imported and domestic spirits under the terms of the statute. However elegant the opinion's demonstration of equality, the absurdity of the conclusion from an international trade perspective is revealed by the court's concession that the foreign distiller could avoid any competitive disadvantage due to the tax assessment system by establishing bottling facilities in the United States. The underlying assumption of the General Agreement—indeed, the argument for free trade in general—is that local laws and regulations should not make the location of industry a factor in trade. To say that part of the foreign industry must be moved to the United States for the foreign product to have the same competitive position as the domestic product is to concede that the legislation in question distorts international trading patterns and serves "to afford protection to domestic production." On the purely technical level, the decision in *Bercut-Vandervoort* may be criticized on the ground that the court considered only the first sentence of paragraph 2 and therefore treated the question as simply one of equal treatment of "like" products. But given its argument that imported bulk liquor is treated equally with domestic bulk liquor, the court acted strangely in not also considering whether, under the second sentence of paragraph 2 (incorporating by reference paragraph 1) and the interpretative note to paragraph 2, the taxation of imported bottled liquor did not serve to "afford protection to domestic production" (paragraph 1) to "a directly competitive or substitutable product which was not similarly taxed" (interpretative note to paragraph 2). The protection accorded the domestic product is the heart of the matter.

Certain internal taxes imposed by European countries on automobiles also played an important role in the Kennedy Round. The United States charged that these taxes were discriminatory against its exports. The taxes were so calculated as to make the internal tax on a U.S. automobile in many cases four or five times that on a locally manufactured automobile. Although U.S. automobiles were generally larger than local automobiles, they were not so much larger as to justify the differential. The Italian internal tax system, for example, imposed a tax on a Chevrolet Corvair which was 336 percent greater

---

26. 46 C.C.P.A. 28 (1958), *cert. den.* 359 U.S. 953 (1959). See also *China Liquor Distribution Co.* v. *United States,* 343 F.2d 1005 (C.C.P.A., 1964).

than the tax on a Fiat 1100-D, despite the fact that the Chevrolet had an engine displacement only 107 percent greater, a curb weight only 25 percent greater, and a list price at the source only 57 percent greater than did the Fiat. Similarly, the tax per fiscal horsepower was $1.71 for a Fiat 600-D, but $6.88 for a Chevrolet Corvair and $11.02 for a Ford Fairlane.[27] The automobile tax negotiations resulted in an agreement by Austria, Belgium, France, and Italy to eliminate certain of the discriminatory aspects of their taxes.[28]

## The GATT Record

Few disputes concerning internal taxes have reached the stage of working party or panel reports in the GATT. That does not necessarily mean, however, that Article III has been ineffectual in combating protectionist internal taxes. On the contrary, a number of complaints registered with the GATT of violation of the internal tax provisions have been settled without the necessity of resorting to the formal GATT dispute-settlement machinery. In 1956 the Department of State was able to list seven different cases in which the United States had been able to secure the elimination of internal taxes discriminating against U.S. exports; in some of these cases representations by the U.S. Embassy to the local government, calling attention to the violation of the General Agreement, had been sufficient to secure elimination of the contested tax.[29] This is important evidence that much of the effectiveness of Article III and of the General Agreement as a whole is not fully revealed by the formal decisions contained in the *Basic Instruments and Selected Documents,* the "reporter system" of GATT cases.

27. Comparison based on statistical information furnished by the U.S. Automobile Manufacturers Association, Inc., to the U.S. Office of the Special Representative for Trade Negotiations on 16 June 1965.
28. Office of the Special Representative for Trade Negotiations, *General Agreement on Tariffs and Trade: Report on U.S. Negotiations: 1964–67 Trade Conference* (1967), I, p. 167.
29. Hearings before the Committee on Ways and Means of the U.S. House of Representatives on H.R. 5500 (84th Cong., 2d Sess., 1956), pp. 58–59.

# 8 Subsidies

The General Agreement is hostile to subsidies. Production subsidies are dealt with less harshly than export subsidies, however, and even among the latter some types escape prohibition. In part the derogations from the strict free-trade position, which views all subsidies as distortions of the market, are attributable to U.S. proposals at the drafting conferences. The U.S. delegation was forced to accommodate its free trade ideology to the domestic political realities of a farm program that relied in the case of certain important products upon a two-price system. The higher domestic price was made possible by government purchase of surpluses, a measure that was in one sense a production subsidy. The surpluses were thereupon sold abroad at the world price through what was in essence an export subsidy. The ambivalent position that the U.S. delegation was forced to take aroused considerable resentment in the ITO Charter negotiations, where the American desire to justify its own subsidy programs while condemning those of other countries was received as proof of hypocrisy.[1]

Even with its qualifications, Article XVI of the General Agreement treats subsidies as, in principle, undesirable interferences with the free flow of goods. Before turning to the complex provisions of the General Agreement, it is worth asking to what extent this antipathy toward subsidies is justified. Subsidies interfere with the efficiency of an otherwise free market and in the case of export subsidies frequently lead to further trade barriers, in the form either of offsetting countervailing duties or of competitive export subsidies in third-country markets. But there are a number of imperfections in the existing international trading system that may introduce certain nuances in one's judgment of subsidies.

---

1. See the discussion in William Adams Brown, *The United States and the Restoration of World Trade* (Washington: Brookings Institution, 1950), pp. 115–19.

## Symptoms and Cures

### Exchange Rates

It is misleading to discuss subsidies without discussing exchange rates. Hostility to subsidies is closely tied to the current preference for fixed unitary exchange rates. In a world where the official fixed exchange rates corresponded to the relative purchasing power of the various currencies, international trade in goods would tend to be similar, from an allocation-of-resources perspective, to purely domestic trade in an internal market. In those circumstances a subsidy would cause a distortion of the competitive situation in the same manner as a domestic subsidy. But if, for example, one currency is substantially overvalued, the artificial disparity in exchange rates may be said to create the distortion of competition, and export subsidies by the country with the overvalued exchange rate may be regarded (at least if they are granted on all exports) as a move away from this distortion and toward the situation that would obtain in an internal market free of subsidies. On a more practical level, a country with a grossly overvalued currency may find it impossible to export without export subsidies. For this reason export subsidies are much more common in less-developed countries, many of which have a penchant for overvalued currencies, than in developed countries. Similarly, export subsidies tend to go hand in hand with blocked currencies and are relatively less common in countries with freely convertible currencies.

Elimination of export subsidies may therefore often be dependent upon an exchange-rate adjustment. For example, in preparing to accede to the GATT, Yugoslavia devalued its currency from 750 to 1250 dinars per U.S. dollar in order to be able to eliminate all export subsidies.[2] But unless the devaluation is adequate, the devaluing country may be forced to continue or to reintroduce its export subsidies. When India devalued the rupee by 36 percent in 1966, it did so with the intention of eliminating export subsidies. When it found that there was still an insufficient incentive to export, it was forced to reintroduce export subsidies on certain products.[3] A generalized export subsidy scheme may even be part of a de facto devaluation. An example is to be found in the across-the-board 20 percent export subsidy, coupled with a 20 percent tariff surcharge, introduced by France in 1957. Both subsidies and surcharges were abolished when the French franc was devalued in June 1958.[4] The primary

2. *Basic Instruments,* 14th Supp. (1966), p. 49, 54.
3. See "India After Devaluation," *The Economist,* CCXX (1966), p. 572; letter to the Editor by Professor Bhagwati, ibid., p. 788; "India Plans for Survival," ibid., p. 1266.
4. The CONTRACTING PARTIES to the General Agreement on Tariffs and Trade, *Commercial Policy: 1957* (1958), p. 48 (hereafter cited as *Commercial Policy: 1957*).

difference between the French subsidy-surcharge scheme and devaluation is that devaluation strikes all transactions, current and capital, whereas subsidies normally affect only current transactions in visibles, such as commodities and industrial products.

## Agriculture

Subsidies are most common in agricultural commodities.[5] This easily observable fact suggests that in the agricultural sector subsidies are more symptoms than causes of an imperfect international market. But here, unlike in the situation of an overvalued currency, only one sector of the world economy is affected. Most countries attempt to insulate their farmers from the vicissitudes of world market prices by subsidies or by measures that are analytically similar to subsidies. Either farmers are paid directly a certain sum per unit of output or acreage, as under the deficiency payments in effect in the United Kingdom; or the government purchases surpluses in order to support the price, as under the price support system in the United States and in most other countries producing temperate agricultural products. In either case, production is higher than it would otherwise be, and under the price support system domestic prices diverge so substantially from world market prices that import and export patterns become distorted.

The international trade consequences of these domestic farm programs will be examined more closely in chapter 15. At the moment it suffices to observe that in countries that are self-sufficient in particular commodities, the surpluses that the government buys, or otherwise causes to increase through its internal subsidy program, must be disposed of abroad. That is accomplished either by a direct export subsidy or simply by export sales by the government at the world market price. Where the government has purchased the domestic production at prices above the world market price, the sale at the latter price must also be considered a subsidy. Whether one treats it as a production subsidy or as an export subsidy depends largely on whether one views the question from the perspective of the subsidizing country or of another exporting country that is trying to compete in third-country markets. When, for example, Malawi complained that a U.S. export subsidy on tobacco was displacing its tobacco exports in third-country markets, the United States replied that the subsidy was merely a necessary consequence of its domestic support programs.[6] But whatever the label, the fundamental point is that the subsidy is only a manifestation of the autarkic policies that most countries pursue in agriculture.

5. *Basic Instruments,* 10th Supp. (1962), p. 201, 203.
6. Ibid., 15th Supp. (1968), pp. 116, 117–18.

Economic Development

Subsidies are also closely related to programs for economic development. Developing countries frequently use subsidies to encourage new industries. These subsidies may be either production subsidies to help the new industries over the high-cost hurdles of the first few years or export subsidies to enable the industries to reach a dimension that permits economies of scale to manifest themselves. In many cases the subsidizing countries may be deceiving themselves about the long-run viability of the industries or may be cynically pursuing, for prestige motives, the development of industries that will never be able to stand on their feet in international competition.

But where the hope is justified that the industries will be able to reduce their costs sufficiently over time to achieve such international viability, the classical infant industry case for tariff protection is presented. As most economists agree, a protective tariff in such a case would not only be beneficial to the country itself but would improve efficiency in the world as a whole. If a tariff would be justified, then so also should a subsidy. Indeed, as suggested below, a subsidy might be preferable to a tariff for all concerned.

**Subsidies versus Tariffs and Quantitative Restrictions**

The infant industry case brings one to a more general point about subsidies and the General Agreement. Since tariffs are considered lawful for protective purposes, should not subsidies (or at minimum, production subsidies intended to permit local industry to compete with imports in the local market) also be considered lawful? One might go even further and argue that production subsidies are better than tariffs and should be encouraged, at least where the alternative is the imposition of a new tariff or the preservation of an existing tariff. A production subsidy coupled with free importation permits the price for the locally-produced goods to find its level in competition with imported goods. Consumption of the goods in question is thereby expanded, which is good for producer and consumer alike, and the increased consumption may hasten the day when the market is sufficiently large to permit the new industry to realize its economies of scale. The production subsidy is thereby more nearly compatible with the free trade ideology than would be a tariff.

This argument was acknowledged by the U.S. negotiators and was indeed used to justify existing U.S. export subsidies—rather incongruously, since those subsidies were, as we have seen, largely in agriculture, where there are few economies of scale to be reaped. To be sure, a subsidy may still be preferable to a tariff as a means of supporting agriculture, but two points should be observed. Since the infant industry argument has little applicability to agriculture, it cannot be argued that an agricultural subsidy serves world efficiency (or, to put the argument in another way, that a subsidy is preferable to unimpeded free trade from the point of view of world efficiency). And, on a more mundane level, its respect for subsidies should have led the U.S. delegation to favor subsidies over tariffs generally and not just in the areas where the United States was already using subsidies.

Export subsidies have the practical disadvantage of leading to further export subsidies by other countries, and the process may easily deteriorate into a competitive subsidization race. While importing countries may impose countervailing duties to offset export subsidies (and are entitled to do so in most cases under Article VI of the General Agreement, whether or not the export subsidy is lawful),[7] other exporting countries have no ready means of protecting their existing markets in third countries against such subsidies. For this reason, the United States introduced export subsidies in 1965 on chicken destined for the Swiss and Austrian markets as a countermeasure to export subsidies accorded by the European Economic Community as part of its Common Agricultural Policy.[8] Moreover, an export subsidy that seems minor to the country introducing it may have a profound effect on smaller competitors whose exports are concentrated in the product in question. A U.S. export subsidy on sultanas, a variety of grape, was alleged by Greece to have undermined a traditional market representing some 8 percent of all Greek exports.[9]

Although the differential treatment of tariffs and subsidies raises some important questions of principle, the differential treatment of quantitative restrictions and subsidies is perhaps of more far-reaching practical importance. Although the General Agreement purports to outlaw quantitative restrictions, the balance-of-payments exception operates perversely as a license for use of such restrictions whenever a currency becomes sufficiently overvalued.[10] No similar balance-of-payments exception was carved out for export subsidies. The consequence of this differential treatment is to encourage countries suffering payments imbalances to seek the requisite adjustment of their international accounts on the import rather than the export side. The volume of world trade is thereby reduced. So long as the payments imbalance stems from a long-term currency overvaluation, the negative effects on the efficiency of the international economic system are likely to be much greater where the necessary adjustment is made on the import rather than the export side.

7. Ibid., 9th Supp. (1961), pp. 194, 200.
8. GATT Document L/2457 (29 Sept. 1965); GATT Document L/2972 (8 Feb. 1968), p. 2.
9. U.S. Tariff Commission, *Operation of the Trade Agreements Program,* 6th Rep. (1954), p. 40.
10. The perverse effect of the balance-of-payments exception is examined in chapter 9, "Quantitative Restrictions," infra.

## Subsidies in the Contemporary World

One of the difficulties in regulating the payment of subsidies is that the classical form of subsidy—that is, a payment of money to someone for doing something—is the exception and not the rule on the current international scene. Certain activities of governments that appear unrelated to typical subsidization motives may have the effect of subsidies. From a legal point of view, this circumstance raises the fundamental problem of the extent to which motive is to be an element of illegality. But motive aside, it raises a question of enforcement, because governments are reluctant to eliminate measures taken to deal with specific problems simply because those measures may, from a GATT perspective, be equivalent to subsidies.

Two illustrations may be drawn from the area of currency practices. Currency retention practices and multiple exchange rates, both responses to balance-of-payments difficulties, are rather clearly subsidies under Article XVI, but are frequently not so thought of by the governments concerned, particularly because they come within the competence of the treasury or the central bank rather than that of trade officials.

Currency retention consists of permitting exporters to retain a portion of scarce foreign exchange proceeds. Depending upon the details of the system, these proceeds may be sold in a free market, where, under scarcity conditions, they will command a price higher than that obtainable under the official exchange rate, or they may be used to import foreign goods for which foreign exchange would otherwise be unavailable under the applicable exchange control regulations. In the latter case, the variations in the details of the systems are wide. Sometimes the retained proceeds must be used to finance imports of raw materials needed for further exports, as under the Japanese "link" system; other times, they must be used to purchase machinery, finished goods, or even, as under a shrewdly conceived Chilean plan, luxury goods.[11] Whatever the details of the system, the possibility of keeping the scarce foreign exchange rather than turning it over to the exchange authorities provides an important incentive to export. From the point of view of third countries, a currency retention system permits the individual exporter to lower his export price while still realizing the same profit measured in domestic currency. And in certain cases a currency retention system may lead to "shunting," which involves the importation of certain goods for reexport to third countries. In "shunting," the trader, permitted to make the purchase at the official rate but to resell the hard currency proceeds at a premium, may gain even though the price is higher in the country of origin than in the country of destination.

11. *Commercial Policy: 1957,* pp. 49–50; The CONTRACTING PARTIES to the General Agreement on Tariffs and Trade, *International Trade: 1955* (1956), p. 181.

Multiple-exchange-rate practices involve the establishment of different official rates for different transactions. Luxury goods or goods that compete with local manufacturing industries may be accorded unfavorable rates for import transactions, and on the export side major export products that encounter stiff competition abroad may receive a favorable rate.[12] The results can be dramatic. Instead of a unitary rate of, for example, 10 units of local currency per dollar, the government may prescribe that henceforth for certain exports the rate will be 15 to 1. Local sellers then will receive 50 percent more local currency for each sale abroad or, perhaps more to the point, will be able to reduce prices up to one-third, thereby expanding sales in highly competitive markets while preserving their per unit margin in terms of local currency. Such practices can be viewed either as a pro tanto devaluation or as an export subsidy. From the latter perspective, the effect is almost precisely the same as a classical export subsidy: local currency proceeds per unit are increased, permitting prices to be lowered in order to sell additional units abroad. To third country competitors the injury is just as serious as in the case of a classical export subsidy. And for countries with overvalued exchange rates, such practices may be justified in the same terms as apply to a classical export subsidy.

Both currency retention practices and multiple-exchange-rate practices fall within the meaning of the term "export subsidies" in Article XVI.[13] But the GATT itself has shown little success in suppressing them, perhaps because both practices are regulated by the International Monetary Fund. In the case of multiple exchange rates, approval by the IMF excludes the possibility of a challenge under Article XVI, although a duty to notify under Article XVI remains.

A quite different group of measures, which fall under the heading of export subsidies in Article XVI[14] but tend not to be viewed by the governments concerned as export subsidies, are the export financing schemes that have been adopted by a steadily growing number of countries since World War II. The fundamental notion behind these plans is that lack of adequate financing is a major barrier to the growth of exports and therefore it is up to the government to assure that the requisite financing is forthcoming. Three basic techniques are involved: (1) credits furnished by the government; (2) government guarantees of commercial bank loans; and (3) government payment of some portion of the costs of commercial bank interest rates, normally that

12. See generally Margaret G. de Vries, "Multiple Exchange Rates: Expectations and Experiences," *International Monetary Fund Staff Papers,* XII (1965), pp. 282–311.
13. On currency retention practices, see *Basic Instruments,* 9th Supp. (1961), pp. 185, 186. On multiple-exchange-rate practices, see Interpretative note, Ad Art. XVI, § B:1; *Basic Instruments,* 9th Supp. (1961), p. 188, 192.
14. *Basic Instruments,* 9th Supp. (1961), pp. 185, 186–87.

portion above the rate for domestic credit. The last is rather clearly a subsidy, but so also may be the other two inasmuch as the interest rate on government loans or on government-guaranteed loans is lower than the free market rate for unguaranteed commercial bank loans. Where commercial bank loans would not be forthcoming in any event, it is difficult to calculate the amount of the subsidy, but a subsidy nevertheless exists.

The reluctance of governments to consider these various measures to be subsidies stems in part from the fact that the scarcity of commercial bank credit for exports is often attributable to noncommercial risks associated with export credits, notably the risks that the goods may be confiscated or that riots or other disturbances may lead to the destruction of the goods. This fact often leads governments to view their own credit activities as noncommercial and hence as not in the nature of a subsidy. A number of governments have established export credit insurance schemes covering noncommercial risks. These also might be considered to constitute subsidies to the extent that the premiums are insufficient to cover claims, but since the risks are not subject to actuarial calculation, it would be difficult to establish the level at which premiums become so low as to constitute subsidies.

A third class of measures raising subsidy questions involves the refund of taxes on the export of goods, including the exemption of taxes that would otherwise be imposed. It is traditional to distinguish the refund of direct taxes from the refund of indirect taxes. In the case of the indirect tax, of which the leading example in the United States is the sales tax and in Europe the turnover tax, a refund is not considered to be a subsidy under the General Agreement so long as the amount refunded does not exceed the amount previously collected. Refund of direct taxes, notably the income tax, is, however, a subsidy under Article XVI. This widely held view concerning the proper construction of the GATT rules was affirmed in 1960 by the Working Party on Subsidies, which, taking a page from the OEEC Code of Liberalization, decided that the "remission, calculated in relation to exports, of direct taxes or social welfare changes on industrial or commercial enterprises" constituted a subsidy under Article XVI.[15]

The distinction between direct and indirect taxes appears to be founded upon the choice of the phrase "duties or taxes borne *by the like product*" to describe the duties and taxes that may be refunded.[16] The basis of the distinction lies primarily in tradition. Governments relying heavily on turnover taxes have traditionally refunded those taxes in order to make export prices more competitive. Income taxes have rarely been refunded. The underlying theoretical argument, for which the empirical evidence is far from convincing, is

15. Ibid.
16. Interpretative note, Ad Art. XVI (emphasis supplied).

that indirect taxes are passed on in the price of the goods while direct taxes are not. Although this subject warrants separate treatment,[17] two general remarks will be made here. First, countries relying primarily on direct taxes frequently consider the distinction unjustly discriminatory. Second, the rule exempting the remission of indirect taxes presents certain difficulties in practice.

The prime difficulty created by the exemption rule is the calculation of the amount of taxes already paid where the goods have incurred taxes at various levels of processing or manufacture. Of the two general systems of turnover taxation, the value-added system and the cascade system, only the former permits a fairly accurate notion of the amount of taxes paid. The difference between the two is, as we have seen, that under the value-added system only the value added at each stage is subject to taxation, whereas under the cascade system the entire value of the goods is subjected to tax at each stage. It was this difficulty of calculation with the consequent danger of unintended subsidization that lead the European Economic Community to require all member states to follow the value-added practice. But even under the value-added practice the goods must be traced through various transformations, a difficult practice for outsiders trying to establish that the authorities of a particular country have refunded more than was justified. The possibility of a subsidy through an excessive refund is similarly presented, it should be noted, where customs duties on import of raw materials are refunded on export of goods.

Another practice that may constitute an export subsidy on goods is a subsidy on inputs, such as raw materials, or on transportation. Transport subsidies are common. Canadian coal destined for points other than the United States, Israeli exports aboard the Israeli national airline, and a wide range of South African exports have benefited from transport subsidies.[18] And in many countries transport subsidies are available for inland domestic producers trying to meet import competition in port areas. These latter subsidies are akin to production subsidies in the sense that they tend to reduce imports into the subsidizing country. Where a mode of transportation is nationalized, the aid is usually in terms of lower rates rather than money payments. That all such differential transport rates designed to aid exports or deter imports should be viewed as subsidies is questionable. Such practices may also be viewed as competitive pricing by transport authorities. In the United States, where transportation facilities are overwhelmingly in private hands, low rates in similar circumstances are common because the transport companies make more money through the additional traffic that the lower rates permit. In the case of rates encouraging exports, the practice is viewed as promotional in the sense that it

17. See discussion in chapter 13, "Border Tax Adjustments," infra.
18. The CONTRACTING PARTIES to the General Agreement on Tariffs and Trade, *International Trade: 1952* (1953), pp. 63–64; *Commercial Policy: 1957,* p. 48.

stimulates additional traffic. In the case of rates discouraging imports, the lower rates are viewed as the meeting of the competition of ocean carriers. Where transport facilities are in public hands, similar pricing practices should not automatically be considered subsidies.[19]

## Production Subsidies

The provisions of Article XVI were substantially revised at the Review Conference in 1955 in an effort to give them more of a cutting edge. All of Section B was added at that time. Until 1955 Article XVI had merely required what is now found in Section A; namely, that contracting parties maintaining subsidies that operate "directly or indirectly to increase exports or . . . reduce imports" are to notify the CONTRACTING PARTIES of such subsidies. Moreover, where "it is determined that serious prejudice to the interests of any other contracting party is caused or threatened," a duty arises to "discuss" the "possibility of limiting the subsidization."

Although the remedy of discussion of possibilities is rather weak, the substantive standard is somewhat more strict than might appear. The CONTRACTING PARTIES determined in 1948 that the term "increased exports" "was intended to include the concept of maintaining exports at a level higher than would otherwise exist in the absence of the subsidy."[20] In 1960 a panel charged with reviewing Article XVI opined that *"mutatis mutandis* this interpretation must apply to the effect on imports" and that in either case the "criterion is therefore what would happen in the *absence* of a subsidy." Although "such a judgment cannot be reached only by reference to statistics, nevertheless a statistical analysis helps to discern the trends of imports and exports and may assist in determining the effects of a subsidy." The panel proposed the adoption of a presumption that a subsidy tending to increase production "will, in the absence of offsetting measures, e.g., a consumption subsidy, either increase exports or reduce imports."[21]

Since Section B is concerned exclusively with export subsidies, Section A remains the crucial provision on production subsidies. It is complemented in practice, however, by Article III:4, which provides that imports "shall be accorded treatment no less favourable than that accorded to like products of national origin in respect of all laws, regulations and requirements affecting their internal sale, offering for sale, purchase, transportation, distribution or

19. It should be noted that the last sentence of paragraph 4, Article III, excludes differential internal transportation charges which are not based solely on "the economic operation of the means of transport" from the national treatment requirement of that paragraph.
20. *Basic Instruments,* Vol. II (1952), p. 39, 44.
21. Ibid., 9th Supp. (1961), pp. 188, 191.

use." Although the scope of this broadly drawn prohibition is drastically restricted, as far as production subsidies are concerned, by paragraph 8(b) of Article III, which provides that the prohibition of paragraph 4 "shall not prevent the payment of subsidies exclusively to domestic producers . . . and subsidies effected through governmental purchases of domestic products," the prohibition remains in effect for subsidies that take other forms. That was the view of a panel for conciliation upholding a U.K. complaint against an Italian statute providing favorable financing to farmers purchasing domestic, but not imported, agricultural machinery. While the applicability of Article III to subsidies is thus limited to certain forms of production subsidies, the provision remains important because it purports to be a flat prohibition and thus gives rise to more than just a duty to consult as under Section A, Article XVI.

## Export Subsidies

Section A of Article XVI applies also to export subsidies, but the more specific provisions on export subsidies are to be found in Section B. The latter Section distinguishes export subsidies on primary products from export subsidies on other products. Contracting parties are to "seek to avoid" subsidies on any primary product and, in any case, are not to apply a subsidy on such products "in a manner which results in [their] having more than an equitable share of world export trade in that product."

## Primary Products

The terms "having," "equitable share," and "world export trade" give rise to several questions of interpretation. The term "having" suggests that an increase in the subsidizing country's share need not be established if the subsidizing country preserves a larger share than it would otherwise have. An export subsidy used to arrest a decline in exports would apparently be prohibited. This conclusion would seem to follow a fortiori from the accepted interpretation of the 'to increase exports" language in Section A, which, as we have seen, makes that which would happen in the absence of a subsidy the crucial factor. Acceptance of this construction, however, makes the meaning of "equitable share" even more indefinite than an equitable standard normally is, because the text of Section B specifically requires that "account [be] taken of the shares of the contracting parties in such trade in the product during a previous representative period." Of what value is comparison with a prior representative period if even holding one's own may constitute a violation? Perhaps the suggestion of the 1960 panel, discussed previously, that statistics "help to discern the trend of imports and exports and may assist in determining the effects of a subsidy" may be read into Section B to make the relationship of current exports to exports in the representative year only one element in determining the "equitable share." A 1958 panel for conciliation had noted that "there is no statistical definition of an 'equitable' share in world exports," but had been able to elude the issue by finding that the subsidy arrangements there in question—arrangements made by France for exports of wheat and wheat flour to Southeast Asia to the injury of Australia's traditional position in that market—had increased French exports so that the French share of world export trade was at that time "more than equitable."[22]

In any case, the additional requirement in Section B that "any special factors which may have affected or may be affecting . . . trade in the product" be taken into account tends to indicate that the determination of an equitable share is much more than a statistical exercise. What those special factors might be is suggested by the statement of the 1955 Review Session Working Party that the CONTRACTING PARTIES "should not lose sight of" the value of economic efficiency or of the influence of export subsidies on trade in the representative period. On the other hand, an interpretative note makes clear that notions of equity require that less-developed countries becoming self-sufficient in primary products be permitted to use export subsidies to enter world markets; the note states that the absence of exports during the representative period "would not in itself preclude . . . [a] right to obtain a share of the trade in the product concerned."[23]

Because few subsidies are so important as to affect substantially world market shares, it is important to know whether an export subsidy that injures substantially the export trade of another contracting party may nevertheless be justified under Article XVI because it does not increase the subsidizing country's share of "world export trade." The 1958 panel for conciliation in the French-Australian case stated that "at both Havana and the Review Session . . . it was implicitly agreed that the concept of 'equitable' share was meant to refer to share in 'world' export trade of a particular product and not to trade in that product in individual markets."[24] The drafting history of Section B is less than conclusive on this question, a point that the GATT Secretariat has underlined by publishing the relevant portions of the summary records of the Review Session discussions.[25] This rather unusual step may suggest the position of the Secretariat. The final resolution of this issue will determine the practical importance of the limitation of export subsidies on primary products.

22. Ibid., 7th Supp. (1959), p. 46, 53. The provisions of Part IV must also be taken into account where export subsidies have the effect of reducing the exports of less-developed country competitors. See 15th Supp. (1968), pp. 116, 123–25.
23. Interpretative note, Ad Art. XVI, para. 3:1. See also *Basic Instruments,* 3d Supp. (1955), p. 222, 226. See also 15th Supp. (1968), pp. 116, 122–23.
24. *Basic Instruments,* 7th Supp. (1959), p. 46, 52.
25. *Analytical Index,* pp. 87–88.

Because under any interpretation the rules on export subsidies of primary products are rather permissive, it is important to examine the definition of the term "primary product." While "any product of farm, forest or fishery, or any mineral" is included, the important problems arise in connection with processed products. The United States has argued that its export subsidies on cotton textiles should be included, but the other contracting parties have not agreed. A primary product may undergo only "such processing as is customarily required to prepare it for marketing in substantial volume in international trade." Since cotton is sold in substantial volume in forms other than textiles, textiles are not included in the definition, even though the U.S. subsidies are calculated according to the raw cotton content of each kind of textile.[26]

## Nonprimary Products

The provisions of Section B dealing with export subsidies in nonprimary products and the steps subsequently taken pursuant to those provisions constitute one of the most interesting attempts at a new approach to the elimination of trade barriers. Simply declaring export subsidies illegal would have been a pious but essentially fruitless step, since Article XVI falls in Part II, and, under the Protocol of Provisional Application, the prohibition would have applied only to export subsidies that were not in effect on 30 October 1947 or on the date of the applicable protocol of accession. Such a step would not have rooted out all existing export subsidies. On the other hand, a separate agreement on illegality, freed of the limitations of Part II, probably could not have been reached, since nations seldom agree that what they are currently doing is illegal if there is the possibility of an effective remedy against the illegality. Both of these pitfalls were avoided by the more expedient and productive approach of an agreement not to introduce new export subsidies, coupled with an agreement to work toward future elimination of existing export subsidies. It was agreed at the 1955 Review Conference (as a part of paragraph 4 of Article XVI) that "as from 1 January, 1958 or the earliest practicable date thereafter" all export subsidies of nonprimary products would be eliminated which resulted in "sale . . . for export at a price lower than the comparable price charged for the like product to buyers in the domestic market." In addition, a standstill on the "introduction of new, or the extension of existing, subsidies" until 31 December 1957 was agreed to. As the interpretative note made clear, the in-

26. Interpretative note, Ad Art. XVI, § B:2; *Third Annual Report of the President of the United States on the Trade Agreements Program* (1959), p. 40. The United States subsequently appended to its signature of the "Giving Effect" Declaration an "understanding" that that Declaration did not prevent a continuation of its cotton textile export payments. The CONTRACTING PARTIES to the General Agreement on Tariffs and Trade, *Status of Multilateral Protocols of which the Director-General Acts as Depositary* (1967), p. 42.01.

tention was to reach agreement before the end of 1957 to abolish all remaining subsidies or, failing such an agreement, to extend the standstill until such time as an abolition agreement could be reached.[27]

An abolition agreement was not reached by 1958, but the consequences were not too serious, because the Organization for European Economic Co-operation was having considerable success in abolishing export subsidies among its members under its liberalization program. In a sense this OEEC success tended to remove the pressure from the GATT, given the fact that the requisite agreement by the developing countries, plagued by overvalued currencies, could hardly have been expected. It is interesting to observe that some of this success may have been attributable to the fact that the OEEC, rather than condemning export subsidies in general terms, specified in some detail the major types of export subsidies that were to be abolished.[28] But the generally improved health of European currencies and the move to free convertibility on current transactions at the end of 1958 also facilitated the elimination of export subsidies.

When the OEEC was transformed into the Organization for Economic Co-operation and Development in 1960 and thereby lost most of its competence in the field of trade, the role of the GATT took on new importance. Following French leadership, a review of the use of subsidies was held in 1960,[29] and a form of declaration was drawn up by the CONTRACTING PARTIES.[30] This Declaration Giving Effect to the Provisions of Article XVI:4 did not, however, bring the prohibition against export subsidies in paragraph 4 into immediate effect. Rather, the "Giving Effect" Declaration, and hence the prohibition, was to become effective only on the date that the more developed European contracting parties plus the United States and Canada all accepted the Declaration, and even then the prohibition was to be effective only for such contracting parties as had accepted the Declaration. In other words, the major industrialized countries were prepared to agree to prohibit export subsidies, but only in a concerted move. It should not be overlooked that this was one of the first times that, Article XVIII aside, the CONTRACTING PARTIES formally recognized that developing countries should be treated differently from developed countries. The Declaration was thus an implicit recognition that the overvalued currencies of some of the developing countries might justify export subsidies.

The standstill provisions of Article XVI had meanwhile been extended from time to time, and in 1960 a further standstill declaration was opened for sig-

---

27. Interpretative note, Ad Art. XVI, para. 4.
28. See Decision of the Council of the OEEC concerning measures designed to aid exports, Organization for European Economic Co-operation, *Code of Liberalisation* (1960), p. 193, for the final form of the OEEC rules.
29. *Basic Instruments,* 9th Supp. (1961), pp. 185–94.
30. Ibid., p. 32.

nature.³¹ This Declaration of Extension of the Standstill Provisions of Article XVI:4 included a "continuous rollback" provision under which any subsidy subsequently reduced or abolished could not be reinstituted. It was of particular significance for those contracting parties that had not signed the "Giving Effect" Declaration, and the hope was that signatories of the former might gradually be persuaded to "move up to" the latter. To induce the developing countries to sign the "Standstill" Declaration, the effectiveness of that declaration was made dependent upon signature by the previously mentioned industrialized countries plus Japan. Both declarations came into effect in due course, and subsequently the "Standstill" Declaration, which unlike the "Giving Effect" Declaration had been temporary, was extended through 31 December 1967.³²

### Reporting Requirements

The declarations showed a good deal of statecraft and suggested a technique that might be used to advantage in other situations, but they were only one string in the GATT's bow. The other was the reporting mechanism, included in the original Article XVI and considerably strengthened through the formulation of a questionnaire requiring detailed information on the amount, nature, incidence, and effects of existing subsidies. For a time filed each year, these questionnaires are now returned once each three years.³³ The results of the reporting mechanism have been disappointing. The information given has been substantially less than demanded and far too general, particularly on the question of trade effects. Some subsidies have not even been reported. For example, despite the availability of financial assistance of one kind or another for shipbuilding in nearly every shipbuilding country and of direct subsidy payments to shipyards in a number of countries, only a single contracting party has mentioned these subsidies in its reports to the GATT.³⁴ There is no evidence that the GATT has done anything of consequence with the information collected, beyond reviewing it and summarizing it for redistribution.

The gathering of information can be of great importance if the information is detailed and is put to use. The futility of the GATT subsidy reporting exercise may be attributed to the failure either to appoint a committee with the compe-

31. Ibid., p. 33.
32. Ibid., 12th Supp. (1964), p. 50. During the period 1964–67 only one country, Finland, was a party to the "Standstill" Declaration. Consequently, that declaration was permitted to lapse at the end of 1967. See Report of the United States Delegation to the Twenty-Fourth Session of the CONTRACTING PARTIES to the General Agreement on Tariffs and Trade (1967) (mimeographed document), Section VIII:a.
33. Ibid., 9th Supp. (1961), pp. 193–94; 11th Supp. (1963), p. 58 .
34. Compare Organization for Economic Co-operation and Development, *The Situation in the Shipbuilding Industry* (1965), with *Basic Instruments,* 10th Supp. (1962), p. 201, 204.

tence and energy to obtain detailed information on the trade effects of subsidies or to adopt a confrontation and justification procedure, a step that might have permitted interested countries to demand the necessary information and to assess the impact of other countries' subsidies on their own trade.

## Trade Negotiations

Beyond the regulation of subsidies in Article XVI (and the supplementary provisions of Article III:4), subsidies may be limited by agreements reached in trade negotiations. First, contracting parties may negotiate about subsidies in the periodic rounds of trade negotiations, even though they rarely do so.[35] A start was made in that direction in the Kennedy Round, where the European Economic Community succeeded partially in focusing agricultural negotiations on the total amount of protection, including subsidies, rather than on tariffs alone. Second, and of greater significance in the past, the binding of a tariff duty may preclude the adoption or increase of a subsidy having the effect of providing protection to domestic production beyond the bound tariff. As has been seen, a production subsidy may be similar to a tariff in its protective effect. Such a subsidy may constitute "nullification or impairment" under Article XXIII, even though it does not violate Article XVI or even give rise to a duty to "discuss" thereunder. This was made clear as early as 1950 in a Chilean-Australian ammonium sulphate dispute, although that case involved rather anomalously the elimination of an existing subsidy for imports of the bound item together with the continuation of subsidies on competing domestically produced items.[36] This interpretation was affirmed by the 1955 Review Session Working Party.[37] At the conclusion of the Kennedy Round, with more items bound and at lower rates than ever before, this interpretation takes on greater significance. Export subsidies, unlike production subsidies, will rarely be affected by the binding of a tariff, however, for their immediate effect is seldom to undercut the limitation on protection implicit in a tariff binding.

35. *Basic Instruments,* 3d Supp. (1955), pp. 222, 225; 8th Supp. (1960), pp. 103, 107–8.
36. Ibid., Vol. II (1952), p. 188.
37. Ibid., 3d Supp. (1955), p. 222, 224: see ibid., 10th Supp. (1962), p. 201, 209.

# 9 Quantitative Restrictions

The American draftsmen of the General Agreement tended to view quantitative restrictions as the incarnation of international commercial evil. They relished the opportunity to condemn them.[1] One of the chief U.S. negotiators, Clair Wilcox, summed up the case against quantitative restrictions in the following undiplomatic terms:

> Quantitative restrictions . . . impose rigid limits on the volume of trade. They insulate domestic prices and production against the changing requirements of the world economy. They freeze trade into established channels. They are likely to be discriminatory in purpose and effect. They give the guidance of trade to public officials; they cannot be divorced from politics. They require public allocation of imports and exports among private traders and necessitate increasing regulation of domestic business. Quantitative restrictions are among the most effective methods that have been devised for the purpose of restricting trade. They make for bilateralism, discrimination, and the regimentation of private enterprise.[2]

As the foregoing excerpt illustrates, quantitative restrictions were seen as having, in contrast to tariffs, at least three undesirable characteristics. First, they permitted the local market to be sealed off to the desired extent from the discipline of the world market. Once the quantity of imports provided for in a restriction had been reached, no degree of increased efficiency in exporting countries or decreased efficiency in the importing country could lead to greater imports. A tariff, on the other hand, was an incentive to efficiency both in exporting countries and in the importing country, since, if the goods could be

---

1. See discussion of the differential treatment in the General Agreement of tariff and nontariff barriers in chapter 4, "The GATT Tariff System," supra.
2. Clair Wilcox, *A Charter for World Trade* (New York: Macmillan, 1949), pp. 81–82. The grounds for preferring tariffs to quotas are analyzed in greater detail and with somewhat greater dispassion by Jacob Viner in *International Economics* (Glencoe, Ill.: Free Press, 1951), pp. 169–72, 356–58.

produced cheaply enough in the former or if the price rose high enough in the latter, trade would occur over the tariff wall. The efficiency-maximizing function of international trade was thus frustrated to a much greater degree by quantitative restrictions than by tariffs.[3] Second, whereas a departure from nondiscriminatory application of tariffs could be relatively easily verified, quantitative restrictions lent themselves peculiarly well to hidden discriminatory application, since administrative discretion normally played a major role in their administration. The third ground for preferring tariffs to quantitative restrictions was somewhat related to the second. Since in the case of quantitative restrictions the quantities that could be imported were determined by administrative officials, those quantities could be rapidly adjusted. If the civil service was skilled, quantitative restrictions permitted a high degree of precision in determining the quantity of imports that would actually be admitted. Since the determination of tariff levels was more likely to be a matter for the legislature, tariffs were not so easily or frequently adjusted and consequently were not so accurate in determining import levels.

In the immediate postwar period, with most of the world suffering from serious payments imbalances vis-à-vis the United States and with many countries full of enthusiasm for economic planning, a principal concern of many of the participants in the ITO negotiations was to preserve the right to impose quantitative restrictions. The three grounds relied upon by the United States for condemning such restrictions were precisely the considerations motivating those countries that sought to retain them. Quantitative restrictions served to isolate the local market from the world market and therefore not only permitted inflationary policies to be pursued but also facilitated economic planning by permitting both the quantity and the content of imports to be controlled. Moreover, in a period of a "dollar shortage," the facility with which quantitative restrictions lent themselves to discrimination, covert if need be, against dollar-area goods was highly prized. Finally, the control that the local administrative officials could exert over quantitative restrictions made those restrictions a much more flexible and precise tool than tariffs for controlling the quantity and direction of international trade.

The U.S. view of quantitative restrictions was rejected by three overlapping groups of countries; namely, those with balance-of-payments problems, those enamored of dirigisme, and those seeking to industrialize. To this list of opponents of the U.S. view one might add those countries that protected domestic agriculture, but for the inconvenient fact that the United States itself fell into that group.

Interestingly enough, the State Department was forced at the outset to modify

3. This point can be exaggerated. If a tariff is high enough—say 1000 percent, for a hypothetical illustration—trade is extremely unlikely to occur for most products.

its position on quantitative restrictions to permit such restrictions when they reinforced certain kinds of domestic agricultural programs designed to increase agricultural incomes.[4] When the United States commenced its informal discussions with the British, it was forced to carve out a balance-of-payments exception. And when the formal multilateral negotiations began, the U.S. quantitative restrictions proposal became the central issue.[5] The final text contained some of the most complex language in the General Agreement, a natural consequence of attempts to spell out and then delimit various exceptions. The political result was a compromise in which the United States succeeded in establishing the general principle that quantitative restrictions were to be eliminated forthwith but in which its negotiating partners obtained a license to continue using such quantitative restrictions so long as they could justify them by payments imbalances.

## The Structure of the GATT Rules

Space does not permit a textual analysis of the dense and lengthy articles on quantitative restrictions or of the substantial number of official interpretations.[6] Nor would such an analysis be of great value. Most of the quantitative restrictions maintained by developed countries today are found in the agricultural sector, where the GATT rules have ceased to exercise a substantial influence and where, as we shall see later, the GATT's efforts to promote liberalization have taken another path.[7] And no serious attempts are made to force less-developed countries to abolish quantitative restrictions.

What are primarily important are not the details of the General Agreement language and interpretations but rather the principal choices that were made at the outset and the ways in which those choices were implemented over the years. As a prelude to pursuit of these latter avenues of inquiry, we shall survey the architecture of that portion of the General Agreement that deals with quantitative restrictions. Thereafter, we shall examine other alternatives that might have been chosen, the techniques adopted by the GATT in seeking compliance with the rules, and the mechanisms for cooperation with the other international institution with competence in the balance-of-payments sphere, the International Monetary Fund.

The fundamental provision of the General Agreement is a flat prohibition. Article XI:1 provides that "no prohibitions or restrictions other than duties,

4. See discussion in chapter 15, "Temperate Agricultural Commodities," infra.
5. Wilcox, writing just after the negotiations, termed quantitative restrictions "the major issue of commercial policy" and "the toughest problem" in the negotiations (Wilcox, p. 82).
6. The best guide to the interpretations is *Analytical Index*, pp. 60–82.
7. See discussion in chapter 15, "Temperate Agricultural Commodities," infra.

taxes or other charges, whether made effective through quotas, import or export licenses or other measures, shall be instituted or maintained" on the "importation" or "exportation" of any product. The language is broad enough to apply to all kinds of nontariff barriers (except perhaps for those that can be said to have their impact after "importation"). However, the heading of the Article, "General Elimination of Quantitative Restrictions," suggests that the prohibition is not intended to overlap the specific provisions in the General Agreement on other types of nontariff barriers.

Of the exceptions to the general prohibition, by all odds the most important is the balance-of-payments exception.[8] Two principal types of balance-of-payments justifications are envisaged in Article XII:2(a). A contracting party may impose quantitative restrictions either "to forestall the imminent threat of, or to stop, a serious decline in its monetary reserves," or, "in the case of a contracting party with very low monetary reserves, to achieve a reasonable rate of increase in its reserves." In theory at least, the right thus granted to impose quantitative restrictions is not unlimited. Such restrictions "shall not exceed those necessary" to accomplish either of the two specified objectives, and, under Article XII:2(b), contracting parties applying such restrictions "shall progressively relax them as . . . conditions improve, maintaining them only to the extent" that the serious decline in reserves or the very low reserves "still justify their application." Under Article XVIII:9 a balance-of-payments exception, framed in substantive terms similar to those of Article XII:2(a) but subject to less strict procedural safeguards, is provided for those less-developed countries that, under paragraph 4(a) of that Article, have an "economy . . . which can only support low standards of living and is in the early stages of development."[9] Article XIII provides that quantitative restrictions, including those imposed for balance-of-payments purposes, are to be maintained on a nondiscriminatory basis. Since quantitative restrictions lend themselves to discrimination in their administration, that article calls on contracting parties, in applying such restrictions on a given product, to "aim at a distribution of trade in such product

---

8. Other exceptions in Article XI permit export restrictions to prevent or relieve critical shortages of certain essentials, import and export restrictions "necessary to the application of standards or regulations for the classification, grading or marketing of commodities in international trade," and certain kinds of agricultural restrictions. The first two classes of exceptions raise relatively few important trade problems. Discussion of agricultural restrictions is deferred to chapter 15, infra. It should be noted that Sections C and D of Article XVIII permit less-developed countries, under certain circumstances, to impose quantitative restrictions for economic development purposes.

9. Slight differences in the formulation of the substantive standards of Articles XII:2(a) and XVIII:9 may be noted. Under the latter provision the threat of a decline in reserves need not be "imminent"; moreover, "inadequate" rather than "very low" reserves may justify restrictions.

approaching as closely as possible the shares which the various contracting parties might be expected to obtain in the absence of such restrictions" (paragraph 2) and to that end to abide by a set of rules regulating the allocation of quotas among supplying contracting parties and requiring public notice and the dissemination of information concerning the details of the restrictions. Article XIV sets forth certain exceptions to the Article XIII principle of nondiscriminatory application of balance-of-payments restrictions.

## The Role of the International Monetary Fund

A major exception to the basic rule against discriminatory application of quantitative restrictions is that a contracting party may discriminate "in a manner having equivalent effect to restrictions on payments and transfers for current international transactions which that contracting party may at that time apply under Article VIII or XIV of the Articles of Agreement of the International Monetary Fund, or under analogous provisions of a special exchange agreement entered into pursuant to paragraph 6 of Article XV."[10] Before exploring the scope of this exception, the interlocking character of the regulation by the IMF and by the GATT must be explored. Whereas the GATT is concerned with trade restrictions, the IMF is concerned with exchange restrictions. These two types of restrictions tend, however, to have similar effects. A rule that forbids a resident from obtaining foreign exchange to purchase foreign goods is, so far as the volume and origin of imports is concerned, functionally equivalent to a rule that forbids the physical import of those goods. It would therefore be fruitless to forbid a contracting party to accomplish through trade restrictions that which it might accomplish through exchange restrictions.

The obligations of IMF members with respect to exchange restrictions on current international transactions depend upon whether the particular member is subject, under the Articles of Agreement of the International Monetary Fund, to the rules of Article VIII or to the rules of Article XIV. Article VIII is the more stringent. Members subject to that Article are prohibited by Section 2 thereof from imposing "restrictions on the making of payments and transfers

10. The quoted language is taken from Article XIV:1 as it has been in effect since 15 February 1961, pursuant to changes adopted at the 1955 Review Session. Previously, Article XIV:1 was more complicated and provided more exceptions legalizing discrimination. For a review of the changes, see George Bronz, "An International Trade Organization: The Second Attempt," *Harvard Law Review,* LXIX (1956), pp. 440, 458–62. In addition to the exception to the principle of nondiscrimination contained in paragraph 1 of Article XIV, paragraph 2 of that article permits discrimination with respect to "a small part of . . . external trade" provided the consent of the CONTRACTING PARTIES is obtained, and provided "the benefits to the contracting party or contracting parties concerned substantially outweigh any injury which may result to the trade of other contracting parties."

for current international transactions."[11] Both of these rules are subject to the exception that the IMF may specifically approve a particular restriction.

The relatively stringent rules of Article VIII are fully applicable only to those members that choose to subject themselves to the regime of that article. Other members may avail themselves of the less stringent provisions of Article XIV. Members availing themselves of the latter article may "maintain and adapt to changing circumstances restrictions on payments and transfers for current international transactions." Indeed, only by an express notification pursuant to Article XIV, Section 3, that it is "prepared to accept the obligations of Article VIII, Sections 2, 3 and 4," does a member lose the benefits of the less stringent rule of Article XIV. Although Article XIV purports to be applicable only in the "postwar transitional period," only 31 of the 106 members of the IMF have elected to be governed by Article VIII.[12]

Although IMF members are sometimes classified for convenience in two categories—namely, Article VIII members and Article XIV members—this categorization oversimplifies the legal relationships. To the extent that Article XIV does not authorize a restriction or practice, Article VIII applies whether or not the member in question has filed an acceptance of the obligations of that Article. Thus, even though Article XIV may authorize a member to "maintain and adapt" existing restrictions on payments or transfers for current international transactions, that member may not introduce new restrictions of that type, except as provided in Article VIII. And once an Article XIV country discontinues such a restriction, it may only revive the restriction under the conditions of Article VIII, which means in practice that it must seek specific authorization from the IMF.[13]

The effect of Article XIV:1 of the General Agreement thus depends upon whether the contracting party in question is, in its capacity as a member of the IMF, an Article VIII or an Article XIV member. In either case, however, the contracting party's right to impose a particular quantitative restriction does not depend upon whether the IMF has actually authorized an exchange restriction having "equivalent effect." The Review Session Working Party agreed

---

11. "The guiding principle in determining whether a measure is a restriction on payments and transfers for current transactions under Article VIII, Section 2, is whether it involves a direct governmental limitation on the availability or use of exchange as such" (International Monetary Fund, *Selected Decisions of the Executive Directors, Third Issue* [1965], pp. 81–82).
12. International Monetary Fund, *Annual Report* (1967), pp. 48, 129. The text states the number of Article VIII notifications filed as of 30 June 1967.
13. On the relationship between Articles VIII and XIV, see generally J. Gold, *The International Monetary Fund and Private Business Transactions* (Washington: International Monetary Fund, 1965), pp. 16–20.

that the issue is whether "corresponding restrictions on payments and transfers *would have been* authorized under the Articles of Agreement of the Fund or approved by the Fund if the contracting party in question had chosen to proceed by way of exchange restrictions rather than trade restrictions."[14] A legal standard based upon what an international organization would have done in a hypothetical situation is, of course, not only unusual but also potentially uncertain in application. The Working Party agreed, however, that a statement by the IMF would be controlling in determining whether Article XIV:1 of the General Agreement had been violated. It will thus be seen that the General Agreement in effect delegates to the IMF some decisions concerning the right of contracting parties to impose quantitative restrictions on trade.[15]

Article XIV:1 of the General Agreement refers not only to Article VIII and XIV of the Articles of Agreement but also to "analogous provisions of a special exchange agreement entered into pursuant to paragraph 6 of Article XV." Such special exchange agreements are required only where a contracting party is not a member of the IMF. A principal function of special exchange agreements is to impose upon the contracting parties obligations with respect to exchange restrictions equivalent to those imposed upon IMF members by the Articles of Agreement. Special exchange agreements thus include the substantive provisions of the Articles of Agreement, with the modification that the CONTRACTING PARTIES are to fulfill the functions of the IMF in approving, for example, the imposition of "restrictions on the making of payments and transfers for current international transactions."[16] Special exchange arrangements are of little importance today. Special exchange agreements were at one time entered into with four contracting parties, but none are currently in effect.[17]

It should be noted that Article XIV:1 of the General Agreement is not a carte blanche to impose quantitative restrictions "having equivalent effect to restrictions on payments and transfers" permitted under Articles VIII and XIV of the Articles of Agreement, but rather authorizes only deviations from the

14. *Basic Instruments,* 3d Supp. (1955), p. 170, 177 (emphasis supplied).
15. An interpretative note makes clear, however, that the reference in Article XIV:1 to the Articles of Agreement of the International Monetary Fund does not preclude, in consultations under the General Agreement, "full consideration . . . of the nature, effects and reasons for discrimination in the field of import restrictions" (Ad Art. XIV, para. 1).
16. See Article VII:1 of the sample text of a special exchange agreement, *Basic Instruments,* Vol. II (1952), pp. 117, 119. See also the two working party reports on procedural arrangements for the implementation of such agreements, ibid., pp. 123-35.
17. Waivers of the obligation to enter into exchange agreements have been granted on a number of occasions. See *Analytical Index,* p. 81. On special exchange arrangements, see generally J. Gold, *The Fund and Non-Member States* (Washington: International Monetary Fund, 1966).

nondiscrimination rule of Article XIII of the General Agreement.[18] However, another provision of the General Agreement, Article XV:9(b), permits the use of quantitative "restrictions or controls . . . to make effective . . . exchange controls or exchange restrictions" that are imposed in accordance with the Articles of Agreement or with a special exchange agreement.[19] Article XV:9(b) differs from Article XIV:1 by requiring exchange restrictions as a prerequisite to trade restrictions. There is no general provision in the General Agreement permitting a contracting party to accomplish by quantitative restrictions whatever can be accomplished under the Articles of Agreement by exchange restrictions.

Since balance-of-payments problems are primarily financial rather than commercial in character, the apparently logical solution of making the GATT the sole institution for interpreting the General Agreement would lead to the practical anomaly that a trade institution would be attempting to make judgments about financial phenomena that can more appropriately be made by a financial institution. Moreover, it would create the possibility that the GATT and the IMF might pursue contradictory policies on balance-of-payments matters, a possibility that is not merely theoretical in view of the fact that the IMF staff has a good deal of autonomy while the GATT is largely an instrument of its contracting parties.

Several substantive provisions of the General Agreement beyond those discussed above are relevant to the division of competence between the GATT and the IMF. One of them, Article XV:4, gives the GATT a certain degree of jurisdiction over exchange controls. It provides that "contracting parties shall not, by exchange action, frustrate the intent of the provisions of . . . [the General] Agreement."[20] An interpretative note seeks, however, to limit the scope of this jurisdiction by making the "intent" rather than the "letter" controlling.[21] And

18. It should also be noted that the drafting of Article XIV:1 of the General Agreement is less than satisfactory because Article VIII of the Articles of Agreement deals not only with "restrictions on payments and transfers for current international transactions" but also with "discriminatory currency practices," activities that are at least equally relevant to discriminatory quantitative restrictions. It is not clear, for example, whether an interference with the free use of foreign exchange that the IMF approves as a "discriminatory currency practice" may justify a quantitative restriction "having equivalent effect" where that interference could have been characterized by the IMF as a "restriction on payments and transfers for current international transactions."
19. Making such exchange controls or restrictions effective must be the "sole effect" of the quantitative "restrictions or controls," except for "effects permitted under Articles XI, XII, XIII and XIV." See Art. XV:9(b).
20. It further provides that "contracting parties shall not . . . frustrate . . . , by trade action, the intent of the provisions of the Articles of Agreement of the International Monetary Fund."
21. Ad Art. XV, para. 4.

paragraph 9(a) of Article XV limits paragraph 4 thereof by providing that nothing in the General Agreement is to preclude "the use by a contracting party of exchange controls or exchange restrictions in accordance with the Articles of Agreement of the International Monetary Fund." Nevertheless, the combination of the jurisdiction granted the GATT by Article XV:4 to deal with exchange restrictions and of the de facto delegation, previously discussed, by the GATT to the IMF of certain competence with respect to trade, increases the chances of a conflict of policies on balance-of-payments matters between the two institutions.

In order to preclude such conflicts and to give the GATT the benefits of the IMF's expertise in balance-of-payments matters, Article XV:2 calls on the CONTRACTING PARTIES to "consult fully" with the IMF whenever they "consider or deal with problems concerning monetary reserves, balance of payments or foreign exchange arrangements." The division of function between the two institutions is set forth in some detail. The CONTRACTING PARTIES are to "accept all findings of statistical and other facts presented by the Fund relating to foreign exchange, monetary reserves and balances of payments" as well as IMF determinations as to the compatibility with the Articles of Agreement and with special exchange agreements of "action . . . in exchange matters." Moreover, the CONTRACTING PARTIES, in reaching decisions under Articles XII:2(a) and XVIII:9, are to accept IMF determinations "as to what constitutes a serious decline in the contracting party's monetary reserves, a very low level of its monetary reserves or a reasonable rate of increase in its monetary reserves and as to the financial aspects of other matters covered in consultation in such cases."

Since "serious decline," "very low level," and "reasonable rate of increase" are the key concepts under the general balance-of-payments exception of Article XII:2(a), as well as the special exception for less-developed countries in Article XVIII:9, the IMF is given competence over a great deal more than fact-finding. The issues that the IMF is to resolve are those that a lawyer would call mixed questions of fact and law; the IMF is given the power to determine not just the facts but also whether the facts fit the legal standard. Although the final decision is retained by the CONTRACTING PARTIES, the division of competence prescribed by those Articles tends to limit greatly the scope for GATT decision. Article XV:3 calls for an agreement with the IMF on procedures for consultation between the two institutions. Although such an agreement was in fact reached, the question of the scope of the competence reserved to the GATT was not defined but rather was left to be worked out on a case-by-case basis. The evidence from those who have followed the GATT-IMF consultations in detail is that the two institutions have avoided giving a particular contracting party conflicting advice.[22] Legal questions aside, that surely is an important accomplishment. It may also reflect, however, a certain passivity on the part of the GATT.

## The Perverse Influence of the GATT Rules

As the foregoing survey of the complex balance-of-payments provisions of the General Agreement indicates, the GATT solution is, in general, to make quantitative restrictions illegal unless those restrictions are "necessary" to accomplish certain balance-of-payments objectives. Although the question of necessity is always lurking in the background, one can probably say with fairness that, once a contracting party has serious balance-of-payments problems, it has broad discretion to impose quantitative restrictions, at least so long as it does so nondiscriminatorily.

One of the reasons that the GATT system is not well designed to permit second-guessing of a contracting party's exercise of this discretion is that Article XII:3(d) precludes the GATT from requiring the withdrawal or the modification of quantitative restrictions on the ground that a change in "domestic policies directed towards the achievement and maintenance of full and productive employment or towards the development of economic resources" would "render unnecessary" such restrictions. Consequently, if a contracting party chooses to pursue inflationary policies, it has what approaches a carte blanche to use whatever quantitative restrictions are necessary to prevent its external balance from becoming a constraint on such policies.

Given the existing international system of fixed exchange rates (backed by IFM's prohibition of floating exchange rates), a differential rate of inflation in various countries tends to produce trade restrictions. Since tariff bindings render tariff surcharges illegal, the GATT rules tend, for countries with balance-of-payments problems, to promote the use of quantitative restrictions and to discourage the use of tariffs. Not only is this result precisely the opposite of that sought by the U.S. draftsmen, but, inasmuch as quantitative restrictions have a more pernicious effect on the volume of international trade and on the allocation of resources than do tariffs, the influence of the GATT rules is perverse.

## The OEEC Approach

In view of the perverse effects of the GATT rules, one may consider an alternative approach that might have been adopted for the elimination of quantitative

22. See the statement of Irving S. Friedman before the Subcommittee on Foreign Economic Policy of the Joint Committee on the Economic Report, reported in *International News Survey*, VIII (1955), p. 175; Gerard Curzon, *Multilateral Commercial Diplomacy* (London: Michael Joseph, 1965), p. 138.

restrictions. The Organization for European Economic Co-operation was faced shortly after the Second World War with the task of liberalizing trade among the principal countries of Western Europe. The OEEC chose to ignore tariffs and to concentrate on the abolition of quantitative restrictions. The latter were not, however, declared illegal as in the General Agreement. Rather, the members were required to abolish quantitative restrictions gradually over a period of years in accordance with a formula.

In November 1949 it was decided that the member countries of the OEEC should abolish, by mid-December of that year, quantitative restrictions on 50 percent of their intermember imports on private account in each of three categories of imports: food and feeding stuffs, raw materials, and manufactured goods.[23] In 1950, after the formation of the European Payments Union making possible multilateral clearing of the then inconvertible currencies of the member countries, the liberalization target was raised to 60 percent for each of the three categories.[24] In 1951 the target was raised to 75 per cent for the three categories taken as a whole, although the 60 per cent figure was retained as a base target for each category in recognition of the difficulties faced in the food and feeding stuffs category.[25] This undertaking was supplemented by a common list of products considered ripe for complete liberalization.[26] In 1955 the overall target was raised to 90 percent, with separate targets of 75 percent for each of the three categories. In addition, unlike the previous measures that had imposed equal obligations whatever the degree of liberalization previously reached, the 1955 revision required that each member country abolish 10 percent of quantitative restrictions in force on 30 June 1954, without regard to the level of liberalization previously attained.[27] The foregoing measures of liberalization were reinforced by a consolidation mechanism under which a product, once freed of quantitative restrictions, could not later be subjected to such restrictions.[28]

The OEEC method differed from the GATT method in a number of ways. Except for the 10 percent increase over 1954 liberalization levels called for in

23. Organization for European Economic Co-operation, *European Recovery Programme: Second Report of the O.E.E.C.* (1950), p. 224.
24. Ibid., p. 226.
25. Organization for European Economic Co-operation, *Economic Progress and Problems of Western Europe* (1951), p. 144. (Although not so entitled, this is the third annual report of the OEEC.)
26. Ibid., p. 145.
27. Organization for European Economic Co-operation, *Seventh Report of the OEEC: Economic Expansion and Its Problems* (1956), p. 66.
28. Organization for European Economic Co-operation, *Code of Liberalisation* (1960 ed.), Art. II.

1955, the OEEC method treated the degree of liberalization already achieved as irrelevant (except for certain derogations considered below). Or, to put the point in another way, it was assumed that all of the member countries were in deficit positions, at least as against the dollar, but that liberalization was nevertheless to be pursued. A formula for increases in the liberalization targets was not, however, worked out when the OEEC liberalization program was first undertaken. Rather, the increases were decided upon only a few months before each new target was to be reached. Thus, the OEEC was able to time the increases with improvements in the state of the member countries' balance of payments. Between 1951 and 1955 the targets were not raised, no doubt because several member countries were in particularly difficult balance-of-payments straits. The liberalization process permitted, however, a certain reciprocity, because the various members' moves toward liberalization were to be taken nearly simultaneously.

Nevertheless, the movement toward liberalization proceeded at quite different rates in different member countries. Some member countries, particularly France, failed rather consistently to meet the liberalization targets. Partly this was due to the extreme liberality of the derogation provisions, which tended to undercut the assumptions of the entire liberalization program. Under the Code of Liberalisation, which had been adopted in 1950 and amended frequently thereafter, a member country was permitted to derogate from the liberalization undertakings (1) "if its economic and financial situation justified such a course" or (2) "if any measures of liberalization of trade . . . result[ed] in serious economic disturbance."[29] Moreover, subject to certain restrictions, a member country was permitted to derogate from those undertakings for up to eighteen months if its "balance of payments position . . . develop[ed] adversely at a rate and in circumstances which it consider[ed] serious in view of the state of its reserves and taking into account the incidence on that balance of payments of specifically European factors."[30] Derogations made under these provisions had to be justified under OEEC procedures.[31]

Despite these derogation provisions, which bore a certain resemblance to the the GATT balance-of-payments exception, the OEEC approach was fundamentally different from that adopted by the GATT. It is therefore worth asking

29. Ibid., Art. 3(a) and (b).
30. Ibid., Art. 3(c) and (d). Further derogations were permitted by Article 4 in the event that a member country was "not in a position to maintain the whole of the measures of liberalisation of trade taken by it . . . because it [was] compelled, in pursuance of its obligations under other international agreements [that is to say, under the General Agreement] to extend to non-member countries those measures." See also ibid., Art. 25 ter.
31. Ibid., Arts. 25–25 bis.

whether the OEEC approach was preferable. Unfortunately, no definite answer can be given to this essentially speculative question. As even former Director-General Wyndham White of the GATT has conceded,[32] the GATT quantitative restriction rules were effectively a "dead letter" with respect to deficit countries during the period in which the OEEC was making substantial progress. Liberalization occurred at a much more rapid rate in the 1950s among the OEEC member countries than among nonmember countries or than between the OEEC member countries and nonmember countries.

There were, however, a multitude of independent factors—monetary, political, and historic—that contributed to the OEEC advance and had nothing to do with the OEEC method. Moreover, certain aspects of the OEEC method resulted in an overstatement of progress actually made and in some cases led to economic distortions.[33] First, the percentages of liberalization were measured by 1948 imports.[34] Owing to war damage, 1948 was a year when there was little intra-OEEC trade in certain products, and there was a tendency in later years to concentrate quantitative restrictions on those products. Not only were such restrictions used to shelter war-torn industries during the period of resuscitation, but, if there were no imports of a particular product from the OEEC member countries in 1948, such restrictions had no effect on the percentages of liberalization achieved as calculated by the OEEC. Second, the liberalization undertakings were phrased in terms of percentages of imports on private account. State trading accounted for a major share of total imports of some OEEC member countries during the early 1950's—in the case of France, some 22 percent of its intra-OEEC imports.[35] And third, the consolidation principle applied only to totally liberalized products. Consequently, it was possible for an OEEC country to improve its liberalization percentage by removing restrictions on one product while tightening restrictions on other already restricted products. Such manipulation of quantitative restrictions for the purpose of establishing a favorable OEEC record may well have had perverse results on the allocation of resources in Europe.

But if the OEEC progress tended to be exaggerated, it was progress nonetheless, and it came at a time when the GATT rules not only did not promote significant liberalization but, as previously discussed, may have had certain

32. Address by Eric Wyndham White, "GATT as an International Organization," Warsaw, 6 June 1961, p. 10.
33. See generally Isaiah Frank, *The European Common Market* (New York: Frederick A. Praeger, 1961), pp. 61–62; Curzon, pp. 160–62.
34. Organization for European Economic Co-operation, *Code of Liberalisation*, Annex A, § 11.
35. Frederick Boyer and J. P. Salle, "The Liberalization of Intra-European Trade in the Framework of OEEC," *International Monetary Fund Staff Papers,* IV (1955), p. 179, 198.

perverse results. To what extent the liberalization of trade was due to the general revival of the European economies and the greater strength of the European currencies rather than to the OEEC rules is, however, a matter for judgment.

Even if one prefers the OEEC method in principle, it is not clear that the OEEC method would have worked well in the period subsequent to 1958, when the major European currencies were externally convertible, when most quantitative restrictions had been eliminated, and when the objective was to abolish all remaining quantitative restrictions. The OEEC method was never put to the test in the later period, because the OEEC Code of Liberalisation was dropped when the OEEC became the Organization for Economic Cooperation and Development in 1960 and because the major OEEC countries had already turned to smaller groupings—the European Economic Community and the European Free Trade Association—in pursuit of their goal of regional trade liberalization. The founding documents of both of these regional groupings contain provisions on the elimination of quantitative restrictions.[36]

## The EEC Approach

The EEC adopted a method that had substantial advantages over the old OEEC method. After requiring that the member states convert all quantitative restrictions into global quotas available to the other five member states on a nondiscriminatory basis, the Rome Treaty, establishing the EEC, required each year a 10 percent increase of the global quota on each product as well as a 20 percent increase of global quotas taken as a whole. Each succeeding 10 and 20 percent increase was to be calculated on the base achieved in the preceding year. The system thus required that substantial progress be made on every product every year and thereby avoided the problem, presented under the OEEC system, that liberalization of one product might be accompanied by a tightening of restrictions on another product. In addition, the system required that exceptional progress be made on at least some products each year so that the overall 20 percent requirement could be fulfilled. To assure that the 20 percent overall increase requirement would be effective and that member states would not use what could be called "paper quotas" to meet that requirement, it was provided that where, for a given product, a global quota exceeded actual imports in two successive years, that quota could no longer be counted for the purpose of determining whether the overall increase exceeded 20 percent. In order to concentrate the attack on those quotas that were most restrictive, the Rome Treaty imposed the further requirement that all global quotas be equal to at least 3 percent of domestic output by the end of the first year, be increased

36. Treaty Establishing the European Economic Community, Arts. 30–37; Convention Establishing the European Free Trade Association, Art. 10.

to 4 and 5 percent of domestic output in the two subsequent years, and be increased by 15 percent each year thereafter.[37]

Favored by steadily improving economic and monetary conditions in the six member states, the EEC provisions on quantitative restrictions enjoyed a considerable success, despite some early technical problems. The provisions had a substantial immediate effect. The total volume covered by France's quotas against other member states increased by 115 percent from 1958 to 1959 and by another 24 percent from 1959 to 1960. The corresponding figures for Italy were even more dramatic: 250 percent and 33 percent.[38] The Italian figures, it should be noted in passing, throw an interesting light on the misleading character of the OEEC liberalization percentages, since Italy had already achieved, by OEEC calculations, a 99.1 percent level of liberalization by the end of 1955.[39]

By May 1960 the EEC program had been so successful that it was decided to seek abolition of all quantitative restrictions in the industrial sector by the end of that year.[40] This objective was achieved, except for certain products in the food processing industry.[41] Quantitative restrictions remained a problem, however, in the agricultural sector and eventually disappeared only in the context of the creation of common agricultural markets in individual agricultural products.

The problems faced by the EEC in the elimination of quantitative restricttions were simpler than those faced by the GATT because of the relative strength of the six currencies concerned, the limited number of countries involved, and the political momentum achieved in the early years of the EEC. But the EEC method warrants study as a technique for eliminating quantitative restrictions in those areas where they still exist. And if balance-of-payments difficulties should force some of the major industrial countries to resort to extensive quantitative restrictions, an adaptation of the EEC formula might be

---

37. The principal Rome Treaty provisions are contained in Article 33.
38. Marc Ouin, "The Establishment of the Customs Union," in *American Enterprise in the European Common Market*, ed. Eric Stein and Thomas L. Nicholson (Ann Arbor: University of Michigan Law School, 1960), Vol. 1, p. 101, 118; Commission of the European Economic Community, *Third General Report of the Community* (1960), p. 86.
39. Organization for European Economic Co-operation, *Seventh Report of the OEEC: Economic Expansion and Its Problems* (1956), p. 67 (Table 17).
40. Commission of the European Economic Community, *Fourth General Report on the Activities of the Community* (1961), pp. 40–41.
41. Commission of the European Economic Community, *Fifth Annual Report on the Activities of the Community* (1962), p. 43. In addition, several governments invoked the temporary safeguard clause of Article 226 of the Rome Treaty for a few other products (ibid.).

more effective in speeding the elimination of those restrictions than the more general standards of the General Agreement.

## Consultation and Waiver Procedures

In evaluating the GATT system for quantitative restrictions, it would be a mistake to limit one's attention to the text of the General Agreement. A number of consultation procedures have been worked out that have transformed that system, especially as it applies to countries that do not have balance-of-payments excuses for imposing such restrictions.

The basis for these new procedures was already contained in the language of the General Agreement. Article XII:4 provides for consultations in a number of situations. First, any contracting party "applying new restrictions or raising the general level of its existing restrictions by a substantial intensification" of Article XII restrictions is required to consult with the CONTRACTING PARTIES immediately after taking such action.[42] Second, if a contracting party can "establish a *prima facie* case" that some other contracting party is maintaining quantitative restrictions in violation of Article XII or XIII and "that its trade is adversely affected thereby," consultations among the contracting parties concerned are to follow. If "direct discussions between the contracting parties concerned have not been successful," then the CONTRACTING PARTIES, upon certain findings of fact, are to "recommend" the elimination of such restrictions and to authorize retaliation. Third, contracting parties maintaining quantitative restrictions under Article XII are required to consult with the CONTRACTING PARTIES annually.[43]

These consultations are wide-ranging and no doubt help to place a certain amount of pressure upon contracting parties to conform to the rules of Article XII, but they fail to come to grips with one of the most troublesome aspects of quantitative restrictions. Although quantitative restrictions may originally be imposed for balance-of-payments reasons, they provide protection for domestic industry. When balance-of-payments considerations no longer justify retention of such restrictions, the domestic firms involved may have become so dependent upon the protection thus afforded that they no longer have the competitive vigor to survive the return of international competition. In some cases balance-of-payments-motivated restrictions may lead to the development of new domestic industries that never could be viable in international competi-

---

42. See *Basic Instruments,* 9th Supp. (1961), pp. 18–20, for the procedures to be followed in such consultations.
43. See ibid., 7th Supp. (1959), pp. 90–98, for the procedures to be followed. Under Article XVIII:12(b), the corresponding periodic reviews of the quantitative restrictions of less-developed countries are to take place only every two years.

tion. An attempt to suspend those restrictions when payments imbalances finally disappear may present political and social problems of major dimensions.

In 1955 the CONTRACTING PARTIES, foreseeing that this problem would be an impediment to full application of the GATT rules when the major European currencies reached the stage of external convertibility, took the unusual step of providing in advance for a type of waiver that would establish a transitional period for the adjustment by domestic firms to the competitive impact of the elimination of quantitative restrictions. The waiver, which became known as the "hard-core waiver," was to afford a transitional period of up to five years, provided that the contracting party concerned could establish that the "sudden removal" of such restrictions "would result in serious injury to a domestic industry having received incidental protection therefrom, and that the temporary maintenance of the restriction is necessary to enable the industry to adjust itself to the situation which would be created by the removal of the restriction."[44] The waiver was to be reviewed annually, and the contracting party concerned was to assure that the measures maintained thereunder did not tend to become more restrictive during the transitional period.

Experience soon showed that the problem was much more serious than had been contemplated. Only one contracting party, Belgium, received the hard-core waiver.[45] In its final, fifth-year report, the working party reviewing the Belgium waiver noted that Belgium had failed to eliminate all of its restrictions within the transitional period and that consequently the "main objective" of the waiver had not been achieved. It also noted that in some cases Belgium had substituted other types of restrictions for the quantitative restrictions in order to continue to afford the same level of protection to domestic industry.[46] The Federal Republic of Germany refused to apply for the hard-core waiver[47] and, after its contention that its restrictions were lawful under the Torquay Protocol had been rejected, it received a less confining waiver.[48] It also failed to remove all quantitative restrictions within the five-year period of its waiver.[49] By permitting the contracting parties that were harmed by such restrictions to examine the specific problems faced by Belgium and Germany and to bring concerted pressure to bear on those two countries, the waiver procedures may nevertheless have accelerated the liberalization process.[50]

44. *Basic Instruments,* 3d Supp. (1965), p. 38, 40.
45. Ibid., 4th Supp. (1956), p. 22; *Analytical Index,* p. 58, n. 2.
46. *Basic Instruments,* 11th Supp. (1963), p. 220, 222.
47. U.S. Tariff Commission, *Operation of the Trade Agreements Program,* 11th Rep. (1960), pp. 50–52.
48. Ibid., 12th Rep. (1961), pp. 41–45; *Basic Instruments,* 8th Supp. (1960), pp. 31, 160.
49. *Basic Instruments,* 11th Supp. (1963), pp. 222, 229–31.
50. See Curzon's "case study" of the German waiver, in *Multilateral Commercial*

However that may be, many contracting parties simply refused to apply for the hard-core waiver while steadfastly maintaining restrictions that, in view of those contracting parties' vastly improved payments positions, were blatantly inconsistent with the General Agreement (although many were no doubt technically lawful under the Protocol of Provisional Application).[51] In a euphemistic phrase that revealed a growing realization that the remaining quantitative restrictions were more products of structural weaknesses in the economies of the countries concerned than of lawlessness on the part of their governments, restrictions that had outlived their balance-of-payments justification became known as "residual" restrictions.

## Residual Restrictions

It became clear that a new approach, focusing on individual products, would be necessary to deal with residual restrictions. The first step was to identify such restrictions. Previously governments had tended to report at most only products that had been liberalized and not products on which quantitative restrictions still existed. Beginning in 1960, all contracting parties were "invited" to file "lists of import restrictions which they are applying contrary to the provisions of the General Agreement and without having obtained the authorization of the CONTRACTING PARTIES," as well as all subsequent changes in such lists.[52] It was specifically agreed that the consultation provisions of Article XXII and the impairment or nullification procedures of Article XXIII might be invoked by contracting parties affected by residual restrictions.

Of the thirty-seven contracting parties that had responded by 1962 to the request for lists, fifteen admitted having residual restrictions. Of the twenty-two contracting parties that stated that they had no residual restrictions, however, sixteen admitted restrictions based on balance-of-payments grounds, and one admitted restrictions based on a hard-core waiver.[53]

The lists of residual restrictions remain depressingly long.[54] Nearly all the major trading nations, including all the EEC member states, the United Kingdom, and the United States, have substantial lists. The consolidated lists run well over one hundred pages. However, the lists reveal that the majority of residual restrictions cover agricultural and food products. The lists have served

---

*Diplomacy,* pp. 146–55. Curzon's review suggests, rather cautiously, that the GATT procedures made a substantial contribution to the liberalization of German trade.
51. See discussion in chapter 19, "The GATT as an International Organization," infra.
52. *Basic Instruments,* 9th Supp. (1961), p. 18, 19.
53. Ibid., 11th Supp. (1963), pp. 206, 211–12.
54. See also U.S. Tariff Commission, *Quantitative Import Restrictions of the United States,* Tariff Commission Publication 243 (1968).

to underline the inferior performance of the GATT system in those sectors and have led to interest in alternative means of promoting international agricultural trade.

Some observers thought that the Kennedy Round would provide an opportunity to deal with residual restrictions. The fact that quotas are expressed in terms of the volume of imports appears to make bargaining feasible; indeed, quotas closely resemble the measures of "trade coverage" that are used in tariff negotiations.[55] But it was decided in the Kennedy Round to deal with quantitative restrictions under the rubric of nontariff barriers. Although a special "group" on quantitative restrictions was established,[56] and although the United States strove to eliminate, for example, quantitative restrictions on coal,[57] little came of the negotiations.

Some progress has been made toward the elimination of quantitative restrictions on products of special export interest to less-developed countries. Through a system of target abolition dates and frequent reviews, a number of significant residual restrictions have been eliminated.[58] It is an open question whether that system would work on products where only developed countries are concerned and therefore the goodwill that sometimes stimulates action toward less-developed countries is absent.

Although the GATT has undeniably accomplished a great deal in the area of quantitative restrictions, the conclusion is inescapable that the developments in that area, more than in any other, have served to undermine the legalistic approach of the draftsmen of the General Agreement. When violations can be listed, one after another, for more than one hundred pages, the concept of illegality loses whatever moral connotations it might ever have had. On the other hand, no effective pragmatic solution to the residual restriction problem has been found. With the Kennedy Round tariff reductions, the problem of residual restrictions has become increasingly significant. The challenge will be to create procedures that lead to further liberalization.

55. See discussion in chapter 5, "Tariff Conferences," supra.
56. GATT Document INT(66)447 (May 1966), p. 6.
57. See address by W. M. Blumenthal, "Commercial Policy and International Politics," at Saint Louis, 7 Dec. 1965 (mimeographed document), p. 5.
58. See discussion in chapter 14, "Less-Developed Countries," infra.

# 10 Antidumping and Countervailing Duties

Although antidumping duties and countervailing duties are treated together in Article VI and in the domestic legislation of some contracting parties, the two types of duties are, as a matter of principle, designed to deal with different problems. Antidumping duties are intended to restrain unfair pricing practices by private exporters. Countervailing duties are intended to offset governmental unfair practices that have their effect on the prices charged by private exporters. The typical situation at which antidumping duties are directed is the charging by a foreign enterprise of lower prices on exports to the duty-imposing country than on sales in the country of export. Countervailing duties, on the other hand, are aimed primarily at subsidies offered a foreign exporter by his government. Until very recently the GATT has been somewhat more concerned with antidumping than with countervailing duties. And antidumping proceedings are more frequent than countervailing duty proceedings. The bulk of the analysis that follows will therefore be devoted to the former.

**The Dumping Problem**

Discussions on antidumping duties frequently do not identify the fundamental problem. Is that problem the private practice of dumping, or the governmental practice of imposing antidumping duties? Both can be attacked and both defended in the name of freer trade. The General Agreement itself rides both horses. The first sentence of Article VI notes that the practice of dumping "is to be condemned" under certain circumstances, but the remainder of the article is concerned primarily with restricting the circumstances under which antidumping duties may be imposed. This contradiction, which is on examination more apparent than real, is to be explained in part by the ambivalence with which the world trading community and responsible government officials regard dumping.

Dumping is conventionally defined as price discrimination among national markets. Price discrimination is usually, but not invariably, regarded as anticompetitive, and therefore dumping can be opposed by governments on antimonopoly, procompetitive grounds. Antidumping duties are almost invariably applied, however, in only one price discrimination situation, and that is where the foreign supplier sells in the duty-imposing country at a lower price than he sells in his home country. The fact that governments act against dumping only when the low price is charged in their own territory reveals that governments are concerned with the welfare of their own enterprises rather than with the protection of their citizens from discriminatorily high prices charged by monopoly sellers. If the problem were really the discrimination itself, then presumably governments would be more concerned to attack high prices than low prices. Where an exporter sold at home at higher prices than he sold abroad, it would be the exporter's government, not the importer's government, that would take coercive action. The General Agreement, like the governments themselves, views the impact in the low-price country as the harmful aspect of dumping; it is only where dumping "causes or threatens material injury to an established industry in the territory of a contracting party or materially retards the establishment of a domestic industry" that, according to Article VI:1, it is to be "condemned."

Rather than being predatory in motivation, the low price in the importing country may be merely an attempt to meet the competition of local firms in the importing country—competition that is not faced at home, often because trade restrictions fence off the exporter's home market from this same international competition. In other cases, the dumping firm may merely be trying to meet the competition in the local market of some third-country exporter who, because his home price is low (as a consequence of domestic competition or of the absence of trade restrictions), cannot be accused of dumping. Here the motivation for the dumping is even more clearly competitive rather than predatory.

The concern with dumping is therefore a concern with the protection of domestic industry from international competition. One coming to the dumping problem with a fresh eye, free of the traditional domestic industry perspective and alert to the pejorative radiations of the expressive term "dumping" (which is so captivating that it has been absorbed without translation into the world's major commercial languages), may find antidumping duties peculiar means for protecting domestic industry. Local firms suffer "injury" (in the sense that they make less, or lose more, money than they otherwise would) whenever the import price is the same or lower than the price they charge. That injury is no greater when dumping is present than when the import price merely reflects the comparative advantage of the exporter. But it is only when consumers in another country are charged a higher price that this injury triggers government action under antidumping laws. And this government action normally occurs, unless the "injury" criterion is unusually stringently construed, whatever the level of efficiency of the local firms. Indeed, the less efficient the local firms, or the greater their local monopoly, the more easily the requisite injury can be shown (even though the local consumer's need for the low-priced imports is comparatively greater).

Economists, free traders, and others who are primarily concerned with the welfare of consumers (and who therefore tend to champion imports at the expense of domestic production) nevertheless normally concede that importing-country measures to offset dumping are justifiable, if not desirable. Sometimes this incongruous concern for the fortunes of domestic producers is based upon the common fallacy that the foreign high price somehow facilitates the low price on imports. The foreign producer is viewed as raising the price in his home market to "subsidize" the low price abroad. This subsidization theory overlooks the foreign producer's incentive to maximize his profits at home by charging an optimum price at all times there; the optimum price at home is, of course, unrelated to the prices charged on his export sales.

A more sophisticated apology for antidumping duties is based on the notion that dumping is a temporary phenomenon. Although consumers benefit from the lower price, the benefit is viewed as being not only ephemeral but also destructive insofar as it weakens or eliminates domestic firms. To this conclusion is often added the assertion that dumping leads to higher prices in the long run, either because a reduced number of domestic firms will remain by the time the dumping ceases or because the foreign firm, having achieved a monopoly by driving local enterprises to the wall, will thereafter charge a monopoly price. In its extreme form this assertion assumes a sequence of events in which a foreign firm, acting with predatory intent, drives local firms out of business through dumping, raises prices to a monopoly level, and maintains those prices at the monopoly level permanently. The proposition that, in the long run, dumping costs consumers more than it saves them is based on certain unarticulated notions as to the restrictions on entry into the industry in the importing country. Specifically, it assumes that firms once having been driven out of that industry will not be able to, or simply will not, reenter, and that the rate of entry into the industry is not responsive to higher prices. These assumptions are, however, likely to represent exaggerations of the consequences of dumping on the fortunes of domestic firms. A review of cases in which dumping duties have been imposed will uncover few cases in which domestic firms have in fact been driven out of business.[1] The usual dumping case pre-

1. See the study by Lowell E. Baier of the evidence constituting injury in recent U.S. antidumping cases, "Substantive Interpretations under the Antidumping Act

sents a situation in which the profits of domestic firms have fallen as their sales and output have been reduced by foreign competition. These firms can quickly expand their output if the dumping ceases. And as long as the foreign dumping does not cease, the domestic consumer is deprived by the antidumping duty of the benefits of the lower price.

The view of dumping as a temporary phenomenon is also based upon the assumption that dumping (except for so-called predatory dumping) occurs because foreign producers regard their exports only as a means of disposing of occasional surpluses that they cannot at any given time sell at home. In many dumping cases, however, the foreign producers sell regularly abroad, and their differential prices reflect differences in competitive conditions in different countries. There may be a monopoly or cartel situation in the foreign producers' home country, protected perhaps by a tariff, while a competitive situation exists in other countries. Where that is so, dumping will tend to be a permanent phenomenon, and antidumping duties may merely serve to protect the monopoly returns of a single domestic seller or the fruits of a domestic cartel. Even where no domestic monopoly or cartel exists, dumping by foreign firms may lead to more effective competition in a local market dominated by a few sellers. Nothing is more threatening to an oligopoly price structure in a particular country than the sudden appearance of foreign competition. The imposition of antidumping duties is such a situation tends to restore the original oligopoly conditions and to permit the few domestic sellers to achieve a higher than competitive rate of return.

Despite the considerations advanced in the preceding paragraphs, most economists nevertheless hold that there is a case for antidumping duties where the dumping is temporary. In part this position is based upon nearly universal and uncritical acceptance of the conclusions of the renowned international trade economist, Jacob Viner, whose exceptionally thorough book published in 1923 recognizes that if dumping is permanent there is no economic case for antidumping duties.[2] He reasons, however, that just as there is a case for tariff protection for infant industries, "there is surely even a stronger case for the temporary protection of an established industry with a long record of successful survival of the test of foreign competition, if such industry is threatened by foreign competition of an abnormal and temporary character."[3] Viner, it should be noted, does not spell out the content of this "stronger case." Nor

---

and the Foreign Trade Policy of the United States," *Stanford Law Review,* XVII (1965), pp. 409, 417–26.
2. Jacob Viner, *Dumping: A Problem in International Trade* (Chicago: University of Chicago Press, 1923).
3. Ibid., p. 146.

does he explain what relation that case may have to the case for tariff protection of infant industries.

Passing such questions of economic theory, a more practical objection to the Viner position is that antidumping duties are the most likely to be imposed precisely where the dumping is a permanent condition. Domestic antidumping laws do not make a showing of temporariness a condition precedent to the imposition of antidumping duties. On the contrary, a flow over a considerable period of time of low-price imports creates the political pressure that may be necessary to motivate a government to impose antidumping duties, and, where an injury criterion is built into domestic law, it may be possible to establish the requisite injury only if the dumping has been in progress for some time. In the United States, for example, the dumper's "capacity and incentive" to continue dumping is considered to be a factor diminishing the domestic industry's burden on the injury issue.[4]

Viner, an economist unusually interested in law and government, is aware of this practical objection to his argument. His response is that the "fact that foreign producers are exporting at dumping prices affords a strong presumption that these prices are temporarily and abnormally low."[5] Viner does not adequately explain why he finds that there is such a "strong presumption." Rather, his illustrations present situations where dumping might be more or less permanent (as where a producer enjoying a monopoly at home sells at a "normal price" abroad, or where he sells abroad at a price "which is lower than the average cost of production but which is nevertheless profitable even in the long run to the dumper"[6]). Nevertheless, Viner believes that, in general, "the evidence strongly supports the conclusion that dumping is likely to be practiced only temporarily, or at least intermittently."[7] Viner does not review the evidence on which he relies (except insofar as isolated bits of relevant information may be scattered through his book). In the absence of access to that specific evidence, one may fairly raise doubts about the conclusion.

On a priori grounds it is as plausible to conclude that dumping, at least of the type against which antidumping duties are going to be imposed, is typically permanent. Since in any case in which antidumping duties are imposed there is local competition in the low-price country (for otherwise no local firm would complain), one may presume that the higher price at home reflects greater market power at home. And where a dumper enjoys market power at

---

4. "Portland Cement from the Dominican Republic," *Federal Register*, XXVIII (1963), p. 4047; "Steel Reinforcing Bars from Canada," ibid., XIX (1964), pp. 3840, 3841.
5. Viner, p. 146.
6. Ibid.
7. Ibid.

home and faces competition abroad, there is little reason to doubt that he will charge more at home than abroad, and do so on a permanent basis. Of course, the differential pricing may be a response to other factors, such as differences in tastes, availability of substitutes, and the like, but that would not lead one to expect the differential pricing to be a temporary phenomenon.

The issue is, as Viner recognizes, empirical. It is somewhat surprising that in an age when economists are wont to frown on any conclusions not based upon quantitative research, the Viner case for antidumping duties is so uncritically accepted.

## Experience under Article VI

In the ITO negotiations there was no challenge to the right of governments to impose antidumping duties. It was agreed that dumping was to be condemned and that the only function of an international agreement was to limit abuses.[8] Since there was no clear understanding of the competitive impact of antidumping duties, the line between abuse and legitimate use was hazy. Consequently, the provisions of Article VI, which were designed to accommodate the U.S. domestic antidumping law,[9] frequently lack precision and specificity. Since the general language of Article VI was made more detailed and precise by the 1967 Agreement on Implementation of Article VI of the General Agreement on Tariffs and Trade (hereafter referred to as the Antidumping Code), little would be gained by extensive consideration of the General Agreement language.[10] And since the Antidumping Code runs fourteen single-spaced pages,[11] a sentence-by-sentence analysis of its provisions would be out of the question here.

It would be gratifying, from the viewpoint of the orderly development of international institutions, to be able to say that the Antidumping Code constitutes a careful reworking of Article VI based upon a detailed review of the shortcomings of the Article VI language as revealed by the twenty years of experience from 1947 to 1967. Although such an explanation could perhaps be defended, it is more realistic to recognize that the Code is the outgrowth of a concrete conflict in the Kennedy Round. A study of the origins and reso-

8. William Adams Brown, Jr., *The United States and the Restoration of World Trade* (Washington: Brookings Institution, 1950), pp. 110–11, 213–14.
9. See the testimony of Harry Hawkins and John Leddy, Hearings before the Committee on Finance, U.S. Sen., 80th Cong., Part 1 (1947), pp. 343, 349.
10. Since the Antidumping Code binds only those contracting parties accepting it, the Article VI provisions on antidumping duties remain important for other contracting parties.
11. GATT Document L/2812 (12 July 1967).

lution of that conflict reveals a good deal about the way in which the GATT has been shaped by the interactions of the policies and actions of individual contracting parties.

Prior to the Kennedy Round, antidumping duties had received little attention from the CONTRACTING PARTIES. At the 1955 Review Session, various amendments to Article VI were considered, but, aside from the addition of an interpretative note on dumping by state-trading enterprises, no changes were made in the antidumping provisions.[12] During the same period only one major dispute concerning the imposition of antidumping duties came before the CONTRACTING PARTIES: that dispute, which concerned a "basic price" system used by Sweden in imposing antidumping duties on Italian exports of nylon stockings, led in 1955 to a lengthy panel report that artfully avoided any clear-cut interpretations of Article VI.[13] The secretariat subsequently conducted a study of the legislative and administrative aspects of antidumping regulations in eight countries.[14] Following the secretariat study, a group of experts was appointed. The group-of-experts reports, issued in 1959 and 1960, elaborated the possible meanings of certain ambiguous terms and provisions in Article VI, but since the group's terms of reference did not call for the giving of authoritative interpretations, the reports made only a modest contribution to resolving those ambiguities.[15]

Although the secretariat study and the group-of-experts reports resulted in a composite juridical analysis of Article VI which, in sheer volume at least, compared favorably with the attention given by GATT organs to other provisions of the General Agreement, that analysis was curiously academic and abstract. The superficiality of the work is attributable to at least two factors. First, until the 1960s the United States and Canada were the principal countries with active antidumping programs, and, as has been seen, Article VI was patterned on the U.S. statute, although departing from it in a number of major respects. Second, since Article VI is in Part II of the General Agreement, that article does not, in light of the Protocol of Provisional Application, invalidate inconsistent provisions of domestic legislation enacted (in the case of original contracting parties) prior to the effective date of the General Agree-

---

12. The provisions of paragraph 6 dealing with countervailing duties were amended.
13. The panel concluded that the Swedish system did not on its face violate Article VI but could do so in its implementation (*Basic Instruments*, 3d Supp. [1955], p. 81). The dispute was subsequently settled when the Swedish government revoked the challenged regulations (U.S. Tariff Commission, *Operation of the Trade Agreements Program*, 9th Rep. [1957], p. 12).
14. *Anti-dumping and Countervailing Duties* (1958), supplemented by GATT Document MGT (59) 122 (1959).
15. *Basic Instruments,* 8th Supp. (1960), p. 145; 9th Supp. (1961), p. 194.

ment or (in the case of acceding contracting parties) prior to the date of the applicable protocol of accession.[16]

## The Antidumping Code

The dumping question came to life, however, in the Kennedy Round. The United States, having introduced the subject of nontariff barriers into the negotiations, was chagrined to find that the nontariff barriers most often singled out by other countries for priority of action were those maintained by the United States, of which one of the most often mentioned was the U.S. antidumping statute. After some hesitation the United States sought to turn the dumping controversy to its advantage through the negotiation of a comprehensive antidumping agreement. The resulting Antidumping Code, while tying the hands of the United States on a number of procedural matters that had given rise to the most vociferous complaints, also affected significantly the United Kingdom and Canada. The latter two countries had procedures that were even less satisfactory to the international trading community than those of the United States. In addition, Canada's substantive law was inconsistent with Article VI in that it did not require a finding of injury as a prerequisite to the imposition of antidumping duties. Because (1) most of Canada's antidumping duties were imposed on imports from the United States, (2) the United Kingdom had begun during the 1960s to initiate a substantial number of antidumping proceedings, and (3) the European Economic Community was in the process of drafting its own antidumping regulations, the United States saw the Antidumping Code as a means to head off future discrimination against U.S. exports under the guise of antidumping proceedings.[17]

It is not entirely clear what institutional lessons should be drawn from this experience. The Code, containing a large number of highly detailed provisions, contrasts sharply with the vague generalities of most recent GATT documents dealing with substantive matters and with the pragmatic predilections of the GATT secretariat. Its form and philosophy are more in the spirit of the GATT's work of the late 1940s and early 1950s. The Antidumping Code was, as has been seen, more of an inspired compromise arising out of trade negotiations among certain contracting parties than a conscious attempt by the GATT as an organization to remedy defects in Article VI. Nevertheless, the studies

---

16. See discussion of the Protocol of Provisional Accession in chapter 19, "The GATT as an International Organization," infra.
17. See William B. Kelly, Jr., "Nontariff Barriers," in *Studies in Trade Liberalization*, ed. Bela Balassa (Baltimore: Johns Hopkins Press, 1967), pp. 265, 295–300. On the Antidumping Code, see generally John B. Rehm, "The Kennedy Round of Trade Negotiations," *American Journal of International Law*, LXII (1968), pp. 403, 427–34.

previously carried on within the organization provided useful background information for the drafting of the Antidumping Code; the GATT furnished a convenient institutional framework for the drafting process; and the General Agreement served as an underlying basis (the Antidumping Code is, it should be recalled, an "agreement on implementation of Article VI"). These facts suggest that the Antidumping Code might provide a precedent for the elaboration of other nontariff-barrier codes where the preconditions for such codification existed. Those preconditions to codification appear to be, if one may judge by the history of the Antidumping Code: first, broad language in the General Agreement that can serve as a basis for detailed negotiations; second, experience with that broad language sufficient to indicate the major ambiguities and lacunae; and third, a coincidence of external circumstances sufficient to lead those contracting parties that are principally concerned to seek jointly a greater degree of specificity and comprehensiveness.

The third factor may be more important than is generally realized. When in the initial drafting of the ITO charter the United States attempted to impose a detailed codification of nontariff-barrier rules on other nations that did not agree on the desirability of those rules, the result in too many instances was simply a codification of a host of exceptions to a basic rule. In the negotiation of the Antidumping Code, there was more general agreement on goals. Those contracting parties that sought to impose limitations on the United States were forced to accept reciprocal limitations on their own freedom of action in antidumping proceedings.

As previously indicated, detailed analysis of the lengthy Antidumping Code is impossible within confines of this study. But several of the Code's provisions are of general interest in any study of nontariff barriers and therefore warrant attention here.

First, the Code's final provisions provide a path around the anomaly, arising out of the Protocol of Provisional Application, that Article VI of the General Agreement does not render illegal any inconsistent national legislation predating the accession to the GATT of the contracting party in question. Each contracting party accepting the Antidumping Code is bound to take the necessary steps to comply with the Code, whatever the vintage of its antidumping legislation.[18] The Code, insofar as it incorporates the provisions of Article VI, thereby places Article VI into full effect. It may be that the other provisions on nontariff barriers found in Part II of the General Agreement can similarly be brought into full effect by separate agreement upon particular

---

18. Agreement on Implementation of Article VI of the General Agreement on Tariffs and Trade, *Basic Instruments*, 15th Supp. (1967), pp. 24–25 (hereafter cited as Anti-Dumping Code). On the Protocol of Provisional Application, see discussion in chapter 19, "The GATT as an International Organization," infra.

provisions among a substantial number of contracting parties, and that the GATT can thus obviate the need for taking what has proved to be all too formidable a step—that is, definitive acceptance of the General Agreement by the contracting parties specified in Article XXVI:6.

Second, the Antidumping Code faces up squarely to the too frequently overlooked legal axiom that the procedures for the enforcement of a statute are often more important than the substantive content of the statute. The U.S. antidumping statute, the Antidumping Act of 1921, was considered by other contracting parties to be a nontariff barrier largely on account of the uncertainties arising out of its procedures rather than on account of the severity of its formal sanctions. Although the U.S. statute required findings both that imports sales were being made at below fair value and that injury to domestic industry was resulting therefrom, the established procedures called for withholding appraisement of the goods in question following a tentative Treasury Department finding of below "fair value" sales without any finding as to injury. The withholding of appraisement was itself a major sanction, since, even though the goods might still be imported under bond, the eventual liability for customs duties was undetermined for the period of the subsequent proceedings before the Treasury and the Tariff Commission. Since the Tariff Commission found injury in only about one-quarter of the cases that were pursued to a final decision,[19] withholding of appraisement was considered by many to be more of a trade barrier than were the antidumping duties themselves.[20]

The Antidumping Code compels a change in the U.S. practice by providing that provisional measures, including withholding of appraisement, can "be taken only when a preliminary decision has been taken that there is dumping and when there is sufficient evidence of injury."[21] The Code further requires that investigations, whether initiated by complaints on the part of a domestic industry or by the local authorities *sua sponte,* may be commenced only if there is evidence of both "dumping" (that is, a sale of an imported good at a price below the price for consumption in the exporting country) and "injury"; moreover, in the course of such investigations, "evidence of both dumping and injury should be considered simultaneously."[22]

---

19. See statistics in Kelly, p. 298, and in Executive Branch Statement on Dumping, Compendium of Papers on Legislative Oversight, Review of U.S. Trade Policies, Committee on Finance, U.S. Sen., 90th Cong., 2d Sess. (1968), I, p. 73, 76.
20. The literature on the U.S. statute is vast. See e.g., James P. Hendrick, "The United States Antidumping Act," *The American Journal of International Law,* LVIII (1964), p. 914.
21. Art. 10(a).
22. Art. 5(a) & (b). Indeed, after a certain stage in the proceedings, evidence of both dumping and injury "shall" be considered simultaneously. For an interpreta-

Although the United States was the target of most of the complaints, the same difficulties were faced in a more exaggerated form by those who became enmeshed in the Canadian or the U.K. antidumping procedures. Since Canada had no injury criterion, antidumping duties might be imposed without regard to injury.[23] And in the United Kingdom antidumping duties could be imposed without notice and without opportunity for the parties to be heard.[24] The Canadian practice was, of course, inconsistent with Article VI, although lawful under the Protocol of Provisional Application. By accepting the Antidumping Code, the Canadian government bound itself to apply an injury criterion.[25] And Article 6 of the Code imposed upon the United Kingdom the obligations of notifying the exporters and importers concerned of the initiation of an investigation and of permitting all parties a full opportunity to defend themselves, including the right to submit whatever evidence those parties considered useful and the right to examine, with certain exceptions, all evidence against them.[26]

Third, the Antidumping Code makes provision for the development of "case law" as to its meaning. A committee on antidumping practices is to meet annually for consultations on the administration of national programs in the light of the Code.[27] If the opportunity is used to develop a set of precedents, the original GATT idea of a code of law in trade matters may become, in the area of antidumping duties at least, more a matter of substance and less a matter of form.

## Countervailing Duties

Countervailing duties bear a resemblance to antidumping duties that was sufficient to lead the draftsmen of the General Agreement to include the two kinds of duties in the same article. But the differences are substantial. Perhaps the primary difference is the ostensible purpose. Unlike antidumping duties, which are designed to offset lower prices attributable to price discrimination by for-

---

tion of this language, see the U.S. Executive Branch Analysis, Hearing on International Dumping Code, Committee on Finance, U.S. Sen., 90th Cong., 2d Sess. (1968), pp. 279, 294–99 (hereafter cited as Hearing on International Dumping Code).

23. Hearing on International Dumping Code, p. 13.
24. See Kelly, p. 300, n. 82.
25. Antidumping Code, Arts. 1, 3. For want of authorizing legislation, the Code did not go into effect domestically in Canada on the Code's effective date of 1 July 1968 (Hearing on International Dumping Code, p. 19).
26. The local authorities are not, however, precluded by these "due process" provisions "from reaching preliminary determinations, affirmative or negative, or from applying provisional measures expeditiously" (Art. 6[i]).
27. Art. 17.

eign private exporters, countervailing duties are designed to offset low prices attributable to subsidies by foreign governments.[28] This difference leads to several observations. The first is that the arguments for permitting countervailing duties are somewhat more forceful, from a free-trade perspective, than the arguments for antidumping duties. From such a perspective countervailing duties merely seek to *offset* the distortion arising from foreign governmental interference in a free international market, whereas antidumping duties *compound* the distortion created by foreign private monopoly in that they assure that local purchasers will also pay the monopoly price.

The second observation, more relevant to the legal interpretation of the General Agreement, is that the permissible scope of countervailing duties cannot be adequately discussed apart from the topic of subsidies, a topic that raises some of the most difficult problems in the General Agreement and is the subject of its own article in the General Agreement, Article XVI.[29] Article VI:3 limits the maximum amount of any countervailing duty to the amount of the foreign subsidy, without regard to whether the foreign subsidy is lawful under Article XVI.[30]

Countervailing duties have never received the same degree of attention in the GATT as have antidumping duties. The panel of experts commissioned to study antidumping and countervailing duties spent most of its time on the dumping question.[31] And no countervailing-duty code came out of the Kennedy Round to take its place beside the Antidumping Code. Perhaps this difference can be explained by the comparatively greater frequency of dumping-duty proceedings than of countervailing-duty proceedings.[32] Perhaps countervailing-duty proceedings are also less often abused for protectionist purposes than are dumping proceedings. It is not clear, however, that the rules in Article

---

28. The General Agreement, although following this distinction in general, sometimes tends to confuse antidumping and countervailing duties. See e.g., interpretative note, Ad Art. VI, paragraphs 2–3, Note 2.
29. Following the General Agreement's lead, the present study devotes a separate chapter (chap. 8) to subsidies. Separation of the discussion of subsidies from that of countervailing duties is dictated by the difficult policy problems posed by the widespread use of subsidies.
30. *Basic Instruments,* 9th Supp. (1961), p. 194, 200.
31. Ibid., 8th Supp. (1960), p. 145; 9th Supp. (1961), p. 194.
32. Compare the statistics in Executive Branch Statement on Dumping, Compendium of Papers on Legislative Oversight, Review of U.S. Trade Policies, Committee on Finance, U.S. Sen., 90th Cong., 2d Sess. (1968), I, p. 73, 76, with those in Executive Branch Statement on Countervailing Duties, ibid., p. 77. Since so few dumping proceedings terminate in final orders, either because of voluntary termination of dumping or because of failure to find injury, the imposition of dumping duties may not be more frequent than the imposition of countervailing duties.

VI are more often followed in the case of countervailing duties. The United States, for example, has no injury criterion in its statute.[33]

At the close of the Kennedy Round it was recognized that, as a question of principle, a countervailing-duty code was fully as warranted as an antidumping code, and a working party was established to undertake preliminary work that might lead to such a code. It remains to be seen whether a countervailing-duty code, which unlike the Antidumping Code would require amendment of the relevant U.S. statute,[34] can be agreed upon in the absence of the compelling pressure of a major round of trade negotiations. The effort to arrive at a countervailing-duty code warrants attention, however, for the light it will throw on the best means of dealing with nontariff barriers. If it is difficult to eliminate such barriers through negotiations, it is likely to be even more difficult to do so where the contracting parties that have to take steps to change their legislation cannot point to direct reciprocal advantages to be obtained. The notion of reciprocity, which has become so deeply engrained in the course of successive rounds of major trade negotiations, may make it necessary to rely on such major negotiations for the opportunity they give to work out agreed "packages" of commitments. If for these reasons the attempt to reach agreement on a countervailing-duty code does not bear fruit, it may also be inferred that codification of stringent rules is no more the road to barrier-free trade than it was at the time of the drafting of the General Agreement.

33. The U.S. statute, dating to 1897, is presumably saved from illegality by the Protocol of Provisional Application.
34. Following the Kennedy Round a dispute erupted between the U.S. administration and certain members of the U.S. Congress over whether the Antidumping Code could be accepted without amendment of the U.S. antidumping statute. The administration took the position that the Antidumping Code required only amendment of certain administrative regulations. See generally Hearing on International Dumping Code.

# 11 Administrative Barriers to Trade

The foregoing chapters of Part II have discussed a number of nontariff devices that interfere with the free flow of goods in the international community. There remain, however, a large number of administrative measures involved in the administration of the tariff, health, and other laws which, to take a phrase from an important book published several decades ago, constitute an "invisible tariff."[1]

Any attempt to eliminate such administrative barriers to trade presents uncommon difficulties. All administrative procedures and requirements affecting international trade constitute, to a greater or lesser extent, a burden on that trade; all of them therefore tend to protect local industry. But customs laws, as well as health regulations and the like, must be administered. Any attempt to deal with such nontariff barriers requires a sorting out of those requirements and procedures that are more burdensome than necessary to accomplish legitimate nonprotective functions. This is not simply a question of identifying the motive for the adoption of such procedures and requirements, even though protectionist forces sometimes find opportunities in this sphere that are denied to them in the formulation of tariff policy. As one customs lawyer has observed, "Let me write the Administrative Act and I care not who fixes the rates of duty."[2]

In view of the increasing optimism, following the conclusion of the Kennedy Round, that GATT's role may shift from the reduction of tariffs to the elimination of nontariff barriers, and in view of the position of administrative barriers as perhaps the most important nontariff barriers, the experience of GATT in dealing with such matters warrants more analysis than it has been

1. Percy W. Bidwell, *The Invisible Tariff* (New York: Council on Foreign Relations, 1939).
2. Benjamin Arthur Levett, *Through the Customs Maze* (New York: Customs Maze Publishing Co., 1923), p. 11.

given. As the discussion below indicates, no single method can be relied upon for the elimination of all such barriers. Rather, each administrative procedure or requirement must be accorded separate study and treatment, and a wide variety of techniques must be used, ranging from multilateral bargaining through the harmonization of laws and regulations to outright prohibition.

The discussion that follows deals with the GATT experience in those areas where the GATT has been most active in the past. No attempt is made to discuss all administrative barriers or even to single out the most important ones. Rather, the emphasis is on the opportunities and the pitfalls involved in attempting to deal with such matters in the GATT, as reflected in the GATT experience to date.

## Formalities

The problem of formalities may be discussed under two headings: fees and documents. Fees are the simpler matter. The fees charged by various countries for documents, forms, visas, approvals, inspections, and so forth in connection with the importation of goods have sometimes exceeded substantially the administrative cost involved. In some cases the fees have been expressed as a percentage of the value of the goods, a formula that causes the amount of the fees to exceed the cost by many times on large shipments. The underlying motive may be of either a revenue or a protective character, but in either case the protective effect may be great.

The formalities problem arises from the documents required by customs officials at the time of importation. Those officials have sometimes required too many documents in too many copies, adding to the importer's costs by typing up administrative employees in mountains of paper work. The officials have in addition sometimes imposed such severe penalties for mistakes and omissions that importers have been discouraged from incurring the attendant risks for small shipments.

On the fees question the General Agreement takes a straightforward prohibitive approach. Article VIII:1 provides that "all fees and charges of whatever character (other than import and export duties and [internal taxes]) . . . shall be limited in amount to the approximate cost of services rendered and shall not represent an indirect protection to domestic products or a taxation of imports or exports for fiscal purposes." The Article VIII provisions are complemented by Article II:2(c), which permits the imposition of "fees or other charges commensurate with the cost of services rendered."

The fees provisions have been of some utility. For example, they were used to bring pressure on France to suspend an increase of a stamp tax from 1.7 percent to 2 percent of the value of imported goods. The weakness of even prohibitory provisions, however, is illustrated by the history of the complaint against France. The complaint, entered in 1954, was successful in little more than obtaining assurance from the French representative that the tax had not been and never would be increased beyond what was necessary to defray the costs of customs services. One year later the French Government increased the tax from 2 percent to 3 percent with the specific provision that the increase was to be used for agricultural family allowances. Upon the amendment of the General Agreement in 1955 to include the more forceful term, "shall," the French delegate conceded that the stamp tax violated the General Agreement, but he argued that there was no other way to finance agricultural family allowances and therefore the tax could not be reduced immediately. Despite repeated assurances that the tax would be reduced, the French Assembly each year continued to reenact the 3 percent tax.[3] It was not until 1 January 1961 that the tax was finally reduced to 2 percent.[4]

France was not the only country to defy the fees provisions of Article VIII. A 1956 GATT survey showed that a number of Latin American countries were imposing fees, calculated on the value of goods, ranging up to 5 percent.[5] But the fact that many such fees had been reduced by the time of a 1962 survey would indicate that the GATT prohibition was not entirely without influence. On the other hand, a certain contempt for the prohibition was reflected in increases of the Nicaraguan and Peruvian fees to 7 percent and 8 percent of the f.o.b. value respectively.[6] A somewhat different approach toward conformity was manifested by Turkey, which sought and received in 1963 a waiver for a 5 percent stamp tax used to provide revenue for its economic development program.[7]

In discussing fees not conforming to the General Agreement, it must be borne in mind that Part II of the General Agreement, which includes the Article VIII rule, has never entered into force definitively with respect to trade restrictions maintained by contracting parties on 30 October 1947 or on the date of the applicable accession protocol. Of course, that fact would surely not justify an increase of an Article VIII fee subsequent to the relevant date. Moreover, the prohibition of Article VIII is in effect picked up in Article II with respect to all bound tariff items. This latter article exempts bound items from all duties and charges other than customs duties, except to the extent

3. U.S. Tariff Commission, *Operation of the Trade Agreements Program,* 12th Rep. (1961), pp. 15–16.
4. The United States accepted a French assurance at a May-June 1960 meeting that the tax was about to be reduced, and the complaint was thereupon withdrawn. U.S. Tariff Commission, *Operation . . . ,* 14th Rep. (1964), p. 27.
5. *Basic Instruments,* 5th Supp. (1957), pp. 102, 112–14.
6. Ibid., 11th Supp. (1963), p. 214, 217.
7. Ibid., 12th Supp. (1964), p. 55.

that such duties and charges are "commensurate with the cost of services rendered."[8]

The documents problem does not lend itself to the prohibitory approach. Burdensome paper work cannot be eliminated by a few words in an international agreement, even with the best of will on all sides. Moreover, it is obviously impracticable to use a major international agreement, dealing with a multitude of topics, as the vehicle for determining how many copies of what documents shall be required in widely varying situations. Article VIII:1 limits itself to a general statement of the need for "decreasing and simplifying import and export documentation requirements." Article VIII goes on, in paragraph 3, to impose a somewhat more definite limitation on "substantial" penalties for "minor" breaches of customs regulations and requirements, particularly omissions and mistakes that are "easily rectifiable and obviously made without fraudulent intent or gross negligence."

In spite of the generality of this language, the GATT record in working toward the simplification of documents has been moderately gratifying. Through the adoption in 1952 of a Code of Standard Practices for Documentary Requirements for the Importation of Goods[9] and through certain other measures to be examined shortly, the GATT was able to induce a number of changes in national practices. It is important to note, however, that the initiative did not come from the GATT Secretariat or from the CONTRACTING PARTIES. Rather, it came from the International Chamber of Commerce, a predominantly private group representing enterprises that had to deal with the "red tape" in consuls' offices and customs sheds. The ICC was the organization that drew up the Code of Standard Practices and presented it to the CONTRACTING PARTIES.[10]

The basic problem to which the Code addressed itself was the existence of the consular invoice. The consular invoice, a manifestation of the bureaucratic penchant of governments, is a heavy burden on international trade. Requiring different and additional information beyond that in the commercial invoice which the seller sends to the buyer, the consular invoice has to be approved by the importing country's consul in the exporting country, usually on forms to be obtained from him. Filling out the forms can in some cases take a skilled administrative employee a day or more. Frequently, the consular invoice has to be certified by the consul a certain number of hours or days before departure of the vessel, and, if the consul cannot be found or is located at a city too

---

8. Arts. II:1(b), II:2(c).
9. *Basic Instruments,* 1st Supp. (1953), pp. 23–25.
10. The CONTRACTING PARTIES to the General Agreement on Tariffs and Trade, *International Trade: 1952* (1953), pp. 105–10; *Basic Instruments,* Vol. II (1952), p. 210.

far from the port to meet this doctrine, the shipment has to be held for the next boat. Aside from the fee charged, the nuisance effect of the consular invoice requirement tends to eliminate commercial shipments of small value. Even where the consular invoice is not required, there may be a requirement that the commercial invoice include a consular certification or visa together with additional information beyond that required in the trade concerned.

The advantages of the consular invoice to the governments concerned are far from obvious, particularly since a large portion of world trade moves without it. But the motivation for the requirement appears to be twofold. First, the fees that consuls charge are for many countries an important source of revenue and, for countries with balance-of-payments problems, an important source of hard currencies. Second, the consular invoice is a useful element in the enforcement of exchange control schemes and discriminatory licensing arrangements insofar as it provides a control on the origin of the goods; transshipment, misstatement of origin, and other ruses can thereby more easily be detected. To the extent that the consular invoice is used for this second purpose, it tends to duplicate the function of certificates of origin, which are often required by the same governments and which are themselves a further burden on trade.

The GATT Code of Standard Practices states that, "in principle," two documents "should suffice" for governmental purposes: (1) a "transport document (bill of lading, consignment note)"; and (2) a "commercial invoice, accompanied where necessary by a packing list." Only in certain circumstances should a certificate of origin or a consular invoice be necessary, and, where either or both of the latter documents are required, the trader should have the option of combining them. The Code goes on to urge governments to limit the number of copies required of each document to a "strict minimum."[11] Together with adopting the Code, the CONTRACTING PARTIES "recommended" the abolition of consular invoices, consular visas, and certificates of origin not later than 31 December 1956. For the interim period they adopted the Standard Practices for Consular Formalities, dealing with certain special burdens arising out of the use of consular invoices and visas.[12]

The results of this international condemnation of consular invoices were gratifying. Before the 1956 deadline, consular invoices were abolished by several countries, including the United States (which retained them only for liquor imported in small boats and for certain special circumstances). Several other

---

11. The Code is set out in *Basic Instruments,* 1st Supp., pp. 23, 24–25. See also the working party report, ibid., p. 100.
12. The rules are set out at ibid., p. 25, 26. The rules also deal with the fees problem insofar as they state that consular fees should not be calculated as a percentage of the value of goods.

countries reduced the number of transactions in which consular invoices were required. It cannot be demonstrated that the GATT alone was responsible for this movement toward suppression of the consular invoice requirement. The assigning of credit is particularly difficult in the case of the United States, which at that time was in the throes of a constitutional battle over presidential powers in the foreign affairs field, a battle that led the administration to downplay its GATT obligations in domestic discussions about trade policy. But the influence of the GATT's efforts, coupled with those of the International Chamber of Commerce, was no doubt considerable.

Nevertheless, several contracting parties (and a number of other countries that had not yet become contracting parties) continued to use consular invoices even after 1956. Consular invoices were particularly popular among Latin American countries, which often administered complicated licensing schemes and appreciated the revenue potentialities of consular fees. The CONTRACTING PARTIES reiterated their 1952 recommendation in 1957[13] and again in 1962,[14] but without exceptional success. Seven Latin American countries and Turkey still used consular invoices or consular legalizations of commercial invoices as late as 1962, and most of them showed little interest in abolition.[15] The question was considered inconclusively in the Kennedy Round by the Group on Administrative and Technical Regulations.

Concurrently, a secondary war was being waged against certificates of origin. In 1953 the CONTRACTING PARTIES adopted a recommendation to supplement the implicit condemnation of certificates of origin as separate documents that was already contained in the Code of Standard Practices. The most important provisions of the 1953 recommendation were that such certificates should be required only where "strictly indispensable" and that "as large a number of competent bodies as possible" should be established to issue such certificates in order to ease the burden of acquisition.[16] It is not clear how strong an influence these recommendations have had, but it is not unlikely that the use of certificates of origin has increased in view of the fact that, although exchange control is less widespread, free trade areas are more common than previously. Since a free trade area involving the elimination of restrictions among member states without the harmonization of external tariffs against third countries creates an incentive for the transshipment of imports from third countries through low-tariff member states into high-tariff member states, certificates of origin are a useful instrument of customs control.

13. Ibid., 6th Supp. (1958), pp. 25–27.
14. Ibid., 11th Supp. (1963), p. 59.
15. Ibid., pp. 214–17.
16. Ibid., 2d Supp. (1954), p. 53, 57. This recommendation was slightly modified in 1956 (ibid., 5th Supp. [1957], p. 33).

## Marks of Origin

Marks of origin, which are affixed on the goods themselves or on their packing, have a quite different function from certificates of origin. Marks of origin are intended for the use of customers, whereas certificates of origin are for the use of government officials. Both requirements are likely to constitute a burden on trade, but protection is the primary purpose only in the case of marks of origin. Marks of origin may lend themselves to protectionist ends in any of three ways: (1) by enabling customers to assert their prejudices against foreign goods in general or against goods from particular countries; (2) by disfiguring consumer luxury goods through the prominence of the mark itself; and (3) by increasing foreign producers' costs through arduous marking requirements. The legitimate function of a mark of origin is to provide consumers with information on which to base their purchases. By making possible more intelligent purchases, this information permits the market to function more efficiently and is thereby consonant with a free trade position. But since the consumer's preference may be merely an expression of xenophobia or a personal foreign policy, many would challenge the legitimacy of marks of origin.

In any event, there is not much doubt that national legislation of this character is generally intended to give indirect protection to domestic goods. What differs is the degree of frankness in conceding this intention. During the protectionist twenties, U.S. officials were quite frank. In 1925 the Board of United States General Appraisers ruled:

> The purpose of Congress in enacting this [marking] provision was to make competition with the domestic manufacturer more difficult and expensive, and, if compliance with its requirements should render articles less desirable to purchasers, or should be more expensive and difficult, such fact could not defeat the intention of Congress which was to reduce, if not prohibit, competition with American manufacturers.[17]

The marks-of-origin question was vigorously debated in the drafting of the Havana Charter.[18] The Americans, with relatively stringent legislation at home, were unable to urge prohibition or even to agree to work toward suppression of marks of origin.[19] Article IX of the General Agreement was consequently aimed only at abuses. It sought to permit marking at the point of importation and thereby to curb the tendency of customs officials to reject automatically goods that arrived without marks that met the local requirements. It further pre-

---

17. *Burstein & Sussman* v. *United States,* Treasury Decision 40771 (1925).
18. William Adams Brown, *The United States and the Restoration of World Trade* (Washington: Brookings Institution, 1950), pp. 105–6.
19. See the elaborations of the U.S. proposals in *Suggested Charter for an International Trade Organization,* Department State Publication 2598, Commercial Policy Series 93 (1946), Art. 14.

scribed that marking requirements "shall be such as to permit compliance without seriously damaging the products, or materially reducing their value, or unreasonably increasing their cost." It was not until the Review Conference in 1955 that the present paragraph 2 was added to Article IX to record agreement that "the difficulties and inconveniences which such measures may cause to the commerce and industry of exporting countries should be reduced to a minimum."

In order to give some substantive content to the amended Article IX, the GATT in 1958 adopted, upon proposal of the International Chamber of Commerce, a series of rules on marks of origin. Contracting parties were not required to follow the rules; it was merely "recommended" that they do so. The United States, faced with domestic legislation at odds with the recommended rules, attached corresponding reservations to its approval.[20]

The new rules urged contracting parties "to limit the requirement of marks of origin to cases where such marks are indispensable for the information of the ultimate purchaser." They condemned the requirement of many countries that the marks be affixed permanently to the goods, a requirement that tended to reduce the value of the goods; it was recommended that "any method of legible and conspicuous marking should be accepted which will remain on the article until it reaches the ultimate purchaser." The rules further permitted abbreviations such as "UK" and "USA," permitted marking in English regardless of the language of the importing country, and otherwise sought to standardize, simplify, and reduce the cost of marking requirements. Although all countries were "invited" to report changes in their legislation and regulations concerning marks of origin, the GATT has not published any summary of these notifications and therefore it is not possible to judge to what extent GATT has been effective in lightening these burdens on international commerce.[21]

## Valuation

A further problem of customs practice that has concerned the GATT is valuation. It is important to distinguish valuation procedures and valuation standards. Delays and harassment in the procedural steps required to obtain a final valuation on goods in customs can discourage international trade quite as effectively, if not more effectively, than can burdensome documents requirements. The staff of the U.S. Commission on Foreign Economic Policy found that as of a certain date in 1953 (before several Customs Simplification Acts were passed) some 313,000 entries, equivalent to about one year of imports, remained unprocessed by the U.S. customs officials. It also found that nearly 5 percent of

20. U.S. Tariff Commission, *Operation* . . . , 12th Rep. (1961), p. 69.
21. The rules are set forth in *Basic Instruments,* 7th Supp. (1959), pp. 30, 31–33.

all entries required forty-eight months or more to liquidate.[22] Prior to customs liquidation, although most goods were released, the amount of duty owed remained uncertain, and the importer had to bear a contingent liability. The impact of this state of affairs on the volume of international trade cannot be definitely ascertained, but it can only be to discourage such trade to some degree.

The GATT has attempted to do very little about procedures. Rather, it has addressed itself largely to the question of valuation standards. Procedures and substantive standards are related, of course, in the sense that much of the delay and complexity of procedures, particularly the U.S. procedures, can be attributed to the concurrent application as alternative bases of valuation of a number of different standards.[23]

The fundamental rule of Article VII is both detailed in its language and uncertain in its application. It requires that "actual value" be used as the base and prohibits assessment "on the value of merchandise of national origin or on arbitrary or fictitious values." Actual value is then defined as "the price at which . . . such or like merchandise is sold or offered for sale in the ordinary course of trade under fully competitive conditions."[24] Article VII leaves to the legislation of the importing country the "time and place" at which such price is to be determined. By delegating this decision to the importing country, Article VII permits use of, among others, the price of the goods in the exporting country, the price in the importing country, or the export price, which may be higher or lower (depending, for example, on the exporter's pricing practices) than the price for like goods on domestic sales in the exporting country. Whatever the place chosen, the time for determining the relevant price may vary from the date of the making of the contract through the date of shipment to the date of clearance through customs. And even if the actual invoice price is chosen, the price may be f.o.b. or c.i.f.

Commercial interests would, in general, prefer to see the invoice price chosen as the basis for valuation, reserving reference to other values for unusual cases such as sales between related companies. An interpretative note takes a step in this direction, but not a conclusive step, by stating that it "would be in con-

22. Randall Commission, *Staff Papers Presented to the Commission on Foreign Economic Policy* (Washington, 1954), pp. 324–25, 337–39. It must be noted, however, that many of the longer delays are attributable to recourse to administrative and judicial review procedures by the importers. Relatively few of the delays are attributable to disputes over valuation as such. It was found that "the most intractable source of delay has been that arising from the need for information from foreign sources required to fix the appropriate valuation" (ibid., p. 339).
23. See ibid., pp. 339–58; G. A. Elliott, *Tariff Procedures and Tariff Barriers* (Toronto: University of Toronto Press, 1955), pp. 142–71.
24. The quoted text reflects certain amendments added at the 1955 Review Session. These amendments were intended to be "improvements in drafting" (*Basic Instruments,* 3d Supp. [1955], p. 205, 212).

formity with Article VII to presume" that the "invoice price" represents "actual value" (with adjustments for any nonincluded legitimate costs and for "any abnormal discount or other reduction from the ordinary competitive price").[25] But to say that invoice price may be used is a long leap from saying that it must be used, and other provisions make clear that the main thrust of Article VII is to place certain limits on the use of values other than the invoice price rather than directly to encourage use of the invoice price. For example, Article VII:2(b) states that, to the extent to which prices other than the invoice price are looked to, and therefore the question of the appropriate quantity becomes important in determining the valuation base, "the price to be considered should uniformly be related to either (i) comparable quantities, or (ii) quantities not less favourable to importers than those in which the greater volume of the merchandise is sold in the trade between the countries of exportation and importation."[26] When the price in the exporting country is used, internal taxes (for example, turnover taxes) refunded on export are to be subtracted.[27]

Article VII is particularly important because of its condemnation of certain valuation bases that discourage international trade. Purely fictional values are, of course, incompatible with the standard of "actual value." But beyond that, use of the price of comparable goods originating in the importing country is incompatible with Article VII under the provision, set out above, that the price chosen "should not be based on the value of merchandise of national origin." The most important example of such a valuation base is the American Selling Price system ("ASP"), which has from the beginning been a major target of criticism in valuation discussions within the GATT.

The United States first adopted ASP in 1922 to give certain portions of the U.S. chemical industry protection from the competition of a resurgent German chemical industry, competition that had not existed during the First World War. The decision was taken to inflate the base rather than to raise the duty, because it was thought that the American public would more easily countenance a "technical" change in the valuation base than they would duty rates in excess of 100 percent.[28] The ASP method was subsequently extended to a few other products, but the benzenoid chemicals sector remained the principal recipient of the added protection involved.

The additional protection granted by ASP does not consist solely in the higher price to be found in the U.S. market as compared with the import price.

25. Interpretative note, Ad Art. VII, para. 2:1.
26. See also interpretative note, Ad Art. VII, paras. 2:2–2:4.
27. Art. VII:3. Also important is Article II:3, which prohibits any change in the method of valuation that would impair the value of a tariff concession.
28. See Elliott, p. 163 (citing "Statement of W. R. Johnson, U.S. House, *On H.R. 1535*, p. 150.")

It consists also in the way in which the U.S. price is calculated. Under Section 402 of the Tariff Act of 1930, as amended,

> the American selling price of any article produced in the United States shall be the price . . . at which such article is freely sold, or in the absence of sales, offered for sale for domestic consumption in the principal market of the United States, in the ordinary course of trade and in the usual wholesale quantities, or the price that the manufacturer, producer, or owner would have received or was willing to receive for such article when sold for domestic consumption in the ordinary course of trade and in the usual wholesale quantities, at the time of exportation of the imported article.[29]

Since under the statute ASP applies only as between the imported product and the identical "article" produced domestically, the domestic industry can obtain protection for a group of functionally related products that are in competition with the imported product through the simple expedient of raising the price on the single domestic product that is identical with the imported product. Moreover, where the product that is imported is not produced domestically, an increase of protection for competitive domestic products can be obtained by going into domestic production of the product identical with the imported product and thereby invoking the ASP system of valuation.[30] Finally, because of the interpretation given the "freely sold . . . or offered" language, U.S. manufacturers have sometimes been able to lead customs officials to accept their list price as the basis for valuation, even though the bulk of their domestic sales take place at substantially lower prices. It suffices that the lower prices are not "freely offered," but rather given only to certain purchasers (whether they purchase large quantities or otherwise), and that some sales take place at the list price. The list price then becomes under the statute "the price that the manufacturer . . . was willing to receive for such article when sold for domestic consumption in the ordinary course of trade and in the usual wholesale quantities."[31] The effect of ASP has in some cases been, according to a U.S. Tariff Commission study, to make the effective rate of duty based on normal methods of valuation at least double the nominal rate and to lead to effective protection based on normal methods of valuation in excess of 100 percent.[32]

The importance of ASP has often been overemphasized, as when ASP became one of the fundamental issues in the Kennedy Round. At the time of

---

29. 19 U.S.C.A. §1401a(e).
30. U.S. Tariff Commission, *Products Subject to Duty on the American Selling Price Basis of Valuation; Conversion of Rates of Duty on Such Products to Rates Based on Values Determined by Conventional Valuation Methods,* Tariff Commission Publication 181 (1966), pp. 53–54.
31. See Randall Commission, p. 342.
32. U.S. Tariff Commission, *Products Subject to Duty. . . .*

those negotiations ASP applied to only about 1 percent of current U.S. imports. It was limited to a few products: coal-tar chemical products, and, by presidential proclamation under the 'flexible tariff" procedure, certain classes of footwear, canned clams, and knit gloves. To know what quantity of potential imports was excluded is, of course, impossible.

In the Kennedy Round the dispute over ASP served to illustrate one of the difficulties that must be faced in negotiations over nontariff barriers that are inconsistent with specific provisions of the General Agreement. The European Economic Community regarded ASP as illegal under Article VII, while the United States took the position that, since the central principle of trade negotiations was a balance of concessions, the Europeans would have to offer something in return for the abolition of ASP—particularly as the application of ASP valuation to a given item was equivalent to a higher rate of duty on an Article VII valuation base.[33] This difference of views tended to poison the atmosphere of the negotiations and threatened for a time to lead to collapse of the entire Kennedy Round.

In a cliff-hanging finale, a package settlement was worked out. The settlement included an unconditional commitment by both the United States and the EEC to reduce duty rates on most chemical products by agreed percentages (50 percent on a large portion of U.S. imports and 20 percent on most EEC imports), together with an agreement providing for certain additional reductions contingent upon abolition of ASP by the U.S. Congress. If the Congress gave the appropriate authorization, the United States would in effect shift to rates on a conventional base that would, in most cases, represent at least 50 percent reductions from the pre-Kennedy Round duty as converted to rates based on normal methods of valuation. The combination of the initial 50 percent reduction together with the conversion and accompanying second reduction would result in an average cut of 48 percent by the United States on imports valued at $325,000,000. At the same time that the United States acted, the EEC would make additional cuts on chemicals in general (that is, on both benzenoid and other chemicals) in order to bring the overall EEC reduction to an average of 46 percent on imports valued at $460,000,000. The effect of the package was to give Congress an incentive to eliminate ASP on benzenoid chemicals. Only thereby could the United States enjoy a full 46 percent reduction by the EEC on chemicals and not merely a 20 percent reduction.[34]

33. Since ASP was in effect in 1947, and since Article VII is in Part II of the General Agreement, ASP falls in a somewhat unusual legal middle ground under the Protocol of Provisional Application. See discussion in chapter 19, "The GATT as an International Organization," infra.
34. For details of the complicated Kennedy Round ASP package agreement, see U.S. Office of the Special Representative for Trade Negotiations, The American Selling Price Issue with Respect to Chemicals (July 31, 1967) (mimeographed docu-

Although the GATT undertook at a relatively early date a major survey of valuation practices,[35] it did not have much success in dealing with valuation malpractices prior to the Kennedy Round. There is some indication, nevertheless, that the GATT may have been of some marginal value in inducing the improvements in the U.S. law brought about by the several Customs Simplification Acts in the 1950s. But there remain provisions in Section 402 of the Tariff Act of 1930, as amended, that are hard to square with Article VII of the General Agreement, notably the use in certain circumstances of the "constructed value" (foreign cost of production) basis.[36]

It is difficult to say whether the GATT would have had more influence on valuation legislation if the Protocol of Provision Application had not made Article VII inapplicable, strictly speaking, to legislation in effect on 30 October 1967 (or the date of the applicable protocol of accession). Whatever value prohibitory rules may have in reducing other barriers to trade, they have less potential value in dealing with valuation problems. By their very nature, valuation legislation and regulations are complex and technical. Moreover, ASP is fundamentally different from other kinds of nontariff barriers. It is actually a tariff barrier in the sense that it permits a very high effective rate of tariff protection. In most cases the official duty rate under ASP can be converted to an effective rate of duty. The U.S. Tariff Commission has in fact made conversion to rates that would yield an equal amount of revenue and would provide approximately, although perhaps not exactly, an equal rate of protection.[37] Such a conversion is not possible with such "invisible" barriers as unnecessary documentary formalities, where there is no objective way of judging the effective rate of protection accorded. Negotiations may thus be less promising in the case of other kinds of administrative barriers to trade.

## Health and Sanitary Regulations

One of the most troublesome administrative barriers to trade arises from health and sanitary regulations. No one disputes that health and sanitary regulations are essential and that they must be enforced with respect to imported as well as

---

ment). The text of the ASP package is contained in Agreement Relating Principally to Chemicals, Supplementary to the Geneva (1967) Protocol to the General Agreement on Tariffs and Trade (June 30, 1967). In addition, an exchange of letters dated 30 June 1967 between the United States and Japan provided for the elimination of ASP on canned clams and wool-knit gloves in return for certain tariff concessions by Japan. See generally John B. Rehm, "The Kennedy Round of Trade Negotiations," *American Journal of International Law*, LXII (1968), pp. 403, 414–20.

35. *Basic Instruments*, 3d Supp. (1955), p. 99.
36. 19 U.S.C.A. §1401a(d).
37. U.S. Tariff Commission, *Products Subject to Duty*. . . .

domestically produced goods if the health of consumers is to be protected. The problem is that such regulations are also rather convenient devices for accomplishing protectionist ends under the banner of health and cleanliness. Any good book on American constitutional law will give more than one example of the use of health requirements by the various states in shielding themselves from sister-state competition. On the international level, the possibilities are illustrated by U.S. embargoes against imports of meat from various Latin American countries because of hoof-and-mouth disease existing in certain localities in those countries.[38] Exclusion by the United States of Canadian imports of Great Lakes fish because of water contamination, coupled with failure to apply similar limitations on the sale in the United States of fish from the same waters when caught by U.S. fishermen, is another example.[39]

Sometimes a national prejudice in a matter of taste and propriety, rather than either health or protectionism, is involved. French canned asparagus has been kept out of U.S. markets by a rule requiring that everything in a can of vegetables must be edible; in France the entire plant is often canned. A shipment of cheese fondue from Switzerland was found unacceptable by U.S. Food and Drug Administration officials because the packages described the conventional manner of eating cheese fondue from a common bowl, a practice considered unsanitary by the inspecting officials.[40]

The latter example suggests one of the difficulties lying in the way of any attempt at international control of the abuses of health and sanitary regulations. The potentially protective effect of such regulations often arises from the manner of administration and cannot be deduced from textual provisions. It would therefore often be difficult for an international organization to verify that an abuse had in fact occurred. Moreover, traders affected by sanitary regulations are sometimes loath to make a public complaint because even if they are successful in official channels, the publicity concerning their difficulties with health officials is not unlikely to leave a question mark in the consumer's mind about the quality of the product.

The General Agreement does not approach health and sanitary regulations in as direct a fashion as it does fees and formalities, marks of origin, and valuation abuses. Rather, health and sanitary regulations, as well as a long list of other "public policy" restrictions listed in Articles XX and XXI, are treated in terms of an exception to the provisions of the General Agreement.[41]

38. See Elliott, p. 321.
39. Ibid., p. 245.
40. Randall Commission, p. 321.
41. Article XX deals with a wide range of restrictions concerning health, morals, industrial property, and the like whereas Article XXI is concerned solely with national security restrictions.

Where the local regulation turns out to be broader than the scope of the exception, the legal situation is not entirely clear. Under Article XX, "nothing in . . . [the General] Agreement shall be construed to prevent . . . measures necessary to protect human, animal or plant life or health." But this exception is made "subject to the requirement that such measures are not applied in a manner which would constitute a means of arbitrary or unjustifiable discrimination between countries where the same conditions prevail, or a disguised restriction on international trade." The natural construction of that language appears to be that if the local requirements "constitute a means of arbitrary or unjustifiable discrimination . . . or a disguised restriction on international trade," the validity of the requirements must be judged under the remaining articles of the General Agreement.

In the case of "discrimination between countries where the same conditions prevail," discrimination among foreign countries seems to be envisaged, and therefore the general most-favored-nation clause would come into play. But what specific prohibitions of the General Agreement might provide the authority for characterizing a health or sanitary requirement as a "disguised restriction"? If the requirement in question applied only to imported products, and not to domestic products, the national treatment provisions of Article III:4 (calling for "treatment no less favorable than that accorded to like products of national origin in respect of all laws, regulations and requirements affecting their internal sale [etc.]") would presumably be applicable. That the notion of "disguised protection" includes failure to accord such national treatment is confirmed by the drafting history of Article XX. A proposal was rejected at the Geneva ITO drafting conference to qualify the health exception of Article XX (but not the other exceptions thereunder) by the phrase, "if corresponding domestic safeguards under similar conditions exist in the importing country." The rejection was based on the ground that the proposed language was "unclear, the meaning being already covered in the headnote to the Article" (covered, that is to say, in the "disguised restriction" language of the preamble).[42]

But what of the situation where national treatment is formally accorded, but there is nevertheless an unnecessary burden on trade? Suppose that a domestic law prescribes the kinds of coloring materials that may be used in food, whether domestic or foreign in origin. These coloring materials are the conventional ones used domestically. Certain foreign producers or canners use, however, other coloring materials. Under these facts it would be stretching the point to say that national treatment is not accorded on food imports. So, too, the asparagus and cheese fondue instances, discussed above, did not involve any failure to grant "national treatment," but the burden to international trade in a multitude of such examples may cumulatively be fairly substantial.

42. *Analytical Index*, p. 110. Article III:1 and XI:1 might also be relevant to the "disguised restriction" standard.

With these limitations in the drafting of the General Agreement, it is not surprising that the GATT has not had any verifiable influence on the use of health and sanitary requirements for protectionist purposes. But here, as in many other areas, it would not necessarily constitute a substantial step forward simply to redraft Article XX. What is required is detailed work, probably product by product, among experts on each of the major problems. If the more common abuses could be identified, and if, for example, a code restricting such abuses could be drafted, substantial progress might be made, even if the code were not mandatory. Care would have to be exercised, however, because the level of health requirements varies not only among countries but also over time, as consumers demand steadily higher standards. An effort to limit abuses should not interfere with a progressive improvement of health standards.

## Technical Conventions

The GATT has also been active in several customs matters not directly covered by the General Agreement. It has cooperated with the International Chamber of Commerce and the Brussels Customs Co-operation Council in drafting and in securing the adoption by contracting parties of several conventions concerning temporary importation. These conventions, although covering rather particular customs problems, would facilitate international trade considerably if universally adopted and followed.

Many different kinds of goods are temporarily imported. If customs duties have to be paid on such goods, importation is less likely to occur, even if the customs duties are refunded on export. Since the kinds of goods that are temporarily imported are subsidiary to other imports or other kinds of economic activity, the denial of duty-free status may have a more than commensurate negative effect on international commerce. The first convention sponsored by the GATT, in this case in connection with the ICC, was the International Convention to Facilitate the Importation of Commercial Samples and Advertising Material.[43] Even in countries providing free importation for salesmen's samples, annoying regulations and stringent penalties in the case of loss or destruction discouraged the importation of samples and thereby reduced the flow of international commerce. Later the GATT jointly sponsored with the ICC three other temporary importation conventions: (1) the Customs Convention on the ATA ("Admission Temporaire–Temporary Admission") Carnet for the Temporary Admission of Goods, which dealt with the temporary, duty-free importation of goods in general in connection with ATA carnets issued by private associations approved by the customs authorities; (2) the Customs Convention on the Importation of Professional Equipment, which was limited to press, radio, television, and cinematographic equipment and to

43. *Basic Instruments,* Vol. II (1952), p. 210; 1st Supp. (1953), p. 94.

equipment used by professionals in connection with the performance of services; and (3) the Customs Convention on the Temporary Importation of Packings, which insofar as it permitted duty-free entry of packing materials and containers may have been the most important of all of these conventions in terms of favorable effect on the volume of international trade.[44]

These conventions reflect a broadening view of the proper role of the GATT. Expanding from its traditional role in the administration of the rules in the General Agreement and the sponsorship of rounds of trade negotiations to a role in the harmonization and simplification of technical legislation affecting trade, the GATT became moderately active in an area of work which, although without glamor, is of potentially great significance in the promotion of international trade. A view of the work that remains to be done may be obtained from the program of the Commission of the European Economic Community for the harmonization of technical legislation and regulations affecting sanitary, health, and safety requirements; customs procedures; road transport; and other matters having an influence on the volume and direction of world trade.[45] It is difficult to judge the potential reward from this kind of work, but one can venture that the results might be fully as productive as attempts to enforce the prohibitory provisions of the General Agreement on the same topics.

If this kind of harmonization work is to be effective, it is necessary that the preparation be conducted by experts and be technically thorough, and that the solutions adopted be specifically directed to individual problems. General language adopted at the international level that leaves the task of interpretation to national customs officials or national legislatures may be more harmful than helpful. An illustration may be drawn from the ill-fated attempt to arrive within the GATT at a uniform definition of nationality.

Nearly every country accepts one or more definitions of nationality for use by customs officials. Wherever any legal right or obligation in customs matters turns on the origin of goods, problems will arise concerning goods that have had contact with more than one foreign country. To take an example, difficult problems of determining nationality may arise in the case of manufactured products where only a part of the cost of manufacturing and processing has been incurred in the country of export. It may be important to national customs authorities to have a formal definition of nationality for the administration of differential tariff rates (including customs unions and free trade areas) or non-global quantitative restrictions or for the compilation of certain kinds of trade statistics.

44. For reports and texts of the conventions, see ibid., 9th Supp. (1961), pp. 201–29; 10th Supp. (1962), pp. 211–36. Also of interest is the UNESCO Proposal Concerning Free Flow of Educational, Scientific and Cultural Materials, *Basic Instruments*, Vol. II (1952), p. 226.

45. See Commission of the European Economic Community, *Ninth General Report on the Activities of the Community,* (1966), pp. 89–105.

Following a recommendation of the International Chamber of Commerce that an internationally accepted definition would be advantageous, the GATT considered the following draft proposed by the French delegation:

> A. The nationality of goods resulting exclusively from materials and labour of a single country shall be that of the country where the goods were harvested, extracted from the soil, manufactured or otherwise brought into being.
>
> B. The nationality of goods resulting from materials and labour of two or more countries shall be that of the country in which such goods have last undergone a *substantial transformation*.
>
> C. A substantial transformation shall—*inter alia*—be considered to have occurred when the processing results in a *new individuality* being conferred on the goods.[46]

This text, any original elegance of which is somewhat obscured by the official English translation, is a good example of what must be avoided in a technical area. It might provide a useful definition if some international body were available to issue official interpretations or to review national interpretations to assure uniformity, but a text on such a level of abstraction can hardly produce uniformity by itself. Furthermore, while general texts of this character may be quite useful if they indicate that a particular practice is to be suppressed, nationality definitions are admitted by all sides to be necessary, and the only question is how to bring them into harmony with one another.

In the case of the French text, it quickly became clear that, whatever meaning the basic terms "substantial transformation" and "new individuality" may have had under French law, they were largely devoid of content in some other legal systems, and many national administrations would have to substitute more precise regulations. An almost unlimited number of differing solutions could be envisaged in that process. The British regarded the definition as "so vague and subjective that it would do no more than set up a facade of general agreement behind which there would be fundamental dis-uniformity in application."[47] The attempt to draft a common definition had to be abandoned.[48]

In considering the fiasco, the International Chamber of Commerce recognized that under the existing system the difficulties in practice were "mainly concerned with matters of detail relating to specific products or even subproducts of a given industry."[49] The ICC therefore came to the conclusion that no common definition was possible.

In the light of the detailed harmonization work of the EEC Commission,

---

46. *Basic Instruments*, 2d Supp. (1954), pp. 53, 55 (emphasis supplied).
47. Ibid., 3d Supp. (1955), p. 94, 98.
48. For working party reports, see ibid., 1st Supp. (1953), pp. 100–106; 2d Supp. (1954), pp. 53–59; 3d Supp. (1955), pp. 94–99.
49. Ibid., 3d Supp. (1955), p. 94, 99.

however, a second conclusion appears more appropriate. Perhaps studies, and eventually definitions, on an industry-by-industry basis, in which an attempt was made to consider the various products and processes in which difficulties arose, would lead to workable solutions. The present difference between the GATT and the EEC Commission is, of course, that the Commission has a large staff working only on the harmonization of technical regulations and in addition calls regularly upon the services of experts from the ranks of national civil services and particular industries concerned. An institutional development of such a character might speed the progress of the GATT in dismantling administrative barriers to world trade.[50]

50. The work of other regional organizations might also provide precedents for new GATT working methods. For example, the experience of the European Free Trade Association in the administration of the origin rules contained in the Stockholm Convention provides an interesting contrast to the abortive GATT efforts in defining the nationality of goods. See Secretariat of the European Free Trade Area, *Building EFTA* (1966), pp. 72–84; S. A. Green and K. W. B. Gabriel, *The Rules of Origin* (Geneva: EFTA, 2d ed., 1967).

# 12 Government Procurement

With the Kennedy Round behind it, the GATT will have to devote increasing attention to nontariff barriers. In this and the following chapter suggestions will be made on how the GATT can most effectively deal with a number of such barriers that have, until now, little concerned it.

In an era when some 25 to 40 percent of the gross national product of most countries passes through public budgets, discrimination against foreign products by government purchasing officials constitutes one of the most important barriers to world trade from a purely quantitative point of view. Although it is difficult to know precisely to what extent governmental restrictions, formal and informal, limit imports destined for governmental use, some notion of that effect may be gained from the following statistics. In 1958 and 1959 the U.S. federal government awarded only 0.05 percent and 0.18 percent, respectively, of the dollar volume of procurement contracts to foreign bidders.[1]

In view of the incontestable impact of government procurement regulations and procedures on international trade, it is striking that the General Agreement does not attempt to control discrimination in procurement. Article III:8 makes clear that the general rule of Article III:4, requiring national treatment for imported products "in respect of all laws, regulations and requirements affecting . . . internal sale, offering for sale, transportation, distribution or use," is not to apply in the case of "procurement by governmental agencies of prod-

1. Since the statistics include only awards in excess of $10,000, the percentages in the text probably tend to overstate the importance of foreign participation in the U.S. procurement programs. The statistics are limited to the ten federal agencies considered the most important in procurement. See Laurence A. Knapp, "The Buy American Act: A Review and Assessment," Columbia Law Review, LXI (1961), p. 430, 450. In 1954 the staff of the Randall Commission estimated that the U.S. Buy American Act was then costing the U.S. government up to $100,000,000 annually in higher prices and another $100,000,000 in foregone customs revenue (*Staff Papers presented to the Commission on Foreign Economic Policy* [Washington,, 1954], pp. 315, 318).

199

ucts purchased for governmental purposes." Only where products are purchased "with a view to commercial resale or with a view to use in the production of goods for commercial sale" does the national treatment clause apply.

The United States had sought in the Havana Charter negotiations to secure a much more limited government procurement exception. Under the draft ITO charter prepared by the United States, only purchases "by and for the military establishment" would have been excluded.[2] This provision was dropped at the London conference because, according to the Preparatory Committee, "an attempt to reach agreement on such a commitment would lead to exceptions almost as broad as the commitment itself."[3] In considering whether the government procurement exception might someday be tightened, it may be profitable to explore the considerations that caused the U.S. proposal to be dropped in London.

## Motives for Procurement Restrictions

The motives for restrictions on governmental purchases are manifold, but they may be classified under three principal headings: (1) balance of payments, (2) national security, and (3) protection for local industry.

Balance-of-payments motives play a large role in discrimination against foreign goods in the procurement context. Government purchasing criteria are viewed as important instruments of national policy. Governments that are fighting payments imbalances and are seeking to put their own houses in order before reducing private expenditures abroad find limitations on foreign procurement to be convenient and politically popular measures, despite the premium that must by definition be paid for domestic supplies. The United States, for example, finds it more convenient to enforce a procurement rule under which domestic goods are preferred unless they cost at least 50 percent more than foreign goods than to impose quantitative restriction on imports.

Restrictions imposed to alleviate balance-of-payments problems would not lend themselves to effective regulation by a government procurement clause in the General Agreement. Since governments are permitted under the General Agreement to impose balance-of-payments restrictions on purchases in the private sector, few would likely be willing to renounce the power to impose such restrictions on their own purchases. Furthermore, any limitations on discrimination in public purchases for balance-of-payments reasons could be circumvented by overall quantitative restrictions or by exchange restrictions that gave the local treasury officials a veto on all foreign purchases. Even under

2. *Suggested Charter for an International Trade Organization,* Department of State Publication 2598, Commercial Policy Series 93 (1946), Art. 9:1.
3. *Analytical Index,* p. 26.

the present GATT regime, residual treasury control tends to inhibit foreign purchases in such countries as the United Kingdom. Nevertheless, there might be some utility in requiring that discriminatory procurement policies imposed for balance-of-payments purposes be submitted to reporting and justification procedures.

The national security justification for discrimination in government procurement is an inescapable fact of contemporary world politics. Even the original U.S. proposal contained, as we have seen, an exception for goods purchased by and for the military establishment. And in any case, Article XXI contains a broadly drafted, self-judging exception to the General Agreement as a whole for all measures which a contracting party "considers necessary for the protection of its essential security interests . . . relating to the traffic in arms, ammunition and implements of war and to such traffic in other goods and materials as is carried on directly or indirectly for the purpose of supplying a military establishment." No one seriously contests the necessity of a national security exception, at least for purchases by governments for their own use. But the national security justification is such an attractive cover for protectionist policies that if the provisions of Article III:8 were to be narrowed, it would be useful to have some way of controlling the inevitable national security exception.

One danger is that the national security argument is almost infinitely expandable. Protectionist claims based on national security interests are put forth not only for products used by the military but also for civilian products. Examples from the U.S. experience are the unsuccessful efforts to secure quantitative restrictions on civilian watches and the successful efforts to secure such restrictions on fuel oil for home use (for which much of the political support comes from the coal industry). The arguments favoring such restrictions are based on the notion that the product in question is produced by an industry that also supplies the military and that would in time of war be called upon greatly to expand its production. The entire infrastructure of a country tends to take on national security aspects: hence the repeated and sometimes successful efforts in the United States to secure special protection for heavy electrical generating equipment used by public utilities. In times of competitive pressure, almost every industry can produce an argument along national security lines. Among the industries that applied to the director of the U.S. Office of Civil and Defense Mobilization for "national security" relief from imports were those manufacturing dental burrs, clinical thermometers, stencil silk, wool felt, and wooden boats.[4] And even in the case of purchases by the military, it is not clear that restrictions on such major budget items as foodstuffs and uniforms (on which the United States has imposed a virtual pro-

4. Knapp, p. 455.

curement embargo under the annual Berry appropriation rider[5]) can be justified under any objective interpretation of national security needs.

But as large as military expenditures are and as important as balance-of-payments constraints on expenditures may be, a major motive for procurement restrictions is protection. This tendency to pursue protectionist ends in procurement is widespread and seemingly instinctive. How is one to explain such curiosities as the "Buy Saskatchewan" program if not by the existence of a universal and deeply engrained feeling that governments ought to help local industry whenever possible?[6] Nevertheless, restrictions imposed to provide protection to local industry may lend themselves to effective regulation by an appropriate government procurement clause in the General Agreement.

## Restrictive Techniques

The most famous, but far from the only or even the most stringent, discriminatory procurement provision is the U.S. "Buy American" Act.[7] As currently interpreted it requires federal agencies to consider a domestic bid unreasonable when that bid exceeds a foreign bid by more than 6 percent (or 10 percent not including customs duty and certain costs). Bids by domestic manufacturers are treated as foreign rather than domestic when domestic materials do not exceed 50 percent of the cost of all materials.[8] This 6 percent price preference is increased to 12 percent for domestic bids by small business firms or for domestic bids from labor surplus areas.[9] The Buy American Act is not, in point of fact, the decisive limitation on U.S. federal government procurement today. With the steady deterioration of the U.S. balance-of-payments position in the early 1960s, the Department of Defense adopted a more stringent set of rules. Similar rules were subsequently extended to other government agencies. The Department of Defense rules call, in general, for a 50 percent price preference when the duty on foreign goods is excluded from the calculation, or for a

---

5. Ibid., pp. 450–51.
6. The Ministry of Industry and Information of Saskatchewan has stated that its policy is to "purchase 'Made in Saskatchewan' goods, providing quality and price are satisfactory." See Memorandum by Joseph W. Marlow, Cravath, Swaine & Moore, New York, p. 22. The Marlow Memorandum (hereafter cited "Marlow") was originally printed in 111 Congressional Record, 27, 28, 29 April, 3, 4, 6, 10, and 11 May (1965), and all citations herein are to a special reprint by Representative John P. Saylor.
7. 41 U.S.C.A. §§ 10a et seq.
8. Executive Order 10582, 19 Federal Register 8723 (1954); Organization for Economic Co-operation and Development, *Government Purchasing* (1966), p. 111 n.
9. *Government Purchasing*, p. 111.

6 percent price preference when the duty on foreign goods is included in the bid price, the more favorable alternative to domestic suppliers to be chosen.[10] Although this 50 percent rule is considered temporary, the Department of Defense has indicated that the rule will remain in effect until the U.S. balance-of-payments deficit is "corrected."[11] The Buy American Act and the supplementary balance-of-payments regulations are complemented by various state Buy American procurement policies.

Although the United States has received most of the international publicity, it is not the only country that pursues autarky in its procurement policies. There is even ground to suspect that the United States may not be the worst offender. Although most countries do not have statutes stating a percentage price preference to be accorded domestic goods, such a preference can be, and often is, accomplished by other means. Among the techniques having that effect are (1) selective tender procedures, in which invitations to bid are sent only to suppliers on preestablished lists; (2) single tender procedures, in which the procuring authority contacts only one supplier; (3) substitution of negotiated contracts for public tenders; (4) limited publicity on public offers; (5) requirements that bidders have branch establishments within the country; and (6) the vesting of discretion in procurement officers to ignore foreign bids. Any attempt to deal on an international plane with government purchases must take these restrictive procedures into account.

For at least the majority of procurement contracts in many countries, the open public tender has been replaced (if it ever existed) by the selective tender, in which invitations to bid are sent only to suppliers on preestablished lists. An extreme variation of the selective tender is the single tender, in which the procurement officer contacts a single supplier and negotiates the contract directly. The criteria for determining admission to the lists of suppliers are often hazy, and even if the lists are not consciously used for protectionist ends, they may have a tendency in that direction. In the United Kingdom open public tender is used with respect to only about 1 percent of contracts, and other contracts are divided between selective tender and single tender procedures. According to information furnished the Organization for Economic Co-operation and Development by the United Kingdom, "foreign firms . . . are not represented on lists in large numbers."[12] In Italy a foreign firm, even if it succeeds in becoming listed, need not be sent an invitation to bid, and in any case listing and delisting is in the unlimited discretion of each domestic agency.[13] The

10. Ibid., p. 113.
11. Ibid.
12. Ibid., p. 105.
13. Ibid., p. 55; Marlow, p. 27.

open public tender is rarely used in the Netherlands, except occasionally in public works contracts, and these contracts are, according to the U.S. Embassy in The Hague, rarely awarded to foreign firms.[14]

Even where open public tender procedures are followed, the method of giving publicity and the length of notice given can be manipulated to favor domestic suppliers. In France open public tenders may be "announced through the medium of posters, the 'Bulletin Officiel des Annonces des Marchés Publics' *or* advertisements in trade journals."[15] But even if all government tenders are regularly announced in a central, easily accessible publication, the announcement of tenders too shortly before the tender date may effectively reduce the number of foreign tenders, particularly in the case of special order goods. Domestic firms are closer to the scene and are thus more likely to have advance knowledge of approaching tender announcements than are foreign forms. Under such circumstances practices such as the German two-to-three-week notice limits, which are applicable even to "special manufactures," are likely to exclude all but the largest and best-organized foreign firms.[16]

Another technique that tends to reduce foreign bidding is the limitation of eligibility to bid to domestic firms and those foreign firms that have branch establishments in the country. In Belgium, bidders may be required to have a "domicile" within the country;[17] for public works, bidders must be of Belgian nationality and, in the case of corporations, at least two-thirds under Belgian ownership.[18] According to information furnished by Italy to the OECD, Italian "government departments do not in principle have any relations with foreign firms or suppliers but with firms legally established in Italy trading in nationalized foreign products."[19] In France the particular minister concerned may decide that bidders must be of French nationality.[20]

The most effective method for discriminating against foreign suppliers is the vesting of discretion in procurement officials to select among bidders on the basis of criteria other than price. The very absence of a statutory price preference may permit the practices of procurement officers to be more protectionist than they otherwise would be. According to a U.S. Foreign Service report, the chief purchasing officer of the French State Railways stated in 1960 that foreign firms would not be seriously considered unless their bids were 20 to

14. *Government Purchasing*, p. 71; Marlow, p. 22.
15. *Government Purchasing*, p. 31 (emphasis supplied).
16. Ibid., p. 36.
17. Ibid., p. 16.
18. Decree-Law of 3 February 1947 (Monitor Belge, 12 Feb. 1947), set forth in Marlow, pp. 19–20.
19. *Government Purchasing*, p. 55.
20. Marlow, p. 23.

30 percent below the lowest French bid.[21] The New Zealand Government Stores Board has stated that it "may . . . in certain cases direct purchase from a local source where this is deemed necessary in the light of current import policy."[22] In Canada a price preference for domestic goods has been established through custom, according to information provided to the OECD by Canadian officials.[23]

The extent to which it is customary in various countries to favor local firms is impossible to determine, because many countries do not normally justify awards and some, such as the Netherlands, do not give information of any kind on either bids or awards.[24] In the United States the formal percentage of preference, coupled with the requirements that all bids be made public and that any unsuccessful bidder be given upon request an explanation of the basis of the award,[25] permits public verification and control of the degree of preference accorded domestic suppliers.

Unofficial and informal devices for restricting foreign competition aside, some countries other than the United States have adopted formal price preference rules. The preferences range up to 15 percent in Norway, 10 percent in South Africa, and 8 percent in Greece.[26] In Spain there is a virtual embargo on procurement of certain types of goods from foreign sources.[27] Preference percentages are often applied after customs duties have been added to the foreign suppliers' prices. And where there are no formal preferences, customs duties are conventionally added to foreign bids in making awards.

Given the similarity of formal price preferences to tariffs, it should not in principle be unduly difficult to negotiate reductions of these preferences in GATT trade negotiations rounds. But such reductions have rarely been negotiated. Although a group on government procurement policies was created in the Kennedy Round, little came of that initiative.

## Experience in Other Organizations

### The OECD

In response to the vacuum created by the Article III:8 exemption in the General Agreement, the Organization for Economic Cooperation and Development in 1963 stepped into the field of government procurement policies. The

21. Ibid., p. 24.
22. Letter from the New Zealand Commissioner of Works, set forth in ibid., p. 57.
23. *Government Purchasing,* p. 23.
24. Ibid., p. 72.
25. Ibid., p. 111.
26. Ibid., pp. 77–78, 45–46; Marlow, pp. 58–62.
27. Marlow, pp. 34–35.

OECD initiated study project culminated in 1966 with the publication of a summary of information by the member governments.[28] As with most information-gathering, the value of the OECD inquiry will depend upon what is done with the information. The danger is, of course, that publication of the information will serve as a substitute for any meaningful progress toward either harmonization of national requirements or reduction in protection. According to the 1966 *Report of the Secretary-General to the Council of Europe,* "Present work in this field explores the possibility of elaborating guidelines which would ensure maximum fairness in the field of government purchasing through limiting discrimination against the suppliers of foreign products." In view of the confidential nature of the work of the OECD Trade Committee, it is too early to judge the efficacy of the OECD approach to this problem.

## The EEC

The Commission of the European Economic Community has been attempting to deal with discrimination in procurement by member states against contractors and suppliers from the other member states. As a preliminary step, it has divided procurement contracts into two categories: public works contracts and supply contracts. Although the Commission has yet to make any proposal to the Council on supply contracts, it has proposed two directives governing public works contracts. Neither of these two proposals has yet been adopted by the Council. Nevertheless, both warrant examination as possible models for use at a latter date in wider economic groupings of nations.

The first proposed directive on public works envisages the elimination of all restrictions, whether formal or resulting from administrative practices, on awards to contracts in the other member states.[29] The second proposed directive deals with more subtle and perhaps quantitatively more important problems: the procedures to be followed in awarding public works contracts.[30]

Although qualified with numerous exceptions, this latter directive would eliminate discriminatory provisions in technical specifications, provide for a system of Community-wide publicity, and establish common criteria for the qualification and selection of contractors. Provisions in technical specifications which would be considered discriminatory would include references to particular trademarks, patents, origins, or other matters that would tend a priori to eliminate or favor particular sources. The problem of de facto discrimination

---

28. *Government Purchasing.* This publication has been used extensively in the preparation of this chapter.
29. *Journal Officiel des Communautés Européennes* (1965), p. 2523/65.
30. Ibid., p. 929/65.

caused through insufficient or tardy publicity on public tenders would be met by the requirement that such tenders be announced in the official journal of the European Communities not later than a fixed number of days prior to the closing date for bids. The common criteria for the qualification and selection of contractors would specify the grounds on which potential bidders might be excluded from the competition and would place some limitations on the use of arbitrary bases for selection of the successful bidder. A presumption would be established that a tender was free of discrimination on the basis of nationality if residents of the other member states constituted one-third of the qualified candidates invited to submit bids; if less than one-third of the qualified candidates were residents of the other member states, there would be a presumption of nondiscrimination only if all qualified residents of the other member states had been invited to bid.

In order to assure compliance with both Community directives by the member states, a consultative committee would be created to assist the Commission. And in order to avoid too great a burden on local authorities, public works contracts not in excess of $100,000 would be exempted from the provisions of the first directive, and those not in excess of $300,000 would be exempted from the second directive.

Aside from their specific provisions, which have been indicated here in the barest outline, the two proposed directives are interesting in several respects. If the EEC member states prove willing to adopt the directives, and if the directives prove successful in promoting international competition in the letting of public works contracts, there is no reason why similar directives could not be adopted, with suitable institutional modifications, by broader groupings of countries, such as the OECD or the GATT. Some other publication could be substituted for the official journal. The absence of such extensive powers as those attributed to the EEC Commission might prove an inconvenience in the event of blatant disregard of the rules by some states, but that is an institutional problem not necessarily relevant in determining whether or not the regulation of national procurement programs is feasible.

In evaluating the EEC performance, one should remember that public works do not constitute a high percentage of total government purchases. Constituting a much higher percentage of total government purchases are supply contracts, and thus far, as indicated above, the Commission has failed to present to the Council any proposal on these modes of government procurement. No official announcement has been made of the reasons for the tardiness here, but the importance of military contracts among the various types of supply contracts and the sensitivity of matters relating to government procurement during the Kennedy Round (when the EEC was scoring negotiating points by attacking the Buy American Act) may help to explain some of the delay.

## The EFTA

Despite the fact that the European Free Trade Area has rather more modest goals for economic integration than the EEC, the EFTA Convention itself contains a provision on the elimination of discrimination in public procurement. Under Article 14 of the Convention, the member states are, during the period from 1960 to 1969, "to ensure the progressive elimination" of certain practices by "public undertakings" (broadly defined to include "central, regional, and local government authorities, public enterprises or any other organization by means of which a Member State, by law or in practice, controls or appreciably influences imports from, or exports to, the territory of a Member State"). Among the practices to be eliminated are "measures the effect of which is to afford protection to domestic production which would be inconsistent with [the EFTA] Convention if achieved by means of a duty or charge with equivalent effect, quantitative restriction or Government aid," and "trade discrimination on grounds of nationality in so far as it frustrates the benefits expected from the removal or absence of duties and quantitative restrictions on trade between Member States." At a 1966 meeting the EFTA Ministers decided that this article meant that, as far as procurement was concerned, "public undertakings shall give equivalent treatment to domestic goods and other goods of EFTA origin and shall award contracts on the basis of commercial considerations."[31] Because such a generalized pronouncement would not have been sufficient by itself to stop discriminatory practices, the ministers agreed to undertake a review of national laws, regulations, and practices, and to submit the results of this review to a group of experts for further study. Not content merely with such a study, however necessary to a final solution of the problem, the ministers also agreed upon several immediate, practical steps. In particular, they agreed that the member governments should take immediate steps to ensure that the relevant governmental agencies made adequate opportunities for bidding available to interested suppliers in the other member countries and to ensure that bids were judged objectively. They further decided that the member countries should exchange "lists" containing "such information as would be of particular interest to potential suppliers in other EFTA countries"; these lists were to be distributed to interested exporters in the various countries.[32]

## A Role for the GATT?

If the measures adopted by the EEC and the EFTA prove successful in promoting international competition in the letting of public contracts, similar mea-

---

31. "Public Undertakings," *EFTA Bulletin,* Vol. VIII, No. 2 (March-April, 1967), pp. 2, 3.
32. Ibid., p. 6.

sures, with suitable institutional modifications, might be attempted in broader groupings of countries, such as the GATT. Moreover, the difficulties, revealed in the Kennedy Round, of dealing with such problems in the context of tariff negotiations suggest that the focus in the GATT may have to be changed in any event from short-term bargaining to a long-term common effort.

The experience of the EEC and the EFTA provides the lesson that the problem of government procurement policies cannot be viewed simply as a question of the prohibition of formally prescribed discrimination but must be attacked affirmatively by stimulating the improvement of procurement procedures and by providing an adequate medium of international publicity—whether a common journal, a system of lists, or something else. This kind of work requires the use of expert groups working toward the common objective of rooting out both formal and informal discrimination and cannot be successful so long as the problem is viewed as one of bargaining over formal restrictions.

# 13 Border Tax Adjustments

It is not unlikely that one of the major commercial policy issues among developed countries in the post-Kennedy Round period will concern border tax adjustments. The principal border tax adjustments in question are refunds of indirect taxes upon export (also called drawbacks or remissions) and equalization charges upon import. The issue has been smoldering for some time and has been the subject of quiet but extensive discussion in the Trade Committee of the Organization for Economic Co-operation and Development. Should the question erupt into a full-scale dispute, the GATT would have the opportunity to play a major conciliatory role; indeed, should retaliation commence, the GATT would be forced to enter the fray. A rethinking of the GATT ground rules concerning border tax adjustments might help to avoid such a major commercial policy confrontation among the major trading nations. The groundwork for such a rethinking was laid in the establishment of a Working Party on Border Tax Adjustments in 1968.[1]

## The GATT Ground Rules

In most of the areas where it has been suggested that the GATT might be active after the Kennedy Round, the rules in the General Agreement are either sketchy or nonexistent. In the area of border tax adjustments, however, the situation is the reverse: the rules are fairly definite, but the content of the rules is frequently viewed as unsatisfactory. The dissatisfaction stems from two major sources: economists who consider that the GATT rules make little economic sense and certain Anglo-Saxon countries, notably the United Kingdom and the United States, which consider that the present rules discriminate against them.

The various GATT rules applicable to border tax adjustments are scattered through the General Agreement and have been discussed above under the con-

---

1. GATT Document L/3009 (17 May 1968).

ventional GATT headings.² It therefore suffices at this point to recall the main principles without entering into an examination of the official interpretations and the residual ambiguities.

When upon export of goods the exporting state refunds indirect taxes (such as turnover or excise taxes) previously paid upon the goods, no problem of violation of the export subsidy provisions of Article XVI arises. Nor does any problem arise in the case of exemption from such taxes of goods destined for export. This conclusion follows from the principle that the "exemption of an exported product from duties or taxes borne by the like product when destined for domestic consumption, or the remission of such duties or taxes in amounts not in excess of those which have accrued, shall not be deemed to be a subsidy."³ This dispensation from the subsidy rules is not considered, however, to extend to direct taxes, such as corporate income taxes.⁴ Refunds of direct taxes on exports therefore not only fall under the export subsidy provisions of Article XVI but also give rise to a right on behalf of any importing country suffering injury to impose countervailing duties under Article VI.

Similarly, when upon import of goods an importing state levies a charge on the imported goods equal to the indirect taxes already imposed upon competitive domestic goods, no violation of the internal tax provisions of Article III arises. Such "equalization charges" may be imposed even if the customs duty on the goods has been bound in GATT tariff negotiations.⁵ Such charges may be designed to equalize taxes not only on "like domestic products" but also "in respect of an article from which the imported product has been manufactured or produced in whole or in part."⁶ But, parallel with the rule on drawbacks, a charge may not be imposed on imported goods to equalize a domestic direct tax, such as a corporate income tax.

The favored treatment granted indirect taxes on both the export and import side is, to be sure, limited by the requirement that neither the export refund nor the import equalization charge exceed the amount of the corresponding domestic indirect tax. But it is in some cases difficult to calculate the total amount of indirect taxes that have been applied in the course of the manufacture of a particular domestic product.⁷ Where taxes are levied on the full value at each of several stages in the manufacturing process, as under a cascade turnover tax, the calculations often encounter difficulties in tracing taxes on raw materials and semifinished goods through to particular finished prod-

2. See discussion in chapters 7, "Internal Taxes," and 8, "Subsidies," supra.
3. Interpretative note, Ad Art. XVI.
4. *Basic Instruments,* 9th Supp. (1961), p. 185, 186.
5. See Arts. II:1(b), II:2(a), III:2.
6. Art. II:2(a).
7. See discussion in chapter 7, "Internal Taxes," supra.

ucts. In the case of certain types of indirect taxes, such as taxes on capital equipment, there is no general agreement on the proper method of treatment. Finally, the tax burden on a particular product may vary widely from manufacturer to manufacturer (depending, where a cascade turnover tax is involved, upon the degree of integration of the various manufacturers) and even from sample to sample produced by the same manufacturer (depending upon such factors as the time elapsed between production runs and the number of purchased component parts used).

Since the total amount of indirect taxes on a particular kind of product is not a constant, calculation of the equalization charge for that product is inherently arbitrary. In the case of the export refund, moreover, administrative considerations may preclude demonstrating for each exported item, or even for each manufacturer, the precise burden of indirect taxation. The common practice is in fact to use an average figure for the product in question in calculating both the equalization charge and the export refund. Under Article 97 of the Treaty of Rome creating the European Economic Community, for example, member states "which levy a turnover tax calculated by a cumulative multi-state system may, in the case of internal charges imposed by them on imported products or of drawbacks granted by them on exported products, establish average rates for specific products or groups of products." Not only may such an average figure diverge sharply from the actual figure in certain instances, but whatever difficulties foreign suppliers or competitors may have in challenging the correctness of a particular equalization charge or export refund are compounded when that equalization charge or export refund purports to be computed in terms of an average figure.

An equalization charge or export refund computed in terms of an average figure is, of course, subject to upward adjustment by the local government. Since an equalization charge inhibits imports as effectively as a customs duty of the same amount, while an export refund promotes exports as efficiently as an export subsidy of the same amount, an increase in an equalization charge or an export refund without any accompanying change in internal taxes is not unlikely to result in an international dispute. In such a dispute the other governments will claim that the increase constitutes a disguised increase in protection (in the case of the equalization tax) or a hidden subsidy (in the case of the drawback).

So too can a dispute arise where, in order to increase its border tax adjustment, a country changes the form of its internal taxation without thereby changing the total tax burden on domestic firms. The impetus for the OECD study of border tax adjustments arose out of a number of such changes in the form of internal taxes within the OECD area. The United Kingdom had begun to rebate certain indirect taxes that had not been eligible for rebate under U.K. law theretofore. And Italy had announced that it was considering converting certain payroll taxes, not considered rebatable under GATT rules, into turnover taxes, eligible for refund on export.

## Present Trends and Omens

One can detect on the political horizon a number of internal tax increases of major proportions which could give rise to disputes over the corresponding border tax adjustments. The plans of the European Economic Community for the harmonization of indirect taxes call for two series of changes in rates. The first series of changes will occur in those countries that currently have a cascade turnover tax—that is to say, in all of the Six except France. These five are to adopt a value-added tax along French lines, a shift that will necessarily result in certain rate changes. In the course of these changes, certain border tax adjustments will doubtless be increased.[8] The first of the five, Germany, approximately doubled its border tax adjustment when it made the change in 1968. The second series of changes will occur when the rates of the six national value-added systems are harmonized. With respect to some systems, this will lead to a considerable increase in rates and hence to a corresponding increase in border tax adjustments toward third countries. Given the internal difficulties that will be encountered in working out the harmonization, the Community will be anxious to avoid embroilment in the GATT. On the other hand, the EEC's trading partners may be suspicious that some of the resulting changes in border tax adjustments are intended to give additional protection to domestic production. It should not be forgotten that all the previously discussed problems of averaging rates and of tracing taxes will arise in the course of these two series of changes.

The potential for acrimonious dispute involved in changes in border tax adjustments is considerably increased by the fact that a number of countries rely mainly on direct, rather than indirect, taxes. These countries consider that they are seriously, if not unjustly, disadvantaged by the prohibition of similar border tax adjustments for direct taxes. Consequently, they do not take kindly to what they regard as the manipulation of drawbacks and equalization charges by their trading partners and competitors. Some direct tax countries, particularly those facing payment imbalances, have considered challenging the GATT rules either directly by commencing rebates of direct taxes ( a step that could well lead to retaliatory action) or indirectly by changing their tax systems in the direction of heavier reliance on indirect taxes in order to create what are euphemistically called "export incentives."

8. See address by Stanley S. Surrey, "Implications of Tax Harmonization in the European Common Market," in New York, 15 Feb. 1968 (mimeographed document), pp. 28–30.

Such considerations led to the formation by the United Kingdom of a commission to study the possibility of introducing a value-added tax[9] and to a campaign by the influential London weekly *The Economist* in favor of such a tax. In the United States, interest in the possibility of moving toward reliance on a value-added tax or some other form of indirect taxation has been evidenced in numerous academic studies and in a major conference sponsored jointly by the National Bureau of Economic Research and the Brookings Institution.[10] The U.S. discussions have often emphasized the international trade advantages to the United States of such a shift.

## The Economic Underpinnings of the GATT Rules

If the GATT rules were universally regarded as just and proper, the potential for international disagreement over changes in border tax adjustments would be considerably attenuated. But informed opinion, and particularly the opinion of professional economists, has come increasingly to question the justification for differential treatment of direct and indirect taxes. Unfortunately, the GATT rules rest on little more than tradition and an economic assumption that is often challenged.

Indirect taxes have traditionally been rebated much more frequently than direct taxes. That tradition may rest, however, on certain factors that are of doubtful importance today. At one time, for example, income taxes, the principal direct taxes, were not sufficiently important to justify the administrative machinery required for border tax adjustments, while today the situation is quite different. Similarly, it was long considered that the calculations required for the remission of direct taxes were too difficult and arbitrary to be undertaken, whereas the present view is that such calculations may be simpler and less arbitrary than the calculations for cascade turnover taxes or indirect taxes on multifunction capital equipment.

The economic assumption upon which the differential treatment of direct and indirect taxes rests is simply that indirect taxes are shifted forward and reflected in the purchase price, whereas direct taxes are absorbed by the seller and are not reflected in the purchase price. This assumption, although still widely held in administrative and governmental circles, has been directly challenged in a host of professional economic articles and books and in studies by certain international groups. Indeed, one can say that although the view that direct taxes are not shifted forward retains some support within the economic fraternity, the view that indirect taxes are fully shifted forward retains no such

9. *Report of the Committee on Turnover Taxation,* Cmnd. 2300 (March 1964).
10. *The Role of Direct and Indirect Taxes in the Federal Revenue System: a Conference Report of the National Bureau of Economic Research and the Brookings Institution* (Princeton: Princeton University Press, 1964).

support. This was explicitly recognized by the Internal Market Committee of the European Parliament in the well-known Deringer Report on the harmonization of indirect taxation in the European Economic Community.[11] One conclusion to be drawn from the economic literature is that full refund of an indirect tax constitutes in fact a subsidy to exports and therefore has the same distorting effect on international trade that any other export subsidy would have. A reciprocal conclusion is that an equalization charge on imported goods equal to the full amount of an internal tax could have a protectionist effect.[12]

As has already been indicated, there is no general agreement among economists on whether direct taxes are shifted forward. Some economists take the view that the corporate income tax is in general passed on to the consumer, and one econometric study goes so far as to conclude that this tax may be fully reflected, if not indeed more than fully reflected, in the price of goods.[13] Other economists hold, however, that direct taxes are not shifted forward or even that they are partly shifted backward to labor and raw materials supplies. Still others take the view that direct and indirect taxes do not differ greatly in this respect and that both types are largely passed on by the seller and reflected in the purchase price.[14] Finally, there are economists who point out that trade effects depend primarily on general price-level changes and that whatever the proper conclusion about shifting in the case of the imposition of an isolated tax, the introduction of a general, across-the-board tax affects the price level only to the extent that governmental authorities adopt inflationary fiscal and monetary policies. Under this analysis, lower prices for the factors of production are an alternative possibility, although some factor prices such as wage rates may be relatively inflexible on the downward side. In the end one must perhaps accept the view of Goode, who concludes that "the case for short-run shifting of a large fraction of the corporation income tax remains unproved," but that the case for some forward shifting is convincing.[15] The relevant question then becomes whether the difference in the degree of shifting is sufficiently

11. Deringer Report (Documents de Séance, European Parliament, Doc. 56, 20 Aug. 1963), para. 164. See also the conclusion of certain experts participating in an OECD symposium, GATT Document L/3009 (17 May 1968), p. 12.
12. Whether an equalization charge will have that effect may depend upon the extent to which it is shifted forward to the purchaser, which is another disputed issue.
13. See Marian Krzyzaniak and Richard A. Musgrave, *The Shifting of the Corporation Income Tax* (Baltimore: The Johns Hopkins Press, 1963).
14. See Earl R. Rolph, *The Theory of Fiscal Economies* (Berkeley: University of California Press, 1965), pp. 123–47; H. G. Brown, "The Incidence of a General Output on a General Sales Tax," *Journal of Political Economy*, XLVII (1939), p. 254; James M. Buchanan, *Fiscal Theory and Political Economy* (Chapel Hill: University of North Carolina Press, 1960), pp. 125–50.
15. Richard Goode, "Who Bears the Corporation Income Tax?" *University of Chicago Law Review*, XXXII (1965), p. 410, 416.

great to justify a diametrically opposite treatment of direct and indirect taxes.

That the rejection of the traditional assumption is to be found not merely in the Anglo-Saxon literature but also in the European thinking is indicated by the studies undertaken within the framework of the European Economic Community's efforts toward harmonization. The Deringer Report of the European Parliament observes that "one believes more and more today that, as a general rule, the income tax is reflected in the price of goods."[16] And the Neumark Report, an expert report prepared for the EEC Commission, concedes that income taxes are shifted forward, albeit to a lesser extent than indirect taxes.[17]

### Prospects and Possibilities for Amendment

For all the difference of opinion on whether direct taxes are shifted forward, it is hard to find authors who support without qualification the assumption behind the GATT rules. The question for statesmen and for international economic institutions is therefore whether that assumption still commands sufficient support to justify the diametrically opposite treatment of direct and indirect taxes or whether it would not be better to seek some formal or informal relaxation of the rigid distinction. Since the degree of shifting of both kinds of taxes is likely to depend upon the particular circumstances, it may well be that a case-by-case approach to the border tax adjustment problem would give not only theoretically more correct results but also results more widely accepted as just and appropriate.

A moment's consideration of the dimensions of the problem that would be involved in reviewing and changing the levels of all equalization charges and drawbacks will indicate that it would be impractical and perhaps politically unwise to attempt any wholesale revision of existing rates. Indeed, the only practical course might be to exclude individual challenges to existing levels (except, of course, on the ground that the drawback or equalization charge in question exceeds 100 percent of the internal indirect tax in violation of the existing rules). GATT review of drawback and equalization charge practices would in that case be limited to changes in levels.

Such a concession to inertia could be justified on theoretical grounds. It appears to be generally conceded by economists that however much the present GATT rules may disadvantage countries relying on direct taxes and favor countries relying on indirect taxes, the distorting effect on international trade

---

16. Deringer Report (Documents de Séance, European Parliament, Doc. 56, 20 Aug. 1963), para. 85. See also Günter Schmölders, *Finanzpolitik* (Berlin: Springer-Verlag, 1955), pp. 229–31.

17. "Report of the Fiscal and Financial Committee," in *The EEC Reports on Tax Harmonization* (Amsterdam: International Bureau of Fiscal Documentation, 1963), pp. 93, 113–15 (unofficial translation).

tends to be ironed out over time by adjustments in exchange rates. Since even the fixed exchange rates of the present international monetary regime tend to be adjusted from time to time, it may be concluded that differential patterns of drawbacks and equalization charges are reflected in existing exchange rates, at least to the extent that no problem of time lag is present. Insofar as these patterns are based upon an inappropriate assumption concerning the shifting of taxes, however, they may tend to distort trade as among different products and as between goods (which are generally subject to border tax adjustments) and services (which are less frequently subject to such adjustments).

Such distortion is beyond the reach of the GATT in the present state of international institutional development. Something that is not reflected in exchange rates under the existing fixed-exchange system but that is surely within the reach of the GATT as an international institution is a change in the rate of drawbacks or equalization charges not associated with any change in the internal tax rate. Because such a change may have trade effects that are similar to those resulting from the increase of a customs duty or an export subsidy, the General Agreement should be amended to provide that contracting parties have the same rights with respect to such a change that they have with respect to the increase of a bound duty or of a subsidy. That is to say, contracting parties suffering trade effects should be able, in the case of a change in equalization charges, to demand compensation and to retaliate in accordance with the provisions of Article XXIII and, in the case of a change in drawbacks, to invoke the subsidy provisions of Article XVI. In view of the trade effects resulting from border tax adjustments, these rights under the General Agreement should be available even though the change in question could theretofore have been defined as only an adjustment to make the drawback or the equalization charge more nearly equal to the internal tax.

GATT procedures to deal with changes in border tax adjustments might be worked out in a number of different ways. What follow are suggested procedures that resemble as closely as possible existing GATT procedures for similar problems and at the same time focus on the essential question of the trade effects of the individual change.

Contracting parties would be free to increase equalization charges without prior approval, but they would be required to give notice to the CONTRACTING PARTIES of any increase. Any contracting party that considered itself injured would be permitted to demand consultations. The contracting party that had increased the equalization charges in question would be required to present not only full information about the legal and administrative issues raised but also complete statistics from which it would be possible to judge what the trade effects of the change might be.

The issues in the ensuing consultations would not be the abstract questions whether the internal tax was shifted and, if so, to what extent it was shifted; rather, the sole issue would be what the protective effect of the change in the equalization charge might be. If the consulting contracting parties agreed that a protective effect was present, the contracting party that had increased the equalization charge would be required to offer appropriate compensation in the form of a reduction either in customs duties or in other equalization charges. If agreement could not be reached on the existence or nonexistence of a protective effect or if the appropriate compensatory adjustment remained at issue, the nullification and impairment procedures of Article XXIII:2 would be available, and, upon authorization by the CONTRACTING PARTIES under that provision, the injured contracting party would be permitted to suspend such concessions or other obligations as the CONTRACTING PARTIES might determine to be appropriate under the circumstances.

In the case of an increase in the export refund on a primary product, the consultations would be designed to determine whether the increase had an effect essentially similar to an export subsidy and, if so, whether the contracting party imposing the increase thereby gained "more than an equitable share of world export trade in that product" under Article XVI, Section B:3. If agreement could not be reached on the effect of the increase or if an increase the effect of which was agreed to be essentially similar to an export subsidy were not revoked, the complaining contracting party could invoke the nullification and impairment procedures of Article XXIII:2. In the case of an increase in the export refund on a nonprimary product, the consultations would turn on whether the increase had an effect essentially similar to an export subsidy and whether the contracting party imposing the increase had signed either the "Giving Effect" Declaration or the "Standstill" Declaration.[18]

The exclusive concern of these procedures would be how far the increase in the border tax adjustment in question had a protective or subsidizing effect. No distinction would be made between the direct and indirect varieties of internal taxes, and the defense that the increased border tax adjustment did no more than compensate for the internal tax would be unavailable.

An alternative solution would be to permit the defense that the increased border tax adjustment did no more than compensate for the internal tax, but to convert the inquiry into an economic inquiry as to the extent of shifting. Whether the border tax adjustment would be held to be no greater than the internal tax would then depend upon the extent to which the border tax adjustment and the internal tax were shifted. It would be necessary to arrive at a determination of "economic" compensation rather than mere "arithmetic" compensation.

This latter alternative would have, in comparison with the first, two practical

---

18. See discussion in chapter 8, "Subsidies," supra.

disadvantages. First, one would be required to attempt to determine just how much particular taxes were shifted in particular situations, a difficult exercise under any circumstances and particularly difficult for an international institution. In view of the technical problems created under the present arithmetic compensation rule of such phenomena as average rates for groups of products, it is unlikely that an economic compensation rule would prove acceptable to governments. Second, whatever advantages that countries relying heavily on indirect taxes might gain from being permitted to increase border tax adjustments in cases of undercompensation would be more than outweighed by the possibility of widespread introduction of new border tax adjustments by direct-tax countries. For this reason, indirect-tax countries would probably consider it wrong to permit the defense that the increased border tax adjustment did no more than compensate for the internal tax.[19]

One problem of the greatest importance, not only in theory but also in the realm of practical politics, is whether an increase in a border tax adjustment that is matched simultaneously and with arithmetic exactitude by an increase in an internal tax should be treated in the same way as other increases in a border tax adjustment. A failure to increase the border tax adjustment to the same extent as the internal tax would constitute a proportional reduction of the adjustment. In view of the frequency of increases of internal taxes under contemporary conditions, a requirement of GATT consultations in the case of any such increase might be considered by many countries to be an improper infringement of their fiscal sovereignty. On the other hand, it must be noted that an increase in a border tax adjustment can match an internal tax increase with mathematical exactitude only in the case of certain kinds of taxes. For example, an increase in a border tax adjustment intended to be equal to an increase in

---

19. It should be noted that the division of the world into indirect-tax and direct-tax countries is an oversimplification. Not only do most, if not all, major trading countries use both kinds of taxes and use border tax adjustments for at least some of their indirect taxes, but the relative revenue balance of direct and indirect taxes may look sharply different when those taxes are related to volumes of international trade. If, to take a strictly hypothetical example, a given country relied on direct taxes for 40 percent of its revenue and on indirect taxes for 60 percent of its revenue, but none of the classes of items subject to indirect taxes were exported, one would make a mistake to classify that country as an indirect-tax country when considering drawbacks. For a statistical comparison of the relative degree of reliance on direct and indirect taxes in various major trading countries, see Otto Eckstein, "Comparison of European and United States Tax Structures and Growth Implications," in *The Role of Direct and Indirect Taxes in the Federal Revenue System: A Conference Report of the National Bureau of Economic Research and the Brookings Institution* (Princeton: Princeton University Press, 1964). The differences between the United States and Europe in this respect can easily be exaggerated. See Robert Z. Aliber and Herbert Stein, "The Price of U.S. Exports and the Mix of U.S. Direct and Indirect Taxes," *American Economic Review,* LIV (1964), p. 703; GATT Document L/3009 (17 May 1968), p. 3.

rates of a cascade turnover tax may or may not be equal in fact, particularly after industry patterns have adjusted to the increase in the turnover tax rates. Similarly, an increase in the border tax adjustment for a particular finished product designed to equal an increase in an indirect tax on capital equipment used in the manufacture of that product may or may not be equal in fact, particularly after the industry has adjusted its relative inputs of the capital equipment and other resources to reflect any resulting shift in comparative costs. Where averaging is used in computing border tax adjustments, moreover, an increase in the border tax adjustment for a particular product may turn out to be unequal to an increase in the internal tax.

It may also be observed that even if mathematical exactitude results, there may be a negative trade effect. That is to say, an equal increase in an equalization charge and in an internal indirect tax may reduce imports by reducing total consumption of the product in question. This trade effect would not in general constitute a protective effect. There might be, however, an intention to protect domestic production of a competitive product; for example, an equal increase in the internal tax and the equalization charge on margarine might be designed to give additional protection to domestic production of butter. In this case Article III:2 (second sentence) might be violated.[20]

A compromise solution to the problem of an increase in a border tax adjustment that was equal to an increase in an internal tax would be to provide that an interested contracting party could demand consultations on any occasion when it was convinced that a particular increase in a border tax adjustment had a protective effect. The contracting parties concerned would be required to consult in accordance with the same procedures used where an increase in a border tax adjustment was not matched by an increase in an internal tax. The question in the consultations, it should be noted, would not be whether there was a trade effect (for any increase in taxes that was shifted forward could be expected to reduce total purchases), but rather whether there was an increase in protective effect.

In the event that the General Agreement could not be amended to make it conform more closely to the state of contemporary economic knowledge, recourse might be had to procedures that are already available under the General Agreement but have not yet been widely used. The nullification and impairment procedures of Article XXIII are available to a contracting party that considers that "any benefit accruing to it directly or indirectly" has been "nullified or impaired" by "the application by another contracting party of any measure, whether or not it conflicts with the provisions" of the General Agreement.[21] Should one contracting party increase an equalization charge in such a way as

20. See discussion in chapter 7, "Internal Taxes," supra.
21. See discussion in chapter 20, "Dispute Settlement," infra.

to increase the protection afforded domestic industry on a bound item (which would be most likely to occur if the increase in the equalization charge were not matched by an internal tax increase, but could occur, as explained above, even if there was a matching internal tax increase), another contracting party that considered that this action "nullified or impaired" a tariff concession previously made to it could invoke the procedures of Article XXIII, even though the equalization charge increase did not violate the General Agreement. Similarly, an increase in a drawback that, in the view of an interested contracting party, had the effect of nullifying or impairing a "benefit" to which that contracting party was entitled under the export subsidy procedures of Article XVI could be challenged under Article XXIII. To be sure, the chances of securing the support of the CONTRACTING PARTIES to retaliatory action as required by Article XXIII:2 might be slight in such a situation, but the right to demand consultations is a weapon of no small utility. In the end the most important point to be made in connection with Article XXIII may be that, since the possibility of demanding consultations exists in all circumstances, it would be desirable to amend the General Agreement to provide for special consultations in connection with changes in border tax adjustments in order to bring the Agreement into better conformity with economic common sense.

# PART 4

**The GATT
and the
Broad
Economic Problems
of Our Time**

# 14 Less-Developed Countries

One of the fields in which the GATT as an institution has experienced the most dramatic change has been the relations between developed and less-developed countries. Not only has the General Agreement been amended several times to elaborate further the rules governing less-developed-country trade, but the GATT as an institution has changed from a passive caretaker of a multilateral legal instrument to an international body affirmatively, and at times agressively, attempting to promote the exports of less-developed countries.

This evolution in GATT's role, which will be traced in this chapter, may be attributed to a number of interrelated factors. In part the change merely reflects a growth of awareness of the economic plight of the less-developed countries. In part the change also reflects an increased emphasis by the less-developed countries on the importance of exports in the development process and a recognition on all sides that a major barrier to development has been the commercial policy of the developed countries themselves. And the change can also be attributed in part to the GATT's efforts to counter the institutional competition of the United Nations Conference on Trade and Development. But to all of these factors must be added a growing appreciation in GATT circles of the limits of substantive rules and of the absolute necessity of improved procedures for the attainment of GATT's objectives.

## The Havana Charter

The original U.S. proposals for an international trade organization did not include more than passing reference to economic development. It was the U.S. position that the less-developed countries could best develop by participating fully in a multilateral nondiscriminatory system with the lowest possible levels of tariffs and no quantitative restrictions. This position proved totally unacceptable to the less-developed world, which sought both affirmative commitments by all member countries to further the process of economic development, and, more important, specific exceptions to many of the prohibitions of the Charter in order to permit the less-developed countries to follow an independent commercial policy. The reigning view in less-developed countries was that economic development—which to those countries meant industrialization—required the creation of import substitution industries. It was asserted that such industries could flourish only behind high tariff walls supplemented, for both security and flexibility, by quantitative restrictions and even by outright embargoes on imports from developed countries. The division on this issue between the United States on the one hand, supported with varying degrees of enthusiasm by Canada, the United Kingdom and certain other developed countries, and, on the other hand, the less-developed countries, supported and at times led by Australia, gave rise to one of the most important disputes in the drafting of the Charter.

When the dust had finally settled, the Havana Charter contained a large number of provisions on economic development of widely disparate character. In general, only the specific exceptions to the commercial policy prohibitions of the Havana Charter were carried over from the Havana Charter to the General Agreement.[1] With the death of the ITO, Chapter III of the Havana Charter, entitled "Economic Development and Reconstruction," slipped into desuetude, with the exception of Article 13, which became Article XVIII of the GATT. Elaborate provisions on the supply of capital funds and other "facilities" for economic development, on international investment and on preferential agreements among less-developed countries were thereby allowed to fall into legal oblivion.[2]

The Havana Charter contained a further chapter of great interest to less-developed countries, namely, the chapter "Intergovernmental Commodity Agreements." Here, however, the U.S. proposals had contained provisions on the subject, and the disagreements were over details.[3] The elaborate provisions, running sixteen articles and constituting a blueprint for the drafting and administration of commodity agreements, were, moreover, to be accorded some status under the General Agreement, even though not incorporated in that instrument. Article XX(h) of the General Agreement (as revised at the 1955 review conference) establishes a general exception to all other obligations and prohibitions in the General Agreement for measures "undertaken in pursuance

---

1. On the history of the dispute and the nature of the compromise, see William Adams Brown, Jr., *The United States and the Restoration of World Trade* (Washington: Brookings Institution, 1950), pp. 97–104; and Clair Wilcox, *A Charter for World Trade* (New York: Macmillan, 1949), pp. 140–52.
2. Havana Charter, Arts. 8–12, 14–15.
3. See Brown, pp. 217–22; Wilcox, pp. 114–25.

of obligations under any intergovernmental commodity agreement which conforms to criteria submitted to the CONTRACTING PARTIES and not disapproved by them or which is itself so submitted and not so disapproved." In an interpretative note that goes well beyond interpretation, it is stated that this provision "extends to any commodity agreement which conforms to the principles approved by the Economic and Social Council in its resolution 30(IV) of 28 March 1947"—a resolution that in turn calls upon members of the United Nations to adopt as a general guide the "principles of the Havana Charter chapter on intergovernmental commodity agreements."[4]

## Article XVIII

Since commodity agreements were mentioned only in a passing reference, Article XVIII was the principal provision in the General Agreement dealing directly with the trade problems of less-developed countries. It represented at one and the same time, almost to the point of caricature, the passive legislative approach to trade problems which was typical of the early GATT. From the viewpoint of economic policy, Article XVIII reflected the predominance of the import substitution approach to economic development.

Even after extensive revision at the 1955 Review Session, Article XVIII retains these essential characteristics. The theory of the article is quite simply that less-developed countries should be freer than developed countries to impose quantitative and other restrictions in order to protect infant industries and to combat payments imbalances.[5] But to prevent abuse of this special dispensation, less-developed countries invoking Article XVIII are to submit such restrictions to regular review by the CONTRACTING PARTIES.

Section B of revised Article XVIII is only a somewhat more flexible version of Article XII, the basic provision on the use of quantitative restrictions for balance-of-payments purposes. Prior to the 1955 revision, balance-of-payments consultations were held under Article XII for developed and less-developed countries alike, but when Article XII was tightened up, it became necessary to provide a safety-valve for less-developed countries under Section B of Article XVIII. Most of this latter provision was copied verbatim from Article XII. Whereas a developed country must show under Article XII:2(a) that restrictions are necessary to "forestall the imminent threat of . . . a serious decline in its monetary reserves," such a threat, even though not "imminent," suffices for

---

4. The reference apparently should have been to resolution 373 (XIII) of 13 September 1951. See Herman Walker, "The International Law of Commodity Agreements," *Law and Contemporary Problems,* XXVIII (1963), p. 392, 401.

5. Section A of Article XVIII further assumes that less-developed countries should have greater freedom to modify and withdraw tariff concessions than do the developed countries. Section A has little practical importance.

a less-developed country under XVIII:9. And consultations are required of less-developed countries only every second year rather than every year, in recognition of the persistent character of their payments imbalances.[6]

More important in principle is Section C of Article XVIII. But it has been invoked so rarely that it would be superfluous to explore this exceedingly complex provision at length. It suffices to say that less-developed countries may impose quantitative restrictions (or any other "specific measure affecting imports") where "required to promote the establishment of a particular industry with a view to raising the general standard of living of its people," provided that "no measure consistent with the other provisions of [the General] Agreement is practicable to achieve that objective."[7]

Less-developed countries have passed up this open invitation to the use of quotas to protect infant industries for perhaps three reasons. First, most of these countries suffer from payments imbalances and may justify their quantitative restrictions under the less rigorous balance-of-payments procedures of Section B. Second, some very early decisions under the pre-1955 Article XVIII made clear that that article was not to be a carte blanche for ignoring tariff concessions or for protecting industries that were merely weak rather than infant.[8] Third, less-developed countries have been reluctant to subject themselves to the searching inquiry and the annual reporting requirement and review that Article XVIII:6 makes a condition for a Section C release. The consequences of these three inhibiting factors is that, except for some reliance on Article XVIII in the early years of the GATT by Cuba, Haiti, and India, Ceylon has (in more recent years) been the only country to make major use of that Article.[9]

## The Panel of Experts and Committee III

Perhaps the turning point in the GATT's relations with less-developed countries was the publication in 1958 of the Report by a Panel of Experts entitled *Trends in International Trade*. The Panel was made up of four world-renowned

---

6. Compare Article XVIII:12(b) with Article XII:4(b).
7. Art. XVIII:13 and 14. After Ceylon discontinued Section C measures on 12 November 1966, no contracting party was applying such measures (*Basic Instruments,* 15th Supp. (1968), p. 65).
8. See the description of the U.K.–Northern Rhodesian and the Cuban textile cases in Gerard Curzon, *Multilateral Commercial Diplomacy* (London: Michael Joseph, 1965), p. 212. On the question of bound duties, see, however, paragraph 18 of the revised Article XVIII.
9. See references to releases and to the annual reviews of the Ceylonese release under "Economic Development," *Basic Instruments,* 15th Supp. (1966), pp. 219–20. Even Ceylon abandoned reliance upon Section C in 1966 (*Basic Instruments,* 15th Supp. [1968], p. 65).

economists—Habeler, Meade, Tinbergen, and Campos. Dubbed the Habeler Report after the chairman of the panel, this searching inquiry into the trade relations of less-developed countries did not mince words. The substance of the report was that the predicament of the underdeveloped countries was due in no small measure to the trade policies of the developed countries.

The GATT reacted quickly and responsibly to the implied criticism of its prior complacent passivity by the inauguration in 1958 of a Programme for Trade Expansion. This was to be a program of action, albeit the means were to be the traditional GATT means of reducing trade barriers. One of the committees established, Committee III, was given responsibility for trade measures restricting less-developed-country exports.[10]

Much of the work of Committee III involved studies of existing barriers. Although these studies resulted—particularly in the first years after 1958—in little progress, they were far from a waste of time. Emphasis was placed upon securing detailed information on the specific products in which the less-developed countries had an export interest, and then, through product-by-product studies, upon obtaining precise information on the nature of the barriers in the developed countries to the importation of those products from the less-developed countries—particularly such barriers as tariffs, quantitative restrictions, revenue and internal fiscal charges, state-trading, and import monopolies. The facts developed by Committee III (and subsequently by its successor organ, the GATT Trade and Development Committee, by the UNCTAD, and by certain scholars) gave a startling view of the extent to which the developed countries were hindering not only some of the traditional exports of the less-developed countries but also, and perhaps more important in view of the latters' interest in industrialization, exports of manufactures.[11]

### Tariffs

Committee III found that high tariffs faced exports of less-developed countries in a wide range of products, particularly vegetable oils, coffee, tea, cocoa products, jute products, cotton products, sporting goods, and leather goods in addition to certain more sophisticated manufactured products. The less-developed countries had experienced particular difficulties in negotiating reductions of those duties, especially because the principal suppliers of some of these products were not less-developed countries and because the less-developed countries often had little to offer in tariff negotiations. They had little to offer

10. *Basic Instruments,* 7th Supp. (1959), p. 27, 29.

11. Except as otherwise indicated, the information in the following paragraphs on specific trade barriers is drawn from the reports of Committee III cited in *Basic Instruments,* 15th Supp. (1968), p. 215.

because the imports of greatest importance to their development programs (such as capital goods) often entered at minimal duties, and because, in the absence of adequate internal tax systems, they were dependent upon customs duties on remaining imports for governmental revenues. Of 4,400 tariff concessions made in the Dillon Round, only 160 were on items then considered to be of export interest to the less-developed countries. Duties on manufactured products of peculiar interest to less-developed countries therefore tended to remain higher than duties on more sophisticated manufactures produced only by developed countries.

But more serious than the absolute level of tariffs in developed countries were two kinds of discrimination—on the basis of origin and on the basis of the degree of processing. Discrimination on the basis of origin was found in a number of products, primarily as a result of arrangements entered into by the then nascent European Economic Community with its African associates. The margin of preference on cocoa beans, for example, was to be 9 percent, a decisive advantage in the large European market for those countries coming within the association arrangements.

Discrimination in tariff rates on the basis of the degree of processing was even more important. The impact of such discrimination was, from the first, one of the major themes of the reports of Committee III. Where the rate for processed products was considerably higher than for the constituent raw materials (as in cocoa, copper, oilseeds and the like), an important impediment to the development of processing industries in the less-developed countries resulted. This was particularly serious because the principal hope for industrialization in those less-developed countries that depended upon one or two major export products was to undertake the first stages of processing before export. Not only was the differential tariff structure in developed countries a powerful disincentive to such a development strategy, but, as later academic commentators made explicit, such a nominal rate structure resulted in startlingly high rates of effective protection for the processing industries in the developed countries. Where raw materials entered duty-free, the effective rate on the value added became even more dramatic. If, for example, the raw material entered duty-free, if the rate of duty on the processed product were 20 percent, and if the value added in processing were 25 percent, the effective rate of protection on the value so added would be 80 percent. Once attention was focused on the effective rather than the nominal rate, it was quickly recognized that reducing rates on raw materials while retaining existing rates for processed products, although perhaps stimulating use of the raw materials, tended to keep the less-developed countries in their traditional position as unindustrialized raw-materials suppliers.

The hypothetical example given is not extreme. A 10 percent tariff differential in favor of copper wire resulted in a 77 percent rate of effective protection for the processing industry in both the United Kingdom and the European Economic Community, and a 3 percent differential resulted in a 23 percent rate of effective protection in Sweden.[12] Similar calculations based on the differential between the rates for shelled groundnuts and for crude oil and cake made therefrom yielded effective rates of protection for the processing industry of 80 percent in the United Kingdom and 140 percent in the European Economic Community.[13] Calculations by D. Gale Johnson showed effective rates of protection in the European Economic Community on the processing of soybeans to be 160 percent.[14] Where processing adds little to the value of the product, the consequences can be extreme. In the case of refined coconut oil a nominal 5.7 percent differential in the United States gives a 57 percent rate of effective protection, and a nominal 15 percent differential in the European Economic Community gives an effective rate of protection of 150 percent.[15] Moreover, if one isolates the value added by labor (which a number of economists have argued is an appropriate approach on the ground that capital can flow much more freely than labor), effective rates of protection on the value added by labor of well over 100 percent can be found on a wide range of products, such as—using statistics for the United States—cutlery, glass containers, products of purchased glass, leather gloves, and tufted carpets and rugs.[16] One must be careful, of course, not to exaggerate by selection of egregious examples the average level of effective protection for processing industries. Nevertheless, for most processed and manufactured products of interest to less-developed countries, effective rates of protection in the United States run as high as 25 to 30 percent and in a great number of cases much higher.[17]

## Quantitative Restrictions

Committee III found quantitative restrictions to be an impediment to less-developed country exports of vegetable seeds and oils, coffee, raw cotton,

12. Curzon, p. 228.
13. Ibid., p. 229.
14. Cited in Harry G. Johnson, "The Theory of Tariff Structure, with Special Reference to World Trade and Development," in Harry G. Johnson and Peter B. Kenen, *Trade and Development* (Geneva: Librairie Droz, 1965).
15. Calculations by Padma Mallampally, in Harry G. Johnson, *Economic Policies toward Less Developed Countries* (Washington: Brookings Institution, 1966), p. 91 (Table 2).
16. Giorgio Basevi, "The United States Tariff Structure: Estimates of Effective Rates of Protection of United States Industries and Industrial Labor," *Review of Economics and Statistics,* XLVIII (1966), p. 147, summarized in Johnson, *Economic Policies,* pp. 100–101 (Table 5).
17. See generally, Basevi; Bela Balassa, "Tariff Protection in Industrial Countries: An Evaluation," *Journal of Political Economy,* LXXIII (1965), p. 573. See also Balassa, "Tariff Protection in Industrial Nations and Its Effects on the Exports of Processed Goods from Developing Nations" (undated mimeographed paper).

tobacco, tropical timber, jute manufactures, cotton manufactures and sewing machines. But the effects of these restrictions were made worse by discrimination similar to that obtaining in tariffs. Discrimination by origin was perhaps more common than in the case of tariffs because of the more prevalent use of discriminatory quantitative restrictions in the 1950s to limit imports from countries, whether less-developed or developed, in other currency groupings. And when the OEEC began to eliminate quantitative restrictions under the Code of Liberalization in the 1950s, the OEEC member countries did not simultaneously extend their liberalization lists to imports from nonmember countries. Committee III found discrimination by origin to be important for such major products as cotton and jute manufactures, vegetable seeds and oils, cocoa, coffee, and copper. Moreover, discriminatory application of quantitative restrictions on the basis of the degree of processing was also common, notably for vegetable oils, cocoa, lead, and copper. When balance-of-payments pressures eased, it was not uncommon for developed countries to eliminate quotas on raw materials while retaining them on processed products. The effect, even more certainly than in the case of differential tariff rates, was to tend to keep the less-developed countries locked into their position as raw materials suppliers. Whatever the nature of the quantitative restrictions, many of them were flatly illegal under the General Agreement.

## Internal Taxes

Less-developed countries were faced with substantial internal taxes in developed countries for a wide range of products of particular export interest to them. Sometimes, as with cotton and jute manufactures, oilseeds, and vegetable oils, these internal taxes were also applicable to domestic products, and so the less-developed countries did not have a strong case. But for many products, notably tropical products, there was no production in the importing developed countries. Such internal taxes were of particular importance for coffee, tea, and cocoa, not only because of the importance of these three products in international trade (where coffee is the second largest product) and in the trade of individual less-developed countries, but also because of the high rate of the internal taxes. Internal taxes and fiscal charges for coffee, measured as a percentage of the import price, reached 89 percent in Germany, 99 percent in Finland, and 101 percent in Italy. Comparable calculations showed tea burdened up to 97 percent in Austria and 112 percent in Germany and cocoa bearing burdens as high as 79 percent in Denmark.

Although the less-developed countries were outraged by the extraordinary level of these taxes, their demands for their diminution met with considerable resistance from European countries that relied on such taxes for revenue. Because of the inelasticity of demand for these products, at least in the short run, it was clear that the immediate effect in most European countries of reducing the taxes would be a greater loss of revenue to the developed importing country than the increase in export earnings. Even if that relationship might have reversed itself over time as consumers acquired a taste for the beverage, the revenue lost would have had to be replaced by some other kind of tax—no doubt harder both to enact and to collect. The less-developed countries, however they might have sympathized with the fiscal problems of the developed European countries, were of the view that it was improper to burden their exports in order to raise revenue that flowed to the developed countries rather than to themselves. The less-developed countries were also angered by the refusal of most developed countries to negotiate on such internal taxes in the regular tariff conferences, although the conference rules permitted such negotiation, as did an interpretative note to Article 17 of the Havana Charter.

### State Trading and Import Monopolies

In a few products the practices of state trading countries and the activities of import monopolies constituted a substantial barrier, although the height of this kind of barrier was uncommonly difficult to measure. For some products—including coffee, cocoa, tea, and tobacco—the difference between the import price and the price to consumers reflected a disguised tax of considerable proportions. For other products—including jute manufactures, tobacco, and vegetable oils—the activities of state agencies suggested protectionist motives. The failure to purchase the full quantity demanded domestically at the import price was, of course, analytically comparable to a quantitative restriction. The efforts to seek out such protectionist uses of import monopolies were handicapped by some countries' failure to submit information on their state-trading activities.[18]

### Other Restrictions

Among other developed country policies found by Committee III to constitute barriers to exports of the less-developed countries were mixing regulations (tobacco), price support programs (cotton), and surplus disposal programs (tobacco).

### The Action Programme

Although the product-by-product inquiries helped to bring about substantial relaxation of developed country restrictions on imports from less-developed

18. See further discussion in chapter 18, "State Trading," infra.

countries[19] and although Committee III began to ask increasingly embarrassing questions of the developing countries and to make steadily more specific recommendations (including a series of principles enshrined in 1961 in a Declaration on Promotion of the Trade of the Less-Developed Countries),[20] the response to the work of Committee III was essentially disappointing. The developed countries undertook no precise commitments and were still too accustomed to viewing the GATT as a passive organization in which barriers to trade were reduced only by quid pro quo negotiations, to be willing to take extensive unilateral steps toward the reduction of barriers to less-developed-country exports. Nor were the less-developed countries able to arrive at any common program that might have aided them in moving simultaneously toward the opening of their domestic markets to less-developed-country products. Finally, in 1963, a group of twenty-one less-developed countries, having decided that five years of study following the Habeler Report were sufficient and that the time for action had come, introduced a resolution calling for what became known as the Action Programme.

The Action Programme was not merely a means of putting pressure on the developed countries but was also, since none of the twenty-one proposing countries were associated with the European Economic Community, a means of by-passing the EEC associated countries. The latter, enjoying their preferences in the EEC, were felt to be responsible for some of the inaction.

The Action Programme was based upon a series of related notions: first, that it was important to obtain specific commitments to eliminate barriers, even barriers that were illegal under the General Agreement; second, that it was better to have a commitment to eliminate a barrier at some future date than no commitment at all; third, that until trade barriers were eliminated, it was important to have a commitment not to introduce new barriers; and fourth, that annual reporting by the developed countries would place continuing pressure upon them and thereby help to assure fulfillment of the commitments.

The Action Programme therefore called for the following measures on exports of less-developed countries: (1) a standstill on all new tariff and non-tariff barriers; (2) elimination within one year, or, in the event of special problems, by the end of 1965 at the latest, of illegal quantitative restrictions; (3) duty-free entry of tropical products by the end of 1963; (4) elimination of tariffs on primary products (date unstated); (5) adoption of a schedule for

---

19. See Staffan B. Linder, "The Significance of GATT for Under-Developed Countries," paras. 186–92, reprinted in *Proceedings of the United Nations Conference on Trade and Development,* Vol. 5 (1964), pp. 502, 529–30, for an attempt to quantify the progress.

20. *Basic Instruments,* 10th Supp. (1962), p. 28.

reduction and elimination of tariffs on semiprocessed and processed products, including a reduction of at least 50 percent over three years; (6) elimination not later than the end of 1965 of internal taxes on products wholly or mainly produced in less-developed countries; and (7) annual reports on steps to be taken under the Action Programme. In addition, an eighth, precatory provision was included calling for urgent consideration of other joint measures.[21]

Because of the inability of the twenty-one moving less-developed countries to secure the full support of all the developed countries, the Action Programme acquired a rather original legal status. The ministers of all industrialized countries, with the exception of the EEC member states, agreed to the Programme. The ministers of the EEC member states "endorsed, in principle, the general objectives of the Programme of Action and declared themselves ready to contribute, for their part, to the fullest extent possible, towards the development of the developing countries."[22] Even the non-EEC ministers hedged their agreement about with a number of important reservations so that their concurrence took on the appearance of an agreement in principle only.[23] The EEC ministers, reflecting hesitations about the effect of the program upon their African associates and influenced by French notions of managed international markets for commodities, attempted to shift the locus of the ministerial debate by arguing that "more positive measures were required to achieve the marked and rapid increase in the export earnings of the developing countries as a whole, which was the fundamental objective."[24] They mentioned commodity agreements and regional arrangements, and the Belgian representative launched the "Brasseur Plan" for preferences by developed countries for less-developed countries.

It is a curious point of history that at the end of 1963, when the less-developed countries urged the developed countries to commit themselves to a GATT-type barrier-lowering approach to the problems of the less-developed countries, the developed countries were unable to give them full satisfaction because some of the developed countries were already interested in more radical ideas that had been advanced by some less-developed countries within the GATT and that were to become the platform of the less-developed countries at the United Nations Trade and Development Conference the following year. In part, the developed countries were only reflecting the ambitions and vested interests of the less-developed countries with which they were most

21. See text of the Action Programme in ibid., 12th Supp. (1964), p. 36.
22. Ibid., p. 38.
23. Ibid., pp. 38–39.
24. Ibid., p. 39; see Commission of the European Economic Community, *Seventh Annual Report on the Activities of the Community* (1964), pp. 253–55.

closely associated. Not many months after the adoption of the Action Programme, the Deputy Executive Secretary, Finn Gundelach, explained some of the difficulties in eliminating tariffs on tropical products:

> Exports from the States associated with the European Economic Community receive preferential treatment in the markets of the Community, as do countries of the Commonwealth in the United Kingdom market. A third category of country, such as those of Latin America, or Indonesia, do not benefit from preferences of this kind. There is thus a cross-current of advantages and disadvantages and of special relationship which tends to add a political ingredient to what is already a difficult economic problem.[25]

But if the Action Programme contained no more than commitments in principle (and was never formally adopted by the CONTRACTING PARTIES), these commitments nevertheless existed, and there was some quickening in the rate of dismantling of the barriers against less-developed country exports.[26] An Action Committee was established to assist in the implementation of the Action Programme; its authority overlapped in many ways with that of Committee III.

Progress was particularly gratifying in the elimination of customs duties on certain tropical products, although the progress could be attributed in part to efforts undertaken by the GATT prior to the adoption of the Action Programme. An extensive study on tropical products had been undertaken by a special group that had been established in 1962.[27] Despite the difficulties involving competition between those less-developed countries that were associated with the EEC and those that were not so associated, all but a few quantitative restrictions had been eliminated, and customs duties on tea and tropical timber had been eliminated or firm commitments for elimination had been given by the end of 1963.[28]

## Part IV of the General Agreement

Before the implementation phase of the Action Programme could succeed or fail, a new set of proposals for institutional change were advanced in the form of proposed amendments of the General Agreement. Sensing that the less-developed countries had to be given "something," thoughts in the capitals of the developed countries turned to additional language in the General Agreement

---

25. Finn Gundelach, "The GATT and the Developing Countries—an Appraisal," Document INT(63)546 (Dec. 1963), p. 4.
26. See Report by the Chairman of the Action Committee, Document L/2307 (17 Nov. 1964) and Document L/2307/Add. 1 (19 Nov. 1964).
27. See The CONTRACTING PARTIES to the General Agreement on Tariffs and Trade, *Trade in Tropical Products* (1963).
28. Gundelach, p. 5.

and, secondarily, to additional institutional machinery. At the May 1963 ministerial meeting—the same meeting at which the Action Programme had been agreed upon—the ministers "recognized the need for an adequate legal and institutional framework to enable the Contracting Parties to discharge their responsibilities in connexion with the work of expanding the trade of less-developed countries"[29] and charged a committee with the task of preparing a draft of the appropriate amendments. There can be little doubt that this step was a reaction to the preparations, already in progress, for the 1964 United Nations Conference on Trade and Development and that the increasing grandeur of the format during the year and one-half of drafting was a reaction to the growth of the UNCTAD from an isolated United Nations conference to a permanent body commanding the allegiance of the entire less-developed world.

First thought of as an amendment to Article XVIII, the work product of the drafting committee became a chapter of Part II[30] and thereafter an independent part on a parity with the three preceding parts of the General Agreement. This latter exalted status was reached just before approval in November 1964 no doubt in order to underline the importance the GATT attached to the problems of the less-developed countries. It became the only part to bear a name, and, it should be noted, this name—"Trade and Development"—was designed to emphasize an interest going beyond trade, the traditional field of GATT activity.

Part IV can be considered from two points of view. It is easy, first of all, to be skeptical of the entire exercise. There is not much doubt that the less-developed countries obtained a great deal of verbiage and very few precise commitments. As an analysis of the language, undertaken below, will show, full implementation of the 1963 Action Programme would have given the less-developed countries much more in concrete terms. On the other hand, the adoption of Part IV was of great symbolic importance in expanding the views of all contracting parties concerning the new role of the GATT in the thorny problem of development. This role had in fact been rehearsed in Committee III but had never received full acceptance in certain governmental quarters. Furthermore, Part IV provided the legal framework for the work of the Trade and Development Committee, and it was this work, together with the Kennedy Round, which was to provide the base for any real progress in the following years.

Part IV is long and complex, and little would be gained by a detailed analysis of the language and the origins of each of the ideas. A brief review of the provisions is useful, however, in indicating how few concrete commitments and

29. *Basic Instruments,* 12th Supp. (1964), p. 36, 45.
30. Document L/2281 (26 Oct. 1964).

how few qualifications of other provisions of the General Agreement are actually involved. It will be noted, as a point of departure, that three articles are included: (1) Article XXXVI on "Principles and Objectives," which is largely preambular in character but contains the provision on reciprocity, a provision which history may show to have been the most important element of Part IV; (2) Article XXXVII on "Commitments," which contains commitments only in highly qualified form; and (3) Article XXXVIII on "Joint Action," which is designed to supplement the "joint action" provisions of Article XXV and which provides an abbreviated work program for the subsequently established Committee on Trade and Development.

Article XXXVI contains the most abstract verbiage. That is perhaps appropriate for an article on "Principles and Objectives." Unfortunately, it is not drafted in a form which throws much light on the substantive provisions of Part IV or on the rest of the General Agreement. Rather, it follows the elegant but indefinite style which has tended to characterize the work of those international organizations where the appearance of action has too often been substituted for action itself. After a long introductory paragraph, the article lists, in succession, a set of agreements as to needs.

Wedged curiously between the listing of agreed needs and a call for "conscious and purposeful effort" is a statement in paragraph 8 on reciprocity:

> The developed contracting parties do not expect reciprocity for commitments made by them in trade negotiations to reduce or remove tariffs and other barriers to the trade of the less-developed contracting parties.[31]

The reciprocity agreement did not, it should be noted, represent a new departure. At the May 1963 ministerial meeting, the ministers had agreed, in the resolution setting forth the principles for the Kennedy Round, that "in the trade negotiations every effort shall be made to reduce barriers to exports of the less-developed countries, but . . . the developed countries cannot expect to receive reciprocity from the less-developed countries."[32] And before the Kennedy Round the European Economic Community had announced in the Dillon Round that it would not expect reciprocity from the less-developed countries. The novelty, other than consecrating the principle in the General Agreement, was to make it specifically applicable, through the interpretative note, to tariff negotiations under Article XVIII, Article XXVIII, Article XXXIII, and "any other procedure" in addition to normal tariff negotiation rounds under Article XXVIII bis.

Article XXXVII on Commitments contains language that recalls certain key

---

31. See discussion in chapter 6, "Technical Tariff Negotiations," supra.
32. *Basic Instruments,* 12th Supp. (1964), p. 36, 48.

paragraphs of the 1963 Action Programme, but the striking aspect of the new article is the substitution, for the precise terminal dates and for the mandatory "shall" of the Action Programme, of a host of drafting techniques tending to water down the substance of the commitments.[33] Paragraph 1 sets forth the substantive commitments of the developed countries. It is qualified at the very beginning by the words "to the fullest extent possible" and, as if to preclude any misapprehension that the notion of possibility is limited to physical impossibility, the quoted language is further qualified by the explanation: "that is, except when compelling reasons, which may include legal reasons, make it impossible." It must be observed, however, that the explanatory language was added at the behest of certain less-developed countries that feared that the words "to the fullest extent possible" might be construed to "leave the applicability of [the substantive commitments] to the judgment of each contracting party subject to them."[34] Thereby qualified within the first paragraph are (in successive subparagraphs) commitments with respect to reduction of barriers, to a standstill on new barriers, and to internal taxes.

Subparagraph (a) deals with the "reduction and elimination of barriers to products currently or potentially of particular export interest to less-developed countries," including, in a specific manifestation of the growing comprehension of the nature of the barriers facing the less-developed countries, "customs duties and other restrictions which differentiate unreasonably between such products in their primary and in their processed forms." But the undertaking is only to "accord high priority" to the reduction or elimination of such barriers. The skeptic may perhaps be forgiven for wondering how much muscle is left in a commitment "to the fullest extent possible [to] accord high priority" to the reduction of trade barriers.

Subparagraph (b) calls for a standstill on introduction or increase of "customs duties or non-tariff import barriers" on less-developed country exports. It also is to be implemented only "to the fullest extent possible."

Subparagraph (c) takes up the thorny question of internal taxes on products "wholly or mainly produced in the territories of less-developed contracting parties"—that is to say, on tropical products. Here one finds a standstill agreement on the imposition of "new fiscal measures," but no specific standstill on the increase of existing fiscal measures, an omission that cannot be an oversight in view of the specific standstill provision in the preceding subparagraph on increases, as well as on the introduction, of import barriers. So far as the reduction of fiscal measures affecting such tropical products is concerned, the commitment here again is only to "accord high priority" to the "fullest extent

33. It must be remembered, of course, that the Action Programme was also qualified by a number of paragraphs in the underlying resolution.
34. Document L/2281 (26 Oct. 1964), p. 2.

possible." Moreover, the commitment to accord high priority to the reduction of internal taxes is to be effective only in the context of "any adjustments of fiscal policy." Room is left for a quarrel over the degree of inelasticity of demand for tropical products by the further limitation of all commitments to those fiscal measures "which would hamper, or which hamper, significantly the growth of consumption." This provision might seem superfluous in view of the dampening effect on consumption of any tax, but having been included, it must presumably be given some scope for application.

The nonbinding character of the undertakings in the first paragraph of Article XXXVII appears in a somewhat different light, however, if one emphasizes the second paragraph, which provides for a system of consultation with respect to all first-paragraph commitments. Any contracting party that considers that "effect is not being given to any of the provisions . . . of paragraph 1" may request the CONTRACTING PARTIES to "consult with the contracting party concerned and all interested contracting parties with respect to the matter with a view to reaching solutions satisfactory to all contracting parties concerned in order to further the objectives set forth in Article XXXVI." Whether the consultations will prove meaningful remains to be seen, but the effort would seem to be to move away from a legality-illegality approach in the assessment of developed country performance toward multilateral efforts to achieving "solutions satisfactory to all . . . concerned." That such consultations might on occasion actually aid the developed countries to live up to their Part IV commitments is suggested by the statement in the succeeding subparagraphs that consultation may "where appropriate" be directed toward "action . . . taken jointly with other developed contracting parties" or toward "joint action" by the CONTRACTING PARTIES.[35] Joint action among developed countries had helped lower some barriers on tropical products. Alternatively, these latter provisions may prove to be an invitation to dilatory tactics by individual developed contracting parties, which may be able to excuse their inaction by the inaction of other developed contracting parties.

Following the specific commitments and the consultation provisions come more general undertakings by both developed and less-developed contracting parties. Of chief interest here is a provision in paragraph 3(a) that attempts to deal with the problems that less-developed countries face when dealing with state-trading countries or with state import monopolies. Where "a government directly or indirectly determines the resale price of products wholly or mainly produced in the territories of less-developed contracting parties," it is to "make

---

35. These two forms of joint action are quite different. The first includes action taken by particular contracting parties outside the institutional framework of the GATT. The latter refers presumably to formal "joint action" taken by the CONTRACTING PARTIES under Articles XXV and XXXVIII.

every effort ...—to maintain trade margins at equitable levels." The very generality of this provision deprives it of its cutting edge, but perhaps more important is the fact that the provision applies only to tropical products; the general problem of protection or discrimination by state-trading countries and by state-import monopolies is left untouched.

"Joint Action" is the subject-matter of Article XXXVIII, and here one finds references to most of the favorite remedies of those who find the barrier-reducing approach of the GATT inadequate. It must be said that this last article reads strangely like an UNCTAD document. Mentioned directly or by inference are international commodity agreements, the UNCTAD itself, development plans, the relationship of trade and financial assistance, reviews of the rate of growth of less-developed country trade, international harmonization and adjustment of national policies and regulations, and export promotion. In addition one finds a specific grant of authority to "establish such institutional arrangements as may be necessary to further the objectives set forth in Article XXXVI and to give effect to the provisions of [Part IV]. The principal significance of this authority, and perhaps of Part IV as a whole, is that it serves as the legal basis for the activities of the Trade and Development Committee, to be discussed at length below.

In order to assess the significance of Part IV, it is useful to examine what is not included. First of all there is no mention of preferences, despite the great interest that was being manifested at the time of the drafting of Part IV to that particular approach to the problems of less-developed country trade. The most-favored-nation clause thus remains formally intact. Specific proposals on preferences by Chile and India were rejected.[36] Similarly, a U.S. proposal to permit certain regional preference arrangements among less-developed countries was dropped from consideration.[37]

Equally important is the absence in Part IV of any specific commitment with respect to agricultural products. To be sure, the general reference in Article XXXVI:4 to the need for "more favourable and acceptable conditions of access to world markets" for "primary products" includes, as the interpretative note indicates, agricultural products. But deleted from the commitment provisions were two alternative draft formulations of a provision that would have required developed countries to modify their internal agricultural policies in order to facilitate exports by less-developed countries.[38] A goodly number of other proposals were rejected, but the deliberate avoidance of any provisions on preferences, agricultural products, and import surcharges would seem to indicate, on the part of the developed countries, both a resolve to preserve the

36. See Document L/2147 (24 Feb. 1964), p. 7.
37. Ibid., pp. 16–17.
38. Document L/2281 (26 Oct. 1964), p. 2, 11.

essential character of the GATT system and an unwillingness to change some of the most objectionable of their commercial practices.

## The Trade and Development Committee

At the special session of the GATT at which the Part IV Protocol was drawn up, the CONTRACTING PARTIES established the Committee on Trade and Development. The new committee, which replaced Committee III, was given a broad mandate over matters falling within the ambit of Part IV.[39]

A large portion of the Trade and Development Committee's efforts has been devoted to the traditional tasks of reducing and eliminating trade barriers, and, since the developed countries were loath to reduce any customs duties except in the context of the Kennedy Round for fear of losing credit for their concessions in the final balancing of bindings, this aspect of the Committee's work has been primarily concerned with quantitative restrictions. Responsibility has been delegated to a special group which has been called, since payments imbalances are no longer the major contributing factor to quantitative restrictions of developed countries, the Group on Residual Restrictions.[40] The work methods of the Group on Residual Restrictions are not different in principle from those followed earlier, although there have been some improvements in application. Attention is devoted to a list of products notified by the less-developed countries as being of special interest to them. Some 250 items were on the list by 1965.[41] Developed contracting parties are required to indicate all restrictions maintained on those products together with the proposed abolition date, if any, and the legal basis, if any, for such restrictions under the General Agreement. Each developed country is summoned before the Group each year. The necessity of explaining restrictive policies before representatives of the major developed and less-developed countries no doubt has some influence on sensitive governments.

Progress has nevertheless been disappointing. Many of the restrictions remaining are clearly illegal under the pre–Part IV General Agreement, but the developed countries in question refuse either to set target abolition dates or to indicate how they intend to solve the underlying domestic economic problem. Others can be justified only on the ground that, under the Protocol of Provisional Application (or applicable protocol of accession), they were "mandatory" restrictions that were already in effect when the developed country in question

39. *Basic Instruments,* 13th Supp. (1965), pp. 75–76 .
40. See the discussion of the concept of "residual" restrictions in chapter 9, "Quantitative Restrictions," supra.
41. The 1967 list ran some forty pages. GATT Document COM.TD/W/60 (11 July 1967).

became a contracting party.⁴² The director-general has taken the position that Part IV does not qualify the legal right of a contracting party to continue to apply Part II restrictions that antedate the General Agreement or the applicable protocol of accession.⁴³ Some developed contracting parties have been satisfied to stand on this interpretation.⁴⁴ France, having in effect rejected Part IV, has boycotted the annual exercises entirely.⁴⁵ It should be noted, however, that many of the products are temperate agricultural commodities and, as will be discussed in a subsequent chapter, the problems with such products are rather unusual.⁴⁶

Although it is natural that progress should become increasingly elusive, with in most cases only the most deeply rooted restrictions representing seemingly intractable domestic problems remaining, some less-developed countries have become disillusioned with Part IV and have urged that a system be introduced, by amendment of the General Agreement, under which developed countries would compensate less-developed countries for remaining residual restrictions.⁴⁷ Other less-developed countries have advocated alternative types of trade controls, such as export controls by the less-developed countries (where there is a legitimate fear that developed country markets may be swamped by less-developed country exports) or discriminatory application of quantitative restrictions in favor of less-developed countries (where the underlying reason for the restriction is a fear of imports from developed countries).⁴⁸

In an attempt to respond to the demands of the less-developed countries and the felt need for more positive efforts toward the expansion of their exports, the Trade and Development Committee has sponsored several different activities. One is a series of studies of the development plans of individual countries. The Trade and Development Committee cannot, however, be credited with originality since these studies were undertaken at the initiative of the GATT secretariat, were authorized before the Trade and Development Com-

42. See discussion of the Protocol of Provisional Application in chapter 19, "The GATT as an International Organization," infra.
43. GATT Document L/2114 (28 Jan. 1964), p. 4.
44. Among the contracting parties citing the Protocol of Provisional Application or a protocol of accession as legal justification in the 1967 review were Austria, Canada, Denmark, Federal Republic of Germany, Sweden, Switzerland, and the United States (GATT Document COM.TD/W/60 [11 July 1967]).
45. See Second Report of the Group on Residual Restrictions, reprinted in General Agreement on Tariffs and Trade, *Expansion of Trade of the Developing Countries (Selected Documents)* (Dec. 1966) (mimeographed), pp. 69, 71.
46. See discussion in chapter 15, "Temperate Agricultural Commodities," infra.
47. See discussion in chapter 20, "Dispute Settlement," infra.
48. Second Report of the Group on Residual Restrictions, p. 71.

mittee was constituted,[49] and were based upon experience obtained in reviewing the Five-Year Plans of India and Pakistan published in 1962.[50] The objective of these Trade and Aid Studies is to assess the likely trade implications of development plans of less-developed countries and to examine the potential role of the export sector of individual countries with a view to improving the plans, coordinating the use of aid with export measures, and familiarizing less-developed countries with one another's import requirements and export targets. The studies are carried on in consultation with the International Bank for Reconstruction and Development and other international agencies with foreign assistance responsibilities in order to improve the coordination of aid and trade efforts.[51]

The first two studies published covered Uganda and Nigeria, and they were reviewed by the Expert Group on Trade and Aid Studies established by the Committee on Trade and Development.[52] These reviews led to certain specific recommendations with respect to the export trade of Uganda and Nigeria, which were subsequently adopted by the CONTRACTING PARTIES.[53]

It is still too early to assess the potential of this kind of effort. It is interesting to observe that in one instance difficulty arose with the less-developed country itself in the review of the final draft. The root of the export difficulties of any particular less-developed country may lie in the internal policies of the country itself. Confrontation with experts from the GATT and other international organizations who are intimately familiar with the local development plan may prove to be a useful stimulus and goad.[54]

## International Commodity Trade

Prior to the adoption of Part IV, the GATT had not been active in the various multilateral activities concerning international commodity trade, such as inter-

49. *Basic Instruments*, 12th Supp. (1963), p. 36, 45.
50. *Study of the Third Five-Year Plan of India* (1962); *Study of the Second Five-Year Plan of Pakistan* (1962).
51. See *The Activities of GATT 1964/65* (1965), pp. 11–13; Eric Wyndham White, "The GATT and Economic Development," address at Karachi (1964), pp. 10–11.
52. *The Uganda Development Plan, 1961–1966* (1966); and *The First Six-Year Plan of Nigeria* (1966).
53. *Basic Instruments*, 14th Supp. (1966), p. 142. Similar studies were undertaken in Kenya and in West Africa generally (GATT Document L/2967 [7 Feb. 1968], p. 10).
54. Another effort to make a positive contribution to the exports of the less-developed countries was the creation of an International Trade Center to provide commercial services to those countries. The Center subsequently became a joint GATT-UNCTAD undertaking (*Basic Instruments*, 15th Supp. (1968), p. 175; GATT Document L/2967 [7 Feb. 1968], pp. 19–22).

national commodity agreements.[55] We have already considered the limited provisions in Article XX(h) under which commodity agreements are considered, at most, permissible exceptions to GATT rules rather than agreements to be promoted and supported by the GATT.[56] But the authorization could nevertheless have been found in the "joint action" provisions of Article XXV if the CONTRACTING PARTIES had regarded such an agreement as "facilitating the operation and furthering the objectives of this Agreement." In part the inaction in the area of international commodity agreements stemmed from a "self-denying attitude" under which the GATT left the negotiation and administration of such agreements to various United Nations organs particularly charged with that responsibility, such as the Interim Co-ordinating Committee for International Commodity Arrangements.[57] But the earlier passivity of the GATT secretariat coincided with the view of certain contracting parties, notably the United States, that some kinds of commodity agreements were hardly consistent with the GATT system.

If one may divide commodity agreements between those that attempt to stabilize fluctuations in price for a commodity around the long-term price trend line and those that attempt to raise the price for the commodity above this line (recognizing that some agreements attempt to accomplish both objectives), it will be seen that agreements directed toward the latter objective are difficult to reconcile with GATT principles. This becomes clearer when one considers the kinds of anticompetitive measures, such as price agreements, export restrictions, and the like, that are necessary to make such an agreement work. Viewed from a traditional GATT perspective, such agreements resemble cartel agreements in which sellers combine to restrict sales and thereby to raise the market price of a product. From this point of view the role of consuming countries as parties to such agreements, as required under the Havana Charter principles, is merely to police the agreement and to assure that nonmember exporters are frozen out of the major consuming markets and thereby prevented from undercutting the cartel price. Commodity agreements are to be viewed as devices to disguise massive aid transfers from consumer to producer countries and are to be considered as inferior to an overt transfer insofar as they reduce competition and lead to a less efficient allocation of resources. Such transfers may also be

---

55. Consideration had been given at the time of the Review Session to a special agreement on commodity arrangements. *Basic Instruments,* 3d Supp. (1955), p. 238. Beginning in 1955, a review of trends in international commodity trade has been held each year, and arrangements have been established for consultation on commodity problems. See 5th Supp. (1957), pp. 26, 87; 7th Supp. (1959), p. 42; 8th Supp. (1960), p. 76; 10th Supp. (1962), p. 83.
56. See discussion in text, supra, at note 4.
57. Statement by Mr. Wyndham White, GATT Press Release No. 839 (9 April 1964), p. 9.

preferable as a technique for accomplishing stabilization. According to this view, a compensatory financing scheme, under which developed importing countries would make periodic financial transfers in the amount of any shortfall of export proceeds of the less-developed exporting countries, would be preferable to a commodity agreement.[58]

A preference on allocation-of-resources grounds for compensatory arrangements is frequently coupled with a belief that, on practical grounds, commodity agreements that attempt to raise price above a competitive level are doomed to failure in any event because they are impossible to enforce over the long term or, if effective in raising the price, only give rise to a shift in consumer preference to competitive products or to the development of synthetics. Mr. Wyndham White, the former director-general of the GATT, expressed this latter opinion as recently as 1964:

> I must say that my own conclusions on this are that, whilst whenever possible it is desirable—indeed, urgent—to enter into and elaborate agreements for the stabilization of prices to prevent violent fluctuations, a solution to this problem is not to be found by attempting to manipulate prices in such a way as to jeopardize the competitive position of primary products; these are already seriously threatened by competitive synthetic products and by technological processes which—at a price—enable considerable economies to be made in the use of primary products in manufacturing processes. Therefore, one form or another of compensatory financing for primary producers is the way to deal with one side of this problem.[59]

Attitudes on the part of the United States and perhaps the GATT Secretariat have nevertheless become somewhat more favorable toward international commodity agreements in recent years. In 1962 the United States entered into the International Coffee Agreement, the first such agreement to which the United States became a party where the commodity was not produced in the United States.[60] The language of Part IV suggests this partial change in attitude. Article XXXVIII:2 specifically provides that the CONTRACTING PARTIES "shall . . . where appropriate, take action, including action through international arrangements, to provide improved and acceptable conditions of access to world markets for primary products of particular interest to less-developed contracting parties and to devise measures designed to stabilize and improve conditions of world markets in these products including measures designed to attain stable,

---

58. For a discussion of how such a compensatory arrangement would work, see International Bank for Reconstruction and Development, *Supplementary Financial Measures* (6 Dec. 1965) (mimeographed).
59. Wyndham White, Statement, p. 10.
60. See Michael Blumenthal, "Commodity Stabilization and Economic Development in Africa," *Department of State Bulletin* 616, XLVII (1962); Walker, p. 414 n. 79.

equitable and remunerative prices for exports of such products." Commodity agreements are thus no longer beyond the GATT pale. Under this authority the Trade and Development Committee has established a Group on International Commodity Problems, which has undertaken intensive discussions of the problems of trade in cocoa, cotton and tropical timber.[61]

The GATT seems nevertheless prepared, for the foreseeable future, to leave the actual responsibility for negotiation of commodity agreements to the UNCTAD and other organizations. The simple truth is that the world community does not at present look to the GATT in connection with commodity agreements. It should be noted, however, that the GATT became involved with commodity agreements in temperate agricultural products in the Kennedy Round as part of the work of the Group on Cereals and the Group on Meats.[62] And in one sense the GATT has already entered the field by its role in the drafting and administration of the Cotton Textiles Agreements.[63]

## Preferences

Perhaps the contemporary movement that most threatens the traditional GATT system is the widespread interest in a system of preferences for less-developed countries. Such a system would tend to make the most-favored-nation principle seem more like an exception than a general rule in the international trading community. The preference question has already been examined in connection with isolated preferences,[64] and will be examined again in connection with the widespread movement in the last decade toward regional arrangements, many of which are little more than preferential trading arrangements.[65] But the proposal for a system of preferences for less-developed countries represents a direct attack on the most-favored-nation principle to a degree that isolated preferences and regional arrangements do not.

Two kinds of preferential systems have been discussed within the GATT: preferences by developed countries in favor of less-developed countries and preferential arrangements among less-developed countries. In the case of the former the dispute is whether such a derogation from the most-favored-nation clause should be permitted at all. In the case of the latter, however, there is general agreement as to the desirability of an exception from the most-favored-

---

61. See Note on the First Meeting of the Group on International Commodity Problems (Document COM.TD/C/2), reprinted in GATT, Expansion of Trade of the Developing Countries (Selected Documents) (1966) (mimeographed document), p. 99.
62. See discussion in chapter 15, "Temperate Agricultural Commodities," infra.
63. See discussion in chapter 17, "Market Disruption and Cotton Textiles," infra.
64. See discussion in chapter 4, "The GATT Tariff System," supra.
65. See discussion in chapter 16, "Regional Economic Arrangements," infra.

nation clause, and the disagreement concerns the breadth of the exception.

Partisans of preferences by developed countries for less-developed countries are divided between those who, on the one hand, favor across-the-board preferences in which all developed countries would grant preferences on all products of interest to those countries (with perhaps some exceptions for some less-developed country exports that are competitive with developed country production or that would cause "market disruption" in developed countries) and those who, on the other hand, favor a selective approach. The first widely discussed plan for selective preferences was the Brasseur Plan, advanced by the Belgian representative at the 1963 ministerial meeting. Under the Brasseur Plan direct negotiations between the party granting and the party receiving preferences, initiated by the latter, would lead to the establishment of "selective, temporary and degressive" preferences on industrial exports of less-developed countries. Although negotiations would in principle be bilateral, "one party or both parties could arrange for a group of Powers acting jointly to serve as their negotiator." The negotiations would deal with the competitiveness of the industry in the less-developed country, the risk of market disruption and the "level, duration and rate of degression of the preference."[66] Such a selective approach is supported with some nuances by the Commission of the European Economic Community, by the French government, and in general by the African countries associated with the EEC, which fear that a system of general, across-the-board preferences offered by developed countries in favor of less-developed countries generally (as favored by the United Kingdom and more recently by the United States) would destroy the value of their own preferences in the EEC.

The subject of preferences by developed countries for less-developed countries is vast and complex and has already received extensive treatment.[67] A consideration of the desirability of such preferential arrangements would be beyond the scope of this study. What is of primary interest here is the attitude that the GATT has demonstrated to date concerning preferences and the role that the GATT would play if the decision were taken to grant such preferences on a broad scale. On the question of desirability it may, however, be noted that there is a general consensus, even among countries such as the United States that originally opposed preferences, that such preferences would be of some benefit to the creation of industries in less-developed countries.

66. "Summary Outline of the Brasseur Plan Machinery," submitted by the Belgium delegation to the Special Committee on Preferences of UNCTAD. See United Nations Conference on Trade and Development, Report of the Special Committee on Preferences, Annex B, TD/B/C.2/1/Add. 1 (8 June 1965), p. 68.
67. See generally Gardner Patterson, *Discrimination in International Trade, The Policy Issues 1945–1965* (Princeton: Princeton University Press, 1966), pp. 323–96; Johnson, *Economic Policies,* pp. 163–211; John Pincus, *Trade, Aid and Development* (New York: Harper & Row, 1968), pp. 284–302.

The debate has to do with the extent of this benefit and with the existence and extent of any undesirable consequences. Those who view preferences as being of great value tend to emphasize the phenomenon of high rates of effective protection for processing industries in developed countries. The skeptics point to the conditions that must be fulfilled simultaneously for each product, each less-developed country and each developed country before a preference will be of value, notably that (1) the industry in the particular less-developed country must be more efficient than the industry in the importing developed country or there will be no incentive to exports, even with duty-free treatment; and (2) the most-favored-nation rate must be sufficiently high after the Kennedy Round reductions become fully effective to leave room for a meaningful preference. The limited gain remaining to the less-developed countries is not viewed as sufficient to compensate for the loss that other countries, developed and less-developed alike, would suffer from the rejection of the most-favored-nation clause and the resulting collapse of the nondiscriminatory GATT approach to world trade.

Since under a selective system those products would tend to be excluded for which less-developed country exports would increase the most, opponents of preferences conclude that the advantages to the less-developed country of any system acceptable to the EEC and their African associates would be more psychological than real. Opponents also stress that where the effect of a preference would be to divert developed country imports from developed country sources to less-developed country sources, world resources would automatically be misallocated since (assuming nondiscrimination previously) the effect would be to shift purchases from relatively low-cost sources to relatively high-cost sources.[68] Where the effect of the preferences would be to replace domestic production in the importing country by imports from less-developed countries, and the preferences would thereby contribute to a better allocation of world resources, the opponents continue, the same effect could be achieved—consistent with the General Agreement—by a most-favored-nation reduction.

The GATT began its studies of preferences before the adoption of Part IV and before the 1964 United Nations Conference on Trade and Development, where the discussions of preferences became one of the great topics of the day and the subject of one of the most important recommendations.[69] At the 1963 ministerial meeting the ministers concluded that a study of preferences should be undertaken. A special working party filed a report in which it discussed the proposals, made by India and the United Arab Republic in the course of drafting Part IV, for automatic, unconditional, across-the-board preferences in

---

68. That is to say, low- and high-cost sources in terms of real resources consumed. See discussion in chapter 16, "Regional Economic Arrangements," infra.

69. See General Principle Eight and Annex A.III.5, *Proceedings of the United Nations Conference on Trade and Development*, Vol. I (1964), pp. 10–11, 39.

favor of all less-developed countries. The working party arrived at no decision, but outlined some of the voiced differences of opinion.[70] When the Trade and Development Committee was created, it formed a Working Group on Preferences, which subsequently discussed the question in an inconclusive fashion.[71]

Interest within the GATT in preferences came to center during this period upon the Australian application for a waiver with respect to its plan for introducing preferences, subject to tariff quotas on some products, for certain less-developed countries. This application was given extended study by a special working party and eventually approved.[72] Since no other contracting parties have followed the Australian example and since the general question of the desirability of preferences has been considered, for better or worse, as falling within the sphere of activities of the UNCTAD, the GATT was not thereafter active in discussions of preferences. The GATT staff did, however, publish a study in 1966 which was critical of preferences insofar as they might not be established on a general nondiscriminatory basis but might be selective in country and commodity coverage.[73] Progress in principle toward a system of preferences was made in the 1968 UNCTAD II, when the United States reversed the hostile stand it took in UNCTAD I, but the crucial issue of a selective versus an across-the-board approach remained unresolved. Disappointing as the results of UNCTAD II were for the less-developed countries, they continued to see their hopes for eventual adoption of preferences better served by keeping the discussions within the UNCTAD. Debates within the GATT on preferences therefore remained perfunctory.

If a consensus should develop among the developed countries to move toward preferences for less-developed countries, the question would immediately arise as to the role of the GATT. The GATT would certainly be involved to some extent since either a waiver or an amendment of the most-favored-nation clauses in Article I and Article II:1 would be required. But if, as now seems likely, only a selective approach would prove universally acceptable, elaborate negotiations would be necessary. Even those developed countries that favor an across-the-board approach would probably, when the chips were down, wish to exclude certain products on the ground of "market disruption." These negotiations would likely be even more complex than the Kennedy Round negotiations, which required more than three years to complete. The number of bilateral negotiations that would be involved is staggering. And the negotiations

70. *Basic Instruments,* 13th Supp. (1965), p. 100.
71. Ibid., pp. 77, 84–87; 14th Supp. (1966), p. 129, 137.
72. Ibid., 14th Supp. (1966), pp. 23, 162. See discussion in chapter 4, "The GATT Tariff System," supra.
73. Preferences and Other Policy Measures to Stimulate Exports of the Less-Developed Countries, Trade Intelligence Paper No. 7 (July 1966).

would become even more complicated if certain of the proposals advanced in the UNCTAD discussions were adopted, such as (1) differentiation of the level of preferences according to the level of development of the preference-receiving country; (2) limitation of the duration of each preference to the time the particular industry in the less-developed country in question would require to become competitive; or (3) the allotment by each developed country of a separate quota for preferential imports from each developing country.[74]

In view of the working methods of the UNCTAD, it might be doubted that that organization would be able to provide as efficient negotiating facilities as the GATT, although UNCTAD would no doubt be capable of laying out ground rules to be followed by individual countries. And while each developed country could introduce its own system of preferences, turning to the GATT only for a waiver when the negotiations were completed (as did Australia), there would be great advantages in bringing the negotiations under a single roof. The advantages would be particularly great for those less-developed countries that do not have the manpower resources to negotiate such specialized matters simultaneously in a dozen or more different capitals.

Certain difficulties would nevertheless be encountered in using the GATT as the negotiating body. Many of the members of the United Nations are not contracting parties of the GATT, but all such members would presumably be entitled to preferences, particularly if the decisive impetus toward preferences should come from UNCTAD deliberations. And some countries, notably France, consider that the GATT would not be an appropriate body for such an exercise.[75]

Proposals for preferential arrangements among less-developed countries command much broader support among GATT contracting parties than do proposals for preferences by developed countries for less-developed countries. An exception to the most-favored-nation clause for regional preference arrangements was included in the Havana Charter. The United States proposed a modified version of the Havana Charter provision in the drafting discussions on Part IV. The GATT working party on preferences reported in 1964 that "there was no disagreement on the principle involved in the granting of preferences between less-developed countries, at least in so far as this was on a regional basis."[76] The support for such preferences by those countries that do

74. See generally United Nations Conference on Trade and Development, Preferences: Review of Discussions (Report by the Secretary-General of the Conference), TD/B/AC.1/1 (23 March 1965).
75. See the observations by the French delegation in United Nations Conference on Trade and Development, Report of the Special Committee on Preferences, TD/B/C.2/1/Add. 1 (8 June 1965), Annex B, p. 40, 43.
76. *Basic Instruments,* 13th Supp. (1965), p. 100, 104. The Japanese delegation reserved its position on the quoted statement.

not support preferences by developed for less-developed countries is based in large part on the belief that less-developed countries do not have a sufficiently large market (considering population and average level of income) to permit self-sustaining economic development leading to industrialization. Paradoxically, preference arrangements among less-developed countries are perhaps more likely to lead to trade diversion on balance than preferences by developed for less-developed countries. In the latter case there is normally a domestic industry that may be displaced. As Patterson has remarked in his review of the discussions of preference arrangements among less-developed countries in the 1964 UNCTAD meeting:

> ... the less-developed countries themselves did not anticipate letting such preferences result in much trade-creation, in the usual sense of changing the locus of production as among themselves. This was made clear by their frequent statements that in any such regional cooperative efforts "due regard" or "careful attention" should be paid to the "individual characteristics" and "different needs" of the members, so as to prevent harm and to assure "equal opportunity" for all.[77]

Most of the discussions in the Trade and Development Committee's Group on Expansion of Trade among the Developing Countries have concerned the types of preferential arrangements that should be permitted. Here the debate has centered upon certain restrictions, urged by the United States, on any such departure from the most-favored-nation clause. The most controversial was a proposed requirement that the less-developed countries be in the same region or have historical ties. The United States argued that such preferential arrangements should be tied to coordinated development of production and trade among the countries involved, and such coordination would normally be possible only within an economic region. Under the U.S. view such preferential arrangements were desirable insofar as they were analogous to customs unions and to free-trade areas. Ad hoc arrangements among isolated developing countries would be different. The United States would also permit deviations from the most-favored-nation clause only where the preferential arrangements "could be expected to lead to a rise in efficiency and productivity in the industries concerned so as to enable it [sic] eventually to withstand foreign competition" and where "they would not cause undue damage to the interests of third countries."[78]

The discussions in the Group on Expansion and Trade, however, made clear that the less-developed countries were hoping for more short-term results,

---

77. Patterson, p. 376, n. 81.
78. Interim Report of the Group on Expansion of Trade among Developing Countries (COM.TD/D/3), reprinted in GATT, Expansion of Trade of the Developing Countries (Selected Documents) (December 1966) (mimeographed document), p. 83, 90.

particularly in view of their payments difficulties, than could be expected in regional integration schemes. Indeed, some of the proposals put forward looked more like bilateral payments arrangements or even bartering than regional integration.[79] The wide differences of opinion in the Group were papered over with a "unanimous conclusion," subsequently endorsed by the Trade and Development Committee as a whole, that "the establishment of preferences among less-developed countries, appropriately administered and subject to the necessary safeguards, can make an important contribution to the expansion of trade among these countries and to the attainment of the objectives of the General Agreement." The Trade and Development Committee went on to note "the view of less-developed countries represented on the Group that such preferences should be granted and applied on a non-discriminatory basis."[80]

Whatever the Committee may have considered a "non-discriminatory" preference to be, it is clear that many less-developed countries have no intention of making any preferences negotiated among several of them open to all less-developed countries. Perhaps the language of the Committee merely represents approval of the provision in the U.S. proposal which would require that any preferential agreement contain, in order to fall within the proposed exception to the most-favored-nation clause, "provisions permitting, on terms and conditions to be determined by negotiation with the parties to the agreement, the adherence of other less-developed countries . . . in the interest of their programmes of economic development."[81] Any semblance of agreement on this point between the United States and the less-developed countries as a group ends at that point, a fact which suggests that the final conclusion of the committee may have within it the seeds of future dispute.

The conclusion, in which the United States apparently acquiesced, was that the less-developed countries should proceed with the negotiation of preferential arrangements before agreement was reached on the scope of the exception to the most-favored-nation clause since "it would be helpful to see what concrete proposals or arrangements might in practice be made or negotiated by less-developed countries acting within the spirit of Part IV."[82] Although a certain diplomatic shrewdness may have dictated this particular form of nonresolution of the issue (in view of the difficulty the less-developed countries will probably have in negotiating any very substantial preferential arrangements), it may also give rise to problems later.

Once a preferential arrangement has been negotiated and perhaps also put into force, it will be difficult for the CONTRACTING PARTIES to withhold their

79. Ibid., pp. 85–88, 90–96.
80. *Basic Instruments,* 14th Supp. (1966), p. 129, 136.
81. Document L/2196/Rev. 1 (1964), p. 27.
82. *Basic Instruments,* 14th Supp. (1966), p. 129, 137.

approval. Yet all the basic issues about the scope of the proposed exception to the most-favored-nation clause remain unresolved:

(1) Should the exception be limited to less-developed countries in the same "economic region," however that intentionally ambiguous term may be interpreted? The United States has strongly favored such a limitation and such countries as India that do not have the best of relations with their closest geographical neighbor have maintained that such a limitation would discriminate against them.

(2) What should be the scope of the GATT review of such preferential arrangements? Assuming that general criteria can be agreed upon (thereby avoiding the waiver procedure), should less-developed countries be required only to notify each arrangement that they enter into, perhaps offering consultations to those contracting parties that allege that they have suffered trade injury? Or should each preferential arrangement be subjected to review by the CONTRACTING PARTIES?

(3) Must the preferences include tariffs, as some developed countries urge? Or may they be limited to quantitative restrictions, as some less-developed countries apparently consider more important in view of their balance-of-payments difficulties? Restrictions of the right to discriminate in the administration of quantitative restrictions have been a continuing source of difficulty under the customs-union and free-trade-area exception of Article XXIV,[83] and the question cannot be avoided in fashioning any new exception to the most-favored-nation clause.

(4) Should some minimum requirement be established for the scope of trade covered and for the percentage cut in tariffs that is required? Under the customs-union and free-trade-area exception of Article XXIV, "substantially all" trade must be covered, and a plan and schedule must be included which provides for the complete elimination of duties. The less-developed countries clearly seek to avoid those requirements. The avowed objectives of the preferential arrangements is "to find larger markets and achieve economies of scale" for manufactures.[84] But less-developed-country exports of manufactures are modest, and there may be no trade at all at present among the countries concerned. A test based upon percentage of trade is therefore irrelevant for such preferential arrangements. On the other hand, it is unlikely that the developed countries will be prepared to approve a preferential arrangement among less-developed countries involving only one or two products.[85] The de-

83. See discussion in chapter 16, "Regional Economic Arrangements," infra.
84. *Basic Instruments*, 14th Supp. (1966), p. 129, 136.
85. At least it is unlikely that they will be prepared to approve such an arrangement unless it is dressed up as a full-fledged free-trade area. See the discussion of the "free trade area" between New Zealand and Australia in chapter 16, "Regional Economic Arrangements," infra.

veloped countries may be more prepared to accept small percentage [cuts on a] wide range of products, particularly as some economists have maintain[ed that] the first percentage cut on a high duty is more likely to improve welf[are than] later cuts when the duty is lower.

Many similar questions will have to be faced if any formal exceptio[n to the] most-favored-nation clause is to be carved out for less-developed cou[ntries.] Simply because of the complexity of the questions, it is not unlikely t[hat the] CONTRACTING PARTIES may elect to avoid the crucial questions by deali[ng with] preferential arrangements on a case-by-case basis in waiver proceedings. [But] experience has shown that it is difficult to refuse a waiver once an agre[ement] has been signed (particularly once it has already gone into effect), su[ch an] election would be unfortunate for the continued vitality of the most-fav[ored-] nation clause and for the authority of the GATT in the future. Howeve[r, the] waiver procedure has traditionally been resorted to only where limited e[xcep]tions have been sought and have normally been granted on defined terms [and] conditions.

### Other Activities

In its efforts to give substance to the vague promises of Part IV, the Trade [and] Development Committee has taken on a number of additional tasks. A sur[vey] was carried out by a group of experts of adjustment assistance measures [in] various developed countries.[87] The Committee reviewed a number of propos[ed] amendments to the General Agreement. One of them, concerning dispu[te] settlement mechanisms, was refined into a decision on Article XXIII pr[o]cedures, which was adopted in 1966.[88] Consideration has also been given to the amendment of Article XVIII to authorize the use of import surcharges by les[s] developed countries for balance-of-payments reasons, an amendment whic[h] would merely tend to legitimate the widespread use of such surcharges. A[t] present the GATT must either grant waivers or stand by without even a waive[r] proceeding when contracting parties, developed and less-developed alike, impose import surcharges in violation of the provisions of Article II concerning bound duties.[89] The review by a working party of the economic problems faced

---

86. For a discussion of the rules that might be adopted, see United Nations Conference on Trade and Development, Trade Expansion and Economic Integration among Developing Countries (Report by the Secretariat of UNCTAD), Document TD/B/85 (2 Aug. 1966), pp. 194–217. Following the Kennedy Round a Trade Negotiations Committee of developing countries was created "to establish a basis" for negotiations of "tariff and trade concessions" among the less-developed countries (*Basic Instruments*, 15th Supp. [1968], p. 67, 71).

87. *Basic Instruments*, 14th Supp., pp. 129, 133–35 (1966).

88. Ibid., p. 18 (1966). See discussion in chapter 20, "Dispute Settlement, infra.

89. See discussions of import surcharges, in chapter 4, "The GATT Tariff System," supra.

... declining world cotton prices suggests a possible new ... procedures.⁹⁰

... dy Round an attempt was made to regain momentum ... riers to less-developed country trade. A review was made ... f the Kennedy Round from the point of view of the less- ...¹ The Trade and Development Committee sought to en- ... plementation of Kennedy Round concessions in favor of ... tries in order to create a significant, albeit short-lived, ... es.⁹² It was also agreed to establish panels of experts for ... roduct groups where less-developed country exports en- ... ons "of a hard-core nature."⁹³

... mportant for the future of the GATT than the actual decisions ... de and Development Committee and its predecessor commit- ... mental change that has come about in the image and role of the ... been seen, a number of different factors have contributed to ... it as new pressures and incentives arise, the origins of this new ... the GATT will be less important than the fact that the GATT is ... rely a trade agreement, administered passively by an embryo ... ut has become de facto an international organization actively ... tain affirmative goals.

... strument, 15th Supp. (1968), pp. 139, 147–48.

... Document COM.TD/48/Rev. 1 (21 Nov. 1967); GATT Document ... 49 (2 Nov. 1967).

... Instruments, 15th Supp. (1968), pp. 143–44, 148–55.

... , pp. 145, 155.

# 15 Temperate Agricultural Commodities

It would be difficult to conclude that the GATT's record in the sphere of temperate agricultural commodities is other than one of failure. Not only is effective protection in all likelihood higher on average than in any other sector of the international economy, but there are many indications that the rate of effective protection is increasing. Domestic prices exceed import prices by as much as 100 percent in some products and in some countries.

If the only thing at stake were high tariffs, one's judgment could be more generous. After all, one can argue from the text of the General Agreement that the GATT merely provides the facilities for negotiations looking toward the reduction of tariffs and that there is nothing in the General Agreement requiring contracting parties to reduce tariffs. Unfortunately for the prestige of the GATT, however, the most important restrictions on international trade in temperate agricultural commodities are nontariff barriers, and a large proportion of these are maintained in blatant violation of the General Agreement. This continued violation of the terms of the General Agreement by a substantial number of contracting parties has become such a way of life that little embarrassment seems to be felt by national representatives and no effort is made to suggest dates on which violations might be terminated.[1]

Committee II of the GATT, reporting upon consultations held with thirty-four contracting parties on a group of major products, found that "in the case of each product a wide variety of nontariff protective devices is in use" and that "one device or another (and sometimes several) is used in practically every

1. Much of what is said here applies also to tropical agricultural products. The problem in tropical products is somewhat different, however, because there is normally no production in the advanced countries, which constitute the major import markets. Some products, notably sugar, raise an intermediate problem. Sugar is produced in the form of cane in semitropical, normally less-developed countries and in the form of beets in temperate, normally developed countries. Problems concerning tropical products are dealt with in chapter 14, on "Less-Developed Countries," supra.

country consulted." In the case of dairy products, all but three of the thirty-four countries consulted applied one form or another of nontariff barriers. For meat, nontariff barriers were used by all but five out of the thirty-four; for fish, by all but six out of the thirty-four. In the case of wheat, nontariff barriers were used "in practically all wheat producing countries," and in the case of sugar "only 5 per cent of imports were not subject to nontariff barriers." Virtually every kind of nontariff barrier known to international trade was used: quantitative restrictions, import levies other than tariffs, state-trading measures, bilateral agreements, deficiency payments, domestic subsidies, and, on the export side, export subsidies. Quantitative restrictions were the most important. They covered 87 percent of production for butter, 84 percent for wheat, 59 percent for cheese, and 52 percent for sugar. More than two-thirds of the countries consulted applied quantitative restrictions on at least some of the products examined.

The fact that the countries consulted had in many cases granted tariff concessions on particular agricultural products did not prevent them from imposing nontariff restrictions on those products and from thereby depriving agricultural exporting countries of the benefit of their tariff bargains. In the case of meat, for example, Committee II found that "one-third of the countries examined were found to have tariff bindings and nearly all of these countries maintained some nontariff device which reduced or even largely nullified the benefit of the binding."[2]

## The Agricultural Provisions of the General Agreement

This extraordinary situation cannot be justified under the provisions of the General Agreement. To be sure, there are several special dispensations for agricultural products in the General Agreement: quantitative restrictions on agricultural products are permitted in some cases under Article XI; subsidies receive special treatment under Article XVI; and export subsidies on agricultural products (as "primary products"[3]) are envisioned under Article XVI. Yet there can be little doubt that few of the nontariff barriers on imports of agricultural commodities can be justified under these special dispensations.

Article XI:2(c) excepts "import restrictions on any agricultural or fisheries product, imported in any form" from the general prohibition of quantitative restrictions, but the exemption applies only where the agricultural import restrictions are "necessary to the enforcement of governmental measures" that impose limits on domestic production or sales. Two types of such internal measures are envisaged. The first comprises measures that "operate . . . to re-

2. The quotations in the foregoing discussion are taken from the third report of Committee II, *Basic Instruments*, 10th Supp. (1962), pp. 135 ff., reprinted in *Trade in Agricultural Products, Second and Third Reports of Committee II* (1962).
3. Interpretative note, Ad Art. XVI, § B:2.

strict the quantities of the like domestic product permitted to be marketed or produced, or, if there is no substantial domestic production of the like product, of a domestic product for which the imported product can be directly substituted." The second is in reality a special case of the first; namely, internal measures that "operate . . . to remove a temporary surplus of the like domestic product, or, if there is no substantial domestic production of the like product, of a domestic product for which the imported product can be directly substituted, by making the surplus available to certain groups of domestic consumers free of charge or at prices below the current market level." Import restrictions justified under Article XI:2(c) must not, however, be so stringent as to "reduce the total of imports relative to the total of domestic production, as compared with the proportion which might reasonably be expected to rule between the two in the absence of restrictions," taking account of historical patterns and special factors, such as changes in relative productive efficiency.[4]

Internal measures of the second type envisioned—consumer-subsidy programs of sufficient scope to "operate to reduce a temporary surplus"—are quite rare. Measures of the first type, entailing the limitation of "quantities . . . marketed or produced," are therefore the principal bases for justifying quantitative restrictions on agricultural imports. But the fact has been that only the United States has attempted with any consistency to restrain domestic *production*. Insofar as restriction of domestic *marketing* is concerned, the term "quantities marketed" appears to refer to marketing by farmers and therefore presumably does not extend to government programs that simply take off the domestic market surpluses created by unrestricted domestic production and either transfer those surpluses to storage or subsidize their sales abroad. This construction is supported by the statement of the responsible subcommittee at Havana that, "in interpreting the term 'restrict' for the purposes of paragraph 2(c), the essential point was that the measures of domestic restriction must effectively keep domestic output below the level which it would have attained in the absence of restrictions."[5] This also appears to have been the implicit construction given the term "quantities marketed" by the government in applying for, and by the CONTRACTING PARTIES in granting, a waiver to impose quantitative restrictions on products for which the U.S. price support system maintained domestic prices above world prices without in all cases imposing production or farm-marketing controls.[6] Furthermore, the agricultural exemption was drafted by the American ITO negotiators, who were keenly aware that

4. Art XI, para. 2, last subpara.; interpretative note thereto. In addition, measures to restrict domestic animal production by restraining imports of particular feedgrains or other animal foodstuffs are permitted, provided domestic production of the restricted commodities is "relatively negligible."
5. *Analytical Index,* p. 53.
6. The waiver is set out in *Basic Instruments,* 3d Supp. (1955), p. 32. See also ibid., p. 141; ibid., Vol. II (1952), p. 16.

no treaty that impinged upon the U.S. farm program could receive the constitutionally-required senatorial approval.

## The GATT versus Agricultural Protection

Only when there emerged domestic pressures to impose import restrictions on dairy products, products on which there were no domestic restrictions, did the United States realize that, although Article XI was "largely tailor-made to United States requirements . . . , the tailors cut the cloth too fine."[7] In 1951 the CONTRACTING PARTIES found that the U.S. import restrictions imposed on dairy products constituted an "infringement" of Article XI.[8] This finding gave rise to the sole invocation in the GATT's history of the retaliation provisions of Article XXIII. The Netherlands secured the authorization of the CONTRACTING PARTIES to limit imports of wheat flour from the United States to 60,000 metric tons per year.[9]

The U.S. government ran into even more trouble with the GATT when Section 22 of the Agricultural Adjustment Act was passed. This statute required the administration to impose quantitative restrictions or special fees (above and beyond customs duties) whenever "any article or articles are being or are practically certain to be imported into the United States under such conditions and in such quantities as to render or tend to render ineffective, or materially interfere with" any U.S. farm program or "to reduce substantially the amount of any product" subject to such a farm program.[10] Pursuant to that requirement, quotas were imposed on cotton, wheat, peanuts, oats, rye, and barley, as well as on certain products processed or manufactured from those commodities and on manufactured dairy products.[11] The CONTRACTING PARTIES granted the United States a waiver that was exceptionally broad, bearing no time limit and requiring only an annual report.[12] The breadth of this waiver, coupled with the fact that the waiver was granted to the contracting party that was at one and the same time the world's largest trading nation and the most vocal proponent of freer international trade, constituted a grave blow to GATT's prestige. The waiver, coming as it did at the same time as the unusually limited grant of authority by the U.S. Congress for the 1955 trade-negotiations round, was

---

7. Address by the then executive secretary of the GATT, Eric Wyndham White, "Europe in the GATT," at Europe House, London, May 1960, p. 5.
8. *Basic Instruments,* Vol. II (1952), p. 16.
9. Ibid., 1st Supp. (1953), p. 32. The authorization covered the year 1953 and was subsequently renewed annually. See, e.g., 4th Supp. (1956), p. 31.
10. 7 U.S.C.A. § 624 (1964).
11. *Basic Instruments,* 3rd Supp. (1955), pp. 141, 145–46.
12. Ibid., p. 32.

profoundly discouraging for many GATT supporters, and the United States was accused of hypocrisy.

The accusation was no doubt justified. But as was to become increasingly clear in the immediately following years, the United States had no monopoly on hypocrisy. The principal continental European contracting parties, which did not so openly espouse the traditional GATT virtues, maintained in many cases even more restrictive import regimes on agricultural commodities. But this fact was obscured by those contracting parties' balance-of-payments difficulties. So long as their currencies remained inconvertible, the continental European countries were able to justify agricultural protectionism under the Article XII balance-of-payments exception.

That it was already well known at the time of the U.S. waiver that payments imbalances alone could not explain the widespread direct controls on agricultural imports was demonstrated by the "hard-core" waiver decision taken the same day as the U.S. waiver decision. This hard-core waiver decision recognized that "some transitional measure of protection by means of quantitative restrictions may be required for a limited period to enable an industry having received incidental protection from those restrictions which were maintained during the period of balance-of-payments difficulties to adjust itself to the situation which would be created by removal of those restrictions" and permitted the continuation of such restrictions under certain rather burdensome conditions.[13] When restrictions that could not be justified under the Article XII balance-of-payments exception began subsequently to be identified and called "residual" restrictions, it became clear that a very high proportion were in agricultural commodity trade. These agricultural restrictions had been introduced in the interwar period, for reasons that in most cases had had little to do with payments imbalances. Countries had desired, for example, to offset grave declines in prices to farmers or to achieve self-sufficiency for defense purposes.[14]

The hard-core decision was a signal that quantitative restrictions in agriculture were no longer to be ignored in GATT proceedings, whether or not the decision was actually to be invoked. Belgium had recourse almost immediately to the hard-core decision to permit it to continue temporarily its quantitative restrictions on a wide range of agricultural products. The contrast between the agricultural and industrial sectors was emphasized by the fact that not a single item on the Belgian list was an industrial product.[15] Luxembourg also applied for a waiver to continue quantitative restrictions in agriculture, but candor compelled the Grand Duchy to admit that the problem was not temporary in

---

13. Ibid., pp. 38, 39. See discussion in chapter 9, "Quantitative Restrictions," supra.
14. See William Adams Brown, *The United States and the Restoration of World Trade* (Washington: Brookings Institution), pp. 39–44.
15. *Basic Instruments,* 4th Supp. (1956), pp. 22, 24–26.

character and that a hard-core waiver was therefore not justified. Not only had agricultural protection existed in Luxembourg at least since 1842, but the problem was so ingrained that the working party was forced to conclude that "no easy, rapid, or perhaps even complete solution can or should be expected."[16] The waiver consequently applied to all existing agricultural restrictions and was indefinite in term.[17]

The Federal Republic of Germany also ran into a major fight in the GATT over its agricultural restrictions. The Federal Republic's list of restricted products contained many more agricultural products than did the lists of Belgium and Luxembourg, and, unlike the latter two lists, it included some industrial products. Caught rather unexpectedly in 1957 and 1958 in the web of GATT consultations demanded by the United States, the Federal Republic at first vaguely suggested continuing balance-of-payments difficulties as a defense. But it subsequently fell back on the defense that the restrictions, as restrictions in effect on the date of the protocol under which the Federal Republic had become a contracting party (the Torquay Protocol), were justified under the provisional-application provision of that protocol.[18] This contention was rejected by the majority of a working party on the ground that the marketing laws in question were not "mandatory" legislation. Some of the members of the working party were of the view, moreover, that the marketing laws were not designed to deal with food shortages and did not authorize import restrictions.[19] The Federal Republic was therefore forced to obtain a waiver.[20] It did not, however, seek a hard-core waiver, since it was unprepared to give any "undertakings or assurances . . . about future commercial policy as it affected agriculture." One important consideration affecting the German government's action was the then recently effective Treaty of Rome, which called for a common market in agriculture among the six member states of the European Economic Community.[21]

Although only Belgium, Luxembourg, and the Federal Republic of Germany sought waivers, other European countries continued to impose restrictions on agricultural imports. As the French balance of payments improved

16. Ibid., p. 102, 111.
17. Ibid., p. 27.
18. The Torquay Protocol is set out at *Analytical Index,* p. 177. See discussion in chapter 19, "The GATT as an International Organization, infra.
19. The working party reports are to be found in *Basic Instruments,* 6th Supp. (1958), p. 55; 7th Supp. (1959), p. 99. The German case is discussed in detail in Gerard Curzon, *Multilateral Commercial Diplomacy* (London: Michael Joseph, 1965), pp. 146–55.
20. *Basic Instruments,* 8th Supp. (1960), p. 31.
21. Ibid., pp. 160, 161.

and the French franc became externally convertible, the French government relaxed restrictions on imports of agricultural commodities from outside the OEEC area at a substantially slower rate than comparable restrictions on industrial imports,[22] thereby underscoring the protectionist effect, if not the protectionist intention, of the agricultural restrictions. The same could be said of the policies of Italy, Austria, and most other European countries.[23]

At the same time that the movement toward external convertibility of most of the major European currencies laid bare the pervasive protection accorded agriculture through quantitative restrictions, other dimensions of the problems of international trade in agriculture became better known through the Habeler Report.[24] The four leading economists who contributed to the Habeler Report emphasized that measures discouraging imports and directly encouraging exports tended to isolate the internal markets of individual countries. An extraordinary degree of protectionism was required to create a situation such as that in wheat, where the prices to Swiss farmers were more than three times the prices to Canadian farmers and approximately twice average world import prices. This protectionism extended to net exporters as well as net importers. In the United States, one of the principal wheat-exporting nations, the prices received by farmers exceeded average world import prices, a situation that added to world surpluses and depressed world prices.[25]

The effect of the protectionism in importing countries was not only to make "net agricultural imports into these countries more and more marginal in relation to their total domestic production and consumption,"[26] but also to reduce the export proceeds of less-developed countries for temperate agricultural commodities. Although less-developed countries are normally thought of as dependent upon exports of tropical agricultural products and nonagricultural primary commodities, the four economists found that temperate agricultural commodities that were subjected to import protection or export subsidization in Europe, Canada, and the United States provided an important source of export revenues for many less-developed countries: wheat, meat, and wool for Argentina and Uruguay; live cattle for Mexico; sugar (produced in temperate developed countries in the form of sugar beets) for Indonesia and the West Indies; tobacco for many countries in Africa, Latin America, and southeastern

22. See U.S. Tariff Commission, *Operation of the Trade Agreements Program,* 12th Rep. (1961), p. 113.
23. Ibid., pp. 111–25.
24. *Trends in International Trade, A Report by a Panel of Experts* (1958).
25. Ibid., p. 85 (Graph III).
26. Ibid., p. 87.

Europe; cotton for Egypt, the Sudan, and Brazil; and oilseeds for many poorer countries in Asia and Africa.[27]

The Habeler Report engendered the GATT Programme for the Expansion of International Trade. The agricultural portion of this program was to be the responsibility of Committee II. That Committee thereupon carried out the series of consultations reviewed at the beginning of this chapter.

The reports of Committee II are revealing documents. Through the mass of diplomatic verbiage seeps a sense of surprise and even shock at the pervasiveness of protection in temperate agricultural commodities. For each of the six commodities studied, "there has been extensive resort to non-tariff devices involving protection to an extent and having consequences which were probably not fully recognized earlier."[28]

The work of Committee II was essentially limited to fact-finding and consultation. There was no attempt (except occasionally in the context of applications for waivers) to set target dates for the elimination of restrictions on agricultural imports, as was done by Committee III and its successor committees in dealing with the exports of less-developed countries.[29] The activities of Committee II were confined to consultations on substantial changes in the agricultural policies of particular contracting parties. Perhaps the most important consultations were held with the European Economic Community in 1962 and concerned the Common Agricultural Policy ("CAP").[30] Further major consultations were carried out in 1965 with the EEC on extensions of the CAP to new products, with the United States on the 1964 Meat Import Law, and with the United Kingdom on changes in its import regime for bacon and cereals.[31] Although the prospect of facing Committee II may have led some contracting parties to alter certain details in their agricultural policies, it is unlikely that this influence was substantial. Certainly no changes were made as direct results of the consultations.

On occasion agricultural problems have been considered within the GATT outside the framework of Committee II. The most important such occasion was the 1961 multilateral consultation on the difficulties experienced by New Zealand in marketing butter in the United Kingdom. This consultation, held under the "joint-action" authorization of Article XXV:1, concerned the de-

---

27. Ibid., pp. 92–93.
28. *Basic Instruments*, 10th Supp. (1962), pp. 135, 140–41.
29. See discussion in chapter 14, "Less-Developed Countries," supra.
30. *Trade in Agricultural Products, Report of Committee II on the Consultation with the European Economic Community* (1962).
31. *Trade in Agricultural Products, Reports of Committee II on Consultations with the European Economic Community, the United States of America and the United Kingdom* (1965).

terioration of the U.K. import price for butter. Protectionism in butter in nearly all countries had caused a concentration by exporters on the only major remaining unprotected market, the United Kingdom. The consultation led to the imposition by the United Kingdom of an import licensing system, a result which could hardly be thought of as progress.[32]

There is every reason to believe that the degree of agricultural protection has increased since the inception of Committee II. This has been particularly the case in the EEC. In many products the only way to achieve agreement on common prices and common systems of market organization has been to agree to align all national policies on those of the most protectionist of the Six for the product in question. Furthermore, in promoting the device of the variable levy to the status of principal weapon in the armory of protection, the EEC has carried to its ultimate conclusion the process of shifting the burden of adjustment from importers to exporters. The variable levy, used for many but not all agricultural products within the EEC, imposes a duty that varies as much and as often as is necessary to span the difference between the internal target price and the world market price. The effect of the variable levy is to make third-country suppliers into residual suppliers: so long as the target price is not reached within the Community, the levy will be sufficient to keep out imports. Any fall in world market prices, even as a result of increased efficiency, will be automatically offset by an increase in the variable levy.[33]

Attempts were made, however, in the context of the Kennedy Round to reduce the level of agricultural protection. In some sectors the duty reductions negotiated were substantial.[34] In other sectors attempts were made to negotiate multilateral commodity arrangements. The grain negotiations, culminating in the International Grains Arrangement ("IGA"), were successful in the sense that an agreement was arrived at. Whether that agreement has the effect of reducing the level of agricultural protection is another question, which will be

---

32. *Basic Instruments,* 10th Supp. (1962), p. 74; Curzon, pp. 198–200. A somewhat similar multilateral consultation on dairy products was commenced after the Kennedy Round. (GATT Document L/2972 [8 Feb. 1968]).

33. The variable levy, and the Common Agricultural Policy in general, is discussed at length in Kenneth W. Dam, "The European Common Market in Agriculture," *Columbia Law Review,* LXVII (1967), pp. 209–65. On the trade effects of the CAP, see Lawrence B. Krause, *European Economic Integration and the United States* (Washington: Brookings Institution, 1968), pp. 75–118. The term "target price" is used for cereals. Other terms are used for some of the other products, but the essential mechanism of the levy remains unchanged. In some sectors other protectionist methods, including tariffs and deficiency payments, are used.

34. On the Kennedy Round agricultural negotiations, see generally Foreign Agricultural Service, U.S. Department of Agriculture, *Report on the Agricultural Trade Negotiations of the Kennedy Round* (1967); and John B. Rehm, "The Kennedy Round of Trade Negotiations," *American Journal of International Law,* LXII (1968), pp. 403, 420–27.

discussed below.[35] Similar efforts in meat and dairy products were unusually modest.[36]

It is likely that further efforts will be made to negotiate agreements in meat and dairy products. If those negotiations are held within a GATT framework, and if they are successful, a decisive turning point in GATT history will have been reached. For agriculture the GATT will have rejected the barrier-reduction approach to trade in favor of a managed-market approach. With wheat as the only commodity now treated in this way, it cannot yet be said that the GATT has abandoned its traditional approach. This is particularly true because, although the IGA was negotiated within the Kennedy Round, it was not entirely a GATT affair. The Kennedy Round resulted only in an agreement in principle, and the details of the IGA were worked out at an International Wheat Conference held in Rome under the joint auspices of the International Wheat Council and the United Nations Conference on Trade and Development.

The IGA is composed of two parts, a Wheat Trade Convention and a Food Aid Convention. The first is a revision of the International Wheat Agreement, which has been in effect in one form or another since 1949. The Wheat Trade Convention is administered by the International Wheat Council. The Food Aid Convention, incorporating multilateral commitments to grant food aid to less-developed countries, is more in the sphere of economic assistance than trade.

The IGA does not, it will be seen, put the GATT in the business of managing markets. Even if the GATT's role in the IGA had gone beyond midwifery, it cannot be taken for granted that the GATT would thereby have signified its abandonment of the goal of freer trade in agriculture. The relation of the IGA to the reduction of import barriers is a complicated matter than can be properly discussed only after the reciprocal problem of export subsidies has been examined.

## Export Subsidies and Concessional Sales

Export subsidies have, within the developed world, been limited principally to agricultural commodities. Within the agricultural sector, however, export subsidies have been common. A panel on subsidies found in 1961 that, "although some subsidies exist on non-primary products, the great bulk of the subsidization measures relate to primary products."[37] Dairy products benefited from export subsidies in ten out of the thirty-four countries surveyed, meat in eight countries, and cereals in seven countries. Production subsidies for agricultural commodities were even more common, with cereals benefiting from production

---

35. See discussion at notes 56–60, infra.
36. See Foreign Agricultural Service, pp. 5–19.
37. *Basic Instruments,* 10th Supp. (1962), p. 201, 203.

subsidies in twenty of the thirty-four countries, dairy products in seventeen, and so forth. To be sure, these production subsidies probably had their major trade impact in reducing imports rather than in stimulating exports.[38] But in a world where the commercial demand for many agricultural products was less than the supply at current prices, the production subsidies doubtless swelled surpluses and tended to lead to the institution or increase of export subsidies in the surplus countries.

The General Agreement does not impose stringent limitations upon the use of export subsidies. Although Article XVI:3 prohibits the use of export subsidies to gain "more than an equitable share of world export trade" of a primary product,[39] export subsidies on agricultural products are usually considered by the GATT only in the context of general reviews of the implementation of that Article. One important exception was the 1958 Australian complaint against France, in which it was charged that France was using export subsidies on wheat and wheat flour to displace Australian exports to Ceylon, Indonesia, and Malaya. The CONTRACTING PARTIES issued a mild recommendation to France, proposing that the "French Government consider appropriate measures to avoid, in the future, that the system of payments . . . to exporters of wheat and wheat flour operates in such a manner as to create adverse effects on normal Australian exports of flour to Southeast Asian markets, and, more generally, on markets of wheat and wheat flour." The recommendation suggested that these measures "might consist of a revision of the methods applied . . . for the financing of French exports of wheat and more particularly of wheat flour, or of an agreement . . . to enter into consultations with the Government of Australia before new contracts are entered into by French exporters of flour to the Southeast Asian markets, with a view to minimizing the impact of such contracts on normal Australian trade channels."[40] However prudent and pragmatic this response to a troublesome dispute may have been, it is doubtful that occasional, isolated interventions of this character can reduce competitive subsidization. So long as a number of major surplus countries employ export subsidies, competitive subsidization is likely to persist.[41]

38. Ibid., pp. 203–4. The panel on subsidies relied upon the work of Committee II for its survey data.
39. See discussion in chapter 8, "Subsidies," supra.
40. *Basic Instruments,* 7th Supp. (1959), pp. 22–23; see also p. 46. During an earlier period the GATT provided the framework for consultations arising out of a Greek complaint concerning U.S. subsidization of sultana exports, as well as consultations arising out of an Italian complaint concerning U.S. subsidization of almonds and oranges. No formal GATT decision was required to settle either of these disputes. See U.S. Tariff Commission, *Operation of the Trade Agreements Program,* 6th Rep. (1954), pp. 39–40; 7th Rep. (1955), pp. 47–50; 8th Rep. (1956), pp. 52–54; 9th Rep. (1957), pp. 12–13.
41. In 1968 the United States filed a request for multilateral consultations concern-

One special aspect of export subsidies that has troubled the GATT at times has been the disposal of surpluses on noncommercial terms. The line between export subsidies and sales on concessional terms may be quite indistinct. Whether the motive of the selling country is to aid its own farmers or to aid the recipient country, food aid that preempts the commercial markets of third-country exporters creates an international trade problem and may in the end be deleterious to the interests not only of the international trading community but even of the recipient country itself. The complaints have usually been against the United States, which until very recently was the only country with a continuing large-scale program of noncommercial disposal in less-developed countries. Although the United States has been, after Canada, the world's second largest *commercial* wheat exporter, its exports on concessional terms have in recent years regularly exceeded its exports on commercial terms.[42] During the 1950s the U.S. food-aid program under Public Law 480 received uniformly critical comments in international trade circles. Only recently has food aid come to seem a duty toward less-developed countries rather than an unfair competitive tactic by a surplus country. Even today highly critical voices are to be heard in exporting countries that feel that their traditional export markets are being preempted by sales on concessional terms. In the 1966 GATT review of the 1955 U.S. waiver, for example, a representative pointed out that his country had been "adversely affected by sales on concessional terms to its traditional markets." As statistical evidence he cited the fact that "since 1954/55, shipments under Public Law 480 to LAFTA-partners had increased more than fourteen times, while in the same period commercial sales from the United States to these countries had increased by 2 per cent only."[43]

A 1955 GATT resolution, the result of a compromise between Australian and U.S. views, called on contracting parties disposing of surplus agricultural products to consult with "principal suppliers of those products and other interested contracting parties" with a view to the "orderly liquidation of such surpluses" and the "avoidance of prejudice to the interests of other contracting parties."[44] This resolution followed on the heels of adoption by the Food and Agricultural Organization in 1954 of a set of principles of surplus disposal. These principles were supplemented shortly thereafter by a set of guiding lines. The greater detail of the FAO principles and guiding lines and the creation of

---

ing competitive subsidization of poultry exports. GATT Document L/2972 (8 Feb. 1968).

42. Hearings on the International Grains Arrangement of 1967, [Ad Hoc] Subcommittee of the Committee on Foreign Relations, U.S. Sen., 90th Cong., 2nd Sess. (1968), p. 138 (Table II) (hereafter cited as "Hearings on International Gains Arrangement of 1967").

43. *Basic Instruments,* 14th Supp. (1966), p. 195, 197.

44. Ibid., 3d Supp. (1955), p. 50.

an FAO consultative subcommittee on surplus disposal, which at times met as often as once a month, led to the transfer of effective responsibility for surplus-disposal consultations to the FAO. GATT activities were thereafter largely limited to annual reviews of actions taken by individual contracting parties during the preceding year.[45]

The FAO principles warrant brief examination here, because they not only form a part of the international legal framework governing trade in temperate agricultural commodities, but they also have an informal status under the GATT resolution in view of the suggestion of the Review Session Working Party "that these principles would be useful to contracting parties engaged from time to time in consultations with respect to the disposal of surpluses."[46] The two central FAO principles are that surpluses are to be disposed of "in an orderly manner so as to avoid any undue pressure resulting in sharp falls of prices on world markets, particularly when prices of agricultural products are generally low," and that disposal on concessional terms is to be "made without harmful interference with normal patterns of production and international trade."[47] The crucial term that must be given content if the principles are to be applied is "harmful interference." In determining whether "harmful interference" exists, "account should be taken of special factors affecting trade in the commodity concerned," including both the new consumption induced and the "danger of displacement of commercial sales of identical or related commodities."[48]

The FAO's consultative subcommittee on surplus disposal was created to act as a "forum to which third-party countries might subsequently refer specific complaints if they did not consider that their views had received sufficient consideration, or if there had been no bilateral consultation." In addition, exporting countries were required to inform the FAO consultative subcommittee "in advance of proposed changes in policy on surplus disposal."[49]

The FAO principles are embellished, at least so far as wheat is concerned, by certain "guidelines" in the International Grains Arrangement of 1967.[50]

45. See e.g., *The Activities of GATT: 1961/62* (1962), p. 27.
46. *Basic Instruments,* 3d Supp. (1955), p. 222, 229. The principles are reviewed at length in an as yet unpublished manuscript by Robert L. Bard.
47. Food and Agriculture Organization, *Disposal of Agricultural Surpluses, Principles Recommended by FAO* (1963), p. 3, paras. 2 and 3. The first of the two undertakings quoted in the text is an undertaking of surplus-exporting countries, and the second is an undertaking of both surplus-exporting and importing countries. Another general principle (para. 1) calls for consumption-increasing rather than supply-restricting solutions to surplus-disposal problems, but this principle is too broadly phrased to be of great importance.
48. Ibid., pp. 3–4, para. 4.
49. Ibid., p. 20.
50. It is not clear whether the concessional-sales provisions of the International Grains Arrangement apply to all grains or only to wheat.

These guidelines call for member countries "to conduct any concessional transactions in grains in such a way as to avoid harmful interference with normal patterns of products and international commercial trade" and "to this end . . . [to] undertake appropriate measures to ensure that concessional transactions are additional to commercial sales which could reasonably be anticipated in the absence of such transactions." Such measures are to be "consistent" with the FAO principles and guiding lines, and they "may provide that a specified level of commercial imports of wheat, agreed with the recipient country, be maintained on a global level by the country." Any such level of commercial imports is to reflect historic commercial import levels and the economic circumstances of the recipient country. The guidelines go on to provide for presale consultations with affected commercial exporting countries.[51]

Evaluation of the GATT-FAO work on surplus disposal is difficult. Interest in the problem of the displacement of commercial exports has declined considerably, but it is not clear whether this decline is to be attributed to (1) improved consultation procedures, (2) recognition that the displacement problem is less serious than was once thought, or (3) the reduction of U.S. surpluses, particularly of wheat, and the greater urgency of providing certain developing countries, most notably India, with wheat on concessional terms. The FAO principles and the International Grains Arrangement guidelines are vague, but the consultative mechanisms apparently work well. The FAO principles tend to follow the original practices of the United States, the first country to initiate a substantial food-aid program. Nevertheless, certain changes in U.S. policies and practices on concessional sales may perhaps be traced to the FAO principles. One example is the 1958 addition to the U.S. authorizing legislation of a requirement that precautions be taken to assure that concessional sales "will not unduly disrupt . . . normal patterns of commercial trade with friendly countries."[52] It is not as clear that the 1967 guidelines merely incorporate existing U.S. practices on concessional sales. The requirement of those guidelines that any commercial-purchase requirements imposed on recipient countries as part of food-aid agreements be on a global basis may preclude the United States from tying food aid to commercial purchases of U.S. commodities; this requirement may be significant if the 1967 guidelines are to be applied to all grains and not just to wheat.[53]

51. The guidelines are to be found in Article 24 of the International Grains Arrangement.
52. Food and Agriculture Organization, "Food Aid and other Forms of Utilization of Agricultural Surpluses: A Review of Programmes, Principles and Consultations," in *Proceedings of the United Nations Conference on Trade and Development,* III (1964), pp. 403, 412–13.
53. International Grains Arrangement, Art. 24.

## The International Grains Arrangement

Agricultural import restrictions and agricultural export subsidies are closely related. In exporting countries, price-support programs, lifting as they do domestic market prices above world market prices, necessitate import restrictions in order to fend off imports attracted to the higher domestic prices; in addition, price-support programs require export subsidies in order to make possible, on the world market, sale of the surpluses created by the high domestic prices. One solution would, of course, be to reduce financial assistance to farmers. That solution is probably not a realistic possibility in view of the political power of farmers and the social problems encountered in transferring farm populations to cities.

Another solution, arguably consistent with the GATT, would be to substitute deficiency payments (that is, direct monetary transfers) for price supports as the principal means of supporting agricultural incomes. Domestic prices would then be equal to world prices. Although deficiency payments are protectionist in the sense that they stimulate local production, they permit the price system to fulfill its allocative function in world markets better than do price supports.[54]

A third, quite different solution would be to transfer the price-support principle from the national to the international level by a concerted effort to raise the world market price to the price-support level of the world's major deficit area. This was in essence the French Plan, which in a greatly watered-down form became the EEC negotiating position in the Kennedy Round.[55] Such a scheme would, of course, be an outright rejection of the GATT system.

A fourth solution, occupying a middle position between the solutions consistent with GATT principles and the French Plan, would be to carve up markets on a multilateral basis—that is, to reach international agreement on the direction and volume of world trade in agricultural commodities. The U.S. proposal in the Kennedy Round was arguably, although not ostensibly, an abbreviated version of this last solution. The United States proposed that guarantees of access be given by importing countries to exporting countries in order to protect traditional exporters' markets against importers' attempts at self-sufficiency. Such an intermediate solution, although giving productive efficiency some room to function, would be hard to square with the GATT system, for it would subject trade flows to agreement rather than to the market and over time would hinder adjustment to new conditions.

54. The differences between price-support and deficiency-payment systems are discussed in Dam, "European Common Market," pp. 215–17.
55. On the French Plan, see ibid., pp. 258–59; and the statements of French officials collected in *Proceedings of the United Nations Conference on Trade and Development* (1964), III, pp. 486–94.

Fortunately for the preservation of the GATT system, the IGA is much less ambitious than either the French or U.S. proposals. The Wheat Trade Convention portion of the IGA is essentially only a continuation of the old International Wheat Agreement. Like the latter, it establishes maximum and minimum prices between which the member countries are to attempt to maintain wheat market prices. The most important tool for maintaining the floor and the ceiling is the agreement of the member importing countries to take a "maximum possible share of its total commercial purchases" from member exporting countries and "when importing wheat from non-member countries . . . to do so at prices consistent with the price range."[56] Member exporting countries agree to supply regularly the commercial needs of the importers at prices within the prescribed range and, when the maximum price is reached, to make immediately available certain quantities at that maximum.[57] There are, however, no fixed commitments as to purchase or sale at the minimum price. Certain review procedures are to be set in motion,[58] but the IGA tacitly relies upon the exporting countries *to agree at the time the minimum price is reached* collectively to hold sufficient supplies off the market to maintain the floor.[59]

There are a number of technical differences between the IGA and the International Wheat Agreement that should permit the former to function more effectively; for example, a schedule of minimum prices for different grades and varieties of wheat is substituted for a single base price. The most important change, however, is that the minimum price is increased by roughly twenty-two cents per bushel. Although the effect of this change cannot be forecast with certainty, it may well be to induce a shift in the function of the IGA from stabilization to price support. Under the International Wheat Agreement wheat almost always traded above the minimum price, largely as a consequence of the operations of the U.S. export authorities. But with the new minimum set at approximately the average market price of past years,[60] it is failure to agree in advance upon the steps to be taken when the minimum much more likely that this minimum will be reached. If that does occur, the price is reached will be crucial. The exporting countries may then arrive at an

56. Wheat Trade Convention, Arts. 4 (2), 4 (5).
57. Ibid., Arts. 4 (3), 5.
58. Ibid., Art. 8.
59. This point was developed at great length by U.S. administration witnesses before the Ad Hoc Senate Subcommittee reviewing the IGA. See Hearings on International Grains Arrangement of 1967, pp. 5–6, 10–14, 16–19, 21. On this point and on the history of the Kennedy Round agricultural negotiations, see generally Irwin R. Hedges, "Kennedy Round Agricultural Negotiations and the World Grains Arrangement," *Journal of Farm Economics*, XLIII (1968), 1332–41.
60. See the statement by Helen C. Farnworth at Hearings on International Grains Arrangement of 1967, pp. 73–74, 145 (Chart A), 147 (Table I).

agreement on effective measures to support the world price, in which case a decisive step away from the GATT system and toward managed international markets will have been taken. Or the exporting countries may not be able to agree, and the price may fall through the floor, in which case some vestige of the GATT system will have been maintained, albeit by default. It is too early to say what will happen, and therefore one cannot yet characterize the IGA as a decisive step toward managed international markets in temperate agricultural commodities.

# 16 Regional Economic Arrangements

The U.S. draftsmen of the ITO Charter did not foresee that post–World War II commercial policy would be dominated by the rise of a multitude of regional arrangements which would challenge the draftsmen's universalist principles in the most fundamental manner. The U.S. Suggested Charter included only a short paragraph on customs unions, a provision that was expanded into the complex provisions on customs unions and free-trade areas presently found in Article XXIV of the General Agreement. This expansion took place at the behest of certain governments interested in European integration and of certain less-developed countries with other goals. The U.S. draftsmen abhorred preferences and endeavored to eliminate them, but they did not seek to prohibit either customs unions or free-trade areas. From one perspective, this differential treatment was plainly inconsistent. What could be more of a preference than lowering a tariff to zero for certain countries while leaving it at its original level for other countries?

The draftsmen's perspective was, however, quite different. So long as a regional arrangement brought about the complete elimination of trade barriers within a multination area, it was viewed as a step toward free trade, partial to be sure but laudable nonetheless. Preferences, which were to be prohibited outright unless saved by a specific exception in Article I,[1] were viewed as different in kind from customs unions and free-trade areas. One prominent State Department official summarized the conventional wisdom of the period:

> A customs union creates a wider trading area, removes obstacles to competition, makes possible a more economic allocation of resources, and thus operates to increase production and raise planes of living. A preferential system, on the other hand, retains internal barriers, obstructs economy in production, and restrains the growth of income and demand.

---

1. See discussion of preferences in chapter 4, "The GATT Tariff System," supra.

... A customs union is conducive to the expansion of trade on a basis of multilateralism and nondiscrimination; a preferential system is not.[2]

Given this point of view, the principal objective in the drafting of the customs union and free-trade area provisions became to tie down, in the most precise legal language possible, the conditions that such regional groupings would have to fulfill in order to escape prohibition under the most-favored-nation clause as preferential arrangements. The unusually complex provisions of paragraphs 4 through 10 of Article XXIV were the consequence.

The effort to attain precision and to force future arrangements into Article XXIV's mold proved to be, as will be seen, a failure, if not a fiasco. Ambiguity rather than precision reigned. The regional agreements that came before the GATT did not conform to the tests of Article XXIV, and in the face of the conflict, the GATT and not the regional groupings yielded. As time passed, the agreements that were placed before the GATT for inspection under Article XXIV came to look more and more like outright preferential arrangements, but the fact that they were defended as being within shouting distance of Article XXIV made it politically difficult to treat them as violations of the most-favored-nation clause. However disappointing these reversals were for the prestige of the General Agreement as the embodiment of a rule of law in international economic life, a more serious flaw in the Article XXIV rules soon became apparent. The supposedly self-evident difference between preferences and customs unions proved to be completely misconceived. Work in economic theory soon demonstrated that customs unions and free-trade areas, far from leading toward freer trade, might lead to results in direct conflict with the resource-allocation raison d'être of freer trade, while preferential arrangements could in some circumstances improve resource allocation. And experience with the customs-union and free-trade-area arrangements coming before the GATT showed that some were in fact disguised preferential arrangements.

Today it is clear that if a single adjective were to be chosen to describe Article XXIV, that adjective would have to be "deceptive." First, the standards established are deceptively concrete and precise; any attempt to apply the standards to a specific situation reveals ambiguities which, to use an irresistible metaphor, go to the heart of the matter. Second, although the rules appear to be based on economic considerations, the underlying principles make little economic sense. Third, the dismaying experience of the GATT has been that, with one possible exception,[3] no customs-union or free-trade-area agreement thus far presented for review has complied with Article XXIV, yet no

2. Clair Wilcox, *A Charter for World Trade* (New York: Macmillan, 1949), pp. 70–71.
3. The possible exception is the United Kingdom/Ireland Free-Trade Area Agreement. See *Basic Instruments,* 14th Supp. (1966), pp. 23, 122.

such agreement has been disapproved. These three weaknesses of Article XXIV will be examined successively.

## The Detailed Rules of Article XXIV

Article XXIV appears on first impression to set forth a precise set of rules for determining the circumstances under which regional arrangements will be permitted. The apparent precision, as in other detailed passages of the General Agreement, is quite illusory.

### Paragraph 4 versus Paragraphs 5–9

Perhaps the principal ambiguity is to be found in the structure of paragraphs 4 through 9 of Article XXIV.[4] Paragraph 4 sets forth what could be considered the principal rule. In that paragraph the contracting parties "recognize that the purpose of a customs union or a free-trade area should be to facilitate trade between the constituent territories and not to raise barriers to the trade of other contracting parties with such territories." This rule, although general, is capable of application; if economic theory is taken into account, the rule is even capable of effective application. But the following paragraph, paragraph 5, introduces the highly detailed rules contained in paragraphs 5 through 9 and starts with the crucial word "Accordingly." The relationship between paragraph 4 and paragraphs 5 through 9 is consequently a fertile source of controversy. If an agreement clearly complies with paragraph 4, is it automatically to be considered as meeting the standards of paragraphs 5 through 9? Or does paragraph 4 really contain only introductory language, and, in view of the word "accordingly," are the substantive rules to be found in paragraphs 5 through 9? Perhaps there are two complementary or additive sets of standards—the "purpose" test of paragraph 4 and the form requirement of the following paragraphs. The number of ways in which paragraph 4 can be related to paragraphs 5 through 9 is limited only by the number and the ingenuity of lawyers involved in the interpretation of Article XXIV.

The relationship between these two parts of Article XXIV became a source of dispute in the review of the Rome Treaty creating the EEC. Although the issue was not formally resolved, the EEC was successful in shifting attention away from paragraph 5 to the more technical criteria of the following paragraphs.[5] The decision thereby implicitly reached has controlled subsequent GATT reviews.

---

4. The remaining paragraphs of Article XXIV, except for the waiver provisions of paragraph 10, do not deal directly with customs unions and free-trade areas.
5. *Basic Instruments,* 6th Supp. (1958), p. 70. Perhaps the most powerful support for the conclusion that paragraphs 5–9 are to control is to be found in paragraph 10.

## The Common External Tariff

Paragraph 4 aside, the detailed rules in the remainder of Article XXIV contain a host of ambiguities. A particularly troublesome ambiguity lies in the requirement that, in the case of a customs union, "duties and other regulations of commerce imposed [on external trade] . . . *shall not on the whole be higher or more restrictive* than the *general incidence* of the duties and regulations of commerce applicable in the constituent territories prior to the formation of such union."[6] The general intent is clear. Although difficult to state in more specific terms than the treaty language itself, that intent is simply to prevent external trade barriers from being raised on balance in the process of creating the customs union.

The process of calculating a common external tariff to be applied to both high-tariff and low-tariff countries gives rise to troublesome problems of interpretation. A principal decision to be made is whether the words "on the whole" and "general incidence" refer to each item in the common external tariff schedule or to the common external tariff schedule as a whole. If the latter alternative is chosen, one must still determine whether the initial step is to calculate the height and restrictiveness of each national tariff schedule and then to strike some kind of average between these national levels (as, for example, by calculating a "height index" for each country, taking an average of these indices in order to determine an index for the common external tariff, and then working backward to calculate a schedule of external duties which will not in the aggregate exceed the height of that average). Or is one first to strike some union-wide average for each tariff classification and then to determine the aggregate height of a common external tariff composed of these union-wide averages, the customs union being free to assign any duties on individual items in the common external tariff as long as the calculated union index is not exceeded?

Whichever alternative is chosen, the unfortunate fact is that one cannot determine from nominal percentage rates the restrictive duty impact that a duty may have. A relatively high duty may provide excess protection in the sense that it may be higher than necessary to eliminate all trade in the commodity in question. When one attempts to reach a judgment as to the overall restrictiveness of a schedule of duties, the assigning of weights to individual duties raises troublesome problems because the most convenient criterion for assign-

---

6. Art. XXIV, para. 5(a) (emphasis supplied). The rule for a free-trade area, or an interim agreement leading to a free-trade area, parallels that for a customs union in most respects, but, because the member states of a free-trade area retain national tariffs, a somewhat different formulation is required. Here the "duties and other regulations of commerce" are not to be "higher or more restrictive than the corresponding duties and other regulations of commerce" previously in effect.

ing weights—the respective volume of trade for each item—tends to be a function of, rather than independent of, the restrictiveness of the duty.

To put these difficulties more concretely, some of the questions that must be answered in any calculation of a common external tariff are: (1) How does one average a tariff and no tariff? For example, if one were determining the height of a two-item schedule, one item having no duty and the other having a 50 percent duty, would the average height be a simple 25 percent? (2) How does one average a protective tariff and a revenue tariff? For example, if in a two-item schedule both items were to bear a 10 percent duty, and if for one item the 10 percent duty were to be sufficient to exclude all imports while for the other item the 10 percent duty were to have little or no effect on the volume of imports (because, for instance, the item could not feasibly be produced domestically), would it be meaningful to say that the average height was 10 percent? And if the protective tariff were to be raised to 50 percent in order to be doubly certain that no imports competed with domestic production, would the average be the arithmetic mean of 30 percent or still only 10 percent on the theory that a 10 percent rate on the protected item would be sufficient to exclude all imports? (3) How does one average tariffs on items with greatly different volumes of imports? For example, should one use a simple average or a weighted average for two items where the volume of imports is much greater for one item than for the other? And if one decides to use a weighted average, how does one weight duties which, for example, are high enough to eliminate all trade? (4) How does one average tariffs among countries? Assuming one takes a weighted average, how does one apply the weights—by the level of actual imports, by the level of potential imports assuming nil tariffs, or by some measure of the size of the national markets such as gross national product?

These questions are not merely statistical puzzlers. The method of calculation can have a dramatic effect on the composition of the common external tariff schedule. Given a customs union composed of several countries, each of a unique economic size and propensity to import, each with a unique combination of items bearing tariffs, and each with a unique mixture of protective and revenue tariffs, it would not be going too far to say that the language of Article XXIV gives no guidance at all. Finally, even if these statistical problems can be solved satisfactorily, and assuming quantitative restrictions are included within the terms "duties and other regulations of commerce," one must weigh quantitative restrictions against tariffs. This task, if not impossible, at least requires an unverifiable estimate of what tariff rate would restrict imports to the levels permitted by particular quotas.

No official interpretation exists. The text of an early draft of Article XXIV uses the phrasing "shall not on the whole be higher or more stringent than the average level." While this phrasing is perhaps slightly more certain of application, it is of little assistance, since we cannot be certain what substantive change was intended by the subsequent amendment. To be sure, the Havana Reports indicate that the intention was that Article XXIV "should not require a mathematical average of customs duties but should permit greater flexibility so that the volume of trade may be taken into account."[7] But to concede that no one method of calculation is required is not to state which methods are forbidden.

These ambiguities plagued the review by the CONTRACTING PARTIES of the EEC Treaty of Rome. The Six, having used an arithmetic average, refused to discuss the best method of calculation, because in their view paragraph 5 did not require any special method. But the discussion of the height of the EEC common external tariff took on a curious unreality, because the EEC had not yet in fact arrived at a definitive agreement on that tariff. In some cases the rates announced were only maximum, "ceiling" rates, and the final duties might be much lower. Under Article 20 and List G of the Treaty of Rome, the rates of duty for products encompassing some 20 percent of total Community imports were left for future agreement. These undetermined duties tended, moreover, to be those on which there was the sharpest conflict of interest among EEC members. The EEC review also raised a quite different legal question: whether the old duty rates with which the new rates were to be compared were the "legal or bound rates on the one hand, or, on the other, rates actually applied."[8]

## Elimination of Internal Barriers

Further ambiguity is to be found in the requirement that, in order for a regional grouping to qualify as a customs union or free-trade area under Article XXIV, "duties and other restrictive regulations of commerce (except, where necessary, those permitted under Articles XI, XII, XIII, XIV, XV and XX) [must be] . . . eliminated with respect to substantially all the trade between the constituent territories."[9] Quite aside from the obvious ambiguity as to what percentage constitutes "substantially all" trade, several more troublesome questions arise. Assume, for example, that the suggestion is correct that "substantially all" means 80 percent.[10] Is the only proper reading of this language that

---

7. Interim Commission for the International Trade Organization, *Reports of Committees and Principal Sub-Committees, United Nations Conference on Trade and Employment held at Havana, Cuba* (ICITO I/8) (1948), p. 51.

8. GATT Documents L/1479 (16 May 1961), pp. 3, 15. The executive secretary subsequently devised a compromise solution which, nevertheless, retained a substantial measure of ambiguity. See L/1979 (14 Nov. 1962), p. 3.

9. Art. XXIV: 8(a)(i); see also para. 8(b).

10. *Basic Instruments,* 6th Supp.(1958), p. 70, 99.

internal tariffs must be eliminated on 80 percent of all trade? Or can the test also be satisfied by reducing all internal tariffs to 20 percent of their earlier levels? Acceptance of the latter possibility would permit the establishment of preferential trading arrangements in derogation of what appears to be the common understanding of the purpose of the General Agreement. Again, assume that tariffs and other restrictions are totally eliminated on 80 percent of internal trade but that several major industries, comprising, say, the remaining 20 percent of internal trade, are totally excluded from the scope of the customs union or free-trade area. Is the "substantially all" test met? As will be seen, an affirmative answer to that question would enlarge the powers of members of regional groupings to benefit themselves and to injure nonmembers.

### Elimination of Internal Quantitative Restrictions

A further ambiguity that has plagued the GATT has arisen in connection with quantitative restrictions. In order for a regional grouping to qualify under Article XXIV, quantitative restrictions, as "restrictive regulations of commerce," must be eliminated on "substantially all" intermember trade, except that "where necessary" quantitative restrictions "permitted under Articles XI, XII, XIII, XIV, XV and XX" may be retained.[11] The ambiguity concerns the right of a member state of a regional grouping to eliminate quantitative restrictions on imports from other member states while retaining them on imports from nonmember countries. It might appear obvious that members of regional groupings are not only permitted but actually required to eliminate quantitative restrictions on "substantially all" intermember trade. Yet Article XIII states that, except in the situations specified in Article XIV, quantitative restrictions must be applied nondiscriminatorily; the elimination of quantitative restrictions against members only entails discrimination; and Article XIV does not refer to Article XXIV customs unions and free-trade areas as authorized exceptions.

The argument that Article XIII prohibits the discrimination entailed in eliminating quantitative restrictions against members only is almost certainly wrong. In the case of tariffs, the most-favored-nation clause of Article I is also silent about customs unions and free-trade areas, but it cannot be doubted that Article XXIV permits the elimination of tariffs against members only. After all, paragraph 5 of Article XXIV states that *"the provisions of this Agreement shall not prevent . . . the formation of a customs union or of a free-trade area"* complying with Article XXIV;[12] it is not merely the most-favored-nation clause that is thereby waived.

11. Art. XXIV: 8.
12. Emphasis supplied.

Nevertheless, a significant legal objection may in fact exist where a member of a customs union or free-trade area applies quantitative restrictions against nonmembers only. Quantitative restrictions may be maintained only for balance-of-payments purposes, and in the situation of application against nonmembers only, the balance-of-payments justification for the quantitative restrictions is likely to be of doubtful validity. If the member country in question were in serious balance-of-payments difficulties, the quantitative restrictions would have to be applied against all foreign currencies, including those of the other member countries. The only other solution consistent with a legitimate balance-of-payments justification would be the adoption of common external quantitative restrictions by the regional grouping as a whole.[13]

The quantitative-restrictions issue was sufficiently important in the review of the EEC for a special subgroup to be established to discuss that issue. The legalistic debates in the subgroup did not lead to any resolution of the issue,[14] and the problem again became a point of controversy in the cases of the European Free Trade Association,[15] the Latin American Free Trade Area,[16] the Association of Greece with the EEC,[17] the Yaounde Convention,[18] and the New Zealand/Australia Free-Trade Agreement.[19] By the time this last agree-

13. However, the latter solution, which would be a possibility for a customs union, would create a further legal question for which the General Agreement has no unambiguous answer. A system in which each member applied identical quantitative restrictions would result in one contracting party's imposing quantitative restrictions to protect the balance-of-payments position of another contracting party, a practice not explicitly authorized either by the quantitative-restrictions provisions of Articles XI–XIV or by the internal-trade-barrier provisions of Article XXIV. Moreover, it is doubtful whether in this situation the provisions of Article XXIV on the external trade barriers of customs unions would provide the requisite authorization. To be sure, under paragraph 8(a)(ii) all member countries may apply "substantially the same duties and other regulations of commerce" to all nonmember countries, but it is possible to argue with considerable textual force that the term "other regulations of commerce" in paragraph 8(a)(ii), unlike the term "other *restrictive* regulations of commerce" in the internal-trade-barrier provisions of paragraph 8(a)(i), does not include quantitative restrictions (emphasis supplied). Without launching into an analysis of the patterns of usage of the noun "regulations" and the adjective "restrictive" in the General Agreement in order to resolve the issue whether the difference between paragraphs 8(a)(i) and 8(a)(ii) is a drafting subtlety or a drafting oversight, it may be observed that the purported precision of Article XXIV proves here, as in the case of the ambiguities discussed in the text, to be illusory.
14. *Basic Instruments,* 6th Supp. (1958), pp. 70, 76–81; Kenneth W. Dam, "Regional Economic Arrangements and the GATT: The Legacy of a Misconception," *University of Chicago Law Review,* XXX (1963), pp. 615, 644–46.
15. *Basic Instruments,* 9th Supp. (1961), pp. 70, 75–78.
16. Ibid., p. 87, 91.
17. Ibid., 11th Supp. (1963), p. 149, 153.
18. Ibid., 14th Supp. (1966), pp. 100, 103–4, 113–14.
19. Ibid., p. 115, 117.

ment was reviewed, however, the legal issue had come to be regarded as insoluble. The working party put the matter aside on the legally extraordinary, but no doubt pragmatically justified, ground that "the issue was one which the [New Zealand/Australian] Agreement raised in common with other regional agreements examined by the CONTRACTING PARTIES, and . . . the different views on this subject were well known to the CONTRACTING PARTIES."[20]

## Interim Agreements

Finally, certain problems have arisen in connection with the requirement of paragraph 5(c) that any "interim agreement" leading to the formation of a customs union or free-trade area shall contain "a plan and schedule for the formation of such a customs union or of such a free-trade area within a reasonable length of time." The difficulty here lies not in the misconceived concreteness of the language but in the conflict between the obvious purpose of the General Agreement to foreclose future preferential arrangements and the pressure of groups of contracting parties to qualify preferential arrangements under the free-trade-area rubric. The draftsmen of the General Agreement knew that it was impracticable to require major regional groupings to spring instantaneously into fully developed form, but, fearing that approval of an "interim agreement" providing for partial freeing of intermember trade would lead to de facto approval of preferences, they required a "plan and schedule." Paragraph 7(b) establishes for the interim agreement a special procedure under which the CONTRACTING PARTIES may "find that such agreement is not likely to result in the formation of a customs union or of a free-trade area within the period contemplated by the parties to the agreement or that such period is not a reasonable one." In the event of such a finding, the CONTRACTING PARTIES shall make recommendations to the parties to the agreement, and "the parties shall not maintain or put into force, as the case may be, such agreement if they are not prepared to modify it in accordance with these recommendations." Nearly all proposals for customs unions and free-trade areas contemplate a transition period, and therefore this special procedure is the usual procedure.

The problems that arise in connection with the "plan and schedule" language are of several kinds. First, the negotiators of a regional grouping invariably find it difficult, and often find it undesirable for their own purposes, to spell out with precision all the steps that must be taken—often years in the future—to bring the customs union or free-trade area to final fruition. Even the elaborate Treaty of Rome creating the European Economic Community left lacunae.[21] Second, where countries at different levels of development are

20. Ibid.
21. Ibid., 6th Supp. (1958), p. 70, 75.

prospective partners, a very long transitional period may be required to permit the domestic industries of the less-developed partners to adjust. In that case a question necessarily arises as to the reasonableness of the time period. No agreement could be reached, for example, on whether the twenty-two year transitional period for the Greek association with the EEC was reasonable.[22] In the case of the Turkish association with the EEC, the possibility that a five-year preparatory stage (which preceded a twelve-year transitional stage) might be extended to eleven years or even longer led two contracting parties to characterize the aggregate period as "indefinite" rather than "reasonable."[23]

As the transitional periods of successive regional agreements reviewed in the GATT became longer, and as the commitments to arrive at completed customs unions or free-trade areas became less definite, the credibility of the legal threat of GATT disapproval vanished. New Zealand and Australia did not bother to set out a plan and schedule in their free-trade-area agreement of 1965. This agreement covered only about 50 percent of current trade between the two countries, and of that 50 percent about 90 percent was already on the free list. The agreement thus involved commitments to eliminate existing restrictions on only about 5 percent of total intermember trade.[24]

## Trade Creation and Trade Diversion

As has been seen, the U.S. draftsmen of the General Agreement viewed customs unions and free-trade areas as constituting movements toward free trade whenever internal tariffs were completely eliminated on substantially all trade. Today it is clear that this view is much too simple. Indeed, when one examines with care the functions of freer trade, it becomes clear that customs unions or free-trade areas complying fully with the requirements of paragraphs 5 through 8 of Article XXIV may be strongly protectionist in effect. One cannot, however, reproach the draftsmen for being bad economists; it was not until 1950 that, under the stimulus of a few pages in a book by Jacob Viner,[25] professional economists began to give serious thought to the conditions under which the allocation of world resources is improved by creation of regional tariff arrangements.

It is important, especially in considering possible improvements in the Article XXIV language and practice, to have a clear view of the key Vinerean

22. Ibid., 11th Supp. (1963), p. 149.
23. Ibid., 13th Supp. (1965), pp. 59, 61–62.
24. GATT Document L/2585 (15 March 1966), p. 2.
25. *The Customs Union Issue* (New York: Carnegie Endowment for International Peace, 1950), pp. 41–56.

concepts of *trade creation* and *trade diversion*.[26] These twin concepts are based essentially on the notion that the function of trade (and, in particular, the function of eliminating trade barriers) is to promote a more rational allocation of resources in the world economy. Without plunging into a full-scale discussion of the conditions for the optimum allocation of resources, it may be observed that in the most general terms a primary criterion is that there be no divergences between the prices paid by consumers and the costs incurred by producers.[27] Such a goal may be achieved only if, among other conditions, (1) consumers make purchases on the basis of relative prices to be paid by them, both as between domestic and foreign sources and as among various foreign sources, rather than on the basis of other criteria—such as might be important, for example, in the case of quantitative controls—and (2) such relative prices paid by consumers do not diverge from the prices received by producers. Assuming the former condition is met, the principal barrier to achievement of the latter condition is the existence of tariffs and quantitative restrictions.[28] While monopolies, cartels, local taxes, and many other internal policies and practices in both importing and exporting countries may create other kinds of divergences between the prices paid by consumers and the costs incurred by producers, the primary international barriers to optimization of the allocation of world resources are tariffs and quantitative restrictions.

## Internal Tariffs

Putting to one side for the moment the question of quantitative restrictions, it is important to observe at the outset that in a tariff-divided world the elimination of any particular tariff or set of tariffs need not, contrary to what might appear to be the common-sense conclusion, lead to an improvement in the allocation of world resources. This fundamental point may be illustrated by taking a hypothetical free-trade area in which we can observe the position of consumers in one member country with respect to purchases of goods from producers in nonmember countries (nonmember goods and producers), from

26. The analysis that follows is based on Dam, "Regional Economic Arrangements," pp. 615, 624 ff., and in turn on the economic literature cited therein.
27. The term "costs" is used here in the broad economic sense to include, for example, returns to capital and management.
28. For example, a tariff produces a divergence between the prices paid by consumers and the prices received by producers which is equal to the amount of the tariff. If in country A producers receive $100 per unit from domestic consumers and country B has a $50 tariff, country B consumers will pay $150 per unit (assuming no price discrimination by country A producers), while country A producers will receive only $100. The divergence is $50 per unit, the amount of the tariff. Quantitative restrictions give rise to a more complicated situation, because, by limiting imports to a specified quantity, country B artificially limits supply and hence induces a disparity between the price in country B and that in country A by an amount that is difficult to determine in advance.

producers in other member countries (member goods and producers), and from producers within the same country (local goods and producers). If the effect of eliminating intermember tariffs is to cause consumers to shift purchases of a particular commodity from relatively low-cost nonmember producers to relatively high-cost member producers, the impact of the creation of the free-trade area will be to that extent unfortunate for the efficiency of allocation of world resources. Before the creation of the free-trade area, tariffs were presumably applied equally against all countries. Therefore, while the prices paid by consumers included the duty, the relative levels of the prices paid by consumers nevertheless reflected the relative prices to all foreign producers. With elimination of the interarea tariffs, it may be that the prices to producers will be identical, yet the prices to consumers will be higher for purchases of nonmember goods (on which a duty must be paid) than for purchases of member goods (on which no duty need be paid).

On the other hand, the elimination of tariffs between members of the free-trade area may tend to shift purchases of a particular commodity from relatively high-cost local producers to relatively low-cost member producers. Thus, the impact of the creation of the free-trade area would be to that extent beneficial for the allocation of world resources. Such a shift would normally occur where prior to the creation of the free-trade area the duty exceeded the difference between the prices received by high-cost local producers and the prices received by low-cost foreign producers.

These two shifts in the source of production—from low-cost nonmember producers to high-cost member producers and from high-cost local producers to low-cost member producers—thus have diametrically opposed consequences for the allocation of world resources, the former unfavorable or trade diverting and the latter favorable or trade creating.

The foregoing is the underlying basis of the ideas of trade creation and trade diversion. Although recognition of these two different effects in the General Agreement and in GATT practice would be a great advance, the Vinerean analysis set out above is not complete. That analysis is limited to what may be called *production effects*. Viner looks only at the impact of the creation of regional arrangements on sources of production, assuming no changes in consumption. These production effects should therefore be contrasted with *consumption effects*, which represent the impact of regional arrangements on consumption. To a certain extent production and consumption effects are merely opposite sides of the same coin. This is the case when we think of consumers' choices between different sources of the same kinds of goods. But when consumption effects refer to consumers' choices among different kinds of goods, those effects describe an impact of regional arrangements upon consumer welfare that goes beyond the impact on production.

The analysis of consumption effects is not essentially different from the analysis of production effects. The structure of prices to local consumers of functionally competitive, albeit not identical, goods from local member and nonmember sources is changed by the elimination of intermember tariffs, the change occurring in such a way that consumers may be led to purchase more member goods than theretofore. Any such increase will come either at the expense of local producers or at the expense of nonmember producers. If it is the local producers that suffer, the effect on the allocation of world resources will be favorable; if the nonmember producers suffer, the effect will be unfavorable. Such consumption effects will, of course, tend to encourage production of the benefited goods in member countries and thereby discourage production of the goods in nonmember countries. Here again there is really no difference in kind between production and consumption effects. Since there is, for the purposes of institution-building, every practical reason for keeping economic concepts simple, it is desirable to use the concepts of trade creation and trade diversion to refer to both production and consumption effects (that is, to the impact on both identical and functionally competitive goods), even though Viner implicitly applies the terms only to production effects.

## Quantitative Restrictions

Insofar as the duty to eliminate barriers to intermember trade is concerned, Article XXIV:8 treats quantitative restrictions as essentially equivalent to tariffs: both are to be eliminated with respect to "substantially all" such trade. The elimination of intermember quantitative restrictions is, however, a quite different matter, so far as the allocation of world resources is concerned, from the elimination of intermember tariffs. The elimination of quantitative restrictions among members will be favorable for the allocation of world resources in all cases, even though quantitative restrictions are retained on imports from nonmember countries. To explain this paradoxical conclusion, it is necessary to note that the elimination of intermember quantitative restrictions, coupled with the retention of quantitative restrictions against nonmember countries, may produce one of two consequences. It may permit additional imports of member goods at the expense of local goods. This result would occur only where the prices to consumers were lower for both member and nonmember goods than for local goods (that is, only where, in the absence of both quantitative restrictions and tariffs, local production would be displaced). Or the elimination of quantitative restrictions against members only may lead to the displacement of nonmember goods by member goods. If this result occurs, it must be either because the prices to producers are lower in member than in nonmember countries or because tariffs against nonmember goods are sufficiently high to offset the lower prices to producers in nonmember countries.

In the former case, trade is created. In the latter case, it is, strictly speaking, the tariff and not the elimination of quantitative restrictions which produces the trade diversion.

## External Tariffs

Where customs unions rather than free-trade areas are concerned, certain additional problems arise. Here the economic literature is of very little assistance, because economists, in that new subdivision of economic theory known as the theory of customs unions, have been dealing with free-trade areas rather than customs unions. The economic impact of discriminatory tariff reduction has been studied to the exclusion of the economic impact of the alignment of external tariffs of two or more countries.

The creation of a common external tariff may entail (1) increasing all duties, (2) increasing some and decreasing other duties, or (3) decreasing all duties. Under Article XXIV, only customs unions of the third category are clearly lawful. Where some external duties are raised and others lowered, the ambiguous "higher-or-more-restrictive" test must be applied. The common-sense notion underlying Article XXIV is, of course, that so long as the common external tariff is no higher than were the members' tariffs collectively, one may conclude that the creation of the common external tariff has not been restrictive. But once we adopt as our principal measure of lawfulness whether the creation of the customs union is a movement toward or away from free trade, we may no longer adhere to such a simplistic notion. A customs union that entails the lowering of all external duties may be a movement away from free trade, whereas a customs union that entails the raising of all external duties may be a movement toward free trade. The direction of the movement depends on the combined effect of eliminating the internal barriers and changing the external barriers.

The task would be simplified if it were certain that, aside from the effects of the elimination of internal barriers, every decrease in an external duty involved a movement toward free trade and every increase a movement away from free trade. But just as we cannot be certain that the elimination of trade barriers between member countries improves the allocation of world resources, so we cannot be certain of the effect that increasing or decreasing any individual duty will have on the efficiency of the allocation of world resources. Given a world economy filled with tariffs, quantitative restrictions, taxes, subsidies, and monopolies, causing divergences between the prices to consumers and the costs to producers, it is not necessarily true that the reduction of any individual tariff (that is, the reduction pro tanto of those divergences) will actually improve the allocation of world resources.

Nevertheless, where one is dealing not with an individual duty but with the entire range of duties of a group of countries (as is inevitably the case in assessing the common external tariff of a customs union), it is likely that a reduction in the external tariff as a whole will be accompanied by an improvement in the allocation of world resources. In that sense Article XXIV's "higher-or-more-restrictive" test may contain a large element of wisdom. But even if it is assumed that a high correlation does exist, one is still left with the conclusion that the effect of the creation of a common external tariff should be placed in the balance with the effect of the elimination of internal barriers in determining whether a customs union is, as a whole, a movement toward or away from free trade. Where the effect of one is favorable, and the effect of the other unfavorable, for the allocation of world resources, there are no developed techniques for striking that balance.[29]

One problem of some practical importance arises from the circumstance that the General Agreement is a multilateral instrument creating mutual rights and obligations. Thus, even where a customs union fully complies with the requirements of Article XXIV, nonmember contracting parties are entitled under paragraph 6 to compensation for any duty that is increased in the process of creating the common external tariff, subject to the general principle that any duties reduced in that process are to be taken into account. The right to such compensation is personal to each contracting party. Normally the compensation will take the form of a reduction of duties on goods that are important exports of the injured contracting party (which reduction must be generalized to all contracting parties under the most-favored-nation principle). Since the decisive question in determining the right to compensation is the impact of the single increase in question with respect to the single contracting party in question, the possibility that the customs union as a whole may constitute a movement on balance toward free trade is irrelevant. One may observe in passing that the present compensation arrangements under Article XXIV, based on the notion of tariff bindings, have a definite bias, since they require customs unions to grant compensation for injuries arising to third parties from the creation of any common external tariff but not for economically similar injuries arising from any discriminatory elimination of internal tariffs.

## Preferential Arrangements

The weaknesses revealed in the underlying principles of Article XXIV throw into question the wisdom of the flat prohibition of preferential arrangements.[30]

29. The relevance of certain offsetting factors (such as the elimination of restrictions on capital and labor, economies of scale, external economies, and the elimination of the resource loss involved in operating a customs system) in judging regional arrangements is considered in Dam, "Regional Economic Arrangements," pp. 632–33.

30. This subject is also considered in chapter 4, "The GATT Tariff System," supra.

Since the tariff reduction inherent in preferential arrangements might be considered a movement toward free trade, albeit not so dramatic a movement as that produced by customs unions or free-trade areas, and since preferential arrangements by definition result in less discrimination against nonmembers than customs unions or free-trade areas, the justification for proscribing such arrangements absolutely is not clear. Certainly it is strange to state, as Article XXIV in effect does, that discrimination is forbidden unless it is 100 percent effective.

At least one can say that the favorable production effects (displacement of local goods by member goods) of any additional unit of trade created between the members of a free-trade area will likely be greater when tariffs are high, as during the first percentage reductions, than when tariffs are low, as during the last few percentage reductions. Any unit of new trade in the former case will be created where the prices to local producers are much higher than the prices to member producers; here again the differences in prices may be measured by the tariff. After most of the scheduled tariff reductions have occurred, however, any subsequent unit of new trade will be created where the prices to local producers and the prices to member producers are less divergent. The displacement of local producers by member producers will thus not produce as favorable an impact on the efficiency of the allocation of world resources as in the former case. This analysis suggests that a good portion of the benefits to the world as a whole to be expected from a given free-trade area could be achieved by a preferential arrangement among the same members.[31]

One basic distinction must be recognized in considering the appropriate treatment of preferential arrangements. There is one enormous practical difference between an arrangement in which, say, all tariffs on intermember trade are reduced by 80 percent and one in which tariffs on 80 percent of intermember trade are totally eliminated. The resource-allocation effects with respect to any given item will be greater in the former case, since early reductions tend to be more beneficial than later reductions. Members of a preferential arrangement are most likely, however, to exclude from the scope of that arrangement those industries where the elimination of intermember tariffs could be expected to have the most favorable production effects. If an economically significant and politically sensitive industry is much less efficient in one member country than in another member country and has therefore received a large measure of tariff and quota protection from the former country, it can be expected that strong

---

31. The resource-allocation effect of a unit of diverted trade will be of equal magnitude, whenever in the process of tariff reduction it occurs, because tariffs against nonmember countries will remain at the same height at all times. Where a customs union rather than a free-trade area is established, the situation is much more complicated, since the creation of the common external tariff will alter tariffs against nonmember countries.

domestic pressure will be exerted to exclude the industry in question from the scope of the preferential arrangement.

The foregoing analysis suggests that the General Agreement's treatment of preferential arrangements may have a perverse impact on the allocation of world resources. Since it requires the complete elimination of tariffs only on "substantially all" commodities (and 80 percent has been suggested as the appropriate measure of "substantially all") but proscribes agreements to reduce all tariffs by, say, 80 percent, Article XXIV may encourage precisely those deviations from the perfect free-trade-area model that minimize favorable resource-allocation effects. The proper conclusion seems to be that preferential arrangements, rather than being absolutely proscribed, should be subjected to the same kinds of analysis as is suggested for free-trade areas and customs unions.

### Application of Article XXIV

Article XXIV may also be judged on its own terms. That is to say, one may legitimately ask whether, even assuming the underlying principles had a sound basis in economics, Article XXIV has been effective in channeling the multitude of post–World War II regional groupings into a GATT-conforming mold.

The record is not comforting. Since it has been reviewed at length in other studies,[32] it need only be summarized here. Perhaps only one of the more than one dozen regional agreements that have come before the GATT complied fully with the Article XXIV criteria. That was the recent United Kingdom/Ireland Free-Trade Area, and even in that case certain doubts were expressed before the working party.[33] In some cases the regional agreements were very wide of the mark. The European Coal and Steel Community, covering only two major product lines, could not even qualify for the special regional-arrangement waiver of Article XXIV:10 but required a general waiver under Article XXV:5. The New Zealand/Australia Free-Trade Agreement, although not purportedly an example of "functional integration," provided for the liberalization of an even smaller percentage of intermember trade.[34] A strong tendency has also been manifested for interim agreements to provide for an even longer transitional period and to contain increasingly fewer detailed commitments for eventual completion of the customs union or free-trade area.[35]

32. Dam, pp. 635–60; Gerard Curzon, *Multilateral Commercial Diplomacy* (London: Michael Joseph, 1965), pp. 260–89; Gardner Patterson, *Discrimination in International Trade: The Policy Issues 1945–1965* (Princeton: Princeton University Press, 1966), pp. 120–270.
33. *Basic Instruments,* 14th Supp. (1966), p. 122.
34. Ibid., pp. 22, 115. See discussion in text, supra, at note 24.
35. See discussion in text, supra, at notes 21–24.

Under these substantive pressures, the formal GATT procedures envisaged by Article XXIV—including "recommendations" under paragraph 7(b) in the event of nonconforming "proposals"—have been shunted aside. For these formal procedures has been substituted what amounts to a tacit waiver in the form of statements, variously formulated, indicating that the regional agreement in question should be subjected to continuing review. This manner of handling the problem of regionalism preserves to individual contracting parties their individual legal rights (at least nominally), while permitting regional groupings to carry out their nonconforming agreements.

To say that the GATT has rarely been successful in forcing regional arrangements entirely into the Article XXIV mold is not to say that it has not had considerable influence at the margin. On the contrary, there is evidence, for example, that the GATT criteria were significant factors in the drafting of the Latin American Free-Trade Association treaty.[36] But the text of some of the newer agreements bespeaks eloquently the loss of credibility that Article XXIV has suffered as a consequence of repeated irresolution and compromise in GATT working parties.

## Some Thoughts on Reform

It is, of course, easier to criticize Article XXIV than to make practicable proposals for change. In considering proposed changes it is necessary to isolate the essential error of the draftsmen of Article XXIV. Those draftsmen thought that it would be possible to impose upon the international legal community a comprehensive set of substantive rules establishing a formal mold into which all regional treaties would have to be forced. Their essential error was thus in their conception of a legal institution as largely a set of substantive prohibitions rather than as largely a set of procedures. That the substantive rules eventually adopted were highly ambiguous and had little relation to the freer-trade goals of the General Agreement as a whole merely exacerbated this error in legal policy.

The draftsmen's error was particularly serious in the case of regional arrangements, for those arrangements were in a sense more powerful than the GATT itself. Patterson's judgment is that if an attempt had been made to block the drive toward regionalism in Europe on the ground that the legal requirements of the General Agreement had not been complied with, "the GATT itself probably would have been destroyed."[37] Although one may doubt that GATT supineness was dictated by such existential considerations in the case of some of the more recent regional groupings, there can be little doubt of the

36. Dam, "Regional Economic Arrangements," p. 661.
37. Patterson, p. 263.

soundness of Patterson's historical assessment in the case of what was in retrospect the crucial test of Article XXIV: namely, the EEC treaty.

The attempt to impose substantive prohibitions has not merely been a failure, but it has had an unfortunate effect on the quality of GATT working party discussions, at least insofar as one can determine from the working party reports. A lawyer cannot read the reports, for example, of the subgroups appointed to study the EEC treaty without a sense of despair at the absurdly legalistic quality of some of the discussion.[38] One carries away from such a reading more than a fleeting impression of diplomats playing at being jurists. Only recently has attention been focused explicitly in the working-party reports on the crucial issues of trade creation and trade diversion.[39]

It has not always been possible, however, to keep practical men from focusing on the heart of the matter. A number of procedural measures that have been utilized on occasion might provide precedents for a more systematic set of procedures that could constitute a basis for more useful and effective GATT reviews of proposed regional arrangements. The two most notable procedural innovations, neither specifically authorized by Article XXIV, have been the product-by-product review of the EEC Association of Overseas Countries and Territories[40] and the annual reviews of interim agreements, instituted in connection with the South African/Rhodesian customs union[41] and utilized for most subsequent regional arrangements.

A product-by-product review would have the advantage of shifting attention from substantive legalisms to the impact of the grouping on the world allocation of resources, the factor of greatest importance to the GATT as an international institution. The EEC product-by-product review is only a limited precedent, however, for that review was severely limited by a number of factors. First, the review was limited by its terms of reference to the effects of the EEC provisions on overseas territories and thus made no attempt to assess the effects of the Community as a whole. Second, only products imported from the overseas territories to the Six were studied; no attention was directed to exports from the Six to the overseas territories or trade among the overseas territories. Third, only twelve commodities were studied, and, although these commodities constituted a very large percentage of total EEC imports from the overseas territories, it is not possible to say that even the total import situa-

38. *Basic Instruments,* 6th Supp. (1958), p. 70.
39. See, for example, the discussions of the Yaounde Convention, ibid., 14th Supp., (1966), pp. 100, 106, 108–9, and of the United Kingdom/Ireland Free-Trade Area Agreement, ibid., p. 122.
40. See GATT Document L/1805/Rev. 1, Adds. 1–12 (1958). See generally Dam, "Regional Economic Arrangements," pp. 649–51.
41. See *Basic Instruments,* Vol. II (1952), p. 29.

tion had been reviewed. Fourth, the Six could not reach agreement with the majority of the working party on the relevant principles to be applied in determining the impact of the association upon world trade in those commodities.

The last of these four limiting aspects of the review is worth more intensive consideration for the light that it throws on the difficulty of assessing the future impact of a given customs union or a free-trade area. The position of most members of the working party was simple and straightforward: the association could necessarily open to the associated territories a vast barrier-free, protected market adequate to absorb not only present production but all foreseeable production by the overseas territories as a whole with respect to each of the twelve commodities. The effect would be, according to this analysis, to permit the associated territories to capture markets currently served by nonassociated areas; to encourage additional, and thus uneconomic, production in the associated territories, thereby necessarily causing even further diversion of exports from nonassociated territories; and, given what would become the inevitable need of nonassociated territories to find markets outside the Six, to depress world market prices.

To the Six, reasoning in this manner was reasoning in a vacuum. Harm to third countries could not be predicted without a forecast of future trends in world prices, at least through the transition period. The association would be only one factor among many that would determine the level of those prices. One could not overlook, the Six argued, the rising world standard of living, the stability of traditional trade patterns, or the physical, climatic, and financial problems affecting production in the overseas territories. More particularly, it would be improper to ignore the rising level of consumption within the Community itself which would result from the creation of the customs union.

The majority of the working party defended on several grounds the procedure of attempting to isolate the influence of the association from all other influences on prices. Third countries would be entitled to participate in the fruits of rising consumption throughout the world if there were no Treaty of Rome. Those countries were, moreover, entitled to participate in the rising consumption of the Six stemming from economic integration, since the expectation of increased consumption was an essential part of the rationale underlying the customs-union and free-trade-area exceptions to the most-favored-nation principle of the General Agreement.[42]

Even with the self-imposed limitations of the twelve-product study, an unprecedented amount of information was gathered and subjected to expert analysis. Most important, this evaluated information was made available to contracting parties which, although being greatly affected by the association,

42. See also the comments on the product-by-product review in Curzon, pp. 276–80.

did not individually have the resources required to gather the kind of detailed information necessary to support an effective negotiating position within the GATT deliberations.

The advantage of a product-by-product review is that such a review alone makes possible an assessment of the degree of trade creation and trade diversion to be expected from the regional grouping in question. Although the difficulties faced in reviewing only twelve commodities in the EEC case suggest that there are some limitations on the results to be expected from such reviews, it is easy to exaggerate those limitations. The process would not always have to be so difficult as it was in the case of the Six. First, agreement that trade creation and trade diversion were the standards to be used in the review would facilitate matters greatly. The disagreements outlined above were primarily differences in standards. Second, the burden of coming forward with the relevant statistical and economic information could be placed squarely on the contracting parties seeking to institute the regional arrangement; if an obligation to show that trade creation exceeded trade diversion were placed unequivocally on the members of the regional grouping, one of the difficulties of obtaining information would be minimized. The GATT secretariat could also play an important role in providing the kind of expert statistical and fact-evaluation services which, for example, the staff of the Commission of the European Economic Community provides in intra-Community matters.[43] Finally, it might be possible, once agreement upon the trade-creation, trade-diversion standard were reached, to arrive at certain rules of thumb that would facilitate the analysis of particular proposals.[44]

The annual reviews of interim agreements have played a useful, though limited, role. At first the members of regional arrangements did not take the annual reviews seriously, but as the reviews became more technical and less political, they became a more important forum for influencing the activities of regional organizations. This was, in particular, the pattern that developed in the European Coal and Steel Community annual reviews.[45] Since interim agreements tend to be more nearly agreements to agree than definitive accords as to the eventual contours of the completed regional groupings, annual reviews can exercise a more effective influence than can initial examination of the founding documents of regional arrangements.

43. The GATT Secretariat did, as a matter of fact, publish a paper on the probable effects of the EEC. See *The Possible Impact of the European Economic Community, in Particular the Common Market, upon World Trade* (Trade Intelligence Paper No. 6, 1957). But since this paper had no official status, it did not become a basis for discussions in the GATT review.
44. See Dam, "Regional Economic Arrangements," pp. 627–28, for certain suggestions.
45. See discussion in ibid., pp. 640–41.

The annual reviews have not been utilized to their full possibilities. In part this has been because there has been no agreement on the standards to be followed. Agreement that the crucial question is not the extent of compatibility with technical legal criteria or the direction of changes in imports and exports, but rather the degree of trade creation versus trade diversion, would provide a basis for more serious reviews. In part the annual reviews have also suffered from neglect. They have not always been taken seriously. The CONTRACTING PARTIES no longer formally require, at the time of the initial consideration of interim agreements, that annual reviews be held, and this failure necessarily affects attitudes toward the legal status of such annual reviews as the regional groupings may choose to subject themselves to voluntarily.

Amendment of Article XXIV would, of course, be difficult. Although such amendment would require acceptance by only two-thirds of the contracting parties, it would, under Article XXX, be effective only with respect to those contracting parties accepting it. But there is no clear indication that the present language of Article XXIV stands in the way of meaningful inquiries into the trade-creating and trade-diverting effects of regional agreements. Such inquiries are surely justified if meaning is to be accorded to paragraph 4 (which provides, it will be recalled, that the contracting parties "recognize that the purpose of a customs union or a free-trade area should be to facilitate trade between the constituent territories and not to raise barriers to the trade of other contracting parties with such territories"). And if paragraph 4 is to be considered the basic test, as its position in Article XXIV surely justifies, the trade-creating, trade-diverting balance of regional agreements becomes crucial.

# 17 Market Disruption and Cotton Textiles

At the same time that the GATT was profoundly changing its procedures to reduce barriers to the exports of less-developed countries and to give affirmative assistance to those exports, there was a strong countercurrent to be observed. This countercurrent led to agreements, entered into within the framework of the GATT, which tended to legitimate existing nontariff restrictions on less-developed country exports of cotton textiles and which in prescribed circumstances permitted additional such restrictions on those exports. The most important agreements, each marking important stages in this offsetting development, were the Decision on the Avoidance of Market Disruption[1] and the Short-Term and the Long-Term Arrangements Regarding International Trade in Cotton Textiles.

These three documents and the countercurrent in general raise certain fundamental questions about the usefulness of law and institutional arrangements in promoting the expansion of international trade. The principal question, which has already been raised in passing in the discussion of the Article XIX escape clause,[2] is whether safeguard measures that legitimate an increase in barriers to trade and that involve a release from solemn undertakings may not paradoxically—particularly if subjected to appropriate procedures and residual supervision by the international community—contribute in an important measure to the reduction of trade barriers and to the promotion of international trade. A subsidiary question is whether, at least with respect to products of unusual import sensitivity, the imposition of quantitative restrictions for protective purposes may not—again when subjected to appropriate procedures and to international supervision—be more favorable to the accomplishment of these goals than is the conventional GATT abstinence from the use of quantitative restrictions for other than balance-of-payments purposes. These questions

1. *Basic Instruments,* 8th Supp. (1960), p. 22.
2. See discussion in chapter 6, "Technical Tariff Negotiations," supra.

can be adequately discussed only in the context of the actual experience of the GATT in recent years, particularly in the implementation of the Long-Term Arrangement.

## The Decision on Market Disruption

The extraordinary growth of Japanese exports in the 1950s gave rise to apprehension in many countries.[3] Those exports were concentrated in a limited number of kinds of manufactures and were often offered at prices well below the prevailing domestic prices in the importing countries. Most countries reacted to this grave threat to some of their most important domestic industries by outright discrimination against Japanese goods. Even after the accession of Japan to the GATT in 1955,[4] many countries continued to discriminate against Japanese goods, either in flagrant violation of the GATT rules or by the invocation of Article XXXV.[5] In some countries this discrimination was justified on the ground that Japan, as a low-wage country, could not be treated in the same way as other exporters of manufacturers. Emphasis was sometimes placed on an alleged lack of "responsibility" on the part of the Japanese government and Japanese industry in permitting sudden increases in exports of particular goods to particular countries, tending thereby to cause severe dislocations in international trading patterns and bankruptcies and unemployment in domestic economies.

As some of the less-developed countries began in the late 1950s to export significant quantities of manufactures, particularly cotton textiles, the fear of "low-wage" imports, long a contributing element in the protectionist policies of the developed countries, became accentuated. Some of the same weapons already used to discourage Japanese imports were thereupon turned on those less-developed countries, with consequences that were extremely serious in the light of the less-developed countries' need for hard currency earnings and the importance of exports of manufactures in any program of industrialization. In the developed countries the dislocation problem began to seem less like a specifically Japanese problem than like a generic problem of international trade in manufactures between countries with different levels of wages. This

3. In 1949 Japan's merchandise exports totaled $533,000,000. By 1959 this figure had increased over 600 percent to 3,413,000,000. See the Japanese balance of payments statistics collected in Warren S. Hunsberger, *Japan and the United States in World Trade* (New York: Harper, 1964), pp. 421–27.
4. See *Basic Instruments*, 4th Supp. (1956), p. 7.
5. Article XXXV is discussed in chapter 19, "The GATT as an International Organization," infra. For the measures taken against Japanese trade and the role of the GATT in reducing the resulting discrimination during the 1950s, see Gardner Patterson, *Discrimination in International Trade, The Policy Issues, 1945–1965* (Princeton: Princeton University Press, 1966), pp. 271–300.

broader problem began to be discussed under the heading of "market disruption."

In 1959 the CONTRACTING PARTIES decided, upon the initiative of the United States, to place the "question of the avoidance of market disruption" on their agenda and to commission the Executive Secretary to submit a factual report based in part on consultations with interested governments.[6] To a certain extent the growing interest in the concept of "market disruption" reflected a search for a legal justification for the retention of quantitative restrictions, which, after the major European currencies became externally convertible in 1958, could no longer be justified on balance-of-payments grounds. A working party was subsequently established to study the market disruption problem. The working party sidestepped the argument that the problem was only one of the appropriate safeguards and that the General Agreement contained sufficient safeguards (such as the escape clause in Article XIX and the renegotiation provisions of Article XXVIII) to protect any legitimate interests of the importing countries. It concluded that "whether or not safeguards against situations of 'market disruption' were already available within the provisions of the General Agreement, there were political and psychological elements in the problem which rendered it doubtful whether such safeguards would be sufficient to lead some contracting parties which are dealing with these problems outside the framework of the General Agreement or in contravention of its provisions to abandon these exceptional methods at this time." The working party advocated a procedural approach to the problem under which (1) explicit recognition would be given to the "existence of a problem which has been called 'market disruption' "; (2) multilateral consultations would be envisaged for arriving at "constructive solutions"; (3) the procedures adopted should lead to "the orderly expansion of international trade"; but (4) "existing rights and obligations under the General Agreement should not be prejudiced."[7]

The CONTRACTING PARTIES thereupon adopted a decision concerning steps to be taken for avoiding "market disruption." The decision commenced with what was in substance if not in form a definition of "market disruption," prepared in this instance by the executive secretary. Following a declaration that "in a number of countries situations occur or threaten to occur which have been described as 'market disruption,' " the CONTRACTING PARTIES continued:

> These situations generally contain the following elements in combination:
>
> (i) a sharp and substantial increase or potential increase of imports of particular products from particular sources;
> (ii) these products are offered at prices which are substantially below

6. *Basic Instruments,* 8th Supp. (1960), p. 22.
7. Ibid., 9th Supp. (1961), pp. 106–7.

those prevailing for similar goods of comparable quality in the market of the importing country;
(iii) there is serious damage to domestic producers or threat thereof;
(iv) the price differentials referred to in paragraph (ii) above do not arise from governmental intervention in the fixing or formation of prices or from dumping practices.

In some situations other elements are also present and the enumeration above is not, therefore, intended as an exhaustive definition of market disruption.[8]

This definition did not, it should be noted, refer to the causes of the exporting country's effectiveness in penetrating the domestic markets of the importing countries. There was no suggestion that the exporting country was doing anything improper. Rather, the principle of comparative advantage was itself being called into question.

If the definition of "market disruption" was somewhat detailed, the measures envisaged for dealing with it were sketchy. The CONTRACTING PARTIES contented themselves with statements that they shared the common objective of finding "constructive solutions consistent with the basic aims of the General Agreement" and that a permanent Working Party on Avoidance of Market Disruption should be established to provide facilities for multilateral consultations and to prepare, with the assistance of the International Labour Office, a report on the factors underlying the "market disruption" problem. The working party was to examine "in particular the relevance to international trade of differences in the costs of various factors of production and marketing, including labour costs."[9]

Interestingly enough, the permanent working party was not called upon to carry out any other specific tasks and in the end it did not even produce a report.[10] One may conjecture that three different factors were involved in this failure to follow up the "market disruption" decision. First, it became increasingly clear that there was but a difference in degree, and not a difference in substance, between the conditions that gave rise to an ordinary increase in international trade and those that gave rise to the economic impact associated with the concept of "market disruption." Second, the Japanese government, continuing a course of action launched early in the 1950s, entered into an increasing number of agreements for "voluntary" export quotas on manufactured products; these bilateral agreements not only provided for Japanese limitations on "sensitive" exports, but also furnished a legal justification for the importing country to restrict imports from Japan where necessary for "orderly market-

8. Ibid., p. 26.
9. Ibid., pp. 26, 27–28.
10. See Patterson, p. 306.

ing."[11] Third, the products tending to cause the greatest dislocations in the importing countries and coming in the highest proportions from the less-developed countries—namely, cotton textiles—were singled out for special attention by the GATT. The developed countries felt that something more than a permanent working party was required to deal with the dramatic increase in textiles imports from certain Asian less-developed countries, such as Hong Kong, Pakistan, and India.

The decisive incident in the movement toward a special international arrangement in textiles came in the spring of 1961 when the newly elected President Kennedy promised the textile industry that he would come to its aid in what then appeared would be a battle for survival. Not long thereafter the United States proposed an international arrangement for the "orderly development" of cotton textile trade. Thereupon followed in short order the negotiation of the Short-Term Arrangement Regarding International Trade in Cotton Textiles, covering the period from 1 October 1961, to 31 September 1962, and the Long-Term Arrangement Regarding International Trade in Cotton Textiles, covering the following five years. In 1967 the Long-Term Arrangement was extended for three years.[12] Since the Long-Term Arrangement incorporates most of the principles contained in the Short-Term Arrangement and since the Short-Term Arrangement no longer has any operative significance, the following discussion will concentrate on the former.

## The Long-Term Arrangement in Cotton Textiles

In considering the provisions of the Long-Term Arrangement, one should bear in mind that the Arrangement was proposed and sold by its proponents as a device for increasing international trade in cotton textiles. The premise was that if trade increased gradually and in an "orderly manner" (the adjective "orderly" came to be as important as the noun "disruption" in the vocabulary of the importing countries), the economic and social costs of the displacement of local production by imports from the less-developed countries and Japan could be reduced to the point where the special measures, often illegal under the General Agreement, then being taken by many importing countries could be eliminated. The argument was that slow but steady growth in less-developed country exports to developed country markets would contribute far more to economic development than would sudden increases, often concentrated in a few products, which merely led to governmental measures closing the developed

---

11. On Japan's voluntary export quotas, see Patterson, pp. 293–300; see generally Hunsberger.
12. The text of the Long-Term Arrangement is set out in *Basic Instruments*, 11th Supp. (1963), p. 25; the text of the Short-Term Arrangement, in 10th Supp. (1962), p. 18. The 1967 extension is in 15th Supp. (1958), p. 56.

country markets to further increases. The preamble to the Long-Term Arrangement was intended to be at least as much in the interest of the less-developed countries as in that of the developed countries. "Disruptive effects," under the preamble, were to be avoided "in individual markets and on individual lines of production in both importing and exporting countries."

The choice of cotton textiles as the first trade sector to be subjected to special multilateral regulation was an important and ironic decision. It was important because cotton textiles made up a large share of total international trade and a particularly large share of exports by certain less-developed countries in Asia. In 1964 world exports of textiles and clothing constituted 10 percent of total world exports of manufactured goods. In 1963 textiles constituted some 44 percent of all Hong Kong exports, 34 percent of all Indian exports, and 34 percent of all Pakistani exports.[13] In the United States, the most active supporter of the GATT initiative in this field, textile products constituted one-fifth of all imports from Asian countries other than Japan.[14] That cotton textiles should have been the first (and thus far the only) field so singled out was ironic because cotton textiles had frequently been the first, and thereafter the major, industry to be found in developing countries (including the developing countries of the nineteenth century), and it is in this field that the comparative advantage of less-developed countries in manufactures had been the most striking. Partly this had been attributable to the labor-intensive structure of the industry, but, as the industry had in recent years become increasingly capital intensive, the new investment in certain less-developed countries had given them more efficient plants and equipment than the old and outmoded facilities in certain developed countries.

The Long-Term Arrangement makes a fundamental distinction between products on which a particular country maintains nontariff restrictions and products on which that country maintains no such restrictions. This fundamental distinction is somewhat obscured by the drafting techniques used, which emphasize countries rather than products. Article 2 imposes certain obligations on countries that maintain nontariff restrictions (the United Kingdom and the six member states of the EEC are such countries), and Article 3 gives certain rights to countries that maintain no nontariff restrictions (the United States is such a country). Despite the fogginess of the language, however, Article 2 countries may enjoy the rights of Article 3 with respect to products on which they maintain no restrictions.

The basic undertaking for Article 2 countries is to expand access to their markets so that at the end of the five-year period imports from other partici-

13. Organization for Economic Co-operation and Development, *Modern Cotton Industry* (Paris, 1965), pp. 62–63.
14. Ibid., p. 68 (Table I).

pating countries of cotton textile "products remaining subject to restrictions . . . taken as a whole" will reach a "level corresponding to the quotas opened in 1962 for such products, as increased by [an agreed] . . . percentage."[15] The agreed percentage in the original Long-Term Arrangement was 15 percent for Norway, Sweden, and Denmark; 88 percent for the European Economic Community; and 95 percent for Austria.[16] The corresponding figures for the 1967 extension were 24, 154 and 152, respectively.[17] The higher figures for the EEC and Austria than for the three Scandinavian countries do not reflect a more onerous undertaking, but, rather, relatively low levels of imports of cotton textiles and relatively stringent import controls.[18]

Although the United Kingdom maintained restrictions on cotton textile imports, it was permitted to attach to its acceptance a reservation that excluded any obligation to increase access to its market. This permission was based on the theory that the United Kingdom met two special criteria set out in the Record of Understandings to the Long-Term Arrangement:

(i) that, in the decade preceding the entry into force of the Arrangement, it had experienced a substantial contraction in its cotton textile industry, and
(ii) that it was importing a substantial volume of cotton textiles, particularly from the less-developed countries and territories and Japan, in relation to its own production of cotton textiles.[19]

Participating countries maintaining restrictions are subject to several further obligations. Where restrictions are maintained contrary to the provisions of the General Agreement, those countries are "to relax those restrictions progressively each year with a view to their elimination as soon as possible,"[20] an obligation that surely adds very little to the basic duty under the General Agreement to eliminate such restrictions forthwith. In addition, participating countries are not to "intensify existing import restrictions," whether or not imposed inconsistently with the General Agreement.[21] They are to administer

15. Art. 2 (3). *Basic Instruments,* 11th Supp. (1963), p. 26.
16. Annex B. Ibid., p. 32. The EEC undertaking was subject to a maximum quantitative limit. See ibid., p. 38.
17. *Basic Instruments,* 15th Supp. (1968), p. 56.
18. See statistics in Organization for Economic Co-operation and Development, *Modern Cotton Industry* (Paris, 1965), p. 70 (Table III). Curzon refers to the policies of the EEC member states as a "practical embargo" and a "virtual lockout." See Gerard Curzon, *Multilateral Commercial Diplomacy* (London: Michael Joseph, 1965).
19. *Basic Instruments,* 11th Supp. (1963), p. 40.
20. Ibid., p. 26, Art. 2(1).
21. Ibid., Art. 2(2).

their remaining restrictions (and to carry out any relaxation of restrictions) "in an equitable manner and with due regard to the special needs and situation of the less-developed countries,"[22] a formula that may be thought to differ markedly from the duty under Article XIII:1 of the General Agreement to administer restrictions in a nondiscriminatory manner.

Participating countries not imposing restrictions on a particular cotton textile product (whether or not they impose restrictions on other cotton textile products) may impose import "restraints" on that product under certain specified conditions. The term "product" is not defined, but the sixty-four "categories" of cotton textiles in the Short-Term Agreement suggest one manner of definition, and the United States has in fact utilized those sixty-four categories. The principal substantive condition for the imposition of these "Article 3 restraints" is that exports by a participating country must be "causing or threatening to cause market disruption."[23]

The standard of "market disruption," set forth in Annex C, is the definition previously laid down by the CONTRACTING PARTIES (set out above), subject to a few qualifications set forth in the Record of Understandings. The price criterion of subparagraph (ii) is changed by the Record of Understandings to require that the prices of the allegedly disruptive imports be compared not only to the prices of the domestic products, but also to "the prices at which other exporting countries also sell their goods in the importing country"; there is, however, no attempt to set forth the relationship that must exist between the prices of the allegedly disruptive imports and those of the third-century imports before a finding of "market disruption" can be justified.[24] The damage criterion in subparagraph (iii) is similarly changed to make clear what was presumably implicit in the earlier definition; namely, that the "damage" must be "caused directly by market disruption and not by any change of consumer taste, technological advance, or similar factors."[25] Finally, the notion of a threat

22. Ibid., pp. 26, 37, Art. 2(4).
23. Ibid., p. 27, Art. 3(1).
24. Record of Understandings, ibid., p. 40, Annex C, para. 26. These understandings were said to be "reached by the Cotton Textiles Committee during its meeting from 29 January to 9 February 1962" and therefore appear to have official status under Article 8 (b) of the Long-Term Arrangement. Other understandings reached at meetings of the Cotton Textiles Committee may also be relevant but are not always made public. The air of secrecy that pervades the meetings of the Committee and, to an even greater extent, the operation of national restraint programs, presents a problem not only for scholars but, more important, for private exporters, who are unable to plan for the future with any measure of security. The secrecy thus contributes to the trade-restraining influence of the Arrangement.
25. Ibid., para. 27.

of disruptive activity, found in the Long-Term Arrangement itself, is limited to refer to "an actual threat and not a potential threat."[26]

When "in the judgment of the importing country" the requisite "market disruption" or threat thereof exists, the importing country may request the exporting country in question to consult. This request must include a "detailed, factual statement of the reasons and justification for the request," and the importing country may indicate in its request the "specific level at which it considers that exports of such products should be restrained."[27] The importing country may indeed request that the exporting country impose export restraints, and, if after sixty days there has been "no agreement either on the request for export restraint or on any alternative solution" (or at any time if "in critical circumstances . . . an undue concentration of imports" threatens "damage difficult to repair"), the importing country may impose a restraint on the product in question.[28] Any such restraint or request for a restraint must conform to the rather complicated provisions of Annex B of the Arrangement.

Annex B constitutes in many ways the heart of the Arrangement, and its provisions on regularly increased access are surely the most original parts of the Arrangement. An Article 3 restraint may not restrain the level of imports (or, in the case of a requested export restraint, the level of exports) of the product in question below the "level of actual imports or exports" during the base period, which is "the twelve-month period terminating three months preceding the month in which the request for consultation is made."[29] Should the restraint remain in effect for more than twelve months, the increased access requirements come into effect. Except in "exceptional cases," the level of restraint in the second twelve-month period "shall not be lower than the level specified for the preceding twelve-month period, increased by 5 percent."[30] And in each subsequent twelve-month period the level of restraint must be increased by not less than 5 percent per year. Moreover, where restraint is exercised for more than one product, "the agreed level for any one product may be exceeded by 5 percent provided that the total exports subject to restraint

---

26. Ibid., para. 28. One crucial ambiguity in the definition of market disruption remains. Although the definition states that market disruption "situations generally contain the following elements in combination" and thereafter lists four factors, it is not clear whether market disruption might exist in the absence of one of those factors, such as, for example, "serious damage to domestic producers or threat thereof." To take a practical example, can restraints be justified where domestic industry is operating at full capacity and low-price imports merely serve to prevent domestic industry from enjoying the firm prices that would otherwise be associated with strong domestic demand?
27. Ibid., p. 27, Art. 3(1).
28. Ibid., pp. 27–28, Art. 3(2) and (3).
29. Ibid., p. 32, Annex B, para. 1(a).
30. Ibid., p. 33, Annex B, para. 2.

do not exceed the aggregate level of all products so restrained."[31] This averaging mechanism gives the exporting country a certain flexibility in the composition of its exports and, one should note, may permit an increase of up to 10 percent in a particular product in a given year. Canada and the United Kingdom were exempted from the annual increase provisions.[32]

The provisions of the Arrangement may be superseded, in part at least, by bilateral arrangements between particular exporting countries. The major limitation on the terms of such bilateral agreements is that, under Article 4, the agreements must not be "inconsistent with the basic objectives of [the] Arrangement."[33] The basic objectives of the Arrangement are not spelled out in Article 4, but presumably they are the goals set out in the preamble, notably the avoidance of "disruptive effects in individual markets and on individual lines of production in both importing and exporting countries."[34] The principal importance of bilateral arrangements is that under Annex B such arrangements may supersede the normal process of determining maximum restraint levels according to base periods. The point is not perfectly clear from the terms of the Arrangement and of Annex B, but apparently bilateral agreements may also exclude the 5 percent yearly increase unless this exclusion may be said to be, under Article 4, "inconsistent with the basic objectives" of the Arrangement.

Bilateral agreements may also affect obligations under Article 2 with respect to products on which restrictions already exist, but on this point the Arrangement is so badly drafted that the permissible scope of bilateral arrangements is far from clear. Despite the broad language of Article 4 concerning the supremacy of bilateral agreements, bilateral arrangements obviously cannot qualify the overall obligation to increase imports over five years by the percentages set forth in Annex A. The language of Article 2:3 suggests that bilateral agreements cannot affect the percentage of increase but at most may affect the distribution of annual increases within the five-year period.

The Long-Term Arrangement is a multilateral arrangement that stands on its own feet, and governments other than GATT contracting parties may accede thereto. Yet the Arrangement was conceived and is administered through a Cotton Textiles Committee entirely within the context of the GATT. The consequence is that there is a curious tension between the terms of the Long-Term Arrangement and the terms of the General Agreement. On the one hand, it is clear that Article 3 restraint orders are inconsistent with the General Agreement and that the undertaking in Article 2:1 to relax *progressively* each year

31. Ibid., p. 28, Art. 3(4).
32. See the protocols relating to the Canadian and United Kingdom reservations, ibid., pp. 35–36.
33. Ibid., Art. 4.
34. Ibid., p. 25.

restrictions that are inconsistent with the General Agreement is an open invitation to continued violation of the General Agreement. On the other hand, Article 1 declares that participating countries "recognize" that the "practical measures of international co-operation" taken under the Long-Term Arrangement "do not affect their rights and obligation under the General Agreement."[35]

When Pakistan refused to accept the reservation of an exemption from any duty to increase imports during the five-year period, the question of the relation of the Long-Term Arrangement to the General Agreement was posed in a particularly difficult fashion. The representative of Pakistan argued in the Cotton Textiles Committee that, although the U.K. reservation applied with respect to the Long-Term Arrangement, the United Kingdom was not exempted from any obligations toward Pakistan under the General Agreement. The representative of Pakistan thereupon argued that the United Kingdom was obligated under the Action Programme to eliminate all quantitative restrictions inconsistent with the terms of the General Agreement within one year or, where special problems existed, by 31 December 1965, at the latest.[36] The chairman of the meeting of the Cotton Textiles Committee, who was none other than the executive secretary of the GATT, agreed that the reservation did not apply as between the United Kingdom and Pakistan. The executive secretary thereupon stated that "it was clear that the reservation attached by the United Kingdom to the Long-Term Arrangement could in no way affect the obligations of the United Kingdom under the General Agreement or the rights of other countries vis-à-vis the United Kingdom under that Agreement."[37]

This studiously vague ruling of the executive secretary leaves open the possibility that the Long-Term Arrangement itself may affect rights under the General Agreement. There is, of course, no doubt that as a practical matter the Agreement shifts from importing countries, at least in part, the traditional burden of adjustment to increased effective exporting capacity. Where a tariff is bound and the traditional GATT rules forbidding nontariff barriers to trade apply, the burden of adjustment to increased effective exporting capacity is upon the importing country. Not only does the Long-Term Arrangement permit the importing country to impose direct restraints in cases of "market disruption," but as a practical matter it makes the importing country the sole judge

---

35. Ibid., p. 26.
36. See discussion of the Action Programme in chapter 14, "Less-Developed Countries," supra.
37. So far as the Action Programme was concerned, the executive secretary stated that it would be inappropriate for the Cotton Textiles Committee to trench upon the prerogatives of the Action Committee. The discussion of the entire matter is set forth in a report of the 1963 meeting of the Cotton Textiles Committee, pp. 16–17, GATT Document COT/M/3 (27 Feb. 1964), attached to GATT Document L/2135 (27 Feb. 1964), pp. 16–17.

of the appropriateness of the restraint. To be sure, the exporting country has the right to demand consultations, to turn to the Cotton Textile Committee for "discussions," and even to have recourse to the dispute settlement procedures of Article XXIII of the General Agreement.[38] But the fact remains that, as we shall see, the United States has used restraint orders to throw the burden of adjustment back on the exporting countries whenever U.S. domestic production has seemed to be unduly threatened. Moreover, there has been no effective multilateral review of the propriety of the various instances of recourse to restraint orders.

The basic question of the relationship of the Long-Term Arrangement to the General Agreement is only in part a question of the locus of the adjustment burden. It is also in part a strictly legal question. That question would arise if an exporting contracting party were to claim, following the imposition of a restraint, that the restraint was an illegal quantitative restriction under the General Agreement and that therefore retaliatory action under Article XXIII was justified. Perhaps this question would be posed most sharply if that exporting contracting party were not a participating country under the Long-Term Arrangement and therefore could not be said to have waived any of its rights under the General Agreement.[39]

## Implementation of the Long-Term Arrangement

The less-developed countries have been disappointed with the implementation of the Long-Term Arrangement. Even if one makes allowance for a certain amount of rhetorical extravagance in the statements by the less-developed countries in the annual reviews before the Cotton Textile Committee, it is clear that many of those countries feel that they have been deprived of many of the benefits that they expected to enjoy as their part of the fundamental bargain. From the first year the less-developed countries have maintained that the importing participating countries have not lived up to the spirit of the Long-Term Arrangement. In their specific criticisms they have suggested, if not asserted, that the letter of the Arrangement has also been neglected.[40]

Part of the less-developed countries' reaction is attributable to U.S. action under the Long-Term Arrangement. First, the United States almost immediately put into effect a far greater number of Article 3 restraint orders than had been

38. *Basic Instruments,* 11th Supp. (1963), pp. 30–31, Arts. 7 and 8.
39. This legal question is perhaps of somewhat limited practical significance in view of the necessity of obtaining the authorization of the CONTRACTING PARTIES prior to retaliation under Article XXIII.
40. Excerpts from the annual reviews of the Cotton Textiles Committee are found in *Basic Instruments,* 12th Supp. (1964), p. 66; 13th Supp. (1965), p. 55; 14th Supp. (1966), p. 65.

anticipated. In the first three years U.S. restraint orders affected imports from seventeen exporting countries and in a total of forty-nine out of the sixty-four categories used in the classification of cotton textile products. Most of these restraints were imposed in the first year. Second, these restraints, or threats of them, were used by the United States in its negotiations with importing countries to reach bilateral agreements replacing the provisions of the Long-Term Arrangement insofar as imports into the United States were concerned. To many less-developed countries, the United States tactics amounted to strong-arm methods.[41]

The less-developed countries have also charged that Article 3 restraint orders have caused severe hardship in many instances. They have asserted that restraints have often been invoked by surprise and that goods unexpectedly refused clearance through customs have had to be sold at distress prices in other countries. Since it is often possible for exporting-country manufacturers to shift rapidly from one textile product to another, imports may build up rapidly in a particular category. When a restraint is imposed immediately under the emergency provisions of Article 3:2, the effect may be to exclude not only goods awaiting clearance through customs, but also a large volume of goods in the "pipeline" between the ports of the exporting and importing countries. Such hardship is almost inevitable under the system adopted because an importing country may not know about a sudden build-up, or may have underestimated its extent, until a particularly large shipment arrives in port. Even where the sixty-day waiting period applies, the "pipeline" problem may be serious. Even though the exporting government is notified, the exporting firms may not learn immediately of a restraint. Moreover, the negotiations between importing and exporting governments that usually precede the imposition of a restraint may proceed without notice to the trade and may continue beyond the sixty-day period, and at that point the restraint may be imposed suddenly and without warning. Finally, even after the restraint is imposed and publicized, private exporters may not be able to determine how much of the quota may be available by the time their exports reach customs in the importing country.

While the United States has taken most of the blame, it has not been the only country to invoke Article 3; in the first three years Article 3 restraints were also imposed by Canada, Italy, and the Federal Republic of Germany. Moreover, the EEC member states, together with several other European countries, have continued to apply the Noordwijk agreement, which discourages certain imports of cotton textiles from less-developed countries by prohibiting reexport of finished textiles made from those imports. And the fact remains that the United States has continued to import more cotton textiles from the

41. Cf. Patterson, p. 313.

Asian less-developed countries than have most other developed countries, and in particular far more on most bases of comparison than have the EEC member states.[42]

The United States has charged in turn that the less-developed countries have not provided the cooperation the Long-Term Arrangement contemplates. Although the United States consulted with the less-developed countries in an attempt to avoid formal restraints, "in only three cases [in the first two years] did the country concerned take steps to insure an orderly development of trade in the product by limiting the rate of exports." The United States has also complained that the less-developed countries have permitted exports in excess of restraint levels as well as the "circumvention and negation of export restraints by transshipments and third-country transactions."[43] Finally, the United States has charged that its record on the number of restraints in effect has been made to look unduly restrictive because certain less-developed countries have resisted the lifting of old restraint orders in order to take advantage of Article 3:4, which in effect permits shortfalls in restrained categories to be transferred to other restrained categories to the extent of a 5 per cent excess in those other categories, so long as the aggregate level of imports does not exceed the aggregate restraint level.

The bilateral agreements between the United States and a particular less-developed country generally provide, it should be observed, for a 5 percent annual increase in the imports in each of a substantial number of classes of textile products. This is more favorable treatment than the less-developed country in question is necessarily entitled to under the Long-Term Arrangement, where the implicit guarantee of the formula in Annex B can be construed as applying to the total number of countries exporting "cotton textile products causing or threatening to cause market disruption," but not to each such country individually. It is, of course, an open question whether the provisions of Article XIII require nondiscriminatory application of quotas established by bilateral agreements under the Long-Term Arrangement.

## The Hong Kong System

The Hong Kong government introduced a special system of export authorization. This system bears examination in some detail, because many less-developed countries feel that a similar system of exporting-country control should be substituted for the present Long-Term Arrangement system of im-

---

42. See the charts contained on pp. 68–75 of Organization for Economic Co-operation and Development, *Modern Cotton Industry* (Paris, 1965).

43. Stanley Nehmer, "Record of U.S. Participation During Second Year of Long-Term Cotton Textile Arrangement," *Department of State Bulletin*, LII (1965), pp. 49, 54–55.

port restraints. In the case of the Hong Kong arrangement, however, the export authorization system does not stand alone, but rather meshes with the import restraints of importing countries, notably the United States under a bilateral agreement,[44] to form a complex system of control over the exports of a large number of Hong Kong firms. Whether or not a quota control system is in effect, the Hong Kong exporter must have both an export authorization and an export license before shipping goods to a country that participates in the Long-Term Arrangement. He must first seek the export authorization. He is entitled to it upon proof that he has entered into a firm contract with a foreign importer for shipment within a prescribed period of time, which varies between three and six months depending upon arrangements made with the importing country. Where no quota control system is in effect, the exporter who has an export authorization is entitled as a matter of course to receive an export license for the particular shipment at any time during the period of validity of the export authorization.

The prime function of the export authorization is statistical; the authorization enables the Hong Kong government to determine with some accuracy the future level of exports for each category and to each importing country. This information, in the form of a month-by-month or a three-monthly forecast, is passed on immediately to each importing country, which is then in a position to determine whether or not to issue a restraint order for each category. In order to receive the forecast, the importing country is supposed to guarantee that it will accept the shipments covered by the export authorizations reflected in the forecast and apply any restraint order only to subsequent shipments. If it issues a restraint order that threatens to restrain substantially the flow of exports, the Hong Kong authorities shift from an export authorization system to a quota control system.

Once a quota control system is in effect for a particular category, export licenses are allocated among exporters, usually on the basis of past shipments in the category. If the quota control system works well, each exporter is reasonably assured that his exports will be admitted into the country imposing the restraint order. Where an existing restraint order appears to the Hong Kong authorities to be in excess of probable shipments in the category in question, there may be a shift back to the export authorization system, in which case export authorizations will be issued on a first-come, first-served basis to both old and new exporters. (Or in the more unlikely case that a new restraint order is in excess of probable shipments, the shift to a quota control system may be avoided.)

The goal of the Hong Kong system is to avoid a problem that has plagued

44. Agreement between the United States of America and Hong Kong, TIAS 6088 (26 Aug. 1966), as amended by Exchange of Notes, TIAS 6290 (31 May 1967).

the functioning of the Article 3 restraint system. As outlined above, the sudden imposition of Article 3 restraints has sometimes had the consequence that shipments made pursuant to firm contracts have been refused entry at the customs shed, to the disappointment and often to the severe financial loss of both the exporting and importing firms. The Hong Kong system, although it may involve direct control of trading patterns when a quota control system is in effect for a particular category, tends to preserve the free market system so long as the export authorization system is in effect. In addition, the system reduces the aura of arbitrariness as well as the losses to private firms that may result from sudden impositions of import restraints. Without such an export authorization system, the importing country may not be aware of a major increase in exports until a number of shipments are already on the dock at the importing port. These affirmative results of the export authorization scheme can be achieved, of course, only so long as the importing country adheres to the basic ground rules and agrees to permit the entry of cotton textiles already covered by export authorizations.[45]

## Criticisms by Less-Developed Countries

Many of the criticisms by the less-developed countries have concerned less the content of the bilateral and other special arrangements than the administration of the import restraint system by the importing countries and particularly by the United States. The less-developed countries have complained, for example, that overcategorization has had the effect of so compartmentalizing the textiles trade that firms in less-developed countries have not been able to diversify their production or make use of manufacturing flexibility in shifting from one product to another. They have charged that the categories have been so narrow that many categories have been underutilized, and therefore, whatever the theoretical increased access and provision for shifts between categories of shortfalls which are written into the Long-Term Arrangement, exports have not been able to expand, as a practical matter, to the contemplated extent. They have also complained of changes in the definitions, which tend to increase the protective effect of the category system. These, and many similar charges, are difficult to evaluate, particularly given the care with which the importing countries shield their cotton textile import programs from public scrutiny.

45. The success of the Hong Kong System depends to a certain extent on the good faith of the importing governments. In the U.S.-Hong Kong bilateral, ibid., the United States retained the right to request consultations in the event of an "undue concentration in exports . . . in any category not given a specific limit," and Hong Kong agreed that it would "not license further exports of the particular product in question" in the course of such consultations. The opportunities for abuse by the United States are evident.

Some of the most severe criticisms have concerned the definition of "market disruption" used in the imposition of import restraints by the importing countries, and by the United States in particular. These criticisms are perhaps of permanent interest, for they suggest difficulties that are bound to arise if the developed countries ever turn to the market disruption concept for additional products. The primary complaint lodged has been that the CONTRACTING PARTIES' three criteria of "market disruption"—"sharp and substantial increase" of quantity, low price, and damage—have been so liberally construed by the importing countries that any increase in imports has been viewed as justifying a restraint order. We have already seen that certain qualifications of the official definition had to be included in the Record of Understandings. In addition, the Cotton Textile Committee was forced, on the occasion of the first annual review of the Long-Term Arrangement, to formulate certain "conclusions" that amounted to informal interpretations or amendments of the official definition.

One conclusion of the Cotton Textiles Committee states that "the question of the relation between the volume of imports and the volume of domestic production of cotton textiles in the importing country [is] . . . clearly relevant" and "is implicit in the definition of market disruption." This suggests that one must measure "sharp and substantial increase" in terms of the volume of domestic production: to the extent that imports are small in relation to domestic production, the increase must be sharper and more substantial.

A second conclusion states that "where the price factor [is] . . . being considered in connection with market disruption, quality differential is a factor which must also be taken into account." The necessity for this conclusion may arise from the fact that, whereas the official definition requires a comparison between the price of the imports to be restrained and the price of "similar goods of comparable quality in the market of the importing country," the imports may be of a lower quality than all domestic goods. The problem is, however, a thorny one. From the point of view of the importing country, a rapid influx of lower-quality goods may tend to depress the demand for higher-quality domestic goods; from the point of view of the exporting country, notions of both justice and free competition support the offering of lower-quality goods at appropriate prices.

A third conclusion of the Cotton Textiles Committee relates to third-country imports: "In determining whether there had been a sharp and substantial increase in imports . . . , it would be appropriate to take due account, *inter alia,* of the past performance of imports from an exporting country concerned as well as total imports from all sources of the particular product or category over a period of years." This conclusion appears to introduce an additional test, since the official definition speaks only of an "increase or potential increase of imports of particular products from particular sources"—that is to say, from the countries against which the restraint is to be imposed—and does not mention third-country imports.

Other conclusions state that the price criterion "is intended to cover the situation where . . . prices are quite clearly out of line with the normal prices prevailing on the market" and that "every attempt to give more precision to the word 'substantial' should be made in the course of the periodic exchanges of view between importing countries and exporting countries when the discussion is likely to be focused on particular countries and particular markets."[46]

### The Cotton Textiles Arrangement as Precedent

Perhaps the most important question about the Long-Term Arrangement is whether or not that Arrangement is to be the forerunner of other such arrangements or whether it is to remain a lone experiment. The participating countries went out of their way to write into the Long-Term Arrangement a declaration that the measures contemplated thereunder "are not to be considered as lending themselves to application in other fields." Thus far the Long-Term Arrangement has produced no offspring. There has been pressure in the United States for the adoption of a similar arrangement for wool textiles, but the Johnson Administration resisted this pressure. Curzon suggests that arrangements for toys, transistors, and typewriters have been considered.[47]

Patterson refers to a number of exports of less-developed countries for which there have been protectionist pressures in developed countries and which therefore may be candidates for such arrangements—woolen textiles, leather and leather manufactures, cutlery, linoleum, many wood and cork manufactures, rugs and carpets, footwear, and various electrical appliances.[48] Patterson also reaches, however, the "tentative, and entirely intuitively derived, conclusion" that there are no goods considered of export interest to the less-developed countries which meet the conditions essential to true market disruption as well as do cotton textiles. These conditions are that the good must be one with respect to which: (1) "labor costs . . . represent a substantial proportion of total costs even under modern production techniques"; (2) "the necessary skills

46. The conclusions of the Cotton Textiles Committee are set out in *Basic Instruments,* 12th Supp. (1964), pp. 66, 70–72. Most of the conclusions relate only to procedures and standards under the Long-Term Arrangement and not to the definition of market disruption. The criticism of the less-developed countries appears to a certain extent in the reports of the Cotton Textiles Committee on the annual review of the arrangement. See, e.g., ibid., 15th Supp. (1968), pp. 125–36.
47. Curzon, p. 256. Article 6(b) itself contemplates the possibility of extending the Long-Term Arrangement to "directly competitive textiles" in order to prevent "circumvention" of the Arrangement. *Basic Instruments,* 11th Supp. (1963), p. 29.
48. Patterson, pp. 321–22.

[are] easily and quickly acquired"; (3) "external economies are relatively unimportant" in production; (4) "frequent style changes" are not characteristic; (5) "quality variations are relatively small"; (6) "the price elasticity of demand in the importing country is high and the income elasticity of demand in the exporting country low"; (7) "brand names are normally not important"; (8) "servicing arrangements are not needed"; and (9) "several of the developing countries already have a domestic industry." Patterson adds that "market disruption is most likely to occur in the industrialized importing country if demand for the product there is relatively stagnant, if the industry has a labor force which is immobile and a physical capital stock specific to the particular function." He further points out that the narrower the domestic industry is defined for policy purposes, "the greater the probability that any given increase in imports will create serious damage."[49]

Patterson's reassuring analysis must, however, be weighed with several other considerations. First of all, Patterson's list of conditions and factors reads suspiciously like a description of the cotton textiles industry, and naturally the cotton textiles industry corresponds better to the description than does any other industry.

Second, the analysis presupposes that there exists an objectively verifiable phenomenon called "market disruption," which has different consequences from ordinary competition. Not only may the existence of such a separate phenomenon (which recalls vaguely the old-fashioned notion of "cutthroat competition" as a phenomenon distinct from ordinary competition) be challenged, but if the competitive threat of less-developed countries becomes severe enough, developed countries may not hesitate to mold the notion of "market disruption" to their desire to impose import controls.

Third, a great deal will depend upon whether the Long-Term Arrangement comes to be considered a success or a failure. That issue is still in doubt. It is in doubt partly because different countries, and different groups within the developed importing countries, tend to have different images of what might constitute success. For the less-developed exporting countries, the Long-Term Arrangement will be a success if it leads to quite substantial and steady increases in their exports of cotton textiles, coupled with the gradual disappearance (hopefully with as limited costs as possible in terms of unemployment and the like) of inefficient textile industries in the developed countries. For some people in the developed importing countries, the Long-Term Arrangement will be a success if it gives their inefficient domestic textile industries the breathing period necessary to carry out the structural adjustments (such as replacement of plant and equipment) necessary to preserve domestic markets. And even if one takes the less-developed countries' standard of success, it is

49. Patterson, pp. 320–21.

not yet clear what the influence of the Long-Term Arrangement has been. On the one hand, it clear that the rate of increase in cotton textile shipments from the less-developed countries to the developed countries has considerably slowed down since the 1950s. But the less-developed countries' share of total world exports by participating countries continues to grow, and total production is growing slightly more rapidly in the less-developed countries than in the developed countries. Finally, there is some basis for asserting that the principal benefit that the less-developed countries have derived from the Long-Term Arrangement has been found in the special shackles that have been placed on Hong Kong and Japanese exports. Some less-developed countries have been able to create an export industry under the resulting protection from Hong Kong and Japanese competition in third-country markets.

The principal difficulty in evaluating the effects of the Long-Term Arrangement is, of course, that it is impossible to determine what would have happened in the absence of such an arrangement. Economic factors alone might have slowed the impressive rates of increase of developing-country exports which were achieved in the 1950s. And one can never know what protectionist measures would have been adopted by certain developed importing countries in the absence of the Long-Term Arrangement. Agreement on the statistical results, even if obtained, could not serve to verify or to disprove the proposition advanced at the beginning of this chapter—that, paradoxically enough, the imposition of certain kinds of direct trade restrictions may, when subjected to appropriate multilateral supervision and control, aid in the long-term effort toward the reduction of overall levels of trade barriers. Most of the criticisms of the Long-Term Arrangement have, as we have seen, involved the administration of the Arrangement by the importing countries. The exporting countries have less often challenged the principle of such an arrangement than the unilateral character of measures taken by the importing countries.

# 18 State Trading

The provisions of Article XVII on State Trading Enterprises (together with the supplementary provisions of Article II:4) apply to two problems that are in practice quite different. The first problem concerns countries that do not have market economies, and the second concerns countries that, although having market economies, grant state-owned or state-controlled enterprises exclusive rights over certain products. In institutional terms, the first problem is how East European countries with centrally planned economies can be brought into the GATT system, and the second is what special GATT arrangements must be made for those products that, in the market-economy countries, are subjected to state monopolies for fiscal, sumptuary, or other reasons.

That the same provisions apply to two relatively disparate situations is an accident of history. The United States draftsmen had originally proposed two separate Havana Charter articles. Article 27 of the U.S. Suggested Charter, which became Article 31 of the Havana Charter and eventually Article XVII of the General Agreement, was entitled "Expansion of Trade of State Monopolies of Individual Products." Article 28 of the U.S. Suggested Charter was entitled "Expansion of Trade by Complete State Monopolies of Import Trade."[1] The latter suggested article was deleted by the Preparatory Committee. The Soviet Union was thought at that early postwar date to be the only important country that was going to maintain a complete monopoly of its import trade, and thus its failure to participate in the work of the Preparatory Committee, which was taken as an indication that it would not become a member of the International Trade Organization, removed the most important reason for this suggested article.[2] Moreover, when no country with a centrally planned econ-

---

1. *Suggested Charter for an International Trade Organization of the United Nations,* Department of State Publication 2598, Commercial Policy Series 93 (1946), p. 22. The related problem of government procurement is discussed in chapter 12, "Government Procurement," supra.

2. William Adams Brown, Jr., *The United States and the Restoration of World*

omy participated in the first round of tariff negotiations, there was little reason to include such a provision in the resulting General Agreement, which at the time was conceived of as only the first of a number of trade agreements to be negotiated under the ITO.

With the assertion of direct control over foreign trade by a number of East European countries and with the growth of interest in some of those countries in becoming GATT contracting parties, Article XVII has had to serve double duty. Article XVII provides the only basis in the General Agreement for dealing with the problems involved in fitting centrally planned economy countries into the GATT system. The consequence has been considerable difficulty in using the GATT as a framework for the reintegration of East European countries into the world economy. Not only has the GATT been deprived of the universal status that the ITO was to have had, but it has been unable to perform a significant role in the fostering of East-West trade, a highly important project for which no other international organization has been prepared to assume responsibility.

Of the East European socialist countries, only two are full contracting parties. Czechoslovakia was a contracting party before it adopted socialist institutions, and since then its participation in GATT affairs has been limited. Yugoslavia's position as a contracting party is, as we shall see later, dependent upon its conversion to a market economy; the history of its relations with the GATT serves to emphasize the practical barriers to bringing other East European countries into the GATT system. Poland, although a contracting party since 1967, has participated in the work of the GATT under special and highly limited arrangements. Hungary and Rumania have been accorded only observer status. And the remaining East European countries maintain no relations with the GATT. Meanwhile, market-economy countries have participated fully in GATT affairs even when the percentage of their imports handled through state-trading agencies has been rather high. In the early 1950s France participated without difficulty in the GATT at a time when its state-trading agencies imported as much as did the state-trading agencies of all of the remaining market-economy European countries combined.[3]

## Centrally Planned and Market Economies

The problem of participation by countries with centrally planned economies goes, of course, beyond mere drafting problems. There is a fundamental diffi-

---

*Trade* (Washington: Brookings Institution, 1950), p. 114; Clair Wilcox, *A Charter for World Trade* (New York: Macmillan, 1949), pp. 101–2.

3. See Marc Ouin, "State Trading in Western Europe," *Law and Contemporary Problems,* XXIV (1959), p. 398, 405. Some 22 percent of France's intra-European imports were subject to state trading. Ibid., p. 401.

culty that concerns the underlying assumption of the GATT tariff system. That system presupposes that importation and exportation are handled by private firms which, stimulated by profit motives, are guided by commercial considerations. The decisions of these firms to import and export are determined by the relation of domestic prices to foreign prices. Given this assumption, the function of the GATT is to limit the influence that governmentally imposed rules may exert upon the private calculus for decision. Only tariffs are to influence the choice between importing and not importing, and since tariffs are to be applied on a most-favored-nation basis, even tariffs are not to influence the determination of source. The many exceptions and shortcomings of the GATT rules that have been considered in prior chapters limit the extent to which the GATT system can carry out this function, but when one considers state trading, the underlying assumption of the GATT system is itself no longer applicable.

The calculus for decision is not the same in centrally planned and in market economies, in part because prices do not have exactly the same functions in the two types of economies. In a market economy the price of a particular product to consumers tends to influence not only the quantities that are consumed but also the quantities that are produced. In a centrally planned economy the price does not typically influence the quantities produced. Rather, the quantities to be produced are stipulated by planning authorities who have previously set economic goals for the country and are seeking the correct allocation of resources to accomplish those goals. The price for a particular product tends to be set after the quantities to be produced have been determined. The price will normally be established at a level that will clear the market. It may, of course, be set at some higher or lower level, either intentionally or because the market clearing level cannot be determined with precision in advance, but in such a case shortages or surpluses of the product will occur.

Just as the plan rather than the price determines production, so the plan determines imports. Planning judgments on imports may be based on the planners' evaluation of the volume and composition of imports that will best serve domestic objectives. These judgments may be based on estimates of comparative advantage (although such judgments cannot rely on the indicia of comparative advantage offered by freely formed prices). Or imports may be viewed as simply compensating for temporary domestic shortages of particular products.

It is not difficult to see that whatever the planners' criteria, tariff rates are likely to have a much more limited influence on the level of imports in a centrally planned economy than in a market-economy country. Since the plan determines the level of imports, the tariff schedule is largely a matter of internal bookkeeping and financial transfers. One consequence is that a tariff reduction by a central-plan country need not lead to an increase in imports.

Relegated to a minor role in determining the level of imports, the tariff schedule of a central-plan country is also unlikely to play a decisive role in determining the origin of imports. A commitment by such a country to give most-favored-nation treatment cannot be discharged simply by imposing identical tariffs on imports from all countries, for where the importing agencies follow political criteria rather than so-called commercial criteria (such as price and quality) in selecting foreign suppliers, uniformity of customs duties is irrelevant. Since commercial policy is often viewed by politicians and civil servants as a weapon of international politics, the source of imports may be influenced by political considerations, particularly where importing decisions are made by the foreign affairs ministry or by a central foreign trade monopoly. Moreover, even if the importing authorities follow purely commercial criteria in determining the source of imports, the planning authorities have the opportunity to influence the choice of these sources through their power over internal prices. This is an important factor in the case of goods that are functionally similar but physically distinguishable. A higher internal price for a type of goods originating in one country than for a competing type of goods originating in another country will tend to discourage importation of the former type of goods because the internal market cannot absorb as great a quantity at the higher price.[4]

Currency factors, although having no necessary theoretical relationship to the distinction between market and centrally planned economies, also tend to make it difficult to fit central-plan countries into the GATT system. Not only are most East European currencies not convertible, but there is no attempt, except in the framework of certain intra–East European arrangements adopted in recent years, to give those currencies any of the indicia of external convertibility. Facilities for multilateral clearing of accounts with Western countries do not normally exist. Transactions with Western countries are usually subject to what might be called total exchange controls. The amounts of each foreign currency that may be used for imports are prescribed in advance, often within the framework of bilateral agreements. The allocation of each currency is, moreover, often made industry by industry, so that the allocation process goes far toward prescribing the volume and source of the imports of each product. Even in Yugoslavia, which as we shall see has instituted a market economy, a large proportion of trade is carried out under bilateral arrangements, and a

---

4. This point applies more broadly to the usual case where the importing authorities are given discretion over the total volume of imports in a particular product category.

substantial number of categories of goods are subject to exchange licensing.[5]

The differences, from a GATT perspective, between state trading in particular industries by market-economy countries, and total control over imports in central-plan countries, must not be overemphasized. Certain similarities are obvious. Since a state-owned or state-controlled enterprise in a market economy is subject to greater political influence than a private firm, such an enterprise may fail to import even if the domestic price exceeds the foreign price by more than the tariff (after taking account of transportation, insurance, etc.). And such an enterprise may favor one foreign source over another for noncommercial reasons. In either case a government subsidy may encourage the pursuit of economically inefficient goals.

These similarities aside, however, the differences between the two cases remain crucial. If a state enterprise in a market economy wishes to follow commercial criteria, its calculus of decision will not be warped by some of the factors present in a centrally planned economy. In the absence of quantitative and exchange restrictions, the volume of imports and exports will not normally be prescribed by a planning authority. Prices will tend to reflect consumers' preferences and will adjust to eliminate shortages and surpluses for all products. The relationship between domestic and foreign prices will provide much better indicia of comparative advantage than in the case of a centrally planned economy. Finally, discrimination among foreign sources will not be a problem, for the structure of prices for functionally similar but physically different goods coming from different foreign sources will reflect conditions of supply and demand with respect to those goods rather than be subject to manipulation by central planning authorities to reflect notions as to the appropriate sources of foreign goods.

Admittedly, the foregoing discussion fails to take account of certain much-discussed institutional changes that have tended to blur the distinction between market and centrally planned economies. But these changes do not affect substantially the differences previously noted. Planning exists in Western countries, but it is usually indicative planning that does not attempt to prescribe the volume of imports and exports. Price regulation also exists, but it is a minor factor today and is in any event rarely designed to influence the volume or direction of foreign trade. In the East European countries a much-discussed trend toward giving firms greater autonomy over prices is evident, and therefore prices are beginning to assume some of the functions that they have in market-economy countries. But decisions on imports and exports normally

5. International Monetary Fund, *Seventeenth Annual Report on Exchange Restrictions* (Washington, 1966), pp. 621–23. On the other hand, exchange controls on the use of foreign currencies by residents for the importation of goods remain extensive in Western countries, even in such important trading countries as the United Kingdom. Ibid., pp. 577–79.

remain in the hands of the foreign trade ministry or industry-wide monopolies operating under guidelines laid down by the foreign trade ministry. Moreover, progress toward making most East European currencies convertible has been slight.

## The Content of the GATT Provisions

The GATT has four principal provisions that are relevant to state trading: Article XVII, which deals primarily with nondiscrimination; Article III:4, which establishes a national treatment standard; Article II:4, which deals with tariff and other concessions; and an interpretative note, which deals with quantitative restrictions.[6]

### Nondiscrimination

Article XVII is ill adapted to centrally planned economies. Its provisions are addressed only to the problem of discrimination and, for all practical purposes, do not deal with the problem of assuring that tariffs constitute the only protection afforded domestic goods. The central obligation imposed upon a contracting party by Article XVII:1 is that state enterprises are to make "purchases and sales involving either imports or exports . . . in a manner consistent with the general principles of non-discriminatory treatment prescribed in . . . [the General] Agreement for governmental measures affecting imports or exports by private traders." This obligation of nondiscrimination is interpreted to mean that "purchases and sales involving either imports or exports" are to be made "solely in accordance with commercial considerations, including price, quality, availability, marketability, transportation and other conditions of purchase or sale, and shall afford other contracting parties adequate opportunity, in accordance with customary business practice, to compete for participation in such purchases or sales."

It is not clear whether the "non-discriminatory treatment" required by paragraph 1 of Article XVII refers only to nondiscrimination as among foreign sources of supply (that is, most-favored-nation treatment) or whether it also refers to nondiscrimination against foreign sources in favor of domestic sources (that is, absence of protection). The concept of "non-discrimination" in other provisions of the General Agreement, such as Article XIII, usually refers to the former type of discrimination. In any event, this question of interpretation is probably of minor importance, since Article III:4, which requires that im-

---

6. Article XXXVII:3(a) is also relevant. It requires contracting parties to "make every effort, in cases where a government directly or indirectly determines the resale price of products wholly or mainly produced in the territories of less-developed contracting parties, to maintain trade margins at equitable levels."

ports be accorded "treatment no less favourable than that accorded to like products of national origin in respect of all laws, regulations and requirements affecting their internal sale, offering for sale, purchase, transportation, distribution or use," appears to prohibit protection in the form of state-enterprise favoritism toward local suppliers. Paragraph 8(a) of Article III, by exempting from paragraph 4 "the procurement by government agencies of products purchased for governmental purposes and *not* with a view to commercial resale or with a view to use in the production of goods for commercial sale,"[7] indicates that state-trading enterprises are subject to the national treatment requirement of paragraph 4.

The obligation of Article XVII:1, which (as in the case of governmental purchases under Article III:4) applies only to importation for resale and for use in production and not to importation for governmental use,[8] is not linked to any rules for determining whether solely commercial considerations have been followed. It is true that paragraph 4 of Article XVII requires contracting parties with state-trading enterprises to furnish certain information, but the kind of detailed information on costs, offers, and so forth that is required to verify a departure from purely commercial considerations is unlikely to be forthcoming. Article XVII thus leaves compliance essentially to the good faith of each contracting party. It is, of course, true that all GATT obligations are in a sense dependent upon the good faith of each contracting party. But where tariffs are concerned, the nondiscriminatory character of a particular tariff is comparatively easy to verify, and the self-interest of private firms, which leads them to buy in markets where prices are lowest and to sell in markets where prices are highest, may be relied upon to assure that the tariff represents the principal noncommercial influence on the sources of imports and the destination of exports.

The drafting of the nondiscrimination obligation creates certain further difficulties that should be noted in passing. A distinction between political and economic discrimination is made but is not applied consistently. A state-trading enterprise normally has a national monopoly of imports or exports and thus may have a degree of monopolistic or monopsonistic power in the world market. (Since consumption of a particular product is likely to be found in more countries than is production of that product, a state-trading enterprise is less likely to have monopsonistic than monopolistic power.) Such market power may permit imports at lower prices from some sellers than from others or exports at higher prices to some buyers than to others. An interpretative note states that the "charging by a state enterprise of different prices for its sales of a product in different markets is not precluded by the provisions of . . .

7. Emphasis supplied.
8. Art. XVII:2.

Article [XVII], provided that such different prices are charged for commercial reasons, to meet conditions of supply and demand in export markets."[9] A state enterprise may thus act as a monopolist seller without violating the nondiscrimination obligation. The negative inference from the absence of any similar provision in the interpretative note for purchases is that the exercise of market power on the buying side is a violation of the nondiscrimination requirement. It is difficult to understand why a distinction between monopoly and monopsony should be made in giving content to the term "commercial considerations."

## Tariff and Other Concessions

The problem of making tariff concessions effective is handled somewhat differently from the problem of preventing discrimination. Article II:4 provides that, where a contracting party maintains a monopoly of importation with respect to a product described in its GATT schedule, "such monopoly shall not, except as provided for in that Schedule or as otherwise agreed between the parties which initially negotiated the concession, operate so as to afford protection on the average in excess of the amount of protection provided for in that Schedule." In other words, a contracting party is not to use a state-trading monopoly in such a way as to afford, in the case of bound items, protection to domestic production beyond that provided for in its tariff schedule. This provision is directed primarily toward state-trading monopolies in market economies. Its relevance to centrally planned economies is limited, since the protection that domestic enterprise receives in such economies stems more directly from the omnipotence of the planning authorities over the volume of imports (or, in those unusual cases where there is no direct regulation of the volume of imports, over domestic prices) than from the manner in which individual importing monopolies operate. Putting the point another way, to ask a country with a centrally planned economy to set forth in its GATT schedule all protection offered to domestic enterprise is to ask it to disband its central planning.

That paragraph 4 of Article II is, nevertheless, intended to mean somewhat more than it says is indicated by an interpretative note requiring that the paragraph be "applied in the light of the provisions of Article 31 of the Havana Charter," unless "otherwise specifically agreed between the contracting parties which initially negotiated the concession" in the GATT schedule of the contracting party with the import monopoly.[10] The meaning of this interpretative note is, to say the least, murky. Article 31 of the Havana Charter dealt primarily with the duty of an ITO Member maintaining an import monopoly to negotiate for the reduction of the protection to domestic production afforded

9. Interpretative note, Ad Art. XVII, para. 1.
10. Interpretative note, Ad Art. II, para. 4.

by that monopoly. Article 31 was thus a counterpart to the general requirement of Article 17 of the Havana Charter that each member of the ITO should, upon request of another member, enter into "negotiations directed to the substantial reduction of the general levels of tariffs and other charges on imports and exports," a requirement that was not carried over to the General Agreement.[11] The interpretative note to Article II:4 is surely not intended to impose upon contracting parties a duty to negotiate with respect to products subject to import monopolies, for such a duty would be inconsistent with the absence in the General Agreement of a general duty to negotiate reductions of protection.

The 1955 Review Session Working Party, "convinced that it would be impossible to obtain general agreement on the precise meaning" of the interpretative note, decided to redraft the note in a form "that is consistent with the obligations of contracting parties with respect to private trade."[12] The revised interpretative note, however, never entered into force, and the entire protocol that contained it was finally abandoned because of the failure of Uruguay to provide the unanimous acceptance that is required by Article XXX for any amendments of Part I.[13]

Since Uruguay's failure to accept was in no way related to the content of the revision, and since the revision represents an important interpretation of Article II:4 and of the interpretative note thereto, the revised version warrants attention. Incorporating certain provisions of Article 31, it provides:

> 1. The protection afforded through the operation of an import monopoly in respect of products described in the appropriate schedule shall be limited by means of:
>
> (a) a maximum import duty that may be applied in respect of the products concerned; or
>
> (b) any other mutually satisfactory arrangement consistent with the provisions of this Agreement; any contracting party entering into negotiations with a view to concluding such an arrangement shall afford to other interested contracting parties an opportunity for consultation.
>
> 2. The import duty mentioned in 1 (a) above shall represent the margin by which the price charged by the import monopoly for the imported product (exclusive of internal taxes conforming to the provisions of Article III, transportation, distribution, and other expenses incident to the purchase, sale or further processing, and a reasonable margin of profit) exceeds the

---

11. See discussion in chapter 5, "Tariff Conferences," supra. It should be noted that Article XVII:3 states that negotiations designed to limit or reduce obstacles to trade created by the operation of state-trading enterprises "are of importance to the expansion of international trade."
12. *Basic Instruments*, 3d Supp. (1955), p. 228.
13. Ibid., 15th Supp. (1968), p. 65.

landed cost; *Provided* that regard may be had to average landed costs and selling prices over recent periods; and *Provided* further that, where the product concerned is a primary commodity which is the subject of a domestic price stabilization arrangement, provisions may be made for adjustment to take account of wide fluxtuations [sic] or variations in world prices, subject to agreement between the countries parties to the negotiations.[14]

The effect of the revised interpretative note would have been, it should be noted, to make the difference between the internal price (less internal costs of distribution) and the landed cost the measure of whether or not a contracting party had abided by a tariff concession granted on a product subject to an import monopoly. Adoption of this measure would obviously have been a step in the direction of realism, even though internal costs of distribution are difficult to measure with any precision. Differences between domestic and foreign prices, after due allowance for costs of importation and distribution, are often used by economists to measure protection.

The crucial factor so far as centrally planned economies as opposed to state-trading, market economies are concerned is that, upon adoption of the revised note, tariff negotiations would necessarily become negotiations over internal price levels and price structures. To central-plan countries this implicit requirement would constitute discriminatory treatment. Not only would contracting parties with market economies not be required to negotiate over domestic prices, even where price controls were in effect,[15] but commitments on prices by such contracting parties could have little value, because the influence of the state over prices in a market economy is necessarily limited.

Perhaps the principal difficulty with negotiations over internal prices would be that, since in a centrally planned economy the plan rather than the margin between import prices and internal prices normally determines the volume of imports, negotiations over prices would be somewhat beside the point. If the importing authorities should not choose to import the bound product, the level of the internal price would be irrelevant. There would simply be a "shortage" of that product, however limited the margin.

This difficulty was recognized when the Havana Charter was drafted. Paragraph 5 of Article 31 sought to deal with it by requiring importing countries, except under certain circumstances, to "import and offer for sale such quantities of the product as will be sufficient to satisfy the full domestic demand for

---

14. The revised interpretative note is included in the Protocol Amending Part I and Articles XXIX and XXX, which is appended to the Final Act of the Ninth Session of the CONTRACTING PARTIES to the General Agreement on Tariffs and Trade (1965), pp. 19, 25–26.
15. See, however, Art. XXXVII:3(a).

the imported product." This provision of Article 31, although arguably still relevant under the existing interpretative note to Article II:4, is not incorporated into the revised interpretative note. Whatever the significance of that deletion, the principle of full satisfaction of domestic demand would be hard to enforce and unlikely to be acceptable to central-plan countries.

A more effective way to deal with the difficulty that in a planned economy the plan rather than the internal price determines the volume of imports would be to institute negotiations on the volume of imports itself. A failure to live up to any undertaking to increase imports of a particular product would be easy to identify. And such an undertaking would be consistent with the practice of planned economy countries negotiating, outside the GATT framework, specific bilateral commitments concerning future imports. The simplest technique in the GATT context would be to negotiate quotas that would represent *minimum* imports per time period.

The objection that is usually raised to any attempt to institute GATT negotiations on import-volume increases is that commitments resulting from such negotiations, in order to be consistent with the multilateral principles of the General Agreement, would have to be on a "global" rather than a bilateral basis. It would be impossible, or so the objection continues, to determine whether such global commitments were administered on a nondiscriminatory (that is, most-favored-nation) basis, and therefore no market-economy country could afford to make significant concessions in order to obtain such global commitments. The same is true, of course, with respect to tariff concessions by central plan countries, for reliance must be placed simply on the "commercial criteria" requirement. Global quota undertakings would not present any most-favored-nation difficulties that are not presented by tariff commitments by central plan countries.

The problems presented by global quota undertakings would, in any event, be analogous to those arising under the requirement of Article XIII that quantitative restrictions be administered in a nondiscriminatory fashion. Indeed, paragraph 2 of that article contains provisions that might well be adapted to the central plan context. Wherever practicable in cases of authorized quantitative restrictions, "quotas representing the total amount of permitted exports" are to be fixed, and import licenses or permits are not to require "importation of the product concerned from a particular country or source." If a quota is nevertheless allocated by source, the allocation is to be made through agreement with all contracting parties having a substantial export interest or, where such agreement is not "reasonably practicable," by allotment to such contracting parties "based upon the proportions, supplied by such contracting parties during a previous representative period, of the total quantity or value of imports of the product, due account being taken of any special factors which may have affected or may be affecting the trade in the product."[16] These provisions do not solve the problems entailed in making global quotas work, but, whatever their intrinsic merits, they at least have the advantage of being applicable to central plan and market-economy countries alike.

The idea of global quotas as the bases for negotiations with central plan countries is not new. The provision in the U.S. Suggested Charter on "complete state monopolies of foreign trade" would have required states maintaining such monopolies to negotiate global quotas:

> *Complete state monopolies of foreign trade.* As the counterpart of tariff reductions and other actions to encourage an expansion of multilateral trade by other members, members having a complete state monopoly of foreign trade should undertake to purchase annually from members, on the nondiscriminatory basis required [by the provision that "state-trading enterprises shall be influenced solely by commercial considerations"], products valued at not less than an aggregate amount to be agreed upon. This global purchase arrangement should be subject to periodic adjustment in consultation with the Organization.

Interest in global quota commitments by central plan countries revived in the Kennedy Round. Poland participated in that tariff conference and undertook, in its protocol of accession, "to increase the total value of its imports from the territories of contracting parties by not less than seven percent per annum."[17] It further committed itself to participate in extensive annual reviews of its trade with other contracting parties. In the event of a failure of Poland to meet its import commitment for reasons other than an "unexpected decline in Polish exports to the territories of contracting parties," the CONTRACTING PARTIES were to "consider the situation, and make such recommendations as they consider appropriate."[18] Provision was also made for bilateral consultations and, under certain circumstances, for the suspension of concessions between Poland and particular contracting parties.[19] The problem of discrimination in the administration of the global commitments was not squarely faced, although the annual reviews and the consultations were to deal with the "geographical distribution" of Polish imports and exports.[20]

16. These provisions are supplemented by requirements as to the furnishing of information, giving of public notice, and so forth.
17. *Basic Instruments,* 15th Supp. (1968), p. 46, 52 (Annex B).
18. Ibid., p. 49.
19. Ibid., p. 49.
20. Ibid., pp. 51–52 (Annex A). In addition, rather elaborate escape provisions were included in response to the fear of some contracting parties that Poland might engage in market-disrupting export pricing (ibid., pp. 48–49).

## Quantitative Restrictions

Since market-economy countries are permitted to impose quantitative restrictions on imports (and sometimes exports) for balance-of-payments, agricultural support, and economic development purposes, it would be inequitable to deny contracting parties that engage in state trading the right to do the same and indeed to do so directly through their purchasing policies (or sales policies). An interpretative note accordingly makes clear that the terms "import restrictions" and "export restrictions" in the relevant Articles "include restrictions made effective through state-trading operations."[21] The application of the interpretative note to the balance-of-payments exception constitutes an important escape provision for central plan countries, since, as noted, those countries do not normally have convertible currencies.

## The GATT Experience

### Central Plan Countries

The difficulties in fitting centrally planned economies into the GATT system are highlighted by the difference between the relationships that Poland and Yugoslavia have been able to work out with the GATT. Both became interested in a formal relationship with the GATT in the late 1950s. Both were given a special, limited status in 1959 by means of Declarations.[22] But Yugoslavia acceded provisionally in 1962 and became a full contracting party in 1966,[23] while Poland did not accede until 1967.[24] The Yugoslav schedule looks much like the schedule of any other contracting party, with precise duty bindings on a wide range of tariff items, while the Polish schedule contains only the annual import increase commitment just described.

The difference in speed and extent between the absorptions of Yugoslavia and Poland into the GATT system is simply explained. Poland had made relatively few changes in the nature of its centrally planned economy. Yugoslavia, on the other hand, had shifted from a centrally planned to something approaching a market economy. Although Yugoslavia had not adopted private enterprise in the Western sense and had retained a considerable degree of state regulation, its enterprises had been given a degree of autonomy over production and pricing not fundamentally different from that enjoyed by privately owned enterprises in market-economy countries. Under Yugoslav law, enterprises were no longer controlled by the state but were controlled by the workers

---

21. Interpretative note, Ad. Arts. XI, XII, XIII, XIV and XVIII.
22. See *Basic Instruments,* 8th Supp. (1960), pp. 12, 17.
23. Ibid., 11th Supp. (1963), p. 50; 15th Supp. (1968), p. 63.
24. Ibid., 15th Supp. (1968), p. 46.

in each enterprise. Perhaps more significant, a number of enterprises normally competed against one another in each industry, and no centralized import and export monopolies provided insulation from the world market. Any enterprise that was properly registered was entitled to import, subject, of course, to exchange controls and quantitative restrictions.[25] Thus, the market-economy assumptions of the GATT had been met by Yugoslavia.

## Market-Economy Countries

Since, as noted, the draftsmen of the General Agreement did not contemplate that there would be any need to worry about the applicability of the GATT rules to centrally planned economies, it would be unfair to criticize the GATT rules for failing to deal with the problem of integrating centrally planned economies into the GATT system. But it is fair to ask how well the GATT rules have functioned in dealing with state monopolies maintained by contracting parties with market economies. A review of the GATT experience reveals a striking absence of discussion and dispute about state monopolies. After the work of the 1955 Review conference resulted in the addition to Article XVII of paragraph 4, requiring notification of state-trading activities, the GATT devoted some attention to obtaining information about state monopolies. But the problems that arose were mainly concerned with obtaining full information from all contracting parties. When the original notification procedures[26] proved inadequate, a panel was appointed to examine the notifications filed.[27] The panel prepared a detailed questionnaire to elicit the information required.[28]

It was not until the GATT became seriously interested in the barriers maintained by developed countries against the exports of less-developed countries that any serious efforts were made to consider the trade implications of state trading. The questionnaire previously developed had to be supplemented to obtain sufficient information for the work of Committee III, which had been

---

25. Yugoslavia, unlike Poland, had become a member of the International Monetary Fund, and therefore its exchange licensing was conducted under the IMF rules and subject to IMF consultations. On the details of the Yugoslav economic reforms, see the following Yugoslav memoranda: "Foreign Trade and Exchange Systems in Yugoslavia," GATT Document L/962 (12 March 1959); "Status of Yugoslav Economic Organization," GATT Document L/961 (11 March 1959), as amended by GATT Document L/1877 (24 Oct. 1962) and by GATT Document L/2488, Annex I (2 Nov. 1965); "Main Features of the Yugoslav Economy and Foreign Trade System," GATT Document L/2488, Annex II. See also the working party report on the provisional accession of Yugoslavia, *Basic Instruments,* 11th Supp. (1963), p. 79.
26. Set out at *Basic Instruments,* 6th Supp. (1958), p. 23.
27. Ibid., 9th Supp. (1961), p. 179.
28. Ibid., p. 184.

charged with investigating barriers to the trade of less-developed countries.[29] From the beginning of the work of Committee III, however, it was clear that state trading had detrimental effects on less-developed-country exports. In 1961 the CONTRACTING PARTIES formally declared:

> Access to markets for products of the type studied by Committee III should not be unnecessarily impeded through the operations of State import monopolies or purchasing agencies. For many products exported by less-developed countries, the prices charged on resale by some State monopolies, whether in countries with centrally-planned economies or in others, involve an implicit heavy taxation of imports. Countries operating State import monopolies or purchasing agencies should endeavour to improve access to their markets for products of less-developed countries by decisions to import larger quantities of the products concerned and, if necessary, by reductions in the difference between import and sales prices.[30]

Although state trading was occasionally the subject of later discussions on barriers facing less-developed countries, as when the practice of the Italian banana import monopoly of importing almost exclusively from former Italian colonies was reviewed,[31] state trading was never the major theme of those discussions.

State trading was also occasionally the topic of discussions on agricultural protectionism. In a 1961 report, Committee II, charged with investigating barriers to agricultural trade, found that state trading was in some cases used as a substitute for quantitative restrictions:

> The activities assigned by some governments to State-trading agencies had the same effect on trade as quantitative restrictions and ... not only buying and selling operations but the quantitative regulation of imports, which was properly a function of government, were being carried out by State-trading agencies.[32]

State-trading practices of certain developed countries also came before the GATT when Uruguay launched a massive attack on practices by developed countries that it deemed to constitute, under Article XXIII, "nullification or impairment" of tariff concessions made to it. The panel appointed to consider the Uruguayan complaint found that, with respect to a number of those practices, "there are *a priori* grounds for assuming that they could have an adverse

---

29. Ibid., 11th Supp. (1963), pp. 176, 184–85, 187–88. See discussion in chapter 14, "Less-Developed Countries," supra.
30. *Basic Instruments,* 10th Supp. (1962), p. 28, 30.
31. First Report of the Group on Residual Restrictions to the Committee on Trade and Development, *Expansion of Trade of the Developing Countries (Selected Documents)* (Dec. 1966) (mimeographed), p. 45, 58.
32. *Basic Instruments,* 9th Supp. (1961), p. 110, 117.

effect on Uruguay's exports."[33] But the panel refrained from passing upon the legality of the state-trading practices under Articles II:4 and XVII.

The relative absence of GATT activity in the area of state trading can be interpreted as indicating that state trading does not consitute a significant barrier to trade. A more plausible interpretation is that the GATT has been primarily concerned with more obvious trade barriers and has failed to come to grips with the state-trading problem. One item of evidence favoring the latter interpretation is the experience of the European Economic Community. When the EEC came into existence, one of the major problems it faced in the creation of a common market was the elimination of the impediments to intra-Community trade stemming from state monopolies. Even today state monopolies present one of the principal barriers to full integration of the economies of the member states.[34]

## The EEC Experience

Since the EEC has had perhaps broader experience with state-trading problems than has the GATT, the EEC record warrants consideration in determining what steps the GATT might take to deal more thoroughly with state trading. The EEC experience throws light, for example, on the question whether the focus of attention should be on amending the GATT rules. The Commission has apparently despaired of following any single set of rules in dealing with the wide variety of state-trading practices in the six member states. It has concluded that the path to integration of those domestic sectors subject to state trading lies in "a pragmatic approach."[35]

The draftsmen of the EEC treaty did not attempt to prescribe the steps to be taken in dealing with state-trading enterprises. Rather, they specified the goal to be reached and left the techniques to the Commission and to the member states. The state-trading problem was viewed as essentially analogous to the problem of eliminating quantitative restrictions. The draftsmen therefore included the article on state monopolies in the Treaty chapter entitled "The Elimination of Quantitative Restrictions as between Member States." The member states were required to "adjust progressively any state monopolies of a commercial character in such a manner as will insure the exclusion, at the date of the expiry of the transitional period [that is, by 1970], of all discrimination between the nationals of member states in regard to conditions of supply or marketing of goods." The "timing" of these adjustments was to be "adapted

33. Ibid., 11th Supp. (1963), pp. 95, 105, 113, 119, 123, 130, 133, 138, 144.
34. See Guido Colonna di Paliano, "State Monopolies and Freedom of Choice," *European Community,* No. 15 (Sept. 1967), p. 4.
35. Europe Economic Community Commission, *Ninth General Report on the Activities of the Community* (1966), p. 51.

to the abolition . . . of the quantitative restrictions on the same products." The Commission was empowered to "make recommendations as to the particulars and the timing according to which the adjustments . . . shall be carried out"; but the final authority on the manner of adjustments was left to the member states.[36]

In carrying out its mission to recommend the procedures to be followed, the Commission has relied on a wide variety of techniques, varying with the product involved and the underlying political and economic situation. In the case of the Italian banana monopoly, the Commission recommended a series of increases in imports and eventually the elimination of state trading entirely.[37] The Commission concluded that the German spirits monopoly could be adjusted simply through the elimination of quantitative restrictions and the automatic grant of import licenses.[38] In the case of the French monopoly of explosives, a special supplementary recommendation on the structure of domestic prices was deemed necessary.[39] Finally, as to French imports of petroleum, which come under a domestic licensing system that results in a state monopoly in substance although not in form, the Commission has apparently concluded that adjustment can take place only within the context of a Community-wide common energy policy.[40]

In the first ten years of the EEC's existence, the accomplishments of the Commission in inducing the member states to adjust their monopolies have been modest in contrast to the outstanding success in eliminating tariffs and quantitative restrictions on intra-Community trade in the private sector. The EEC experience cautions against expecting the GATT to accomplish very much at its present stage of institutional development. And that experience indicates that progress in the GATT, if it is to take place at all, must be based on special procedures designed to deal with the differential character of the various state-trading practices of the contracting parties. The GATT rules alone do not provide an adequate framework for an attack on protectionism in the guise of state trading.

36. Treaty of Rome, Art. 37. State monopolies are also subjected by Article 90 to the rules of competition applicable to private firms. On the meaning of Article 37, see Ernst-Joachim Mestmäcker, "State Trading Monopolies in the European Economic Community," *Vanderbilt Law Review,* XX (1967), p. 321; G. van Hecke, "Government Enterprises and National Monopolies under the E.E.C. Treaty," *Common Market Law Review,* III (1966), p. 450; and the references cited in those two articles.
37. European Economic Community Commission, *Fifth General Report on the Activities of the Community* (1962), p. 45; *Seventh General Report on the Activities of the Community* (1964), p. 39; *Eighth General Report on the Activities of the Community* (1965), p. 46.
38. *Eighth General Report on the Activities of the Community* (1965), p. 46.
39. *Tenth General Report on the Activities of the Community* (1967), p. 72.
40. Ibid., p. 20.

# PART 5

### The Institutional Arrangements

# 19 The GATT as an International Organization

The title of this chapter is not one that will be acceptable to many of the "old GATT hands." For some purists it is an article of faith that the GATT is not an organization. Indeed, it can be argued that there is no such thing as "the GATT," but rather that there is merely a multilateral agreement, the General Agreement, which provides in Article XXV:1 for "joint action" of its contracting parties to give effect to its provisions and to further its objectives. When the contracting parties take joint action, the action is designated as action of the (uppercase) "CONTRACTING PARTIES." Nothing in the General Agreement refers to the GATT as an organization or to the concept of membership.

Whether the GATT should nevertheless be viewed as an "organization" is a futile and abstruse question, which need not detain us here.[1] But this fine point for the initiated serves to highlight the peculiar character of the GATT. In legal and institutional patrimony, the GATT is one of the most humble, if not deprived, of the multitude of international bodies on the current world scene. But in positive accomplishments, the GATT must surely rank near the top. In large measure this initial handicap has been overcome through the persistence and resourcefulness of a dedicated and pragmatic secretariat and through the will of the leading contracting parties. But a number of institutional arrangements adopted over the past twenty years have also contributed to the accomplishments of the GATT.

1. Eric Wyndham White, then executive secretary of the GATT, perhaps put this insiders' question to rest in a speech entitled "GATT as an International Trade Organization," in which he stated: "The General Agreement on Tariffs and Trade, as its name clearly indicates, is, juridically speaking, a trade agreement and nothing more. But because it is a multilateral agreement and contains provisions for joint action and decision it had the potentiality to become, and has in fact become, an international 'organization' for trade cooperation between the signatory States" (address at the Polish Institute of International Affairs, Warsaw, 6 June 1961, p. 3.

The unusual legal status of the GATT developed out of the peculiar circumstances in which the General Agreement came into existence. Since the General Agreement was to be only a recordation of the results of the first round of tariff negotiations within the framework of the International Trade Organization and a stopgap set of rules pending the coming into effect of the Havana Charter, no thought was given to institutional problems. Although the General Agreement contained substantive provisions essentially similar to those of the Havana Charter chapter on commercial policy, the permanent institution was to be the ITO. The Havana Charter contained elaborate provisions in Chapter VII for a conference, an executive board, commissions, a director-general, and a staff. Chapter VII provided for a relatively elaborate system for dispute settlement. The General Agreement, on the other hand, was innocent of institutional provisions and, so far as dispute settlement was concerned, contained relatively modest procedures.

### Intersessional Procedures

The early GATT suffered from a number of institutional weaknesses. One of the most serious was the collegial character of action by the CONTRACTING PARTIES, given the long periods that elapsed between sessions. Since the authority for such action was that contained in the "joint action" provisions of Article XXV, special steps had to be taken to permit action during periods between sessions. There was not sufficient business to justify full-dress meetings more than once or twice a year, but some items of business could not easily be postponed until the next meeting. For example, under Article XII:4(a) as then drafted, any contracting party that was not currently applying quantitative restrictions but that was "considering the need to do so" was required to consult with the CONTRACTING PARTIES before instituting such restrictions or, if prior consultation was impracticable, immediately thereafter. If such consultation could only take place during the regular sessions, which were then normally held only once a year, the consultation requirement usually could not be carried out, because the country faced with the balance-of-payments crisis would not usually consider itself in a position to postpone restrictive action.

In 1949 certain special arrangements for action between sessions by th' chairman of the CONTRACTING PARTIES were made with respect to vario: kinds of balance-of-payments matters. The chairman was given the power convene special sessions of the CONTRACTING PARTIES, to entrust consul tions to an ad hoc committee, and to canvass the contracting parties to obt a consensus that consultations should be commenced in those circumstar where the General Agreement gave the initiative to the CONTRACTING PART

In addition, a "selected committee" was established for certain types of intersessional balance-of-payments consultations.[2]

The necessity for a general intersessional body became increasingly clear, but progress was slow. A working party on the continuing administration of the General Agreement recommended in 1950 the establishment of a standing committee with intersessional powers over matters going well beyond balance-of-payments restrictions.[3] But it was not until the sixth session in 1951 that a committee for agenda and intersessional business was formed, and even then the life of the committee was limited to one intersessional period.[4] But the life of the Intersessional Committee, as it became known, was extended regularly at the end of each session.

The Intersessional Committee originally had two functions: first, to meet some four to six weeks before each session to fix the agenda and, second, to consider urgent and unforeseen matters.[5] With the growth of the secretariat and the establishment by the major contracting parties of permanent representations to the GATT, the function of fixing the agenda was transferred in 1958 from the Intersessional Committee to "informal contact" between the executive secretary and the permanent representatives.[6] The functions of the Intersessional Committee with respect to matters other than the agenda had been spelled out in increasing detail over the years,[7] and in 1958 its functions with respect to balance-of-payments problems were transferred to a standing balance-of-payments committee.[8] The scope of intersessional work had meanwhile been enlarged by extending the authorization for airmail and telegraphic voting between sessions to all issues designated by the chairman of the CONTRACTING PARTIES, as opposed to only those issues concerning balance-of-payments restrictions.[9]

In 1955 a major effort was made to remedy the weaknesses of the intersessional arrangements and to strengthen the secretariat through the establishment of an Organization for Trade Cooperation (OTC). This organization, which was designed to pick up the ITO institutional pieces, would have been a full-scale international organization with an assembly, an executive committee, and a secretariat. It would have been empowered to carry out many of the functions of the CONTRACTING PARTIES, including the granting of waivers and

2. *Basic Instruments,* Vol. II (1952), pp. 89–103; Vol. I (1952), p. 101.
3. *Ibid.,* Vol. II (1952), p. 197.
4. Ibid., p. 205.
5. Ibid., p. 206.
6. Ibid., 7th Supp. (1959), pp. 108, 109–10.
7. Compare ibid., 1st Supp. (1953), p. 7, with 5th Supp. (1957), p. 17.
8. Ibid., 7th Supp. (1959), p. 108, 110.
9. Compare ibid., 1st Supp. (1963), pp. 7, 8–9, with 2nd Supp. (1954), p. 8, 13.

the authorization of suspension of obligations under the nullification or impairment provisions of Article XXIII.[10] The OTC, however, met the same fate as the ITO—stillbirth through the failure of the Congress to ratify the underlying agreement.

When it became clear that the OTC was never to become a reality, attention turned to the possibilities for improving the intersessional procedures. After extensive discussions, the Council of Representatives was created in 1960 to replace the Intersessional Committee. The Council differs from the Committee in several ways. Whereas the Committee was limited in membership in order that it might become "an effective Committee," the Council is "composed of representatives of all contracting parties willing to accept the responsibility of membership therein."[11] In part, this is merely a change in form. A major restraining influence on the number of members of the Committee used to be the number of countries with permanent representatives in or near Geneva who were in a position to attend sporadic intersessional meetings. As the GATT grew in importance and as the creation of the European Economic Community and the European Free Trade Association enhanced the desirability for small countries of having high-level trade representatives located in Europe, an increasingly large number of countries were in a position to assume continuing GATT responsibilities. The limitation on the membership of the Committee was, in any event, of minimal importance, because arrangements were made to permit participation, in the case of particular issues, by countries claiming a substantial interest and wishing to be represented.[12]

Fuller membership became important because of a major expansion of the authority granted for intersessional work. The Intersessional Committee had been limited to those functions specified in advance by the CONTRACTING PARTIES, but the Council has broad powers, including the power "to deal with such other matters with which the CONTRACTING PARTIES may deal at their sessions."[13] Only the power to grant waivers under Article XXV:5 is specifically withheld, and the Council may pass upon requests for waivers. Where the Council approves a waiver, the vote on the waiver can be taken by postal or telegraphic ballot without the necessity of waiting for the next regular session.[14] In order to protect individual contracting parties from unexpected

---

10. See The Agreement on the Organization for Trade Cooperation annexed to the Final Act adopted at the Ninth Session of the CONTRACTING PARTIES (1955); see generally G. Bronz, "An International Trade Organization: The Second Attempt," *Harvard Law Review,* LXIX (1956), pp. 440, 473–79.
11. *Basic Instruments,* 9th Supp. (1961), p. 7, 8.
12. Ibid., 5th Supp. (1957), p. 17, 20.
13. Ibid., 9th Supp. (1961), p. 7, 8.
14. Ibid., pp. 8–9. See GATT Document L/2607 (23 March 1966), p. 3, for a description by the Council of Representatives of the handling of one waiver during a period between sessions.

intersessional action, each contracting party is granted the power to "suspend the operation of such action by the Council through the submission of a written appeal to the CONTRACTING PARTIES."[15]

The Council has a number of other functions. It supervises the agenda of the sessions and the work of working parties and other bodies established by the CONTRACTING PARTIES. Most technical matters are handled by the Council, followed by CONTRACTING PARTY action through postal ballot or in a subsequent session. Reports of working parties and other subsidiary bodies not requiring action are reviewed by the Council, and the CONTRACTING PARTIES are asked simply to adopt Council reports noting those reports or recommending their adoption.[16] The agenda of the sessions, fixed by the Council, can thereby be limited to broad questions with a substantial policy component and to matters which for one reason or another are not ripe for Council action prior to the sessions.[17] The effect of this greatly expanded intersessional authority, coupled with the growing GATT workload, is to make the Council the central organ of the GATT and to turn the sessions into appellate bodies for issues that are too delicate or too important to be definitively resolved by operating-level civil servants.

The creation of the Council has permitted the GATT to complete its transformation from a collegial body meeting at widely spaced intervals to a full-time international "organization." It has had the collateral effect of inducing a further increase in the quality of the national representations to the GATT, since the continuing business requires the presence of permanently stationed personnel.

## The Secretariat

It would be difficult to describe the secretariat of the GATT in a few summary paragraphs and perhaps even harder to do so in a book. On the one hand, difficulty of description is inherent in the nature of international secretariats. Such secretariats do not operate by rules that can be summarized and analyzed. They are administrative bodies that contribute interstitially to policy decisions as they respond to individual challenges and opportunities. They frequently reflect the goals and personality of their chief. Perhaps nowhere is this personal influence more marked than in the GATT, where the skill and prestige of the first director-general, Eric Wyndham White, was a predominant and omnipresent factor in GATT affairs from the beginning until his retirement in 1968. At every major turning point and in every major success in GATT history has figured an imaginative compromise, an unexpected initiative, or a face-saving

---

15. *Basic Instruments,* 9th Supp. (1961), p. 7, 9.
16. See GATT Document L/2607 (23 March 1966), pp. 6–8.
17. Ibid., pp. 9–17.

formula originated by Wyndham White. His personal style has been reflected less in broad principles of administration and leadership than in pragmatic responses to individual situations. What is needed for an understanding of the GATT is perhaps a biography of this singularly effective international civil servant. But one who has not lived through the GATT years in the secretariat or in one of the more active national delegations is not in a position to tell the story properly, because that story is to be found less in documents and in speeches than in private conversations.

But some observations can be made about the secretariat as an institution. One has to do with the modesty of its size and financial resources. There was a time when the GATT secretariat consisted of nothing more than three or four professional people and a handful of typists and file clerks. That the secretariat existed at all was to be credited to the secretariat of the Interim Commission for the International Trade Organization (ICITO), which was kept alive even after the ITO had been left by the United States to perish. Since the ICITO was alimented by loans from the United Nations Working Capital Fund, it was able to delegate a small number of civil servants to the GATT. Although the embryo GATT staff had to be supplemented at the complex Annecy negotiations in 1949,[18] not until 1951 did the contracting parties begin to make contributions for the secretariat.[19] The pretense of using the ICITO or its secretariat as the source of the GATT secretariat continued, even though the ICITO had no function but to provide services for the GATT.[20]

The secretariat remained miniscule, and the budget for the GATT as a whole did not climb above one-half million dollars until 1958.[21] In 1965 the GATT was able to accomplish its work with 179 full-time employees, including typists and file clerks. The International Labor Organization, a few blocks away in Geneva, required some 1,547 employees, and the International Monetary Fund, whose functions are in some ways comparable to those of the GATT, had some 773 employees. Most independent observers would probably agree that the GATT's accomplishments compare favorably with those of the Food and Agricultural Organization, which provided employment for a full-time staff of 4,261.[22] The GATT's budget remains similarly unpretentious. For 1966 the GATT budgeted $2,233,000, which compared, for example, to the IMF's forecast of $15,160,000 for administrative salaries and expenses alone.[23] The United Nations Conference on Trade and Development, fresh in the budgetary

18. See William Adams Brown, *The United States and the Restoration of World Trade* (Washington: Brookings Institution, 1950), pp. 295–96.
19. See *Yearbook of the United Nations* (1951), p. 965.
20. See e.g., *Basic Documents,* 12th Supp. (1964), p. 10, 12.
21. U.S. Tariff Commission, *Operation of the Trade Agreements Program,* 11th Rep. (1960), p. 76.
22. *Yearbook of the United Nations* (1965), pp. 709, 716, 761, 795.
23. Ibid., pp. 761, 795.

race as it was, had already lapped the GATT with a 1966 budget of $5,971,500.[24]

Another characteristic of the GATT secretariat is, paradoxically enough, its dramatic growth. The GATT budget increased fivefold from 1958 to 1966.[25] The increase was attributable to two factors other than any Parkinsonian phenomenon that might have been operative. The first was that the Dillon and Kennedy Rounds were long and complex and required extensive staff support. The second and more important factor was the publication in 1958 of the expert report "Trends in International Trade," which, although perhaps not seen at the time, marked a decisive turning point in the history of the GATT. As previously described,[26] the events engendered by that report led to a steady expansion of the GATT's activities. In physical terms that expansion included the construction of a new building to house the newer activities, including most recently the staff for the Trade and Development Committee and the International Trade Center. This new building was constructed just above the Villa le Bocage, a compact but ample country house that had housed the GATT secretariat for years. There was more than a little symbolism in the decision to keep the old GATT in the traditional, albeit slightly faded, elegance of the Villa while housing the new GATT in an antiseptically modern building smacking of the prefabricated, if not of the temporary.

**Provisional Application**

If the GATT has transcended the bounds of the General Agreement to become an international institution with a life of its own, it is nonetheless a product and in many ways a captive of the restrictive terms of that founding document. One of the principal limitations arises from the limited legal application of Part II of the General Agreement arising out of the provisions of the Protocol of Provisional Application and similar provisions in subsequent protocols of accession. In order to understand the limitations imposed by those provisions, it is necessary to consider the arrangement of the General Agreement.

The General Agreement is divided into four parts. Part I consists of only the first two articles; it thus contains principally the most-favored-nation obligation and the provisions on bindings. Part II, including Articles III through XXIII, contains the commercial policy provisions that constitute the GATT's substantive code of good behavior in trade matters. Until the 1964 effort to placate the less-developed countries by giving them their own "part," Part III contained the remainder of the original General Agreement. It includes most of the procedural provisions and certain miscellaneous substantive provisions,

24. Ibid., p. 668.
25. Compare *Basic Instruments,* 6th Supp. (1958), p. 131, with 14th Supp. (1966), p. 157.
26. See discussion in chapter 14, "Less-Developed Countries," supra.

such as the material in Article XXIV on customs unions and free-trade areas.

This tripartite division was not a mere editing convenience. Rather, it had an explicit legal purpose. And it created one of the principal weaknesses of the General Agreement as a codification of a rule of law in economic affairs.

When the General Agreement was drafted in 1947, a number of nations realized that some of their existing domestic legislation was in conflict with specific prohibitions contained in what is now Part II. Not only would efforts to amend that domestic legislation have delayed the bringing into effect of the General Agreement, but any attempt in some countries to eliminate certain trade restrictions that were dear to the hearts of powerful domestic economic interests might have led to the outright rejection of the General Agreement. An imaginative legal device was adopted to circumvent these difficulties.

The General Agreement was applied only "provisionally." This was achieved through the Protocol of Provisional Application.[27] The fact that Parts I and III were applied only provisionally had no important operative significance.[28] But the Protocol of Provisional Application contained a clause that provided that Part II was to be applied "to the fullest extent not inconsistent with existing legislation." Existing legislation conflicting with specific provisions of Part II would thus not constitute a violation of the General Agreement.[29]

Provisional application of the General Agreement was to be terminated upon definitive acceptance of the General Agreement pursuant to Article XXVI. But the General Agreement remains applicable to the original contracting parties only provisionally. And the contracting parties that have acceded to the GATT have done so under protocols of accession that contain language on Part II similar to that contained in the Protocol of Provisional Accession. In the case of the accession protocols, however, the cut-off date is the date of the accession protocol rather than 30 October 1947, which has been interpreted to be the cut-off date for the original contracting parties.[30]

The importance of these "grandfather clauses," as measured by the amount

---

27. The Protocol of Provisional Application is reproduced in the Appendix, infra.

28. One minor difference is that paragraph 5 of the Protocol of Provisional Application provides for a sixty-day waiting period for withdrawals whereas Article XXXI provides for a six-months period.

29. An interpretative note makes clear that "the obligations incorporated in paragraph 1 of Article I by reference to paragraphs 2 and 4 of Article III and those incorporated in paragraph 2(b) of Article II by reference to Article VI shall be considered as falling within Part II for the purposes of the Protocol of Provisional Application." Interpretative note, Ad Art. I, para. 1. Paragraph 1(b) of Article II contains its own saving clause with respect to "other duties and charges" on bound items.

30. See, e.g., the Annecy and Torquay protocols, *Analytical Index*, pp. 173, 177. On the selection of 30 October 1947, as the relevant date, see *Basic Instruments*, Vol. II (1952), p. 35.

of legislation that is saved, is difficult to assess. Certainly many of the residual restrictions still in effect are illegal, even taking into account the saving provisions of the various protocols. Several attempts have been made to induce the various contracting parties to report the legislation that they consider to be saved, but these attempts, though resulting in lists of impressive length, have not received unanimous cooperation.[31] The result is, in any case, an unsatisfactory situation in which trade restrictions are often discussed in a legal half-light; practices that are clearly inconsistent with GATT principles can nevertheless be defended as lawful because they have been in effect since pre-GATT days. Those contracting parties that have fully complied with Part II sometimes regard the reliance by other contracting parties on the saving clause as evidence of bad faith.

The saving clause is ambiguous in one important respect: there is authority for the interpretation that only "mandatory" legislation is saved. Under this interpretation, pre-1948, or pre-accession, legislation that merely authorizes the executive authorities of a country to impose a trade restriction will not save a restriction imposed thereunder. This interpretation is open to the objection that the word "mandatory" is not in fact to be found in the Protocol of Provisional Application. A working party report adopted by the CONTRACTING PARTIES in 1949 stated that a trade measure would be saved only if "the legislation on which it is based is by its terms or expressed intent of a mandatory character—that is, it imposes on the executive authority requirements which cannot be modified by executive action."[32] The Review Session Working Party agreed, substituting assertion for proof in concluding that "it is plain from the wording of the Protocol of Provisional Application that the exception can only be applicable to legislation which is, by its terms or expressed intent, of a mandatory character."[33]

An attempt was made in the 1955 Review Session to induce governments to accept the General Agreement definitively. The same considerations that had led to the device of provisional application in 1947 were, however, still operative. Many governments were not even willing to agree to a Scandinavian proposal for a transitional period of fixed duration during which all legislation would be brought into conformity with Part II.[34]

In an effort to deal with the form rather than the substance of the problem, there was agreed upon at the Review Session a formula which, it was hoped, would encourage contracting parties to adopt the General Agreement defini-

31. See GATT Document L/2375/Add. 1 (19 March 1965).
32. *Basic Instruments,* Vol. II (1952), p. 49, 62. See also 1st Supp. (1953), p. 59, 61.
33. Ibid., 3d Supp. (1955), pp. 231, 249–50.
34. Ibid., p. 248.

tively. The CONTRACTING PARTIES unanimously agreed that an acceptance under Article XXVI might be accompanied "by a reservation to the effect that Part II of the General Agreement will be applied to the fullest extent not inconsistent with legislation which existed on 30 October 1947 or, in the case of a contracting party which since 30 June 1949 has acceded to the Agreement, the date of the Protocol providing for such accession."[35] In other words, definitive application of the General Agreement would not preclude continued application of the same nonconforming legislation that had been saved by the Protocol of Provisional Application. It was thought that through annual reviews and through a major review three years after the General Agreement came into definitive force it would be possible to induce contracting parties to bring their domestic legislation largely into conformity with Part II.

The 1955 plan did not work. When the director-general issued a call in 1965 for an end to the anomaly of provisional application, he could report only a single case in which a contracting party had deposited an instrument of acceptance.[36] Since the General Agreement was not to enter into force definitively until, pursuant to Article XXVI:6, instruments of acceptance had been deposited on behalf of that proportion of thirty-four named contracting parties that accounted for 85 percent of the total external trade of those contracting parties, it was clear that definitive application was still some years away.

## Amendment of the General Agreement

Since amendments to the General Agreement frequently concern major issues of commercial policy, contracting parties have sometimes been slow to accept proposed amendments. Article XXX provides that even those amendments that do not require unanimity and that become effective upon acceptance by two-thirds of the contracting parties are, nevertheless, to be effective only "in respect to those contracting parties which accept them." Thus no contracting party can be bound by an amendment unless it specifically accepts that amendment. In this respect Article XXX differs from Article 108 of the United Nations Charter, under which an amendment to the Charter comes into force when adopted and ratified by two-thirds of the membership, provided that all the permanent members of the Security Council adopt it.

The technique that is adopted for GATT amendments is to place them in documents called protocols. Each protocol states the terms and conditions upon which it shall become effective, those terms and conditions being subject, of course, to the explicit requirements of Article XXX. It is thus possible,

---

35. Ibid., p. 48.
36. GATT Document L/2375 (5 March 1965), p. 2. Haiti had much earlier accepted the General Agreement definitively (GATT Document L/2375/Add. 1 [19 March 1965], p. 20).

although not necessarily easy, to determine which protocols are in effect with respect to which contracting parties. From time to time a GATT document is circulated to the various contracting parties on the status of GATT protocols.[37]

One inconvenience in the GATT arrangement is that it is sometimes a considerable challenge to determine which GATT rights are enforceable by which contracting parties at any given point in time. Another kind of inconvenience is produced by the dilatoriness of certain contracting parties in accepting technical protocols that they have no policy grounds for opposing. A device used with some success to deal with the latter problem is the inclusion of a list of such protocols in the protocol embodying the results of a round of major tariff negotiations, with the provision that acceptance of the latter constitutes acceptance of the former in the absence of notice by a contracting party to the contrary.[38]

A different kind of problem has arisen from the requirement of Article XXX that amendments to Part I gain unanimous acceptance. Some such amendments never entered into force because of the refusal of Uruguay to deposit an instrument of acceptance of a protocol containing the amendments. The CONTRACTING PARTIES repeatedly extended the time period for accepting the relevant protocol while urging unanimous acceptance, but were finally obliged to abandon the protocol.[39]

## Accession

Accession to the GATT entails bringing the new contracting party into a network of protocols. The problems that arise are somewhat different from those faced by other international organizations, because an entrant to the GATT automatically becomes the beneficiary of a large number of tariff concessions through the operation of Article II:1. In order to assure that the new contracting party gives something of value for these benefits, the institution of "entrance-fee" negotiations has arisen.

New states may sometimes be able to avoid entrance-fee negotiations with their ensuing complexity and delay. Article XXVI:5(c) provides that if a contracting party previously accepted the General Agreement with respect to

37. Information on protocols was at one time published in the *Basic Instruments*. See, e.g., *Basic Instruments*, 5th Supp. (1957), p. 9. For more recent information, see THE CONTRACTING PARTIES to the General Agreement on Tariffs and Trade, *Status of Multilateral Protocols of which the Director-General Acts as Depositary* (1967).
38. See Protocol Embodying the Results of the 1960–61 Tariff Conference, para. 7(b), *Basic Instruments*, 11th Supp. (1963), p. 8, 11.
39. See, for example of the extensions, ibid., 14th Supp. (1966), p. 17, and for the abandonment, 15th Supp. (1968), p. 65.

the territory of a new state, that new state "shall, upon sponsorship through a declaration by the responsible contracting party . . . be deemed to be a contracting party." Since many colonial powers accepted the General Agreement with respect to their colonies, this alternative path to contracting party status has been available to many former colonies.[40] The new state thus becomes a contracting party "on the terms and conditions previously accepted by the metropolitan government on behalf of the territory in question,"[41] and it is bound by any tariff concessions that may have been made on behalf of its customs territory by the sponsoring contracting party.[42]

Contracting party status is not, however, automatic for a state qualifying under Article XXVI:5(c). Although the General Agreement requirement that a declaration of sponsorship be filed has in effect been dropped,[43] the new state itself must indicate its intention to be a contracting party. Since a new state is likely to have more pressing problems than whether or not to participate in GATT affairs and since the theory of Article XXVI:5(c) is that the application of GATT commitments with respect to the customs territory of the new state continue without interruption, there may result immediately following independence an awkward interregnum in which it is not clear whether or not commitments made by the former colonial power are applicable. To bridge that gap, a system of de facto application has been established. Not specifically authorized by the General Agreement, this system illustrates another pragmatic adaption of GATT practices to deal with dilemmas not clearly foreseen by the drafters of the General Agreement. De facto application refers simply to a "recommendation" by the CONTRACTING PARTIES that, with respect to the customs territory in question, contracting parties "should continue to apply *de facto* the Agreement in their relations with that territory, *provided* that that territory also continues to apply *de facto* the Agreement to them."[44] Since tariff schedules are an integral part of the General Agreement, this language refers not only to rules of commercial policy but also to tariff concessions. The period of de facto application is two years, but the CONTRACTING PARTIES, anxious to promote widespread participation of the less-developed countries in the GATT and faced with a good deal of indifference toward the GATT on the part of those countries, have frequently extended the period of de facto

40. For a detailed description of the GATT practice under this provision, see Tatsuro Kunugi, "State Succession in the Framework of GATT," *American Journal of International Law,* LIX (1965), pp. 268–90. See also the discussion of accession in chapter 6, "Technical Tariff Negotiations," supra.
41. *Basic Instruments,* 10th Supp. (1962), p. 69, 73.
42. Some dispute on the implications of this principle arose in the case of Gabon. See ibid., 12th Supp. (1964), pp. 73, 75–76.
43. See GATT Documents C/30 (26 April 1963), and C/M/15 (15 May 1963).
44. Ibid., 6th Supp. (1958), p. 11, 12.

application and in 1967 decided to make de facto application a more or less permanent status.[45]

Another kind of pragmatic adjustment, in this case designed to deal with the delays required to conclude entrance-fee negotiations, is the institution of provisional accession. Under the provisional accession procedure the General Agreement is made applicable to the commercial relations between the provisionally acceding state and those contracting parties accepting the particular declaration of provisional accession. When the tariff negotiations are concluded, the status of the acceding government is changed from provisional accession to full accession through a protocol of accession under Article XXXIII.

A problem over reservations has sometimes arisen in connection with provisional accession. Certain provisionally acceding countries have not been able to bring their commercial policies with respect to such matters as quantitative restrictions into conformity with the rules of Part II of the General Agreement. In some instances the provisional status has consequently had to be extended beyond the completion of the entrance-fee negotiations. The decision to permit Switzerland to accede provisionally was taken in 1958, after some years of discussions concerning such matters as the incompatibility between Swiss agricultural policy and Article XI, but it was not until 1966 that the CONTRACTING PARTIES decided that full accession should occur, and even then Switzerland's accession was subject to certain reservations to permit it to continue to protect its agriculture.[46] The dangers are, of course, that provisional status may become permanent and that it may be used to circumvent the general GATT policy against reservations to the General Agreement.

## Nonapplication between Particular Contracting Parties

Occasionally some contracting parties do not wish to grant an acceding contracting party all of the benefits usually accorded contracting parties under the General Agreement. The motivation for this reluctance is usually economic: namely, the fear of low-wage competition, as in the case of the Japanese accession. But the motivation may be political, as in the case of the Portuguese accession.

Article XXXIII makes a two-thirds majority vote sufficient for the accession of a new contracting party, but each existing contracting party is given the privilege under Article XXXV of refusing to apply the General Agreement (or alternatively, refusing to apply only Article II thereof) to the acceding country. The acceding country, having been thereby deprived of rights against the re-

---

45. See, for extensions of de facto application, ibid., 10th Supp. (1962), p. 17; 14th Supp. (1966), p. 12. For the 1967 decision, see 15th Supp. (1967), p. 64.

46. See ibid., 5th Supp. (1957), p. 40; 7th Supp. (1959), pp. 18, 19; 14th Supp. (1966), pp. 6, 13.

fusing contracting party, is freed of any obligations toward that party. The General Agreement simply does not apply between the two countries. This arrangement tends to encourage accession while preserving the position of existing contracting parties vis-à-vis the newcomer. Its original purpose, however, appears primarily to have been to avoid difficulties that arise when accession occurs before accession negotiations have been undertaken with all contracting parties[47] and it was not contemplated that nonapplication would became a quasi-permanent relation. As a further measure to promote accession, an acceding party may elect to render the General Agreement inapplicable with respect to its relations with an existing contracting party. The election, whether made by an existing contracting party or an acceding party, must be made before the two countries have "entered into tariff negotiations with each other"[48]—that is, before the entrance-fee negotiations between them have begun.

The most extensive use that has been made of the election machinery was the invocation of Article XXXV against Japan in 1955 by fourteen countries representing about 40 percent of the foreign trade of GATT contracting parties.[49] This massive decision to discriminate was motivated largely by a fear of low-wage competition in manufactured goods, although fears of "unfair competition" and political factors no doubt also played a part.[50]

The Japanese case illustrates one of the major difficulties with the Article XXXV rule. The ease of invoking that Article was responsible for the success of the efforts to bring Japan into the GATT system and thereby to contribute not only to Japan's growth but also to that country's sense of international responsibility in trade matters. But if it was easy to invoke Article XXXV, it was also difficult to induce the withdrawal of such invocations as wages rose in Japan and the fear of "unfair competition" proved largely groundless. Relatively few contracting parties chose to withdraw their invocation of Article XXXV in the years immediately following Japanese accession. Meanwhile, a large number of new contracting parties that acceded via the sponsorship route simply continued the invocation that they had inherited. And one country, Portugal, invoked Article XXXV against Japan at the time of the former's accession under Article XXXIII. A total of forty-three different contracting parties invoked Article XXXV against Japan, either directly or by succession, although

47. *Analytical Index,* p. 159.
48. Art. XXXV:1(a). See also *Analytical Index,* p. 160.
49. *Analytical Index,* pp. 161–62.
50. See generally on the problems entailed in bringing Japan into the GATT, Gardner Patterson, *Discrimination in International Trade: The Policy Issues 1945–1965* (Princeton: Princeton University Press, 1966), pp. 271–88. See also Warren S. Hunsberger, *Japan and the United States in World Trade* (New York & Evanston: Harper & Row, 1964), pp. 231–39.

not that many invocations were in effect at any one time.[51] The numerous invocations of Article XXXV led to a number of difficult questions concerning Japan's right to participate in GATT affairs when, for example, a question involving the rights or duties of a contracting party that had invoked Article XXXV came before a GATT organ.[52]

In 1960 a working party was appointed to review the Japanese situation.[53] It found that the principal use of the invocations was to impose special discriminatory restrictions on imports from Japan rather than to deny Japan the benefits of the most-favored-nation clause on tariffs. It also found that some contracting parties that had not invoked Article XXXV also discriminated, but it pointed out that at least in those situations Japan had available the dispute-settlement remedies built into the General Agreement. The Article XXXV invocations might also have led Japan to maintain more import restrictions than it otherwise would have done. This consequence might have arisen not only from the limitation on Japan's export receipts deriving from the foreign restrictions but also from a reluctance to throw away a bargaining counter that might be useful in securing withdrawal of Article XXXV invocations.

A major problem arising from the numerous invocations of Article XXXV was that Japan was hampered in its participation in tariff negotiations. Although the working party was neither specific nor precise in its discussion of this point, it is worth noting that Japan could not effectively negotiate at tariff conferences with those countries that had invoked Article XXXV. Moreover, where Japan was the principal supplier of a product, the consequence of the "principal-supplier" rule might be that tariffs on that product would remain high against imports from other exporting countries. And according to the working party, since Japanese exports tended to be concentrated in the markets of countries that had not invoked Article XXXV, those countries would be hesitant to reduce tariffs on products exported by Japan.

The 1960 working party suggested that the need for Article XXXV would tend to disappear if "satisfactory multilateral solutions" could be found to the problem of "market disruption."[54] In retrospect that suggestion seems to underestimate the diversity of the protectionist influences driving governments to discriminate against Japan. As late as 1966 only fourteen contracting parties had withdrawn their Article XXXV invocation, while another twenty-nine had continued their invocation of that Article.[55] Most of the latter countries, how-

51. *Analytical Index,* pp. 161–62.
52. See Patterson, pp. 288–89.
53. *Basic Instruments,* 10th Supp. (1962), p. 69. The authority for the review was contained in Art. XXXV:2.
54. Ibid., p. 73.
55. *Analytical Index,* pp. 161–62.

ever, were smaller countries from Asia and Africa, and it may be that indifference was a major factor. Almost all the contracting parties that had continued their invocation of Article XXXV were ones that had succeeded to the invocation of a sponsoring contracting party; interestingly enough, they had continued their invocation even after their sponsoring contracting party had withdrawn *its* invocation. This anomalous situation suggests that an automatic withdrawal of Article XXXV invocations after a fixed period, coupled with the right to renew the invocations by special notice, might help reduce the number of invocations in effect without infringing on any country's sovereignty.

Japan's experience with Article XXXV may be an indication that some contracting parties do not find the General Agreement's safeguard arrangements, such as the "escape clause" of Article XIX and the compensatory adjustment system of Article XXVIII, to be wholly satisfactory for dealing with unanticipated increases in imports from a particular country. Or it may mean that some contracting parties do not find the Article XXII consultation procedures and the Article XXIII nullification or impairment procedures to be satisfactory means for dealing with governmental assistance to exports. But it seems more likely that the Japanese experience reflects a general insecurity on the part of developed contracting parties toward low-wage exporters of manufactures. The Japanese experience is closely connected with the history of the notion of "market disruption," which led to the Long-Term Arrangement in Cotton Textiles.[56] With the transition of other developing countries to the status of exporters of manufactures, the Japanese experiences may be seen as only the first in a series of related events that are going to place a special strain on the GATT system. A more optimistic view is that the Japanese experience is unique. The proponents of this view stress that the fear of Japanese exports engendered by Japanese trading practices in the pre–World War II period has no parallel in recent commercial history.

56. See discussion in chapter 17, "Market Disruption and Cotton Textiles," supra.

# 20 Dispute Settlement

The General Agreement is a legal document. Disputes frequently arise concerning the legal rights and obligations of various contracting parties. The GATT as an institution, consciously or by force of circumstance, has established customary ways of handling those disputes.

The fundamental decision was taken at the very beginning to refrain from the adjudicatory approach to dispute settlement. The General Agreement contains no provision for reference of either actual disputes or questions of interpretation to the International Court of Justice.[1] In this respect it differs from other founding documents of international organizations, such as the United Nations Charter, which provides that "the General Assembly or the Security Council may request the International Court of Justice to give an advisory opinion on any legal question."[2]

Nor is there any provision in the General Agreement for the establishment of an internal tribunal to resolve actual disputes or to promulgate authoritative interpretations on questions of interpretation. To some extent the CONTRACTING PARTIES, acting jointly under Article XXV:1 or under more specific provisions of the General Agreement, exercise the functions of a tribunal. And, as will be further described, the CONTRACTING PARTIES have delegated to subsidiary bodies, such as working groups and panels of experts, the task of exercising those functions, at least as a preliminary matter. But the final decision in those instances is taken by the entire membership and is therefore a con-

---

1. Individual contracting parties may, of course, refer disputes to the International Court of Justice if the requisites of International Court jurisdiction are otherwise present. Nothing in the General Agreement prohibits such reference. But the General Agreement is not a source of such jurisdiction. Nor can International Court of Justice proceedings be considered an appeal from any GATT decision. See the interpretation of the chairman of the CONTRACTING PARTIES, *Analytical Index*, p. 133.

2. Art. 96, para. 1.

sciously political rather than a judicial decision. Indeed, as we shall see the provisions of the General Agreement authorizing the CONTRACTING PARTIES to pass on disputes are so drafted as to make clear that decisions are not to be taken on narrow legalistic grounds.

The system of sanctions built into the General Agreement conditions not only the manner of resolving disputes but also attitudes toward violations by a contracting party of the General Agreement. "Illegality" is an uncertain and ambiguous concept when applied to the General Agreement. Although the substantive provisions of the General Agreement are drafted in conventional terms, including a rather liberal use of prohibitory language, the remedy provisions are not drawn in terms of sanctions. Rather, the organizing principle is that the General Agreement, and the GATT as a whole, is a system of reciprocal rights and obligations to be maintained in balance. This is particularly the case with respect to tariff concessions, where "reciprocity" is viewed as essential not only to the conclusion of tariff agreements but also to adjustments and withdrawals of bindings. A failure to respect a tariff concession is usually regarded not as a transgression to be punished but rather as an event giving affected parties the privilege, subject to the approval of the CONTRACTING PARTIES, of suspending reciprocal concessions.

To a certain extent this philosophy carries over, both in the language of the General Agreement and even more strikingly in practice, to GATT obligations other than tariff concessions. If a contracting party fails to live up to substantive obligations or violates a substantive prohibition, the most that the CONTRACTING PARTIES can do is to authorize affected contracting parties, pursuant to Article XXIII, to suspend the application to the offending contracting party "of such concessions or other obligations . . . as they determine to be appropriate in the circumstances." Thus, even in cases of flagrant violations the General Agreement appears to contemplate the role of the CONTRACTING PARTIES as tribunal to be the maintenance of a balance of concessions and other obligations among the contracting parties.[3] The limited role accorded sanctions in promoting respect for the substantive rules of the General Agreement contrasts strikingly with the use of sanctions by domestic courts to enforce compliance with the substantive prohibitions of domestic law and with the power of the United Nations Security Council to impose sanctions upon members of the United Nations in the event of failure to abide by the principles of the Charter concerning the use of force.[4]

---

3. Although Article XXIII does not require the concessions suspended to be of equal value to the concessions nullified or impaired, there is evidence that such a test is considered appropriate in GATT circles. See the reference to "equivalent obligations or concessions" in *Basic Instruments,* 11th Supp. (1963), p. 95.
4. United Nations Charter, Arts. 2, 39–51.

## The Range of Dispute Settlement Procedures

In view of the uncertain and ambiguous nature of the concept of "illegality" in the General Agreement, it would be a mistake to limit a consideration of the GATT's dispute-settlement mechanisms to the procedures provided for in the central remedy provision, Article XXIII:2. Although that article establishes procedures of last resort in the event of "nullification or impairment" of GATT obligations, related retaliation provisions are to be found in Articles XII:4(c) and XVIII:12(c). There are, moreover, a wide variety of other procedures established by the General Agreement for the resolution of disputes before the Article XXIII stage is reached. Most notable are the consultation provisions of Article XXII, which may be invoked by any contracting party "with respect to any matter affecting the operation of the [General] Agreement," and the preretaliation consultation procedures of Article XXIII:1. And there is a series of more particularized consultation arrangements. Some have already been discussed in connection with technical tariff negotiations; these include the consultations called for by the provisions on escape-clause action under Article XIX and on modification of schedules under Article XXVIII.[5] In the much publicized "Chicken War" between the United States and the European Economic Community, the United States withdrew concessions in retaliation after submitting the issue of the "trade coverage" of the EEC withdrawal to a special GATT panel.[6] Other procedures are more particularized, including the consultations envisaged by Article XXXVII:2 in the event of any failure of developed contracting parties to carry out certain special commitments toward less-developed countries contained in Part IV and the subsidy consultations provided for in Article XVI.

It would be too narrow a view to limit one's attention to those procedures concerning specific allegations of violations of the General Agreement. Restrictions imposed by one contracting party on its imports injure the export prospects of other contracting parties, whether or not those restrictions are lawful under the General Agreement. Thus all GATT consultation procedures must be examined in any realistic assessment of the GATT's contribution to the resolution of international disputes. For example, one should consider the annual balance-of-payments reviews of the quantitative restrictions imposed by individual contracting parties. Although the question of the formal compatibility of existing quantitative restrictions with the balance-of-payments provisions of the General Agreement is a relevant question in those annual reviews, the reviews are directed more toward a general examination of the trade and

---

5. See discussion in chapter 6, "Technical Tariff Negotiations," supra.
6. See U.S. Tariff Commission, *Operation of the Trade Agreements Program,* 16th Rep. (1966), pp. 46–47; *Basic Instruments,* 12th Supp. (1964), p. 65; GATT Document L/2088 (21 Nov. 1963).

payments policies of the contracting party in question and of the rate of trade liberalization it has achieved. In that sense the balance-of-payments reviews are more prophylactic than punitive. Aside from their primary function of affirmatively promoting trade liberalization, they serve to avoid disputes by identifying and exposing to collective examination those quantitative restrictions that might otherwise lead to serious disputes.

These annual balance-of-payments reviews can be a useful instrument for achieving a greater understanding of the underlying structural and economic problems that lead to the imposition of trade restrictions, and they can thereby promote a considerably improved climate for discussion of trade differences. A concrete example arose out of the continuation by certain European governments of discriminatory restrictions on U.S. goods even after those European governments had reached the stage of full convertibility. The United States was able to make substantial progress toward the elimination of that discriminatory treatment, without the necessity of poisoning the diplomatic atmosphere through charges of illegality, simply by focusing attention in the annual reviews on the absence of a balance-of-payments justification for restrictions that may previously have been justified.

In addition to conducting the annual balance-of-payments reviews, the GATT sometimes serves as the framework for broad-ranging discussions of international trade problems relating to a specific economic sector. An example is the series of consultations held in 1960 on butter marketing in the United Kingdom. There the interests of a number of countries conflicted, and the consultations helped to focus attention on the multilateral aspects of what could have been considered merely a bilateral affair.[7]

The waiver procedures of Article XXV:5 also constitute an important aspect of the dispute-settlement mechanisms of the GATT. It became clear rather early that full compliance with all provisions of the General Agreement by all contracting parties was not politically possible. In some specific cases domestic protectionist sentiment and pressures were simply too great to permit local governments to comply. In other cases the violation of the General Agreement was more technical than substantial. And in still other cases it was generally agreed by the various contracting parties that compliance with the General Agreement in the situation at hand was not particularly desirable; that situation might be one where the GATT rules were out of harmony with economic principles or where certain overriding considerations of political or social policy led the contracting parties as a group to subordinate economic efficiency to other goals.

Waivers help to avoid disputes because so long as a particular restriction remains nominally illegal, a contracting party whose exports are affected has

7. *Basic Instruments,* 10th Supp. (1962), pp. 74, 77.

the option of complaining, and indeed may even feel compelled by domestic pressures from the affected export industry to precipitate a trade dispute. To be sure, some waivers include provisions preserving the right of affected contracting parties to resort to Article XXIII,[8] but resort to retaliation under those circumstances is rare. A waiver settles the rights of complaining parties de facto, if not de jure. The waiver procedures warrant an oblique analogy to declaratory judgment actions under domestic law insofar as they provide a vehicle for clarifying legal relationships and thereby eliminate an irregular situation that might give rise to future disputes. The waiver procedures differ from declaratory judgment actions, of course, in the sense that a waiver—like special legislation—changes the rules of the game in favor of the party receiving the waiver. In a system where the most important value may be to preclude the type of retaliation which leads to trade wars, waivers must certainly be regarded as dispute-avoidance mechanisms.

Aside from their role in the avoidance of disputes, the waiver procedures also help to settle existing disputes. A contracting party seeking a waiver knows that a measure it has instituted or proposes to institute violates the General Agreement. It may already have received protests from other contracting parties. The ensuing discussions of the benefits and costs of the measure to the world trading community as a whole provide a more favorable atmosphere for accommodations of differences than would discussions carried on in terms of legality and illegality. Although it is true that applications for waivers are almost always granted, it is also true that important conditions are sometimes placed on the terms of waivers. These conditions, often buried in a whereas clause or in a statement in a working party report, constitute the core of a number of important settlements of trade differences.[9]

As the foregoing review of GATT procedures suggests, it would be possible to distinguish three kinds of activities that have here been thrown together under the general heading of dispute settlement. Those three would be (1) treaty enforcement; (2) dispute avoidance; and (3) dispute settlement, narrowly defined. This author's taxonomic propensities are not sufficiently strong for him to undertake to classify GATT activities under those three heads, but it is worth noting that treaty enforcement is not regarded in GATT circles as an important function. Neither the CONTRACTING PARTIES as a group nor the secretariat views its task as the enforcement of the General Agreement in the sense that prosecuting agencies enforce the criminal law. This circumstance is both an illustration and a result of, on the one hand, the strongly pragmatic, antilegalistic style of the secretariat and, on the other hand, the underlying

8. See e.g., ibid., 3d Supp. (1955), p. 32, 35.
9. See, e.g., the discussion of the United Kingdom waiver in chapter 4, "The GATT Tariff System," supra.

principle that the GATT is essentially designed to preserve a balance of concessions and obligations. Dispute avoidance is, as has been seen, an important function of many of the procedures outlined. Dispute settlement, narrowly defined, is also an important objective.

In early years the notion of the CONTRACTING PARTIES functioning as an objective, independent body for the settlement of disputes between particular countries had some currency in GATT circles. In a speech in 1956 Wyndham White outlined the GATT system for "settlement of disputes."[10] In recent years, however, the tendency has been to use the term "conciliation" to describe the same GATT activities.[11] It is unlikely that mere chance is involved in this change of terms. Rather, as part of the increasingly pragmatic policies of the secretariat and the recognition by all contracting parties that legalism does not contribute to trade liberalization, emphasis has shifted from the formal role of the GATT as third-party arbiter to its informal role as catalyst for the resolution of disputes by the disputing parties themselves. This verbal difference may mask a growing recognition that once a dispute erupts, governments are not prepared to view the substantive provisions of the General Agreement as setting forth the applicable principles of decision. Beyond this, governments may believe that disputes should be settled by compromising differences rather than by the winner-take-all approach that characterizes formal adjudication by tribunals. If that is so, then the GATT's only function can be to provide the framework for conciliation of differences. But, as will be seen later, conciliation has certain disadvantages that warrant consideration.

## Rights and Remedies

Despite the many aspects of the General Agreement that are relevant to a balanced view of the GATT dispute-settlement mechanisms, Article XXIII remains the key provision. Not only does it furnish the remedy of last resort in any dispute, but also its field of application in turn delimits and defines the true scope of all of the substantive provisions of the General Agreement. Its provisions on "nullification or impairment" therefore warrant intensive analysis.[12]

Lawyers are fond of saying, when discussing domestic law, that there is no right without a remedy. In GATT affairs this observation has a particular bite. To begin with, Article XXIII gives the affected contracting party a sole remedy—

10. Address by Mr. Eric Wyndham White at the Graduate Institute of International Studies, Geneva, December 1956 (mimeographed document), p. 15.
11. See, e.g., *Basic Instruments,* 14th Supp. (1966), p. 18.
12. See generally Walter Hollis, "Dispute Settlement under the General Agreement on Tariffs and Trade," in *International Trade Arbitration,* ed. Martin Domke (New York: American Arbitration Association, 1958), pp. 77–84.

the withdrawal of "such concessions or other obligations as [the CONTRACTING PARTIES] determine to be appropriate in the circumstances." This remedy then reintroduces the paradoxical consequences of the reciprocity principle of tariff negotiations: the retaliatory withdrawal of a tariff concession, for example, is a measure that imposes a substantial detriment on the "guilty" contracting party, which thereupon finds its export prospects restricted, but such a withdrawal does not accord the injured contracting party a comparable benefit. Although an industry in the injured country may receive additional protection as a result of retaliation, the consumers of that country have to pay more for the item on which the retaliation occurs. If that item is a raw material, semifinished product, or capital good, the exporting position of the injured contracting party is further compromised. And the protection afforded the domestic industry is fortuitous, because the tariff category on which retaliation occurs is unlikely to be related to any need of that industry for protection.

Moreover, where the retaliating contracting party seeks to avoid introducing an element of discrimination into its tariff schedule, it is even more likely that an industry not specially deserving protection will nevertheless fortuitously receive such protection, while the industry injured by the violation of the General Agreement is not benefited at all. When, for example, a German concession on poultry was withdrawn as part of an increase in duties involved in the creation of the Common Agricultural Policy by the European Economic Community, the United States retaliated by increasing duties on a number of products, principally brandy valued over $9 per gallon and automobile trucks valued at $1,000 or more.[13] The obvious basis for these choices was that those products (1) had, together with the other products, a "trade coverage" approximately equal to the $26,000,000 that had been agreed upon as the volume of U.S. poultry exports to the EEC; (2) were of importance to the EEC countries (affecting principally French brandy and German Volkswagens, respectively); and (3) were not products of major export interest to non-EEC countries. The United States was quite explicit about the rationale of its selection:

> In selecting the articles on which to increase duties, the United States chose commodities of interest chiefly to the EEC countries; nevertheless, such articles were also affected when imported into the United States from third countries entitled to trade-agreement rates of duty. U.S. imports of the articles from the European Economic Community in 1962 were valued at about $24 million, and those from all other countries, at about $1 million.[14]

13. Other products subjected to retaliation were potato starch, dextrine, and soluble or chemical treated starches. U.S. Tariff Commission, *Operation* . . . , 16th Rep. (1966), p. 47.
14. Ibid.

U.S. poultry producers were not benefited in the slightest, nor were U.S. consumers. At the same time, U.S. producers of, for example, panel trucks enjoyed unmerited and doubtless unexpected insulation from foreign competition.

The principle of no right without a remedy has, however, a peculiar twist in the GATT. In an important sense Article XXIII gives a remedy without a right. In order to understand how this occurs, it is important to note that Article XXIII grants three different kinds of jurisdiction. In all three cases a prerequisite to GATT action is a complaint by a contracting party that "any benefit accruing to it directly or indirectly under this Agreement is being nullified or impaired or that the attainment of any objective of the Agreement is being impeded." But only paragraph 1(a), the first of the three bases of jurisdiction, assumes a violation of the General Agreement; it refers to complaints concerning "the failure of another contracting party to carry out its obligations under this Agreement." Paragraph 1(b), on the other hand, covers complaints concerning "the application by another contracting party of any measure, whether or not it conflicts with the provisions of this Agreement." And paragraph 1(c), even more wide-ranging, simply refers to complaints concerning "the existence of any other situation."

Under Article XXIII "any measure" or "any other situation" thus has a status comparable to the "failure of another contracting party to carry out its obligations under this Agreement." What is crucial, under the language of Article XXIII, is not whether the action alleged to give rise to the right to retaliate is a violation of the Agreement, but rather whether: first, as a result of such action, a "benefit accruing" under the Agreement is being "nullified or impaired" or the "attainment of any objective of the Agreement is being impeded" (these two criteria being thrown together, in accordance with the title of Article XXIII, under the heading of "nullification or impairment"); second, the CONTRACTING PARTIES "consider that the circumstances are serious enough to justify" the retaliation; and third, the CONTRACTING PARTIES determine that the proposed retaliatory measure is "appropriate in the circumstances." By placing infringing and noninfringing activity on a par, the language of Article XXIII underscores the fundamental notion that the function of the GATT is to maintain a balance of advantages among individual contracting parties.

In 1950 the CONTRACTING PARTIES adopted a working party report that dealt with an Australian subsidy arrangement and that relied upon the "any measure" authority. Australia had maintained subsidies on both imported sodium nitrate and domestic ammonium sulphate, which were competitive products. It then granted Chile a duty-free binding on sodium nitrate. Thereafter, Australia discontinued the subsidy on the imported sodium nitrate while maintaining the one on domestically produced ammonium sulphate. The working party was forced to conclude that no violation of the General Agreement had been committed by Australia.[15] It concluded, however, that under the particular circumstances of the case the removal of the import subsidy impaired a benefit—the tariff binding—accruing to Chile under the General Agreement. The members of the working party agreed that the test for impairment was whether the "action of the Australian Government which resulted in upsetting the competitive relationship between sodium nitrate and ammonium sulphate *could not reasonably have been anticipated* by the Chilean Government, taking into consideration all pertinent circumstances and the provisions of the General Agreement, at the time it negotiated for the duty-free binding on sodium nitrate," and they therefore concluded that impairment had occurred.[16] The working party thereby apparently imported a reasonable expectations test into Article XXIII for disputes in which an actual infringement of the General Agreement is not involved.[17]

The problem of the circumstances justifying retaliation against activity that is lawful under the General Agreement was presented in somewhat more extreme form in connection with a 1960 study of restrictive business practices. Certain appointed experts considered the question whether restrictive business practices of nationals of one contracting party might permit retaliation by another contracting party. The question was particularly difficult because, in addition to the circumstance that restrictive business practices were not prohibited by the General Agreement, the experts had to face the subsidiary issue whether acts of private parties can ever justify retaliation. The experts divided on the overall question, the majority pleading their incompetence with respect to such an issue of legal interpretation and the minority concluding that Article XXIII could be applied by the CONTRACTING PARTIES.[18] In their decision following consideration of the group-of-experts, the CONTRACTING PARTIES skirted the entire issue by recommending a system of consultation for disputes involving restrictive business practices.[19] The group of experts rather clearly had no authority to issue a binding pronouncement on the issue, but the discussions served to illustrate how far the departure from the concept of illegality could eventually carry the GATT.

The breadth of jurisdiction conferred by the "any measure" language by

15. *Basic Instruments,* Vol. II (1952), pp. 188, 192, 194.
16. Ibid., p. 193 (emphasis supplied).
17. The case was somewhat unusual because Chile, although relying on Article XXIII, did not seek to retaliate. Rather, it sought an adjustment of the Australian subsidy arrangements to remove any impartiality of treatment. Such an adjustment was recommended for "the sole reason . . . that, in this particular case, it happens that such action appears to afford the best prospect of an adjustment of the matter satisfactory to both parties" (ibid., p. 195).
18. Ibid., 9th Supp. (1961), pp. 170, 172, 177.
19. Ibid., p. 28.

paragraph 1(b)—and for that matter by the "any other situation" language of paragraph 1(c)—creates, for the panels that pass on Article XXIII complaints, problems of a jurisprudential order, even though the diplomats and trade experts who struggle with those complaints may not recognize their dilemma as jurisprudential in character.

Although laymen engaged in dispute settlement sometimes like to think that they decide cases without reference to "law" (or, as the quaint phrase sometimes runs, "on the merits"), such decisions are, in the nature of things, impossible. Even the resolution of disputes by compromise—by splitting the difference between the two opposed views—is the application of a rule for decision. To rely on paragraph 1(b) jurisdiction is to attempt to resolve disputes without reference to specific substantive rules. If substantive rules are to be avoided, then one must turn, for a standard of decision, to the generalities of the preamble of the General Agreement—which reduce essentially to the twin goals of maintaining a balance of advantages and promoting world trade.

Such standards are unsatisfactory bases for decision. To rest a decision solely upon the preservation of a balance of advantages is in most cases to rely on the most elusive of criteria; as we shall see, the panels have shrunk from such a difficult exercise. And although use of the promotion of world trade as a criterion (which would mean applying Article XXIII whenever an importing country's trade restriction inhibited international trade) would provide a concrete rule for decision, it would be a highly unsatisfactory rule. Such a rule would undermine the notion that the General Agreement constitutes a code for world trade, distinguishing those trade restrictions that are permissible from those that are not. All nonfrivolous cases would have to be decided in favor of the complaining party. The panels, faced with these dilemmas, have intuitively drawn back from the bases of jurisdiction contained in paragraphs 1(b) and 1(c), in favor of an approach that would make the legality of the trade measure under the substantive provisions of the General Agreement the crucial factor in determinations of nullification or impairment.

The entire question assumed great importance in a broad-scale attack launched by Uruguay in the early 1960s against the policies of developed countries toward less-developed-country exports. A panel, appointed to pass upon the Uruguayan complaint, reviewed each of the national policies attacked by Uruguay to determine whether they conformed with the General Agreement. Where the policies were lawful but were calculated to reduce Uruguayan exports, the panel suggested that the parties should resort to Article XXII consultations. The following formulation was used:

> In this connexion the Panel recalled the provisions of Article XXII pursuant to which the Government of [the importing country] would no doubt accord sympathetic consideration to any concrete representations

which Uruguay might wish to make concerning these measures, or their administration, with a view to minimizing any such adverse effects.[20]

The result was not, however, to relegate all allegations of nullification or impairment not involving a violation to Article XXII consultations. Rather, the panel chose to manipulate the burden of proof requirements. In certain specific instances the following formulation was adopted in order to make Article XXIII applicable even though there was no showing of a violation:

> As regards [certain specified measures], the Panel considers that, insofar as it has not been established that these measures are being applied consistently with the provisions of the General Agreement or are permitted by the terms of the Protocol under which [the importing country] applies the GATT, it has to proceed on the assumption that their maintenance can nullify or impair the benefits accruing to Uruguay under the Agreement.[21]

But the panel did not consistently shift the burden of proof on legality to the accused contracting party. With respect to certain kinds of measures, and particularly variable taxes and charges, it chose simply not to pass upon the issue, thereby effectively deciding against Uruguay.[22]

The panel rejected Uruguay's basic contention that, in view of the language of Article XXIII, what was important was not whether a particular measure violated the General Agreement, but rather whether that measure "had the effect of restricting the access to the [importing country's] market for a number of Uruguayan products which together constituted a considerable proportion of Uruguay's total exports,"[23] The panel did not believe that any measure having the consequence of substantially restricting the exports of a contracting party necessarily resulted in nullification or impairment under Article XXXIII:

> In [the panel's] view impairment and nullification in the sense of Article XXIII does not arise merely because of the existence of any measures; the nullification or impairment must relate to benefits accruing to the contracting party "under the General Agreement."
>
> * * * While it is not precluded that a *prima facie* case of nullification or impairment could arise even if there is no infringement of GATT provisions, it would be in such cases incumbent on the country invoking Article XXIII to demonstrate the grounds and reasons for its invocation.

20. E.g., ibid., 11th Supp. (1963), p. 95, 105.
21. E.g., ibid., p. 108.
22. E.g., ibid., pp. 104–5. The panel gave, as excuses for these dispositions in favor of importing countries, the difficulty of the issues and the fact that "at the nineteenth session of the CONTRACTING PARTIES . . . it was pointed out that such measures raised serious questions which had not been resolved" (ibid., p. 100).
23. E.g., ibid., p. 105.

Detailed submissions on the part of that contracting party on these points were therefore essential for a judgment to be made under this Article.[24]

The weakness of the Uruguayan case was thus a failure to specify what affirmative benefits under the General Agreement had been denied Uruguay. It will be noted that the approach of the panel came close to emasculating the "any measure" authority of paragraph 1(b). It might be argued, for example, that no measure can deny a conferred benefit without constituting a violation of the General Agreement—in which case the authority of paragraph 1(b) is irrelevant. There appears to be one area in which a measure not violating the General Agreement may nevertheless lead to nullification or impairment. That is the situation presented in the previously discussed Chile-Australian dispute.[25] If a tariff concession has been granted, that concession may be the kind of benefit accruing under the General Agreement that the panel had in mind. A restrictive measure may render the concession meaningless in trade terms and thereby, at least if the reasonable expectations test of the Australia-Chile case is applied, constitute nullification or impairment.

The hesitancy of the panel in the Uruguayan case to give any scope to the "any measure" jurisdiction of Article XXIII:1(b) contrasted strangely with the report of another panel, adopted by the CONTRACTING PARTIES on the same day that they adopted the report of the Uruguayan panel. This report concerned a dispute between Canada and the United States over Canadian valuation of potato imports. The Canadian system was designed to discourage imports from the United States at that time each year when, the U.S. harvest having preceded the Canadian harvest by a few weeks owing to climatic factors, the U.S. domestic price was at its lowest levels and the Canadian domestic price was relatively high. The Canadian valuation system consisted of taking a three-year average of actual prices on imports into Canada from the United States rather than taking the price at the time of the immediate transaction. The effect was, of course, a substantially higher valuation base at that time of year than the actual value rule of Article VII would have provided.[26]

The panel appointed to consider the U.S.-Canadian dispute determined that "the concept of value for duty as applied presently on import of potatoes . . . was different from the concept of value for customs purposes, which the CONTRACTING PARTIES had in mind in drafting the provisions of Article VII."[27]

24. Ibid., pp. 99–100. This position was reiterated in a later report of the panel, also adopted by the CONTRACTING PARTIES (ibid., 13th Supp. [1965], p. 45, 47).
25. See discussion in text, supra, at notes 15–17.
26. See discussion of Article VII in chapter 11, "Administration Barriers to Trade," supra.
27. *Basic Instruments,* 11th Supp. (1963), p. 88, 93.

The panel did not, however, find that Canada had violated the General Agreement, although such a conclusion was seemingly implicit from the foregoing determination. Rather, the panel stated that it "did not consider that the provisions of Article VII were relevant in the context of its examination."[28]

The panel was able to sidestep the difficult question whether nullification or impairment under the "any measure" jurisdiction of Article XXIII existed, by treating the higher duty that resulted from the increased valuation as a violation of the tariff-binding provisions of Article II:1(a). Although the panel was perhaps to be commended for cutting through the form of the Canadian device to its substance (that is, a higher effective rate of protection), it should be noted that Article II:1(a) merely provides that "each contracting party shall accord to the commerce of the other contracting parties treatment no less favourable than that provided for in the [tariff concession]." Less favorable "treatment," viewed in pragmatic terms, can, of course, result from any type of trade restriction imposed on a bound item and not just from a restriction that can be converted into money terms. Article II:1(a) could thus provide a basis, when coupled with the reasonable expectations test of the Australian-Chile case, for finding a nullification or impairment in cases of restrictions imposed on bound items. Once an item was bound, any additional restriction would represent a violation of Article II:1(a) and would thereby provide the basis for a finding of nullification or impairment under paragraph 1(a) of Article XXIII.

Both the Uruguayan and the U.S.-Canadian panel reports reveal a great hesitancy to find nullification or impairment in the absence of activity by the importing state that could be characterized as a violation of the General Agreement. Although this hesitancy is difficult to reconcile with the express terms of Article XXIII, it probably represents a sound approach to dispute settlement. It surely reveals a conservative and traditional instinct towards dispute settlement on the part of the panel members. Despite the tendency to view the panels' function as one of conciliation rather than arbitration, the panel members intuitively seek the certainty that comes from explicit legal rules.

Contracting parties have filed a substantial number of Article XXIII complaints. Although published sources do not reveal the total number of complaints registered, the number of disputes resolved by the GATT compares favorably with the record of other postwar international institutions. Some eighteen different disputes have reached the stage of panel or working-party reports that have been included in the *Basic Instruments and Documents* of the

---

28. Ibid. It is not clear why the panel did not consider the relevance of Article II:3, which prohibits changes in valuation methods impairing the value of concessions. The duty had been bound in 1957, and the new valuation was introduced in 1962 (ibid., pp. 88–89).

GATT.[29] These eighteen undoubtedly represent a minor proportion of the disputes that have been discussed formally or informally in one GATT forum or another.

It is a striking fact that in only a single case has the dispute proceeded to the stage where the CONTRACTING PARTIES have specifically authorized the withdrawal of concessions or obligations under Article XXIII:2.[30] The CONTRACTING PARTIES have manifested a great reluctance to authorize the act—retaliation—that constitutes the heart of the GATT enforcement system. In several cases they have found nullification or impairment but have avoided authorizing retaliation.[31] Two considerations appear to have been particularly significant in dictating this sparing recourse to the principal form of coercion available to the GATT. First, the desire to act as conciliators rather than as arbitrators has led the CONTRACTING PARTIES to seek to delay as long as possible the imposition of the GATT's ultimate sanction. And second, within the context of a concrete dispute it often becomes painfully obvious that no one gains by retaliation; as previously argued, the retaliating party loses just as much as the party retaliated against.

Article XXIII is drafted with a bias toward delay by the CONTRACTING PARTIES in authorizing retaliation—and in some respects even with a bias toward outright refusal to grant such authorization. That article lays down both procedural prerequisites and substantive conditions for the authorization of retaliation. The CONTRACTING PARTIES have made use of both categories of limitations to further the conciliatory aspect of their role in dispute settlement.

## Procedural Limitations on Retaliation

A contracting party wishing to proceed under Article XXIII must, under the

---

29. The figure of eighteen is based on the list of sixteen in the 1966 *Analytical Index,* p. 123, plus two cases in *Basic Instruments,* 15th Supp. (1968), pp. 113–16. Not all these eighteen disputes, however, involved formal recourse to Article XXIII.

30. That case involved the imposition of quantitative restrictions by the Netherlands upon imports of wheat from the United States in retaliation against certain U.S. restrictions on dairy products. See *Basic Instruments,* 1st Supp. (1953), p. 32. This authorization to the Netherlands was subsequently renewed from year to year. In another case the CONTRACTING PARTIES played a role in retaliation by the United States against the EEC, under Article XXVIII, which does not require authorization by the CONTRACTING PARTIES of retaliation, as does Article XXIII. The retaliation occurred in the so-called Chicken War. See ibid., 12th Supp. (1964), p. 65. There is no way of knowing how many contracting parties may have had recourse to self-help in withdrawing concessions or obligations outside the framework of Article XXIII procedures.

31. These include the Australian fertilizer case, ibid., Vol. II, p. 188; the French compensatory tax case, ibid., 3d Supp. (1955), p. 26; and the French import restrictions case, ibid., 11th Supp. (1963), pp. 55, 94. See also the Canadian potato case, ibid., pp. 55, 88.

terms of paragraph 1, first "make written representations or proposals to the other contracting party or parties which it considers to be concerned." Thereupon, "any contracting party thus approached shall give sympathetic consideration to the representatives or proposals made to it." Only after this process is completed and only "if no satisfactory adjustment is effected between the contracting parties concerned within a reasonable time" may the dispute be referred to the CONTRACTING PARTIES.[32] The practice appears to have developed of consulting with the GATT secretariat during this preliminary period. The secretariat has on occasion been able to resolve disputes at this early stage.

Once the reference to the CONTRACTING PARTIES is made, the usual practice is to refer the dispute to a panel on complaints. In the early days of the GATT, the reference was to a working party. A working party differs from a panel insofar as the former is composed of representatives of individual contracting parties whereas the latter is composed of individuals chosen in their personal capacities and for their personal qualities. The men who sit on panels are, of course, representatives of contracting parties, but the difference is not merely one of form. Since they are acting in their own right and are not merely carrying out a function assigned to their delegations, panel members appear to consider themselves freer to exercise the functions of dispassionate mediators than they would be if they sat as representatives of their governments. Such, at any rate, is the theory behind the change from working parties to panels.

The chairman of the panel, who is selected by the chairman of the CONTRACTING PARTIES, is normally a senior official who has long experience in GATT affairs and who is a representative of a country that is of secondary importance in world trade and that is not a party to the dispute. The effort is to find a man with great prestige within the GATT "club" who will be able to act as a neutral party. The goal appears to be to enhance the conciliatory role of the panel and to deemphasize the legal and technical aspects of the dispute.

Although the panel is likely to meet in intersessional periods, a good deal of time may elapse between the date of the formal reference of the dispute to the CONTRACTING PARTIES and the conclusion of the panel proceedings. During this period the panel meets one or more times with the disputing parties, and a panel report is drafted. If the dispute raises balance-of-payments problems, the advice of the International Monetary Fund must be sought—a process that can consume some months. The effect of the delay is sometimes to reduce the emotional content of the dispute and thereby to promote a compromise between the parties.

The report of the panel, whenever it may be issued, must await the next

---

32. Art. XXIII:2. If the "any other situation" jurisdiction of Article XXIII:1(c) is invoked, the reference to the CONTRACTING PARTIES need not be deferred for the specified "reasonable time."

session of the CONTRACTING PARTIES to be adopted. And the panel report, if it adheres to current practice, contains only draft recommendations to be formally issued under the aegis of the CONTRACTING PARTIES. These recommendations normally call on the disputing contracting parties to settle their dispute by some means short of retaliation. One form of recommendation calls, in polite language, on the offending contracting party to eliminate the practice in question.[33] Indeed, the requirement, to be discussed below, that retaliation may be authorized only when the circumstances are "serious enough to justify such action" has been construed to limit such authorization to situations where the CONTRACTING PARTIES have sought to resolve the dispute by other means, such as "withdrawal of the measures causing the damage [or] the substitution of other concessions."[34] It is only after the recommendations have failed to lead to a resolution of the dispute that the CONTRACTING PARTIES have authorized retaliation.

Although the Council may, under the terms of the decision creating it,[35] have the authority to authorize retaliation, the final authorization is almost certain to be put over to a session of the CONTRACTING PARTIES. The minimum time that must elapse between the recommendations and the authorization of retaliation is thus at least six months (the shortest period between sessions of the CONTRACTING PARTIES). In the case of the sole example of authorized retaliation, the Netherlands' retaliation against the United States, the U.S. restrictions were introduced on 9 August 1951, and, despite the fact that the panel device was not used, the final authorization to retaliate was not issued until 8 November 1952.[36] In some cases retaliation has been deferred for an impressive period. The Brazilian internal tax dispute, which first came before the CONTRACTING PARTIES in 1949, was finally settled with the abolition by Brazil of the disputed practice in 1958, all without any retaliation being authorized.[37] The eventual success of the GATT in eliminating the unlawful measure in such cases rests, of course, upon the patience of the affected contracting parties and upon the general awareness that retaliation will help no one. Thus, the "all deliberate speed" of the GATT procedures contributes to the avoidance of retaliatory action.

33. See, e.g., *Basic Instruments,* 7th Supp. (1959), p. 22. Article XXIII also envisages the possibility of a GATT "ruling" and of consultations with "the Economic and Social Council of the United Nations and with any other appropriate intergovernmental organization."
34. *Basic Instruments,* 3d Supp. (1955), p. 231, 250.
35. The Council is empowered "to deal with such other matters with which the CONTRACTING PARTIES may deal at their sessions" (ibid., 9th Supp. [1961], p. 8).
36. See ibid., 1st Supp. (1953), pp. 31, 32; U.S. Tariff Commission, *Operation . . . ,* 6th Rep. (1954), pp. 43–45.
37. See *Basic Instruments,* Vol. II (1952), p. 181; 7th Supp. (1959), p. 68.

## Substantive Limitations on Retaliation

The substantive standards also promote resolution of disputes by means other than retaliation. The preliminary jurisdictional requirements of paragraph 1 have already been discussed. Beyond these, paragraph 2 sets out additional standards specifying the conditions under which retaliation may be authorized. It may be authorized only where "the circumstances are serious enough to justify such action." Moreover, the type and extent of retaliation must be "appropriate in the circumstances."

The meaning of these standards was considered by the Review Session Working Party upon the occasion of a joint proposal by Denmark, Norway, and Sweden to add an interpretative note to the effect that action under Article XXIII "should be directed towards the maintenance of a general level of reciprocal and mutually advantageous concessions not less favourable to trade than that provided for in the original situation" and that "it was, therefore, desirable that resort should be had to retaliatory action only when all other possibilities had been explored."[38] The Review Session Working Party concluded that "the principle set out in the proposed interpretative note conformed with both the intention of the Article and the practice the CONTRACTING PARTIES had hitherto followed in applying its provisions."[39] The Scandinavian countries thereupon withdrew their proposal.

Although this restrictive interpretation might seem to be a gloss on the Agreement language, the Review Session Working Party argued that the interpretation was to be drawn from the "serious enough" requirement that limits retaliation

> to cases where endeavours to solve the problem through the withdrawal of the measures causing the damage, the substitution of other concessions, or some other appropriate action have not proved to be possible, and where there is considered to be a substantial justification for retaliatory action, as in cases in which such authorization appears to be the only means either of preventing serious economic consequences to the country for which a benefit has been nullified or impaired, or the only means of restoring the original situation.[40]

The report went on to reject the notion said to be implicit in the Scandinavian proposal that a compensatory reduction by the offending contracting party of some other trade restriction was as satisfactory as elimination of the illegal measure. Compensatory adjustments, which play a major role in other provi-

38. Ibid., 3d Supp. (1955), p. 231, 250. It should be noted not only that this report of the Review Session Working Party was officially adopted by the CONTRACTING PARTIES, but also that the Review Session Working Party's views have been especially important in GATT affairs.
39. Ibid.
40. Ibid., pp. 250–51.

sions of the General Agreement, such as Articles XIX and XXVII, "should be resorted to only if the immediate withdrawal of the measures was impracticable and only as a temporary measure pending the withdrawal of the measures which were inconsistent with the Agreement."[41] The Review Session Working Party, it will be seen, established a hierarchy of solutions: first, withdrawal of the illegal measure; second, compensatory adjustment; and last, retaliation.

The self-abnegating role of the panels and of the CONTRACTING PARTIES has certain advantages. One is the modest extent of the pressure that can be brought to bear upon contracting parties engaging in illegal action. So long as conciliation continues, an obstinate government or a government faced with strong protectionist pressures at home is under little compulsion to lift the illegal restriction. And even retaliation itself may prove to be a relatively weak sanction where the injured contracting party is not a major customer for a major product of the offending contracting party. Many less-developed countries have felt powerless to influence the restrictive commercial policies of developed countries because they did not consume enough of any of the latters' exports. This circumstance may explain the existence of the large number of "residual" quantitative restrictions that are maintained in open violation of the General Agreement.

## The Uruguay-Brazil Plan

Uruguay, which received little satisfaction from its 1961 broad-scale attack on developed-country policies, thereafter teamed up with Brazil to attempt to put more "muscle" into the Article XXIII procedures. The Uruguay-Brazil Plan would have provided less-developed countries financial compensation for violations of the General Agreement by developed countries:

> In the event that the measures complained of have been applied by a developed contracting party and it is established that they are adversely affecting the trade and the economic prospects of the less-developed contracting party or parties concerned, the panel may recommend, where it is not possible to eliminate the measures complained of or to obtain an adequate commercial remedy, that the damage caused should be compensated by means of an indemnity of a financial character on mutually acceptable terms.[42]

A large number of objections were lodged against this financial liability proposal. As summarized in the report of the Ad Hoc Committee on Legal

---

41. Ibid., p. 251.
42. Report of the Ad Hoc Group on Legal Amendments to the General Agreement, reprinted in "Expansion of Trade of the Developing Countries," December 1966 (mimeographed document), p. 112, 119.

Amendments, which was charged with passing upon the plan, financial compensation would, in addition to being an "entirely new concept," be subject to the practical objections

> that it would be impossible to evaluate the loss incurred by a contracting party in its export opportunities in money terms or to work out an appropriate level of financial compensation in each case; that although a country might be affluent and capable of making cash payments, any requirement on it to assume such an obligation would seem to require more authority than a mere finding by a panel of experts; that even if the assessment question could be solved, the problem of enforcing the payment of such an assessment would remain; that it was inconceivable that national legislatures would be willing to vote budgetary provisions for this purpose; that it was unreasonable to expect that a sovereign country would agree to be fined for its action; that it was difficult to see how a fine could be imposed on "mutually satisfactory terms" and that the most effective redress might be the removal of the measure complained of rather than some form of compensation.[43]

These objections are difficult to assess. A lawyer would find the principle of financial liability to injured parties for unlawful activity to be quite congenial. That principle is central to the institution of civil liability in domestic law. Taking a different point of view, an economist would find a financial remedy superior to retaliation. The party injured by the illegal trade measures would receive a benefit through a financial transfer, whereas retaliation grants that party nothing of value. To be sure, the possibility of retaliation may give the injured party a bargaining counter to induce the offending party to withdraw the illegal trade measure. The retaliation itself tends, however, to worsen the position of the injured party. And this fact tends to lessen the deterrent value of the threat of retaliation: a man standing near a dynamite plunger is unlikely to be able to ward off an armed robber by threatening to "blow us both up." Moreover, the problem has arisen within the GATT precisely because less-developed countries allegedly have no effective power of retaliation.

If a system of financial compensation could be based upon sufficiently clear and definite standards that the amount of compensation could be measured in advance with some precision, financial compensation would surely be superior to retaliation as a deterrent. A government that chose, or felt impelled for reasons of domestic politics, to violate a GATT provision would have to calculate the injury caused to other contracting parties. That international calculus of benefit and injury would become the private calculus for the acting government. The government would presumably impose that measure only if the benefit that the acting government calculated it would receive by imposing the restrictive measure exceeded the compensation it would have to pay. This

---

43. Ibid., p. 115.

would be an application of the social cost principle that has been a rationale for the imposition of liability for certain so-called international torts in domestic law.

Professor Ronald Coase has shown in another context that it does not really matter upon whom the legal system imposes liability. That is to say, it does not matter whether liability for a loss is imposed on the party causing that loss (the "financial liability" system) or is permitted to remain on the party suffering the loss, because in either event the same final result will be achieved.[44] Applying this insight to the problem at hand, if the loss to the exporting country is *greater* than the gain to the importing country from an import restriction, it is to the advantage of the exporting country to compensate the importing country for the elimination of the trade restriction (the "private compensation" system). The trade restriction will thus be eliminated whether or not financial liability is imposed. On the other hand, if the loss to the exporting country is *less* than the gain to the importing party from the trade restriction, it is to the advantage of the importing country to maintain the restriction whether or not financial liability is imposed. Financial liability will therefore be no deterrent. Similarly, under the private compensation system the exporting country would have to pay the importing country more than the amount of the loss in order to induce the latter to eliminate the trade restriction (since, by hypothesis, the gain to the importing country exceeds the loss to the exporting country); this the exporting country would not, of course, be willing to do.

One should not conclude, however, that there will be no difference between a system in which financial liability is imposed and one in which it is not. It is true that the number and incidence of trade restrictions will tend to be the same under either system. But the wealth of exporters and importers will differ. Financial liability will entail transfer payments from importing countries to exporting countries, whereas a private compensation system will entail transfer payments from exporting countries to importing countries. To less-developed exporting countries the financial liability system may be more palatable than the private compensation system (even though many less-developed countries —particularly those that receive foreign aid—tend to import more goods than they export).

On the other hand, one major advantage of the financial liability system over the private compensation system in many domestic law situations is of little importance in many international situations. In domestic law the number of parties injured by the pollution of water or air by a particular manufacturing company, for example, may be so great that it is impracticable for them to

44. Ronald Coase, "The Problem of Social Cost," *Journal of Law and Economics,* III (1960), p. 1. Coase's position is summarized in George J. Stigler, *The Theory of Price* (New York: Macmillan, 3d ed., 1966), pp. 104–14.

pool their efforts to compensate the manufacturer to cease the pollution; the costs of contracting would be so great as to preclude a result that could be achieved by, let us say, a tax on the manufacturer equal to the injury to the community. But in the international trade arena the number of countries with an export interest in a particular product is normally rather small. Those exporting countries are, moreover, normally in constant diplomatic contact with each importing country and are often in the throes of negotiating over a variety of arrangements (foreign aid, state trading contracts, defense cost sharing, other trade restrictions, and so forth). Thus private compensation can, and probably often does, take place through appropriate adjustments in those other arrangements.

Discussions of the relative advantages of financial liability and private compensation take place within an unusual context in the international arena, where states may be more intent on maximizing prestige, influence, security, and the like than on maximizing wealth. Moreover, the institutional arrangements within a particular country may be such that it is difficult to think of that country's government making rational, or even reasoned, decisions on certain kinds of trade issues. Critics of the role of Congress in trade matters often take this view. It must be clearly seen that trade restrictions tend to increase the real incomes of certain groups within the country imposing the restrictions and at the same time to reduce the incomes of other groups. It is doubtful that most governments, in determining whether to impose a particular trade restriction, make serious efforts to measure those effects in order to identify and pursue that policy which maximizes the incomes of the country as a whole. The differential political effectiveness of various domestic groups often plays a role on a given issue that is out of proportion to the differential financial stake of those groups in that issue. It is less than clear that a government behaves in economic affairs in the same way that a firm does.

Whatever may be one's views on the relative superiority of the financial-liability and private-compensation systems, one is led to suspect that the determinative argument leading the GATT to reject the Uruguay-Brazil Plan was the traditionalist argument that financial liability was an "entirely new concept" which was out of harmony with the traditional GATT system. To adopt a financial liability system would require a revolution in attitudes toward the function of the GATT, a revolution that would be unacceptable to those contracting parties—a clear majority—that have preferred to pursue their national interest in trade matters without too many scruples concerning the effects on other contracting parties. That revolution would also place a strain on existing GATT institutional arrangements. It is probable that conciliation would come to seem inappropriate for the imposition of what would be viewed as a fine. Financial liability would therefore provoke a movement toward an adjudicatory approach, which might require the establishment of a more formal dispute-settlement tribunal. Such a development would please those who favor the growth of international judicial institutions, but it seems unlikely to occur, at least within the GATT context, in the current state of world organization.

Although a financial liability system was the most dramatic aspect of the Uruguay-Brazil plan, that plan contained a number of other important proposals. One that was rejected by the ad hoc group would have accorded less-developed contracting parties the right, pending action by the CONTRACTING PARTIES, to take immediate provisional retaliatory action.[45] The proponents of this change argued that

> while it was true that the right to take automatic retaliatory action might not be necessary in ordinary cases, the same could not be said of the present situation in which some developed contracting parties had ignored some of their explicit obligations under the GATT. Many less-developed countries were suffering damage from measures applied inconsistently with the GATT provisions and the countries affected were obliged to honour their own obligations without any protection from the damage that they suffered. The present system . . . was in fact one in which GATT obligations could be violated unilaterally by some countries because the countries affected by such illegal action lacked sufficient bargaining power to protect their legitimate interests.[46]

The essence of this argument was that the existing pattern of illegal trade restrictions by developed countries against less-developed country exports could be traced to defects in the remedies system. In this form the argument was surely considerably overdrawn. As the GATT Trade and Development Committee found in its efforts to eliminate residual restrictions against less-developed countries, such restrictions had deep-seated causes within the domestic economies of the developed countries. No tinkering with the GATT remedies system would have been likely to eradicate those restrictions. But if the proponents over-argued their case, they nevertheless had a point. The delays built into Article XXIII tended to favor those countries that took their GATT obligations lightly.

The criticisms of the proposal by the developed countries were also exaggerated. They argued that the proposed right of provisional retaliation "could lead to a chaotic situation" and "would lead to a scaling down of GATT obligations."[47] Although unilateral action is dangerous, even if subject to subsequent review by the CONTRACTING PARTIES, the provisions in Article XXVIII:3 on unilateral retaliatory withdrawals of concessions were not shown to have created undue difficulties. The developed countries did not make the point,

45. Report of the Ad Hoc Group, p. 112, 120.
46. Ibid., p. 116.
47. Ibid.

but the most weighty objection to the proposed provisional retaliation system is that such a system would lead to more retaliation and hence to higher levels of duties and to additional direct restrictions in less-developed countries, a result that would be unlikely to redound to those countries' economic benefit. The moral may be that an inherently unsatisfactory remedy cannot be improved by being made more readily available.

## The Reform of GATT Procedures

Although the ad hoc group rejected the two most radical proposals in the Uruguay-Brazil plan, much of the plan was approved and finally officially promulgated in a 1966 decision of the CONTRACTING PARTIES.[48] The new rules are designed to promote prompter disposition of Article XXIII complaints filed by less-developed contracting parties. The essence of the new rules, which apply only to complaints by less-developed contracting parties against developed contracting parties, is, first, to bring the director-general of the GATT formally into the consultation procedures "so that . . . he may use his good offices with a view to facilitating a solution"[49] and, second, to set a series of deadlines to be met by the various organs of the GATT in their consideration of complaints and requests for authorization to retaliate. The substantive standards remain unchanged.

One of the new rules points Article XXIII in a new and hopeful direction. The panel appointed to review a complaint is called upon to "take due account of all the circumstances and considerations relating to the application of the measures complained of, and their impact on the trade and economic development of affected contracting parties." In order to assure that the panel's judgment in this respect is informed, the director-general is to submit a report "with all background information." The director-general is empowered to require the contracting parties concerned to "furnish all relevant information."[50] Here one may detect a first step toward an Article XXIII procedure that could well be adopted for all disputes, whether or not involving a less-developed country.

Although the reports by Article XXIII panels are not normally sufficiently detailed to form a solid judgment as to what actually happened in the proceedings, it seems fairly clear that the discussions, however frank and informal, do not normally probe into the actual effects of the challenged trade measures on the complaining party and on the world trading community as a whole. Just as has been the case in other GATT proceedings, such as the working party

48. *Basic Instruments,* 14th Supp. (1966), p. 18.
49. Ibid., p. 19.
50. Ibid.

reviews of proposed free-trade areas and customs unions under Article XXIV,[51] the economic analysis of the production and consumption effects of the restrictions tends to be superficial or nonexistent. This is particularly true when the question of the appropriate degree of retaliation is under discussion. Here the artificial notion of the "trade coverage" of the illegal restriction and of the proposed retaliatory restriction seems to dominate the discussions. In the "Chicken War" dispute between the United States and the EEC, the discussions under Article XXVIII deteriorated into a silly and essentially meaningless battle over the monetary value to be assigned to the withdrawn poultry concessions.[52]

The blame for the superficiality of panel investigations may not fairly be laid at the panels' door. In part the fault lies in the notion of conciliation, which seems to invoke images of friendly, general discussions among members of the GATT "club." And more important, the panels have no explicit authority to demand the necessary background information, and the contracting parties concerned often have no incentive to provide that information.

At least two institutional paths to the acquisition of the necessary background information are available. One is to phrase the substantive and procedural standards in such a way that certain parties have to produce that information. The reference in the new rules to "the circumstances and considerations relating to the application of the measures complained of, and their impact on the trade and economic development of affected contracting parties" moves in the right direction but fails to allocate the burden of coming forward with the information to the contracting parties in possession of the information.

The second institutional path to the acquisition of the necessary background information is to charge the director-general with the duty of preparing a report and to require the contracting parties to provide such relevant information as he may need. If the director-general were to take advantage of this opportunity, a very considerable improvement in the dispute settlement procedures of the GATT might be achieved. Much would, of course, depend on the skill and resourcefulness of the secretariat. But the director-general has certain advantages that the panels do not have. He is independent in a way in which no national representative can be, however neutral the representative's government may be in the dispute at hand. Here the independence that is important is not merely independence from the influence of a national government but also, and more significant, independence arising from long experience in viewing trade problems from the perspective of the entire world trading community and not just from the perspective of a particular country. In international trade questions, more than in most international problems, there is an international

---

51. See discussion in chapter 16, "Regional Economic Arrangements," supra.
52. See discussion in chapter 6, "Technical Tariff Negotiations," supra. In that case Article XXVIII:3 rather than Article XXIII retaliation was involved.

perspective that is more than just the sum of the national perspectives. Whether a particular trade measure leads to an improvement in the world allocation of resources, for example, is not merely a question of balancing the gain to one party against the loss to another.

The director-general has the possibility of calling upon a trained and experienced staff, and where necessary upon consultants, for the preparation of detailed reports. The panels have no staffs at all. It is true that a national representative called upon to sit on a panel may be able to gain some assistance from subordinates in his national delegation, but the difference in training and resources available is none the less significant. Panel members frequently are chosen from small countries (since it is usually thought that size and dispassion are inversely related), and those countries normally have small trade staffs in Geneva and even in their home capitals.

The analogy between the role that the Commission of the European Economic Community plays and the role that the director-general of the GATT could play should not be overlooked. One of the major institutional lessons of European integration is the contribution that can be made by an independent "secretariat" staffed with highly trained personnel dedicated to presenting a "community" viewpoint on all important issues. This contribution is embodied not only in triumphs of the "community perspective" over national solutions, but also, through the intellectual influence of the secretariat's reports, in the growth of a community perspective in the organs of opinion—newspapers, magazines, and scholarly publications—in the member states. The success of the EEC Commission is obviously related to the powers of initiative and enforcement granted the Commission under the Treaty of Rome, but it is in no sense solely dependent upon those powers. If the CONTRACTING PARTIES were to require detailed studies by the GATT secretariat and were to commit themselves to furnish the necessary background data for such studies, and if the GATT secretariat were to produce work of the quality of the EEC Commission, there is every reason to believe that there would be a substantial development of an "international perspective" in GATT discussions—at first in GATT proceedings and subsequently in national discussions of trade problems.

# 21 The Institutional Environment: The UNCTAD and the OECD

One of the most distinctive features of the post–World War II scene has been the proliferation of international economic organizations. Three of those organizations have extensive competence in trade matters: the GATT, the United Nations Conference on Trade and Development, and the Organization for Economic Co-operation and Development.[1] The existence of three such organizations has important implications for the GATT.

In this institutional environment the GATT tends to be regarded by its contracting parties as only one forum among several for the discussion of trade questions. Less-developed countries may find the UNCTAD a more congenial forum than the GATT for the articulation of aspirations and demands. Developed countries may feel more comfortable in discussing delicate issues within the intimacy of the OECD. And, of course, bilateral negotiations would be of major importance as an alternative to the GATT even if these competing trade organizations did not exist.

Since positions on issues of any significance must be decided in the national bureaucracies and not by national representatives sitting at a GATT table, GATT meetings frequently become an arid exercise of casting decisions taken elsewhere in official GATT form. For example, if the decision has been taken elsewhere by affected contracting parties to ignore the GATT rules with respect to a particular matter, then a working party must be appointed to work out the terms of an Article XXV:5 waiver.

A corollary is that the GATT secretariat, and to a certain extent Geneva-stationed national representatives to the GATT, become something like profes-

1. Other international organizations have limited competence in particular fields. Examples are the Food and Agriculture Organization in agriculture and the Economic Commission for Europe in East-West trade.

sional lawyers or doctors seeking clients. Their codes of ethics forbid them to advertise openly, but if they do not make some efforts to cultivate new business, they may find interesting questions being treated in other organizations. It would be instructive to consider from this perspective the institutional history of such recent issues as preferences for less-developed countries.

Another quite different consequence of the existence of multiple trade organizations is that since each has different institutional strengths, biases and clienteles, each organization is to some degree the competitor, if not the foe, of another.

With the creation in 1964 of the UNCTAD as a permanent organ of the General Assembly, the GATT's competence in the field of international trade was directly challenged, and it was widely thought that the GATT might not survive this challenge with its principles and procedures unscathed. Some representatives of developed countries feared that the GATT might tend to become a quasi-UNCTAD in which the less-developed countries would use their superior voting position to attempt to bring pressure on developed countries and would thereby dilute the effectiveness of the GATT in dealing with trade relations among developed countries. This fear gave rise to a good deal of informal talk about the desirability of creating a new trade organization, with only developed countries as members, for dealing with problems involving only developed countries, or, alternatively, of using the OECD for that purpose. Since the GATT could have been effectively undermined simply by a concerted shift by the developed countries of the locus of discussion of such trade problems from the GATT to the OECD without any formal transfer of competence, the very existence of the OECD constituted a latent threat to the GATT's preeminence in the trade field. Thus, the existence of competing organizations may shape the form of the GATT either by causing the GATT to become more like them in order to maintain the GATT's influence, or by a shift of effective competence from the GATT to another organization by collective tacit decision to discuss particular questions in those other organizations.

A short look at the UNCTAD and the OECD may serve not only to aid understanding of the GATT in its institutional environment but also to cast new light on the changes that might be made in the structure and processes of the GATT. A short look at the competitors may also reveal something about the fundamental question of the role of substantive and procedural rules in international organizations. Among the factors to be considered in each case are the history of the organization insofar as it shapes the attitudes and philosophy of its secretariat and the image of the organization's role held by its member states, the breadth and nature of its membership, the range of its competence, and its structure and working methods.

## The UNCTAD

The UNCTAD, perhaps even more than the GATT, is the institutional expression of the talent and energy of one dedicated man. In the UNCTAD case, the man is Raul Prebisch, its first secretary-general. Prebisch, unlike Wyndham White, exercised a decisive influence even before the organization came into existence. It was Prebisch who, in large measure, conceived the idea of a United Nations conference on the massive scale of the 1964 UNCTAD conference and who created the intellectual framework within which the 1964 conference was held and which has dominated the UNCTAD's work since then. Without going into the details of Prebisch's economic philosophy, which has been set out in detail by Prebisch and examined in detail by numerous authors, one can in barest summary say that Prebisch believed that the less-developed countries could not develop properly unless those countries were able to earn added foreign exchange through an increase in the volume and prices of their exports sufficient to close a "trade gap" estimated to be about $20 billion per year, and that this increase could only be brought about by concerted international measures, largely of an institutional nature.[2]

The 1964 conference was called to discuss this thesis and was so organized and directed as to lead to "recommendations" by the conference of the measures proposed by Prebisch. The dynamics of the conference were simple. The seventy-five less-developed countries voted unanimously in the vast majority of cases for recommendations which, following the guidelines drawn by Prebisch, had been prepared within five major substantive committees, in each of which the less-developed countries also had a dominant position. The developed countries were split, with the United States in the forefront of those defending the traditional nondiscriminatory trade position usually associated with the GATT, and with the French (and to a certain extent the EEC as a whole) in the vanguard of those espousing managed international markets and discriminatory trade arrangements as the means best calculated to close the "trade gap."

The recommendations, embodied in the Final Act of the Conference, called for a large number of specific actions (some of which, such as preferences for less-developed countries, have already been examined above) by developed countries or by United Nations members acting collectively. Also recommended was the establishment of "continuing machinery" to continue the work of the conference and to encourage and supervise the implementation of the conference's substantive recommendations. The General Assembly gave effect to this institutional desire for a longer life by establishing the United Nations

2. The basic paper, "Towards a New Trade Policy," is most easily available in *Proceedings of the United Nations Conference in Trade and Development,* Vol. II (1965), p. 5.

Conference on Trade and Development as a "permanent organ" of the General Assembly.[3] Prebisch was named the secretary-general of the resuscitated UNCTAD, and the organization has continued to reflect his views as well as the 1964 conference's character as a forum in which less-developed countries exercise pressure on developed countries.

The 1964 UNCTAD meeting in Geneva was a major success for Prebisch for, if precious few concrete substantive advances were made, the less-developed countries had demonstrated unanticipated solidarity in rhetoric and voting. Prebisch's ideas became institutionalized, and the extent to which the trade policies of developed countries impeded development was dramatized in a way that GATT procedures had never permitted. But the second meeting in 1968 in New Delhi (or UNCTAD II as it has come to be known) was a disaster for the prestige of the UNCTAD. The meeting lasted for months, and little was accomplished. In part the fate of UNCTAD II was sealed in the many doctrinaire resolutions that were passed in UNCTAD I at the behest of the seventy-five less-developed countries over the opposing votes or the abstentions of the countries that would have to take the action demanded. When the action was not taken between the two meetings, the less-developed countries had little choice but to force through the fruitless resolutions once more or to desist entirely. The pattern that was so successful in UNCTAD I could not be repeated in UNCTAD II without conceding failure, and the developed countries, upon whose affirmative measures any realization of the less-developed countries' demands depended, were no more prepared to undertake those measures than they had been in 1964.

The growing institutionalization of pressure group politics, which was perhaps inevitable given the origins of the UNCTAD and the trend of contemporary events, was consciously encouraged by the "group system" of organization. Member states were divided into four groups, constituted (roughly) as follows: Group A—Asian and African less-developed countries; Group B—developed Western countries; Group C—Latin American less-developed countries; and Group D—Eastern state-trading countries, whether or not developed. Not only was there an attempt to distribute positions among the countries on the basis of this division, but efforts were made to induce each group, and particularly Groups A and C, to arrive at a common position before definitive votes were taken on major issues. This induced splintering of the world trading community was called by Presbisch the "principle of co-ordinated action by groups of

3. U.N. General Assembly, Resolution 1995 (XIX). The word "permanent" does not appear in the General Assembly's grant of the status of an "organ" to the UNCTAD but has been added by the UNCTAD's secretary-general in describing the General Assembly's grant of power. See the Report by the Secretary-General, Institutional Arrangements, Review of International Trade and Development 1966, Part Three, Document TD/B/82/Add. 3 (1966), p. 5.

countries," and, according to a 1966 report by him, this principle has been "applied continuously" in all subsidiary bodies of the UNCTAD since its inception.[4]

After the failure of UNCTAD II, Prebisch was considerably less sanguine about the group system. Although insisting that the "group system has proved to be very useful and has great potentialities," he argued that its "shortcomings . . . were accentuated at the last Conference, seriously jeopardizing its efficient functioning and unduly extending its duration." The cult of unanimity made it possible for laggard developed countries to force agreement in Group B to the "lowest common denominator" and for the most militant less-developed countries to compel agreement in their groups to their "maximum demands." "It was enough that one or a few countries inside the group had a dissenting attitude to unduly delay or even paralyze not only the decisions of the group but also the progress of the whole Conference."[5] Prebisch concluded his indictment of the unanimity principle by noting that it often made impossible effective negotiation with a view to compromise agreements between groups. Although Prebisch does not spell out his solution, he apparently favors retention of the group system while introducing the principle of majority or qualified majority voting within groups.

The contrast between the UNCTAD's group system, based on unanimity, and the GATT procedures is great. The GATT protocol system aids progress toward trade liberalization by facilitating general agreement upon commitments that will only be binding upon those parties that thereafter specifically agree to be bound. Protectionist contracting parties thereby find it more difficult to block progress by other countries toward freer trade. Similarly, the GATT frowns upon the formation of blocks for the purpose of putting pressure on other contracting parties. The experience of UNCTAD II suggests that the GATT's procedures have in this respect been sound.

At the same time the differences between the UNCTAD and the GATT should not be exaggerated; the GATT works on a de facto unanimity principle within a certain sphere. It is rare that a contracting party with a significant interest in a trade matter will be required to undertake effective affirmative action through GATT decisions taken by majority vote. In the GATT, too, a recalcitrant country may find it possible to impose its will upon the majority that seeks affirmative section. The status quo is hard to change. Where a contracting party plans to take protectionist measures, a fait accompli yields tactical advantages. The adoption of Part IV also tended to reshape the GATT in the image of the UNCTAD, so far as less-developed countries were concerned,

4. Report by the Secretary-General, Institutional Arrangements, p. 14.
5. Prebisch, The Significance of the Second Session of UNCTAD, Document TD/96 (1968), pp. 9–11.

by casting aside the notion of give-and-take between equal sovereign states (a notion which finds expression in the reciprocity principle) in favor of the principle that less-developed countries are entitled to demand unilateral trade liberalization by developed countries.

The UNCTAD proper, that is to say the Conference, is to meet "at intervals of not more than three years,"[6] although four years passed between UNCTAD I and UNCTAD II. When the Conference is not in session, the Trade and Development Board is to "carry out the functions that fall within the competence of the Conference."[7] Membership on the Board is so distributed that less-developed countries maintain a majority; Group A alone is entitled to twenty-two of the fifty-five seats and Group C is entitled to another nine seats.[8] Although decisions of the Conference of substance are to be taken by a two-thirds majority of representatives present and voting at meetings of the Conference (with the one-state, one-vote principle applying), all decisions of the Board, whether or not involving matters of substance, may be taken by a simple majority of representatives present and voting.[9] To reduce the possibility that the less-developed countries may, through their voting dominance, use the Board to score easy, meaningless victories that do not reflect any measure of agreement on the part of developed countries, conciliation procedures have been introduced to encourage adequate consultation among groups before votes on matters of substance are taken.[10]

The structure of the subsidiary bodies of the Board gives a better idea of the sphere of effective competence of the UNCTAD than does the broadly drafted statement of the Conference's (and, derivatively, of the Board's) "principal functions."[11] The Board has four principal committees (the Committees on Commodities, on Manufactures, on Shipping, on Invisibles and Financing related to Trade) as well as an Advisory Committee to the Board and to the Committee on Commodities. In addition, the Board has from time to time created special committees, the names of which suggest its preoccupations—notably, the Special Committee on Preferences, the Expert Committee on the Expansion of Trade among Developing Countries and on Regional Development, and the Expert Group on International Monetary Issues.[12]

The Committee on Commodities is concerned, as the name suggests, with the general field of primary commodities. In its role as successor to the United

6. U.N. General Assembly, Resolution 1995 (XIX), para. II(2).
7. Ibid., para. II (14).
8. Ibid., para. II (5).
9. Ibid., para. II (24).
10. Ibid., para. II (25).
11. The "principal functions" are listed in ibid., para. II (3).
12. See Report of Secretary-General, Institutional Arrangements, p. 11.

Nations Commission on International Commodity Trade, it has been concerned with the negotiation of international commodity agreements on tropical products. The Advisory Committee to the Board and to the Committee on Commodities is a group of experts that has replaced the former Interim Coordinating Committee for International Commodity Arrangements and is intended to provide expert guidance in this area. The Committee on Commodities does not itself sponsor the negotiations; rather, they are carried out in separate United Nations conferences under the auspices of the UNCTAD. The UNCTAD, "convinced that the securing of an International Agreement on Cocoa will demonstrate beyond all possible doubt the instrumentality of the United Nations Conference on Trade and Development for practical solution of the problems of trade and development of the developing countries," sponsored the 1966 United Nations Cocoa Conference.[13] Since this was the one major opportunity for the UNCTAD to accomplish something specific in a negotiating context, the failure of the 1966 United Nations Cocoa Conference, followed by the failure of a second cocoa conference in 1967, left intact the UNCTAD's image as a talking, nonacting body.[14] Nevertheless, the UNCTAD has a more secure institutional position in the field of international commodity agreements than the GATT, which (ignoring cotton textiles) entered the field only in the context of the Kennedy Round and then only for certain temperate products. Moreover, the GATT achieved success only in wheat and left the final negotiations of the International Grains Arrangement to an International Wheat Conference.[15] Although the GATT has established a Group on International Commodity Problems within the context of Part IV of the General Agreement, it seems likely that the UNCTAD will continue to be the more directly involved in negotiations for commodity arrangements in tropical products.

A large proportion of the energies of the UNCTAD Committee on Manufactures has been devoted to preferences for underdeveloped countries. A Group on Preferences and a Special Committee on Preferences were established to study the question. At UNCTAD II a major, albeit inconclusive, agreement was reached on preferences. Although the GATT has also studied preferences,[16] it seems likely that, given the intellectual origin and the history of the proposal, the UNCTAD will continue to dominate the stage. Should, however, the stage of country-by-country and product-by-product negotiations

13. See Trade and Development Board Resolution 25(III), Resolutions and Decisions, Supp. No. 1, Document TD/B/74 (1965).
14. The UNCTAD has been successful in extending, in one form or another, preexisting international arrangements in tin, sugar, and olive oil. See Report of the United Nations Conference on Trade and Development on its Second Session, Document TD/L.37 (1968), pp. 8–9, n. 14.
15. See discussion in chapter 15, "Temperate Agricultural Commodities," supra.
16. See discussion in chapter 14, "Less-Developed Countries," supra.

be reached, an institutional struggle between the UNCTAD and the GATT might develop. The most-favored-nation clause of the General Agreement would be called into question, as was the case in the Australian waiver for its preferences for less-developed countries.[17] Even if the UNCTAD were to sponsor the negotiations, a GATT waiver, with perhaps periodic reviews of the waiver, would be necessary. Moreover, some contracting parties would no doubt consider the GATT a more appropriate framework than the UNCTAD for the highly technical negotiations that would arise in any attempt to institute a system of selective, individually negotiated preferences on a broad scale.

The UNCTAD Committee on Shipping deals with a subject well beyond the scope of the GATT's activities. Shipping is nevertheless an activity of great economic importance, and by excluding this kind of commerce the GATT has left untouched an item constituting a significant percentage of total trade in invisibles. Shipping would present an unusual subject-matter for the GATT insofar as many of the restraints on competition in shipping are private in character. To undertake to deal with such private restraints would no doubt involve the GATT in difficulties similar to those encountered in the field of restrictive trade practices, a field that the GATT has, after a few limited forays, elected not to enter.[18] Nevertheless, there remain a number of government-created restrictions on shipping that might be appropriate for GATT review, such as subsidies to shipbuilding and nationality restrictions on certain kinds of carriage.

The UNCTAD Committee on Invisibles and Financing related to Trade also deals with matters almost entirely beyond the scope of traditional GATT activities. The portion of the work of this committee that deals with development assistance—that is to say, with aid rather than trade—is beyond the scope of the GATT for rather obvious reasons.[19] But it is not so clear that the GATT should consider governmental restrictions on certain other forms of commerce within the terms of reference of this UNCTAD committee—such as insurance, transportation, and tourism—as foreign to its concerns. The limitation of the terms of the General Agreement largely to trade in visibles is an obvious, but a not entirely sufficient, ground for the GATT's inactivity in the field of invisibles. In 1959 the CONTRACTING PARTIES recommended that governments avoid limitations on the freedom of traders to purchase transport insurance on the most economic basis available. To be sure, the recommenda-

17. *Basic Instruments,* 14th Supp. (1966), p. 23.
18. Ibid., 9th Supp. (1961), pp. 28, 170; The CONTRACTING PARTIES to the General Agreement on Tariffs and Trade, *Restrictive Business Practices* (1959), and *The Activities of GATT 1960/61* (1961), pp. 29–30.
19. The GATT's interest in financial assistance has been limited almost exclusively to the relationship between trade and aid. See *Basic Instruments,* 12th Supp. (1964), pp. 135, 137; and discussion in chapter 14, "Less-Developed Countries," supra.

tion was stated to be justified by the restrictive effect on international trade in goods that limitations on free competition in transport insurance might have.[20] But in 1955 the CONTRACTING PARTIES recommended the stimulation of the international flow of capital through bilateral and multilateral agreements concerning "security for existing and future investment, the avoidance of double taxation, and facilities for the transfer of earnings upon foreign investments," and this resolution was not based on any alleged relation to international trade in goods.[21] Whether or not restrictions on invisibles and on trade financing could be attacked under the present terms of the General Agreement, it has been amended in the past and could be amended once more to expand the range of the GATT's interest within the field of international commerce beyond the present preoccupation with visibles.

An expansion of the GATT's activities to include a range of commercial matters as broad as that dealt with by the UNCTAD would carry with it serious risks. One of the GATT's strengths over the years has been that it has stuck to its knitting—tariffs and certain blatant nontariff restrictions on trade in goods—and has not permitted itself to become embroiled in each new commercial policy and economic development fad that has appeared on the international scene. It should not be overlooked that the extraordinary breadth of its agenda contributed significantly to the failure of UNCTAD II. Prebisch commented that "it proved to be practically impossible to deal with all of [the items on its agenda] seriously and in an orderly fashion, and to effectively negotiate on so many items."[22] Foreseeing this difficulty, he had attempted to focus UNCTAD II on certain "points of crystallization," but to no avail.[23]

One major advantage of the UNCTAD over the GATT is the former's broader membership. Not only does the UNCTAD (including in its membership all United Nations members plus members of all the U.N. specialized agencies plus the International Atomic Energy Agency) encompass almost all the less-developed world but it includes as well many more of the Eastern European state-trading nations. The difference in breadth of membership of the two institutions is narrowing as the GATT begins to have closer relations with Eastern Europe and as more less-developed countries become contracting parties. Sheer numbers are not, of course, an advantage. The fact that 133 countries had to be heard contributed to the cumbersomeness of UNCTAD II. Meetings of the Board, with 55 members, and the various UNCTAD com-

20. *Basic Instruments,* 8th Supp. (1960), p. 26; for the history of the recommendation, see U.S. Tariff Commission, *Operation of the Trade Agreements Program,* 12th Rep. (1961), pp. 66–67.
21. *Basic Instruments,* 3d Supp. (1955), pp. 49–50.
22. Prebisch, Significance of Second Session, p. 10.
23. Ibid., and Report of the United Nations Conference, pp. 22–24.

mittees, with 45 to 55 members each, are more like plenary meetings of international conferences than informal executive meetings.[24] The GATT has been fortunate in keeping most of its meetings smaller, in part through the device of the ad hoc working party.

At the same time the GATT has one strong card in its competition with the UNCTAD. That is its great experience in handling complicated trade negotiations. The sheer complexity of the Kennedy Round surpassed that of any other trade negotiations in history. Perhaps a division of labor might develop in which the grand outlines of commercial policy issues involving less-developed countries would be debated in the UNCTAD until a consensus was reached among the most important countries of both the developed and less-developed worlds, and thereafter the necessary negotiations for the implementation of the solutions, particularly if they involved tariffs, could be negotiated within the GATT.

Another strong GATT card is that the GATT continues to have the confidence of many, if not most, developed countries. This confidence is based in part upon GATT's working methods. Even when major issues of policy have arisen, there has been little tendency to resort to verbose speeches or to steamroller tactics. Rather, the informal rules of the "club" have required that such issues be resolved informally, amicably and if possible without undue recourse to international public opinion. With the less-developed countries having reached a majority position in the GATT, this situation might change rapidly if they should decide to use the GATT—as they have used the UNCTAD—as an instrument for putting pressure on the developed countries. In that event the developed countries might choose to rely more often on the OECD as the major forum for the resolution of commercial policy issues, particularly for those issues that involve relations among the developed countries themselves. In that event the OECD would be less of a threat to the GATT as a direct institutional competitor than as a developed-countries' alternative, to coin a word, to an UNCTADization of the GATT.

## The OECD

The role of the OECD in trade matters has been growing steadily. At the time of its creation it was thought that the OECD would have no significant trade role. Its predecessor, the Organization for European Economic Co-operation, had played a major role in the suppression of quantitative restrictions in intra-European trade through its Code of Liberalisation.[25] But by 1960 the success of the OEEC and the achievement of convertibility by the major European

24. Prebisch, Significance of Second Session, p. 10.
25. See discussion in chapter 9, "Quantitative Restrictions," supra.

currencies had reduced the need for continuing efforts along OEEC lines. Moreover, the United States, as an entering member of the transformed organization, was at once unwilling to undertake specific OEEC commitments in the trade field and more interested in a universalist approach to the reduction of trade barriers under the GATT than in a regional approach within the OECD.

Largely at the insistence of the United States the trade function of the OECD was limited. The Code of Liberalisation dealing with goods was suspended while the Code of Liberalisation of Current Invisible Operations and the Code of Liberalisation of Capital Movements remained in force to be administered by the OECD. A Trade Committee of high-level national officials was formed, however, and a General Working Party composed of working-level representatives was created to assist it. The tasks assigned to the Trade Committee soon grew to the point where the General Working Party was "in practically permanent session."[26] And other OECD committees, such as the Committee on Invisible Transactions, have dealt with certain aspects of commercial policy.

The OECD has been as institutional competitor of the GATT in several fields. It has dealt with a number of concrete problems that have also been before the GATT. Among such topics are government purchasing, border tax adjustments, antidumping legislation, preferences for less-developed countries, customs formalities, import surcharges, classification and valuation of goods for tariff purposes, and procedures for delivering import licenses.[27] These exercises have seldom led, however, to relatively concrete undertakings or changes of national policies. That is not surprising because many of these problems have shown themselves intractable, and it can also be said that the GATT has not made much more progress on these problems during the period in which the OECD Trade Committee has been in existence.

In one sense the OECD has gone beyond the GATT in encouraging trade in visibles. It has adopted an affirmative approach to the expansion of trade in certain sectors through the harmonization of technical laws and regulations in such fields as the registration and labeling of pharmaceutical products and the establishment of quality standards for fruits and vegetables and of safety standards for welded gas cylinders.[28] It has sought to reduce certain fiscal restraints on trade through the OECD Draft Convention on Double Taxation.

26. Organization for Economic Co-operation and Development, *The OECD at Work* (1964), p. 42.
27. Ibid., pp. 42–45. The confidentiality of the work of the Trade Committee makes it difficult to follow the OECD's work in the trade field. Perhaps the best guide is the annual reports of the secretary-general of the OECD to the Council of Europe. Occasional articles in the OECD *Observer* also provide some insight. On the OECD generally, see Henry G. Aubrey, *Atlantic Economic Cooperation* (New York: Frederick A. Praeger, 1967).
28. *The OECD at Work*, p. 44.

And it has turned its attention to sectors of international commerce left untouched by the GATT, such as coordination of national energy policies and of national policies toward international fisheries.[29]

The OECD has also dealt with a wide range of commercial policy questions that the GATT has left virtually untouched. In this sense the OECD, like the UNCTAD, has adopted a broader view of its competence than has the GATT. In the field of trade in invisibles it has considered shipping, insurance, advertising, business travel, and tourism. In these areas the Code of Liberalisation of Current Invisible Operations has been of particular importance.[30]

The limited membership and the working methods of the OECD have had a decisive influence on the treatment of the problems that have come before it. The membership, being that of the old OEEC plus the United States, Canada, and Japan,[31] includes relatively few less-developed countries. This limitation of membership therefore leads, even more than in the GATT, to a club atmosphere (sometimes derisively referred to as a "rich man's club") and thereby affects its working methods.[32]

The informality of the OECD procedures can be attributed not only to the more limited membership but also to the OECD's special goals. The OECD is, in most domains, less interested in binding commitments than in joint study of problems leading at most to coordination of national policies. Coordination of national policies has seldom been an interest of the GATT. The GATT's activities have been in the direction of discouraging governmental activities that could distort trade rather than of coordinating those governmental activities. This distinction is of little significance in most areas of the GATT's work, but it could come to be highly important if the GATT were to turn its attention, for example, toward the imperfections in the international monetary system that lead to certain kinds of trade barriers, or toward restrictions in international commerce other than trade in goods. Even within the scope of the GATT's traditional activities, it can be argued that the GATT has been ineffective in agriculture because it has tried to separate the international trade aspects of agriculture from the internal policies that lead to restrictions on international trade in agricultural products. In any event, the OECD policy, in rather sharp contrast to the undeclared but nevertheless persistently pursued GATT policy, emphasizes the necessity of approaching economic problems from all relevant

29. Ibid., pp. 78–82, 95–99.
30. Ibid., pp. 51–56.
31. Yugoslavia and Finland have a special status, less than full membership. The United States and Canada had associate status in the OEEC. Spain had a special membership status in the OEEC.
32. Even in a small, informal organization like the OECD the necessity of holding plenary sessions of committees representing the active membership reduces the effectiveness of the work. See Aubrey, p. 124.

perspectives simultaneously. As set forth in one OECD publication, the OECD has carried over from the OEEC an emphasis on "the inter-relatedness of all economic problems in a network of mutual implication, the consequent necessity of interdependence in policy formation, and the need for all possible knowledge that could be brought to bear on economic issues."[33] This emphasis was particularly marked in the paper agreed upon within the framework of the Economic Policy Committee of the OECD on The Balance of Payments Adjustment Process. It emphasized that such commercial policy questions as the use of quantitative restrictions, the timing of unilateral tariff reductions, the timing of changes in border tax adjustments, and the use of import surcharges and of export subsidies were inextricably involved in the general question of the proper methods of adjusting to payments imbalances.[34]

The informality of OECD working parties is also sometimes a limitation. Some kinds of problems can be dealt with only through binding arrangements. When the OEEC dealt with the quantitative restrictions problem, it relied upon the binding Code of Liberalisation. The Code of Liberalisation of Current Invisible Operations, carried over from the OEEC, is also a binding document. Informal methods have been possible because the OECD, in the view of its member countries, "is not a regulatory body but rather a forum for the exchange of informed views on policy questions."[35] Thus, the developed countries could hardly shift the focus of action on commercial policy questions involving their own trade to the OECD without a substantial change in the character and the working methods of that organization.

Another difficulty that would be encountered in such a shift of developed country trade problems to the OECD is the unanimity rule. Under the convention establishing the OECD, "unless the Organisation otherwise agrees unanimously for special cases, decisions shall be taken and recommendations shall be made by mutual agreement of all the Members."[36] In point of fact, the unanimity rule does not make the OECD sharply different from the GATT because "if a Member abstains from voting on a decision or recommendation, such abstention shall not invalidate the decision or recommendation, which shall be applicable to the other Members but not to the abstaining Member."[37] This arrangement has some obvious parallels to the GATT protocol system under which most new commitments are enshrined in protocols or declarations

---

33. *The OECD at Work*, p. 4.
34. See OECD, *The Balance of Payments Adjustment Process* (Aug. 1966), especially pp. 23–24.
35. *The OECD at Work*, p. 6.
36. Convention on the Organization for Economic Co-operation and Development, Art. 6(1).
37. Ibid., Art. 6(2).

and are made applicable only to those contracting parties that agree to be bound by them. Nevertheless, in the General Agreement, unlike the OECD Convention, certain major commitments on a broad range of commercial policy issues are already contained in the founding document. A revision of the OECD Convention or at least a change in the unanimity rule would therefore probably be necessary if the OECD were to take over the present role of the GATT for developed country trade.

# Appendix

Text of the General Agreement, as in force on 1 March 1969, including interpretative notes and Protocol of Provisional Application. Reprinted from The CONTRACTING PARTIES to the General Agreement on Tariffs and Trade, *Basic Instruments and Selected Documents,* Volume IV (Geneva, 1969), pages 1–78. The reader should note that the asterisks, inserted by the original publisher, mark the portions of the text that should be read in conjunction with the interpretative notes in Annex I. The appendix to Volume IV, not reproduced here, contains a useful summary of the source and effective date of GATT provisions.

# THE GENERAL AGREEMENT ON TARIFFS AND TRADE

The Governments of the COMMONWEALTH OF AUSTRALIA, the KINGDOM OF BELGIUM, the UNITED STATES OF BRAZIL, BURMA, CANADA, CEYLON, the REPUBLIC OF CHILE, the REPUBLIC OF CHINA, the REPUBLIC OF CUBA, the CZECHOSLOVAK REPUBLIC, the FRENCH REPUBLIC, INDIA, LEBANON, the GRAND-DUCHY OF LUXEMBURG, the KINGDOM OF THE NETHERLANDS, NEW ZEALAND, the KINGDOM OF NORWAY, PAKISTAN, SOUTHERN RHODESIA, SYRIA, the UNION OF SOUTH AFRICA, the UNITED KINGDOM OF GREAT BRITAIN AND NORTHERN IRELAND, and the UNITED STATES OF AMERICA:

Recognizing that their relations in the field of trade and economic endeavour should be conducted with a view to raising standards of living, ensuring full employment and a large and steadily growing volume of real income and effective demand, developing the full use of the resources of the world and expanding the production and exchange of goods,

Being desirous of contributing to these objectives by entering into reciprocal and mutually advantageous arrangements directed to the substantial reduction of tariffs and other barriers to trade and to the elimination of discriminatory treatment in international commerce,

Have through their Representatives agreed as follows:

# PART I

## Article I

### General Most-Favoured-Nation Treatment

1. With respect to customs duties and charges of any kind imposed on or in connection with importation or exportation or imposed on the international transfer of payments for imports or exports, and with respect to the method of levying such duties and charges, and with respect to all rules and formalities in connection with importation and exportation, and with respect to all matters referred to in paragraphs 2 and 4 of Article III, * any advantage, favour, privilege or immunity granted by any contracting party to any product originating in or destined for any other country shall be accorded immediately and unconditionally to the like product originating in or destined for the territories of all other contracting parties.

2. The provisions of paragraph 1 of this Article shall not require the elimination of any preferences in respect of import duties or charges which do not exceed the levels provided for in paragraph 4 of this Article and which fall within the following descriptions:

   (a) Preferences in force exclusively between two or more of the territories listed in Annex A, subject to the conditions set forth therein;
   (b) Preferences in force exclusively between two or more territories which on July 1, 1939, were connected by common sovereignty or relations of protection or suzerainty and which are listed in Annexes B, C and D, subject to the conditions set forth therein;
   (c) Preferences in force exclusively between the United States of America and the Republic of Cuba;
   (d) Preferences in force exclusively between neighbouring countries listed in Annexes E and F.

3. The provisions of paragraph 1 shall not apply to preferences between the countries formerly a part of the Ottoman Empire and detached from it on July 24, 1923, provided such preferences are approved under paragraph 5 † of Article XXV, which shall be applied in this respect in the light of paragraph 1 of Article XXIX.

---

† The authentic text erroneously reads " sub-paragraph 5 (a) ".

4. The margin of preference * on any product in respect of which a preference is permitted under paragraph 2 of this Article but is not specifically set forth as a maximum margin of preference in the appropriate Schedule annexed to this Agreement shall not exceed:

(*a*) in respect of duties or charges on any product described in such Schedule, the difference between the most-favoured-nation and preferential rates provided for therein; if no preferential rate is provided for, the preferential rate shall for the purposes of this paragraph be taken to be that in force on April 10, 1947, and, if no most-favoured-nation rate is provided for, the margin shall not exceed the difference between the most-favoured-nation and preferential rates existing on April 10, 1947;

(*b*) in respect of duties or charges on any product not described in the appropriate Schedule, the difference between the most-favoured-nation and preferential rates existing on April 10, 1947.

In the case of the contracting parties named in Annex G, the date of April 10, 1947, referred to in sub-paragraphs (*a*) and (*b*) of this paragraph shall be replaced by the respective dates set forth in that Annex.

## Article II

### *Schedules of Concessions*

1. (*a*) Each contracting party shall accord to the commerce of the other contracting parties treatment no less favourable than that provided for in the appropriate Part of the appropriate Schedule annexed to this Agreement.

(*b*) The products described in Part I of the Schedule relating to any contracting party, which are the products of territories of other contracting parties, shall, on their importation into the territory to which the Schedule relates, and subject to the terms, conditions or qualifications set forth in that Schedule, be exempt from ordinary customs duties in excess of those set forth and provided for therein. Such products shall also be exempt from all other duties or charges of any kind imposed on or in connection with importation in excess of those imposed on the date of this Agreement or those directly and mandatorily required to be imposed thereafter by legislation in force in the importing territory on that date.

(*c*) The products described in Part II of the Schedule relating to any contracting party which are the products of territories entitled under Article I to receive preferential treatment upon importation into the territory to which the Schedule relates shall, on their importation into such territory, and subject to the terms, conditions or qualifications set forth in that Schedule, be exempt from ordinary customs duties in excess of those set forth and provided for in Part II of that Schedule. Such products shall also be exempt from all other duties or charges of any kind imposed on or in connection with importation in excess of those imposed on the date of this Agreement or those directly and mandatorily required to be imposed thereafter by legislation in force in the importing territory on that date. Nothing in this Article shall prevent any contracting party from maintaining its requirements existing on the date of this Agreement as to the eligibility of goods for entry at preferential rates of duty.

2. Nothing in this Article shall prevent any contracting party from imposing at any time on the importation of any product:

(a) a charge equivalent to an internal tax imposed consistently with the provisions of paragraph 2 of Article III * in respect of the like domestic product or in respect of an article from which the imported product has been manufactured or produced in whole or in part;

(b) any anti-dumping or countervailing duty applied consistently with the provisions of Article VI;*

(c) fees or other charges commensurate with the cost of services rendered.

3. No contracting party shall alter its method of determining dutiable value or of converting currencies so as to impair the value of any of the concessions provided for in the appropriate Schedule annexed to this Agreement.

4. If any contracting party establishes, maintains or authorizes, formally or in effect, a monopoly of the importation of any product described in the appropriate Schedule annexed to this Agreement, such monopoly shall not, except as provided for in that Schedule or as otherwise agreed between the parties which initially negotiated the concession, operate so as to afford protection on the average in excess of the amount of protection provided for in that Schedule. The provisions of this paragraph shall not limit the use by contracting parties of any form of assistance to domestic producers permitted by other provisions of this Agreement.*

5. If any contracting party considers that a product is not receiving from another contracting party the treatment which the first contracting party believes to have been contemplated by a concession provided for in the appropriate Schedule annexed to this Agreement, it shall bring the matter directly to the attention of the other contracting party. If the latter agrees that the treatment contemplated was that claimed by the first contracting party, but declares that such treatment cannot be accorded because a court or other proper authority has ruled to the effect that the product involved

cannot be classified under the tariff laws of such contracting party so as to permit the treatment contemplated in this Agreement, the two contracting parties, together with any other contracting parties substantially interested, shall enter promptly into further negotiations with a view to a compensatory adjustment of the matter.

6. (*a*) The specific duties and charges included in the Schedules relating to contracting parties members of the International Monetary Fund, and margins of preference in specific duties and charges maintained by such contracting parties, are expressed in the appropriate currency at the par value accepted or provisionally recognized by the Fund at the date of this Agreement. Accordingly, in case this par value is reduced consistently with the Articles of Agreement of the International Monetary Fund by more than twenty per centum, such specific duties and charges and margins of preference may be adjusted to take account of such reduction; *Provided* that the CONTRACTING PARTIES (*i.e.*, the contracting parties acting jointly as provided for in Article XXV) concur that such adjustments will not impair the value of the concessions provided for in the appropriate Schedule or elsewhere in this Agreement, due account being taken of all factors which may influence the need for, or urgency of, such adjustments.

(*b*) Similar provisions shall apply to any contracting party not a member of the Fund, as from the date on which such contracting party becomes a member of the Fund or enters into a special exchange agreement in pursuance of Article XV.

7. The Schedules annexed to this Agreement are hereby made an integral part of Part I of this Agreement.

# PART II

## Article III *

*National Treatment on Internal Taxation and Regulation*

1. The contracting parties recognize that internal taxes and other internal charges, and laws, regulations and requirements affecting the internal sale, offering for sale, purchase, transportation, distribution or use of products, and internal quantitative regulations requiring the mixture, processing or use of products in specified amounts or proportions, should not be applied to imported or domestic products so as to afford protection to domestic production.*

2. The products of the territory of any contracting party imported into the territory of any other contracting party shall not be subject, directly or indirectly, to internal taxes or other internal charges of any kind in excess of those applied, directly or indirectly, to like domestic products. Moreover, no contracting party shall otherwise apply internal taxes or other internal charges to imported or domestic products in a manner contrary to the principles set forth in paragraph 1.*

3. With respect to any existing internal tax which is inconsistent with the provisions of paragraph 2, but which is specifically authorized under a trade agreement, in force on April 10, 1947, in which the import duty on the taxed product is bound against increase, the contracting party imposing the tax shall be free to postpone the application of the provisions of paragraph 2 to such tax until such time as it can obtain release from the obligations of such trade agreement in order to permit the increase of such duty to the extent necessary to compensate for the elimination of the protective element of the tax.

4. The products of the territory of any contracting party imported into the territory of any other contracting party shall be accorded treatment no less favourable than that accorded to like products of national origin in respect of all laws, regulations and requirements affecting their internal sale, offering for sale, purchase, transportation, distribution or use. The provisions of this paragraph shall not prevent the application of differential internal transportation charges which are based exclusively on the economic operation of the means of transport and not on the nationality of the product.

5. No contracting party shall establish or maintain any internal quantitative regulation relating to the mixture, processing or use of products in specified amounts or proportions which requires, directly or indirectly, that any specified amount or proportion of any product which is the subject of the regulation must be supplied from domestic sources. Moreover, no contracting party shall otherwise apply internal quantitative regulations in a manner contrary to the principles set forth in paragraph 1.*

6. The provisions of paragraph 5 shall not apply to any internal quantitative regulation in force in the territory of any contracting party on July 1, 1939, April 10, 1947, or March 24, 1948, at the option of that contracting party; *Provided* that any such regulation which is contrary to the provisions of paragraph 5 shall not be modified to the detriment of imports and shall be treated as a customs duty for the purpose of negotiation.

7. No internal quantitative regulation relating to the mixture, processing or use of products in specified amounts or proportions shall be applied in such a manner as to allocate any such amount or proportion among external sources of supply.

8. (*a*) The provisions of this Article shall not apply to laws, regulations or requirements governing the procurement by governmental agencies of products purchased for governmental purposes and not with a view to commercial resale or with a view to use in the production of goods for commercial sale.

(*b*) The provisions of this Article shall not prevent the payment of subsidies exclusively to domestic producers, including payments to domestic producers derived from the proceeds of internal taxes or charges applied consistently with the provisions of this Article and subsidies effected through governmental purchases of domestic products.

9. The contracting parties recognize that internal maximum price control measures, even though conforming to the other provisions of this Article, can have effects prejudicial to the interests of contracting parties supplying imported products. Accordingly, contracting parties applying such measures shall take account of the interests of exporting contracting parties with a view to avoiding to the fullest practicable extent such prejudicial effects.

10. The provisions of this Article shall not prevent any contracting party from establishing or maintaining internal quantitative regulations relating to exposed cinematograph films and meeting the requirements of Article IV.

## Article IV

*Special Provisions relating to Cinematograph Films*

If any contracting party establishes or maintains internal quantitative regulations relating to exposed cinematograph films, such regulations shall take the form of screen quotas which shall conform to the following requirements:

(*a*) Screen quotas may require the exhibition of cinematograph films of national origin during a specified minimum proportion of the total screen time actually utilized, over a specified period of not less than one year, in the commercial exhibition of all films of whatever origin, and shall be computed on the basis of screen time per theatre per year or the equivalent thereof;

(*b*) With the exception of screen time reserved for films of national origin under a screen quota, screen time including that released by administrative action from screen time reserved for films of national origin, shall not be allocated formally or in effect among sources of supply;

(*c*) Notwithstanding the provisions of sub-paragraph (*b*) of this Article, any contracting party may maintain screen quotas conforming to the requirements of sub-paragraph (*a*) of this Article which reserve a minimum proportion of screen time for films of a specified origin other than that of the contracting party imposing such screen quotas; *Provided* that no such minimum proportion of screen time shall be increased above the level in effect on April 10, 1947;

(*d*) Screen quotas shall be subject to negotiation for their limitation, liberalization or elimination.

## Article V

*Freedom of Transit*

1. Goods (including baggage), and also vessels and other means of transport, shall be deemed to be in transit across the territory of a contracting party when the passage across such territory, with or without trans-shipment, warehousing, breaking bulk, or change in the mode of transport, is only a portion of a complete journey beginning and terminating beyond the frontier of the contracting party across whose territory the traffic passes. Traffic of this nature is termed in this Article " traffic in transit ".

2. There shall be freedom of transit through the territory of each contracting party, via the routes most convenient for international transit, for traffic in transit to or from the territory of other contracting parties. No distinction shall be made which is based on the flag of vessels, the place of origin, departure, entry, exit or destination, or on any circumstances relating to the ownership of goods, of vessels or of other means of transport.

3. Any contracting party may require that traffic in transit through its territory be entered at the proper custom house, but, except in cases of failure to comply with applicable customs laws and regulations, such traffic coming from or going to the territory of other contracting parties shall not be subject to any unnecessary delays or restrictions and shall be exempt from customs duties and from all transit duties or other charges imposed in respect of transit, except charges for transportation or those commensurate with administrative expenses entailed by transit or with the cost of services rendered.

4. All charges and regulations imposed by contracting parties on traffic in transit to or from the territories of other contracting parties shall be reasonable, having regard to the conditions of the traffic.

5. With respect to all charges, regulations and formalities in connection with transit, each contracting party shall accord to traffic in transit to or from the territory of any other contracting party treatment no less favourable than the treatment accorded to traffic in transit to or from any third country.\*

6. Each contracting party shall accord to products which have been in transit through the territory of any other contracting party treatment no less favourable than that which would have been accorded to such products had they been transported from their place of origin to their destination without going through the territory of such other contracting party. Any contracting party shall, however, be free to maintain its requirements of direct consignment existing on the date of this Agreement, in respect of any goods in regard to which such direct consignment is a requisite condition of eligibility for entry of the goods at preferential rates of duty or has relation to the contracting party's prescribed method of valuation for duty purposes.

7. The provisions of this Article shall not apply to the operation of aircraft in transit, but shall apply to air transit of goods (including baggage).

## Article VI

*Anti-dumping and Countervailing Duties*

1. The contracting parties recognize that dumping, by which products of one country are introduced into the commerce of another country at less than the normal value of the products, is to be condemned if it causes or threatens material injury to an established industry in the territory of a contracting party or materially retards the establishment of a domestic industry. For the purposes of this Article, a product is to be considered as being introduced into the commerce of an importing country at less than its normal value, if the price of the product exported from one country to another

   (*a*) is less than the comparable price, in the ordinary course of trade, for the like product when destined for consumption in the exporting country, or,

   (*b*) in the absence of such domestic price, is less than either

      (i) the highest comparable price for the like product for export to any third country in the ordinary course of trade, or

      (ii) the cost of production of the product in the country of origin plus a reasonable addition for selling cost and profit.

Due allowance shall be made in each case for differences in conditions and terms of sale, for differences in taxation, and for other differences affecting price comparability.*

2. In order to offset or prevent dumping, a contracting party may levy on any dumped product an anti-dumping duty not greater in amount than the margin of dumping in respect of such product. For the purposes of this Article, the margin of dumping is the price difference determined in accordance with the provisions of paragraph 1.*

3. No countervailing duty shall be levied on any product of the territory of any contracting party imported into the territory of another contracting party in excess of an amount equal to the estimated bounty or subsidy determined to have been granted, directly or indirectly, on the manufacture, production or export of such product in the country of origin or exportation, including any special subsidy to the transportation of a particular product. The term " countervailing duty " shall be understood to mean a special duty levied for the purpose of offsetting any bounty or subsidy bestowed, directly or indirectly, upon the manufacture, production or export of any merchandise.*

4. No product of the territory of any contracting party imported into the territory of any other contracting party shall be subject to anti-dumping or countervailing duty by reason of the exemption of such product from duties or taxes borne by the like product when destined for consumption in the country of origin or exportation, or by reason of the refund of such duties or taxes.

5. No product of the territory of any contracting party imported into the territory of any other contracting party shall be subject to both anti-dumping and countervailing duties to compensate for the same situation of dumping or export subsidization.

6. (a) No contracting party shall levy any anti-dumping or countervailing duty on the importation of any product of the territory of another contracting party unless it determines that the effect of the dumping or subsidization, as the case may be, is such as to cause or threaten material injury to an established domestic industry, or is such as to retard materially the establishment of a domestic industry.

(b) The CONTRACTING PARTIES may waive the requirement of sub-paragraph (a) of this paragraph so as to permit a contracting party to levy an anti-dumping or countervailing duty on the importation of any product for the purpose of offsetting dumping or subsidization which causes or threatens material injury to an industry in the territory of another contracting party exporting the product concerned to the territory of the importing contracting party. The CONTRACTING PARTIES shall waive the requirements of sub-paragraph (a) of this paragraph, so as to permit the levying of a countervailing duty, in cases in which they find that a subsidy is causing or threatening material injury to an industry in the territory of another contracting party exporting the product concerned to the territory of the importing contracting party.*

(c) In exceptional circumstances, however, where delay might cause damage which would be difficult to repair, a contracting party may levy a countervailing duty for the purpose referred to in sub-paragraph (b) of this paragraph without the prior approval of the CONTRACTING PARTIES; *Provided* that such action shall be reported immediately to the CONTRACTING PARTIES and that the countervailing duty shall be withdrawn promptly if the CONTRACTING PARTIES disapprove.

7. A system for the stabilization of the domestic price or of the return to domestic producers of a primary commodity, independently of the movements of export prices, which results at times in the sale of the commodity for export at a price lower than the comparable price charged for the like commodity to buyers in the domestic market, shall be presumed not to result in material injury within the meaning of paragraph 6 if it is determined

by consultation among the contracting parties substantially interested in the commodity concerned that:

(a) the system has also resulted in the sale of the commodity for export at a price higher than the comparable price charged for the like commodity to buyers in the domestic market, and

(b) the system is so operated, either because of the effective regulation of production, or otherwise, as not to stimulate exports unduly or otherwise seriously prejudice the interests of other contracting parties.

## Article VII

### Valuation for Customs Purposes

1. The contracting parties recognize the validity of the general principles of valuation set forth in the following paragraphs of this Article, and they undertake to give effect to such principles, in respect of all products subject to duties or other charges * or restrictions on importation and exportation based upon or regulated in any manner by value. Moreover, they shall, upon a request by another contracting party review the operation of any of their laws or regulations relating to value for customs purposes in the light of these principles. The CONTRACTING PARTIES may request from contracting parties reports on steps taken by them in pursuance of the provisions of this Article.

2. (a) The value for customs purposes of imported merchandise should be based on the actual value of the imported merchandise on which duty is assessed, or of like merchandise, and should not be based on the value of merchandise of national origin or on arbitrary or fictitious values.*

(b) "Actual value" should be the price at which, at a time and place determined by the legislation of the country of importation, such or like merchandise is sold or offered for sale in the ordinary course of trade under fully competitive conditions. To the extent to which the price of such or like merchandise is governed by the quantity in a particular transaction, the price to be considered should uniformly be related to either (i) comparable quantities, or (ii) quantities not less favourable to importers than those in which the greater volume of the merchandise is sold in the trade between the countries of exportation and importation.*

(c) When the actual value is not ascertainable in accordance with sub-paragraph (b) of this paragraph, the value for customs purposes should be based on the nearest ascertainable equivalent of such value.*

3. The value for customs purposes of any imported product should not include the amount of any internal tax, applicable within the country of

origin or export, from which the imported product has been exempted or has been or will be relieved by means of refund.

4. (*a*) Except as otherwise provided for in this paragraph, where it is necessary for the purposes of paragraph 2 of this Article for a contracting party to convert into its own currency a price expressed in the currency of another country, the conversion rate of exchange to be used shall be based, for each currency involved, on the par value as established pursuant to the Articles of Agreement of the International Monetary Fund or on the rate of exchange recognized by the Fund, or on the par value established in accordance with a special exchange agreement entered into pursuant to Article XV of this Agreement.

(*b*) Where no such established par value and no such recognized rate of exchange exist, the conversion rate shall reflect effectively the current value of such currency in commercial transactions.

(*c*) The CONTRACTING PARTIES, in agreement with the International Monetary Fund, shall formulate rules governing the conversion by contracting parties of any foreign currency in respect of which multiple rates of exchange are maintained consistently with the Articles of Agreement of the International Monetary Fund. Any contracting party may apply such rules in respect of such foreign currencies for the purposes of paragraph 2 of this Article as an alternative to the use of par values. Until such rules are adopted by the CONTRACTING PARTIES, any contracting party may employ, in respect of any such foreign currency, rules of conversion for the purposes of paragraph 2 of this Article which are designed to reflect effectively the value of such foreign currency in commercial transactions.

(*d*) Nothing in this paragraph shall be construed to require any contracting party to alter the method of converting currencies for customs purposes which is applicable in its territory on the date of this Agreement, if such alteration would have the effect of increasing generally the amounts of duty payable.

5. The bases and methods for determining the value of products subject to duties or other charges or restrictions based upon or regulated in any manner by value should be stable and should be given sufficient publicity to enable traders to estimate, with a reasonable degree of certainty, the value for customs purposes.

## Article VIII

*Fees and Formalities connected with Importation and Exportation* \*

1. (*a*) All fees and charges of whatever character (other than import and export duties and other than taxes within the purview of Article III) imposed by contracting parties on or in connexion with importation or exportation shall be limited in amount to the approximate cost of services rendered and shall not represent an indirect protection to domestic products or a taxation of imports or exports for fiscal purposes.

(*b*) The contracting parties recognize the need for reducing the number and diversity of fees and charges referred to in sub-paragraph (*a*).

(*c*) The contracting parties also recognize the need for minimizing the incidence and complexity of import and export formalities and for decreasing and simplifying import and export documentation requirements.\*

2. A contracting party shall, upon request by another contracting party or by the CONTRACTING PARTIES, review the operation of its laws and regulations in the light of the provisions of this Article.

3. No contracting party shall impose substantial penalties for minor breaches of customs regulations or procedural requirements. In particular, no penalty in respect of any omission or mistake in customs documentation which is easily rectifiable and obviously made without fraudulent intent or gross negligence shall be greater than necessary to serve merely as a warning.

4. The provisions of this Article shall extend to fees, charges, formalities and requirements imposed by governmental authorities in connexion with importation and exportation, including those relating to:

(*a*) consular transactions, such as consular invoices and certificates;
(*b*) quantitative restrictions;
(*c*) licensing;
(*d*) exchange control;
(*e*) statistical services;
(*f*) documents, documentation and certification;
(*g*) analysis and inspection; and
(*h*) quarantine, sanitation and fumigation.

## Article IX

*Marks of Origin*

1. Each contracting party shall accord to the products of the territories of other contracting parties treatment with regard to marking requirements no less favourable than the treatment accorded to like products of any third country.

2. The contracting parties recognize that, in adopting and enforcing laws and regulations relating to marks of origin, the difficulties and inconveniences which such measures may cause to the commerce and industry of exporting countries should be reduced to a minimum, due regard being had to the necessity of protecting consumers against fraudulent or misleading indications.

3. Whenever it is administratively practicable to do so, contracting parties should permit required marks of origin to be affixed at the time of importation.

4. The laws and regulations of contracting parties relating to the marking of imported products shall be such as to permit compliance without seriously damaging the products, or materially reducing their value, or unreasonably increasing their cost.

5. As a general rule, no special duty or penalty should be imposed by any contracting party for failure to comply with marking requirements prior to importation unless corrective marking is unreasonably delayed or deceptive marks have been affixed or the required marking has been intentionally omitted.

6. The contracting parties shall co-operate with each other with a view to preventing the use of trade names in such manner as to misrepresent the true origin of a product, to the detriment of such distinctive regional or geographical names of products of the territory of a contracting party as are protected by its legislation. Each contracting party shall accord full and sympathetic consideration to such requests or representations as may be made by any other contracting party regarding the application of the undertaking set forth in the preceding sentence to names of products which have been communicated to it by the other contracting party.

## Article X

*Publication and Administration of Trade Regulations*

1. Laws, regulations, judicial decisions and administrative rulings of general application, made effective by any contracting party, pertaining to the classification or the valuation of products for customs purposes, or to rates of duty, taxes or other charges, or to requirements, restrictions or prohibitions on imports or exports or on the transfer of payments therefor, or affecting their sale, distribution, transportation, insurance, warehousing, inspection, exhibition, processing, mixing or other use, shall be published promptly in such a manner as to enable governments and traders to become acquainted with them. Agreements affecting international trade policy which are in force between the government or a governmental agency of any contracting party and the government or governmental agency of any other contracting party shall also be published. The provisions of this paragraph shall not require any contracting party to disclose confidential information which would impede law enforcement or otherwise be contrary to the public interest or would prejudice the legitimate commercial interests of particular enterprises, public or private.

2. No measure of general application taken by any contracting party effecting an advance in a rate of duty or other charge on imports under an established and uniform practice, or imposing a new or more burdensome requirement, restriction or prohibition on imports, or on the transfer of payments therefor, shall be enforced before such measure has been officially published.

3. (*a*) Each contracting party shall administer in a uniform, impartial and reasonable manner all its laws, regulations, decisions and rulings of the kind described in paragraph 1 of this Article.

(*b*) Each contracting party shall maintain, or institute as soon as practicable, judicial, arbitral or administrative tribunals or procedures for the purpose, *inter alia*, of the prompt review and correction of administrative action relating to customs matters. Such tribunals or procedures shall be independent of the agencies entrusted with administrative enforcement and their decisions shall be implemented by, and shall govern the practice of, such agencies unless an appeal is lodged with a court or tribunal of superior jurisdiction within the time prescribed for appeals to be lodged by importers; *Provided* that the central administration of such agency may take steps to obtain a review of the matter in another proceeding if there is good cause to believe that the decision is inconsistent with established principles of law or the actual facts.

(c) The provisions of sub-paragraph (b) of this paragraph shall not require the elimination or substitution of procedures in force in the territory of a contracting party on the date of this Agreement which in fact provide for an objective and impartial review of administrative action even though such procedures are not fully or formally independent of the agencies entrusted with administrative enforcement. Any contracting party employing such procedures shall, upon request, furnish the CONTRACTING PARTIES with full information thereon in order that they may determine whether such procedures conform to the requirements of this sub-paragraph.

## Article XI *

### *General Elimination of Quantitative Restrictions*

1. No prohibitions or restrictions other than duties, taxes or other charges, whether made effective through quotas, import or export licences or other measures, shall be instituted or maintained by any contracting party on the importation of any product of the territory of any other contracting party or on the exportation or sale for export of any product destined for the territory of any other contracting party.

2. The provisions of paragraph 1 of this Article shall not extend to the following:

(a) Export prohibitions or restrictions temporarily applied to prevent or relieve critical shortages of foodstuffs or other products essential to the exporting contracting party;

(b) Import and export prohibitions or restrictions necessary to the application of standards or regulations for the classification, grading or marketing of commodities in international trade;

(c) Import restrictions on any agricultural or fisheries product, imported in any form,* necessary to the enforcement of governmental measures which operate:

   (i) to restrict the quantities of the like domestic product permitted to be marketed or produced, or, if there is no substantial domestic production of the like product, of a domestic product for which the imported product can be directly substituted; or

   (ii) to remove a temporary surplus of the like domestic product, or, if there is no substantial domestic production of the like product, of a domestic product for which the imported product can be directly substituted, by making the surplus available

(iii) to restrict the quantities permitted to be produced of any animal product the production of which is directly dependent, wholly or mainly, on the imported commodity, if the domestic production of that commodity is relatively negligible.

Any contracting party applying restrictions on the importation of any product pursuant to sub-paragraph (*c*) of this paragraph shall give public notice of the total quantity or value of the product permitted to be imported during a specified future period and of any change in such quantity or value. Moreover, any restrictions applied under (i) above shall not be such as will reduce the total of imports relative to the total of domestic production, as compared with the proportion which might reasonably be expected to rule between the two in the absence of restrictions. In determining this proportion, the contracting party shall pay due regard to the proportion prevailing during a previous representative period and to any special factors* which may have affected or may be affecting the trade in the product concerned.

## Article XII *

*Restrictions to Safeguard the Balance of Payments*

1. Notwithstanding the provisions of paragraph 1 of Article XI, any contracting party, in order to safeguard its external financial position and its balance of payments, may restrict the quantity or value of merchandise permitted to be imported, subject to the provisions of the following paragraphs of this Article.

2. (*a*) Import restrictions instituted, maintained or intensified by a contracting party under this Article shall not exceed those necessary:

(i) to forestall the imminent threat of, or to stop, a serious decline in its monetary reserves, or

(ii) in the case of a contracting party with very low monetary reserves, to achieve a reasonable rate of increase in its reserves.

Due regard shall be paid in either case to any special factors which may be affecting the reserves of such contracting party or its need for reserves, including, where special external credits or other resources are available to it, the need to provide for the appropriate use of such credits or resources.

(*b*) Contracting parties applying restrictions under sub-paragraph (*a*) of this paragraph shall progressively relax them as such conditions improve, maintaining them only to the extent that the conditions specified in that sub-paragraph still justify their application. They shall eliminate the restrictions when conditions would no longer justify their institution or maintenance under that sub-paragraph.

3. (*a*) Contracting parties undertake, in carrying out their domestic policies, to pay due regard to the need for maintaining or restoring equilibrium in their balance of payments on a sound and lasting basis and to the desirability of avoiding an uneconomic employment of productive resources. They recognize that, in order to achieve these ends, it is desirable so far as possible to adopt measures which expand rather than contract international trade.

(*b*) Contracting parties applying restrictions under this Article may determine the incidence of the restrictions on imports of different products or classes of products in such a way as to give priority to the importation of those products which are more essential.

(*c*) Contracting parties applying restrictions under this Article undertake:

> (i) to avoid unnecessary damage to the commercial or economic interests of any other contracting party;*
>
> (ii) not to apply restrictions so as to prevent unreasonably the importation of any description of goods in minimum commercial quantities the exclusion of which would impair regular channels of trade; and
>
> (iii) not to apply restrictions which would prevent the importation of commercial samples or prevent compliance with patent, trade mark, copyright, or similar procedures.

(*d*) The contracting parties recognize that, as a result of domestic policies directed towards the achievement and maintenance of full and productive employment or towards the development of economic resources, a contracting party may experience a high level of demand for imports involving a threat to its monetary reserves of the sort referred to in paragraph 2 (*a*) of this Article. Accordingly, a contracting party otherwise complying with the provisions of this Article shall not be required to withdraw or modify restrictions on the ground that a change in those policies would render unnecessary restrictions which it is applying under this Article.

4. (*a*) Any contracting party applying new restrictions or raising the general level of its existing restrictions by a substantial intensification of the measures applied under this Article shall immediately after instituting or intensifying such restrictions (or, in circumstances in which prior consultation is practicable, before doing so) consult with the CONTRACTING

PARTIES as to the nature of its balance of payments difficulties, alternative corrective measures which may be available, and the possible effect of the restrictions on the economies of other contracting parties.

(b) On a date to be determined by them,* the CONTRACTING PARTIES shall review all restrictions still applied under this Article on that date. Beginning one year after that date, contracting parties applying import restrictions under this Article shall enter into consultations of the type provided for in sub-paragraph (a) of this paragraph with the CONTRACTING PARTIES annually.

(c) (i) If, in the course of consultations with a contracting party under sub-paragraph (a) or (b) above, the CONTRACTING PARTIES find that the restrictions are not consistent with the provisions of this Article or with those of Article XIII (subject to the provisions of Article XIV), they shall indicate the nature of the inconsistency and may advise that the restrictions be suitably modified.

(ii) If, however, as a result of the consultations, the CONTRACTING PARTIES determine that the restrictions are being applied in a manner involving an inconsistency of a serious nature with the provisions of this Article or with those of Article XIII (subject to the provisions of Article XIV) and that damage to the trade of any contracting party is caused or threatened thereby, they shall so inform the contracting party applying the restrictions and shall make appropriate recommendations for securing conformity with such provisions within a specified period of time. If such contracting party does not comply with these recommendations within the specified period, the CONTRACTING PARTIES may release any contracting party the trade of which is adversely affected by the restrictions from such obligations under this Agreement towards the contracting party applying the restrictions as they determine to be appropriate in the circumstances.

(d) The CONTRACTING PARTIES shall invite any contracting party which is applying restrictions under this Article to enter into consultations with them at the request of any contracting party which can establish a *prima facie* case that the restrictions are inconsistent with the provisions of this Article or with those of Article XIII (subject to the provisions of Article XIV) and that its trade is adversely affected thereby. However, no such invitation shall be issued unless the CONTRACTING PARTIES have ascertained that direct discussions between the contracting parties concerned have not been successful. If, as a result of the consultations with the CONTRACTING PARTIES, no agreement is reached and they determine that the restrictions are being applied inconsistently with such provisions, and that damage to the trade of the contracting party initiating the procedure is caused or threatened thereby, they shall recommend the withdrawal or modification of the restrictions. If the restrictions are not withdrawn or modified within such time as the CONTRACTING PARTIES may prescribe, they may release the contracting party initiating the procedure from such obligations under this Agreement towards the contracting party applying the restrictions as they determine to be appropriate in the circumstances.

(*e*) In proceeding under this paragraph, the CONTRACTING PARTIES shall have due regard to any special external factors adversely affecting the export trade of the contracting party applying restrictions.*

(*f*) Determinations under this paragraph shall be rendered expeditiously and, if possible, within sixty days of the initiation of the consultations.

5. If there is a persistent and widespread application of import restrictions under this Article, indicating the existence of a general disequilibrium which is restricting international trade, the CONTRACTING PARTIES shall initiate discussions to consider whether other measures might be taken, either by those contracting parties the balances of payments of which are under pressure or by those the balances of payments of which are tending to be exceptionally favourable, or by any appropriate intergovernmental organization, to remove the underlying causes of the disequilibrium. On the invitation of the CONTRACTING PARTIES, contracting parties shall participate in such discussions.

## Article XIII *

### Non-discriminatory Administration of Quantitative Restrictions

1. No prohibition or restriction shall be applied by any contracting party on the importation of any product of the territory of any other contracting party or on the exportation of any product destined for the territory of any other contracting party, unless the importation of the like product of all third countries or the exportation of the like product to all third countries is similarly prohibited or restricted.

2. In applying import restrictions to any product, contracting parties shall aim at a distribution of trade in such product approaching as closely as possible the shares which the various contracting parties might be expected to obtain in the absence of such restrictions, and to this end shall observe the following provisions:

(*a*) Wherever practicable, quotas representing the total amount of permitted imports (whether allocated among supplying countries or not) shall be fixed, and notice given of their amount in accordance with paragraph 3 (*b*) of this Article;

(*b*) In cases in which quotas are not practicable, the restrictions may be applied by means of import licences or permits without a quota;

(c) Contracting parties shall not, except for purposes of operating quotas allocated in accordance with sub-paragraph (d) of this paragraph, require that import licences or permits be utilized for the importation of the product concerned from a particular country or source;

(d) In cases in which a quota is allocated among supplying countries, the contracting party applying the restrictions may seek agreement with respect to the allocation of shares in the quota with all other contracting parties having a substantial interest in supplying the product concerned. In cases in which this method is not reasonably practicable, the contracting party concerned shall allot to contracting parties having a substantial interest in supplying the product shares based upon the proportions, supplied by such contracting parties during a previous representative period, of the total quantity or value of imports of the product, due account being taken of any special factors which may have affected or may be affecting the trade in the product. No conditions or formalities shall be imposed which would prevent any contracting party from utilizing fully the share of any such total quantity or value which has been allotted to it, subject to importation being made within any prescribed period to which the quota may relate.*

3. (a) In cases in which import licences are issued in connection with import restrictions, the contracting party applying the restrictions shall provide, upon the request of any contracting party having an interest in the trade in the product concerned, all relevant information concerning the administration of the restrictions, the import licences granted over a recent period and the distribution of such licences among supplying countries; *Provided* that there shall be no obligation to supply information as to the names of importing or supplying enterprises.

(b) In the case of import restrictions involving the fixing of quotas, the contracting party applying the restrictions shall give public notice of the total quantity or value of the product or products which will be permitted to be imported during a specified future period and of any change in such quantity or value. Any supplies of the product in question which were *en route* at the time at which public notice was given shall not be excluded from entry; *Provided* that they may be counted so far as practicable, against the quantity permitted to be imported in the period in question, and also, where necessary, against the quantities permitted to be imported in the next following period or periods; and *Provided* further that if any contracting party customarily exempts from such restrictions products entered for consumption or withdrawn from warehouse for consumption during a period of thirty days after the day of such public notice, such practice shall be considered full compliance with this sub-paragraph.

(c) In the case of quotas allocated among supplying countries, the contracting party applying the restrictions shall promptly inform all other contracting parties having an interest in supplying the product concerned of the shares in the quota currently allocated, by quantity or value, to the various supplying countries and shall give public notice thereof.

4. With regard to restrictions applied in accordance with paragraph 2 (d) of this Article or under paragraph 2 (c) of Article XI, the selection of a representative period for any product and the appraisal of any special factors * affecting the trade in the product shall be made initially by the contracting party applying the restriction; *Provided* that such contracting party shall, upon the request of any other contracting party having a substantial interest in supplying that product or upon the request of the CONTRACTING PARTIES, consult promptly with the other contracting party or the CONTRACTING PARTIES regarding the need for an adjustment of the proportion determined or of the base period selected, or for the reappraisal of the special factors involved, or for the elimination of conditions, formalities or any other provisions established unilaterally relating to the allocation of an adequate quota or its unrestricted utilization.

5. The provisions of this Article shall apply to any tariff quota instituted or maintained by any contracting party, and, in so far as applicable, the principles of this Article shall also extend to export restrictions.

### Article XIV *

*Exceptions to the Rule of Non-discrimination*

1. A contracting party which applies restrictions under Article XII or under Section B of Article XVIII may, in the application of such restrictions, deviate from the provisions of Article XIII in a manner having equivalent effect to restrictions on payments and transfers for current international transactions which that contracting party may at that time apply under Article VIII or XIV of the Articles of Agreement of the International Monetary Fund, or under analogous provisions of a special exchange agreement entered into pursuant to paragraph 6 of Article XV.*

2. A contracting party which is applying import restrictions under Article XII or under Section B of Article XVIII may, with the consent of the CONTRACTING PARTIES, temporarily deviate from the provisions of Article XIII in respect of a small part of its external trade where the benefits to the contracting party or contracting parties concerned substantially outweigh any injury which may result to the trade of other contracting parties.*

3. The provisions of Article XIII shall not preclude a group of territories having a common quota in the International Monetary Fund from applying against imports from other countries, but not among themselves, restrictions in accordance with the provisions of Article XII or of Section B of Article XVIII on condition that such restrictions are in all other respects consistent with the provisions of Article XIII.

4. A contracting party applying import restrictions under Article XII or under Section B of Article XVIII shall not be precluded by Articles XI to XV or Section B of Article XVIII of this Agreement from applying measures to direct its exports in such a manner as to increase its earnings of currencies which it can use without deviation from the provisions of Article XIII.

5. A contracting party shall not be precluded by Articles XI to XV, inclusive, or by Section B of Article XVIII, of this Agreement from applying quantitative restrictions:

(*a*) having equivalent effect to exchange restrictions authorized under Section 3 (*b*) of Article VII of the Articles of Agreement of the International Monetary Fund, or

(*b*) under the preferential arrangements provided for in Annex A of this Agreement, pending the outcome of the negotiations referred to therein.

## Article XV

### *Exchange Arrangements*

1. The CONTRACTING PARTIES shall seek co-operation with the International Monetary Fund to the end that the CONTRACTING PARTIES and the Fund may pursue a co-ordinated policy with regard to exchange questions within the jurisdiction of the Fund and questions of quantitative restrictions and other trade measures within the jurisdiction of the CONTRACTING PARTIES.

2. In all cases in which the CONTRACTING PARTIES are called upon to consider or deal with problems concerning monetary reserves, balances of payments or foreign exchange arrangements, they shall consult fully with the International Monetary Fund. In such consultations, the CONTRACTING PARTIES shall accept all findings of statistical and other facts presented by the Fund relating to foreign exchange, monetary reserves and balances of payments, and shall accept the determination of the Fund as to whether action by a contracting party in exchange matters is in accordance with the Articles of Agreement of the International Monetary Fund,

or with the terms of a special exchange agreement between that contracting party and the CONTRACTING PARTIES. The CONTRACTING PARTIES, in reaching their final decision in cases involving the criteria set forth in paragraph 2 (*a*) of Article XII or in paragraph 9 of Article XVIII, shall accept the determination of the Fund as to what constitutes a serious decline in the contracting party's monetary reserves, a very low level of its monetary reserves or a reasonable rate of increase in its monetary reserves, and as to the financial aspects of other matters covered in consultation in such cases.

3. The CONTRACTING PARTIES shall seek agreement with the Fund regarding procedures for consultation under paragraph 2 of this Article.

4. Contracting parties shall not, by exchange action, frustrate * the intent of the provisions of this Agreement, nor, by trade action, the intent of the provisions of the Articles of Agreement of the International Monetary Fund.

5. If the CONTRACTING PARTIES consider, at any time, that exchange restrictions on payments and transfers in connexion with imports are being applied by a contracting party in a manner inconsistent with the exceptions provided for in this Agreement for quantitative restrictions, they shall report thereon to the Fund.

6. Any contracting party which is not a member of the Fund shall, within a time to be determined by the CONTRACTING PARTIES after consultation with the Fund, become a member of the Fund, or, failing that, enter into a special exchange agreement with the CONTRACTING PARTIES. A contracting party which ceases to be a member of the Fund shall forthwith enter into a special exchange agreement with the CONTRACTING PARTIES. Any special exchange agreement entered into by a contracting party under this paragraph shall thereupon become part of its obligations under this Agreement.

7. (*a*) A special exchange agreement between a contracting party and the CONTRACTING PARTIES under paragraph 6 of this Article shall provide to the satisfaction of the CONTRACTING PARTIES that the objectives of this Agreement will not be frustrated as a result of action in exchange matters by the contracting party in question.

(*b*) The terms of any such agreement shall not impose obligations on the contracting party in exchange matters generally more restrictive than those imposed by the Articles of Agreement of the International Monetary Fund on members of the Fund.

8. A contracting party which is not a member of the Fund shall furnish such information within the general scope of section 5 of Article VIII of the Articles of Agreement of the International Monetary Fund as

the CONTRACTING PARTIES may require in order to carry out their functions under this Agreement.

9. Nothing in this Agreement shall preclude:

(*a*) the use by a contracting party of exchange controls or exchange restrictions in accordance with the Articles of Agreement of the International Monetary Fund or with that contracting party's special exchange agreement with the CONTRACTING PARTIES, or

(*b*) the use by a contracting party of restrictions or controls on imports or exports, the sole effect of which, additional to the effects permitted under Articles XI, XII, XIII and XIV, is to make effective such exchange controls or exchange restrictions.

## Article XVI *

### *Subsidies*

#### Section A—Subsidies in General

1. If any contracting party grants or maintains any subsidy, including any form of income or price support, which operates directly or indirectly to increase exports of any product from, or to reduce imports of any product into, its territory, it shall notify the CONTRACTING PARTIES in writing of the extent and nature of the subsidization, of the estimated effect of the subsidization on the quantity of the affected product or products imported into or exported from its territory and of the circumstances making the subsidization necessary. In any case in which it is determined that serious prejudice to the interests of any other contracting party is caused or threatened by any such subsidization, the contracting party granting the subsidy shall, upon request, discuss with the other contracting party or parties concerned, or with the CONTRACTING PARTIES, the possibility of limiting the subsidization.

#### Section B—Additional Provisions on Export Subsidies *

2. The contracting parties recognize that the granting by a contracting party of a subsidy on the export of any product may have harmful effects for other contracting parties, both importing and exporting, may cause undue disturbance to their normal commercial interests, and may hinder the achievement of the objectives of this Agreement.

3. Accordingly, contracting parties should seek to avoid the use of subsidies on the export of primary products. If, however, a contracting

party grants directly or indirectly any form of subsidy which operates to increase the export of any primary product from its territory, such subsidy shall not be applied in a manner which results in that contracting party having more than an equitable share of world export trade in that product, account being taken of the shares of the contracting parties in such trade in the product during a previous representative period, and any special factors which may have affected or may be affecting such trade in the product.*

4. Further, as from 1 January 1958 or the earliest practicable date thereafter, contracting parties shall cease to grant either directly or indirectly any form of subsidy on the export of any product other than a primary product which subsidy results in the sale of such product for export at a price lower than the comparable price charged for the like product to buyers in the domestic market. Until 31 December 1957 no contracting party shall extend the scope of any such subsidization beyond that existing on 1 January 1955 by the introduction of new, or the extension of existing, subsidies.*

5. The CONTRACTING PARTIES shall review the operation of the provisions of this Article from time to time with a view to examining its effectiveness, in the light of actual experience, in promoting the objectives of this Agreement and avoiding subsidization seriously prejudicial to the trade or interests of contracting parties.

## Article XVII

### *State Trading Enterprises*

1.* (*a*) Each contracting party undertakes that if it establishes or maintains a State enterprise, wherever located, or grants to any enterprise, formally or in effect, exclusive or special privileges,* such enterprise shall, in its purchases or sales involving either imports or exports, act in a manner consistent with the general principles of non-discriminatory treatment prescribed in this Agreement for governmental measures affecting imports or exports by private traders.

(*b*) The provisions of sub-paragraph (*a*) of this paragraph shall be understood to require that such enterprises shall, having due regard to the other provisions of this Agreement, make any such purchases or sales solely in accordance with commercial considerations,* including price, quality, availability, marketability, transportation and other conditions of purchase or sale, and shall afford the enterprises of the other contracting parties adequate opportunity, in accordance with customary business practice, to compete for participation in such purchases or sales.

3

(c) No contracting party shall prevent any enterprise (whether or not an enterprise described in sub-paragraph (a) of this paragraph) under its jurisdiction from acting in accordance with the principles of sub-paragraphs (a) and (b) of this paragraph.

2. The provisions of paragraph 1 of this Article shall not apply to imports of products for immediate or ultimate consumption in governmental use and not otherwise for resale or use in the production of goods * for sale. With respect to such imports, each contracting party shall accord to the trade of the other contracting parties fair and equitable treatment.

3. The contracting parties recognize that enterprises of the kind described in paragraph 1 (a) of this Article might be operated so as to create serious obstacles to trade; thus negotiations on a reciprocal and mutually advantageous basis designed to limit or reduce such obstacles are of importance to the expansion of international trade.*

4. (a) Contracting parties shall notify the CONTRACTING PARTIES of the products which are imported into or exported from their territories by enterprises of the kind described in paragraph 1 (a) of this Article.

(b) A contracting party establishing, maintaining or authorizing an import monopoly of a product, which is not the subject of a concession under Article II, shall, on the request of another contracting party having a substantial trade in the product concerned, inform the CONTRACTING PARTIES of the import mark-up * on the product during a recent representative period, or, when it is not possible to do so, of the price charged on the resale of the product.

(c) The CONTRACTING PARTIES may, at the request of a contracting party which has reason to believe that its interests under this Agreement are being adversely affected by the operations of an enterprise of the kind described in paragraph 1 (a), request the contracting party establishing, maintaining or authorizing such enterprise to supply information about its operations related to the carrying out of the provisions of this Agreement.

(d) The provisions of this paragraph shall not require any contracting party to disclose confidential information which would impede law enforcement or otherwise be contrary to the public interest or would prejudice the legitimate commercial interests of particular enterprises.

## Article XVIII *

*Governmental Assistance to Economic Development*

1. The contracting parties recognize that the attainment of the objectives of this Agreement will be facilitated by the progressive development

of their economies, particularly of those contracting parties the economies of which can only support low standards of living\* and are in the early stages of development.\*

2. The contracting parties recognize further that it may be necessary for those contracting parties, in order to implement programmes and policies of economic development designed to raise the general standard of living of their people, to take protective or other measures affecting imports, and that such measures are justified in so far as they facilitate the attainment of the objectives of this Agreement. They agree, therefore, that those contracting parties should enjoy additional facilities to enable them (*a*) to maintain sufficient flexibility in their tariff structure to be able to grant the tariff protection required for the establishment of a particular industry\* and (*b*) to apply quantitative restrictions for balance of payments purposes in a manner which takes full account of the continued high level of demand for imports likely to be generated by their programmes of economic development.

3. The contracting parties recognize finally that, with those additional facilities which are provided for in Sections A and B of this Article, the provisions of this Agreement would normally be sufficient to enable contracting parties to meet the requirements of their economic development. They agree, however, that there may be circumstances where no measure consistent with those provisions is practicable to permit a contracting party in the process of economic development to grant the governmental assistance required to promote the establishment of particular industries\* with a view to raising the general standard of living of its people. Special procedures are laid down in Sections C and D of this Article to deal with those cases.

4. (*a*) Consequently, a contracting party the economy of which can only support low standards of living\* and is in the early stages of development\* shall be free to deviate temporarily from the provisions of the other Articles of this Agreement, as provided in Sections A, B and C of this Article.

(*b*) A contracting party the economy of which is in the process of development, but which does not come within the scope of sub-paragraph (*a*) above, may submit applications to the CONTRACTING PARTIES under Section D of this Article.

5. The contracting parties recognize that the export earnings of contracting parties, the economies of which are of the type described in paragraph 4 (*a*) and (*b*) above and which depend on exports of a small number of primary commodities, may be seriously reduced by a decline in the sale of such commodities. Accordingly, when the exports of primary commodities by such a contracting party are seriously affected by measures taken

by another contracting party, it may have resort to the consultation provisions of Article XXII of this Agreement.

6. The CONTRACTING PARTIES shall review annually all measures applied pursuant to the provisions of Sections C and D of this Article.

## Section A

7. (*a*) If a contracting party coming within the scope of paragraph 4 (*a*) of this Article considers it desirable, in order to promote the establishment of a particular industry * with a view to raising the general standard of living of its people, to modify or withdraw a concession included in the appropriate Schedule annexed to this Agreement, it shall notify the CONTRACTING PARTIES to this effect and enter into negotiations with any contracting party with which such concession was initially negotiated, and with any other contracting party determined by the CONTRACTING PARTIES to have a substantial interest therein. If agreement is reached between such contracting parties concerned, they shall be free to modify or withdraw concessions under the appropriate Schedules to this Agreement in order to give effect to such agreement, including any compensatory adjustments involved.

(*b*) If agreement is not reached within sixty days after the notification provided for in sub-paragraph (*a*) above, the contracting party which proposes to modify or withdraw the concession may refer the matter to the CONTRACTING PARTIES, which shall promptly examine it. If they find that the contracting party which proposes to modify or withdraw the concession has made every effort to reach an agreement and that the compensatory adjustment offered by it is adequate, that contracting party shall be free to modify or withdraw the concession if, at the same time, it gives effect to the compensatory adjustment. If the CONTRACTING PARTIES do not find that the compensation offered by a contracting party proposing to modify or withdraw the concession is adequate, but find that it has made every reasonable effort to offer adequate compensation, that contracting party shall be free to proceed with such modification or withdrawal. If such action is taken, any other contracting party referred to in sub-paragraph (*a*) above shall be free to modify or withdraw substantially equivalent concessions initially negotiated with the contracting party which has taken the action.*

## Section B

8. The contracting parties recognize that contracting parties coming within the scope of paragraph 4 (*a*) of this Article tend, when they are in rapid process of development, to experience balance of payments difficulties arising mainly from efforts to expand their internal markets as well as from the instability in their terms of trade.

9. In order to safeguard its external financial position and to ensure a level of reserves adequate for the implementation of its programme of economic development, a contracting party coming within the scope of paragraph 4 (*a*) of this Article may, subject to the provisions of paragraphs 10 to 12, control the general level of its imports by restricting the quantity or value of merchandise permitted to be imported; *Provided* that the import restrictions instituted, maintained or intensified shall not exceed those necessary:

  (*a*) to forestall the threat of, or to stop, a serious decline in its monetary reserves, or

  (*b*) in the case of a contracting party with inadequate monetary reserves, to achieve a reasonable rate of increase in its reserves.

Due regard shall be paid in either case to any special factors which may be affecting the reserves of the contracting party or its need for reserves, including, where special external credits or other resources are available to it, the need to provide for the appropriate use of such credits or resources.

10. In applying these restrictions, the contracting party may determine their incidence on imports of different products or classes of products in such a way as to give priority to the importation of those products which are more essential in the light of its policy of economic development; *Provided* that the restrictions are so applied as to avoid unnecessary damage to the commercial or economic interests of any other contracting party and not to prevent unreasonably the importation of any description of goods in minimum commercial quantities the exclusion of which would impair regular channels of trade; and *Provided* further that the restrictions are not so applied as to prevent the importation of commercial samples or to prevent compliance with patent, trade mark, copyright or similar procedures.

11. In carrying out its domestic policies, the contracting party concerned shall pay due regard to the need for restoring equilibrium in its balance of payments on a sound and lasting basis and to the desirability of assuring an economic employment of productive resources. It shall progressively relax any restrictions applied under this Section as conditions improve, maintaining them only to the extent necessary under the terms of paragraph 9 of this Article and shall eliminate them when conditions no longer justify such maintenance; *Provided* that no contracting party shall be required to withdraw or modify restrictions on the ground that a change in its development policy would render unnecessary the restrictions which it is applying under this Section.*

12. (*a*) Any contracting party applying new restrictions or raising the general level of its existing restrictions by a substantial intensification

of the measures applied under this Section, shall immediately after instituting or intensifying such restrictions (or, in circumstances in which prior consultation is practicable, before doing so) consult with the CONTRACTING PARTIES as to the nature of its balance of payments difficulties, alternative corrective measures which may be available, and the possible effect of the restrictions on the economies of other contracting parties.

(*b*) On a date to be determined by them,* the CONTRACTING PARTIES shall review all restrictions still applied under this Section on that date. Beginning two years after that date, contracting parties applying restrictions under this Section shall enter into consultations of the type provided for in sub-paragraph (*a*) above with the CONTRACTING PARTIES at intervals of approximately, but not less than, two years according to a programme to be drawn up each year by the CONTRACTING PARTIES; *Provided* that no consultation under this sub-paragraph shall take place within two years after the conclusion of a consultation of a general nature under any other provision of this paragraph.

(*c*) (i) If, in the course of consultations with a contracting party under sub-paragraph (*a*) or (*b*) of this paragraph, the CONTRACTING PARTIES find that the restrictions are not consistent with the provisions of this Section or with those of Article XIII (subject to the provisions of Article XIV), they shall indicate the nature of the inconsistency and may advise that the restrictions be suitably modified.

(ii) If, however, as a result of the consultations, the CONTRACTING PARTIES determine that the restrictions are being applied in a manner involving an inconsistency of a serious nature with the provisions of this Section or with those of Article XIII (subject to the provisions of Article XIV) and that damage to the trade of any contracting party is caused or threatened thereby, they shall so inform the contracting party applying the restrictions and shall make appropriate recommendations for securing conformity with such provisions within a specified period. If such contracting party does not comply with these recommendations within the specified period, the CONTRACTING PARTIES may release any contracting party the trade of which is adversely affected by the restrictions from such obligations under this Agreement towards the contracting party applying the restrictions as they determine to be appropriate in the circumstances.

(*d*) The CONTRACTING PARTIES shall invite any contracting party which is applying restrictions under this Section to enter into consultations with them at the request of any contracting party which can establish a *prima facie* case that the restrictions are inconsistent with the provisions of this Section or with those of Article XIII (subject to the provisions of Article XIV) and that its trade is adversely affected thereby. However, no such invitation shall be issued unless the CONTRACTING PARTIES have ascertained that direct discussions between the contracting parties concerned have not been successful. If, as a result of the consultations with the CONTRACTING PARTIES no agreement is reached and they determine that the restrictions are being applied inconsistently with such provisions, and that damage to the trade of the contracting party initiating the procedure is caused or threatened thereby, they shall recommend the withdrawal or modification of the restrictions. If the restrictions are not withdrawn or modified within such time as the CONTRACTING PARTIES may prescribe, they may release the contracting party initiating the procedure from such obligations under this Agreement towards the contracting party applying the restrictions as they determine to be appropriate in the circumstances.

(*e*) If a contracting party against which action has been taken in accordance with the last sentence of sub-paragraph (*c*) (ii) or (*d*) of this paragraph, finds that the release of obligations authorized by the CONTRACTING PARTIES adversely affects the operation of its programme and policy of economic development, it shall be free, not later than sixty days after such action is taken, to give written notice to the Executive Secretary [1] to the CONTRACTING PARTIES of its intention to withdraw from this Agreement and such withdrawal shall take effect on the sixtieth day following the day on which the notice is received by him.

(*f*) In proceeding under this paragraph, the CONTRACTING PARTIES shall have due regard to the factors referred to in paragraph 2 of this Article. Determinations under this paragraph shall be rendered expeditiously and, if possible, within sixty days of the initiation of the consultations.

## Section C

13. If a contracting party coming within the scope of paragraph 4 (*a*) of this Article finds that governmental assistance is required to promote the establishment of a particular industry * with a view to raising the general standard of living of its people, but that no measure consistent with the other provisions of this Agreement is practicable to achieve that objective, it may have recourse to the provisions and procedures set out in this Section.*

14. The contracting party concerned shall notify the CONTRACTING PARTIES of the special difficulties which it meets in the achievement of the objective outlined in paragraph 13 of this Article and shall indicate the specific measure affecting imports which it proposes to introduce in order to remedy these difficulties. It shall not introduce that measure before the expiration of the time-limit laid down in paragraph 15 or 17, as the case may be, or if the measure affects imports of a product which is the subject of a concession included in the appropriate Schedule annexed to

---

[1] See Preface.

this Agreement, unless it has secured the concurrence of the CONTRACTING PARTIES in accordance with the provisions of paragraph 18; *Provided* that, if the industry receiving assistance has already started production, the contracting party may, after informing the CONTRACTING PARTIES, take such measures as may be necessary to prevent, during that period, imports of the product or products concerned from increasing substantially above a normal level.*

15. If, within thirty days of the notification of the measure, the CONTRACTING PARTIES do not request the contracting party concerned to consult with them,* that contracting party shall be free to deviate from the relevant provisions of the other Articles of this Agreement to the extent necessary to apply the proposed measure.

16. If it is requested by the CONTRACTING PARTIES to do so,* the contracting party concerned shall consult with them as to the purpose of the proposed measure, as to alternative measures which may be available under this Agreement, and as to the possible effect of the measure proposed on the commercial and economic interests of other contracting parties. If, as a result of such consultation, the CONTRACTING PARTIES agree that there is no measure consistent with the other provisions of this Agreement which is practicable in order to achieve the objective outlined in paragraph 13 of this Article, and concur * in the proposed measure, the contracting party concerned shall be released from its obligations under the relevant provisions of the other Articles of this Agreement to the extent necessary to apply that measure.

17. If, within ninety days after the date of the notification of the proposed measure under paragraph 14 of this Article, the CONTRACTING PARTIES have not concurred in such measure, the contracting party concerned may introduce the measure proposed after informing the CONTRACTING PARTIES.

18. If the proposed measure affects a product which is the subject of a concession included in the appropriate Schedule annexed to this Agreement, the contracting party concerned shall enter into consultations with any other contracting party with which the concession was initially negotiated, and with any other contracting party determined by the CONTRACTING PARTIES to have a substantial interest therein. The CONTRACTING PARTIES shall concur * in the measure if they agree that there is no measure consistent with the other provisions of this Agreement which is practicable in order to achieve the objective set forth in paragraph 13 of this Article, and if they are satisfied:

(*a*) that agreement has been reached with such other contracting parties as a result of the consultations referred to above, or

(b) if no such agreement has been reached within sixty days after the notification provided for in paragraph 14 has been received by the CONTRACTING PARTIES, that the contracting party having recourse to this Section has made all reasonable efforts to reach an agreement and that the interests of other contracting parties are adequately safeguarded.*

The contracting party having recourse to this Section shall thereupon be released from its obligations under the relevant provisions of the other Articles of this Agreement to the extent necessary to permit it to apply the measure.

19. If a proposed measure of the type described in paragraph 13 of this Article concerns an industry the establishment of which has in the initial period been facilitated by incidental protection afforded by restrictions imposed by the contracting party concerned for balance of payments purposes under the relevant provisions of this Agreement, that contracting party may resort to the provisions and procedures of this Section; *Provided* that it shall not apply the proposed measure without the concurrence * of the CONTRACTING PARTIES.*

20. Nothing in the preceding paragraphs of this Section shall authorize any deviation from the provisions of Articles I, II and XIII of this Agreement. The provisos to paragraph 10 of this Article shall also be applicable to any restriction under this Section.

21. At any time while a measure is being applied under paragraph 17 of this Article any contracting party substantially affected by it may suspend the application to the trade of the contracting party having recourse to this Section of such substantially equivalent concessions or other obligations under this Agreement the suspension of which the CONTRACTING PARTIES do not disapprove; * *Provided* that sixty days' notice of such suspension is given to the CONTRACTING PARTIES not later than six months after the measure has been introduced or changed substantially to the detriment of the contracting party affected. Any such contracting party shall afford adequate opportunity for consultation in accordance with the provisions of Article XXII of this Agreement.

## Section D

22. A contracting party coming within the scope of sub-paragraph 4 (b) of this Article desiring, in the interest of the development of its economy, to introduce a measure of the type described in paragraph 13 of this Article in respect of the establishment of a particular industry * may apply to the CONTRACTING PARTIES for approval of such measure. The CONTRACTING PARTIES shall promptly consult with such contracting party

and shall, in making their decision, be guided by the considerations set out in paragraph 16. If the CONTRACTING PARTIES concur * in the proposed measure the contracting party concerned shall be released from its obligations under the relevant provisions of the other Articles of this Agreement to the extent necessary to permit it to apply the measure. If the proposed measure affects a product which is the subject of a concession included in the appropriate Schedule annexed to this Agreement, the provisions of paragraph 18 shall apply.*

23. Any measure applied under this Section shall comply with the provisions of paragraph 20 of this Article.

## Article XIX

### *Emergency Action on Imports of Particular Products*

1. (*a*) If, as a result of unforeseen developments and of the effect of the obligations incurred by a contracting party under this Agreement, including tariff concessions, any product is being imported into the territory of that contracting party in such increased quantities and under such conditions as to cause or threaten serious injury to domestic producers in that territory of like or directly competitive products, the contracting party shall be free, in respect of such product, and to the extent and for such time as may be necessary to prevent or remedy such injury, to suspend the obligation in whole or in part or to withdraw or modify the concession.

(*b*) If any product, which is the subject of a concession with respect to a preference, is being imported into the territory of a contracting party in the circumstances set forth in sub-paragraph (*a*) of this paragraph, so as to cause or threaten serious injury to domestic producers of like or directly competitive products in the territory of a contracting party which receives or received such preference, the importing contracting party shall be free, if that other contracting party so requests, to suspend the relevant obligation in whole or in part or to withdraw or modify the concession in respect of the product, to the extent and for such time as may be necessary to prevent or remedy such injury.

2. Before any contracting party shall take action pursuant to the provisions of paragraph 1 of this Article, it shall give notice in writing to the CONTRACTING PARTIES as far in advance as may be practicable and shall afford the CONTRACTING PARTIES and those contracting parties having a substantial interest as exporters of the product concerned an opportunity to consult with it in respect of the proposed action. When such notice is given in relation to a concession with respect to a preference, the notice

shall name the contracting party which has requested the action. In critical circumstances, where delay would cause damage which it would be difficult to repair, action under paragraph 1 of this Article may be taken provisionally without prior consultation, on the condition that consultation shall be effected immediately after taking such action.

3. (*a*) If agreement among the interested contracting parties with respect to the action is not reached, the contracting party which proposes to take or continue the action shall, nevertheless, be free to do so, and if such action is taken or continued, the affected contracting parties shall then be free, not later than ninety days after such action is taken, to suspend, upon the expiration of thirty days from the day on which written notice of such suspension is received by the CONTRACTING PARTIES, the application to the trade of the contracting party taking such action, or, in the case envisaged in paragraph 1 (*b*) of this Article, to the trade of the contracting party requesting such action, of such substantially equivalent concessions or other obligations under this Agreement the suspension of which the CONTRACTING PARTIES do not disapprove.

(*b*) Notwithstanding the provisions of sub-paragraph (*a*) of this paragraph, where action is taken under paragraph 2 of this Article without prior consultation and causes or threatens serious injury in the territory of a contracting party to the domestic producers of products affected by the action, that contracting party shall, where delay would cause damage difficult to repair, be free to suspend, upon the taking of the action and throughout the period of consultation, such concessions or other obligations as may be necessary to prevent or remedy the injury.

## Article XX

### *General Exceptions*

Subject to the requirement that such measures are not applied in a manner which would constitute a means of arbitrary or unjustifiable discrimination between countries where the same conditions prevail, or a disguised restriction on international trade, nothing in this Agreement shall be construed to prevent the adoption or enforcement by any contracting party of measures:

(*a*) necessary to protect public morals;
(*b*) necessary to protect human, animal or plant life or health;
(*c*) relating to the importation or exportation of gold or silver;
(*d*) necessary to secure compliance with laws or regulations which are not inconsistent with the provisions of this Agreement, including

those relating to customs enforcement, the enforcement of monopolies operated under paragraph 4 of Article II and Article XVII, the protection of patents, trade marks and copyrights, and the prevention of deceptive practices;

(e) relating to the products of prison labour;

(f) imposed for the protection of national treasures of artistic, historic or archaeological value;

(g) relating to the conservation of exhaustible natural resources if such measures are made effective in conjunction with restrictions on domestic production or consumption;

(h) undertaken in pursuance of obligations under any intergovernmental commodity agreement which conforms to criteria submitted to the CONTRACTING PARTIES and not disapproved by them or which is itself so submitted and not so disapproved;*

(i) involving restrictions on exports of domestic materials necessary to ensure essential quantities of such materials to a domestic processing industry during periods when the domestic price of such materials is held below the world price as part of a governmental stabilization plan; *Provided* that such restrictions shall not operate to increase the exports of or the protection afforded to such domestic industry, and shall not depart from the provisions of this Agreement relating to non-discrimination;

(j) essential to the acquisition or distribution of products in general or local short supply; *Provided* that any such measures shall be consistent with the principle that all contracting parties are entitled to an equitable share of the international supply of such products, and that any such measures, which are inconsistent with the other provisions of this Agreement shall be discontinued as soon as the conditions giving rise to them have ceased to exist. The CONTRACTING PARTIES shall review the need for this sub-paragraph not later than 30 June 1960.

## Article XXI

### Security Exceptions

Nothing in this Agreement shall be construed

(a) to require any contracting party to furnish any information the disclosure of which it considers contrary to its essential security interests; or

(b) to prevent any contracting party from taking any action which it considers necessary for the protection of its essential security interests

    (i) relating to fissionable materials or the materials from which they are derived;

    (ii) relating to the traffic in arms, ammunition and implements of war and to such traffic in other goods and materials as is carried on directly or indirectly for the purpose of supplying a military establishment;

    (iii) taken in time of war or other emergency in international relations; or

(c) to prevent any contracting party from taking any action in pursuance of its obligations under the United Nations Charter for the maintenance of international peace and security.

## Article XXII

### Consultation

1. Each contracting party shall accord sympathetic consideration to, and shall afford adequate opportunity for consultation regarding, such representations as may be made by another contracting party with respect to any matter affecting the operation of this Agreement.

2. The CONTRACTING PARTIES may, at the request of a contracting party, consult with any contracting party or parties in respect of any matter for which it has not been possible to find a satisfactory solution through consultation under paragraph 1.

## Article XXIII

### Nullification or Impairment

1. If any contracting party should consider that any benefit accruing to it directly or indirectly under this Agreement is being nullified or impaired or that the attainment of any objective of the Agreement is being impeded as the result of

(a) the failure of another contracting party to carry out its obligations under this Agreement, or

(b) the application by another contracting party of any measure, whether or not it conflicts with the provisions of this Agreement, or

(c) the existence of any other situation,

the contracting party may, with a view to the satisfactory adjustment of the matter, make written representations or proposals to the other contracting party or parties which it considers to be concerned. Any contracting party thus approached shall give sympathetic consideration to the representations or proposals made to it.

2. If no satisfactory adjustment is effected between the contracting parties concerned within a reasonable time, or if the difficulty is of the type described in paragraph 1 (*c*) of this Article, the matter may be referred to the CONTRACTING PARTIES. The CONTRACTING PARTIES shall promptly investigate any matter so referred to them and shall make appropriate recommendations to the contracting parties which they consider to be concerned, or give a ruling on the matter, as appropriate. The CONTRACTING PARTIES may consult with contracting parties, with the Economic and Social Council of the United Nations and with any appropriate inter-governmental organization in cases where they consider such consultation necessary. If the CONTRACTING PARTIES consider that the circumstances are serious enough to justify such action, they may authorize a contracting party or parties to suspend the application to any other contracting party or parties of such concessions or other obligations under this Agreement as they determine to be appropriate in the circumstances. If the application to any contracting party of any concession or other obligation is in fact suspended, that contracting party shall then be free, not later than sixty days after such action is taken, to give written notice to the Executive Secretary[1] to the CONTRACTING PARTIES of its intention to withdraw from this Agreement and such withdrawal shall take effect upon the sixtieth day following the day on which such notice is received by him.

---

[1] See Preface.

# PART III

## Article XXIV

*Territorial Application—Frontier Traffic—Customs Unions and Free-trade Areas*

1. The provisions of this Agreement shall apply to the metropolitan customs territories of the contracting parties and to any other customs territories in respect of which this Agreement has been accepted under Article XXVI or is being applied under Article XXXIII or pursuant to the Protocol of Provisional Application. Each such customs territory shall, exclusively for the purposes of the territorial application of this Agreement, be treated as though it were a contracting party; *Provided* that the provisions of this paragraph shall not be construed to create any rights or obligations as between two or more customs territories in respect of which this Agreement has been accepted under Article XXVI or is being applied under Article XXXIII or pursuant to the Protocol of Provisional Application by a single contracting party.

2. For the purposes of this Agreement a customs territory shall be understood to mean any territory with respect to which separate tariffs or other regulations of commerce are maintained for a substantial part of the trade of such territory with other territories.

3. The provisions of this Agreement shall not be construed to prevent:

   (*a*) Advantages accorded by any contracting party to adjacent countries in order to facilitate frontier traffic;

   (*b*) Advantages accorded to the trade with the Free Territory of Trieste by countries contiguous to that territory, provided that such advantages are not in conflict with the Treaties of Peace arising out of the Second World War.

4. The contracting parties recognize the desirability of increasing freedom of trade by the development, through voluntary agreements, of closer integration between the economies of the countries parties to such agreements. They also recognize that the purpose of a customs union or of a free-trade area should be to facilitate trade between the constituent territories and not to raise barriers to the trade of other contracting parties with such territories.

5.  Accordingly, the provisions of this Agreement shall not prevent, as between the territories of contracting parties, the formation of a customs union or of a free-trade area or the adoption of an interim agreement necessary for the formation of a customs union or of a free-trade area; *Provided* that:

   (a) with respect to a customs union, or an interim agreement leading to the formation of a customs union, the duties and other regulations of commerce imposed at the institution of any such union or interim agreement in respect of trade with contracting parties not parties to such union or agreement shall not on the whole be higher or more restrictive than the general incidence of the duties and regulations of commerce applicable in the constituent territories prior to the formation of such union or the adoption of such interim agreement, as the case may be;

   (b) with respect to a free-trade area, or an interim agreement leading to the formation of a free-trade area, the duties and other regulations of commerce maintained in each of the constituent territories and applicable at the formation of such free-trade area or the adoption of such interim agreement to the trade of contracting parties not included in such area or not parties to such agreement shall not be higher or more restrictive than the corresponding duties and other regulations of commerce existing in the same constituent territories prior to the formation of the free-trade area, or interim agreement, as the case may be; and

   (c) any interim agreement referred to in sub-paragraphs (a) and (b) shall include a plan and schedule for the formation of such a customs union or of such a free-trade area within a reasonable length of time.

6.  If, in fulfilling the requirements of sub-paragraph 5 (a), a contracting party proposes to increase any rate of duty inconsistently with the provisions of Article II, the procedure set forth in Article XXVIII shall apply. In providing for compensatory adjustment, due account shall be taken of the compensation already afforded by the reductions brought about in the corresponding duty of the other constituents of the union.

7.  (a) Any contracting party deciding to enter into a customs union or free-trade area, or an interim agreement leading to the formation of such a union or area, shall promptly notify the CONTRACTING PARTIES and shall make available to them such information regarding the proposed union or area as will enable them to make such reports and recommendations to contracting parties as they may deem appropriate.

   (b) If, after having studied the plan and schedule included in an interim agreement referred to in paragraph 5 in consultation with the parties to that agreement and taking due account of the information made available in accordance with the provisions of sub-paragraph (*a*), the CONTRACTING PARTIES find that such agreement is not likely to result in the formation of a customs union or of a free-trade area within the period contemplated by the parties to the agreement or that such period is not a reasonable one, the CONTRACTING PARTIES shall make recommendations to the parties to the agreement. The parties shall not maintain or put into force, as the case may be, such agreement if they are not prepared to modify it in accordance with these recommendations.

(*c*) Any substantial change in the plan or schedule referred to in paragraph 5 (*c*) shall be communicated to the CONTRACTING PARTIES, which may request the contracting parties concerned to consult with them if the change seems likely to jeopardize or delay unduly the formation of the customs union or of the free-trade area.

8. For the purposes of this Agreement:

(*a*) A customs union shall be understood to mean the substitution of a single customs territory for two or more customs territories, so that

  (i) duties and other restrictive regulations of commerce (except, where necessary, those permitted under Articles XI, XII, XIII, XIV, XV and XX) are eliminated with respect to substantially all the trade between the constituent territories of the union or at least with respect to substantially all the trade in products originating in such territories, and,

  (ii) subject to the provisions of paragraph 9, substantially the same duties and other regulations of commerce are applied by each of the members of the union to the trade of territories not included in the union;

(*b*) A free-trade area shall be understood to mean a group of two or more customs territories in which the duties and other restrictive regulations of commerce (except, where necessary, those permitted under Articles XI, XII, XIII, XIV, XV and XX) are eliminated on substantially all the trade between the constituent territories in products originating in such territories.

9. The preferences referred to in paragraph 2 of Article I shall not be affected by the formation of a customs union or of a free-trade area but may be eliminated or adjusted by means of negotiations with contracting parties affected.* This procedure of negotiations with affected contracting parties shall, in particular, apply to the elimination of preferences required to conform with the provisions of paragraph 8 (*a*) (i) and paragraph 8 (*b*).

10. The CONTRACTING PARTIES may by a two-thirds majority approve proposals which do not fully comply with the requirements of paragraphs 5 to 9 inclusive, provided that such proposals lead to the formation of a customs union or a free-trade area in the sense of this Article.

11. Taking into account the exceptional circumstances arising out of the establishment of India and Pakistan as independent States and recognizing the fact that they have long constituted an economic unit, the contracting parties agree that the provisions of this Agreement shall not prevent the two countries from entering into special arrangements with respect to the trade between them, pending the establishment of their mutual trade relations on a definitive basis.*

12. Each contracting party shall take such reasonable measures as may be available to it to ensure observance of the provisions of this Agreement by the regional and local governments and authorities within its territory.

## Article XXV

### *Joint Action by the Contracting Parties*

1. Representatives of the contracting parties shall meet from time to time for the purpose of giving effect to those provisions of this Agreement which involve joint action and, generally, with a view to facilitating the operation and furthering the objectives of this Agreement. Wherever reference is made in this Agreement to the contracting parties acting jointly they are designated as the CONTRACTING PARTIES.

2. The Secretary-General of the United Nations is requested to convene the first meeting of the CONTRACTING PARTIES, which shall take place not later than March 1, 1948.

3. Each contracting party shall be entitled to have one vote at all meetings of the CONTRACTING PARTIES.

4. Except as otherwise provided for in this Agreement, decisions of the CONTRACTING PARTIES shall be taken by a majority of the votes cast.

5. In exceptional circumstances not elsewhere provided for in this Agreement, the CONTRACTING PARTIES may waive an obligation imposed upon a contracting party by this Agreement; *Provided* that any such decision shall be approved by a two-thirds majority of the votes cast and that such majority shall comprise more than half of the contracting parties. The CONTRACTING PARTIES may also by such a vote

(i) define certain categories of exceptional circumstances to which other voting requirements shall apply for the waiver of obligations, and

(ii) prescribe such criteria as may be necessary for the application of this paragraph.†

## Article XXVI

*Acceptance, Entry into Force and Registration*

1. The date of this Agreement shall be 30 October 1947.

2. This Agreement shall be open for acceptance by any contracting party which, on 1 March 1955, was a contracting party or was negotiating with a view to accession to this Agreement.

3. This Agreement, done in a single English original and in a single French original, both texts authentic, shall be deposited with the Secretary-General of the United Nations, who shall furnish certified copies thereof to all interested governments.

4. Each government accepting this Agreement shall deposit an instrument of acceptance with the Executive Secretary[1] to the CONTRACTING PARTIES, who will inform all interested governments of the date of deposit of each instrument of acceptance and of the day on which this Agreement enters into force under paragraph 6 of this Article.

5. (*a*) Each government accepting this Agreement does so in respect of its metropolitan territory and of the other territories for which it has international responsibility, except such separate customs territories as it shall notify to the Executive Secretary[1] to the CONTRACTING PARTIES at the time of its own acceptance.

(*b*) Any government, which has so notified the Executive Secretary[1] under the exceptions in sub-paragraph (*a*) of this paragraph, may at any time give notice to the Executive Secretary[1] that its acceptance shall be effective in respect of any separate customs territory or territories so excepted and such notice shall take effect on the thirtieth day following the day on which it is received by the Executive Secretary.[1]

(*c*) If any of the customs territories, in respect of which a contracting party has accepted this Agreement, possesses or acquires full autonomy in the conduct of its external commercial relations and of the other matters

---

† The authentic text erroneously reads " sub-paragraph ".
[1] See Preface.

provided for in this Agreement, such territory shall, upon sponsorship through a declaration by the responsible contracting party establishing the above-mentioned fact, be deemed to be a contracting party.

6. This Agreement shall enter into force, as among the governments which have accepted it, on the thirtieth day following the day on which instruments of acceptance have been deposited with the Executive Secretary[1] to the CONTRACTING PARTIES on behalf of governments named in Annex H, the territories of which account for 85 per centum of the total external trade of the territories of such governments, computed in accordance with the applicable column of percentages set forth therein. The instrument of acceptance of each other government shall take effect on the thirtieth day following the day on which such instrument has been deposited.

7. The United Nations is authorized to effect registration of this Agreement as soon as it enters into force.

## Article XXVII

### *Withholding or Withdrawal of Concessions*

Any contracting party shall at any time be free to withhold or to withdraw in whole or in part any concession, provided for in the appropriate Schedule annexed to this Agreement, in respect of which such contracting party determines that it was initially negotiated with a government which has not become, or has ceased to be, a contracting party. A contracting party taking such action shall notify the CONTRACTING PARTIES and, upon request, consult with contracting parties which have a substantial interest in the product concerned.

## Article XXVIII *

### *Modification of Schedules*

1. On the first day of each three-year period, the first period beginning on 1 January 1958 (or on the first day of any other period * that may be specified by the CONTRACTING PARTIES by two-thirds of the votes cast) a contracting party (hereafter in this Article referred to as the "applicant contracting party") may, by negotiation and agreement with any contracting party with which such concession was initially negotiated and with any other contracting party determined by the CONTRACTING PARTIES to have a principal supplying interest* (which two preceding categories of contracting

---

[1] See Preface.

parties, together with the applicant contracting party, are in this Article hereinafter referred to as the "contracting parties primarily concerned"), and subject to consultation with any other contracting party determined by the CONTRACTING PARTIES to have a substantial interest* in such concession, modify or withdraw a concession* included in the appropriate Schedule annexed to this Agreement.

2. In such negotiations and agreement, which may include provision for compensatory adjustment with respect to other products, the contracting parties concerned shall endeavour to maintain a general level of reciprocal and mutually advantageous concessions not less favourable to trade than that provided for in this Agreement prior to such negotiations.

3. (a) If agreement between the contracting parties primarily concerned cannot be reached before 1 January 1958 or before the expiration of a period envisaged in paragraph 1 of this Article, the contracting party which proposes to modify or withdraw the concession shall, nevertheless, be free to do so and if such action is taken any contracting party with which such concession was initially negotiated, any contracting party determined under paragraph 1 to have a principal supplying interest and any contracting party determined under paragraph 1 to have a substantial interest shall then be free not later than six months after such action is taken, to withdraw, upon the expiration of thirty days from the day on which written notice of such withdrawal is received by the CONTRACTING PARTIES, substantially equivalent concessions initially negotiated with the applicant contracting party.

(b) If agreement between the contracting parties primarily concerned is reached but any other contracting party determined under paragraph 1 of this Article to have a substantial interest is not satisfied, such other contracting party shall be free, not later than six months after action under such agreement is taken, to withdraw, upon the expiration of thirty days from the day on which written notice of such withdrawal is received by the CONTRACTING PARTIES, substantially equivalent concessions initially negotiated with the applicant contracting party.

4. The CONTRACTING PARTIES may, at any time, in special circumstances, authorize* a contracting party to enter into negotiations for modification or withdrawal of a concession included in the appropriate Schedule annexed to this Agreement subject to the following procedures and conditions:

(a) Such negotiations* and any related consultations shall be conducted in accordance with the provisions of paragraphs 1 and 2 of this Article.

(b) If agreement between the contracting parties primarily concerned is reached in the negotiations, the provisions of paragraph 3 (b) of this Article shall apply.

(c) If agreement between the contracting parties primarily concerned is not reached within a period of sixty days* after negotiations have been authorized, or within such longer period as the CONTRACTING PARTIES may have prescribed, the applicant contracting party may refer the matter to the CONTRACTING PARTIES.

(d) Upon such reference, the CONTRACTING PARTIES shall promptly examine the matter and submit their views to the contracting parties primarily concerned with the aim of achieving a settlement. If a settlement is reached, the provisions of paragraph 3 (b) shall apply as if agreement between the contracting parties primarily concerned had been reached. If no settlement is reached between the contracting parties primarily concerned, the applicant contracting party shall be free to modify or withdraw the concession, unless the CONTRACTING PARTIES determine that the applicant contracting party has unreasonably failed to offer adequate compensation.* If such action is taken, any contracting party with which the concession was initially negotiated, any contracting party determined under paragraph 4 (a) to have a principal supplying interest and any contracting party determined under paragraph 4 (a) to have a substantial interest, shall be free, not later than six months after such action is taken, to modify or withdraw, upon the expiration of thirty days from the day on which written notice of such withdrawal is received by the CONTRACTING PARTIES, substantially equivalent concessions initially negotiated with the applicant contracting party.

5. Before 1 January 1958 and before the end of any period envisaged in paragraph 1 a contracting party may elect by notifying the CONTRACTING PARTIES to reserve the right, for the duration of the next period, to modify the appropriate Schedule in accordance with the procedures of paragraphs 1 to 3. If a contracting party so elects, other contracting parties shall have the right, during the same period, to modify or withdraw, in accordance with the same procedures, concessions initially negotiated with that contracting party.

## Article XXVIII bis

### Tariff Negotiations

1. The contracting parties recognize that customs duties often constitute serious obstacles to trade; thus negotiations on a reciprocal and mutually advantageous basis, directed to the substantial reduction of the general level of tariffs and other charges on imports and exports and in particular to the reduction of such high tariffs as discourage the importation even of minimum quantities, and conducted with due regard to the objectives of this Agreement

and the varying needs of individual contracting parties, are of great importance to the expansion of international trade. The CONTRACTING PARTIES may therefore sponsor such negotiations from time to time.

2. (*a*) Negotiations under this Article may be carried out on a selective product-by-product basis or by the application of such multilateral procedures as may be accepted by the contracting parties concerned. Such negotiations may be directed towards the reduction of duties, the binding of duties at then existing levels or undertakings that individual duties or the average duties on specified categories of products shall not exceed specified levels. The binding against increase of low duties or of duty-free treatment shall, in principle, be recognized as a concession equivalent in value to the reduction of high duties.

(*b*) The contracting parties recognize that in general the success of multilateral negotiations would depend on the participation of all contracting parties which conduct a substantial proportion of their external trade with one another.

3. Negotiations shall be conducted on a basis which affords adequate opportunity to take into account:

(*a*) the needs of individual contracting parties and individual industries;

(*b*) the needs of less-developed countries for a more flexible use of tariff protection to assist their economic development and the special needs of these countries to maintain tariffs for revenue purposes; and

(*c*) all other relevant circumstances, including the fiscal,* developmental, strategic and other needs of the contracting parties concerned.

## Article XXIX

### *The Relation of this Agreement to the Havana Charter*

1. The contracting parties undertake to observe to the fullest extent of their executive authority the general principles of Chapters I to VI inclusive and of Chapter IX of the Havana Charter pending their acceptance of it in accordance with their constitutional procedures.*

2. Part II of this Agreement shall be suspended on the day on which the Havana Charter enters into force.

3. If by September 30, 1949, the Havana Charter has not entered into force, the contracting parties shall meet before December 31, 1949, to agree whether this Agreement shall be amended, supplemented or maintained.

4. If at any time the Havana Charter should cease to be in force, the CONTRACTING PARTIES shall meet as soon as practicable thereafter to agree whether this Agreement shall be supplemented, amended or maintained. Pending such agreement, Part II of this Agreement shall again enter into force; *Provided* that the provisions of Part II other than Article XXIII shall be replaced, *mutatis mutandis*, in the form in which they then appeared in the Havana Charter; and *Provided* further that no contracting party shall be bound by any provisions which did not bind it at the time when the Havana Charter ceased to be in force.

5. If any contracting party has not accepted the Havana Charter by the date upon which it enters into force, the CONTRACTING PARTIES shall confer to agree whether, and if so in what way, this Agreement in so far as it affects relations between such contracting party and other contracting parties, shall be supplemented or amended. Pending such agreement the provisions of Part II of this Agreement shall, notwithstanding the provisions of paragraph 2 of this Article, continue to apply as between such contracting party and other contracting parties.

6. Contracting parties which are Members of the International Trade Organization shall not invoke the provisions of this Agreement so as to prevent the operation of any provision of the Havana Charter. The application of the principle underlying this paragraph to any contracting party which is not a Member of the International Trade Organization shall be the subject of an agreement pursuant to paragraph 5 of this Article.

## Article XXX

### *Amendments*

1. Except where provision for modification is made elsewhere in this Agreement, amendments to the provisions of Part I of this Agreement or to the provisions of Article XXIX or of this Article shall become effective upon acceptance by all the contracting parties, and other amendments to this Agreement shall become effective, in respect of those contracting parties which accept them, upon acceptance by two-thirds of the contracting parties and thereafter for each other contracting party upon acceptance by it.

2. Any contracting party accepting an amendment to this Agreement shall deposit an instrument of acceptance with the Secretary-General of the United Nations within such period as the CONTRACTING PARTIES may specify. The CONTRACTING PARTIES may decide that any amendment made effective under this Article is of such a nature that any contracting party

which has not accepted it within a period specified by the CONTRACTING PARTIES shall be free to withdraw from this Agreement, or to remain a contracting party with the consent of the CONTRACTING PARTIES.

## Article XXXI

### *Withdrawal*

Without prejudice to the provisions of paragraph 12 of Article XVIII, of Article XXIII or of paragraph 2 of Article XXX, any contracting party may withdraw from this Agreement, or may separately withdraw on behalf of any of the separate customs territories for which it has international responsibility and which at the time possesses full autonomy in the conduct of its external commercial relations and of the other matters provided for in this Agreement. The withdrawal shall take effect upon the expiration of six months from the day on which written notice of withdrawal is received by the Secretary-General of the United Nations.

## Article XXXII

### *Contracting Parties*

1. The contracting parties to this Agreement shall be understood to mean those governments which are applying the provisions of this Agreement under Articles XXVI or XXXIII or pursuant to the Protocol of Provisional Application.

2. At any time after the entry into force of this Agreement pursuant to paragraph 6 of Article XXVI, those contracting parties which have accepted this Agreement pursuant to paragraph 4 of Article XXVI may decide that any contracting party which has not so accepted it shall cease to be a contracting party.

## Article XXXIII

### *Accession*

A government not party to this Agreement, or a government acting on behalf of a separate customs territory possessing full autonomy in the conduct of its external commercial relations and of the other matters provided for in this Agreement, may accede to this Agreement, on its own behalf or on behalf of that territory, on terms to be agreed between such government and the CONTRACTING PARTIES. Decisions of the CONTRACTING PARTIES under this paragraph shall be taken by a two-thirds majority.

## Article XXXIV

*Annexes*

The annexes to this Agreement are hereby made an integral part of this Agreement.

## Article XXXV

*Non-application of the Agreement between
particular Contracting Parties*

1. This Agreement, or alternatively Article II of this Agreement, shall not apply as between any contracting party and any other contracting party if:

   (*a*) the two contracting parties have not entered into tariff negotiations with each other, and

   (*b*) either of the contracting parties, at the time either becomes a contracting party, does not consent to such application.

2. The CONTRACTING PARTIES may review the operation of this Article in particular cases at the request of any contracting party and make appropriate recommendations.

# PART IV*

## TRADE AND DEVELOPMENT

### Article XXXVI

*Principles and Objectives*

1.* The contracting parties,

(*a*) recalling that the basic objectives of this Agreement include the raising of standards of living and the progressive development of the economies of all contracting parties, and considering that the attainment of these objectives is particularly urgent for less-developed contracting parties;

(*b*) considering that export earnings of the less-developed contracting parties can play a vital part in their economic development and that the extent of this contribution depends on the prices paid by the less-developed contracting parties for essential imports, the volume of their exports, and the prices received for these exports;

(*c*) noting, that there is a wide gap between standards of living in less-developed countries and in other countries;

(*d*) recognizing that individual and joint action is essential to further the development of the economies of less-developed contracting parties and to bring about a rapid advance in the standards of living in these countries;

(*e*) recognizing that international trade as a means of achieving economic and social advancement should be governed by such rules and procedures—and measures in conformity with such rules and procedures—as are consistent with the objectives set forth in this Article;

(*f*) noting that the CONTRACTING PARTIES may enable less-developed contracting parties to use special measures to promote their trade and development;

agree as follows.

2. There is need for a rapid and sustained expansion of the export earnings of the less-developed contracting parties.

3. There is need for positive efforts designed to ensure that less-developed contracting parties secure a share in the growth in international trade commensurate with the needs of their economic development.

4. Given the continued dependence of many less-developed contracting parties on the exportation of a limited range of primary products,* there is need to provide in the largest possible measure more favourable and acceptable conditions of access to world markets for these products, and wherever appropriate to devise measures designed to stabilize and improve conditions of world markets in these products, including in particular measures designed to attain stable, equitable and remunerative prices, thus permitting an expansion of world trade and demand and a dynamic and steady growth of the real export earnings of these countries so as to provide them with expanding resources for their economic development.

5. The rapid expansion of the economies of the less-developed contracting parties will be facilitated by a diversification * of the structure of their economies and the avoidance of an excessive dependence on the export of primary products. There is, therefore, need for increased access in the largest possible measure to markets under favourable conditions for processed and manufactured products currently or potentially of particular export interest to less-developed contracting parties.

6. Because of the chronic deficiency in the export proceeds and other foreign exchange earnings of less-developed contracting parties, there are important inter-relationships between trade and financial assistance to development. There is, therefore, need for close and continuing collaboration between the CONTRACTING PARTIES and the international lending agencies so that they can contribute most effectively to alleviating the burdens these less-developed contracting parties assume in the interest of their economic development.

7. There is need for appropriate collaboration between the CONTRACTING PARTIES, other intergovernmental bodies and the organs and agencies of the United Nations system, whose activities relate to the trade and economic development of less-developed countries.

8. The developed contracting parties do not expect reciprocity for commitments made by them in trade negotiations to reduce or remove tariffs and other barriers to the trade of less-developed contracting parties.*

9. The adoption of measures to give effect to these principles and objectives shall be a matter of conscious and purposeful effort on the part of the contracting parties both individually and jointly.

## Article XXXVII

*Commitments*

1. The developed contracting parties shall to the fullest extent possible—that is, except when compelling reasons, which may include legal reasons, make it impossible—give effect to the following provisions:

   (*a*) accord high priority to the reduction and elimination of barriers to products currently or potentially of particular export interest to less-developed contracting parties, including customs duties and other restrictions which differentiate unreasonably between such products in their primary and in their processed forms;*

   (*b*) refrain from introducing, or increasing the incidence of, customs duties or non-tariff import barriers on products currently or potentially of particular export interest to less-developed contracting parties; and

   (*c*) (i) refrain from imposing new fiscal measures, and

   (ii) in any adjustments of fiscal policy accord high priority to the reduction and elimination of fiscal measures,

   which would hamper, or which hamper, significantly the growth of consumption of primary products, in raw or processed form, wholly or mainly produced in the territories of less-developed contracting parties, and which are applied specifically to those products.

2. (*a*) Whenever it is considered that effect is not being given to any of the provisions of sub-paragraph (*a*), (*b*) or (*c*) of paragraph 1, the matter shall be reported to the CONTRACTING PARTIES either by the contracting party not so giving effect to the relevant provisions or by any other interested contracting party.

   (*b*) (i) The CONTRACTING PARTIES shall, if requested so to do by any interested contracting party, and without prejudice to any bilateral consultations that may be undertaken, consult with the contracting party concerned and all interested contracting parties with respect to the matter with a view to reaching solutions satisfactory to all contracting parties concerned in order to further the objectives set forth in Article XXXVI. In the course of these consultations, the reasons given in cases where effect was not being given to the provisions of sub-paragraph (*a*), (*b*) or (*c*) of paragraph 1 shall be examined.

   (ii) As the implementation of the provisions of sub-paragraph (*a*), (*b*) or (*c*) of paragraph 1 by individual contracting parties may in some cases be more readily achieved where action is taken jointly with other developed contracting parties, such consultation might, where appropriate, be directed towards this end.

(iii) The consultations by the CONTRACTING PARTIES might also, in appropriate cases, be directed towards agreement on joint action designed to further the objectives of this Agreement as envisaged in paragraph 1 of Article XXV.

3. The developed contracting parties shall:

(*a*) make every effort, in cases where a government directly or indirectly determines the resale price of products wholly or mainly produced in the territories of less-developed contracting parties, to maintain trade margins at equitable levels;

(*b*) give active consideration to the adoption of other measures * designed to provide greater scope for the development of imports from less-developed contracting parties and collaborate in appropriate international action to this end;

(*c*) have special regard to the trade interests of less-developed contracting parties when considering the application of other measures permitted under this Agreement to meet particular problems and explore all possibilities of constructive remedies before applying such measures where they would affect essential interests of those contracting parties.

4. Less-developed contracting parties agree to take appropriate action in implementation of the provisions of Part IV for the benefit of the trade of other less-developed contracting parties, in so far as such action is consistent with their individual present and future development, financial and trade needs taking into account past trade developments as well as the trade interests of less-developed contracting parties as a whole.

5. In the implementation of the commitments set forth in paragraphs 1 to 4 each contracting party shall afford to any other interested contracting party or contracting parties full and prompt opportunity for consultations under the normal procedures of this Agreement with respect to any matter or difficulty which may arise.

## Article XXXVIII

### *Joint Action*

1. The contracting parties shall collaborate jointly, within the framework of this Agreement and elsewhere, as appropriate, to further the objectives set forth in Article XXXVI.

2. In particular, the CONTRACTING PARTIES shall:

(a) where appropriate, take action, including action through international arrangements, to provide improved and acceptable conditions of access to world markets for primary products of particular interest to less-developed contracting parties and to devise measures designed to stabilize and improve conditions of world markets in these products including measures designed to attain stable, equitable and remunerative prices for exports of such products;

(b) seek appropriate collaboration in matters of trade and development policy with the United Nations and its organs and agencies, including any institutions that may be created on the basis of recommendations by the United Nations Conference on Trade and Development;

(c) collaborate in analysing the development plans and policies of individual less-developed contracting parties and in examining trade and aid relationships with a view to devising concrete measures to promote the development of export potential and to facilitate access to export markets for the products of the industries thus developed and, in this connexion, seek appropriate collaboration with governments and international organizations, and in particular with organizations having competence in relation to financial assistance for economic development, in systematic studies of trade and aid relationships in individual less-developed contracting parties aimed at obtaining a clear analysis of export potential, market prospects and any further action that may be required;

(d) keep under continuous review the development of world trade with special reference to the rate of growth of the trade of less-developed contracting parties and make such recommendations to contracting parties as may, in the circumstances, be deemed appropriate;

(e) collaborate in seeking feasible methods to expand trade for the purpose of economic development, through international harmonization and adjustment of national policies and regulations, through technical and commercial standards affecting production, transportation and marketing, and through export promotion by the establishment of facilities for the increased flow of trade information and the development of market research; and

(f) establish such institutional arrangements as may be necessary to further the objectives set forth in Article XXXVI and to give effect to the provisions of this Part.

## ANNEX A

### List of Territories referred to in Paragraph 2 (*a*) of Article I

United Kingdom of Great Britain and Northern Ireland
Dependent territories of the United Kingdom of Great Britain and Northern Ireland
Canada
Commonwealth of Australia
Dependent territories of the Commonwealth of Australia
New Zealand
Dependent territories of New Zealand
Union of South Africa including South West Africa
Ireland
India (as on April 10, 1947)
Newfoundland
Southern Rhodesia
Burma
Ceylon

Certain of the territories listed above have two or more preferential rates in force for certain products. Any such territory may, by agreement with the other contracting parties which are principal suppliers of such products at the most-favoured-nation rate, substitute for such preferential rates a single preferential rate which shall not on the whole be less favourable to suppliers at the most-favoured-nation rate than the preferences in force prior to such substitution.

The imposition of an equivalent margin of tariff preference to replace a margin of preference in an internal tax existing on April 10, 1947 exclusively between two or more of the territories listed in this Annex or to replace the preferential quantitative arrangements described in the following paragraph, shall not be deemed to constitute an increase in a margin of tariff preference.

The preferential arrangements referred to in paragraph 5 (*b*) of Article XIV are those existing in the United Kingdom on April 10, 1947, under contractual agreements with the Governments of Canada, Australia and New Zealand, in respect of chilled and frozen beef and veal, frozen mutton and lamb, chilled and frozen pork, and bacon. It is the intention, without prejudice to any action taken under sub-paragraph (*h*) † of Article XX, that these arrangements shall be eliminated or replaced by tariff preferences, and that negotiations to this end shall take place as soon as practicable among the countries substantially concerned or involved.

The film hire tax in force in New Zealand on April 10, 1947, shall, for the purposes of this Agreement, be treated as a customs duty under Article I. The

---

† The authentic text erroneously reads " part I (*h*) ".

renters' film quota in force in New Zealand on April 10, 1947, shall, for the purposes of this Agreement, be treated as a screen quota under Article IV.

The Dominions of India and Pakistan have not been mentioned separately in the above list since they had not come into existence as such on the base date of April 10, 1947.

## ANNEX B

### List of Territories of the French Union referred to in Paragraph 2 (b) of Article I

France
French Equatorial Africa (Treaty Basin of the Congo [1] and other territories)
French West Africa
Cameroons under French Trusteeship [1]
French Somali Coast and Dependencies
French Establishments in Oceania
French Establishments in the Condominium of the New Hebrides [1]
Indo-China
Madagascar and Dependencies
Morocco (French zone) [1]
New Caledonia and Dependencies
Saint-Pierre and Miquelon
Togo under French Trusteeship [1]
Tunisia

## ANNEX C

### List of Territories referred to in Paragraph 2 (b) of Article I as respects the Customs Union of Belgium, Luxemburg and the Netherlands

The Economic Union of Belgium and Luxemburg
Belgian Congo
Ruanda Urundi
Netherlands
New Guinea
Surinam
Netherlands Antilles
Republic of Indonesia

For imports into the territories constituting the Customs Union only.

## ANNEX D

### List of Territories referred to in Paragraph 2 (b) of Article I as respects the United States of America

United States of America (customs territory)
Dependent territories of the United States of America
Republic of the Philippines

---

[1] For imports into Metropolitan France and Territories of the French Union.

The imposition of an equivalent margin of tariff preference to replace a margin of preference in an internal tax existing on April 10, 1947, exclusively between two or more of the territories listed in this Annex shall not be deemed to constitute an increase in a margin of tariff preference.

## ANNEX E

### List of Territories covered by Preferential Arrangements between Chile and Neighbouring Countries referred to in Paragraph 2 (*d*) of Article I

Preferences in force exclusively between Chile on the one hand, and

1. Argentina
2. Bolivia
3. Peru

on the other hand.

## ANNEX F

### List of Territories covered by Preferential Arrangements between Lebanon and Syria and Neighbouring Countries referred to in Paragraph 2 (*d*) of Article I

Preferences in force exclusively between the Lebano-Syrian Customs Union, on the one hand, and

1. Palestine
2. Transjordan

on the other hand.

## ANNEX G

### Dates establishing Maximum Margins of Preference referred to in Paragraph 4 † of Article I

| | |
|---|---|
| Australia | October 15, 1946 |
| Canada | July 1, 1939 |
| France | January 1, 1939 |
| Lebano-Syrian Customs Union | November 30, 1938 |
| Union of South Africa | July 1, 1938 |
| Southern Rhodesia | May 1, 1941 |

## ANNEX H

### Percentage Shares of Total External Trade to be Used for the Purpose of Making the Determination referred to in Article XXVI

(based on the average of 1949-1953)

If, prior to the accession of the Government of Japan to the General Agreement, the present Agreement has been accepted by contracting parties the external

---

† The authentic text erroneously reads "Paragraph 3".

trade of which under column I accounts for the percentage of such trade specified in paragraph 6 of Article XXVI, column I shall be applicable for the purposes of that paragraph. If the present Agreement has not been so accepted prior to the accession of the Government of Japan, column II shall be applicable for the purposes of that paragraph.

|  | *Column I* (Contracting parties on 1 March 1955) | *Column II* (Contracting parties on 1 March 1955 and Japan) |
|---|---|---|
| Australia | 3.1 | 3.0 |
| Austria | 0.9 | 0.8 |
| Belgium-Luxemburg | 4.3 | 4.2 |
| Brazil | 2.5 | 2.4 |
| Burma | 0.3 | 0.3 |
| Canada | 6.7 | 6.5 |
| Ceylon | 0.5 | 0.5 |
| Chile | 0.6 | 0.6 |
| Cuba | 1.1 | 1.1 |
| Czechoslovakia | 1.4 | 1.4 |
| Denmark | 1.4 | 1.4 |
| Dominican Republic | 0.1 | 0.1 |
| Finland | 1.0 | 1.0 |
| France | 8.7 | 8.5 |
| Germany, Federal Republic of | 5.3 | 5.2 |
| Greece | 0.4 | 0.4 |
| Haiti | 0.1 | 0.1 |
| India | 2.4 | 2.4 |
| Indonesia | 1.3 | 1.3 |
| Italy | 2.9 | 2.8 |
| Netherlands, Kingdom of the | 4.7 | 4.6 |
| New Zealand | 1.0 | 1.0 |
| Nicaragua | 0.1 | 0.1 |
| Norway | 1.1 | 1.1 |
| Pakistan | 0.9 | 0.8 |
| Peru | 0.4 | 0.4 |
| Rhodesia and Nyasaland | 0.6 | 0.6 |
| Sweden | 2.5 | 2.4 |
| Turkey | 0.6 | 0.6 |
| Union of South Africa | 1.8 | 1.8 |
| United Kingdom | 20.3 | 19.8 |
| United States of America | 20.6 | 20.1 |
| Uruguay | 0.4 | 0.4 |
| Japan | — | 2.3 |
|  | 100.0 | 100.0 |

*Note:* These percentages have been computed taking into account the trade of all territories in respect of which the General Agreement on Tariffs and Trade is applied.

# ANNEX I

### Notes and Supplementary Provisions

## Ad *Article I*

*Paragraph 1*

The obligations incorporated in paragraph 1 of Article I by reference to paragraphs 2 and 4 of Article III and those incorporated in paragraph 2 (*b*) of Article II by reference to Article VI shall be considered as falling within Part II for the purposes of the Protocol of Provisional Application.

The cross-references, in the paragraph immediately above and in paragraph 1 of Article I, to paragraphs 2 and 4 of Article III shall only apply after Article III has been modified by the entry into force of the amendment provided for in the Protocol Modifying Part II and Article XXVI of the General Agreement on Tariffs and Trade, dated September 14, 1948. [1]

*Paragraph 4*

The term " margin of preference " means the absolute difference between the most-favoured-nation rate of duty and the preferential rate of duty for the like product, and not the proportionate relation between those rates. As examples:

(1) If the most-favoured-nation rate were 36 per cent *ad valorem* and the preferential rate were 24 per cent *ad valorem*, the margin of preference would be 12 per cent *ad valorem*, and not one-third of the most-favoured-nation rate;

(2) If the most-favoured-nation rate were 36 per cent *ad valorem* and the preferential rate were expressed as two-thirds of the most-favoured-nation rate, the margin of preference would be 12 per cent *ad valorem*;

(3) If the most-favoured-nation rate were 2 francs per kilogramme and the preferential rate were 1.50 francs per kilogramme, the margin of preference would be 0.50 franc per kilogramme.

The following kinds of customs action, taken in accordance with established uniform procedures, would not be contrary to a general binding of margins of preference:

(i) The re-application to an imported product of a tariff classification or rate of duty, properly applicable to such product, in cases in which the application of such classification or rate to such product was temporarily suspended or inoperative on April 10, 1947; and

(ii) The classification of a particular product under a tariff item other than that under which importations of that product were classified on April 10, 1947, in cases in which the tariff law clearly contemplates that such product may be classified under more than one tariff item.

---

[1] This Protocol entered into force on 14 December 1948.

## Ad *Article II*

*Paragraph 2* (a)

The cross-reference, in paragraph 2 (*a*) of Article II, to paragraph 2 of Article III shall only apply after Article III has been modified by the entry into force of the amendment provided for in the Protocol Modifying Part II and Article XXVI of the General Agreement on Tariffs and Trade, dated September 14, 1948.[1]

*Paragraph 2* (b)

See the note relating to paragraph 1 of Article I.

*Paragraph 4*

Except where otherwise specifically agreed between the contracting parties which initially negotiated the concession, the provisions of this paragraph will be applied in the light of the provisions of Article 31 of the Havana Charter.

## Ad *Article III*

Any internal tax or other internal charge, or any law, regulation or requirement of the kind referred to in paragraph 1 which applies to an imported product and to the like domestic product and is collected or enforced in the case of the imported product at the time or point of importation, is nevertheless to be regarded as an internal tax or other internal charge, or a law, regulation or requirement of the kind referred to in paragraph 1, and is accordingly subject to the provisions of Article III.

*Paragraph 1*

The application of paragraph 1 to internal taxes imposed by local governments and authorities within the territory of a contracting party is subject to the provisions of the final paragraph of Article XXIV. The term " reasonable measures " in the last-mentioned paragraph would not require, for example, the repeal of existing national legislation authorizing local governments to impose internal taxes which, although technically inconsistent with the letter of Article III, are not in fact inconsistent with its spirit, if such repeal would result in a serious financial hardship for the local governments or authorities concerned. With regard to taxation by local governments or authorities which is inconsistent with both the letter and spirit of Article III, the term " reasonable measures " would permit a contracting party to eliminate the inconsistent taxation gradually over a transition period, if abrupt action would create serious administrative and financial difficulties.

*Paragraph 2*

A tax conforming to the requirements of the first sentence of paragraph 2 would be considered to be inconsistent with the provisions of the second sentence

---

[1] This Protocol entered into force on 14 December 1948.

only in cases where competition was involved between, on the one hand, the taxed product and, on the other hand, a directly competitive or substitutable product which was not similarly taxed.

*Paragraph 5*

Regulations consistent with the provisions of the first sentence of paragraph 5 shall not be considered to be contrary to the provisions of the second sentence in any case in which all of the products subject to the regulations are produced domestically in substantial quantities. A regulation cannot be justified as being consistent with the provisions of the second sentence on the ground that the proportion or amount allocated to each of the products which are the subject of the regulation constitutes an equitable relationship between imported and domestic products.

## Ad *Article V*

*Paragraph 5*

With regard to transportation charges, the principle laid down in paragraph 5 refers to like products being transported on the same route under like conditions.

## Ad *Article VI*

*Paragraph 1*

1. Hidden dumping by associated houses (that is, the sale by an importer at a price below that corresponding to the price invoiced by an exporter with whom the importer is associated, and also below the price in the exporting country) constitutes a form of price dumping with respect to which the margin of dumping may be calculated on the basis of the price at which the goods are resold by the importer.

2. It is recognized that, in the case of imports from a country which has a complete or substantially complete monopoly of its trade and where all domestic prices are fixed by the State, special difficulties may exist in determining price comparability for the purposes of paragraph 1, and in such cases importing contracting parties may find it necessary to take into account the possibility that a strict comparison with domestic prices in such a country may not always be appropriate.

*Paragraphs 2 and 3*

1. As in many other cases in customs administration, a contracting party may require reasonable security (bond or cash deposit) for the payment of anti-dumping or countervailing duty pending final determination of the facts in any case of suspected dumping or subsidization.

2. Multiple currency practices can in certain circumstances constitute a subsidy to exports which may be met by countervailing duties under paragraph 3 or can constitute a form of dumping by means of a partial depreciation of a country's currency which may be met by action under paragraph 2. By " multiple

currency practices " is meant practices by governments or sanctioned by governments.

*Paragraph 6* (b)

Waivers under the provisions of this sub-paragraph shall be granted only on application by the contracting party proposing to levy an anti-dumping or countervailing duty, as the case may be.

## Ad *Article VII*

*Paragraph 1*

The expression " or other charges " is not to be regarded as including internal taxes or equivalent charges imposed on or in connexion with imported products.

*Paragraph 2*

1. It would be in conformity with Article VII to presume that " actual value " may be represented by the invoice price, plus any non-included charges for legitimate costs which are proper elements of " actual value " and plus any abnormal discount or other reduction from the ordinary competitive price.

2. It would be in conformity with Article VII, paragraph 2 (*b*), for a contracting party to construe the phrase " in the ordinary course of trade ... under fully competitive conditions ", as excluding any transaction wherein the buyer and seller are not independent of each other and price is not the sole consideration.

3. The standard of " fully competitive conditions " permits a contracting party to exclude from consideration prices involving special discounts limited to exclusive agents.

4. The wording of sub-paragraphs (*a*) and (*b*) permits a contracting party to determine the value for customs purposes uniformly either (1) on the basis of a particular exporter's prices of the imported merchandise, or (2) on the basis of the general price level of like merchandise.

## Ad *Article VIII*

1. While Article VIII does not cover the use of multiple rates of exchange as such, paragraphs 1 and 4 condemn the use of exchange taxes or fees as a device for implementing multiple currency practices; if, however, a contracting party is using multiple currency exchange fees for balance of payments reasons with the approval of the International Monetary Fund, the provisions of paragraph 9 (*a*) of Article XV fully safeguard its position.

2. It would be consistent with paragraph 1 if, on the importation of products from the territory of a contracting party into the territory of another contracting party, the production of certificates of origin should only be required to the extent that is strictly indispensable.

## Ad *Articles XI, XII, XIII, XIV and XVIII*

Throughout Articles XI, XII, XIII, XIV and XVIII, the terms " import restrictions " or " export restrictions " include restrictions made effective through state-trading operations.

## Ad *Article XI*

*Paragraph 2* (c)

The term " in any form " in this paragraph covers the same products when in an early stage of processing and still perishable, which compete directly with the fresh product and if freely imported would tend to make the restriction on the fresh product ineffective.

*Paragraph 2, last sub-paragraph*

The term " special factors " includes changes in relative productive efficiency as between domestic and foreign producers, or as between different foreign producers, but not changes artificially brought about by means not permitted under the Agreement.

## Ad *Article XII*

The CONTRACTING PARTIES shall make provision for the utmost secrecy in the conduct of any consultation under the provisions of this Article.

*Paragraph 3* (c) (*i*)

Contracting parties applying restrictions shall endeavour to avoid causing serious prejudice to exports of a commodity on which the economy of a contracting party is largely dependent.

*Paragraph 4* (b)

It is agreed that the date shall be within ninety days after the entry into force of the amendments of this Article effected by the Protocol Amending the Preamble and Parts II and III of this Agreement. However, should the CONTRACTING PARTIES find that conditions were not suitable for the application of the provisions of this sub-paragraph at the time envisaged, they may determine a later date; *Provided* that such date is not more than thirty days after such time as the obligations of Article VIII, Sections 2, 3 and 4, of the Articles of Agreement of the International Monetary Fund become applicable to contracting parties, members of the Fund, the combined foreign trade of which constitutes at least fifty per centum of the aggregate foreign trade of all contracting parties.

*Paragraph 4* (e)

It is agreed that paragraph 4 (*e*) does not add any new criteria for the imposition or maintenance of quantitative restrictions for balance of payments reasons.

It is solely intended to ensure that all external factors such as changes in the terms of trade, quantitative restrictions, excessive tariffs and subsidies, which may be contributing to the balance of payments difficulties of the contracting party applying restrictions, will be fully taken into account.

## Ad *Article XIII*

*Paragraph 2* (d)

No mention was made of " commercial considerations " as a rule for the allocation of quotas because it was considered that its application by governmental authorities might not always be practicable. Moreover, in cases where it is practicable, a contracting party could apply these considerations in the process of seeking agreement, consistently with the general rule laid down in the opening sentence of paragraph 2.

*Paragraph 4*

See note relating to " special factors " in connexion with the last sub-paragraph of paragraph 2 of Article XI.

## Ad *Article XIV*

*Paragraph 1*

The provisions of this paragraph shall not be so construed as to preclude full consideration by the CONTRACTING PARTIES, in the consultations provided for in paragraph 4 of Article XII and in paragraph 12 of Article XVIII, of the nature, effects and reasons for discrimination in the field of import restrictions.

*Paragraph 2*

One of the situations contemplated in paragraph 2 is that of a contracting party holding balances acquired as a result of current transactions which it finds itself unable to use without a measure of discrimination.

## Ad *Article XV*

*Paragraph 4*

The word " frustrate " is intended to indicate, for example, that infringements of the letter of any Article of this Agreement by exchange action shall not be regarded as a violation of that Article if, in practice, there is no appreciable departure from the intent of the Article. Thus, a contracting party which, as part of its exchange control operated in accordance with the Articles of Agreement of the International Monetary Fund, requires payment to be received for its exports in its own currency or in the currency of one or more members of the International Monetary Fund will not thereby be deemed to contravene Article XI or Article XIII. Another example would be that of a contracting party which specifies on an import licence the country from which the goods may be imported, for the purpose not of introducing any additional element of discrimination in its import licensing system but of enforcing permissible exchange controls.

### Ad *Article XVI*

The exemption of an exported product from duties or taxes borne by the like product when destined for domestic consumption, or the remission of such duties or taxes in amounts not in excess of those which have accrued, shall not be deemed to be a subsidy.

*Section B*

1. Nothing in Section B shall preclude the use by a contracting party of multiple rates of exchange in accordance with the Articles of Agreement of the International Monetary Fund.

2. For the purposes of Section B, a " primary product " is understood to be any product of farm, forest or fishery, or any mineral, in its natural form or which has undergone such processing as is customarily required to prepare it for marketing in substantial volume in international trade.

*Paragraph 3*

1. The fact that a contracting party has not exported the product in question during the previous representative period would not in itself preclude that contracting party from establishing its right to obtain a share of the trade in the product concerned.

2. A system for the stabilization of the domestic price or of the return to domestic producers of a primary product independently of the movements of export prices, which results at times in the sale of the product for export at a price lower than the comparable price charged for the like product to buyers in the domestic market, shall be considered not to involve a subsidy on exports within the meaning of paragraph 3 if the CONTRACTING PARTIES determine that:

   (*a*) the system has also resulted, or is so designed as to result, in the sale of the product for export at a price higher than the comparable price charged for the like product to buyers in the domestic market; and

   (*b*) the system is so operated, or is designed so to operate, either because of the effective regulation of production or otherwise, as not to stimulate exports unduly or otherwise seriously to prejudice the interests of other contracting parties.

Notwithstanding such determination by the CONTRACTING PARTIES, operations under such a system shall be subject to the provisions of paragraph 3 where they are wholly or partly financed out of government funds in addition to the funds collected from producers in respect of the product concerned.

*Paragraph 4*

The intention of paragraph 4 is that the contracting parties should seek before the end of 1957 to reach agreement to abolish all remaining subsidies as from 1 January 1958; or, failing this, to reach agreement to extend the application of the standstill until the earliest date thereafter by which they can expect to reach such agreement.

## Ad *Article XVII*

*Paragraph 1*

The operations of Marketing Boards, which are established by contracting parties and are engaged in purchasing or selling, are subject to the provisions of sub-paragraphs (*a*) and (*b*).

The activities of Marketing Boards which are established by contracting parties and which do not purchase or sell but lay down regulations covering private trade are governed by the relevant Articles of this Agreement.

The charging by a state enterprise of different prices for its sales of a product in different markets is not precluded by the provisions of this Article, provided that such different prices are charged for commercial reasons, to meet conditions of supply and demand in export markets.

*Paragraph 1* (a)

Governmental measures imposed to ensure standards of quality and efficiency in the operation of external trade, or privileges granted for the exploitation of national natural resources but which do not empower the government to exercise control over the trading activities of the enterprise in question, do not constitute " exclusive or special privileges ".

*Paragraph 1* (b)

A country receiving a " tied loan " is free to take this loan into account as a " commercial consideration " when purchasing requirements abroad.

*Paragraph 2*

The term " goods " is limited to products as understood in commercial practice, and is not intended to include the purchase or sale of services.

*Paragraph 3*

Negotiations which contracting parties agree to conduct under this paragraph may be directed towards the reduction of duties and other charges on imports and exports or towards the conclusion of any other mutually satisfactory arrangement consistent with the provisions of this Agreement. (See paragraph 4 of Article II and the note to that paragraph.)

*Paragraph 4* (b)

The term "import mark-up" in this paragraph shall represent the margin by which the price charged by the import monopoly for the imported product (exclusive of internal taxes within the purview of Article III, transportation, distribution, and other expenses incident to the purchase, sale or further processing, and a reasonable margin of profit) exceeds the landed cost.

## Ad *Article XVIII*

The CONTRACTING PARTIES and the contracting parties concerned shall preserve the utmost secrecy in respect of matters arising under this Article.

*Paragraphs 1 and 4*

1. When they consider whether the economy of a contracting party " can only support low standards of living ", the CONTRACTING PARTIES shall take into consideration the normal position of that economy and shall not base their determination on exceptional circumstances such as those which may result from the temporary existence of exceptionally favourable conditions for the staple export product or products of such contracting party.

2. The phrase " in the early stages of development " is not meant to apply only to contracting parties which have just started their economic development, but also to contracting parties the economies of which are undergoing a process of industrialization to correct an excessive dependence on primary production.

*Paragraphs 2, 3, 7, 13 and 22*

The reference to the establishment of particular industries shall apply not only to the establishment of a new industry, but also to the establishment of a new branch of production in an existing industry and to the substantial transformation of an existing industry, and to the substantial expansion of an existing industry supplying a relatively small proportion of the domestic demand. It shall also cover the reconstruction of an industry destroyed or substantially damaged as a result of hostilities or natural disasters.

*Paragraph 7* (b)

A modification or withdrawal, pursuant to paragraph 7 (*b*), by a contracting party, other than the applicant contracting party, referred to in paragraph 7 (*a*), shall be made within six months of the day on which the action is taken by the applicant contracting party, and shall become effective on the thirtieth day following the day on which such modification or withdrawal has been notified to the CONTRACTING PARTIES.

*Paragraph 11*

The second sentence in paragraph 11 shall not be interpreted to mean that a contracting party is required to relax or remove restrictions if such relaxation or removal would thereupon produce conditions justifying the intensification or institution, respectively, of restrictions under paragraph 9 of Article XVIII.

*Paragraph 12 (b)*

The date referred to in paragraph 12 (*b*) shall be the date determined by the CONTRACTING PARTIES in accordance with the provisions of paragraph 4 (*b*) of Article XII of this Agreement.

*Paragraphs 13 and 14*

It is recognized that, before deciding on the introduction of a measure and notifying the CONTRACTING PARTIES in accordance with paragraph 14, a contracting party may need a reasonable period of time to assess the competitive position of the industry concerned.

*Paragraphs 15 and 16*

It is understood that the CONTRACTING PARTIES shall invite a contracting party proposing to apply a measure under Section C to consult with them pursuant to paragraph 16 if they are requested to do so by a contracting party the trade of which would be appreciably affected by the measure in question.

*Paragraphs 16, 18, 19 and 22*

1. It is understood that the CONTRACTING PARTIES may concur in a proposed measure subject to specific conditions or limitations. If the measure as applied does not conform to the terms of the concurrence it will to that extent be deemed a measure in which the CONTRACTING PARTIES have not concurred. In cases in which the CONTRACTING PARTIES have concurred in a measure for a specified period, the contracting party concerned, if it finds that the maintenance of the measure for a further period of time is required to achieve the objective for which the measure was originally taken, may apply to the CONTRACTING PARTIES for an extension of that period in accordance with the provisions and procedures of Section C or D, as the case may be.

2. It is expected that the CONTRACTING PARTIES will, as a rule, refrain from concurring in a measure which is likely to cause serious prejudice to exports of a commodity on which the economy of a contracting party is largely dependent.

*Paragraphs 18 and 22*

The phrase " that the interests of other contracting parties are adequately safeguarded " is meant to provide latitude sufficient to permit consideration in each case of the most appropriate method of safeguarding those interests. The appropriate method may, for instance, take the form of an additional concession to be applied by the contracting party having recourse to Section C or D during such time as the deviation from the other Articles of the Agreement would remain in force or of the temporary suspension by any other contracting party referred to in paragraph 18 of a concession substantially equivalent to the impairment due to the introduction of the measure in question. Such contracting party would have the right to safeguard its interests through such a temporary suspension of a concession; *Provided* that this right will not be exercised when, in the case of a measure imposed by a contracting party coming within the scope of paragraph 4 (*a*), the CONTRACTING PARTIES have determined that the extent of the compensatory concession proposed was adequate.

*Paragraph 19*

The provisions of paragraph 19 are intended to cover the cases where an industry has been in existence beyond the " reasonable period of time " referred to in the note to paragraphs 13 and 14, and should not be so construed as to deprive a contracting party coming within the scope of paragraph 4 (*a*) of Article XVIII, of its right to resort to the other provisions of Section C, including paragraph 17, with regard to a newly established industry even though it has benefited from incidental protection afforded by balance of payments import restrictions.

*Paragraph 21*

Any measure taken pursuant to the provisions of paragraph 21 shall be withdrawn forthwith if the action taken in accordance with paragraph 17 is withdrawn or if the CONTRACTING PARTIES concur in the measure proposed after the expiration of the ninety-day time limit specified in paragraph 17.

## Ad *Article XX*

*Sub-paragraph* (h)

The exception provided for in this sub-paragraph extends to any commodity agreement which conforms to the principles approved by the Economic and Social Council in its resolution 30 (IV) of 28 March 1947.

## Ad *Article XXIV*

*Paragraph 9*

It is understood that the provisions of Article I would require that, when a product which has been imported into the territory of a member of a customs union or free-trade area at a preferential rate of duty is re-exported to the territory of another member of such union or area, the latter member should collect a duty equal to the difference between the duty already paid and any higher duty that would be payable if the product were being imported directly into its territory.

*Paragraph 11*

Measures adopted by India and Pakistan in order to carry out definitive trade arrangements between them, once they have been agreed upon, might depart from particular provisions of this Agreement, but these measures would in general be consistent with the objectives of the Agreement.

## Ad *Article XXVIII*

The CONTRACTING PARTIES and each contracting party concerned should arrange to conduct the negotiations and consultations with the greatest possible secrecy in order to avoid premature disclosure of details of prospective tariff changes. The CONTRACTING PARTIES shall be informed immediately of all changes in national tariffs resulting from recourse to this Article.

*Paragraph 1*

1. If the CONTRACTING PARTIES specify a period other than a three-year period, a contracting party may act pursuant to paragraph 1 or paragraph 3 of Article XXVIII on the first day following the expiration of such other period and, unless the CONTRACTING PARTIES have again specified another period, subsequent periods will be three-year periods following the expiration of such specified period.

2. The provision that on 1 January 1958, and on other days determined pursuant to paragraph 1, a contracting party "may ... modify or withdraw a concession" means that on such day, and on the first day after the end of each period, the legal obligation of such contracting party under Article II is altered; it does not mean that the changes in its customs tariff should necessarily be made effective on that day. If a tariff change resulting from negotiations undertaken pursuant to this Article is delayed, the entry into force of any compensatory concessions may be similarly delayed.

3. Not earlier than six months, nor later than three months, prior to 1 January 1958, or to the termination date of any subsequent period, a contracting party wishing to modify or withdraw any concession embodied in the appropriate Schedule, should notify the CONTRACTING PARTIES to this effect. The CONTRACTING PARTIES shall then determine the contracting party or contracting parties with which the negotiations or consultations referred to in paragraph 1 shall take place. Any contracting party so determined shall participate in such negotiations or consultations with the applicant contracting party with the aim of reaching agreement before the end of the period. Any extension of the assured life of the Schedules shall relate to the Schedules as modified after such negotiations, in accordance with paragraphs 1, 2 and 3 of Article XXVIII. If the CONTRACTING PARTIES are arranging for multilateral tariff negotiations to take place within the period of six months before 1 January 1958, or before any other day determined pursuant to paragraph 1, they shall include in the arrangements for such negotiations suitable procedures for carrying out the negotiations referred to in this paragraph.

4. The object of providing for the participation in the negotiations of any contracting party with a principal supplying interest, in addition to any contracting party with which the concession was initially negotiated, is to ensure that a contracting party with a larger share in the trade affected by the concession than a contracting party with which the concession was initially negotiated shall have an effective opportunity to protect the contractual right which it enjoys under this

Agreement. On the other hand, it is not intended that the scope of the negotiations should be such as to make negotiations and agreement under Article XXVIII unduly difficult nor to create complications in the application of this Article in the future to concessions which result from negotiations thereunder. Accordingly, the CONTRACTING PARTIES should only determine that a contracting party has a principal supplying interest if that contracting party has had, over a reasonable period of time prior to the negotiations, a larger share in the market of the applicant contracting party than a contracting party with which the concession was initially negotiated or would, in the judgment of the CONTRACTING PARTIES, have had such a share in the absence of discriminatory quantitative restrictions maintained by the applicant contracting party. It would therefore not be appropriate for the CONTRACTING PARTIES to determine that more than one contracting party, or in those exceptional cases where there is near equality more than two contracting parties, had a principal supplying interest.

5. Notwithstanding the definition of a principal supplying interest in note 4 to paragraph 1, the CONTRACTING PARTIES may exceptionally determine that a contracting party has a principal supplying interest if the concession in question affects trade which constitutes a major part of the total exports of such contracting party.

6. It is not intended that provision for participation in the negotiations of any contracting party with a principal supplying interest, and for consultation with any contracting party having a substantial interest in the concession which the applicant contracting party is seeking to modify or withdraw, should have the effect that it should have to pay compensation or suffer retaliation greater than the withdrawal or modification sought, judged in the light of the conditions of trade at the time of the proposed withdrawal or modification, making allowance for any discriminatory quantitative restrictions maintained by the applicant contracting party.

7. The expression " substantial interest " is not capable of a precise definition and accordingly may present difficulties for the CONTRACTING PARTIES. It is, however, intended to be construed to cover only those contracting parties which have, or in the absence of discriminatory quantitative restrictions affecting their exports could reasonably be expected to have, a significant share in the market of the contracting party seeking to modify or withdraw the concession.

*Paragraph 4*

1. Any request for authorization to enter into negotiations shall be accompanied by all relevant statistical and other data. A decision on such request shall be made within thirty days of its submission.

2. It is recognized that to permit certain contracting parties, depending in large measure on a relatively small number of primary commodities and relying on the tariff as an important aid for furthering diversification of their economies or as an important source of revenue, normally to negotiate for the modification or withdrawal of concessions only under paragraph 1 of Article XXVIII, might cause them at such a time to make modifications or withdrawals which in the long

run would prove unnecessary. To avoid such a situation the CONTRACTING PARTIES shall authorize any such contracting party, under paragraph 4, to enter into negotiations unless they consider this would result in, or contribute substantially towards, such an increase in tariff levels as to threaten the stability of the Schedules to this Agreement or lead to undue disturbance of international trade.

3. It is expected that negotiations authorized under paragraph 4 for modification or withdrawal of a single item, or a very small group of items, could normally be brought to a conclusion in sixty days. It is recognized, however, that such a period will be inadequate for cases involving negotiations for the modification or withdrawal of a larger number of items and in such cases, therefore, it would be appropriate for the CONTRACTING PARTIES to prescribe a longer period.

4. The determination referred to in paragraph 4 (*d*) shall be made by the CONTRACTING PARTIES within thirty days of the submission of the matter to them, unless the applicant contracting party agrees to a longer period.

5. In determining under paragraph 4 (*d*) whether an applicant contracting party has unreasonably failed to offer adequate compensation, it is understood that the CONTRACTING PARTIES will take due account of the special position of a contracting party which has bound a high proportion of its tariffs at very low rates of duty and to this extent has less scope than other contracting parties to make compensatory adjustment.

## Ad *Article XXVIII* bis

*Paragraph 3*

It is understood that the reference to fiscal needs would include the revenue aspect of duties and particularly duties imposed primarily for revenue purposes or duties imposed on products which can be substituted for products subject to revenue duties to prevent the avoidance of such duties.

## Ad *Article XXIX*

*Paragraph 1*

Chapters VII and VIII of the Havana Charter have been excluded from paragraph 1 because they generally deal with the organization, functions and procedures of the International Trade Organization.

## Ad *Part IV*

The words " developed contracting parties " and the words " less-developed contracting parties " as used in Part IV are to be understood to refer to developed and less-developed countries which are parties to the General Agreement on Tariffs and Trade.

## Ad *Article XXXVI*

*Paragraph 1*

This Article is based upon the objectives set forth in Article I as it will be amended by Section A of paragraph 1 of the Protocol Amending Part I and Articles XXIX and XXX when that Protocol enters into force. [1]

*Paragraph 4*

The term " primary products " includes agricultural products, *vide* paragraph 2 of the note ad Article XVI, Section B.

*Paragraph 5*

A diversification programme would generally include the intensification of activities for the processing of primary products and the development of manufacturing industries, taking into account the situation of the particular contracting party and the world outlook for production and consumption of different commodities.

*Paragraph 8*

It is understood that the phrase " do not expect reciprocity " means, in accordance with the objectives set forth in this Article, that the less-developed contracting parties should not be expected, in the course of trade negotiations, to make contributions which are inconsistent with their individual development, financial and trade needs, taking into consideration past trade developments.

This paragraph would apply in the event of action under Section A of Article XVIII, Article XXVIII, Article XXVIII *bis* (Article XXIX after the amendment set forth in Section A of paragraph 1 of the Protocol Amending Part I and Articles XXIX and XXX shall have become effective [1]), Article XXXIII, or any other procedure under this Agreement.

## Ad *Article XXXVII*

*Paragraph 1* (a)

This paragraph would apply in the event of negotiations for reduction or elimination of tariffs or other restrictive regulations of commerce under Articles XXVIII, XXVIII *bis* (XXIX after the amendment set forth in Section A of paragraph 1 of the Protocol Amending Part I and Articles XXIX and XXX shall have become effective [1]), and Article XXXIII, as well as in connexion with other action to effect such reduction or elimination which contracting parties may be able to undertake.

*Paragraph 3* (b)

The other measures referred to in this paragraph might include steps to promote domestic structural changes, to encourage the consumption of particular products, or to introduce measures of trade promotion.

---

[1] This Protocol was abandoned on 1 January 1968.

# PROTOCOL OF PROVISIONAL APPLICATION OF THE GENERAL AGREEMENT ON TARIFFS AND TRADE

1. The Governments of the COMMONWEALTH OF AUSTRALIA, the KINGDOM OF BELGIUM (in respect of its metropolitan territory), CANADA, the FRENCH REPUBLIC (in respect of its metropolitan territory), the GRAND-DUCHY OF LUXEMBURG, the KINGDOM OF THE NETHERLANDS (in respect of its metropolitan territory), the UNITED KINGDOM OF GREAT BRITAIN AND NORTHERN IRELAND (in respect of its metropolitan territory), and the UNITED STATES OF AMERICA, undertake, provided that this Protocol shall have been signed on behalf of all the foregoing Governments not later than 15 November 1947, to apply provisionally on and after 1 January 1948:

   (a) Parts I and III of the General Agreement on Tariffs and Trade, and
   (b) Part II of that Agreement to the fullest extent not inconsistent with existing legislation.

2. The foregoing Governments shall make effective such provisional application of the General Agreement, in respect of any of their territories other than their metropolitan territories, on or after 1 January 1948, upon the expiration of thirty days from the day on which notice of such application is received by the Secretary-General of the United Nations.

3. Any other government signatory to this Protocol shall make effective such provisional application of the General Agreement, on or after 1 January 1948, upon the expiration of thirty days from the day of signature of this Protocol on behalf of such Government.

4. This Protocol shall remain open for signature at the Headquarters of the United Nations (a) until 15 November 1947, on behalf of any government named in paragraph 1 of this Protocol which has not signed it on this day, and (b) until 30 June 1948, on behalf of any other Government signatory to the Final Act adopted at the conclusion of the Second Session of the Preparatory Committee of the United Nations Conference on Trade and Employment which has not signed it on this day.

5. Any government applying this Protocol shall be free to withdraw such application, and such withdrawal shall take effect upon the expiration of sixty days from the day on which written notice of such withdrawal is received by the Secretary-General of the United Nations.

6. The original of this Protocol shall be deposited with the Secretary-General of the United Nations, who will furnish certified copies thereof to all interested Governments.

IN WITNESS WHEREOF the respective Representatives, after having communicated their full powers, found to be in good and due form, have signed the Protocol.

DONE at Geneva, in a single copy, in the English and French languages, both texts authentic, this thirtieth day of October one thousand nine hundred and forty-seven.

American Selling Price (ASP)
  effective rate of protection of, 192
  in the Kennedy Round, 191
  as a violation of Article VII, 189–92
Antidumping Code, 175–76
Antidumping duties
  Article VI accomodates U.S. law, 172
  definition of, 168
  economic rationale of, 169–72
  implementation of, 172–77
  problem with, 167–68
  protectionist elements of, 168–69
  as punishing consumers, 168–70
  purpose of, 167
  *See also* Countervailing duties
Argentina, 263
Aubrey, Henry G., 386n
Australia
  complaint about French wheat export subsidies, 143, 267
  dispute with Chile over ammonium sulphate, 147
  dispute with Chile over sodium nitrate binding, 358–59
  free-trade area with New Zealand, 282–83
  less-developed countries, position on, 52–55, 226, 250
  safeguard clause, Article XIX, use of, 106
Austria
  discriminatory taxes on U.S. automobiles, 131

Note: The Appendix has not been indexed.

**469**

Austria—*Continued*
retention of trade restriction not justifiable, 263
safeguard clause, Article XIX, use of, 106

Baier, Lowell F., 169n
Balance-of-payments. *See* Quantitative restrictions
Balassa, Bela, 231n
Baldwin, Robert E., 74n
Bard, Robert L., 269n
Basevi, Giorgio, 231n
Belgium
Brasseur plan sponsor, 235
discriminatory taxes on U.S. automobiles, 131
governmental restrictive procurement practices, 204
waiver, hard-core, 165, 261
Benelux countries, 108
Bhagwqti, Professor, 133n
Bidwell, Percy W., 180n
Blumenthal, W. Michael, 57n, 73n, 166n, 246n
Border tax adjustments, 210–21
economic rationale, 214–16
mechanics of, 211
preferential treatment of indirect taxes, 210–12
problems of calculating proper amount, 211–12
protectionist elements, 212, 215
recommended procedures for handling, 217–21
subsidy effects of, 212, 215
trade effects of, as violating Article III, 220
Working Party on, 210
Boyer, Frederick, 160n
Brasseur Plan, 235, 248
Brazil
internal tax case, 120–21
restrictions on temperate agricultural products, 264
Uruguay-Brazil Plan for Article XXIII, 368–73
waiver, Article XXV, pending Article XXVIII renegotiations, 98–99

Bronz, George, 103n, 152n, 338n
Brown, H. G., 215n
Brown, William Adams, Jr., 43n, 132 172n, 186n, 226n, 261n, 316n,
Brussels Customs Co-operation Counc 195
Buchanan, James M., 215n

Cambodia, 110
Canada
agricultural restrictions harming less-developed countries, 263–64
Antidumping Code, effect of, 173–7 177
"Buy Saskatchewan" program, 202
Canadian-U.S. Automotive Products Agreement, 49–51
Cotton Textiles Arrangement, 305,
Havana Charter position on less-developed countries, 226
import surcharges, maintenance of, 2 32
potato valuation dispute with Unite States, 362–63
restrictive health and safety regula- tions, effect on, 193
restrictive procurement practices, pr preference as, 205
safeguard clause, Article XIX, use of, 106
tariff negotiations, out-of-season authorization, 96
Centrally-planned economies. *See* State trading
Ceylon
Article XVIII, use of to protect infa industry, 228
Article XXVIII, use of for renegotiat 98
Article XXV, waiver to impose impo surcharges, 29
Chicken War, 87–91, 357–58. *See* als Germany, Federal Republic of; United States
Chile
currency retention practices, 137
disputes with Australia, 147, 358–5
proposed preferences, 241

waiver, Article XXV, for import surcharges, 29
Coase, Ronald, 370
Committee III
  Programme for Trade Expansion, 229
  Report on nontariff barriers, 229, 231–32
  Report on state-trading country obstacles, 329–30
Committee II
  agriculture section, Programme for Expansion of International Trade, 264
  consultations with United Kingdom, EEC, and United States, 264
  reporting on nontariff protective measures, 257–58
  state-trading, 330
Commodity Agreements
  International Coffee Agreement, 246
  International Grains Arrangement, 265–66, 271–73
  in the Kennedy Round, 247
  resemblance of, to cartels, 245
  United Nations Interim Co-ordinating Committee for International Commodity Agreements, 245
Compensatory adjustment
  Article XIX, none required, 100–101
  Article XXVIII, 85
  See also Retaliation.
Consultation, provision in General Agreement on, 21, 221
Consumer protection, 50–51. See also Antidumping duties
Cooper, Richard N., 74n
Cortney, Phillip, 14n
Cotton textiles
  arrangements, 296, 300–307
  benefits of, 314–15
  consultation requirements, 303
  damage criteria, 303
  implementation of, 307–9
  increased access requirements, 303
  market disruption, 297–303
  other arrangements proposed, wool, 313–14
  quantitative restrictions as forwarding goals of, 296–97

relation to Article XIII, 309
  relation to Article XXIII rights, 306–7
  restraint orders, 306–7
  tension with General Agreement, 305–6
Council of Representatives, 338–39
Countervailing duties
  code, lack of, 179
  compared with antidumping duties, 177–78
  economic theory, 178
  in the Kennedy Round, 178
  purpose of, 167, 178
  relation to subsidies, 178
  See also Antidumping duties
Cuba, 228
Curzon, Gerard, 57n, 164n, 228n, 231n, 290n, 293n, 302n, 313
Customs unions. See Free-Trade Areas
Czechoslovakia
  dispute with United States, 101–3
  state-trading, 317

Dairy products and nontariff protection, 258
Dam, Kenneth W., 38n, 265n, 271n, 281n, 284n, 288n, 290n, 294n
Denmark
  internal taxes, 232
  tariff negotiations, 96
Deringer Report, 215–16
De Vries, Margaret G., 138n
Dillon Round, 56. See also Tariff negotiations
Dispute Settlement
  annual reviews of quantitative restrictions, 353
  conciliatory rather than ajudicatory approach, 356
  differences with United Nations, 351–52
  general provisions in the General Agreement, 353
  political solutions, 352
  sectors, economic, 354
  waiver procedures of Article XXV as, 355
Drawbacks and Equalization Charges, 217, 220–21. See also Taxes, internal
Dumping. See Antidumping Duties

Eckstein, Otto, 219n
Economic Development
  Article XVIII as remnant of Havana Charter, 226-28
  economic efficiency as a conflicting value, 6-7
  exception to prohibition on quantitative restrictions, 21
  import substitution approach toward, 227
Economic Theory, 5-6. *See also* Anti-dumping duties; Border-Tax adjustments; Cotton textiles; Countervailing duties; Free-Trade areas; Part IV; Preferences; Subsidies; Taxes; Trade Creation
Egypt, 264
Elliott, G. A., 188n, 189n, 193n
European Coal and Steel Community, Article XXV waiver, 290
European Economic Community
  agricultural protectionism, 265
  agricultural sector negotiations, 70-71
  border tax adjustments, 212-14
  bypassed by Action Programme, 234
  consultations with Committee II, 264
  cotton textiles, 301
  effective rate of protection, 231
  harmonizing technical requirements, 196
  overcoming restrictive governmental procurement practices, 206
  preferences for less-developed countries, 248
  quantitative restrictions, elimination of, 161-63
  residual restrictions of, 165
  safeguard clause, use of Article XIX, 107
  state-trading problems, 331-32
  tariff averaging, 279
  Value-added taxes, 140. *See also* Free-trade areas.
European Free Trade Area (EFTA), 208. *See also* Free-trade areas
Evans, John W., 65n
Exchange arrangements, 154
Exchange Rates
  fixed, as favored by IMF, 15
  multiple, as outlawed by the General Agreement, 28-29

Exchange restrictions, 152-53

Federal states
  discrimination under Article XXIV:12, 128-29
Finland
  Brazilian Article XXV waiver compensation, 99
  Brazilian internal taxes case, 129
  internal taxes, 232
  party to Standstill Declaration, 146n
Food and Agricultural Organization (FAO)
  consultative mechanisms, 270
  International Grains Arrangement guidelines, 270
  surplus disposal, principles of, 268-70
France
  Brasseur Plan, support for, 248
  dispute with Australia over wheat, 143
  French Plan, 66-67, 271
  governmental restrictive procurement practices 204-5
  Greek internal tax, challenge to, 116-17
  harmonization of border tax adjustments, 213
  health and safety regulations, 193
  monopolies, approach by EEC, 332
  negotiations with United States, Article II:5, 108
  negotiations with United States, Article XXVIII, 94
  OEEC liberalization targets, failure to meet, 159
  Part IV of General Agreement, rejection of, 243
  preference negotiations, 48
  residual restrictions, 262-63
  safeguard clause, Article XIX, use of, 106
  stamp tax, increase in import fees, 180-81
  subsidies, export, on wheat sales, 267
  taxes on U.S. automobiles, 131
  technical conventions proposals, 197
Free-trade areas, 274-95
  annual reviews, importance of, 294-95
  Article XXIV, 274-95
  economic theory of, 275, 283-90
  European Economic Community, 282-83

exception to most-favored-nation obligation of Article I, 275
interim agreements, 282–83
ITO negotiations concerning provisions, 274
New Zealand/Australia free-trade area, 283
Paragraph 4 of Article XXIV, 295
Paragraphs 5–9 of Article XXIV, 296
preferences, 47, 275
quantitative restrictions, most-favored-nation problems, 280–82
substantially all trade, meaning of, 279–80
tariff, calculating common external, 277
tariff height, determining, 278
Friedman, Irving S., 157n

Gardner, Richard, 42n
Germany, Federal Republic of
agricultural protection, waiver application, 262
border tax adjustments, 213
cotton textiles, 308
governmental restrictive procurement practices, 204
internal taxes, 232
safeguard clause, Article XIX, use of, 106
spirits monopoly, 332
turnover taxes, 122–23
waiver, hard-core, refusal to apply for, 164
Giving Effect Declaration, for Article XVI, 145
Gold, J., 154n
Goode, Richard, 215
Governmental restrictive procurement practices, in the Kennedy Round, 199, 207, 209
Greece
internal tax dispute with France and the United Kingdom, 116–17
price preference, 205
safeguard clause, Article XIX, use of, 100, 106
Gunndelach, Finn, 236

Habeler Report
agricultural protection, dimensions of, 263
Programme for Expansion of International Trade, stimulus for, 264
trade relations of less-developed countries, 229, 234
Haiti
definitively adopting the General Agreement, 344
protection of infant industries, 228
Havana Charter
commodity agreement provisions, 226, 241, 244–47
as final version of ITO Charter, 11
government procurement clause negotiations, 200
General Agreement, what it did not incorporate from, 11
less-developed-country proposals, 225
state-trading provisions, 323–26
tariff conferences, rules governing, 57–58. See also International Trade Organization (ITO)
Hawkins, Harry, 172n
Hecke, G. van, 332n
Hedges, Irwin R. 272n
Heilperin, Michael A., 14n
Hendrick, James P., 176n
Hexner, Ervin, 40n
Holborn, Hajo, 12n
Holborn, Louise W., 12n
Hong Kong, 300–301
Hong Kong System, 309–11
Hull, Cordell, 14n, 65
Hungary, 317
Hunsberger, Warren S., 297n, 300n, 348n

India
cotton textiles, 300–301
infant industries, 228
preference proposals, 241, 249–50
renegotiations under Article XXVIII, 98
review of its Five-Year Plan, 244
Indonesia
renegotiations under Article XXVIII, 98
restrictions on temperate agricultural products as harmful, 263

Institutional weakness of the GATT, 336–39
Internal Taxes. *See* Taxes, internal
International Bank for Reconstruction and Development (IBRD), 244
International Chamber of Commerce
  Code of Standard Practices, 182, 185
  marks-of-original rules, 187
  technical conventions, role in adoption of, 195, 197
International Coffee Agreement, 246
International Grains Arrangement, 265–66, 271–73
International Monetary Fund (IMF)
  balance-of-payments cooperation with GATT, 150, 152–57
  division of competence with GATT, 156
  exchange taxes, authority over, 125–26
  fixed exchange rates, problem of, 15
International organization, GATT as, 335
International Trade Organization (ITO)
  antidumping negotiations, 172
  commercial policy provisions incorporated by GATT, 11
  need for, 16
  negotiations, 10
International Wheat Conference, 266
Italy
  border tax adjustments, 213
  banana import monopoly, 330
  cotton textiles, use of restraint orders, 308
  discriminatory taxes on U.S. automobiles, elimination of, 131
  dispute with Sweden, 173
  governmental restrictive procurement practices, 203–4
  internal taxes, 232
  negotiations, Article II:5, with the United States, 108
  safeguard clause, Article XIX, use of, 106
  subsidies for farmers disputed by United Kingdom, 142
  trade barrier restrictions, no longer justified, 263

Japan
  Accession, nonapplication of most-favored-nation benefits, 347–50

  link system of currency retention, 137
  market disruption, 297
  voluntary export limits, 299
Johnson, D. Gale, 231
Johnson, Harry G., 65n, 231n
Johnson, W. R., 189n

Kelly, William B., Jr., 174n, 176n, 177n
Kennedy Round, 57, 68–77
  linear method, exceptions to, 69–71
  nonlinear countries, 71–72
  reciprocity in, 69
  results of, 77
  role of Article XXVIII bis in, 68–69
Knapp, Laurence A., 199n, 201n
Krause, Lawrence B., 265n
Krzyzaniak, Marian, 215n
Kunugi, Tatsuro, 346n

Latin American Free-Trade Association, 291
Law, procedural and substantive, 4–5
Lebanon, 48
Leddy, John, 172n
Legalism in GATT, 3–4
Legal status of GATT, 336
Less-developed countries, 225–56, 311–13
  *See also* Part IV
Levett, Benjamin Arthur, 180n
Linder, Staffan B., 98n, 99n, 110, 234n
Low Tariff Club, 66
Low-tariff countries, 60–64, 97. *See also* under individual countries
Luxembourg, 261–62

McEwen, Rt. Hon. J., 52n
Malawi, 134
Marks of origin, 20. *See also* Nontariff barriers to trade.
Marlow, Joseph W., 202n
Mestmacker, Ernst-Joachim, 332n
Mexico, 263
Modification and rectification
  Article XXVIII, 85–86
  compensation for, 86
  nomenclature changes as, 35
Most-favored-nation
  customs unions and free trade areas, as exceptions, 19

effect of, when coupled with tariff
reduction, 26
meaning of, 18–19
spill-over effect of, 62–63
Musgrave, Richard A., 215 n

Nehmer, Stanley, 309 n
Netherlands, the
governmental restrictive procurement practices, 204–5
retaliation against United States, 260, 366
Neumark Report, 216
New Zealand
consultations with United Kingdom concerning butter, 264–65
free-trade area with Australia, 283, 290
governmental restrictive procurement policy, 205
Nicaragua, 181
Nigeria
safeguard clause, Article XIX, use of, 106
Trade and Aid Study, 244
Nontariff barriers
administrative or judicial decisions as, 108, 180–81
agricultural, types of, 258
antidumping and countervailing duties as, 20
customs service fees as, 20
documents as, 182–83, 185
export restrictions as, 21
formalities as, 181–85
government procurement as, 199–205
health and safety regulations as, 191–95
internal taxes as, 20
marks of origin as, 186–87
mixing regulations as, 233
price-support programs as, 233
prohibitory approach of Article XI, 19
technical conventions, to overcome, 195–98
types of, 20–22
Noordwijk agreement concerning cotton textiles, 308
Norway
price preference, 205

Tariff negotiations, out-of-season, authorization to conduct, 96
Nullification and impairment, 21. *See also* Retaliation
Nurske, Ragnar, 9

Organization for Economic Cooperation and Development (OECD)
border tax adjustments, 210
Code of Liberalisation, 386
committees of, 33, 386, 388
competition for GATT, 386
Draft Convention on Double Taxation, 386–87
governmental restrictive procurement practices, 205–6
preferences for less-developed countries, 55
regional approach within, 386
role in trade matters, as increasing, 385
Trade Committee, 386
unanimity rule, 388
Organization for European Economic Cooperation (OEEC), 145
Organization for Trade Cooperation (OTC), 337–38

Pakistan
cotton textile arrangement, 300–301, 306
review of Five-Year Plan, 244
tariff negotiations, under Article XXVIII, with United States, 94
Paliano, Guido Colonna di, 331 n
Part IV
commodity agreements, GATT change of position, 246
effect of, 91–94
effect of, on Article XXVIII negotiations, 91–92
emphasis on trade and development, 237
as incompatible with free-trade goal of GATT, 93
joint action, Article XXXVIII, 240–41
nonbinding character of Article XXXVII undertakings, 240
Peruvian waiver, 91–92
provisions of, 238
reciprocity, as not expected from less-developed countries, 73, 91–94, 238

Part IV—*Continued*
  reduction and elimination of barriers for less-developed countries, 239
  as a response to less-developed countries, 236–42
  standstill provisions, 239
  state trading and import monopolies, 240
  Trade and Development Committee, 238
  what is not included in, 241
Patterson, Gardner, 248n, 252, 290n, 291–92, 297n, 300n, 308n, 313–14, 348n, 349n
Penrose, E. F., 61n
Peru
  high import fees as violating Article VIII, 181
  renegotiations under Article XXVIII, 98
  safeguard clause, Article XIX, use of, 106
  waiver applications, 29, 91–93
Pincus, John, 248n
Poland
  associating with GATT, problems of, 328–29
  discrimination in meeting its quotas, 327
  Kennedy Round, participation in, 327
  state-trading problems, 317
Portugal, 347–48
Pragmatism, as an approach to GATT, 3–4
Prebisch, Raul, 378–80, 384–85
Preferences
  different treatment from tariffs, 43
  economic development, use of to attain, 13
  exceptions to the most-favored-nation clause, 19, 254
  for less-developed countries, 51–55, 249
  margin of preference, 43–44
  problem of nondiscrimination, 253
  trade creation and diversion, 288–90
  types of, 247–55
  United Kingdom waiver, 45–47
  UNCTAD's competence, 250–51
  United States views, 42–55
Principal-supplier rule, 61–62
Primary products, 144
Procedures of the GATT
  poorly designed to analyze waiver applications, 53–54
  proper focus of Article XXIV, 291
  role in Kennedy Round, 77–78
Provisional accession. *See* Accession, provisional
Provisional application, 341–44
  breadth of saving clause, 343
  failure to gain definitive acceptance, 344
  importance of grandfather clauses, 342–43
  as principal weakness of the General Agreement, 342
  terminated upon acceptance of Article XXVI, 342

Quantitative restrictions, 148–66
  agriculture, 20–21, 258–61
  balance-of-payments exception, 20–21, 149–50
  in the Chicken War, 88
  consultations required for imposition of, 163–64, 227–32
  contrast to tariffs, 148
  deviation from nondiscrimination rule of Article XIII, 151–52
  discriminatory application, 149
  exceptions, 151–52
  exchange controls, 155
  less-developed countries' use of, 20–21, 150
  negotiations, ITO, 149
  OEEC approach to, 158–61
  prohibition by Article XI, 150–51
  reporting requirements, 146–47
  standstill provisions, 146
  waiver, 163–64

Ray, Jean, 70n
Reciprocity
  exceptions to rule for less-developed countries, 59
  principle of, 17, 58–59
Rectifications and modifications, 34–35
Reform proposals
  adoption of linear method, 64
  low-tariff country complaints, 64
Rehm, John B., 68n, 174n, 265n

Remedies. See Retaliation
Renegotiations under Article XXVIII, 97–99
Residual restrictions, 165–67
Retaliation
 Article XXVIII, as central remedy provision, 352, 356
 bias toward delay, 364, 372
 burden of proof under Article XXIII, 361
 compensatory adjustment, 367–68
 conciliatory aim of, 365
 financial compensation as, 368–73
 hesitancy to authorize, 363–64
 justification for acts of private parties, 41, 359–60
 as an organizing principle, 81
 reasonable expectations test, 359, 362
 reforms of, 373–75
 remedy without a right, 358–59
 rights and obligations, as reciprocal, 352
 self-help as a remedy, 86
 substantially equivalent concessions, meaning of, 87–91
 substantive limits on, 367
 use of, 366
Rhodesia-Nyasaland, 106
Rolph, Earl R., 215n
Roth, W. M., 57n
Rules, in the Kennedy Round, 77–78
Rumania, 317

Safeguard clause, Article XIX
 different treatment of original and retaliatory suspensions, 105
 duration of, 100
 emergency provision, 104
 importance of, 99
 invocation, frequency of, 106
 justification required, 101–2
 most-favored-nation problems, 104–5
 negotiations, 99–107
 obligations other than tariffs, 105–6
 other economic treaties, use in, 107
 procedures, 103–4
 provisions of, 98
 scope of, 100
 substantially equivalent concessions, 104–5

unforeseen developments requirement, 99, 101–2
Salle, J. P., 160n
Sanctions. See Retaliation
Schmölders, Günter, 216n
Secretariat
 antidumping regulations study, 173
 commodity agreements, passivity, 245–46
 initiating Trade-and-Aid studies, 243
 providing information, potential role, 294, 374–75
 responsible for GATT accomplishments, 335–41
 role of, in tariff negotiations, 57
 role, not as enforcer of the General Agreement, 355–56
 views on equitable share of world export trade, 143–44. See also Wyndham White, Eric
Sector discussions, 78
South Africa, restrictive government procurement practices, 205
South African/Rhodesian Customs Union, 292
Spain, restrictive procurement practices, 205
Standstill Agreement, on drawbacks, 216
State trading and import Monopolies, 316–32
 accession problems, 111, 316
 as barriers to trade of less-developed countries, 233
 differences with market economies, 318–21
 interpretative note, 324–28
 nondiscrimination under Article XVII, 321–23
 as a nontariff barrier, 20
 quantitative restrictions, use of, 328
 regulation of, 317–32
Stein, Herbert, 219n
Steinberger, Helmut, 48n
Subsidies, 132–48
 agricultural, 134, 258
 balance-of-payments exception, 136
 currency retention practices as, 137
 as de facto devaluation, 133–34

Subsidies—*Continued*
  detrimental effects of, on world efficiency, 136
  differential treatment for tariffs and quantitative restrictions, 135–36
  disposal of surpluses as, 268
  economic development, use for, 135
  economic theory, 132–48
  exchange rates having the effect of, 133–34, 138–42
  export, 142–46, 266–70
  export-financing schemes as, 138–39
  measures having the effect of, 137–38
  negotiation limits on, 147
  on nonprimary products, 144–45
  production, 20–21, 141–42
  protective effect of, 147
  refund of taxes as, 139
  reporting requirements, 146–47
  similarity of export and production subsidies, 134
Sudan, 264
Surcharges, import
  IMF approval required for waiver, 30
  inconsistent treatment relative to quantitative restrictions, 33
  limitation on bindings, 32–33
  waiver, 29
Surplus disposal programs, 233
Surrey, Stanley S., 213 n
Sweden
  antidumping duties, basic price system, 173
  effective rates of protection, 231
Switzerland
  accession reservations, 347
  health and safety regulations, effect on, 193
  protection of its wheat farmers, 263
Syria, 48

Tariffs
  bindings, 17, 25–26, 30–31
  concessions, 17
  differential treatment from other barriers, 26–27
  disparities, 73–76
  duties, 35–37, 38
  external, 287–88
  functions, of GATT, beyond negotiation, 80
  harmonization, 73
  indirect increases in protection, 39
  internal, 284–86
  limitations of Article II on revision of bound duties, 36
  negotiations, 17, 57–59, 61–64
  open-season negotiations, 81–95
  out-of-season negotiations, 95–97
  protective effect of, 89
  ratchet effect of Article XXVIII, 85
  rounds, 56–57
  schedules, 31–32
  as stumbling blocks for less-developed countries, 107–8, 229–31
Taxes
  cascade system of turnover, 140
  direct, 124–25, 139–40
  direct-tax countries, 213
  exchange, 125–28
  indirect, 139–40
  internal, 40, 115–32. *See also* Taxes, turnover
  shifting of, 216
  turnover, 121–24, 140
  value-added system of turnover, 140
Trade and Development Committee
  compensation for less-developed countries for violations of GATT obligations, 243
  foundation of discrimination against less-developed countries, 372
  Group on International Commodity Problems, 247
  Group on Preferences, Working, 250
  position on preferences for less-developed countries, 253
  review of Article XXIII mechanisms for dispute settlement, 255
  review of Kennedy Round, 256
  studies of development plans, 243
Trade barrier effect, 20
Trade coverage
  in the Chicken War, 88–89
  meaning of, 59–60
  use of, 61
Trade creation and diversion
  consumption effects of, 285

Index 479

in free-trade areas, 283–90
key issue in Article XXIV waivers, 48
preferences for less-developed
  countries, 51–52, 252
production effects of, 285
of quantitative restrictions, 286–87
United Kingdom waiver application, 45
United States–Canadian Automotive
  Products Agreement, 50
Turkey
  Article XIX safeguard clause, 100
  renegotiations, Article XXVIII, 98
  waiver for fees in violation of Article
    VIII, 181

Uganda, 244
United Arab Republic, 249–50
United Kingdom
  Antidumping Code, effect on, 174–77
  balance-of-payments exception, 150
  border tax adjustments, 210, 212–13
  Committee II, consultations with, 264
  cotton textile arrangement, 301–3
  deficiency payments as agricultural
    subsidy, 134
  effective rate of protection, 231
  Greek internal tax dispute, 116–17
  import surcharges, in violation
    of Article II, 29, 32
  Ireland/United Kingdom
    Free-Trade Area, 290
  Italian production subsidy
    complaint, 142
  less-developed countries, position
    at Havana Charter, 226
  New Zealand's problem of marketing
    butter, 264–65
  preferences for less-developed
    countries, 248
  residual restrictions, list of, 165
  restrictive governmental procurement
    practices, 201–3
  value-added tax, 214
United Nations Cocoa Conference, 382
United Nations Conference on Trade
  and Development (UNCTAD)
  advantages relative to the GATT,
    384–85

committees, 383–84
commodity agreements, responsibility
  for negotiating, 247
competence shared with the GATT, 8
institutional competition for the GATT,
  225, 376–85
International Wheat Conference,
  sponsor, 266
preferences for less-developed countries,
  55
problems of less-developed countries, 22
United Nations Conference on Trade
  and Employment, 10n
United States
  Agricultural Adjustment Act, 260
  agricultural production restraints, 259–60
  Antidumping Code, effect on, 174
  antidumping program, 173
  border tax adjustments, 210
  "Buy American" Act, 202
  Canadian–U.S. Automotive Products
    Agreement, 49–51
  Commodity agreements, attitude
    toward, 245–46
  consular invoice, abolishment of, 184
  consultations with Committee II, 264
  Cotton Textiles Arrangement, 298,
    307–9
  countervailing duties, 179
  dairy product import restrictions, 260
  effective rates of protection, 231
  European taxes on automobiles, 131
  FAO guidelines, 270
  government purchases from foreign
    bidders, 199
  health and safety regulations, 193
  influence on GATT drafting, 10, 12
  Kennedy Round, agricultural position
    in, 70–71
  less-developed countries, position on,
    225–26, 241, 248
  Malawi, dispute with, 134
  marks of origin, 186–87
  most-favored-nation clause, 252
  objection to border tax adjustments, 210
  potato valuation dispute with Canada,
    362–63
  proposal for guaranteed access to world
    agricultural markets, 271

United States—*Continued*
  quantitative restrictions, views on at ITO, 149
  residual restrictions, list of, 165
  restrictions on temperate agricultural imports, 262–64
  retaliation against, by the Netherlands, 366
  safeguard clause, Article XIX, use of, 100–103, 106
  subsidy, farm price supports as a form of, 134
  surplus agricultural commodities, 268
  tariff reductions prior to GATT, 64
  Tariff Commission on Trade Agreements Program, 89
  tax on distilled spirits, 129–30
  Trade Expansion Act of 1962, 67
  treatment of turnover taxes, 122–23
  value-added turnover tax system, 214
  Wheat prices, 263
Uruguay
  attack on policies of developed countries, 360–61
  import surcharge waiver, 29
  recommendation of Article XXII consultations, 360–61
  state-trading, position on, 324, 330–31
  temperate agricultural products, 263
  Uruguay–Brazil Plan for Article XXIII, 368–73

Valuation, 187–89
Viner, Jacob, 148n, 170–72, 283, 285–86

Waiver
  case-by-case approach, 255
  hard-core, 261–62
  reporting requirements, 47–48
Walker, Herman, 227n
West Indies, 263
Wilcox, Clair, 148, 150n, 275n, 317n
Withdrawal from GATT, 22
Withdrawal of tariff concessions, 18, 85–86
Wyndham White, Eric, 78, 160, 245n, 246, 260n, 335n, 339–40, 356, 378. *See also* Secretariat

Yugoslavia, 317, 319, 328–29